SAGE DIRECTIONS IN EDUCATIONAL PSYCHOLOGY

SAGE LIBRARY OF EDUCATIONAL THOUGHT AND PRACTICE

SAGE DIRECTIONS IN EDUCATIONAL PSYCHOLOGY

VOLUME III

Edited by

Neil J. Salkind

Los Angeles | London | New Delhi
Singapore | Washington DC

SAGE Publications Ltd
1 Oliver's Yard
55 City Road
London EC1Y 1SP

SAGE Publications Inc.
2455 Teller Road
Thousand Oaks, California 91320

SAGE Publications India Pvt Ltd
B 1/I 1, Mohan Cooperative Industrial Area
Mathura Road
New Delhi 110 044

SAGE Publications Asia-Pacific Pte Ltd
33 Pekin Street #02-01
Far East Square
Singapore 048763

British Library Cataloguing in Publication data

A catalogue record for this book is available from the
British Library

ISBN: 978-0-85702-178-6 (set of five volumes)

Library of Congress Control Number: 2010923776

Typeset by Mukesh Technologies Pvt. Ltd., Pondicherry, India.
Printed on paper from sustainable resources
Printed in Great Britain by the MPG Books Group, Bodmin and King's Lynn

Mixed Sources
Product group from well-managed
forests and other controlled sources
www.fsc.org Cert no. SA-COC-1565
© 1996 Forest Stewardship Council
FSC

Contents

Volume III

Section II: Curriculum, Instruction and Learning (*Continued*)

Section III: Motivation

Section II: Curriculum, Instruction and Learning (*Continued*)

Human Intelligence: An Introduction to Advances in Theory and Research

David F. Lohman

What is intelligence? How does it develop? Does it decline? Has cognitive science really changed our understanding of this construct? Old questions about intelligence have been raised with a renewed vigor, and new questions have been posed. In short, there has been a remarkable resurgence of research on human abilities in the past 15 years, fueled in part by legal challenges to intelligence tests, but in even larger measure by a renewed interest in cognition in psychology. New methods of investigation and theories of cognition have been applied to old tests and theories of individual differences. Although the results have not met the loftier expectations of some advocates, progress has been made. The purpose of this paper is to provide a sampling of this progress, to note some of the problems that have attended it, and to suggest some research strategies for future research on human intelligence.

I focus on three research traditions: trait theories of intelligence, information-processing theories of intelligence, and general theories of thinking. The discussion of trait theories of intelligence focuses on Cattell's (1963) theory of fluid and crystallized abilities, particularly the elaborations of this theory proposed by Horn (1985) and by Snow (1981). Their work provides a convenient framework for the discussion of information-processing theories of intelligence. First, I summarize attempts to build process theories of the major factors identified in Horn's (1985) model, such as the work of Jensen (1982) and Eysenck (1982) on mental speed, of Hunt (1985) and Frederiksen (1982) on verbal-crystallized abilities, of Sternberg (1977) on fluid-reasoning abilities,

Source: *Review of Educational Research*, 59(4) (1989): 333–373.

and of Pellegrino and Kail (1982) and Lohman (1988) on spatial-visualization ability. This section concludes with a discussion of Sternberg's (1984, 1985) recent attempts to develop a comprehensive theory of intelligence. I then turn the problem around. Instead of asking how cognitive science might help us understand existing tests or ability constructs, I ask how a theory of intelligence might be derived from the sort of general theories of thinking currently advanced in cognitive psychology and artificial intelligence (AI). Here the discussion emphasizes Anderson's (1983) ACT* theory (the latest version of his Adaptive Control of Thought system) and the "New Connectionism" of Rumelhart, McClelland, and the PDP (Parallel Distributed Processing) Research Group (1986). The paper concludes with some speculations about the meaning of the construct *intelligence* and some suggestions for research on it.

The resurgence of general ability.   Several developments converged in the early 1970s to renew interest in the construct intelligence. First, there was the growing realization that the ability profiles provided by multiple-aptitude batteries were not as useful for prediction as many had hoped (McNemar, 1964). Although there were exceptions, the predictive validities of the several scores from multiple-aptitude batteries were repeatedly found to be little better than the corresponding validity of one general factor estimated from the same battery.[1] Nor were the specific abilities that Thurstone (1938) and Guilford (1959) had identified of much use in attempts to adapt instructional methods to the ability profile of the learner. Instead, general ability accounted for most of the findings. In their summary of 20 years of research on Aptitude X Treatment interactions, Cronbach and Snow (1977) concluded:

> It has become fashionable to decry the use of measures of general ability, and sometimes their use has been prohibited in school systems. The attackers usually insist that the tests do not assess ability to learn, and it is often proposed to substitute measures of achievement or "learning styles."...
> While we see merit in a hierarchical conception of abilities, with abilities differentiated at coarse and fine levels, we have not found Guilford's subdivision a powerful hypothesis....Instead of finding general abilities irrelevant to school learning, we find nearly ubiquitous evidence that general measures predict amount learned or rate of learning or both. And, whereas we had expected specialized abilities rather than general abilities to account for interactions, the abilities that most frequently enter into interactions are general. Even in those programs of research that started with specialized ability measures and found interactions with treatment, the data seem to warrant attributing most effects to general ability, (pp. 496–497)

Thus, on one hand, special abilities failed either to predict educational outcomes better than general ability or to predict which students would profit from specialized educational interventions designed to match their particular patterns of abilities. On the other hand, American theorists gradually adopted a hierarchical model of abilities which, while allowing for both broad and narrow abilities, clearly emphasized the role of general ability.

The cognitive revolution. The second development was an outgrowth of the cognitive revolution in psychology. From Watson (1925) until Skinner (1953), American psychology was dominated by the belief that mind was not the proper subject matter for psychology. Studies of animal learning or conditioning were the norm. Thinking and reasoning were considered complex behaviors that would be explained sometime in the future after elementary mechanisms of learning were adequately understood. By the mid-1960s, however, this promise was wearing thin. Psychology seemed not to be building toward the explanation of complex phenomena but, if anything, was digging increasingly deeper into reductionism. Some had already called for a rejection of radical behaviorism on theoretical grounds (Chomsky, 1959). But it was the emergence of the computer as a metaphor for mind and as a vehicle for testing theories about thinking that finally dethroned behaviorism. Rather swiftly, the mainstream of psychology moved from conditioning to perception and then to thinking and problem solving. By 1985, in the first paragraph of his introductory text on cognitive psychology, Anderson was proclaiming, "the goal of cognitive psychology is to understand human intelligence and how it works" (p. 1). Thus, in 2 decades, the word *intelligence* moved from the periphery of American psychology to its center.[2]

The cognitive revolution had two rather different influences on theories of human intelligence. There were some who saw that the methods and theories of the cognitive psychologists provided a new way to understand what intelligence and other ability tests were really measuring. Carroll (1976), Glaser (1972), Hunt (e.g., Hunt, Frost, & Lunneborg, 1973), Sternberg (1977), and Snow (e.g. Snow, Marshalek, & Lohman, 1976) were leaders in this effort. There were others, however, who were not at all concerned with intelligence as an individual difference construct. These investigators sought to develop theories of human cognition and, at times, to simulate their theories in computer programs that then displayed AI. Both of these efforts will be briefly reviewed in this paper.

The Challenge of Process

Although most research on intelligence has focused on the products of intelligence, both theoreticians and clinicians have long called for greater attention to the process of intelligent thinking.[3]

> Nobody has ever made an inventory of tasks [that define the universe of intellectual tasks], determined the correlation of each with intellect, selected an adequate battery of them, and found the proper weights to attach to each...If anybody did this wisely, a large fraction of his labor would be precisely to find out what abilities our present instruments did measure, and how these abilities were related to intellect; or to find out what abilities

constituted intellect, and how these abilities were measured by our present instruments. (E. L. Thorndike, Bregman, Cobb, & Woodyard, 1926, p. 2)

Three decades later in his call for the unification of the two disciplines of scientific psychology – the correlational psychology of mental testing and the experimental psychology of learning – Cronbach (1957) argued

> Sophistication in data analysis has not been matched by sophistication in theory. The correlational psychologist was led into temptation by his own success, losing himself first in practical prediction, then in a narcissistic program of studying his tests as an end in themselves. A naive operationism enthroned theory of test performance in the place of theory of mental processes. (p. 675)

In this Cronbach echoed Thurstone (1947), who considered a factor-analytic study of abilities only the first step in a research program. Ability factors identified in such studies should be investigated in experiments designed to manipulate and thus identify "the processes which underlie" the factors (p. 55). But such experiments had little appeal in a psychology dominated by behaviorism, and so the research program Thurstone advocated had to await the rediscovery of mental process by the mainstream of American experimental psychology.

Cognitive Science and the Computer Metaphor

Recent research on intelligence has been driven by a renewed interest in cognition in psychology and in many other fields. *Cognitive science* is the term now commonly used to refer to this new blend of computer science, cognitive psychology, linguistics, neuropsychology, philosophy, and instructional psychology. Although roots of the cognitive revolution may be traced to many earlier sources, several observers see 1956 as the pivotal year in the development of cognitive science. In that year, Newell and Simon (see Newell, Shaw, & Simon, 1957) reported their success in devising a computer program that could actually prove theorems in logic. In the same year, Bruner, Goodnow, and Austin published their *Study of Thinking*, and Miller published a seminal paper on short-term memory in which he argued that the capacity of this memory store seemed to be limited by "the magic number seven" (Newell & Simon, 1972, p. 4). The cognitive revolution gathered momentum in the 1960s and achieved ascendency during the 1970s (see Gardner, 1985).

The computer has contributed importantly to this revolution in at least two ways. The most obvious contribution of the computer has been as a metaphor for human cognition.[4] This metaphor has taken several forms. At the simplest level, direct analogies have been made between the hardware of the computer and the human cognitive system. Computers have devices for encoding information from external sources (card readers, keyboards), temporarily storing it (memory buffers), transforming it (central processors), retaining it on long-term storage devices (tapes, disks), and producing output (printers, video displays). Early models of human information processing relied heavily on this analogy in positing similar structures in the human cognitive system. When used in this way, the computer is but the latest mechanical metaphor for mind in psychology (Marshall, 1977). Although more sophisticated than previous metaphors such as the wax tablet or the hydraulic pump, the computer metaphor is incomplete and even misleading. For example, some researchers have begun to question the extent to which theorizing has been artificially constrained by the serial-processing, digital computer. New research programs based on parallel processing may circumvent some of these problems, particularly for modeling perception and other nonlinguistic processes. But, as will be explained, these theories have their critics too.

Some analogies between computers and human cognition go considerably beyond comparisons of the superficial characteristics of system hardware. In particular, it is argued that similar principles govern the functioning of any system that processes information. Fodor (1981) and others who espouse this computational metaphor for thought treat the mind as a device for manipulating symbols. At this level of abstraction, differences in hardware, whether electronic or neurophysiological, are thought to be irrelevant. Whether such an assumption is tenable is a hotly debated issue in cognitive science.

However, all would agree that the contribution of the computer has far exceeded its admittedly limited value as a metaphor for the human cognitive system. The greater contribution of the computer has been as a tool for developing and testing theories of cognition or, as Anderson and Bower (1973) put it, for experimenting on the nature of the connection between stimulus and response. In this way, the computer has changed the evidentiary base to include something other than human behavior. Theories of thinking and learning can be formalized as computer programs. Programs gain a measure of plausibility if they solve problems using sequences of steps that are similar to the steps used by successful human problem solvers or if, when failing to solve problems, they make errors that mimic human errors. A constant exchange between those who study human problem solving in the psychological laboratory and those who attempt to develop computer programs that display AI serves to refine and extend both efforts.

Some would object that such comparisons between humans and computers diminish human dignity. However, cognitive science makes no pretense that computational theories completely account for human cognition. Computational models of thought are in principle no different from computational models of the weather (Miller, 1981). Yet, as Miller observes, no one fears that a tornado might destroy the computer center when the computer is used to model the behavior of tornadoes. Nor do we dismiss efforts to model the weather because such models will never produce rain. Perhaps we expect more from computational models of thought because "the brain is itself a computer in a sense in which the weather is not," and so a "computer that models an intelligent brain is expected to be a brain" (p. 220).

Contributions of Cognitive Research

Cognitive science has contributed to the understanding of human intelligence in three ways. First, methods and theories of cognitive science have been applied to existing tests of intelligence, either through experimental analysis of tasks taken from intelligence and other ability tests, or through careful study of the problem-solving or other information-processing characteristics of individuals identified as more or less able by existing tests. In this way, cognitive psychology offers a new source of evidence on the construct validity of tests and the ability factors they define. Second, tests of intelligence and narrow abilities are often used to predict performance in some non–test situation (e.g., conventional schooling). Careful study of the knowledge and processing demands of these criterial performances has led to the development of new measurement strategies and suggestions for the refinement of existing measures (Frederiksen, 1984; Snow & Lohman, 1989). Third, cognitive science has sought to move beyond existing definitions of intelligence grounded in individual differences to develop general theories of thinking and learning. New measures are then developed to estimate particular processes or knowledge structures hypothesized by these theories. Patterns of individual differences on these new measures are then investigated, usually by determining relationships between new measures and scores on existing tests or experimental tasks.

The following section contains a brief review of attempts to understand intelligence through the study of existing tests or ability constructs defined by such tests. Cattell's theory of fluid and crystallized abilities has had a major impact on these efforts, particularly the theories of Horn (1985), Snow (1981), and Sternberg (1985), and so his theory and recent extensions of it are summarized first. Then, experimental research on four of the major ability constructs identified by Cattell, Horn, and other theorists is summarized. The four constructs are verbal-crystallized (Gc) ability, spatial-visualization (Gv) ability, fluid-reasoning (Gf) ability, and mental speed (Gs).

Controversies about Intelligence

Controversies about the nature of intelligence seem to repeat themselves. Two of the most important controversies relate to the question of whether the general (sometimes called g) factor that is commonly equated with intelligence should be viewed as a psychological entity, or whether it is merely a mathematical abstraction. E. L. Thorndike (see E. L. Thorndike et al., 1926) and Thomson (1920) were early advocates of the view that responses to items on intelligence tests represent a particular sample of mental bonds, and thus intelligence was better understood as a mathematical abstraction than as a psychological entity. Humphreys (1985) gives a modern statement of this view. Spearman, on the other hand, interpreted the g factor as the ability to reduce relations and correlates. Sternberg's (1977) early work on analogical reasoning constitutes a modern version of this view. This controversy has important implications for the potential contributions of cognitive theory to a theory of intelligence. If the ubiquitous general factor is simply a mathematical dimension (Humphreys, 1985), then analyses of tasks used on intelligence tests are unlikely to isolate a particular set of mental processes that are the core of intelligence. In fact, tests that are a good measure of this dimension should be composed of maximally heterogeneous items and thus would be psychologically complex (Humphreys, 1986). However, higher order processes such as coordination of existing routines or assembly of new routines (Snow, 1981) might still emerge across diverse performances (see Butcher, 1968, p. 25).[5]

The second controversy, often correlated with the first, is whether intelligence is an innate cognitive capacity or, instead, an acquired set of cognitive competencies.[6] Hereditarians such as Burt (1958), Terman (1922), Jensen (1980), and Eysenck (1982) argue that good intelligence tests are – or should be – measures of this basic, biologically-based capacity. Others, such as Humphreys (1986) and Cronbach (1972), claim that potential and capacity are pie-in-the-sky concepts with no place in a scientific account of human ability. In fact, both argue that the psychology of individual differences would be well rid of the term *intelligence*. This controversy is reflected in the search for neurological correlates of intelligence test scores among the hereditarians and perhaps in the search for an explanation of intelligence in terms of structural differences (e.g., capacity of working memory, rate of information transfer in memory) by like-minded cognitive psychologists.[7] On the other hand, those who believe that abilities are acquired competencies tend to emphasize the importance of knowledge in thinking (Glaser, 1984), to study the development of abilities rather than attempt to explain individual differences at a particular point in time (Kail & Pellegrino, 1985), and to view intelligence as a product of formal schooling, not simply as a predictor of success in that medium (Snow & Yalow, 1982).

The third perennial controversy concerns the question of whether intelligence is unitary, as Spearman emphasized, or has multiple dimensions, as E. L. Thorndike, Thurstone, and Guilford emphasized.

The Theory of Fluid and Crystallized Abilities

It is fitting that the most popular current resolution to the debate between Spearman, Thorndike, and Thurstone about the dimensions of intelligence was proposed by an Englishman who received his PhD under Spearman (in 1929), completed a postdoctoral fellowship under E. L. Thorndike (in 1937), conducted research with both Burt and Thurstone (Cattell, 1971, p. ix), and eventually took up permanent residence in the United States. In 1941, shortly after accepting a position at Harvard, Cattell proposed a quasi-hierarchical model of human abilities with two general factors at the apex (rather than the one advocated by Spearman). Each was defined by several of the primary factors Thurstone had identified. Cattell called these two factors fluid intelligence (Gf) and crystallized intelligence (Gc).

In the earliest published account of the theory, Cattell (1943) argued that fluid ability was "a purely general ability to discriminate and perceive relations between any fundaments, new or old" (p. 178). Fluid ability was hypothesized to increase until adolescence and then slowly decline. It was thought to represent the "action of the whole cortex" (p. 178). Further, fluid intelligence was thought to be the cause of the general factor found among ability tests administered to children and among the "speeded or adaptation-requiring" (p. 178) tests administered to adults. Crystallized intelligence, on the other hand, was thought to consist of "discriminatory habits long established in a particular field" that were originally acquired through the operation of fluid ability but that no longer required "insightful perception" (p. 178). The empirical facts Cattell hoped to explain by this theory were the relative independence of individual differences in speed and power in adult intellectual performance and their different patterns of growth and decline. The important psychological distinction in the theory was between process (fluid intelligence) and product (crystallized intelligence) (Cattell, 1963).

The theory of fluid and crystallized ability attracted little attention, possibly because Cattell soon left Harvard for a research professorship at the University of Illinois. There he turned away from the study of human abilities and returned to his earlier research interest of applying the methods of factor analysis to the study of personality. He later wrote, "I had not learned...that more original and vital ideas than mine have collected dust on bookshelves for lack of exegesis by their parent or some scholarly leader" (Cattell, 1971, p. x). Twenty years were to elapse before Cattell was to return to the theory of fluid and crystallized abilities with new data. In the 1963 formulation of the theory, Gf was hypothesized to reflect the physiological integrity of the organism useful for adapting to novel situations that, when invested in particular learning experiences, produced Gc. Thus, Gf was now hypothesized to be physiologically determined, whereas Gc was "a product of environmentally varying, experientially determined investments of Gf." (Cattell, 1963, p. 4)

Although intuitively appealing, the hypothesis that Gf reflects physiological influences and is thus a better measure of the true intelligence of an individual is perhaps the most controversial aspect of the theory. Several prominent theorists accept the fluid-crystallized distinction, and some also subscribe to the investment theory of aptitude. But they do so without assuming that fluid ability represents something more innate than crystallized ability. For example, Cattell's student and collaborator, Horn (1976), interpreted Gf simply as "facility in reasoning, particularly in figural or non-word symbolic materials" (p. 445). Cronbach (1977) went even further and argued that "fluid ability is itself an achievement" that reflects the "residue of indirect learning from varied experience" (p. 287). More recently, Horn (1985) echoed the same theme: "There are good reasons to believe that Gf is learned as much as Gc, and that Gc is inherited as much as Gf" (p. 289). Gc, said Horn, reflects individual differences in "acculturation learning" whereas Gf reflects individual differences in "casual learning" and "independent thinking" (Horn, 1985, pp. 289–290). Horn and others point out that, if tests of fluid abilities were somehow better estimates of the physiological integrity of the organism and if achievement tests were more a product of experience, then scores on tests of fluid abilities should show relatively higher heritabilities, which they do not (Horn, 1985; Humphreys, 1981; Scarr & Carter-Saltzman, 1982). These theorists also reject using tests of fluid ability as measures of "capacity" or "potential" against which achievement can be gauged (Cronbach, 1977; Humphreys, 1985; R. L. Thorndike, 1963). On the contrary, some argue that fluid abilities are among the most important products of education and experience (Snow & Yalow, 1982).

Recent Changes in Gf–Gc Theory

The most important change in Gf–Gc theory in recent years has been the addition of several other second-order factors to the model. These developments are summarized somewhat differently by Cattell (1971) and by Horn (1985). Horn identified 10 second-order factors: two deep processing factors (Fluid Ability and Crystallized Ability), three perceptual organization factors (Visualization, Clerical Speed, and Auditory Thinking), three associational processing factors (Short-Term Acquisition and Retrieval, Long-Term Storage and Retrieval, and Correct Decision Speed), and two sensory reception factors (Visual Sensory Detection and Auditory Sensory Detection). Figure 1 shows how these factors can be arrayed along a continuum that progresses from surface to deep processing or from infancy to adulthood.

The model is frankly speculative. "I know very little about human abilities," writes Horn (1985). "All I can do is write articles about them, talk about them, and specify models for them. The more I talk and write and model, the more I realize how little I really know about this complex realm of human functioning" (p. 293). Nevertheless, the model summarizes much of what is known about the organization of human abilities, and it is, in the main, consistent with the abilities Carroll (in press) has thus far identified in his massive review and reanalyses of 60 years of factor-analytic studies of human abilities. Recent research on the four most widely studied broad factors in this model is presented in the next section.

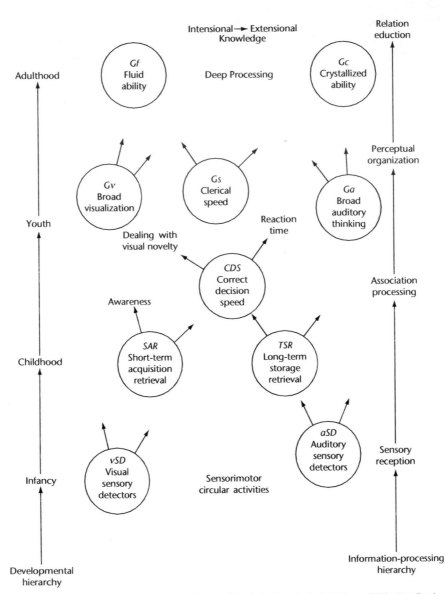

Note: From "Remodeling Old Models of Intelligence" by J. L. Horn in B. B. Wolman (Ed.), *Handbook of Intelligence* (p. 295). New York: John Wiley & Sons. Copyright 1985 by John Wiley & Sons, Inc. Reprinted by permission.

Figure 1: A model of ability organization within developmental and information processing hierarchies

Unpacking Existing Tests and Constructs

Tests of Fluid and Crystallized Abilities

Tests of fluid ability require novel problem solving, much like many of the intelligence tests developed during the first half of the century – particularly the so-called nonverbal or performance tests such as matrices or block design. These tests require subjects to reason with moderately novel figural or symbolic stimuli. For this reason, complex spatial tests often load strongly on the Gf factor (Lohman, 1979). Span tests and other measures of what Jensen (1969) calls *Level I* ability also often load significantly on the Gf factor (Horn, 1985). Tests of crystallized ability, on the other hand, require the examinee to display an understanding of concepts and skills taught in some domain, particularly in school. Verbal knowledge and skills are emphasized, although numerical computation and mechanical knowledge tests often load significantly on Gc factors.

Recently the Stanford-Binet was revised along the lines of the theory of fluid and crystallized abilities. The particular version of Gf–Gc theory on which the new Stanford-Binet is based combines the hierarchical model of intelligence of Vernon (Vernon, 1950) and the quasi-hierarchical model of intelligence of Cattell (1963). The three-level hierarchy includes a General Reasoning factor, G, at the top. Three broad group factors – Crystallized Abilities, Fluid-Analytic Abilities, and Short-Term Memory – constitute the second level. Three more specific factors make up the third level. G is interpreted "as consisting of the cognitive assembly and control processes that an individual uses to organize adaptive strategies for solving novel problems" (R. L. Thorndike, Hagen, & Sattler, 1986, p. 3). Thus, the authors adopt Snow's (1981) definition of Gf as their definition of G. This is a reasonable equation since the Gf factor is invariably highly (Cattell, 1971; Lohman, 1979), or even perfectly (Gustafsson, 1984), correlated with G. Crystallized abilities are represented by both verbal and quantitative reasoning tasks. These abilities "are greatly influenced by schooling, but they are also developed by more general experiences outside of school" (p. 4). Fluid-analytic abilities are estimated by figural and spatial tasks. Fluid abilities are thought to involve "the flexible reassembly of existing strategies to deal with novel situations." Further, the authors acknowledge that these abilities are also developed, but they are developed from more general experiences than schooling. Finally, the Short-Term Memory factor is represented by tests requiring memory for beads, sentences, digits, or objects. Thus, the new Stanford-Binet attempts to fit old tasks into a more recent theory of intelligence. But do we really understand these tasks well enough to defend the inference that different combinations of them reflect different abilities? What happens when we try to look at the processes subjects use when solving test items or when acquiring the knowledge they sample? In other words, is it possible to develop process theories of abilities?

Verbal-Crystallized Ability

Specific verbal processes.   Verbal abilities hold a prominent place in all theories of intelligence. It is not surprising, then, that some of the first efforts to understand intelligence in terms of cognitive processes focused on verbal abilities. Hunt and his colleagues have reported several studies of the information-processing characteristics of subjects who differed in verbal-crystallized abilities. Their work is of particular interest because it deals with an important facet of intelligence and because it shows the strengths and weaknesses of both the newer cognitive-experimental approach and the traditional correlational approach to the study of intelligence. The aim of this line of research is aptly summarized in the question, "What does it mean to be high verbal?" which was the title of a report by Hunt, Lunneborg, and Lewis (1975). The method used in this and several other studies was to select college students with extremely high or low scores on the verbal section of a college entrance examination, to administer to these subjects a battery of presumably well understood experimental tasks, to estimate information-processing scores for each subject on each experimental task, and then to relate these scores to scores on the reference verbal-ability tests using some type of correlational analysis.

For example, in one experimental task, subjects were required to compare pairs of letters of the alphabet, and to respond "yes," if the two letters were physically identical (as in "aa" or "AA"), or "no", if they were different (as in "aA" or "ab"). In a second task, similar pairs of letters were presented, but this time pairs were to be judged according to their names. Thus, in Task 1, the correct answer to the pair "Aa" would be "no," whereas in Task 2, the correct answer would be "yes." An information-processing model for Task 1 (Physical Comparison) would posit processes for encoding the appearance of the two letters, comparing these representations, and then responding. A model for Task 2 (Name Comparison) would include all of the processes required by Task 1 plus an additional process to retrieve the name codes. Thus, the difference between the time to respond to a given pair of letters in Task 2 and the same pair of letters in Task 1 provides an estimate of the time needed to perform this additional process. The resulting score is called the NIPI (Name Identity minus Physical Identity) difference and has been widely studied as a measure of the speed of accessing overlearned name codes. Correlations between the NIPI score and measures of verbal comprehension are typically about $r = -.3$, suggesting that subjects high in verbal ability access name codes faster than subjects low in verbal ability.[8]

These and other results are consistent with both a hierarchical model of human abilities and with current theories of the way knowledge is represented in memory. In particular, the information-processing tasks used by Hunt et al. (1975) appear to measure specific verbal abilities found in the lower branches of hierarchical models of abilities. Performance on many of these tasks depends on the subject's ability (a) to produce a rapid, fluent response and/or (b) to remember the order in which information was presented. This latter ability is sometimes represented in models of memory by a special type of memory code called a *linear order* (Anderson, 1983). Such a code preserves the sequential structure of an event: what came first, then next, then next, and last. Spelling tests require this sort of memory code; one must not only remember the correct letters but also their proper sequence. Similarly, sequencing arbitrary phonemes into words, such as when learning a new language, or sequencing arbitrary words into strings of words, such as when memorizing the names of the letters of the alphabet, days of the week, or lines in a poem, seems to depend in part on the ability to code information in this way.

Research relating scores on experimental tasks to scores on verbal ability tests also has revealed important limitations in efforts to generalize from laboratory tasks to test behavior. First, seemingly simple experimental tasks can measure different abilities in different subjects. For example, Hunt and others (see, e.g., Hunt, Lunneborg, & Lewis, 1975) have used a sentence verification task in which subjects are shown a phrase such as "star above plus" and a picture which either conforms with or contradicts the sentence. Subjects must determine whether the picture and sentence agree. However, minor variations in procedure can substantially alter the way subjects solve this task (Glushko & Cooper, 1978). More importantly, in any given procedure, subjects can differ in the way they solve the task: some create a mental picture from the phrase and compare it with the picture, and some convert the picture to a verbal description and compare that description with the phrase (Macleod, Hunt, & Mathews, 1978).

A second limitation stems from the low correlations between scores representing particular information processes on experimental tasks and scores on reference tests of verbal abilities. Keating and MacLean (1987) argue that the main contribution of the information-processing approach to the analysis of intelligence is that it permits investigators to identify particular mental processes such as rate of rotation or speed of lexical access. The value of the process approach diminishes quickly when these parameters show low correlations with other measures or with similarly labeled parameters derived from other tasks. Keating and MacLean are particularly critical of studies in which Hunt abandoned process parameters and instead defined latent "process factors" based on correlations among total reaction time (RT) or errors on experimental tasks. Using composite indices in this way, they claim, comes close to "dismissing the logic of the original cognitive correlates approach" (p. 259). Such composite indices cannot be used to "explain" composite indices computed in the same way on ability tests.

Part of the confusion here surely stems from different expectations about what process parameters represent. It is commonly assumed that, by fitting an information-processing model to a task and by decomposing a composite index (total correct or total latency) into component indices, one has also decomposed individual differences on the task into cleaner components. This is not the case. Actually, individual differences in component scores (e.g., rate of rotation) salvage individual differences relegated to the error term when performance for each individual is summarized in a single score such as number of problems solved correctly, or mean response latency. Recapturing variance from the error term might be a profitable activity but only when items on the task show poor internal consistency. Even then, it must be recognized that such scores do not represent a decomposition of the individual differences variance reflected in total or average scores.

Low correlations between scores thought to represent particular verbal processes and reference verbal-ability tests may also mean that much of the knowledge or some of the cognitive processes that account for general crystallized abilities (Gc) as measured by tests are not required by the experimental tasks. Experimental tasks in which subjects are required to infer the meaning of unfamiliar words from context sometimes show much higher correlations than do simple laboratory tasks with both Gc scores and general reasoning scores (Sternberg & Powell, 1983). This suggests that the low correlations obtained by Hunt et al. (1975) may estimate the contribution of specific verbal processes to Gc. Much of the remaining variability in Gc is better attributed to the ability to apply general reasoning skills and prior knowledge to the task of understanding verbal material and learning from it.

Reading comprehension.   Nowhere is this interdependence of specific component processes, general reasoning abilities, and prior knowledge better demonstrated than in reading. Reading comprehension is highly correlated with general verbal abilities, particularly in school-age populations. Thus, research on reading comprehension not only illuminates an important aspect of Gc but also shows how diagnostically useful tests can be derived from theory and how studies of individual differences can in turn reveal needed changes in the theory. J. R. Frederiksen's (1982) work is perhaps the best example of this reciprocity. Frederiksen began by developing a general model of reading from his own research and that of many other investigators. He eventually distinguished three types of information-processing skills used in reading: *word-analysis processes* (e.g., encoding single- and multiletter units, using phonics skills), *discourse analysis processes* (e.g., retrieving word meanings, resolving problems of reference), and *integrative processes* (e.g., combining information from pictures and text). Frederiksen then constructed a test battery to measure some of these skills. Measures were validated by using both experimental and correlational techniques. Later, training tasks were devised to assist poor readers in acquiring deficient skills.

Other theories of reading ability have been advanced in recent years. For example, Perfetti (1986) distinguishes three types of component processes in his theory: lexical access, proposition encoding, and text modeling. Lexical access refers to the process by which word meanings are activated in long-term memory. Individual word meanings are then combined and retained in working memory in predicate-like structures called propositions. These in turn are combined with the reader's prior schematic knowledge to form a text model. This model, then, represents the reader's understanding of the text. Kintsch (1986), in another theory of text comprehension, argues that two types of mental models must be coordinated: a text model, which contains the reader's representation of the propositions embedded in the text, and a situation model, which might be a mental image of the situation described by the text. For example, in following directions to assemble a toy, the text model might represent the ideas implied by the words, "Attach wheel K to spindle Q using two 5/16 washers and a large hex nut." The situation mental model might be represented by an image of what one is supposed to do. Pictures, illustrations, good description, metaphor, and analogy facilitate the generation of good situation models. A well structured text that follows a familiar schema and uses familiar words facilitates the construction of a coherent text model.

Mental models may be an important link in the individual difference equation as well. A central problem in the definition of verbal abilities has been the overlap between measures of reasoning abilities and measures of verbal comprehension. However, theories of reasoning (Holland, Holyoak, Nisbett, & Thagard, 1987; Johnson-Laird, 1983) also emphasize the construction and the coordination of mental models. Thus, process analyses reveal commonalities between tasks (and the ability constructs they define) not apparent in armchair analyses.

A similar argument may account for the high correlation between reasoning and vocabulary scores. The meaning of an unfamiliar word is usually inferred from the contexts in which the word has been embedded. (Daalen-Kapteijns & Elshout-Mohr, 1981; Marshalek, 1981; Sternberg & Powell, 1983). This process is most successful when the learner generates a good schema (or model or working hypothesis) about the meaning of an unfamiliar word when it is first encountered. This schema can then be confirmed or contradicted by evidence from subsequent contexts. Low-verbal subjects are less likely to use this strategy than are high-verbal subjects. Thus, vocabulary tests that use abstract words (i.e., words whose meanings are difficult to infer from a single context) show higher correlations with reasoning than do vocabulary tests of comparable difficulty composed of infrequent words (Marshalek, 1981).

Spatial-Visualization Ability

Spatial tasks have long been used as psychological tests. Before 1915, Porteus had used such "performance" tasks to estimate the intelligence of linguistically different or disabled examinees. Spearman also originally used such "performance" tests as a measure of g, a tradition he attributes to Itard (1801, cited in Spearman & Wynn Jones, 1950). Spatial tasks also figured prominently in the Army Beta examinations of World War I. However, beginning with Kelley (1928) and then El Koussy (1935), such tasks were studied in their own right, and several specific spatial abilities were identified (Smith, 1964). Nevertheless, spatial or figural reasoning tasks have continued in their role as measures of general abilities, particularly Gf.

As with verbal abilities, cognitive research on spatial abilities may be divided into (a) attempts to develop general theories of spatial thinking that ignore individual differences (e.g., Pinker, 1984; Shepard & Cooper, 1982), and (b) attempts to explain individual differences on existing tests of spatial abilities, either through correlations between scores on spatial tests and performance on laboratory tasks or through the construction of information-processing models for particular spatial tests. In contrast to recent research on verbal abilities, however, only a few studies have examined correlations between scores from laboratory tasks and scores from existing tests. Instead, most effort has been directed toward attempts to build information-processing models that describe how subjects solve particular spatial tests (see, e.g., Pellegrino & Kail, 1982). This is because most spatial tests are process-intensive in the same way that most verbal tests are knowledge-intensive. In other words, although some interesting processing occurs when subjects take a vocabulary test (Sternberg & McNamara, 1985), most of the complex processing occurred at the time the words were learned. Conversely, although spatial knowledge has an important impact on spatial problem solving (Lohman, 1988), whether subjects solve such problems depends heavily on the processes they employ during the test.

Theories of spatial thinking (e.g., Kosslyn, 1980) distinguish two types of spatial knowledge: knowledge best modeled by quasi-pictorial mental representations (e.g., appearance of a particular object) and knowledge best modeled by abstract, proposition-based memory representations (concepts of symmetry, proportionality, closure, etc.). Each type of representation can be transformed by a different class of mental operators or procedural knowledge. Quasi-pictorial representations can be subjected to various analog transformations such as a rotation or synthesis (Shepard & Cooper, 1982). Propositional representations can be subjected to the same general and specific cognitive operators (e.g., means ends analysis) that can be applied to propositional knowledge derived from other sources (e.g., linguistic inputs). Transformations such as rotation, then, are of interest primarily for the constraints they place on the type of mental representation used. Thus, many spatial-ability tests present items which seem to require for their solution analog transformations such as rotation, reflection, transposition, or synthesis.

Research on how subjects solve spatial tests has turned up several surprises. One persistent finding has been that all subjects rarely solve figural tasks in the same way. For example, in a series of experiments on visual comparison processes, Cooper (1982) identified two markedly different strategies. Some subjects appeared to rely on a serial, analytic process to compare forms whereas others relied on a parallel, holistic process. Complex tasks – such as the paper-folding tasks or form-board tasks commonly seen in mental tests – elicit an even wider range of alternative solution methods. Some subjects solve items on such tests by generating mental images that they then transform holistically. These high-spatial subjects excel in generating, retaining, and transforming mental representations that preserve information about the configuration of a figure. They also use their spatial knowledge to decompose unfamiliar visual shapes into simpler, more familiar shapes. Other subjects rely on general reasoning skills or external aids (such as line drawings) to solve problems. Others use still different processes. But most subjects use more than one type of processing, generally shifting from one strategy to another as problems increase in difficulty (Lohman, 1988). Such within-subject variability in solution strategy challenges simple information-processing models of spatial tests. Strategy shifting may partially explain why complex spatial tests are often good measures of g or Gf. Appropriate flexibility in adapting solution methods to meet personal limitations and changing item demands appears to be a central aspect of any process theory of Gf (Snow & Lohman, 1989).

Fluid-Reasoning Ability

There has been considerably more research on reasoning or general fluid ability than on either general crystallized or general visualization abilities. However, attempts to understand how subjects solve Gf tasks such as analogies, classification, and series completion that have ignored differences in processing strategy (by averaging over items) or reduced the need for alternative strategies (by drastically simplifying items) have generally produced experimental tasks that show little relationship with scores on reference Gf tests. Put another way, simple items that are all solved in the same way by all subjects probably require little of what we call intelligence.

The effects of simplifying a complex task so that it could be studied experimentally and ignoring within-person strategy shifts were perhaps most evident in Sternberg's (1977) first investigation of analogical reasoning. Sternberg hypothesized that subjects use several different or "component" processes when solving analogies such as "Up is to down as left is to (a) back (b) right" or A:B::C:D1, D2. According to Sternberg's theory, subjects (a) first read and understand each term in the analogy (*encoding*), (b) determine the relationship between the A and B terms (*inference*), (c) infer the relationship between the A and C terms (*mapping*), (d) generate an ideal answer by applying the A-B relationship to C (*application*), and (e) compare their ideal answer with the options provided (*comparison*). If none of the presented options meet the subjects' criterion for acceptability, they then recycle through some or all of the preceding steps (*justification*) and finally choose an option and respond (*response*). Component processes were assumed to be executed serially. Different models were then formulated by deleting particular processes (e.g., mapping, justification) and by specifying different modes of execution for a given process (e.g., self-terminating or exhaustive). Three important results were obtained. First, models were quite successful in accounting for variabilities in response latencies and, to a lesser extent, in response errors. Second, the data from most subjects were well fitted by a single model, suggesting that most subjects used the same strategy. Third, estimates of speed of executing particular component operations showed small and inconsistent relationships with reference reasoning tests. Unexpectedly, the highest correlations were observed for the preparation-response component. Thus, the componential analysis appeared successful, but those components hypothesized to reflect the essence of reasoning seemed not to measure reasoning at all.

Later studies in which better practiced subjects attempted more complex items did show significant correlations between component scores and scores on reasoning tests (Bethell-Fox, Lohman, & Snow, 1984; Sternberg & Gardner, 1983). It appears that problems must be more than trivially difficult before individual differences in reasoning are observed. Further, items must also vary somewhat in the processing demands they place on examinees.[9] This means that problems must be moderately novel.

Novelty is an ancient theme in the psychology of individual differences. From Stern (1912/1914) to Sternberg (1985), theorists have argued that intelligence is best displayed when tasks are relatively novel. Cognitive psychologists are only beginning to understand how subjects transfer prior learning to analogous situations (Gick & Holyoak, 1983). The problem, of course, is that what is novel for one person may not be novel for another person or even for the same person at a different time. It appears that inferences about how subjects solve items that require higher level processing must be probabilistic, since the novelty of each item varies for each person.

Snow (1981) has integrated these and other research results in the following hypothesis on the nature of fluid and crystallized abilities.

> Gc may represent prior assemblies of performance processes retrieved as a system and applied anew in instructional or other performance situations not unlike those experienced in the past, while Gf may represent new assemblies of performance processes needed for more extreme adaptations to novel situations. The distinction is between long-term assembly for transfer to familiar situation vs. short-term assembly for transfer to unfamiliar situations. Both functions develop through exercise, and perhaps both can be understood as variations on a central production system development. (p. 360)

The point about "exercise" derives from E. L. Thorndike's (1903) theory of learning whereas the point about "production system" derives from the ACT* model of Anderson (1983), which is discussed later.

Mental Speed

The fourth and last broad factor in Horn's (1985) model that will be examined here is sometimes called General Speed, sometimes Clerical Speed, or sometimes simply, Mental Speed. There is a new interest in this construct, whatever it is called. However, like most other ability constructs, mental speed has a long history in educational and psychological measurement. E. L. Thorndike, Spearman, and Thurstone all addressed the question of whether mental speed should be distinguished from power (or altitude). For example, although mental speed was one of the four dimensions of his model of intelligence, E. L. Thorndike considered speed less important than altitude (see E. L. Thorndike et al., 1926). On the other hand, Spearman (1927), citing studies which showed high correlations between scores on a time limit test and scores on the same test after an extended period of time, concluded (erroneously) that speed and power (or altitude) were interchangeable. Thurstone (1937) proposed a three-dimensional model that related ability, speed, and motivation. Like E. L. Thorndike, he defined ability in terms of power or altitude in his model (although many of the ability factors he identified in his empirical studies were based on simple, highly speeded tests).

Individual differences in mental speed have been studied in several paradigms, two of which are summarized here. Research in the first paradigm at first sought to estimate the subjects' "natural" rate of thinking (Hunsicker, 1925). This search led to the identification of several personality factors such as Carefulness, Persistence, and Impulsivity that described subjects' typical trade-off between speed and accuracy. It also led to the identification of several cognitive speed factors, such as Perceptual Speed, Clerical Speed, and eventually, to claims of a General Speed factor.

Research in the second paradigm, which may be traced back to Galton (1869) has sought to define intelligence as a physiological rather than as a psychological or sociocultural construct. Thus, the aim is to determine the integrity and efficiency of neurological mechanisms thought to underlie intelligent thought and action. Preferred indicators of intelligence in this paradigm are measures of sensory acuity, speed of detecting a stimulus or discriminating between two stimuli, and, in more recent work, patterns in recordings of electrical activity in the brain. Correlations are then computed between these measures and more global indices of intelligence, such as teacher ratings, course grades, or scores on existing intelligence tests. Work in this paradigm had hardly begun when it was abandoned by most psychologists, partly because of studies like that of Wissler (1901), but perhaps in larger measure because of the success of Binet's test. Wissler, working under the direction of James McKeen Cattell at Columbia (who had in turn worked with Galton for a short time), found that a measure of RT was uncorrelated with grade point average in a sample of university students. The RT paradigm has recently been revived by Jensen, Eysenck, and others.

Speed factors.   Variation in the relative emphasis tests placed on speed or level of performance is an important confound in much of the literature on human abilities. The primary factors identified by Thurstone and his followers, particularly Guilford, were often defined by tests that contained simple, similar, highly speeded items. Complex versions of the same tests administered under conditions which emphasize level or altitude invariably show stronger loadings on the general factor and little evidence of the fractionalization of ability that occurs when simple, speeded tests are administered (Lohman, 1979). This is because individual differences in the speed with which subjects can solve relatively simple problems in a domain show only weak correlation with the complexity of a problem of the same type which subjects can solve when time is not a factor (Horn, 1985; Kyllonen, 1985).

The question remains, though, whether some or all of these various speed primaries may define a higher order or General Speed factor. Although several investigators have claimed to have identified a General Speed factor, closer examination shows that such factors are often little more than overblown Clerical Speed or Perceptual Speed factors. General differences in speed of processing may well exist, but they are difficult to identify by factor analyzing speed scores from a battery of tests. The major reasons are that one cannot make unambiguous comparisons of response latencies across individuals unless (a) all subjects correctly solve all items, (b) all subjects adopt the same trade-off between speed and accuracy, and (c) neither of these factors vary systematically across tasks. One way to avoid these problems would be to use a single task that is so simple that everyone can solve it and that is not much influenced by the individual's decision to emphasize speed or accuracy. Recent studies of reaction time aim to fit both of these criteria.

Recent research on reaction time.   The primary dependent measure in much cognitive research is response latency, usually on simple tasks. Those who study individual differences raised the question of whether individual differences in latencies on these laboratory tasks would show any relationship with individual differences on other tasks that presumably required the same processes (Underwood, 1975) or with ability variables commonly assessed by mental tests (Hunt et al., 1973; Snow et al., 1976). But the main goal of researchers like Hunt, Snow, and Sternberg was to develop and test information-processing models of theoretically interesting cognitive tasks or of tests commonly used to estimate important ability constructs, not to propose new measures of mental speed. However, this was precisely the goal of another group of researchers. Led by Jensen in the United States and Eysenck in the United Kingdom, these researchers saw possibilities for new measures of intelligence in response latencies on simple tasks and other indices of cognitive efficiency presumably unaffected by intention or experience.

Jensen's work.   Jensen sparked new interest in the relationship between RT and G (intelligence) by showing significant correlations between choice (or discrimination) RT and measures of G. Jensen's work has generated much discussion. In part this is because his goal seems to be to isolate a culture-free measure of intelligence. Individual and group differences on such a measure could then not be interpreted "as reflecting only differences in cognitive contents and skills that persons have chanced to learn in school or acquire in a cultured home" (Jensen, 1980, p. 704).

The apparatus Jensen has used in his studies contains a center "home button" surrounded by 8 light/button pairs. Different light/button pairs can be covered to manipulate the number of stimulus–response pairs between 1 and 8. The task is to hold a finger on the home button until one of the exposed lights is activated and then turn it off as quickly as possible by moving the finger from the home button to the button directly below the activated light. Two time intervals are recorded: (a) the time between the onset of the stimulus light and the release of the home button (called RT), and (b) the additional time required to move the finger to the button below the activated light and press it (called movement time). In a typical experiment, subjects receive a few practice trials, followed by 15 trials at each of four levels of task complexity: 1, 2, 4, or 8 light/button pairs exposed. Typically, RT increases linearly with the log of the number of buttons exposed. Jensen found that the slope of this function, which is taken as an estimate of the rate at which a person processes a single unit of information, and G correlated negatively, with. $r = -.41$ being the most often cited correlation. In addition, the correlation between RT and G increases as task complexity is increased from 1 to 8 light/button pairs, suggesting that the greater the information-processing burden, the greater the demand on G.

Jensen's work has been praised by some (e.g., Eysenck, 1982) and criticized by others (e.g., Longstreth, 1984; Carroll, 1987). In particular, Jensen's claim that performance on the choice RT task is not influenced by practice, motivation, or instructions to alter speed-accuracy trade-off has been questioned (Carroll, 1987; Longstreth, 1984). Longstreth also raises a number of fundamental questions about Jensen's procedure, such as the routine confounding of practice with task complexity. Carroll questions the replicability and interpretation of Jensen's results. He suggests that differences between individuals in average RT may better be described as differences in the variability in RT for a given person over trials. This is because RTs have a lower limit, and thus individuals with more variable RTs would tend to have higher mean RTs because they are more likely to deviate upward from the lower limit. This suggests that the observed correlation between RT and G may in part reflect differences in attentional control and not simply differences in the speed of neural conduction or the rate of neural oscillation, as Jensen hypothesizes.

Attempts to replicate Jensen's findings usually find some relationship between RT and G (most often between the variability of RTs for individual subjects and G, with lower G subjects having more variable RTs). But replications consistently fail to find that low G subjects show greater increases in RT with increases in the number of exposed light/button pairs than do high G subjects (Barrett, Eysenck, & Lucking, 1986; Carlson, C. M. Jensen, & Widaman, 1983; Jensen, 1987).

Although controversy about Jensen's work continues, there is some consensus on the main findings. First, correlation between G and RT is generally somewhat lower for the simple RT condition (one light/button pair exposed) than for the discriminative RT conditions (two or more light/button pairs exposed). Second, correlations between discrimination RT and G vary widely. However, replicable correlations are generally in the −.2 to −.4 range. Conditions with more light/button pairs (e.g., 8) do not yield dependably higher correlations with G than conditions with fewer light/button pairs (e.g. 2). Indeed, it is a common finding that correlations between RT and G decline as more and more complex information processing is required. More complex tasks allow multiple strategies and are prone to differences in the speed–accuracy trade-off subjects adopt. Third, the variability in RT over trials often correlates as highly with G as does mean or median RT. Thus, attention control (or, conversely, distractibility) may be as important as speed of processing in this task. Fourth, Jensen's claim that RT increases linearly with the log of the number of exposed light/button pairs has been repeatedly confirmed. However, other investigators have not been able to confirm his claim that individual differences in the slope of this line correlate with G. It is unclear whether this is due to persistent methodological inadequacies in these studies (which usually follow Jensen's procedures), as Longstreth (1984) notes, or whether this reflects a more fundamental error in Jensen's theory, as Eysenck (1987b) now claims.

Eysenck's work. Eysenck (1982; 1988) has proposed a theory of intelligence with an even stronger physiological flavor. Following Hebb (1949), Eysenck (1988) distinguished among biological intelligence, psychometric intelligence, and social intelligence. Biological intelligence "refers to the structure of the human brain, its physiology, biochemistry, and genetics which are responsible for the possibility of intelligent action" (p. 3). Eysenck considers biological intelligence to be the purest, most fundamental intelligence because it is "least adulterated by social factors." He claims it can be measured by the electroencephalogram (EEG), evoked potentials, galvanic skin responses, and perhaps reaction times.

Psychometric intelligence is defined as that intelligence which is measured by psychometric tests. In addition to the core of biological intelligence, is determined by cultural factors, education, family upbringing, and socioeconomic status. However, since only a fraction of the variance in psychometric intelligence (i.e., IQ) can be attributed to genetic factors (Eysenck estimates 70%), IQ should not be confused with biological intelligence.

Social intelligence reflects the ability to solve problems an individual encounters in life. But since so many noncognitive factors are reflected in such performances, Eysenck (1988) argues that "social intelligence is far too inclusive a concept to have any kind of scientific meaning" (p. 45). Thus, for Eysenck, intelligence is a concept that is best studied at the physiological (or even neurological) level, only indirectly represented in intelligence tests, and obscured almost entirely in performances in the real world. This is an extreme view and is not widely shared, at least not by American academics.

As with Jensen's work, much of the controversy surrounding Eysenck's work has centered not so much on the finding of significant correlations between G and EEGs, cortical evoked potentials, and other physiological indices but on the reported magnitude of the correlations. For example, Eysenck's colleague, Hendrickson (1982), reported a correlation of $r = .83$ between a measure of evoked potentials and Wechsler IQ for a sample of 219 15-year old children. In 1984, Eysenck claimed that "several replications... have shown the results are essentially reproducible" and that these results were "a most important validation of Galton's concept" of intelligence (published in Eysenck, 1987a, p. 359). However, by 1988, presumably on the basis of new evidence, Eysenck had changed his mind. "It seems unlikely that the correlation between IQ and a physiological measurement of biological intelligence... can exceed the square root of the heritability of IQ," and thus correlations such as those obtained by Hendrickson (1982) are "inherently improbable and unlikely to be replicated" (Eysenck, 1988, p. 12).

Inspection time. A similar history attends the reports on correlations between inspection time and IQ. Inspection time is the minimum duration for which two different stimuli must be presented if they are to be perceived as different. Nettelbeck and Lally (1976) reported a correlation of $r = -.92$ between the Wechsler Adult Intelligence Scale performance scale and inspection time, but, for a sample of only 10 subjects, 2 of which were retarded. The magnitude of the reported correlations gradually declined as larger and less wide-ranging samples were tested. By 1984, Irwin reported correlations of $r = -.32$ and $r = -.09$ for auditory and visual inspection times with a verbal intelligence test and correlations of $r = -.23$ and $r = -.27$ for those same inspection times with a nonverbal intelligence test for a sample of 50 12-year-old children.

In the meantime, Nettlebeck and Kirby (1983) had gathered new data on a large sample of adults and had reanalyzed data from one of their earlier studies. This time they found no correlation between G and slope in the Jensen task and a weak correlation between inspection time and G ($r = -.3$) when retarded subjects were excluded. They therefore concluded that their earlier correlations had been inflated by the inclusion of retarded subjects, who were "markedly less efficient" (p. 39) on these tasks. Their conclusions run completely counter to earlier claims:

> This outcome raised doubt about the validity of combining data from retarded and nonretarded subjects. Our results ran counter to claims that tasks of the kind used [in this study] are largely uninfluenced by cognitive

variables [such as strategy], so that findings are not necessarily explained satisfactorily in terms of a mental speed factor. These measures of timed performance do not, at this time, provide a basis from which a reliable, culture-fair measure of intelligence might be devised. (p. 39)

Summary. Critics of studies that report correlations between measures such as RT, inspection time, evoked potentials, and G cynically argue that the best predictor of the correlation obtained is the date of the study. The first correlation reported is usually strikingly high, but then the magnitude of the reported correlation declines almost linearly with year of publication, eventually stabilizing on a value in the $-.1$ to $-.4$ range. Such correlations are theoretically interesting, but they do not justify attempts to replace existing intelligence tests with RT measures, or interpretations of G as a purely physiological phenomena.

One need not descend to the level of neurons to find a plausible account of the role of mental speed in models of intelligence. For example, the rate at which activation spreads through regions of memory, the rate at which an activated memory loses its activation, and the level of activation needed to allow further processing are all important constructs in modern theories of memory (Anderson, 1983). Direct study of these variables would seem more useful than the study of isolated tasks that have not been designed to estimate specific cognitive processes. Even then, variables thought to reflect the physiological action of the cortex are useful only to the extent that they predict individual differences in behavior labeled "intelligent" in the culture. E. L. Thorndike saw this clearly:

> Psychologists would of course assume that differences in intelligence are due to differences histological or physiological, or both, and would expect these physical bases of intelligence to be measurable.... [However], even if one aimed at discovering the physiological basis of intellect and measuring it in physiological units, one would have to begin by measuring the intellectual products produced by it. For our only means of discovering physiological bases is search for the physiological factors which correspond to intellectual production. (E. L. Thorndike et al., 1926, p. 12)

Individual differences in mental speed have an important impact on all of cognition. But neither theory nor empirical evidence justifies attempts to define G in terms of speed, while ignoring the larger contributions of level or altitude in both process and knowledge to this construct we call intelligence.

Attempts to Move Beyond Existing Tests

It has long been recognized that theories of human intelligence have been limited by the selection of tasks included in particular intelligence tests or in factor-analytic studies of abilities. Several theorists (e.g., Cattell, 1971;

Guilford, 1959) have proposed schemes for defining the universe of intelligent behaviors, cognitive functions or tasks. The framework can then be used to select or construct tests of different facets of intelligence. In this section, I briefly survey two rational models of this sort; Guilfor's (1959, 1985) structure of the intellect (SOI) model and Sternberg's (1985) triarchic theory of intelligence.

Guilford's SOI Model

As director of the Aviation Psychology Research Unit during World War II, Guilford saw the number of factorially defined abilities grow as tests were developed to measure abilities hypothesized to be important in the training and performance of air crews. After the war, he continued to investigate new abilities in his Aptitudes Research Project at the University of Southern California. By the mid-1950s, approximately 40 ability factors had been identified in one or both of these efforts (Guilford, 1985). In searching for a way to organize these factors and guide the search for new abilities, Guilford hit upon the idea of grouping abilities by a three-way classification: by the kind of mental process required, by the kind of information processed, and by the mental products generated. The combination of five types of mental processes, four types of content, and six types of product defined the 120 abilities in the structure of the intellect model.[10]

Although the model has generated considerable research, it has declined in influence in recent years. Questions have been raised about the factor-analytic methods used to identify factors (Horn & Knapp, 1973), about the seeming fractionation of ability (McNemar, 1964, called the scheme "scatter-brained"), and about the adequacy of the SOI model itself. Some of these challenges have been countered. Elshout, van Hemert, and van Hemert (1975) showed that Guilford's Procrustean factor-analytic methods were not as bad as Horn and Knapp (1973) had claimed. Following Humphreys' (1962) suggestion, Guilford (1985) countered criticisms of fractionation by agreeing that higher order abilities may be defined by averaging over cells within the SOI model. In addition, he countered objections that the model did not include auditory abilities by adding another level to the content facet for auditory abilities – raising the total number of cells in the model from 120 to 150. Nevertheless, levels of facets have no convincing foundation other than rational appeal, and the entire product dimension remains poorly validated (Cronbach & Snow, 1977). Excepting the addition of 30 new auditory abilities, over 20 years of research has produced no substantive changes in the model. Perhaps this is because research sought to demonstrate the validity of the model rather than to identify and correct its weaknesses.

Triarchic Theory

Overview of the theory.   Sternberg's (1985) theory of intelligence contains three subtheories: a contextual subtheory, an experiential subtheory, and a componential subtheory. The contextual subtheory attempts to specify those behaviors that would be considered intelligent in a particular culture. Sternberg argues that, in any culture, contextually intelligent behavior involves purposeful adaptation to the present environment, selection of an optimal environment, or shaping of the present environment to fit better one's skills, interests, and values. The nature of the adaptation, selection, or shaping can vary importantly across cultures. For example, navigational skills, hunting skills, and academic skills are highly valued as markers of intelligence in different cultures.

However, even if a particular task is thought to require intelligence, contextually appropriate behavior is not equally "intelligent" at all points along the continuum of experience with that class of tasks. According to the experiential subtheory, intelligence is best demonstrated when the task or situation is relatively novel or when learners are practicing their responses to the task so that they can respond automatically and effortlessly. Although many have suggested that tasks must be moderately novel to measure intelligence, Sternberg's theory is unique in its claim that the ability to automatize processing is also a good indicator of intelligence. To date, no convincing evidence has been advanced to support this hypothesis.

In the componential subtheory, Sternberg attempts to specify the cognitive structures and processes that underlie all intelligent behavior. Contextually appropriate behavior at relevant points in the experiential continuum is said to be intelligent to the extent to which it involves certain types of processes. Three types of processes are hypothesized: *metacomponents*, which control processing and enable one to monitor and evaluate it; *performance components*, which execute plans assembled by the metacomponents; and *knowledge acquisition components*, which selectively encode and combine new information and selectively compare new information to old information.

Thus, Sternberg's contextual subtheory describes what types of tasks, situations, and behaviors might be considered intelligent. It is relativistic with respect to individuals and to the sociocultural settings in which they live. In the United States, the prevailing contextual theory of intelligence involves problem-solving, or fluid abilities; knowledge-based, or crystallized abilities; and social and practical abilities. The experiential subtheory claims that intelligence is relative to each individual's experience with the task or situation. Only the componential subtheory claims to describe the mechanisms of thought that would be used in any intelligent act.

Evaluation of the Triarchic Theory.   Some argue that intelligence as measured in the tradition of Binet and Wechsler is best construed as scholastic aptitude. This tendency to narrow the scope of intelligence tests has been countered repeatedly by those who would extend measurement to domains such as social intelligence (E. L. Thorndike, 1920), creativity (Guilford, 1959), or musical ability (Gardner, 1983) that are sampled inadequately or not at all by existing tests. Those who would extend the purview of existing tests tend to view *intelligence* as an adjective rather than a noun and argue that tests of intelligence should sample all domains of activity that are valued as intelligent in the culture. Sometimes these unmeasured abilities are essential features of the theorist's implicit theory of intelligence or that of a larger social group.

Those who view *intelligence* as a noun usually equate intelligence with individual differences in a particular type of cognition, such as "eduction of relations and correlates" (Spearman, 1927) or "judgment" (Binet & Simon, 1905). However, others view the noun as a shorthand expression for all individual differences in cognition and argue that a good test of intelligence presupposes a good theory of cognition (Hunt, 1986) or at least a good sample of "the repertoire of intellectual skills and knowledge available to the person at a particular point in time" (Humphreys, 1986, p. 98). Sternberg's triarchic theory attempts to satisfy both of these demands. His contextual theory recognizes the cultural relativity implied when intelligence is treated as an adjective, and his componential theory "[covers] most if not all of the territory of cognitive psychology" (Carroll, 1986, p. 325).

Reactions to Sternberg's theory have been mixed. Some argue that his triarchic theory is not a theory at all but a "conceptualization" of intelligence (Humphreys, 1984). Sternberg's theory for testing implies that one should model individual performance on cognitive tasks that represent fluid and crystallized abilities, so that component scores and solution strategy may be estimated for the individual; recognize that comparisons of individuals and especially of groups may be misleading, because tasks are differentially novel or practiced for different individuals and groups; and broaden the sample of tasks included on intelligence tests to better represent skills in adapting to the environment, shaping the environment, or selecting new environments. Here, Sternberg (1985) sees a special need for tests that measure "real-world" or practical intelligence. In several studies, questionnaires designed to assess repondents' tacit knowledge about managing self, others, and career have shown moderate correlations with various objective criteria of success in the domain (Wagner & Sternberg, 1986). Cronbach (1986) agrees that this is a worthwhile goal for measurement, but he is unimpressed with the verbal tests of practical intelligence Sternberg has thus far developed. He claims that Sternberg's tests are "quizzes on gamesmanship" (p. 24). Sternberg counters that scores on his questionnaires are generally uncorrelated with measures of verbal intelligence.

Perhaps Ford's (1986) research on the measurement of social intelligence can provide some useful cues for the measurement of practical intelligence. He argues that better measures can be obtained when social intelligence is defined in terms of outcomes (i.e., social competencies) rather than in terms of social cognition (e.g., understanding verbal or pictorial displays of social events). However, practical and social intelligence differ in several respects, and each has its roots in a different tradition. Whereas research on social intelligence stemmed from the observation that academic intelligence was no guarantee of social competence, research on practical intelligence began with the observation that academic intelligence was also no guarantee of "common sense." Thus, studies of social intelligence are rooted in the research on social judgments, whereas studies of practical intelligence developed from research on "tacit" knowledge – that is, knowledge that is not explicitly taught or discussed but that may facilitate performance or even be necessary for success in some domain.

Whether or not Sternberg succeeds in his efforts to develop new measures of practical intelligence or better measures of other aspects of intelligence, he has clearly succeeded in unifying diverse – even antagonistic – traditions in research on intelligence.

> With his prolific research, writing, and editing activities, Robert Sternberg has probably done more than any other contemporary psychologist to bring back into attention fundamental questions about intelligence – what it is, how it can best be observed and measured, and how it relates to other domains of behavior. (Carroll, 1986, p. 325)

Integrative Theories in Cognitive Science

All of the research efforts described to this point have involved the study of individual differences, either in existing tests of intelligence or achievement, or in tasks taken from the laboratories of experimental cognitive psychologists. However, there is an obvious circularity in attempts to understand the nature of intelligence by studying existing tests of intelligence or by identifying the information-processing characteristics of people who have been labeled high or low ability because of their scores on existing tests. Attempts to specify the cognitive character of the target behaviors or achievements such tests aim to predict expand the circle significantly but do not remove the circularity. What is needed is a general theory of human cognition. Measurements of individual differences could then be derived from this theory rather than in a theoretical vacuum. There have been several attempts to put theory before assessment, particularly in the measurement of reading disabilities (Frederiksen, 1982) and (less successfully) in the measurement of spatial abilities (Poltrock & Brown, 1984). But the term *intelligence* connotes a much broader effort.

A central question in cognitive science is whether human cognition is best modeled as a unitary system or as a collection of independent systems or modules. This debate parallels the Spearman-Thorndike/Thurstone controversy over g versus multiple factors in differential psychology (see R. M. Thorndike & Lohman, 1989). Much early theorizing presumed a unitary system, as Newell and Simon (1972) advocated in their General Problem Solver. This program aimed to solve a broad array of reasoning problems using general heuristics. By the late 1970s, however, the pendulum was beginning to swing the other way. Led by Chomsky (1980) and Fodor (1981), a modular view of cognition gained popularity. Modularists argue that the mind is best construed as a collection of independent information-processing systems, including systems for language, visual processing, music, and other specialized mental contents. Chomsky even describes such faculties as "mental organs," analogous to physical organs such as the heart. Modularists point to findings from neuropsychology on apparent localization of different mental functions in different regions of the brain and to factor-analytic and other studies of individual differences which show that musical, spatial, numerical, and other abilities can be distinguished (Gardner, 1983). Most modularists deny the need for a central or executive processor. Some recognize these higher thought processes but argue that cognitive science cannot explain them (Fodor, 1981). [Modularists recognize higher thought processes, but they deny the need for a central or executive processor and argue that cognitive science also cannot explain them (Fodor, 1981)].

Anderson's ACT* Theory

Several research efforts, most notably that of Anderson and his colleagues, have opposed this side of modularity. In a series of monographs (Anderson & Bower, 1973; Anderson, 1976, 1983), Anderson has developed and refined his Adaptive Control of Thought (ACT) system, culminating in the latest version, ACT*. The system is too complex to describe more than its general features here. (The reader is referred to Chap. 1 of Anderson, 1983.)

First, Anderson (1983) claims that all "higher cognitive processes, such as memory, language, problem solving, imagery, deduction, and induction, are different manifestations of the same underlying system" (p. 1). Nevertheless, ACT* posits special-purpose "peripheral systems" that convert information presented to the senses into distinctive perception-based memory representations or codes, such as images (that preserve information about configuration) and temporal strings (that preserve information about temporal order). Other perception-based memory codes (e.g., olfactory, kinesthetic) seem likely, but they have not been much studied. The peripheral systems that create and process these perception-based codes function like the modules Fodor posits.

Higher cognitive processes, however, are thought to depend more heavily on a different type of memory representation that preserves the meaning of an event. Indeed, Anderson (1983, 1985) argues that this type of abstract code dominates long-term memory, even for memories that might appear to be more perception based. For example, much of what we remember about a visual scene depends on our interpretation and understanding of the visual display. On this view, meaning-based representations (such as the idea of roundness) are derived from particular perception-based memories (such as memories for many particular round objects).

This multicode theory of memory has several interesting analogs in research on individual differences. For example, specific learning disabilities may be caused by a dysfunction in one or more peripheral systems that encode information from the environment into memory or decode the products of thinking into particular responses. Conversely, the dominance of the meaning-based code in human cognition corresponds to the dominance of the general factor in individual differences on complex tasks that seemingly emphasize different mental contents or processes. Indeed, general ability – as typically estimated – may reflect the ability to create, transform, and retain meaning-based mental representations (Snow & Lohman, 1989).

A second feature of Anderson's ACT* theory that can inform theorizing about intelligence is the distinction between declarative and procedural knowledge. These two types of knowledge are posited in many, although certainly not all, AI theories. Declarative knowledge is knowing that something is the case. Procedural knowledge is knowing how to do something.[11] Declarative knowledge is represented by a network in which nodes are like idea units, and procedural knowledge is represented by conditional imperatives of the form, "If a certain condition holds, then perform a certain action." Thus, procedural knowledge is dynamic; declarative is static. Procedural knowledge can be executed automatically, even unconsciously; declarative knowledge is often accessed slowly and consciously. Each is also acquired with different proficiency and by different methods. On one hand, new declarative knowledge can be acquired relatively quickly (often in a single trial), often by elaborating relationships with previously acquired knowledge. On the other hand, proceduralization generally requires more extensive practice.

The declarative-procedural distinction has several implications for a theory of intelligence. First, cognitive skills are modeled as forms of procedural knowledge in ACT*. Therefore, those parts of the theory which describe how declarative knowledge is converted to procedural knowledge also describe an important aspect of ability development. Second, the theory predicts the gradual differentiation of abilities some have hypothesized (Garrett, 1946; Anastasi, 1970), and it can explain how the same task (e.g., division) can require general problem-solving skills for the inexperienced examinee and specific problem-solving skills for the more experienced examinee. Third, attempts to measure declarative and procedural knowledge suggest new ways to separate students' factual knowledge in a domain from their ability to solve unfamiliar problems in the domain. This is an old (Lindquist, 1948) but seldom attained goal in educational measurement. Attempts to assess declarative knowledge usually involve the construction of a map of the examinee's factual knowledge base. Attempts to assess procedural knowledge emphasize speed of solving problems, methods of classifying them, or errors made in such processing.

Kyllonen and Christal (1989a) have shown that Anderson's theory can be used as a general framework for the assessment of individual differences. They argue that individual differences on a wide variety of cognitive tasks arise from differences in four primary sources: cognitive processing speed, working memory capacity, breadth and pattern of declarative knowledge, and breadth and pattern of procedural knowledge. Working memory occupies a central position in ACT* and in applications of the four-sources framework to problems of skill acquisition (Woltz, 1988) and reasoning abilities (Kyllonen & Christal, 1989b). For example, in one series of studies, Kyllonen and Christal (1989b) found strikingly high correlations between theory-based measures of working memory capacity and traditional measures of reasoning ability (or Gf). While acknowledging that such correlations are open to multiple interpretations, they argue that individual differences in working memory capacity cause individual differences in reasoning. One interesting implication of this view is that attempts to localize reasoning ability in a particular component process (e.g., inference) are bound to fail since working memory capacity affects success across all component stages of reasoning tasks.

These are but a few of the sorts of connections that can be made between a general theory of cognition and concepts familiar in measurement, particularly educational measurement. Some of these hypotheses may prove useful; others will surely be discarded. Nevertheless, it would appear that any good theory of intelligence must distinguish between higher level cognitive representations and the processes that operate on them and lower level representations and the processes that mediate between the world and the individual. Such a differentiation may take the form of a hierarchical system: a base of built-in, primitive mechanisms that operate in parallel with processes not accessible to introspection and a second level of processing that is serial, often open to introspection, and can be modified with some flexibility (Gardner, 1985). A good theory of intelligence must also acknowledge the crucial role of knowledge in all of cognition (Glaser, 1984). A major implication of Anderson's theory of research on skill acquisition and of research on expertise is that aspects of thinking that were once considered elementary, wired-in processes are now understood to be knowledge that has been automatized ("compiled" or "proceduralized") through practice. Thus, understanding abilities means understanding individual differences in learning and development.

The "New Connectionism"

Critics of the computer metaphor for human thought have long pointed to the discrepancy between the serial, digital "Von Neumann" computer and the parallel, analog nature of much human thought. Cognitive psychologists countered that it was often impossible to distinguish between a serial model, in which one stage of processing follows on the heels of another, and a parallel model for the same task, in which all processes start at the same time, run in parallel, but finish at different times. Further, it was argued that parallel processing could be simulated – albeit clumsily – on a serial computer.

These arguments began to lose their appeal as parallel processing computers were constructed and as deliberate efforts were made to make computational models of thought conform better to biological theories of brain function. This new breed of neurally inspired models of cognition is best exemplified in the work of Rumelhart, McClelland, and the PDP Research Group (1986) and their Parallel Distributed Processing (PDP) approach. Instead of a series of operations on symbols, a PDP model contains thousands of connections among hundreds of cognitive units. Excitations or inhibitions are signaled from one unit to another until the network momentarily achieves a stable state. "Thinking" or "action" occurs as strengths of the connections among units are momentarily altered. Memory is thus modeled as the set of relationships among aspects of events encoded in groups. The pattern of connections and their strengths allow particular "memories" to be recreated when the network is activated.

The PDP approach signals a significant shift from purely serial models of thinking to parallel models. Some have already suggested that a comprehensive account of thinking will require both types of processing – for example, a richly interconnected hierarchy with parallel-processing modules at the base that are dedicated to particular sensory inputs or response systems and a serial, limited capacity system at the apex to model higher order thinking (Gardner, 1985). Such a system mirrors the sort of hierarchial model of human intelligence advocated in various guises by Spearman, Burt, Vernon, and Cattell.

The PDP approach also reflects a shift from theories rich in process but short on knowledge to theories that are rich in knowledge but short on process. There has been a gradual realization in all of cognitive science of the importance of an extensive, accessible, and well organized knowledge base for intelligent performance. In AI, early efforts to avoid knowledge in the interest of simplification only served to make the task of modeling human reasoning "harder than it needed to be" (Dehn & Schank, 1982, p. 373). Similarly, there has been a gradual shift in cognitive psychology from the sort of knowledge-free information-processing models that can be neatly summarized in a flow chart to the study of the role of prior knowledge represented as scripts (Schank & Abelson, 1977), schema (Rumelhart & Ortony, 1977), mental models (Johnson-Laird, 1983), and belief systems (Carey, 1986). The importance of knowledge has even emerged in process-intensive tasks, such as those used to estimate spatial abilities. Further, many functions formerly represented as wired-in processes in information-processing models are now seen as acquired proficiencies (i.e., procedural knowledge). Indeed, the goal of measuring knowledge- or experience-free cognitive processes may be a measurement pipe dream, as E. L. Thorndike et al. (1926) suggested. In a way, this newfound role of knowledge in cognitive science parallels the gradual realization by differential psychologists that intelligence is not an innate characteristic of the person but an acquired set of competencies (Anastasi, 1986; Cronbach, 1984).

Future Directions

Including Affect

Kant popularized Aristotle's threefold categorization of mental faculties: cognitive, affective, and conative (knowing, feeling, and willing). By this account, a complete theory of mind must explain not only the cognitive dimension but also the emotional and intentional dimensions as well. Attempts to simply the task of understanding intelligence by ignoring emotion and intention may prove as ineffective as early attempts to ignore knowledge in AI. Indeed, theorists are once again beginning to argue that affect must be included in accounts of learning and cognition (Snow & Farr, 1987). Thus, one direction research on intelligence seems to be taking is to expand its horizons to include affective dimensions long recognized as central to intelligence (e.g. Wechsler, 1939) but rarely combined with the systematic study of the cognitive dimensions (see Royce, 1979, however, for one effort). A theory of intelligence thereby becomes more than an account of human cognition. It becomes an account of affect and perhaps even volition as well. Even when *intelligence* is treated as a noun, its purview knows no bounds.

From Crystallized to Fluid

A second trend in research on intelligence is moving in the opposite direction. Binet's test was originally designed to predict performance in school. Whatever larger purposes he might have hoped the test might serve, or that others have actually used tests for, it is clear that intelligence tests have always been most heavily used as measures of scholastic aptitude. Researchers have begun to uncover the reasons why such tests predict success in conventional forms of schooling as they have begun to understand the nature of the knowledge and thinking skills that are required by school-learning tasks that are also estimated by intelligence tests. Items on intelligence tests often appear to differ markedly from the sort of school-learning tasks they predict. For example, matrix completion problems and/or paper folding problems do not appear to have much in common with understanding a story or solving an algebra word problem. Yet intensive analyses reveal a commonality in the processes students use to solve both test problems and school-learning tasks (Snow & Lohman, 1984).

Analyses of existing intelligence tests and of the school-learning tasks such tests were originally designed to predict will continue to be important activities in measurement and instructional psychology. However, the study of school-learning tasks is now viewed by some as the research activity most likely to produce useful results (Cronbach, 1984, p. 300). In fact, there has been a subtle shift in recent years from the study of intelligence to the study of achievement, particularly the acquisition, organization, and use of knowledge in particular domains such as science, mathematics, and literature (Glaser, Lesgold, & Lajoie, 1987). Thus, somewhat paradoxically, new developments in the measurement of intelligence – particularly the sort of intelligence required by and developed through formal schooling – may well come about more through the careful study of achievement than through continued scrutiny of tasks modeled after existing intelligence tests. And there are reasons to be optimistic that such research may produce intelligence tests that are useful for instruction in more ways than are existing tests.

This possibility can be better understood if intelligence and achievement are viewed as points on a continuum of transfer or novelty rather than as qualitatively distinct constructs. Figure 2 shows one such continuum. The horizontal line symbolizes the amount of transfer required by the test or the average novelty of the problems for the typical examinee. At the far left, problems on the test duplicate those taught. As one moves to the right, problems become increasingly novel and require increasing transfer. For example, if students have learned to add numbers in columns, then one could present these same addition facts in column format to require minimum transfer. Presenting the same facts horizontally would require a bit of transfer; embedding the problems in a sentence would require more transfer; and embedding them in a matrix problem in which the rule is "add row 1 to row 2" requires even more transfer. Perhaps creating the matrix items in the first place requires the most transfer. As this example demonstrates, the continuum of novelty in Figure 2 is not limited to general ability but can apply to narrower ability constructs as well. It also illustrates the principle that the same task can elicit different processes from different people, depending on their prior experience.

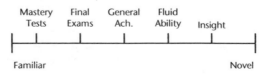

Figure 2: Hypothetical continuum of transfer for general achievement and ability tests

Important educational objectives may be identified all along this line (Elshout, 1987). Students must learn specific skills, but they must also learn to transfer their learnings to unfamiliar situations and to be creative. Unfortunately, measurement problems increase as one moves from left to right on this scale. Tests that sample no more than those facts and skills explicitly taught are relatively easy to defend, especially when only limited inferences are made from test scores. Tests that require transfer are more difficult to defend because problem novelty varies from individual to individual and because such tests are usually constructed in ways that encourage grander inferences. Some argue that defensible tests of insight (on the far right) are nonexistent.

Much of the research on intelligence and intelligence tests conducted by Sternberg, Snow, Hunt, Pellegrino and others during the 1970s could be seen as an effort to start in the middle of Figure 2 and move to the left. Both Snow (1978) and Glaser (1976) argued that the ultimate goal of their research on intelligence was to discover how the thinking skills required by such tests are also required for learning in schools. Although much has been learned from these efforts, dependable methods for encouraging the development of fluid abilities have not been discovered, even though many recommendations have been made (e.g., Wagner & Sternberg, 1984). In part, this may be an inevitable consequence of studying tests that were designed to work rather than to reflect a particular theory of cognition. A more fruitful avenue, for education at least, might be to begin somewhere near the left of Figure 2 and work toward the right. Perhaps then educators might finally learn what to teach the so-called "overachiever," who scores higher on tests of crystallized abilities than on tests of fluid abilities. The recent work of Brown and Ferrera (1985) in estimating a student's "zone of proximal development" exemplifies one effort toward this goal.

Process Sensitive Tasks

A third trend in research on intelligence is a renewed emphasis on the contextual foundation of the concept "intelligence" in the culture and life-history of the individual. In part, this represents a rediscovery of the fact that, as E. L. Thorndike et al. (1926) put it, "measurements of intelligence rest on judgements of value" (p. 12). But it also represents a breaking down of artificial barriers within psychology, such as between learning and the context in which learning occurs (Brown, Collins, & Duguid, 1989; Greeno, 1989) or between learning and development (Chi, 1978; Glaser, 1984).

Renewed linkages between the psychologies of learning and development are particularly noteworthy. Understanding how abilities develop is central to the task of understanding what abilities are. It is no accident that qualitative advances in our understanding of the mental processes which produce intelligent performances have come from those who studied the development of intelligence rather than those who focused exclusively or primarily on the organization of individual differences at a particular point in time. Much of this can be explained by a closer examination of the type of task typically studied by the developmentalist.

> All scientific measurements of intelligence that we have at present are measures of some product produced by the person or animal in question, *or of the way in which some product is produced* [italics added]. A is rated as more intelligent than B because he produces a better product, essay written, answer found, choice made, completion supplied or the like, *or produces an equally good product in a better way, more quickly or by inference rather than by rote memory, or by more ingenious use of the material at hand* [italics added]. (E. L. Thorndike et al., 1926, p. 11–12)

Thorndike et al. (1926) here describe two types of tasks: tasks which permit inferences about the nature of intelligence from the type of response made (often a qualitative judgment) and tasks which permit inferences about the rank order of individuals in ability by counting up the number of responses scored "correct" (usually a quantitative judgment). Psychometrics has understandably followed the quantitative route. Items are scaled for difficulty and examinees are ranked by how far up the ladder they can climb. Developmentalists from Piaget to Siegler have followed the qualitative path. The same problem is presented to all children and their developmental level is inferred from the sophistication of the response given. Indeed, early efforts to develop tests which provided a qualitative assessment of intelligence, such as the tests of Healy and Fernald (1911) or even the Binet scale of 1905, "did not emphasize the objective score which the child made so much as his general behavior and the way in which he went about the tasks which were set him" (Freeman, 1926, p. 108). However, judgments about process were clearly less dependable than judgments about whether the subject gave a keyed response, and so qualitative assessments of process were quickly displaced by quantitative assessments of product. Furthermore, tests which provided a score that could be immediately ranked better fit the requirements of a burgeoning test industry that was more interested in identifying who was intelligent than in understanding what intelligence was.

By the 1970s, however, cognitive psychologists had developed new methods for testing inferences about process – methods that were more sophisticated and objective than clinical judgments. Many tried to apply these new methods for detecting process to experimental tasks modeled after existing intelligence tests. Of all the "strange ironies" which have attended the history of mental testing (Cronbach, 1975), none is stranger than the attempt to apply powerful methods for detecting individual differences in processing strategy to a class of test-like tasks carefully pruned of such differences. It is a tribute to the power of the methods and the ingenuity of the researchers who employed them that anything interesting was found at all. Perhaps process analyses would be more successful in revealing interesting individual differences in process if they were to be applied to tasks deliberately designed to elicit such differences than to tasks modeled after existing mental tests.

Summary and Evaluation

Summaries broader than the scope of this paper are available (see Snow & Lohman, 1989; Sternberg, 1985), but several themes emerge in all of them.

First, much of the optimism about the potential impact of cognitive psychology on the study of human intelligence (e.g., Hunt et al., 1973; Sternberg, 1977) has been tempered by experience. Hunt now sees some fundamental incompatibilities between the correlational and experimental camps in psychology. He notes:

> Cronbach [1957] thought that general theories of psychological process ought not to ignore individual differences, and vice versa. He was right, and in a general sense the union of the camps is well underway. In my opinion...the way to achieve the scientific union is to concentrate on understanding how individual differences variables, such as age, sex, genetic constitution, and education, influence the processes of cognition. It does not seem particularly fruitful to try to derive the dimensions of... [a trait model] of abilities from an underlying process theory. (Hunt, 1987, p. 36)

Like Hunt, Sternberg has also modified his views, although he sees more compatibility than Hunt. In 1977, Sternberg described a method for testing information-processing models of tasks that he called componential analysis. He then compared his method of componential analysis with factor-analytic methods for understanding abilities and found the latter seriously wanting. More recently, he has claimed that "cognitive approaches to intelligence are basically compatible with psychometric and other approaches" (1985, p. 108), each better suited to addressing different questions about the same phenomenon. Sternberg (1985) argues that his triarchic theory recognizes the contributions not only of the correlational and the information-processing approaches to the study of intelligence but also of theorists such as Berry (1972) and E. L. Thorndike et al. (1926) who point out that the list of behaviors and accomplishments valued as "intelligent" varies over cultures and contexts.

The conclusion that trait and process approaches are in some ways fundamentally incompatible may seem overly pessimistic. Nevertheless, it at least acknowledges that the two approaches make completely different demands on the basic person by item data matrix. Each partitions the data matrix in completely different ways. The trait theorist focuses on variation in row means whereas the experimentalist focuses on variation in column means. The trait theorist is concerned with covariances computed over persons whereas the experimentalist should be more concerned with covariances computed over items. It is possible – even likely – to propose a processing model that does an excellent job of accounting for variability in item difficulties or latencies, either for all subjects or separately for each subject, and yet have no explanation for individual differences on the task. On the other hand, the trait theorist constructs measures of broad abilities by making items (or subtests) as heterogeneous as possible (Spearman, 1927; Humphreys, 1985), thereby making a process analysis of the test either impossible or so general that it is uninformative.[12] Thus, the two approaches are in some ways complementary but in other ways incompatible (Ippel & Lohman, 1990).

There has been a similar tempering of enthusiasm about the prospects for an easy victory over the problem of human intelligence in other quarters of cognitive science – particularly AI. Increasingly, those who have attempted to develop artificially intelligent systems have come to question their efforts and the constraints that the digital computer has placed on their work. In a summary of this recent history of AI, Dehn and Schank (1982) note, "Arrogance about the potential superiority of machine-specific intelligence slowly gave way to a growing respect for human intelligence and its operation. Characteristics of human intelligence…that had at first seemed to be weaknesses began to be recognized as strengths" (p. 354). For example, humans tend not to consider all aspects of a problem or to generate and evaluate all possible answers to a problem before deciding upon a course of action. Computers are easily programmed with algorithms that painstakingly consider all factors in a problem before choosing the best answer. However, the computer begins to drown in computation as problems increase in complexity, such as when the input is a visual scene or when the number of alternatives that could be generated is unlimited, as in a chess game. Further, this problem will not be solved by building computers with greater computational speed and power. Therefore, AI has shifted from programs that solve problems by brute force to programs modeled after the "satisficing" sort of rules of thumb humans use – balancing effort and time against expected payoff – in complex situations.

The recent shift to parallel-processing computers and to models of cognition that conform to current theories of brain function takes an even larger step away from the conventional digital computer and the constraints it imposes on efforts to model human cognition. However, some predict that even these efforts are doomed to fail, either because human cognition is not rule bound (Dreyfus & Dreyfus, 1986) or because higher level cognitive processes such as judgment and reasoning can be influenced by one's beliefs, values, and intentions (Pylyshyn, 1984; Fodor, 1981).

In short, there has been a growing respect for human intelligence, and a realization that it will not yield to ready explanation by the methods of cognitive science any more than it yielded to ready explanation by the method of factor analysis. Yet factor analysis contributed – and continues to contribute (Carroll, in press; Gustafsson, 1984) – to our understanding of human intelligence. Cognitive science will also continue to contribute to our understanding in spite of the dire warnings of the pessimists and in spite of difficulties already encountered. But it will do so with a little less arrogance and, hopefully, with a little greater appreciation for the contributions of Binet, E. L. Thorndike, and others who have traveled this path before.

Notes

1. Special abilities often improve the prediction when samples are large or restricted on general ability (R. L. Thorndike, 1986). Note, too, that the issue is not general versus special abilities but whether to give each ability factor a unique weight or to give all the same weight in forming a single composite to be correlated with a criterion. It has long been known that a weighted average differs little from a simple average (Burt, 1907, cited in Butcher, 1968, p. 68). Instability of regression weights for correlated predictors demands it. Pooling correlations from different studies (e.g., Hunter, 1986) further exaggerates the role of general abilities (Linn, 1986). Finally, multiple aptitude batteries can still provide important information for guidance (Tyler, 1986).
2. Like many cognitive psychologists, Anderson (1985) usually uses the word *intelligence* as a synonym for cognition, not the individual difference construct associated with intelligence tests. The implications of this view for an individual difference interpretation are outlined in the third section of this paper.
3. For example, Freeman (1926) notes the need "to identify the mental processes which are measured by [existing ability tests]" (p. 127). He also provides a remarkably balanced summary of early research on intelligence.
4. Norman (1986) claims that the architecture of the digital computer was heavily influenced by the designers' tacit theories of human cognition. Nevertheless, many who came later turned the metaphor around and looked for parallels between physical structures in the computer and psychological structures.
5. There are several intermediate cases as well. For example, Cronbach (1977) argues that "intelligence" is an abstraction much like "efficiency". On this view, one cannot locate production efficiency in a particular department of a factory: rather, it is a term that describes the overall functioning of the system relative to comparable factories. Another possibility is that intelligence is something like Spearman's (1927) mental energy or Jensen's (1982) neural efficiency. Once again, one could not isolate "intelligence" in particular processes, but one might equate it with some general characteristics of cognition, such as attentional resources or speed of processing.
6. Fancher (1985) offers a fascinating historical perspective on the controversy. Using biographical sources, he traces the conflict from the disparate life experiences of John Stuart Mill and Frances Galton, through the lives of the major players in this controversy, to the recent debates between Kamin and Eysenck.
7. Humphreys (1986) aptly describes those who openly espouse environmental explanations for intelligence but who then assume some biological capacity not measured by existing intelligence tests that would be assessed by a properly constructed test as "closet hereditarians". The description seems also to apply to some cognitive scientists.
8. Carroll (1980) suggests that the correlation with verbal ability may be more parsimoniously attributed to a general or perceptual speed dimension. In a hierarchical model, however, factors such as perceptual (or clerical) speed, memory span, and fluency are

located below verbal comprehension and thus represent specific verbal abilities. Carroll's critique is troublesome only if one views verbal comprehension as the sole verbal ability (see Snow & Lohman, 1989).

9. Low correlations with external criteria for all component scores except the intercept parameter is a statistical necessity unless task scores have poor internal consistency. This point is discussed below and in greater detail in Ippel and Lohman (in preparation). Thus, low correlations between components and other variables do not invalidate the models, although they do challenge the goal of estimating component scores for individuals.

10. For the there-is-nothing-new-under-the-sun folks, E. L. Thorndike et al. (1926) proposed that the various "products" of the human intellect be more systematically sampled from tests that differed in content ("including situations containing other human beings," p. 20) that required different "internal...processes" or "operations performed with the words, numbers, pictures, and other content" (p. 21).

11. Although procedural knowledge is said to be developed out of declarative knowledge, Anderson uses the term "procedural knowledge" more restrictively than some theorists. Knowledge of how to do something that is not yet compiled (or automatized) would be called declarative knowledge. Clearly, one can have declarative knowledge of a procedure or can have proceduralized that knowledge and not have a declarative representation of it, or one could have both.

12. As previously suggested, more informative process analyses demand tasks that allow ready inference of how subjects solved a problem, or what knowledge they brought to bear on it by the type of response they gave, not by the presence or absence of a correct response. In other words, the fundamental problem should be one of response categorization, not response scoring. Analyses of individual differences in response latencies introduce even more problems, such as what to do with error-response latencies or how to equate subjects on speed-accuracy trade-off. These problems are routinely ignored or incorrectly dismissed (for further discussion, see Lohman, 1989).

References

Anastasi, A. (1970). On the formation of psychological traits. *American Psychologist, 25,* 899–910.

Anastasi, A. (1986). Intelligence as a quality of behavior. In R. J. Sternberg & D. K. Detterman (Eds.), *What is intelligence? Contemporary viewpoints on its nature and definition* (pp. 19–21). Norwood, NJ: Ablex.

Anderson, J. R. (1976). *Language, memory, and thought.* Hillsdale, NJ: Erlbaum.

Anderson, J. R. (1983). *The architecture of cognition.* Cambridge, MA: Harvard University Press.

Anderson, J. R. (1985). *Cognitive psychology and its implications* (2nd ed.). New York: W. H. Freeman.

Anderson, J. R., & Bower, G. H. (1973). *Human associative memory.* Washington, DC: Winston.

Barrett, P., Eysenck, H. J., & Lucking, S. (1986). Reaction time and intelligence: A replicated study. *Intelligence, 10,* 9–40.

Berry, J. W. (1972). Radical cultural relativism and the concept of intelligence. In L. J. Cronbach & P. Drenth (Eds.), *Mental tests and cultural adaptation* (pp. 77–89). The Hague: Mouton.

Bethell-Fox, C. E., Lohman, D. F., & Snow, R. E. (1984). Adaptive reasoning: Componential and eye movement analysis of geometric analogy performance. *Intelligence, 8,* 205–238.

Binet, A., & Simon, T. (1905). New methods for the diagnosis of the intellectual level of subnormals. *L'Annee Psychologique, 11,* 245–336.

Brown, A. L., & Ferrara, R. A. (1985). Diagnosing zones of proximal development. In J. Wertsch (Ed.), *Culture, communication and cognition: Vygotskian perspectives* (pp. 273–305). Cambridge, MA: Cambridge University Press.

Brown, J. S., Collins, A., & Duguid, P. (1989). Situated cognition and the culture of learning. *Educational Researcher, 18*, 32–42.

Bruner, J. S., Goodnow, J., & Austin, G. (1956). A study of thinking. New York: Wiley.

Burt, C. (1958). The inheritance of mental ability. *American Psychologist, 13*, 1–15.

Butcher, H. J. (1968). *Human intelligence: Its nature and assessment.* London: Methuen.

Carey, S. (1986). Cognitive science and science education. *American Psychologist, 41*, 1123–1130.

Carlson, J. S., Jensen, C. M., & Widaman, K. F. (1983). Reaction time, intelligence, and attention. *Intelligence, 7*, 329–344.

Carroll, J. B. (1976). Psychometric tests as cognitive tasks: A new "structure of the intellect." In L. B. Resnick (Ed.), *The nature of intelligence* (pp. 27–56). Hillsdale, NJ: Erlbaum.

Carroll, J. B. (1980). *Individual differences in psychometric and experimental cognitive tasks* (NU 150–406 ONR Final Report). Chapel Hill, NC: University of North Carolina, L. L. Thurstone Psychometric Laboratory.

Carroll, J. B. (1986). Beyond IQ is cognition. A review of Beyond IQ: A triarchic theory of human intelligence by R. J. Sternberg. *Contemporary Psychology, 31*, 325–327.

Carroll, J. B. (1987). Jensen's mental chronometry: Some comments and questions. In S. Modgil & C. Modgil (Eds.), *Arthur Jensen: Consensus and controversy* (pp. 297–307). New York: The Falmer Press.

Carroll, J. B. (in press). Factor analysis since Spearman: Where do we stand? What do we know? In R. Kanfer, P. L. Ackerman, & R. Cudeck (Eds.), *The Minnesota symposium on learning and individual differences: Abilities, motivation, and methodology.* Hillsdale, NJ: Erlbaum.

Cattell, R. B. (1943). The measurement of adult intelligence. *Psychological Bulletin, 40*, 153–193.

Cattell, R. B. (1963). Theory of fluid and crystallized intelligence: A critical experiment. *Journal of Educational Psychology, 54*, 1–22.

Cattell, R. B. (1971). *Abilities: Their structure, growth, and action.* New York: Houghton Mifilin.

Chi, M. T. H. (1978). Knowledge structures and memory development. In R. S. Siegler (Ed.), *Children's thinking: What develops?* (pp. 73–96). Hillsdale, NJ: Erlbaum.

Chomsky, N. (1959). A review of B. F. Skinner's Verbal behavior. *Language, 35*, 26–58.

Chomsky, N. (1980). *Rules and representations.* New York: Columbia University Press.

Cooper, L. A. (1982). Strategies for visual comparison and representation: Individual differences. In R. J. Sternberg (Ed.), *Advances in the psychology of human intelligence* (Vol. 1, pp. 77–124). Hillsdale, NJ: Erlbaum.

Cronbach, L. J. (1957). The two disciplines of scientific psychology. *American Psychologist, 12*, 671–684.

Cronbach, L. J. (1972). Judging how well a test measures: New concepts, new analyses. In L. J. Cronbach & P. Drenth (Eds.), *Mental tests and cultural adaptation* (pp. 413–427). The Hague: Mouton.

Cronbach, L. J. (1975). Five decades of public controversy over mental testing. *American Psychologist, 30*, 1–14.

Cronbach, L. J. (1977). *Educational psychology* (3rd ed.). New York: Harcourt, Brace, Jovanovich.

Cronbach, L. J. (1984). *Essentials of psychological testing* (4th ed.). New York: Harper and Row.

Cronbach, L. J. (1986). Signs of optimism for intelligence testing. *Educational Measurement: Issues and Practice, 5*, 23–24.

Cronbach, L. J., & Snow, R. E. (1977). *Aptitudes and instructional methods: A handbook for research on interactions.* New York: Irvington.

Daalen-Kapteijns, M. M. van, & Elshout-Mohr, M. (1981). The acquisition of word meanings as a cognitive learning process. *Journal of Verbal Learning and Verbal Behavior, 20*, 386–399.

Dehn, N., & Schank, R. (1982). Artificial and human intelligence. In R. J. Sternberg (Ed.), *Handbook of human intelligence* (pp. 352–391). Cambridge, MA: Cambridge University Press.

Dreyfus, H. L., & Dreyfus, S. E. (1986). *Mind over machine.* New York: Free Press.

Elshout, J. J. (1987). Problem solving and education. In E. de Corte, H. Lodewijks, R. Parmentier, & P. Span (Eds.), *Learning and instruction: European research in an international context* (Vol. 1, pp. 259–274). Oxford, UK: Leuven University Press and Pergamon Press.

Elshout, J. J., Hemert, N., A. van, & Hemert, M., van (1975). Comment on Horn and Knapp on the subjective character of the empirical base of Guilfor's structure-of-intellect model. *Onderwijsresearch, 1*, 15–25.

Eysenck, H. J. (1982). *A model for intelligence.* New York: Springer.

Eysenck, H. J. (1987a). A general systems approach to the measurement of intelligence and personality. In S. H. Irvine & S. E. Newstead (Eds.), *Intelligence and cognition: Contemporary frames of reference* (pp. 349–376). Dordrecht, Netherlands: Martinus Nijhoff.

Eysenck, H. J. (1987b). Intelligence and reaction time: The contribution of Arthur Jensen. In S. Modgil & Modgil (Eds.), *Arthur Jensen: Consensus and controversy* (pp. 285–296). New: The Falmer Press.

Eysenck, H. J. (1988). The concept of "intelligence": Useful or useless? *Intelligence, 12*, 1–16.

Fancher, R. E. (1985). *The intelligence men: Makers of the IQ controversy.* New York: W. W. Norton & Co.

Fodor, J. A. (1981). *Representations: Philosophical essays on the foundations of cognitive science.* Cambridge, MA: MIT Press.

Ford, M. E. (1986). A livings systems conceptualization of social intelligence: Outcomes, processes, and developmental change. In R. J. Sternberg (Ed.), *Advances in the psychology of human intelligence* (Vol. 3, pp. 119–171). Hillsdale, NJ: Erlbaum.

Frederiksen, J. R. (1982). A componential theory of reading skills and their interactions. In R. J. Sternberg (Ed.), *Advances in the psychology of human intelligence* (Vol. 1, pp. 125–180). Hillsdale, NJ: Erlbaum.

Frederiksen, N. (1984). The real test bias: Influences of testing on teaching and learning. *American Psychologist, 39*, 193–202.

Freeman, F. N. (1926). *Mental tests: Their history, principles and application.* Boston: Houghton Mifflin.

Galton, F. (1869). *Hereditary genius.* London: Macmillan.

Gardner, H. (1983). *Frames of mind: The theory of multiple intelligences.* New York: Basic Books.

Gardner, H. (1985). *The mind's new science.* New York: Basic Books.

Garrett, H. E. (1946). A developmental theory of intelligence. *American Psychologist, 1*, 372–378.

Gick, M., & Holyoak, K. (1983). Schema induction and analogical reasoning. *Cognitive Psychology, 15*, 1–38.

Glaser, R. (1972). Individuals and learning: The new aptitudes. *Educational Researcher, 1*, 5–12.

Glaser, R. (1976). The processes of intelligence and education. In L. B. Resnick (Ed.), *The nature of intelligence* (pp. 341–352). Hillsdale, NJ: Erlbaum.

Glaser, R. (1984). Education and thinking: The role of knowledge. *American Psychologist, 39*, 93–104.

Glaser, R., Lesgold, A., & Lajoie, S. (1987). Toward a cognitive theory for the measurement of achievement. In R. R. Ronning, J. A. Glover, J. C. Conoley, & J. Witt (Eds.),

The influence of cognitive psychology on testing and measurement: The Buros-Nebraska symposium on measurement and testing (Vol. 3, pp. 41–86). Hillsdale, NJ: Erlbaum.

Glushko, R. J., & Cooper, L. A. (1978). Spatial comprehension and comparison processes in verification tasks. *Cognitive Psychology, 10*, 391–421.

Greeno, J. G. (1989). A perspective on thinking. *American Psychologist, 44*, 134–141.

Guilford, J. P. (1959). Three faces of intellect. *American Psychologist, 14*, 459–479.

Guilford, J. P. (1985). The structure-of-intellect model. In B. B. Wolman (Ed.), *Handbook of intelligence* (pp. 225–266). New York: Wiley.

Gustafsson, J. E. (1984). A unifying model for the structure of intellectual abilities. *Intelligence, 8*, 179–203.

Healy, W., & Fernald, G. M. (1911). Tests for practical mental classification. *Psychological Monographs, 13* (2).

Hebb, D. (1949). *The organization of behavior.* New York: Wiley.

Hendrickson, D. E. (1982). The biological basis of intelligence: Part 2. Measurement. In H. J. Eysenck (Ed.), *A model for intelligence* (pp. 197–228). New York: Springer.

Holland, J. H., Holyoak, K. J., Nisbett, R. E., & Thagard, P. R. (1987). *Induction: Processes of inference, learning, and discovery.* Cambridge, MA: MIT Press.

Horn, J. L. (1976). Human abilities: A review of research theory in the early 1970s. *Annual Review of Psychology, 27*, 437–485.

Horn, J. L. (1985). Remodeling old models of intelligence. In B. B. Wolman (Ed.), *Handbook of intelligence* (pp. 267–300). New York: John Wiley & Sons.

Horn, J. L., & Knapp, J. R. (1973). On the subjective character of the empirical base of Guilford's structure-of-the-intellect model. *Psychological Bulletin, 80*, 33–43.

Humphreys, L. G. (1962). The organization of human abilities. *American Psychologist, 17*, 475–483.

Humphreys, L. G. (1981). The primary mental ability. In M. P. Friedman, J. P. Das, & N. O'Connor (Eds.), *Intelligence and learning* (pp. 87–102). New York: Plennum.

Humphreys, L. G. (1984). A rose is not a rose: A rival view of intelligence. Comment on R. J. Sternberg's "Toward a triarchic theory of human intelligence." *The Behavioral and Brain Sciences, 7*, 292–293.

Humphreys, L. G. (1985). General intelligence: An integration of factor, test, and simplex theory. In B. B. Wolman (Eds.), *Handbook of intelligence* (pp. 201–224). New York: Wiley.

Humphreys, L. G. (1986). Describing the elephant. In R. J. Sternberg & D. K. Detterman (Eds.), *What is intelligence? Contemporary viewpoints on its nature and definition* (pp. 97–100). Norwood, NJ: Ablex.

Hunsicker, L. M. (1925). A study of the relationship between rate and ability. *Contributions to Education, No. 185.* New York: Columbia University, Teachers College.

Hunt, E. (1985). Verbal ability. In R. J. Sternberg (Ed.), *Human abilities: An information-processing approach* (pp. 31–58). New York: Freeman.

Hunt, E. (1986). The heffalump of intelligence. In R. J. Sternberg & D. K. Detterman (Eds.), What is intelligence? Contemporary viewpoints on its nature and definition (pp. 101–108). Norwood, NJ: Ablex.

Hunt, E. (1987). Science, technology, and intelligence. In R. R. Ronning, J. A. Glover, J. C. Conoley, & J. C. Witt (Eds.), *The influence of cognitive psychology on testing: The Buros-Nebraska symposium on measurement and testing* (Vol. 3, pp. 11–40). Hillsdale, NJ: Erlbaum.

Hunt, E. B., Frost, N., & Lunneborg, C. (1973). Individual differences in cognition: A new approach to intelligence. In G. Bower (Ed.), *The psychology of learning and motivation* (Vol. 7, pp. 87–122). New York: Academic Press.

Hunt, E. B., Lunneborg, C., & Lewis, J. (1975). What does it mean to be high verbal? *Cognitive Psychology, 7*, 194–227.

Hunter, J. E. (1986). Cognitive ability, cognitive aptitudes, job knowledge, and job performance. *Journal of Vocational Behavior, 29*, 340–362.

Ippel, M. J., & Lohman, D. F. (1990). *Cognitive diagnosis: From statistically-based assessment to theory-based assessment.* Unpublished manuscript.

Irwin, R. J. (1984). Inspection time and its relation to intelligence. *Intelligence, 8*, 47–66.

Jensen, A. R. (1969). How much can we boost IQ and scholastic achievement? *Harvard Educational Review, 39*, 1–123.

Jensen, A. R. (1980). *Bias in mental testing.* New York: The Free Press.

Jensen, A. R. (1982). Reaction time and psychometric g. In H. J. Eysenck (Ed.), *A model for intelligence* (pp. 93–132). Prenger-Verlag.

Jensen, A. R. (1987). Process differences and individual difference in some cognitive tasks. *Intelligence, 11*, 107–136.

Johnson-Laird, P. N. (1983). *Mental models: Towards a cognitive science of language, inference, and consciousness.* Cambridge, MA: Harvard University Press.

Kail, R., & Pellegrino, J. W. (1985). *Human intelligence: Prospectives and prospects.* New York: Freeman.

Keating, D. P., & MacLean, D. J. (1987). Cognitive processing, cognitive ability, and development: A reconsideration. In P. A. Vernon (Ed.), *Speed of information-processing and intelligence* (pp. 239–270). Norwood, NJ: Ablex.

Kelley, T. L. (1928). *Crossroads in the mind of man.* Stanford, CA: Stanford University Press.

Kintsch, W. (1986). Learning from text. *Cognition and instruction, 3*, 87–108.

Kosslyn, S. M. (1980). *Image and mind.* Cambridge, MA: Harvard University Press.

Koussy, A. A. H. El. (1935). The visual perception of space. *British Journal of Psychology, 7* (Whole No. 20).

Kyllonen, P. C. (1985). *Dimensions of information processing speed.* (AFHRL-TP-84-56). Brooks AFB, TX: Air Force Human Resources Lab.

Kyllonen, P. C., & Christal, R. E. (1989a). Cognitive modeling of learning abilities: A status report of LAMP. In R. Dillon & J. W. Pellegrino (Eds.), *Testing: Theoretical and applied issues* (pp. 146–173). New York: Freeman.

Kyllonen, P. C., & Christal, R. E. (1989b). *Reasoning ability is (little more than) working memory capacity.* Manuscript submitted for publication.

Lindquist, E. F. (1948). *The nature and purposes of the Iowa Tests of Educational Development.* Unpublished manuscript.

Linn, R. L. (1986). Comments on the g factor in employment testing. *Journal of Vocational Behavior, 29*, 438–444.

Lohman, D. F. (1979). *Spatial ability: A review and reanalysis of the correlational literature* (Tech. Rep. No. 9). Stanford, CA: Stanford University, School of Education. (NTIS No. AD-A075 972)

Lohman, D. F. (1988). Spatial abilities as traits, processes, and knowledge. In R. J. Sternberg (Ed.), *Advances in the psychology of human intelligence* (Vol. 4, pp. 181–248). Hillsdale, NJ: Erlbaum.

Lohman, D. F. (1989). Individual differences in errors and latencies on cognitive tasks. *Learning and Individual Differences, 1*, 179–202.

Longstreth, L. E. (1984). Jensen's reaction-time investigations of intelligence: A critique. *Intelligence, 8*, 139–160.

Macleod, C. M., Hunt, E. B., & Mathews, N. N. (1978). Individual differences in the verification of sentence-picture relationships. *Journal of Verbal Learning and Verbal Behavior, 17*, 493–508.

Marshalek, B. (1981). *Trait and process aspects of vocabulary knowledge and verbal ability* (Tech. Rep. No. 15). Stanford, CA: Stanford University, Aptitude Research Project, School of Education. (NTIS No. AD-A102 757).

Marshall, J. C. (1977). Minds, machines and metaphors. *Social Studies of Science, 7*, 475–488.

McNemar, Q. (1964). Lost: Our intelligence? Why? *American Psychologist, 19*, 871–882.

Miller, G. A. (1956). The magical number seven, plus or minus two: Some limits on our capacity for processing information. *Psychological Review, 63*, 81–97.

Miller, G. A. (1981). Trends and debates in cognitive psychology. *Cognition, 10*, 215–225.

Nettelbeck, T., & Kirby, N. H. (1983). Measures of timed performance and intelligence. *Intelligence, 7*, 39–52.

Nettelbeck, T., & Lally, M. (1976). Inspection time and measured intelligence. *British Journal of Psychology, 67*, 17–22.

Newell, A., Shaw, J. C., & Simon, H. A. (1957). Empirical explorations with the logic theory machine. *Proceedings of the Western Joint Computer Conference, 15*, 218–239.

Newell, A., & Simon, H. A. (1972). *Human problem solving.* Englewood Cliffs, NJ: Prentice-Hall.

Norman, D. A. (1986). Reflections on cognition and parallel distributed processing. In D. E. Rumelhart, J. L. McClelland, and the PDP Research Group (Eds), *Parallel distributed processing: Vol. 2. Psychological and biological models* (pp. 531–546). Cambridge, MA: MIT Press.

Pellegrino, J. W., & Kail, R. (1982). Process analyses of spatial aptitude. In R. J. Sternberg (Ed.), *Advances in the psychology of human intelligence* (Vol. 1, pp. 311–366). Hillsdale, NJ: Erlbaum.

Perfetti, C. A. (1986). *Reading ability.* New York: Oxford University Press.

Pinker, S. (1984). Visual cognition: An introduction. *Cognition, 18*, 1–63.

Poltrock, S. E., & Brown, P. (1984). Individual differences in visual imagery and spatial ability. *Intelligence, 8*, 93–138.

Porteus, S. D. (1915). Mental tests for the feebleminded: A new series. *Journal of Psycho-Asthenics, 19*, 200–213.

Pylyshyn, Z. W. (1984). *Computation and cognition.* Cambridge, MA: MIT Press.

Royce, J. R. (1979). Toward a viable theory of individual differences. *Journal of Personality and Social Psychology, 37*, 1927–1931.

Rumelhart, D. E., McClelland, J. L., and the PDP Research Group. (1986). *Parallel distributed processing: Vol. 1. Foundations.* Cambridge, MA: MIT Press.

Rumelhart, D. E., & Ortony, A. (1977). The representation of knowledge in memory. In R. C. Anderson, R. J. Spiro, & W. E. Montague (Eds.), *Schooling and the acquisition of knowledge* (pp. 99–136). Hillsdale, NJ: Erlbaum.

Scarr, S. & Carter-Saltman, L. (1982). Genetics and intelligence. In R. J. Sternberg (Ed.), *Handbook of human intelligence* (pp. 792–896). Cambridge, MA: Cambridge University Press.

Schank, R. C., & Abelson, R. P. (1977). *Scripts, plans, goals, and understanding.* Hillsdale, NJ: Erlbaum.

Shepard, R. N., & Cooper, L. A. (1982). *Mental images and their transformations.* Cambridge, MA: MIT Press.

Skinner, B. F. (1953). *Science and human behavior.* New York: Macmillan.

Smith, I. M. (1964). *Spatial ability.* San Diego: Knapp.

Snow, R. E. (1978). Theory and method for research on aptitude processes. *Intelligence, 2*, 225–278.

Snow, R. E. (1981). Toward a theory of aptitude for learning: Fluid and crystallized abilities and their correlates. In M. P. Friedman, J. P. Das, & N. O'Connor (Eds.), *Intelligence and learning* (pp. 345–362). New York: Plenum Press.

Snow, R. E., & Farr, M. J. (Eds.). (1987). *Aptitude, learning, and instruction: Vol. 3, Conative and affective process analyses.* Hillsdale, NJ: Erlbaum.

Snow, R. E., & Lohman, D. F. (1984). Toward a theory of cognitive aptitude for learning from instruction. *Journal of Educational Psychology, 76*, 347–376.

Snow, R. E., & Lohman, D. F. (1989). Implications of cognitive psychology for educational measurement. In R. Linn (Ed.), *Educational Measurement* (3rd ed.) (pp. 263–331). New York: Macmillan.

Snow, R. E., Marshalek, B., & Lohman, D. F. (1976). *Correlation of selected cognitive abilities and cognitive processing parameters: An exploratory study* (Tech. Rep. No. 3). Stanford, CA: Stanford University, School of Education.

Snow, R. E., & Yalow, E. (1982). Education and intelligence. In R. J. Sternberg (Ed.), *Handbook of human intelligence* (pp. 493–585). Cambridge, MA: Cambridge University Press.

Spearman, C. E. (1927). *The abilities of man.* London: Macmillan.

Spearman, C. E., & Wynn Jones, L. L. (1950). *Human ability.* London: Macmillan.

Spencer, H. (1855). *The principles of psychology.* London: Williams and Norgate.

Stern, W. (1914). *The psychological method of testing intelligence* (G. M. Whipple, Trans.). Baltimore: Warwick & York. (Original work published 1912)

Sternberg, R. J. (1977). *Intelligence, information processing, and analogical reasoning: The componential analysis of human abilities.* Hillsdale, NJ: Erlbaum.

Sternberg, R. J. (1984). Toward a triarchic theory of human intelligence. *The Behavioral and Brain Sciences, 7,* 269–315.

Sternberg, R. J. (1985). *Beyond IQ: A triarchic theory of human intelligence.* Cambridge, MA: Cambridge University Press.

Sternberg, R. J., & Gardner, M. K. (1983). Unities in inductive reasoning. *Journal of Experimental Psychology: General, 112,* 80–116.

Sternberg, R. J., & McNamara, T. P. (1985). The representation and processing of information in real-time verbal comprehension. In S. E. Embretson (Ed.), *Test design: Developments in psychology and psychometrics* (pp. 21–43). Orlando, FL: Academic Press.

Sternberg, R. J., & Powell, J. S. (1983). Comprehending verbal comprehension. *American Psychologist, 38,* 878–893.

Terman, L. M. (1922). The great conspiracy. *New Republic, 33,* 116–120.

Thomson, G. H. (1920). General versus group factors in mental activities. *Psychological Review, 27,* 173–190.

Thorndike, E. L. (1903). *Educational psychology.* New York: The Science Press.

Thorndike, E. L. (1920). Intelligence and its uses. *Harper's Magazine, 140,* 227–235.

Thorndike, E. L., Bregman, E. O., Cobb, M. V., & Woodyard, E. (1926). *The measurement of intelligence.* New York: Columbia University, Teachers College.

Thorndike, R. L. (1963). *The concepts of over- and under-achievement.* New York: Columbia University, Teachers College.

Thorndike, R. L. (1986). The role of general ability in prediction. *Journal of Vocational Behavior, 29,* 332–339.

Thorndike, R. L., Hagen, E. P., & Sattler, J. M. (1986). *The Stanford-Binet intelligence scale: Fourth edition technical manual.* Chicago: The Riverside Publishing Company.

Thorndike, R. M., & Lohman, D. F. (1989). *A century of ability testing.* Chicago: The Riverside Publishing Company.

Thurstone, L. L. (1937). Ability, motivation, and speed. *Psychometrika, 2,* 249–254.

Thurstone, L. L. (1938). Primary mental abilities. *Psychometric Monograph, 1.*

Thurstone, L. L. (1947). *Multiple factor analysis.* Chicago: University of Chicago Press.

Tyler, L. (1986). Back to Spearman? *Journal of Vocational Behavior, 29,* 445–450.

Underwood, B. J. (1975). Individual differences as a crucible in theory construction. *American Psychologist, 30,* 128–134.

Vernon, P. E. (1950). *The structure of human abilities.* London: Methuen.

Wagner, R. K., & Sternberg, R. J. (1984). Alternative conceptions of intelligence and their implications for education. *Review of Educational Research, 54,* 179–224.

Wagner, R. K., & Sternberg, R. J. (1986). Tacit knowledge and intelligence in the everyday world. In R. J. Sternberg & R. K. Wagner (Eds.), *Practical intelligence: Nature and origins of competence in the everyday world* (pp. 51–83). Cambridge, MA: Cambridge University Press.

Watson, J. B. (1925). *Behaviorism.* New York: Norton.

Wechsler, D. (1939). *The measurement of adult intelligence.* Baltimore: Williams & Wilkins.

Wissler, C. (1901). The correlation of mental and physical tests. *Psychological Monographs, 3* (6, Whole No. 16).

Woltz, D. J. (1988). An investigation of the role of working memory in procedural skill acquisition. *Journal of Experimental Psychology: General, 117,* 319–331.

37

Cognitive Demands of New Technologies and the Implications for Learning Theory

Richard J. Torraco

A t a basic level, learning to perform work-related activities requires the engagement of one's cognitive processes with the task to be accomplished. Few studies trace prescriptions for learning all the way back through human cognitive processes to the specific characteristics of the tasks that determine what should be learned in the first place. This study identifies the cognitive demands of new technologies by first examining the specific requirements of tasks involving the use of new technologies. These tasks are shown to place unique cognitive demands on those who use new technologies. Then, the question is raised, How well do current theories of learning address these cognitive demands? Four theories – those of Scribner, Schon, Wenger, and Hutchins – are analyzed for their power to explain human cognition and learning as they relate to the use of new technologies. Finally, the article offers new directions for future research on learning theory, studies of workplace learning, and theory building.

Although the primary focus of this article is the need for better theory to explain learning at work, I start by addressing the nature of the task itself. This honors Gagne's (1962) seminal admonition that scholars should first examine the task to be learned in order to specifically address what learning should accomplish and Hackman's (1969) treatise on the centrality of the task to research on work behavior. The concept of task remains a prominent construct in models of work design (Campion & Medsker, 1992; Hackman & Oldham, 1980; Smith,

Source: *Human Resource Development Review*, 1(4) (2002): 439–466.

Henning, & Smith, 1994), work motivation (Locke & Latham, 1990), work complexity (Campbell, 1988; Khurana, 1999; Weick, 1990), and human cognition (Engestrom & Middleton, 1996; Hutchins, 1995; Simon, 1981).

Characteristics of Tasks Involving New Technologies

Any meaningful discussion of task characteristics must be framed in the context of a work or organizational environment. For the purpose of this article, the work environment is composed of the immediate physical environment of the worker and the organizational demands placed on the worker. The immediate physical environment is constituted by the tools, equipment, electronic devices, and other material resources needed by the worker to accomplish the task. Organizational demands relate to work requirements placed on the individual that go beyond one's immediate responsibilities such as project deadlines, the need for administrative approvals, expected rates of transaction, and other requirements imposed on the individual by the organization that indicate how one's job activities fit with process requirements.

Technology is also a key concept in this discussion. Like other tools, technology is a means through which work is accomplished. Berniker's (1987) definition of technology is adopted for this discussion. Berniker embedded the concept of technology within the larger structure of a technical system, which is

> a specific combination of machines, equipment, and methods used to produce some valued outcome.... Every technical system embodies a technology. It derives from a large body of knowledge which produces the basis for design decision. Technology refers to a body of knowledge about the means by which we work on the world, our arts and our methods. (p. 10)

Four specific characteristics of tasks involving the use of new technologies are described next. These concepts – contingent versus deterministic tasks, distancing technologies, stochastic events, and systemic interdependence – compose a proposed model of task characteristics associated with new technologies. These concepts were identified as elements of the model through a comprehensive review of the literature that sought task characteristics distinctively associated with the use of new technologies. These four characteristics are central to understanding the unique cognitive demands faced by users of new technologies and are not meant to be an exhaustive review of constructs related to the use of new technologies. Mindful of the need for balance between a model's comprehensiveness and parsimony, I developed two concepts to explain new phenomena (contingent versus deterministic tasks and distancing technologies), whereas two others are adapted from existing theories (stochastic events and systemic interdependence). Thus, all concepts in the model are either developed and justified by the author or grounded in existing literature.

- Contingent versus deterministic tasks: When applied to what were once routine, predictable tasks (deterministic tasks), new technologies have substantially increased the contingency of these tasks by increasing their complexity and speed (Pentland, 1997).
- Distancing technologies such as digital displays, controls, and sensor technologies, remove the operator from the operating location and eliminate the physical cues and sentient information from which knowledge can be derived (Woods, O'Brien, & Hanes, 1987; Zuboff, 1988).
- Stochastic events are randomly occurring and unpredictable events that are properties of new technologies (Weick, 1990) and flexible manufacturing systems (Norros, 1996).
- Systemic interdependence is the system of relationships needed to ensure that one's work is coordinated with that of others within the work system (Adler, 1986).

These four task characteristics of new technologies place unique cognitive demands on those who use them. The next section discusses the cognitive demands associated with each task characteristic. The task characteristics and the cognitive demands associated with them are listed in Table 1.

Cognitive demands of contingent tasks. New technologies have fundamentally changed the character of technical work by removing it further than ever from its historical and deterministic origins. The work of technicians and craftsmen has always been contingent on contextual factors because task execution is frequently altered by temporal, material, social, economic, and other factors that reflect the changing properties of the task environment. However, new

Table 1: The cognitive demands of task characteristics

Task characteristic	Cognitive demand
Contingent versus deterministic tasks Unanticipated problems Expanded menu of solutions	• Mental reconstruction of problem and causes • Capability for systematic search and pragmatic solutions • Ability to go beyond scripted procedures
Distancing technologies Physical separation Psychological separation	• Capabilities for inference, imagination, and mental modeling to understand what is going on elsewhere • Reconciliation of mental representation of work process with actual work process
Stochastic events Disruptions to work process Premature task termination	• Movement from emotional arousal to constructive thought and action • Memory (information storage and retrieval) to reconsider means-ends relationships and desired end states • Improvisation – the abilities of the bricoleur
Systemic interdependence Partial versus complete knowledge Transforming inputs to outputs	• Interpersonal skills • Transactive memory

technologies have substantially increased task contingency by reducing their transparency, increasing their speed, and expanding the menu of options available for task accomplishment. Work processes that were formerly transparent (i.e., separate, observable, and easily deconstructed into their systemic components) have been combined through process engineering (Davenport, 1993) and have disappeared into computer-controlled machines and communication technology (Weick, 1990), thereby reducing their transparency and complicating efforts to discern process interactions. Technicians and customers can no longer see the flow of information and materials and must infer from outputs what occurred earlier in the work process. Replacing the industrial-era belief in "one best method" for each operation (Woodward, 1994), the reduced transparency of technology now masks an Internet-like network of possible paths for processing materials and information. These factors contribute directly to the contingency of tasks associated with the use of new technologies.

New technology also feeds social pressures for rapid transactions, especially in customer service situations. Predetermined procedures are frequently abandoned to expedite customer requests. Expanded options for task accomplishment within and among distinct technologies further contributes to the contingent nature of work strategies. Although the Internet offers alternative paths for processing information (e-mail, Web sites), it can be circumvented altogether through the use of the phone, facsimile, satellite links, paper, or personal contact for communication. As witnessed in equipment repair (Orr, 1996), software support (Pentland, 1997), science laboratories (Barley & Bechky, 1994), insurance claim processing (Wenger, 1998), automobile assembly (Graham, 1993), and military operations (Hutchins, 1995; Weick & Roberts, 1993), new technologies have made technical tasks more contingent than ever.

Because technical work is filled with novel or poorly defined problems that cannot be fully anticipated in advance (Barley & Orr, 1997), technicians are often confronted by technology breakdowns of ambiguous origins that cannot be resolved with schematics and procedural knowledge alone. Because their problem-solving algorithms are inadequate for the variety and unpredictability of these problems, technicians must rely instead on pragmatic rules of thumb and other shortcuts afforded by the task environment. Thus, successful performance requires employees to go beyond scripted procedures to resolve problems in innovative ways. This does not mean that job aids, operating procedures, and training in the use of such resources are of no value. Effective work systems should provide such technical assistance in ways that are easily referenced to minimize mental and computational loads, so workers are free to do higher level evaluation and problem solving (Norman, 1988). However, to understand and respond to ambiguous situations, workers must make use of improvised materials, local conditions, and social circumstances, thus deploying contingent work strategies that reflect the changing properties of the task environment.

The cognitive demands faced by those who deal with these problems include a considerable amount of systematic mental search to identify pragmatic solutions. Workers frequently must reconstruct the situation that led to the problem, identify the causes, develop a solution strategy, and ensure that the proposed solution is satisfactory and feasible. Assistance in this regard from the information storage and retrieval capabilities of technology may not always help workers deal with these cognitive demands. Technology-based troubleshooting aids that provide workers with problem-solving heuristics, algorithms, and databases are just as likely to hinder as help the worker's problem-solving efforts (Norman, 1993). Moreover, as Griffith and Northcraft (1996) demonstrated, the implementation of technologies may be better served when less, rather than more, information about the technology is provided to users. Regardless of whether the technology itself is seen as valuable or detrimental, the contingency of tasks associated with new technologies places important cognitive demands on those who must use them. This characteristic of new technologies (contingent vs. deterministic tasks) and the cognitive demands associated with it are listed in Table 1.

Cognitive demands of distancing technologies. Distancing technologies are present in work environments ranging from industrial factories (Zuboff, 1988) to high technology settings (Pentland, 1997). Digital displays, controls, and sensor technologies at the operator's workstation are symbolic representations that distance workers from the physical and sensory referents present at the actual sites of operation. In the pulp and paper mills studied by Zuboff (1988), instrumentation formerly was located on or close to the operating equipment, allowing the operator to combine data from an instrument reading with data from his or her own senses. Distancing technologies removed the operator from the operating location and eliminated the physical cues and sentient information in which knowledge was based. In addition to physical distance from customers, the software support technicians studied by Pentland (1997) were expected to solve software problems over the telephone despite customers' diverse software and hardware configurations. Problem solving was difficult due to the ambiguity of the problems as described by customers, who were unable to identify specific conditions that were relevant to troubleshooting the problems. Technicians had difficulty visualizing the situations that gave rise to the problems.

The problems created by physical distance are magnified by the computer controls of most distancing technologies that display information on separate screens of a computer monitor. To recognize irregular patterns among the data or to initiate novel search sequences, the technician must remember what earlier screens have shown and hope that the readings have not changed while subsequent screens are accessed. However, human factors research has shown that it is easier to recognize patterns when data are presented simultaneously rather than serially. Technicians in production control rooms who use technology based on this research can easily create novel search sequences when they are able to sweep visually across an array of indicators that present data at the lowest level of detail (Woods, O'Brien, & Hanes, 1987). Similar principles of task design have been applied to high-technology work settings. For example, Gill (1996) showed that changing the task characteristics of expert information systems to enhance the user's sense of control over task activities and their own performance increased the intrinsic motivational character of these tasks, which, in turn, enhanced the workers' motivation to increase their use of these expert systems.

Separation from the operating environment requires workers to interpret symbolic, electronically presented data. The ability to make sense of what is going on at remote operating sites is vital to competent performance in these work environments. Software support technicians and production control room operators have to imagine the conditions in the operating environment that cannot be displayed by their information systems. Before attempting to solve problems, they must first mentally visualize the conditions that give rise to the problems. Thus, the physical and psychological separation created by distancing technologies increases cognitive demands for inference, imagination, and mental modeling to understand what is happening elsewhere.

Human-computer-robot manufacturing systems, known as automatic manufacturing technology, provide an example of the performance problems associated with distancing technologies. Early automatic manufacturing technology systems provided the operator with a televised view of the robot's actions at the point of manufacturing located away from the operator's control panel. But because the televised view distorted the spatial properties of visual feedback to the operator, control panels were relocated closer to the point of operation to allow direct viewing of the automatic manufacturing technology robot by the operator, thus reducing the cognitive demands on the operator (Smith, Henning, & Smith, 1994). The physical and psychological distance from one's work caused by these technologies can be reduced by designing work environments according to principles of human factors and ergonomics (Salvendy, 1987) and by giving more attention to the importance of inference and mental modeling in employee training and development. A discussion of how well these employee needs are addressed in current theories of learning is presented later in the article. This characteristic of new technologies (distancing technologies) and the cognitive demands associated with it are listed in Table 1.

Cognitive demands of stochastic events. Complexity is added to the task when it is interrupted by stochastic events. Stochastic events are randomly occurring and unpredictable events that are properties of new technologies (Weick, 1990) and flexible manufacturing systems (Norros, 1996). When new technologies are implemented in industrial work processes, they frequently produce system disturbances to which operators must respond, even though they have not yet developed expertise in the use of these technologies (Norros, 1996). Pre–industrial era technologies were predictable and easily understood because key operating mechanisms followed clear cause-effect relationships. However, today's technologies are more complex and present problems due to their instability, reduced transparency, and tendency to break down.

New technologies have always been accompanied by problems. Early mass production lines were plagued by incessant breakdowns. Although stochastic events are not new, Weick (1990) noted that new technologies are unique in that the uncertainties are permanent rather than transient. Many software-dependent systems are intentionally pushed through product development and quickly delivered to market. Product testing is short-circuited because implementation is often the means by which the technology itself is designed. Such development-delivery tradeoffs result in "buggy" software, incomplete information networks, and password-activated technologies that will not start. Even common technologies are not free of breakdowns (e.g., disconnection from the Internet, power failures, being cut off during telephone calls). Dealing with the disruptions from unfinished technologies and prototypes increases the cognitive demands placed on technicians who must use them.

When a sudden, unpredictable event disrupts a task, it triggers emotional arousal (Weick, 1990). Once emotion is stimulated, it increases as long as the interruption remains unexplained, especially when work stoppage is costly or risky. Stochastic events require rapid movement from emotion to action, that is, from arousal, to the search for explanations, to actions that produce information about possible causes. This occurs as the worker tries to subdue emotional interference with thought and action.

Sudden work stoppage also forces the reconsideration of means-ends relationships and of desired end states. Are alternative paths available for project completion that circumvent the disabled technology? Can the project be completed elsewhere, by someone else, or at a later time? How much can the desired end state of the transaction be modified? The cognitive demands on memory (information storage and retrieval) and search for additional information from such disruptions can be considerable. A sudden system failure challenges workers to make do with the tools and materials at hand. As they improvise to complete their tasks, they invoke the skills of contemporary *bricoleurs* – resourceful craftsmen who make use of whatever materials are available to complete the project (Levi-Strauss, 1966). This characteristic of new technologies (stochastic events) and the cognitive demands associated with it are listed in Table 1.

Cognitive demands of systemic interdependence. The interdependencies needed to ensure that one's work is coordinated with the work of others have been termed "systemic interdependence" by Adler (1986). Systemic interdependence requires

> ongoing and flexible integration of hitherto distinct functions of operations, systems, design, and training. The reciprocal nature of this interdependence in operations is exemplified in the reliance on common databases. Users thereby become dependent on other users' data input accuracy. (p. 19)

Systemic interdependence requires interpersonal skills and the ability to work effectively with others on the same project despite different social and technical backgrounds. Such interdependence is strengthened through the use of transactive memory systems (Wegner, Erber, & Raymond, 1991). Transactive memory is based on the premise that we need not know a particular subject ourselves if we know where to find information about it. Transactive memory systems are integrated and differentiated structures in which related information is held by different group members working on a common project. It is the sharing of relevant data that yields the higher order insights and generalizations that are valued in these work environments. Workers who contribute to transactive memory systems participate in the sharing and integration of technical knowledge and, in turn, further develop their networks of social and technical interdependencies. This characteristic of new technologies (systemic interdependence) and the cognitive demands associated with it are listed in Table 1.

These four characteristics – contingent versus deterministic tasks, distancing technologies, stochastic events, and systemic interdependence – are fundamental elements of new technologies that place unique cognitive demands on those who use them. How well do current theories of learning address these cognitive demands? The next section discusses the extent to which four selected theories explain human cognition and learning as they relate to working with new technologies.

Theories of Learning and Cognitive Demands

The theories of Scribner (Tobach, Falmagne, Parlee, Martin, & Kapelman, 1997), Schon (1983, 1987), Wenger (1998), and Hutchins (1995) are analyzed for their power to explain human cognition as it relates to the use of new technologies. These four learning theories provide comprehensive and meaningful explanations of how learning occurs in the type of work settings discussed here. The criteria used for selecting these theories for this discussion are that each theory (a) describes specific cognitive processes, (b) addresses learning as both an enabler and product of work practices, (c) explains how learning occurs in authentic work settings, (d) is comprehensive in its treatment of the behavioral and environmental influences on learning, and (e) offers propositions that can be generalized to other settings. Because these four theories explain the phenomena discussed in this article better than most other theories, these five selection criteria are discussed in more detail in the final section of the article as desirable characteristics of sound theory.

Scribner's model of practical thinking at work.   Scribner used activity theory as developed by Leont'ev (1981) to bridge the conceptual relationship between knowing and doing in her cognitive studies of work. Activity theory explains purposeful behavior by focusing on the structure of the activity itself. For Leont' ev, the activity is the appropriate unit of analysis for human behavior. An activity can be analyzed at three levels. First, at the highest level of organization is the motivation of the activity, which provides coherence to the other levels. At the next level are goal-directed actions, carried out in the service of the activity. At the third level are operations, or the specific conditions under which actions are carried out. For example, if our action is traveling from one place to another in the service of some activity (e.g., pursuing leisure and recreation), whether we walk, drive, or use some other means of transportation is an operation that depends on distance and other specific conditions related to the action.

Because dynamic relationships exist among the three elements of the theory, the theory presents different levels of analysis for studying work activity. Activities, actions, and operations may change positions in the hierarchy relative to one another according to changing situations, new knowledge, and the intentions of the human agent. Because motivated activities, actions, and operations are defined according to their functions rather than properties inherent in the elements themselves, an activity can lose its motivating force and become an action in the service of another activity (e.g., losing interest in the intrinsic value of one's job and performing it primarily for income). Hence, questions about performance or the structure of work in different environments can be asked at the level of the activity, the action, and the operation. Because an activity is a dynamic system, methods of studying the activity can change as the activity changes and as new questions about it emerge.

Scribner's model of practical thinking is strongly influenced by the notion of activities as mediators of knowing and doing. The collection of Scribner's cognitive studies of work concludes with a paper that presents her model of practical thinking (Tobach et al., 1997). The model is organized around four principles synthesized from Scribner's studies of dairy workers (Scribner, 1984), industrial machinists (Martin & Scribner, 1991), bartenders (Scribner & Beach, 1993), indigenous literacy in West Africa (Scribner & Cole, 1981), and practical and theoretical arithmetic (Scribner & Fahrmeier, 1983). Scribner's research sought support for the premise that cognitive skills take shape in the course of participation in socially organized practices. The results of her work are embodied in the four principles of her model: (a) economy of effort functioned as a criterion distinguishing skilled from amateur performance – the "least-effort strategy" was consistently followed by skilled performers whether mental or physical effort was minimized and regardless of resource constraints in the work environment; (b) problem-solving strategies were dependent on specific knowledge about materials and conditions in the immediate task environment; (c) diversity and flexibility of solution modes distinguished expert problem solvers from beginners; and (d) more experienced workers replaced all-purpose algorithms with a menu of solution modes fitted to properties of specific problems in changing environments. Scribner (cited in

Tobach et al., 1997) summarized the four principles in this way: "Thinking in the dairy was goal-directed and regulated by a principle of economy which, operating under changing conditions and on the basis of knowledge and information in the environment, generated flexible solution procedures adapted to particular occasions of use" (p. 380).

Scribner's work and the cognitive demands of new technologies.   Scribner's work demonstrated that workers seek pragmatic solutions through economy of effort regardless of the contingent or deterministic structure of the task. Her study of working intelligence (Scribner, 1984) fully accounts for task unpredictability and the need to go beyond scripted procedures to accommodate the changing demands of the task environment. For example, because each dairy order was different, delivery drivers modified their problem framing and arithmetic solutions to conform to the benefits of either their calculators or paper-and-pencil computations. Ways of solving problems followed means of arriving at solutions.

Systemic interdependence requires knowledge of how one's work fits in with the work of others and the ability to work with others on interdependent tasks. Scribner's theory emphasizes workers' ability to capitalize on available resources to find successful work strategies, including the efficiencies and reduced effort of relying on one's coworkers to accomplish related tasks. However, a dominant theme in Scribner's work, the importance of contextual factors in cognitive studies, is reflected in her theory as a multiplicity of influences, both social and material, on the cognitive strategies people adopt to accomplish their work. Interpersonal relations and interdependencies among workers is one of several key factors identified by Scribner that shape one's repertoire of work behaviors.

Scribner's model emphasizes that successful work strategies are goal directed and vary adaptively with the changing properties of the problems and resources encountered by workers in the task environment. The model explains how workers might respond to stochastic events by relying on flexible solution strategies and improvising with available tools and materials. Task disruptions might trigger the reassessment of means-ends relationships, and solutions would reflect Scribner's concept of mental and physical effort saving. Contextual factors would strongly influence how workers in a production environment learn and adapt their skills on the job. The power and endurance of Scribner's model are evident. Even though it was developed 20 years ago, before technologies considered new today were developed, her theory explains how workers adapt to task contingency and respond to stochastic events. Although today's workers might use Scribner's least-effort strategies and context-specific solutions to achieve competence in today's high-technology work environments, it is not known how well Scribner's model of practical thinking addresses the cognitive demands of distancing technologies or explains the roles of inference and mental modeling to enable more effective use of these technologies. A summary of how Scribner's theory addresses the cognitive demands of new technologies is given in Table 2.

Schon's theory of reflection in action. Schon (1983) argued for a new epistemology of practice that takes as its point of departure the competence and artistry already embedded in skillful practice – especially, the reflection in action through which professionals think about what they are doing while they are doing it. Reflection in action is a theory of learning that explains how reflective practitioners use knowledge and problem solving in their work. Reflection in action is an iterative process that moves through the stages of (a) assessment of the situation, (b) testing of one's preliminary sense of the problem through experiments, (c) examination of results, and (d) reassessment leading to another cycle of problem reformulation. Learning occurs through an iterative process of purposeful actions, discovered consequences, implications, reassessments, and further actions. Using reflection in action, we conduct experiments to examine the validity of our judgments and, in the process, expose ourselves to new possibilities for learning. According to Schon (1983), "the situation talks back, the practitioner listens, and as he appreciates what he hears, he reframes the situation once again" (p. 131). This theory of learning prompted Schon to raise a critical question: What kind of professional education would be appropriate to an epistemology of practice based on reflection in action?

His subsequent work (Schon, 1987) answered this question by proposing that university-based professional schools should learn from such deviant traditions of education for practice as studios of art and design, conservatories of music and dance, athletic coaching, and apprenticeship in the crafts, all of which emphasize coaching and learning by doing. Professional education, Schon (1987) argued, should be redesigned to combine the teaching of applied science with coaching in the use of reflection in action strategies. He proposed a generalized educational setting, the reflective practicum, as a model for professional development in which learning occurs by doing, with the help of coaching, especially through a dialogue of reciprocal reflection in action between coach and student.

The reflective practicum is a methodology for implementing reflection in action in the sense that it brings together the necessary material and contextual resources, along with the coach's personal and technical support for critical reflection. It provides an environment in which students can learn by doing, not simply through trial and error, but through critical refection as students are coached in refection in action strategies.

Reflection in action begins with a situation that yields spontaneous routinized responses. As long as the situation appears normal, our responses are tacit and spontaneously delivered without conscious deliberation. Yet routine responses sometimes produce a surprise – an unexpected outcome, pleasant or unpleasant, that does not fit our present knowledge schema. This unexpected consequence triggers reflection. We think about the consequence and

Table 2: Summary of learning theories and the cognitive demands of new technologies

Task characteristic	Theory of learning			
	Scribner	Schon	Wenger	Hutchins
• Contingent versus deterministic tasks	• Problem-solving strategies are adaptive and dependent on specific knowledge of materials and changing conditions in the task environment. • Workers seek pragmatic solutions that reflect economy of mental and physical effort.	• Reflection in action enables workers to spontaneously construct solutions to problems that cannot be fully anticipated in advance.	• Communities of practice allow workers to reach pragmatic solutions through mutual engagement. • Communities of practice legitimize peripheral learning and foster adaptation and sense making in changing work environments.	• In Hutchins's model of cultural cognition, practice, learning, and work environment are all simultaneously transformed. • Workers use tools to transform the (navigation) task by mapping it into a domain, using representations and heuristics, where the answer or the path to the solution is apparent.
• Distancing technologies	• Although Scribner's principle of context-dependent problem solving has been broadly applied to work settings, it is not known how well the theory addresses the cognitive demands of distancing technologies.	• Reflection in action is a means for making sense of new situations through an iterative process of purposeful action, discovered consequences implications, reconstruction of our understanding, and further actions.	• Communities of practice provide a social context for learning about distancing technologies and enable the sharing of representations of these technologies among members across locations.	• Hutchins's model explains how workers' mental representations of their work allow navigation at night when navigators are "distanced" from the sentient cues that relate the ship's position to its environment.

	Scribner's model	Schön's model	Communities of practice	Hutchins
• Stochastic events	• Scribner's model explains how workers improvise with available tools and materials and use flexible solution strategies to respond to task disruptions and stochastic events.	• Workers respond to stochastic events through reflection in action. Reflection in action probes the unexpected disruption and allows for tentative understanding, testing, and reframing of the event to reach a resolution.	• Communities of practice strive to make sense of stochastic events as members exchange individual perspectives on their meaning. • The sharing of interpretations of stochastic events is likely to include explanations for successfully resolving these disruptions.	• Hutchins describes how workers in crisis overcome emotional arousal and construct solutions from procedural knowledge, environmental shortcuts, and bricolage. In these situations, practice, learning, and work environment are all simultaneously transformed.
• Systemic interdependence	• Scribner's model identifies mutual dependencies among colleagues as means for adapting to the changing demands of the task environment.	• Relationships among coaches and students based on reciprocal reflection in action are central to professional development in Schön's model.	• Communities of practice build support and interdependencies that foster the sharing of members' insights and generalizations. • Membership in a community of practice provides access to the knowledge of individuals and of the community of practice.	• Hutchins's conception of distributed cognition reflects the overlapping knowledge among navigation team members and emphasizes networks of interdependence and shared expertise.

ponder why it occurred and, at the same time, we ask, "How have I been thinking about this?" Our thoughts turn back on the surprising phenomenon and, at the same time, back on themselves. Thus, reflection in action is a critical function through which we consciously or unconsciously question the assumptions of our present knowledge.

Schon contrasts reflection in action with the technical rationality of prevailing curricula for professional education. Technical rationality is based on an objectivist view of practice that posits that reality can be known objectively – the reality to be known is distinct from the practitioner's knowing. According to this view, professional knowledge is founded on facts and data; formal inquiry serves to measure, predict, and control the phenomenon of interest.

On the other hand, reflection in action rests on a constructivist view of the reality that professionals face in practice. Reality and its meaning are negotiable, and what is known is influenced by the process of coming to know it. The dynamics of reflection in action cut across the positivist dichotomies of research-practice, means-ends, and knowing-doing. For the reflective professional, practice is researchlike, means and ends are interdependent and may be transformed depending on how the problem is framed, and practice involves personal interaction with the situation in which knowing and doing are inseparable.

Schon's work and the cognitive demands of new technologies. Schon's theory accounts for contingent tasks by acknowledging that professionals are frequently confronted by novel situations and must construct their interpretations and responses accordingly. Schon recognized that procedural knowledge and problem-solving algorithms have limited applications in practice, where most problems are contextual and difficult to predict. The capability for reflection in action addresses these cognitive demands by allowing workers to bypass scripted procedures to arrive at solutions for problems that cannot be fully anticipated in advance.

Reflection in action also explains the cognitive processes needed to respond effectively to stochastic events. A sudden disruption arouses emotion and triggers reassessment of means-ends relationships. Schon's discussion of mental experimentation explains how workers might respond to a sudden systems failure by probing the unexpected disruption, forming a tentative understanding of the event, testing their understanding, and reframing the problem to arrive at a solution. Thus, workers respond to emergent situations by constructing new knowledge through reflection in action.

Reflective practitioners are continuous learners, and those involved in professional practice are regularly confronted by new situations that may be uncertain, ill defined, and incoherent. Problem novelty and ambiguity are among the challenges facing those using distancing technologies that separate people from the physical cues and information present at the operating location. Those who have embraced reflection in action for solving problems and making sense of new situations come to rely on their cognitive strategies for constructing understandings of the new problems confronted in practice. Although referring to the problem solving used to resolve architectural problems of an ambiguous nature, the following statement by Schon (1987) applies to other reflective practitioners, including those who use new technologies: "Their designing is a web of projected moves and discovered consequences and implications, sometimes leading to reconstruction of the initial incoherence – a reflective conversation with the materials of a situation" (p. 42).

Because relationships among coaches and students based on reciprocal reflection in action are central to professional development in Schon's model, the theory reflects the systemic interdependence involved in work situations that include the use of new technologies. One learns and refines reflection in action strategies through ongoing exchanges of reciprocal reflection in action with others. As colleagues in a network of practitioners, those working with new technologies share in shaping each other's problem-solving strategies during reflective practice. A summary of how Schon's theory addresses the cognitive demands of new technologies is given in Table 2.

Communities of practice. Communities of practice are informal associations of workers who share common work problems and seek the benefits of learning from one another. In such communities, learning occurs primarily through participation in social practice (Wenger, 1998).

Underlying communities of practice as an observable phenomenon is Wenger's theory of social learning. The theory embodied in communities of practice builds on previous work in social learning theory and situated cognition. Social learning theory explains learning as a product of the reciprocal interactions among behavior, cognition, and environmental factors. Learning can occur directly, especially when one's learning self-efficacy is high, or vicariously through behavior modeling by others (Bandura, 1977). Situated cognition originates with engagement in the activity itself, not with a preconceived model of how learning should occur. Situated cognition follows an "activity-perception-representation" model, in which the cognitive dynamics of learning appear less open to the predetermined knowledge schemas that are dominant in formal instruction (Brown, Collins, & Duguid, 1989). When people lack experience with a situation or are introduced to a new concept, presenting a relevant model may catalyze the formation of mental representations of what is learned. Along with new perceptions and relevant past experiences, the model becomes part of the present context for learning, in which the learner's activities and perceptions precede mental representation.

Four constructs compose the framework for Wenger's theory of learning: practice, the shared historical and social resources, frameworks, and perspectives that can sustain mutual engagement in action; community, the social configurations in which our enterprises are defined as worth pursuing and our participation is recognizable as competence; identity, how learning changes who we are and creates personal histories of becoming in the context of our communities; and meaning, the ability to experience our life and world as meaningful. Wenger's assumptions about learning and the nature of knowledge include the premise that meaning – our ability to experience the world and our engagement with it as meaningful – is ultimately what learning is to produce. Another assumption that grounds communities of practice is that engagement in social practice is the fundamental process by which we learn and so become who we are. Thus, communities of practice provide a broad conceptual framework for thinking about learning as a process of social participation.

The concept of practice is carefully defined by Wenger as experiences that include both the explicit and the tacit. Practice involves the language, tools, documents, images, symbols, well-defined roles, specified criteria, codified procedures, regulations, and contracts that various practices make explicit for a variety of purposes. But practice also includes the implicit relations, tacit conventions, subtle cues, untold rules of thumb, and so on. Most of these are never articulated, yet they are unmistakable signs of membership in communities of practice and are crucial to the success of their organizations. Learning in practice addresses the need for members to acquire skills and information, but learning goes beyond gaining competence. Members use competence to form an identify of participation. "Practice connotes doing, but not just doing in and of itself. It is doing in a historical and social context that gives structure and meaning to what we do. In this sense, practice is always social practice" (Wenger, 1998, p. 47).

The central issue in learning is becoming a member of a community of practice, not simply learning about practice. A community of practice is a learning community to the extent that it is able to continuously reconfigure the identities of its members and of itself. This flexibility of organization allows it to negotiate and renegotiate the nature of its practice.

Identity in a community is fostered by allowing members to participate peripherally, yet legitimately, in practice. Legitimacy and peripheral participation in practice are often mutually exclusive. Newcomers seeking to participate in the work of a community of practice are granted peripherality (e.g., as students) but denied legitimacy. Conversely, newcomers may be granted legitimacy but are denied the opportunity for development through peripheral participation. The periphery of practice not only is an important site for learning but can be a valuable source of innovation. Sustaining the peripherality of members' perspectives is sought increasingly as a way to generate fresh insights for practice and new directions for the future.

Wenger's work and the cognitive demands of new technologies. Participation in communities of practice allows each member to draw on collective knowledge to construct responses to unanticipated or poorly structured problems, thus enabling members to respond effectively to contingent tasks associated with new technologies. Wenger (1998) illustrated his theory with ethnographic accounts of insurance claims processors who had to respond to customers' questions about claims coverage given only standardized forms and procedures and without full knowledge of how contested claims were ultimately resolved. The tasks they faced were made more contingent by customers' concerns about copayments and company concerns about overpayments, especially in cases of multiple coverages. Workers tried to make sense of these ambiguous situations primarily through social configurations – the networks that claims processors spontaneously formed with each other, not by following claims processing procedures. Communities of practice allowed workers to go beyond standardized procedures and reach pragmatic solutions through mutual engagement.

Stochastic events interrupt work, trigger affective responses, and challenge workers to make sense of unexplained disruptions. Members of a community of practice have the advantage of drawing on collective experiences and emotional support from other members to arrive at explanations and responses for stochastic events. A defining feature of communities of practice is the ability to generate fresh perspectives on practice from members who each develop unique identities within their community of practice. Because unexplained events elicit perspectives from members, some who are central to practice, and others, as newer members, who are more peripheral to practice, responses to a stochastic event are diverse and more likely to include a strategy for explaining and resolving the disruption.

Communities of practice are manifestations of Wenger's theory of social learning, and the relationships and expertise acquired by employees at work are explained in terms of social learning dynamics. This process of social learning helps meet the cognitive demands of distancing technologies, which require users to possess the capabilities for inference, imagination, and mental modeling to understand what is going on elsewhere. Communities of practice have emerged in high technology environments where distancing technologies are present (Marshall & Shipman, 1995; Orr, 1996). Communities of practice enable members to make sense of distancing technologies by supporting a communal memory that allows individuals to understand these technologies without needing to know everything about them and by sharing representations of these technologies among members across locations. Communities of practice provide a social context for learning about new technologies that gives structure and meaning to this process for members.

The creation of identity is at the core of how communities of practice enable members to meet the cognitive demands of new technologies. Wenger (1998) maintained that who we are and what we can do are transformed through the process of becoming members of communities of practice. Identity and membership permit further engagement in social practice and access to collective knowledge, thus providing the basis for establishing the systemic interdependencies needed by users of new technologies. Although a member may lack specific knowledge about a problem, communities of practice provide collective knowledge that enables a response to the unpredictability and ambiguity of new technology (Orr, 1996). Legitimate peripheral participation (Lave & Wenger, 1991) and identity (Wenger, 1998) allow members of communities of practice to share their insights and generalizations and foster the development of systemic interdependence. Thus, communities of practice can build support and personal interdependencies that help to meet the cognitive demands of new technologies (Weick & Roberts, 1993). A summary of how Wenger's theory addresses the cognitive demands of new technologies is given in Table 2.

Cultural cognition.   Hutchins conceptualized cognition as a complex phenomenon in which practice, learning, and the work environment are all simultaneously transformed. Hutchins (1995) stated, "The very same processes that constitute the conduct of activity and that produce changes in the individual practitioners of navigation also produce changes in the social, material, and conceptual aspects of the setting" (p. 374). These changes occur at different rates and degrees of intensity and reflect histories of different lengths, but they all intersect during any moment in human practice. In the course of task performance, learning occurs and subsequent actions are carried out that create elements of representational structure (e.g., written notes or an improvised tool) that survive beyond the end of the task. The artifacts of learning become elements of the environment, just as the environment influences the nature of learning. It is because these processes interact simultaneously that Hutchins considered cognition at work a fundamentally cultural process.

Hutchins (1995) argued that as sociocultural systems, work environments have cognitive properties that are distinct from the cognition of those who perform the work. He confronted contemporary thinking in cognitive science by challenging the adequacy of symbolic processing alone to explain how we use cognitive abilities to solve environmental problems. In this regard, Hutchins stated,

> Notice that when the symbols are in the environment of the human and the human is manipulating the symbols, the cognitive properties of the human are not the same as the properties of the system that is made up of the human in interaction with these symbols. The properties of the human in interaction with the system produce some kind of computation. But that does not mean that the computation is happening inside the person's head. (p. 361)

This premise that knowledge can only be created through human interaction with a sociocultural system that includes environmental artifacts is the foundation for Hutchins's theory of cognition.

Hutchins's work and the cognitive demands of new technologies.   Hutchins (1995) opened *Cognition in the Wild by* describing a stochastic event – the *USS Palau* loses all power and risks running aground in a narrow channel while entering San Diego harbor. Only through expert navigational skills and some luck is the crew able to recover the vessel and safely come to anchor. To meet the cognitive demands of these situations, workers must quickly overcome emotional arousal and construct solutions from procedural knowledge, environmental shortcuts, and bricolage (Levi-Strauss, 1966). Hutchins showed that this process is strongly shaped by the tools and techniques of practice, themselves historically developed. Learning is made easier in work settings where tools are used in public and the details of technology are observable, as they are in the practice of navigation. Hutchins described how the difficulty of piloting large ships is made easier by implementing the fix cycle – a series of procedures in which representations of the position of the ship in its environment are propagated across a series of representational media from initial telescope sightings to the actions taken to correct the ship's course. These tools transform the complex task of navigation by mapping it into a domain, using the navigation chart and other artifacts, where the answer or the path to the solution is apparent.

The fix cycle and other strategies allow navigation at night when navigators are distanced from the sentient cues that relate the ship's position to its environment. They must rely on radar and limited environmental prompts to inform actions to maintain the ship's course. Navigators' mental representations of the ship's position in oceanic darkness strongly influence the nature of the activities navigators use to monitor the ship's course during their watch. The likelihood of encountering unanticipated contingent tasks increases when navigating through infrequently traveled waters and especially when piloting ships in the restricted waters of harbors and coastlines. Contingent tasks require the generation of novel responses (e.g., altering course and speed in response to approaching pleasure craft or changing weather) that may not be part of established procedures, because this type of navigation requires both adherence to restricted waters protocol (i.e., more frequent implementation of the fix cycle) and a collective awareness among navigation team members of the possibility of encountering an unscripted situation. Hutchins's model of cultural cognition explains how navigators learn and adapt to rapidly changing navigation conditions through a process in which practice, learning, and the work environment are all simultaneously transformed.

Systemic interdependence is accounted for in Hutchins's model by overlapping distributions of knowledge among members of the navigation team and by the structure of shipboard authority and decision making. Hutchins clearly described the areas of overlapping knowledge among navigation team members, showed how the career trajectories of navigators are advanced through mastering ever-increasing areas of knowledge, and emphasized a decision-making process in which key personnel and environmental cues interact simultaneously, especially during crisis. Hutchins's notion of distributed cognition reflects the network of interdependencies and the sharing of expertise associated with systemic interdependence.

The fix cycle also illustrates a central premise of Hutchins's theory of cultural cognition – technology is best used to address the cognitive demands of complex tasks by using it to simplify the task, not to amplify cognitive ability. Illustrating the same point, Norman (1997) gave the example of using a computer for writing. Instead of designing computers and software programs to help the author create ideas with dialog boxes, menu choices, and other symbolic clutter, the computer should be used as a word processor to simplify the output process. Rather than attempting to use technology to extend one's cognitive abilities, technology should transform what are normally difficult cognitive tasks into easy ones. A summary of how Hutchins's theory addresses the cognitive demands of new technologies is given in Table 2.

Implications for Further Research

This section summarizes key ideas from the preceding discussion and offers directions for further research on learning theory, future studies of workplace learning, and theory building.

Implications for research on learning theory. Several implications for further research emerge from this examination of learning theory and the cognitive demands of new technologies. First, the four theories examined in the article address some of the cognitive demands of new technologies discussed more completely than others. All four theories explain cognitive mechanisms related to how workers deal with the cognitive demands of contingent versus deterministic tasks, stochastic events, and systemic interdependence, albeit from different theoretical perspectives (see Table 2). However, the task characteristic of distancing technologies is only partially addressed by these theories. Hutchins's theory offers the most complete treatment of this task characteristic with its explicit description of the cognitive strategies and navigation techniques used by navigators to pilot ships in unknown waters at night. In addition, the theories of Wenger and Schon offer plausible explanations of how one might adapt to the cognitive demands of distancing technologies. However, the relevance of Scribner's theory to this task characteristic is speculative. Distancing technologies separate the worker physically and psychologically from elements of the task environment and require capabilities for inference, imagination, and mental modeling to understand what is going on elsewhere. Technologies with distancing properties such as those enabled by the Internet and satellite technology are among the most recent, complex, and rapidly developing of technologies affecting the workplace. Because technologies with distancing properties are complex and have very short design-implementation cycles (i.e., they quickly become obsolete and replaced by newer technologies), there is little time to assimilate considerations from new users and applications before the next generation of technologies is introduced. Thus, the turnover, complexity, and rapid development cycles associated with these technologies account, in part, for why they are incompletely addressed by theories of learning. Future research is needed to further examine the requirements these technologies place on users. Moreover, we need to know more about the human and environmental factors that support effective learning in this context. How do users develop the capabilities for inference, imagination, and mental modeling associated with the effective use of these technologies? What resources and environmental conditions are most conducive to developing expertise in the use of distancing technologies? Research to address these and other questions is needed to formulate new or revised theoretical explanations of effective learning in the use of these technologies.

Future research is also needed to examine questions specific to other learning theories examined in this article. Schon's theory of reflection in action reconceptualized teaching and learning in the professions. Although it explains how professionals engage in reflective practice, its applicability to nonprofessionals (technicians, supervisors, and skilled personnel who may not be considered professionals) is less apparent. Are skilled nonprofessionals included among those for whom learning through reflection in action is intended to apply? Although there is ample evidence that the capability for reflective practice is not limited to professionals, the scope and application of this theory to various populations of employees and occupations remains a question open to further study.

Those who have closely studied communities of practice have raised some concern about their nebulous nature. Wenger and Snyder (2000) stated that "the organic, spontaneous and informal nature of communities of practice makes them resistant to supervision and interference" (p. 141). This makes communities of practice difficult to identify, assess, and cultivate. Thus, their existence in organizational contexts presents a paradox. Communities of practice create a type of value increasingly sought by organizations, yet the active development of such communities by organizations destroys them. How can communities of practice be fostered if their organic, spontaneous, and informal nature makes them resistant to supervision and interference?

Further research might also attempt to extend Scribner's model of practical thinking. Although Scribner's least-effort strategies and context-specific solutions provide valuable insights into the cognitive strategies used by those in the work settings she studied, how well does Scribner's model explain the contingent, stochastic, interdependent nature of today's work? Further research to address these questions promises to yield valuable revisions and extensions of these theoretical explanations of how learning occurs in contemporary work environments.

What can we learn from these theories? The learning theories examined in this article are but four among many theories that have been developed to explain learning in a variety of contexts including experiential learning,

learning in formal educational settings, workplace learning and on-the-job training, informal and incidental learning, role- and occupation-specific learning, and other types of learning. The ubiquity of learning and the broad range of contexts in which it occurs constrain the ability of learning theories to explain more than a particular domain within this diverse phenomenon. Even so, a class of learning theories is available to those seeking theoretical explanations of learning in work settings, and from among these, specific theories are available that adequately address the types of work settings and technical tasks discussed in this article. A central contention of this article is that relatively few learning theories that have been applied by scholars to work settings fully capture the behavioral and environmental dynamics of this distinctive phenomenon. Because the four theories selected for discussion here explain this phenomenon better than other theories, their attributes merit further examination. What is noteworthy here is not which of these four theories (Scribner's, Schon's, Wenger's, or Hutchins's) is the best or right theory for explaining this type of learning but the acknowledgment that this class of theories has theoretical properties that enable them to provide effective explanations of work-related learning and that distinguish them from other learning theories.

Some features of sound theories.   The four theories discussed in this article provide meaningful explanations of how learning occurs in the type of work settings discussed here. Why is this? Considering the need to reflect the workplace, what are the features of a good theory of learning? Five attributes embodied in the four theories covered in this article are summarized next.

1. Each theory describes specific cognitive processes. All the theories make explicit the cognitive processes for learning and describe the dynamics of learning in particular environments. Schon described the dynamics of learning as iterative cycles of reflection in action. Hutchins explained learning as a sociocultural process that occurs simultaneously with the activities of practice and changes in the environment. Scribner described specific solution strategies and how they were derived through learning by experienced workers. Wenger described how learning in practice is generated by the dynamic tension between experience and competence. All four theories describe specific cognitive processes and clearly explain how the dynamics of learning relate to other aspects of their theories.
2. Each theory addresses learning as an enabler and product of work practices. Rather than treating either learning or work practice as dominant, each theory reflects their reciprocal relationship by grounding learning in the conduct of practice. Work practice is one of four central concepts in Wenger's theory of social learning; Schon proposed the reflective practicum as the setting to operationalize his theory of learning; Scribner showed how cognitive skills were dependent on the materials and conditions of practice; and

Hutchins proposed practice as the intersection of work activity, learning, and the environment, where all are simultaneously transformed.

3. Each theory explains how learning occurs in authentic work settings. Each theorist relied on ethnography or intimate knowledge of practice to describe the work settings and define the tasks in which learning was studied. None of the studies from which these theories were derived were purely theoretical or carried out in laboratories or other experimental settings.

4. Each theory is comprehensive in its treatment of the multiple ways in which knowledge can be generated. Rather than conceptualizing working knowledge as arising from cognitive or environmental sources alone, each theory accounts for multiple way s in which knowledge about work is generated and used. The theories explain how working knowledge can emerge from personal reflection and experience; from practice-specific tools, techniques, and conditions; through relationships with others; and through associations with other elements of the system and the environment.

5. Each theory offers propositions that can be generalized to other settings. Although each theory was based in studies of specific work environments and occupations, all theories offer principles of learning that have been applied elsewhere. Scribner's "least-effort strategy" has been demonstrated in nonindustrial settings (Scribner & Cole, 1981; Scribner & Fahrmeier, 1983). Schon's reflection in action has been applied to the preparation of architects, urban planners, artists, musicians, and athletes (Schon, 1987). Wenger's theory has been used to explain communities of practice among photocopier repair technicians (Orr, 1996), refrigeration technicians (Henning, 1998), and insurance claims processors (Wenger, 1998). Hutchins's original work on navigation technology has been applied to airline pilots (Hutchins & Klausen, 1996) and to the design of the human-computer interface (Hutchins, Hollan, & Norman, 1986). Each theory offers new knowledge about learning that can be applied and extended through further research.

These five features of the learning theories discussed in this article provide a basis for developing better theories of learning. In addition to the criteria for evaluating theory offered by Bacharach (1989), Patterson (1983), and Whetten (1989) that can be applied to all theories, the features listed above are specifically applicable to theories intended to model the dynamics of learning and working. An additional distinction that cuts across these five features is also present in the four theories discussed here – the theories of Scribner, Schon, Wenger, and Hutchins conceptualize learning and working as phenomena that occur simultaneously.

Learning and working are inseparable.   Judging from the volume and variety of such studies, research on workplace learning is appealing to many researchers from a variety of disciplines. Many of these studies focus primarily or exclusively on the phenomenon of learning and give secondary or cursory consideration to work activity. How appropriate is such an approach for the study of learning and working? The four theorists discussed in this article provide a clear, coherent response to this question – studies of learning and working should treat these as phenomena that occur simultaneously. The four theories examined here ground learning in the conduct of work practice and emphasize their reciprocal relationship. This important premise is the basis for the following model for studies of learning and working.

The fabric of work activity is woven with fibers of work and fibers of learning (see Figure 1). Although learning and working are inseparable during most work activity, there are periods during which one or the other is the dominant or exclusive activity, such as during routine tasks that are performed unconsciously or during periods when learning is uninterrupted by task demands. These separations of learning from working are shown in Figure 1 as discontinuities in the fabric of work activity. However, much work activity can be characterized generally as a phenomenon in which learning and working are inseparable. This feature of work activity is evident in Scribner's model of practical thinking, Schon's reflection in action, Wenger's concept of practice, and Hutchins's cultural cognition.

Future studies of learning and working need to treat these as phenomena that occur simultaneously. This requires giving greater attention to the basic questions such studies seek to answer. Research questions such as, How does learning occur in a particular setting? generally examine only the learning fibers of the fabric of work activity. Although such studies may include references to the conditions or context of the work itself, they do so in a way that marginalizes these factors and provides a central focus on learning. Unlike questions that probe learning only, broader questions that examine the entire fabric of work activity might ask, What is happening as someone works through a task or project? Such a question is more likely to reveal how the fibers of learning and working are woven together to constitute the type of work activity described in this article. Because the theories

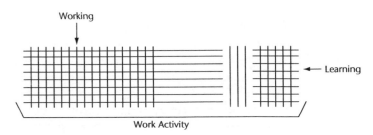

Figure 1: The fabric of work activity

of Scribner, Schon, Wenger, and Hutchins conceptualize learning and working as phenomena that occur simultaneously, this represents an additional feature that distinguishes these from other learning theories and can be added to the five distinctions previously discussed. Those interested in developing broader, more integrative theories of how learning and working occur in contemporary work environments might arrive at better theories of learning and working using this perspective.

Implications for theory-building research. Precise and logical conceptual development is the theorist's central task when working back and forth from general domains to specific concepts and from existing knowledge to new theory. Just as the empirical researcher provides a detailed account of all data sources, instrumentation, and methods of data collection and analysis, the theorist allows other scholars to replicate the theorizing process by explicitly tracing all paths from existing knowledge to new theory. In short, clearly stated relationships among carefully selected concepts produces better theory. Theorizing that is replicable and provocative is more likely to advance our knowledge by stimulating further inquiry that leads to new knowledge. But how does a theory become provocative?

Provocativeness (or fruitfulness) is the capacity of a theory to change research and/or practice in the field. A theorist who wishes to accurately model a cross-disciplinary phenomenon such as the cognitive demands of new technologies must confront the limits of her or his own discipline in relation to the cross-disciplinary system being modeled by the theory. Theorists who are interested in cross-disciplinary phenomena, but who venture too far away from domains they understand in attempting to explain these phenomena, risk developing theory that is poorly informed in unfamiliar domains. On the other hand, theorists who embrace the multiple content domains needed to model cross-disciplinary phenomena are likely to produce provocative theory.

So the theorist (or cross-disciplinary theory-building team) starts with the accumulated knowledge from fields related to the phenomenon of interest. In the case of the model proposed in this article, relevant knowledge was needed from human factors/ergonomics, industrial engineering, information technology, psychology, cognitive science, and education. The model presented here was constructed to be a carefully selected combination of ideas synthesized from knowledge in all of these areas. Mindful of the need for balance between a theory's comprehensiveness and parsimony, specific concepts – some created to explain new phenomena and others adapted from existing theories, were integrated into the full model. Because the new model contains thinking from several disciplines, it is more likely to stimulate new ideas within the theorist's own discipline. New theories are provocative, in part, because they stretch our thinking across existing paradigms and beyond the boundaries of our discipline.

References

Adler, P. S. (1986). New technologies, new skills. *California Management Review, 29*(1), 9–28.

Bacharach, S. B. (1989). Organizational theories: Some criteria for evaluation. *Academy of Management Review, 14*(4), 496–515.

Bandura, A. (1977). *Social learning theory*. Englewood Cliffs, NJ: Prentice Hall.

Barley, S. R., & Bechky, B. A. (1994). In the backrooms of science: The work of technicians in science labs. *Work and Occupations, 21*(1), 85–126.

Barley, S. R., & Orr, J. E. (1997). *Between craft and science: Technical work in U.S. settings.* Ithaca, NY: ILR Press.

Berniker, E. (1987, November). *Understanding technical systems*. Paper presented at the Symposium on Management Training Programs: Implications of New Technologies, Geneva, Switzerland.

Brown, J. S., Collins, A., & Duguid, P. (1989). Situated cognition and the culture of learning. *Educational Researcher, 18*(1), 32–42.

Campbell, D. J. (1988). Task complexity: A review and analysis. *Academy of Management Review, 13*(1), 40–52.

Campion, M. A., & Medsker, G. J. (1992). Job design. In G. Salvendy (Ed.), *Handbook of human factors*. New York: John Wiley.

Davenport, T. H. (1993). *Process innovation: Reengineering work through information technology*. Boston: Harvard Business School Press.

Engestrom, Y., & Middleton, D. (1996). *Cognition and communication at work*. New York: Cambridge University Press.

Gagne, R. M. (1962). Military training and principles of learning. *American Psychologist, 17*, 83–91.

Gill, T. G. (1996). Expert systems usage: Task change and intrinsic motivation. *MIS Quarterly, 20*, 301–329.

Griffith, T. L., & Northcraft, G. B. (1996). Cognitive elements in the implementation of new technology: Can less information provide more benefits? *MIS Quarterly, 20*, 99–110.

Graham, L. (1993). Inside a Japanese transplant: A critical perspective. *Work and Occupations, 20*(2), 147–173.

Hackman, J. R. (1969). Toward understanding the role of tasks in behavioral research. *Acta Psychologica, 31*, 97–128.

Hackman, J. R., & Oldham, G. R. (1980). *Work redesign*. Reading, MA: Addison-Wesley.

Henning, P. H. (1998). Ways of learning: An ethnographic study of the work and situated learning of a group of refrigeration service technicians. *Journal of Contemporary Ethnography, 27*(1), 85–136.

Hutchins, E. (1995). *Cognition in the wild.* Cambridge, MA: MIT Press.

Hutchins, E., Hollan, J., & Norman, D. A. (1986). Direct manipulation interfaces. In D. A. Norman & S. Draper (Eds.), *User centered system design: New perspectives in human-computer interaction*. Hillsdale, NJ: Lawrence Erlbaum.

Hutchins, E., & Klausen, T. (1996). Distributed cognition in an airline cockpit. In Y. Engestrom & D. Middleton (Eds.), *Cognition and communication at work*. New York: Cambridge University Press.

Khurana, A. (1999). Managing complex production processes. *Sloan Management Review, 40*(2), 85–97.

Lave, J., & Wenger, E. (1991). *Situated learning: Legitimate peripheral participation*. New York: Cambridge University Press.

Leont'ev, A. N. (1981). *Problems of the development of mind*. Moscow: Progress.

Levi-Strauss, C. (1966). *The savage mind.* Chicago: University of Chicago Press.

Locke, E. A., & Latham, G. P. (1990). *A theory of goal setting and task performance.* Englewood Cliffs, NJ: Prentice Hall.

Marshall, C. C., & Shipman, F. M. (1995). Making large-scale information resources serve communities of practice. *Journal of Management Information Systems, 11*(4), 65–87.

Martin, L. M. W., & Scribner, S. (1991). Laboratory for cognitive studies of work: A case study of the intellectual implications of new technology. *Teachers College Record, 92*(4), 582–602.

Norman, D. A. (1988). Knowledge in the head and in the world. In *The psychology of everyday things.* New York: Basic Books.

Norman, D. A. (1993). *Things that make us smart: Defending human attributes in the age of the machine.* Reading, MA: Addison-Wesley.

Norman, D. A. (1997). Melding mind and machine. *Technology Review, 100,* 29–31.

Norros, L. (1996). System disturbances as springboard for development of operators' expertise. In Y. Engestrom & D. Middleton (Eds.), *Cognition and communication at work.* New York: Cambridge University Press.

Orr, J. E. (1996). *Talking about machines: An ethnography of a modern job.* Ithaca, NY: ILR Press.

Patterson, C.H.(1983). *Theories of counseling and psychotherapy.* Philadelphia: Harper and Row.

Pentland, B. T. (1997). Bleeding edge epistemology: Practical problem solving in software support hot lines. In S. R. Barley & J. E. Orr (Eds.), *Between craft and science: Technical work in U.S. settings.* Ithaca, NY: ILR Press.

Salvendy, G. (1987). *Handbook of human factors.* New York: John Wiley.

Schon, D. A. (1983). *The reflective practitioner: How professionals think in action.* New York: Basic Books.

Schon, D. A. (1987). *Educating the reflective practitioner.* San Francisco: Jossey-Bass.

Scribner, S. (1984). Studying working intelligence. In B. Rogoff & J. Lave (Eds.), *Everyday cognition: Its development in social context.* Cambridge, MA: Harvard University Press.

Scribner, S., & Beach, K. D. (1993). An activity theory approach to memory. *Applied Cognitive Science, 7,* 185–190.

Scribner, S., & Cole, M. (1981). *The psychology of literacy.* Cambridge, MA: Harvard University Press.

Scribner, S., & Fahrmeier, E. (1983). *Practical and theoretical arithmetic* (Working Paper No. 3). New York: Industrial Literacy Project, City University of New York.

Simon, H. A. (1981). *The sciences of the artificial* (2nd ed.). Cambridge, MA: MIT Press.

Smith, T. J., Henning, R. A., & Smith, K. U. (1994). Sources of performance variability. In G. Salvendy & W. Karwowski (Eds.), *Design of work and development of personnel in advanced manufacturing.* New York: Wiley-Interscience.

Tobach, E., Falmagne, R. J., Parlee, M. B., Martin, L. M. W., & Kapelman, A. S. (1997). *Mind and social practice: Selected writings of Sylvia Scribner.* New York: Cambridge University Press.

Wegner, D. M., Erber, R., & Raymond, P. (1991). Transactive memory in close relationships. *Journal of Personality and Social Psychology, 61*(6), 923–929.

Weick, K. A. (1990). Technology as equivoque: Sensemaking in new technologies. In P. S. Goodman & L. S. Sproull and Associates (Eds.), *Technology and organizations.* San Francisco: Jossey-Bass.

Weick, K. A., & Roberts, K. H. (1993). Collective mind in organizations: Heedful interrelating on flight decks. *Administrative Science Quarterly, 38,* 357–381.

Wenger, E. (1998). *Communities of practice: Learning, meaning, and identity.* New York: Cambridge University Press.

Wenger, E., & Snyder, W. M. (2000). Communities of practice: The organizational frontier. *Harvard Business Review, 78*(1), 139–145.

Whetten, D. A. (1989). What constitutes a theoretical contribution? *Academy of Management Review, 14*(4), 490–495.

Woods, D. P., O'Brien, J. F., & Hanes, L. F. (1987). Human factors challenges in process control: The case of nuclear power plants. In G. Salvendy (Ed.), *Handbook of human factors*. New York: John Wiley.

Woodward, J. (1994). *Industrial organization: Theory and practice* (4th ed.). London: Oxford University Press.

Zuboff, S. (1988). *In the age of the smart machine: The future of work and power*. New York: Basic Books.

38

Cognitive Conceptions of Learning

Thomas J. Shuell

P sychologists and educators have long been interested in understanding how people learn, for the concept of learning is central to many different human endeavors. Teaching, child rearing, counseling, and a wide variety of training situations, to name just a few areas, are all concerned in one way or another with individuals learning new knowledge and/or behavior. There is, of course, a long history of empirical research on learning dating back to the classic research of Ebbinghaus (1913) first published in 1885. During the first half of the present century, research on learning flourished (nearly all of it within the behavioral tradition of psychology), and learning theory exerted a strong influence on research and practice in many different spheres of psychology and education.

This influence and interest in learning remained strong well into the 1960s. During the late 1960s and early 1970s, however, the *zeitgeist* of psychology began to change from a behavioristic to a cognitive orientation. Concern for the mind and the way it functions returned to scientific psychology. This cognitive orientation was clearly evident in research on topics such as meaningful verbal learning (Ausubel, 1962, 1963), discovery learning (e.g., Bruner, 1957, 1961), imagery (Paivio, 1969, 1971), "mathemagenic" behaviors (behaviors that give birth to learning) (Rothkopf, 1965, 1970), generative learning (Wittrock, 1974, 1978), and mnemonics (e.g., Bower, 1970).

Nevertheless, during the period from about 1960 to 1980, research on learning per se – that is, a concern for those factors that produce *changes* in an individual's behavior and/or knowledge – diminished drastically. For a variety of reasons (some of which will be discussed below), cognitive psychologists' interest in learning gave way to other concerns. Cognitive psychologists occasionally

Source: *Review of Educational Research*, 56(4) (1986): 411–436.

acknowledged the importance of learning, but little effort was devoted to furthering our understanding of how learning occurs. In appraising this situation, Voss (1978) concluded that "although the concept of learning may be found in cognitive psychology, it also must be conceded that the cognitive view of learning is vague, is abstract, and, most important, is lacking a substantive data base" (p. 13). Similar conclusions were voiced by other cognitive psychologists (e.g., J. R. Anderson, 1982; Greeno, 1980a; Langley & Simon, 1981).

Since about 1975, however, cognitive psychologists have shown a growing interest in learning, and a new era of research on learning may be at hand. Much, but certainly not all, of this more recent research represents an information-processing orientation and involves sophisticated computer models of learning. As one might expect, these cognitive conceptions of learning (both the earlier and the more recent ones) differ from traditional, behavioristic conceptions of learning in ways that enrich our understanding of how humans acquire new knowledge and new ways of doing things.

The purpose of this article is to examine current conceptions of learning, primarily from the vantage point of modern-day cognitive psychology. To provide an appropriate perspective, however, similarities and differences between traditional and cognitive conceptions of learning will be discussed. After first highlighting some characteristics of traditional conceptions of learning, ways in which cognitive psychology has influenced research on learning will be considered. Next, several cognitive theories of learning will be described. Finally, implications for future research on learning and for educational practices will be outlined.

Traditional Conceptions of Learning

During the 100 years since Ebbinghaus' pioneering research, nearly all research on learning has been conducted within a behavioral framework. Although the Gestalt psychologists of the 1910s to 1930s (perhaps the chief forerunners of modern-day cognitive psychology) occasionally discussed learning, they were more interested in perception than in learning, and they usually interpreted learning in terms of perceptual principles of organization. For a variety of reasons (see, e.g., Stevenson, 1983), traditional research on learning focused primarily on animal learning rather than human learning (although this research has not been totally void of cognitive influence – see, e.g., Kimble, 1984). As a result, most research on learning has involved relatively simple forms of learning. Even in the case of human learning, most traditional studies of learning have employed simple tasks that involve memorization more than comprehension. But before continuing, perhaps it would be useful to consider what we normally mean by the term learning.

The Concept of Learning

The concern for learning, of course, focuses on the way in which people acquire new knowledge and skills and the way in which existing knowledge and skills are modified. Nearly all conceptions of learning have involved – either explicitly or implicitly – three criteria for defining *learning* (see, e.g., Shuell & Lee, 1976): (a) a change in an individual's behavior or ability to do something, (b) a stipulation that this change must result from some sort of practice or experience, and (c) a stipulation that the change is an enduring one. The primary purpose of the latter two qualifications is to exclude certain types of behavioral changes that do not seem to represent what we mean by learning (maturation, temporary changes due to drugs, etc.).

Although there appears to be general agreement among behavioral and cognitive conceptions of learning with regard to the defining characteristics of the underlying phenomenon, there are also a number of important differences between the two orientations. The only formal definition of learning from a cognitive perspective that I have been able to find (Langley & Simon, 1981) fits the above criteria almost perfectly: "Learning is any process that modifies a system so as to improve, more or less irreversibly, its subsequent performance of the same task or of tasks drawn from the same population" (p. 367). The main difference appears to be the emphasis on the performance of a system rather than on the behavior of an individual. Cognitive conceptions of learning, however, focus on the acquisition of knowledge and knowledge structures rather than on behavior per se, on "...discrete change between states of knowledge rather than [on] change in probability of response" (Greeno, 1980a, p. 716). The significance of this difference is not as minor as it might appear, for if it is knowledge that one learns, "...then behavior must be the *result* of learning, rather than that which itself is learned" (Stevenson, 1983, p. 214).

There also tends to be general (although not complete) agreement among behavioral and cognitive conceptions of learning that both environmental factors and factors internal to the learner contribute to learning in an interactive manner (e.g., Brown, Bransford, Ferrara, & Campione, 1983). As one might expect, however, the different positions disagree on which side of this learner-environment equation is most important. For example, behavioral approaches focus on changing the environment in order to influence learning (e.g., by providing reinforcement when the appropriate response is made), whereas cognitive approaches focus more on changing the learner (e.g., by encouraging the person to use appropriate learning strategies). There are also considerable differences with regard to both what is learned (e.g., behavior vs. structured knowledge) and the factors that influence the learning process (e.g., reinforcement vs. strategies for obtaining feedback).

The Transition Begins

Although the seeds of modern-day cognitive psychology were present during the 1930s (e.g., Bartlett, 1932; Tolman, 1932), they did not grow to fruition, especially with regard to learning, for many years. During the 1960s, research on learning, especially verbal learning (the main body of research on human learning during this period), began to undergo a change that reflected views more consistent with cognitive interpretations of behavior. Investigators began to question, for example, whether simple conceptions of learning could adequately handle the more complex forms of learning encountered in real-life situations such as the classroom. The debate about whether classical conditioning and operant conditioning represent one or two different types of learning (see Kimble, 1961) was extended by Gagné's (1962, 1965) postulation of eight types of learning, including complex forms of learning such as concept learning and problem solving. People started to realize that even simple learning materials (e.g., nonsense syllables, isolated words) have meaning and that this meaningfulness can influence the learning process (e.g., Underwood & Schulz, 1960).

The realization that learners were not passive during learning (e.g., Bruner, 1957; Miller, Galanter, & Pribram, 1960) began to spread. For example, subjects often selected a stimulus (the "functional stimulus") that differed from the one intended by the experimenter (the "nominal stimulus") (Underwood, 1963), and when allowed (e.g., the free-recall paradigm), they organized the material being learned in meaningful ways, even in the absence of obvious bases of organization (Shuell, 1969; Tulving, 1968). Thus, a transition had begun from a strictly behavioristic orientation to one that involved more cognitive activities. But somewhere in the transition the concern for learning got set aside.

There are many reasons for the demise of interest in learning. Among the more obvious reasons are the following:

1. The appearance of experimental data that were difficult to reconcile with existing theories of learning (see Stevenson, 1983; White, 1970). Included among the many examples of this problem are age changes in the solution of reversal-nonreversal shift problems (Kendler & Kendler, 1962), the presence of organizational patterns in free recall (Shuell, 1969), and the transfer data that led to the notion of the functional stimulus (Underwood, 1963).
2. The feeling that one must understand the nature of the performance system before one can investigate learning (Newell & Simon, 1972). It is difficult to study transitions between knowledge states without first knowing something about the knowledge states between which the transition is being made, a problem directly analogous to the classical requirements for operational definitions and criterion specification.

3. The realization that the laws of learning depend on the context in which it occurs and the prior knowledge of the learner (for a good discussion of this point, see Siegler, 1983).
4. The ability of fresh ideas to capture the interest of investigators becoming bored with decades of traditional thinking about learning – that is, the *zeitgeist* of cognitive psychology.

In addition, the cognitive psychologists of the 1960s and 1970s became interested in identifying and describing the various stages and processes involved in human information processing. This focus led naturally to a concern for the nature of the memory system rather than learning – that is, how knowledge is represented in memory rather than how changes in knowledge take place. Different research questions were being asked; different paradigms were being employed; different assumptions were being made; and different theories were being developed.

The Influence of Cognitive Psychology

Cognitive psychology is concerned with various mental activities (such as perception, thinking, knowledge representation, and memory) related to human information processing and problem solving, and it presently represents the mainstream of thinking in both psychology and education. The emphasis is no longer strictly on behavior, but on the mental processes and knowledge structures that can be inferred from behavioral indices and that are responsible for various types of human behavior. Thus, with regard to learning, the search by learning psychologists of the 1950s and 1960s for atheoretical, functional relationships (Underwood, 1964) has shifted to a concern for the thought processes and mental activities that mediate the relationship between stimulus and response (see, e.g., Wittrock, 1986).

Nevertheless, cognitive psychology has influenced learning theory and research in several significant ways, including (a) the view of learning as an active, constructive process; (b) the presence of higher-level processes in learning; (c) the cumulative nature of learning and the corresponding role played by prior knowledge; (d) concern for the way knowledge is represented and organized in memory; and (e) concern for analyzing learning tasks and performance in terms of the cognitive processes that are involved.

Learning as an Active Process

Cognitive approaches to learning stress that learning is an active, constructive, and goal-oriented process that is dependent upon the mental activities of the learner. This view, of course, contrasts with the behavioral orientation that focuses on behavioral changes requiring a predominantly passive response from the learner to various environmental factors. Although operant conditioning requires the learner to make an overt response (so that it can be reinforced), the active nature of learning suggested by cognitive psychologists is very different. The cognitive orientation, for example, focuses on the mental activities of the learner that lead up to a response, and it explicitly acknowledges the following: (a) the role of metacognitive processes such as planning and setting goals and subgoals (e.g., Brown et al., 1983; Flavell, 1981); (b) the active selection of stimuli (e.g., the distinction between functional and nominal stimuli; Underwood, 1963); (c) the attempt by learners to organize the material they are learning, even when no obvious bases of organization are present in the materials being learned (e.g., Shuell, 1969; Tulving, 1968); (d) the generation or construction of appropriate responses (e.g., Wittrock, 1974); and the use of various learning strategies (e.g., Weinstein & Mayer, 1986).

The suggestion that memory (e.g., Bartlett, 1932; Cofer, 1973; Jenkins, 1974) and learning (e.g., Wittrock, 1974) both require the learner to actively construct new knowledge and strategies is appealing to many cognitive psychologists, but these views are plagued with a theoretical paradox (see, e.g., Bereiter, 1985). The problem arises when a learner acquires a new cognitive structure that is more advanced or complex than the structures that are presently possessed. The paradox involves the need to explain how the learner can acquire the new cognitive structure without already having an existing cognitive structure more advanced or complex than the one being acquired – a situation that is easier to explain in terms of innate mental structures than in terms of learning. Bereiter (1985) suggests 10 "resources" that permit one to avoid this "learning paradox," but few studies currently support their validity.

Higher-Level Processes in Learning

Most cognitive conceptions of learning acknowledge the hierarchical nature of the psychological processes responsible for learning. Miller, Galanter, and Pribram's (1960) book, *Plans and the Structure of Behavior*, proved very influential in popularizing the notion that behavior is hierarchically organized. Since the late 1970s, the higher-level (superordinate, executive) processes of learners have typically been referred to as metacognition (see, e.g., Brown, 1978; Brown et al., 1983; Flavell, 1979). Although such analyses raise the homunculus or "inner man" problem, such concerns need not be fatal. (For a discussion of this problem, see Brown et al., 1983.)

Generally, two types of metacognitive activities are involved in learning. The first involves regulation and orchestration of the various activities that must be carried out in order for learning to be successful (planning, predicting what information is likely to be encountered, guessing, monitoring the learning process, etc.) (e.g., Brown, 1978). Since learning is goal oriented, the learner must somehow organize his or her resources and activities in order to achieve the goal. The second is concerned with what one does and does not know about the material being learned and the processes involved in learning it. Flavell and Wellman (1977) suggest four general classes of metacognitive knowledge: (a) tasks – knowledge about the way in which the nature of the task influences performance on the task; (b) self – knowledge about one's own skills, strengths, and weaknesses; (c) strategies – knowledge regarding the differential value of alternative strategies for enhancing performance; and (d) interactions – knowledge of ways in which the preceding types of knowledge interact with one another to influence the outcome of some cognitive performance.

An example of the hierarchical nature of learning is Sternberg's (1984a, 1984b) componential theory of knowledge acquisition. Sternberg suggests that performance is regulated by nine metacomponents (executive processes) such as "recognition of just what the problem is that needs to be solved" (Sternberg, 1984b, p. 165). These metacomponents operate on lower-level performance components (processes used in the execution of a task, such as encoding and comparison) and three knowledge-acquisition components:

1. *Selective encoding* (sifting out relevant information from irrelevant information, in the stimulus environment, in order to select information for further processing).
2. *Selective combination* (combining selected information in such a way as to render it interpretable; that is, integrating it in some meaningful way).
3. *Selective comparison* (rendering newly encoded or combined information meaningful by perceiving its relations to old information previously stored). (Sternberg, 1984b, p. 168)

These knowledge-acquisition components operate on a variety of cues present in the material being learned, although cue utilization is affected by moderating variables such as number of occurrences, variability of contexts, location of cues, importance of the to-be-learned information, and density of the information to be learned (Sternberg, 1984a).

The Role of Prior Knowledge

Learning is cumulative in nature; nothing has meaning or is learned in isolation. Cognitive conceptions of learning place considerable importance on the role played by prior knowledge in the acquisition of new knowledge. Whereas traditional research on verbal learning was concerned with transfer and the effect of proactive inhibition on retention, concern for what the learner had already acquired focused on associations between individual stimuli and responses rather than on the acquisition of meaning from organized bodies of knowledge.

In the early 1970s, several studies (Bransford & Johnson, 1972; Dooling & Lachman, 1971) demonstrated that what the learner already knows and the extent to which this knowledge is activated at the time of learning has important implications for what will be acquired and for whether or not the material being studied will make any sense to the learner. Realizations such as these led to the development of schema theory (e.g., R. C. Anderson, 1984), which stresses that the organized, structured, and abstract bodies of information (known as schemata) that a learner brings to bear in learning new material determine how the task is interpreted and what the learner will understand and acquire from studying the task.

The traditional concept of transfer was concerned with the way prior learning influences later learning, and this influence was explained in terms of the similarity between stimuli and responses in the two situations. The newer cognitive concern for the role of prior knowledge in learning, however, recognizes that for meaningful forms of learning this process is more complex than the one suggested by earlier approaches to transfer. For example, Bransford and Franks (1976) suggest that the role of prior knowledge is to establish "boundary constraints" for identifying both the "sameness" and the "uniqueness" of novel information: "From the present perspective, growth and learning do not simply involve an expansion of some body of interconnected facts, concepts, etc. Learning involves a change in the form of one's knowledge so that it can set the stage for new discoveries" (p. 112). Likewise, within the context of cognitive development, Siegler (1983) and Siegler and Klahr (1982), among others, have emphasized the importance of prior knowledge (especially the rules used to perform various tasks) in determining when children are ready to learn new material.

Another change that has occurred recently is an emphasis on domain-specific knowledge and learning skills (e.g., Glaser, 1984). Although this change in thinking cannot be attributed directly to the rise of cognitive psychology, it has had a substantial influence on cognitive conceptions of learning. Traditional research on learning sought general laws applicable to all individuals and all subject-matter areas. However, recent research on individuals with differing levels of expertise in a particular subject, such as physics (e.g., Chi, Glaser, & Rees, 1982), has shown convincingly that experts and novices solve problems in fundamentally different ways. Although controversy remains over the relative importance of domain-specific knowledge and general, domain-independent learning strategies (e.g., Block, 1985; Glaser, 1984; Sternberg, 1985), it is generally recognized (e.g., Glaser, 1985; Keil, 1984) that both are important in most learning situations. Consequently, there is an important relationship between the emphasis on domain-specific knowledge and the concern for prior knowledge that is evident in research on cognitive learning.

The Question of What is Learned

One major difference between behavioral and cognitive conceptions of learning concerns the nature of what an individual learns. Behavioral approaches typically suggest either that the learner acquires associations or "bonds" between a stimulus and a response (e.g., Thorndike, 1913) or that the issue of what an individual might acquire internally (i.e., "theories" of learning) is totally irrelevant for understanding the factors responsible for learning (i.e., changes in behavior) (Skinner, 1950).

Cognitive psychologists, on the other hand, are primarily concerned with meaning rather than with behavior per se – that is, a concern for the manner in which an individual extracts meaning from some experience. The emphasis is on understanding, not merely on learning how to perform a task, and on the acquisition of knowledge rather than on the acquisition of behavior. If knowledge is what an individual learns, then behavior is the *result* of learning rather than what an individual acquires (Stevenson, 1983). Generally, this knowledge is best represented by complex knowledge structures rather than by simple associations.[1]

These knowledge structures are usually conceptualized as networks of information specifying the relationship among various facts and actions (e.g., J.R. Anderson, 1980; Norman et al., 1975). There are, however, other ways of conceptualizing what an individual acquires in cognitive learning. For example, both Scandura (1970, 1977) and Siegler (1983) have suggested that rules are useful units for characterizing what people learn. Actually, it seems likely that humans have several different ways and/or modes for representing knowledge. For example, a distinction is frequently made in cognitive psychology between propositional (or declarative) and procedural knowledge, and it appears likely that there are several additional forms of knowledge representation (e.g., Gagné & White, 1978; Shuell, 1985) and several different memory systems (Tulving, 1985).

Cognitive Process Analysis

One important consequence of the cognitive influence on learning has been an interest in analyzing performance and cognitive abilities in terms of the cognitive processes involved in performing a cognitive task, including performance on tests of mental ability such as intelligence (e.g., Carroll, 1976; Snow & Lohman, 1984; Sternberg, 1979), inductive reasoning (e.g., Pellegrino & Glaser, 1982), and deductive reasoning (e.g., Johnson-Laird, 1985). For example, Sternberg (1977) proposed that analogical reasoning – which some (e.g., Rumelhart & Norman, 1981) have suggested is the basis of cognitive learning – involves six cognitive processes: (a) encoding the various terms that make up the analogy, (b) inferring the relationship between the first two terms of the analogy, (c) mapping or discovering a higher-order rule that relates the first and third terms of the analogy, (d) applying the results of the inferring and mapping components to the third term in order to generate an appropriate fourth term, (e) an optional justification process in which one of the answers provided is selected as being the closest to the "ideal" answer produced by the application process, and (f) a response process whereby the solution is translated into a response.

This type of cognitive process analysis also has been applied to various types of instructional tasks such as the learning of geometry (e.g., Greeno, 1978, 1980b), physics (e.g., Champagne, Klopfer, & Gunstone, 1982; Heller & Reif, 1984), reading (e.g., Omanson, Beck, Voss, & McKeown, 1984), and addition and subtraction (e.g., Carpenter, Moser, & Romberg, 1982). Such analyses can help us to better understand both the cognitive processes involved in learning and the instructional techniques most likely to facilitate that learning.

Cognitive Theories of Learning

Most cognitive conceptions of learning reflect an overriding concern for the more complex forms of learning, that is, the types of learning frequently characterized as "meaningful" or where one "learns for understanding." For the most part, cognitive psychologists have been interested in the latter approach. As Norman (1978) put it:

> I do not care about simple learning.... that only takes 30 minutes. I want to understand real learning, the kind we all do during the course of our lives.... I want to understand the learning of complex topics.... [those] with such a rich set of conceptual structures that it requires learning periods measured in weeks or even years. (p. 39)

One problem with meaningful learning is that it is difficult to define. Although an operational definition is not readily available, it is possible to provide examples of the differences that concern many investigators. It makes little sense to most people, for example, to say that one "understands" his or her phone number; we "can learn, know, or remember a phone number, but not understand one" (Markman, 1981, p. 63). Only information that is structured or organized can be thought of as being meaningful and can serve as an object of understanding (Bransford & McCarrell, 1974; Moravcsik, 1979). Although some investigators would apparently limit cognitive learning to the acquisition of information that is structured or organized, higher-order thought processes are involved in many forms of simpler learning as well (e.g., when elaboration occurs or when mnemonics are used – see Pressley & Levin, 1983a, 1983b). It seems reasonable to suggest that all of these different types of situations fall within the domain of cognitive learning.

Various attempts have been made over the years to articulate the role of learning from a cognitive or human information-processing perspective (for a detailed discussion of these approaches, see Bower and Hilgard, 1981). The following discussion will focus on those theories that have most influenced current thinking and research on cognitive learning.

Early Conceptions

During the late 1950s and early 1960s, several writers began to formulate cognitive theories of learning. For example, Bruner (1957, 1961) talked about learning in terms of "discovery" and "going beyond the information given." According to Bruner (1957), learning occurs when an "organism ... code[s] something in a generic manner so as to maximize the transferability of the learning to new situations" (p. 51). He goes on to identify four general sets of conditions under which such learning will occur: (a) the "set to learn" or "attitude toward learning", (b) an appropriate need state (in which an "optimal" level of motivation is discussed), (c) prior mastery of the original learning (and its importance for generic coding), and (d) diversity of training.

The first systematic model of cognitive learning, however, was Ausubel's (1962, 1963) subsumption theory of meaningful verbal learning. Ausubel makes clear that the theory is concerned only with "meaningful" (as opposed to "rote"), "reception" (as opposed to "discovery") learning. According to this theory, new, potentially logical information is subsumed (incorporated) into the learner's existing cognitive structure. The availability of an existing cognitive structure – hierarchically organized with progressive differentiation within a given field of knowledge from more inclusive concepts to less inclusive subconcepts – is seen as the major factor affecting meaningful learning, and the use of "advance organizers" (models or other types of representation that provide a structured overview of the material to be learned) can help ensure that such availability exists. Another major factor is the extent to which the new material is discriminable from the existing cognitive structure that subsumes it. This discriminability can be facilitated by repetition and/or by explicitly pointing out the similarities and differences between the new materials and their presumed subsumers in cognitive structure. Finally, the retention of meaningful material was thought to be influenced by repetition, the length of time that relevant subsuming concepts had been part of the learner's cognitive structure, the use of appropriate exemplars, and multi-contextual exposure.

Another early theory of cognitive learning was Wittrock's (1974) model of generative learning. According to this model (Wittrock, 1974, 1978), people learn meaningful material by generating or constructing relationships among new information and knowledge already stored in long-term memory. These verbal and imaginal elaborations occur as the learner seeks to discover the underlying rule or relationship "by drawing inferences [about the rule], applying it, testing it, and relating it to other rules and to experience" (Wittrock, 1978, p. 26). It was recognized that individuals might proceed differently and that different instructional adjuncts could elicit the appropriate cognitive processes. It appears that the primary mechanisms of learning, according to the generative model, consist of the learner making inferences about potential relationships and then actively seeking feedback on the adequacy of these relationships.

Bransford and Franks (1976) suggested that understanding or comprehension involves the acquisition of novel information that is difficult, if not impossible, for the traditional, "memory metaphor" model of learning to explain. They suggest that learning that involves understanding (i.e., comprehension) occurs via a process of decontextualization. That is, knowledge is initially acquired in a specific context; in order for understanding to occur, this knowledge must become more abstract so that it can be related to a variety of different situations. A mechanism for this decontextualization process is not suggested, but Bransford and Franks suggest that concepts and knowledge become abstract by virtue of being used to clarify a number of situations, and thus stress the importance of the learner encountering relevant examples.

Most of the more recent work on cognitive learning has occurred within the area of artificial intelligence (AI), where the goal has been to develop computer programs that can learn. A concern for simulating learning was present in some of the early work on AI – for example, the EPAM model (Feigenbaum, 1959; Simon & Fiegenbaum, 1964). Since about 1975, this interest has intensified, especially with regard to J. R. Anderson's (1982, 1983) ACT theory. The programs of interest here are those intended to serve as models or theories of human cognitive learning. In general, attempts to define cognitive learning have emphasized a system of processes, relationships among concepts and/or facts, and the restructuring of schemata. The similarities and differences between behavioral and cognitive conceptions of learning can be illustrated by considering several prominent theories of cognitive learning and the mechanisms considered to be responsible in the psychological changes we refer to as learning.

Rumelhart and Norman

The first comprehensive theory of cognitive learning was Rumelhart and Norman's (1978) attempt to account for the process of learning within a schema-based theory of long-term memory, although they emphasized that "learning is not a unitary process: No single mental activity corresponding to learning exists.... and no single theoretical description will account for the multitude of ways by which learning might occur"

(p. 50).[2] Rumelhart and Norman suggest three qualitatively different kinds of learning: (a) *accretion*, or the encoding of new information in terms of existing schemata; (b) *restructuring or schema creation*, or the process whereby new schemata are created; and (c) *tuning or schema evolution*, or the slow modification and refinement of a schema as a result of using it in different situations.

Most models of memory involve learning by accretion. New information is interpreted in terms of preexisting schemata, and this process occurs most readily when the material being learned is consistent with schemata already available in memory. The new information is added to knowledge already in memory without any changes being made in the way that knowledge is organized. Accretion involves the acquisition of factual information that some people might refer to as memorization. Resnick (1984) refers to this type of learning as schema instantiation and suggests that it is similar to the Piagetian concept of assimilation. Norman (1978) suggests that "...accretion learning requires study, probably with the use of mnemonic aids (and deep levels of processing). It can be tested by conventional recall and recognition techniques" (p. 40). Interference from related topics tends to be high and transfer to related topics tends to be low.

Tuning and restructuring are similar to the Piagetian concept of accommodation (Resnick, 1984). Restructuring may occur without any formal addition of new knowledge – that is, the learner may already have all of the necessary information and the only thing that occurs is a reorganization of existing knowledge. Rumelhart and Norman (1978) suggest two basic ways for restructuring to occur: (a) *schema induction*, which is a form of learning by contiguity in which certain spatial or temporal co-occurrence of schemata results in the formation of a new schema, and (b) *patterned generation*, in which a new schema is patterned (copied with modifications) on an old schema. Restructuring occurs as a result of encountering examples, analogies, and metaphors, as well as through tutorial interactions such as Socratic dialogue. Tests of restructuring should include conceptual tests and questions that require inference or problem solving (Norman, 1978). Generally, learning that involves the creation of new schemata occurs as the result of analogical processes – that is, we learn new schemata by relating new information to old schemata in analogical ways (Rumelhart & Norman, 1981).

Tuning involves the slow and gradual refinement of existing schemata, a process that lasts a lifetime. Norman (1978) suggests that tuning is "...best accomplished by practice at the task or in using the concepts of the topic matter. Tests of tuning should be measures of speed and smoothness, [including] performance under stress or pressure" (p. 42). With tuning there is low interference from related topics, and transfer to related topics is high with regard to general knowledge and very low with regard to specific (tuned) knowledge.

John Anderson's ACT

Most cognitive psychologists distinguish between declarative and procedural knowledge. *Declarative knowledge* is our knowledge about things and is usually thought to be represented in memory as an interrelated network of facts (e.g., $2 + 3 = 5, 5 \times 4 = 20$) that exist as propositions. *Procedural knowledge* is our knowledge of how to perform various skills (e.g., produce the correct sum when given an addition problem, solve a word problem). John Anderson (1982, 1983) has developed a computer program (i.e., a theory) called ACT (or ACT*, as the current version is called) that is capable of learning procedural knowledge such as solving geometry proofs and other types of problems. In contrast to Rumelhart and Norman's (1978) belief that there are many forms of learning, ACT is based on the presumption that a single set of learning processes is "...involved in the full range of skill acquisition, from language acquisition to problem solving to schema abstraction" (Anderson, 1983, p. 255). Since ACT is the most explicit and comprehensive of current cognitive theories of learning, it will be described in some detail.

The distinction between declarative and procedural knowledge is a fundamental part of the ACT theory. Declarative knowledge is represented in ACT as a *network of propositions* (i.e., statements of relationships among concepts, events, etc.), and procedural knowledge is represented as a *system of productions* (i.e., statements of the circumstances under which a certain action should be carried out and the details of what should be done when that action is appropriate). The theory is concerned with the acquisition of both declarative and procedural knowledge, as well as the transition between the two, although the emphasis is more on the latter than the former.

According to ACT, knowledge in a new domain always begins as declarative knowledge; procedural knowledge is learned by making inferences from facts available in the declarative knowledge system. Anderson (1982, 1983) suggests that three stages are involved in learning procedural knowledge: the declarative stage, the knowledge compilation stage, and the procedural stage. These stages are similar to the three phases of skill learning suggested by Fitts (1964). The ACT theory is basically organized for problem solving in the belief that problem solving is the basic mode of cognition (Anderson, 1982; Newell, 1980). Consequently, the ACT system is organized in a hierarchical, goal-structured manner, with both performance and the various learning mechanisms operating under the control of some goal or subgoal.

When new information is encountered, it is coded probabilistically into a network of existing propositions as declarative knowledge. The activation of various propositions in this network is determined by the strength of nodes – that is, points in the knowledge structure representing specific concepts, relationships among concepts (propositions), or images – which varies directly with practice and inversely with the passage of time. This declarative knowledge has little, if any, direct control on behavior. Rather, the impact of declarative knowledge on behavior, according to Anderson (1982), is

> filtered through an interpretive system that is well oiled in achieving the goals of the system.... New information should enter in declarative form because one can encode information declaratively without committing control to it and because one can be circumspect about the behavioral implications of declarative knowledge. (pp. 380–381)

During the declarative stage, general problem-solving procedures are used to interpret new information in a way that directs the learner's behavior toward dealing with the task at hand. At some point this declarative knowledge is compiled into higher-order procedures (productions) that apply the knowledge and increase efficiency in dealing with the learning task (e.g., problem). Finally, ACT uses an adaptive production system that engages in the type of learning referred to in the preceding section (on Rumelhart and Norman) as tuning, a process that refines the procedure. Three learning mechanisms are used as the basis of this tuning: (a) *generalization,* a process by which production rules become broader in their range of applicability; (b) *discrimination,* a process by which production rules become narrower in their range of applicability; and (c) *strengthening,* a process by which better rules are strengthened and poorer rules are weakened.

An example of how the ACT theory would explain the way a child learns to do addition problems would begin with statements (perhaps spoken by the teacher or read in a textbook) of certain facts such as: "In addition problems, one first adds the numbers in the rightmost column;" "Next, you add the numbers in the second column"[3] and so forth. With some practice (and perhaps examples by the teacher), these statements of fact are transformed into the ability to actually do what these statements say need to be done. (While many educators are aware that knowing about something does not necessarily mean that the student has acquired the procedures for translating that knowledge into practice, this distinction is made explicitly by cognitive psychology.) The ability to carry out the actions specified might be represented as productions (P) such as the following:[4]

P1.   IF   the goal is to do an addition problem,
         THEN   add the numbers in the rightmost column.
P2.   IF   the goal is to do an addition problem and the rightmost column has already been added,
         THEN   add the numbers in the second column.

With additional experience, these (along with other productions) might be compiled into the following, higher-order productions taken from J. Anderson (1982, p. 371):

P3.　　　IF　the goal is to do an addition problem,
　　　THEN　the subgoal is to iterate through the columns of the problem.
P4.　　　IF　the goal is to iterate through the columns of an addition prob-
　　　　　　lem and the rightmost column has not been processed,
　　　THEN　the subgoal is to iterate through the rows of the rightmost
　　　　　　column and set the running total to zero.

These and other productions would then be compiled into yet other, more general productions that would enable the student to solve addition problems smoothly and efficiently. As other tasks are encountered, however, generalization may occur with the result that various production rules will become broader in their range of applicability. Generalization in ACT is similar to the traditional concept of generalization, except that in ACT generalization involves the learner (i.e., the program) searching for appropriate similarities among production rules and then creating a new production rule that combines those features that the two rules have in common. The search for rules is, of course, the feature that distinguishes this cognitive version of generalization from more traditional behavioristic ones. For example, in learning to solve addition problems, the student acquired production P3 above. Later, in learning to solve subtraction problems, the following production may be acquired:

P5.　　　IF　the goal is to do a subtraction problem,
　　　THEN　the subgoal is to iterate through the columns of the problem.

The similarity between productions P3 and P5 are noticed, and the following generalization is formed:

P6.　　　IF　the goal is to do an LV problem,
　　　THEN　the subgoal is to iterate through the columns of the problem.

LV is a "local variable" defined by the specific instances in which the production might apply. The new, more general production would not replace the two original ones; they would continue to apply in special circumstances. Transfer is facilitated, according to ACT, if the same components are taught in two different procedures so that the commonality is more likely to be noticed and generalization can occur. Thus, the transfer involved in learning to drive a new car will be greater if the individual has previously driven several different cars rather than only a single car, a position that is consistent with the results of a number of transfer studies (see e.g., Shuell & Lee, 1976, pp. 71–72) and more recent work on cognitive learning (e.g., Sternberg, 1984a).

There are, of course, many situations in which the range of applicability of a production needs to be limited – that is, discrimination needs to occur if the learner is to produce appropriate behavior. For example, in learning to solve addition problems, the student may have acquired the following production:

P7.   IF   the goal is to iterate through the rows of a column and the top row has not been processed,

       THEN   the subgoal is to add the digit of the top row into the running total.

Through the use of this production in a variety of different types of addition problems, generalization may have occurred. In fact, when first encountering subtraction problems, the learner may attempt to employ this production, which has worked in the past. Obviously, if the student is to be successful in solving subtraction problems, he or she must learn to discriminate between production P7 and a similar production in which the action specified involves subtracting (rather than adding) the digit from the running total.

Discrimination in ACT depends on the learner experiencing both correct and incorrect application of the production, a requirement that is consistent with the well documented need for the learner to encounter both positive and negative exemplars in concept learning (see, e.g., Tennyson & Park, 1980). Two types of discrimination are involved in ACT: *action discrimination* involves learning a new action and can occur only when feedback is obtained about what action is correct in the situation being considered. *Condition discrimination* involves restricting the conditions under which the old action was carried out, although the new, more restrictive productions coexist with the original production rather than replacing it.

Generalization and discrimination are viewed as the inductive components of the learning system embodied in ACT. Due to the nature of induction, generalization and discrimination will err and produce incorrect and/ or inappropriate productions – for example, overgeneralizations and useless discriminations. A mechanism that strengthens successful productions will help to ensure that appropriate behavior will occur. While the strengthening mechanism in ACT is fairly complex, it functions basically by modifying the probability attached to a given production, depending on the positive and negative feedback it receives.

Implications for Future Research

A new wave of research on learning is beginning within the various cognitive sciences. Although much of this research holds promise for new and more powerful theories of human learning, considerable work remains to be done before a truly viable and comprehensive theory (or theories) of learning (i.e., capable of accounting for both simpler and more complex forms of learning) is available. As might be expected, given its relative newness, much of this research has focused on theoretical discussions of its nature and empirical demonstrations that certain types of processes and factors have been overlooked in traditional research on human learning – e.g., learners construct appropriate responses rather than merely react to environmental stimuli (see Wittrock, 1974) and encoding plays a crucial role in learning; see Siegler, 1983 and Sternberg, 1984a. A number of problems should be addressed by future research, and some of the challenges will be discussed in terms of: (a) variables that affect the learning process; (b) the relationship between knowledge and learning, including the role of prior knowledge and domain-specific versus domain-independent (general) aspects of learning; and (c) phases of learning.

Variables Affecting Learning

Little is known about the specific variables (e.g., environmental events) that influence the learning process. Future research should develop more precise, operational definitions of variables that can influence cognitive learning (e.g., those that a teacher or counselor might use in trying to facilitate the learning of a student or client) so that they can be systematically investigated. Current theories of cognitive learning have identified various functions that must be performed if learning is to occur. For example, Sternberg (1984a) suggests that many, if not all, cognitive theories of learning incorporate three functions that must be performed if learning is to occur: (a) the collection of new information (encoding), (b) the combination of disparate pieces of new information, and (c) the relating of new to old information. It seems to me that several other functions, such as evaluation, are also involved.

Little research has been done on variables that affect these factors within a complex learning situation (e.g., the specific variables that determine what does and what does not get encoded), although Sternberg (1984a) identifies and discusses five variables that appear to affect the learning of verbal concepts: (a) the number of occurrences of the new item of knowledge, (b) the variability of contexts in which multiple occurrences of the new item of knowledge occur, (c) location of cues relative to the to-be-learned item of knowledge, (d) importance of the to-be-learned item of knowledge, and (e) density of items of knowledge to be learned. It is interesting to note how similar most of these variables are to those variables responsible for more traditional types of learning (e.g., practice, contiguity, and reinforcement). (For a discussion of how these variables provide the basic conditions for learning to occur, see Shuell and Lee, 1976.)

In fact, it should be evident from the preceding sections that many of the current theories use traditional concepts from the psychology of learning to explain cognitive learning – for example, generalization. It has been suggested that new schemata are learned by establishing analogies between old and new schemata (Rumelhart & Norman, 1981). If such is the case, it seems likely that the process is one of generalization and transfer. But generalizations based on analogies may be rather different from traditional conceptions of generalization, since analogies involve structured relationships whereas traditional conceptions typically involve unidimensional stimuli and responses.

Tversky (1977) has proposed a contrast model of similarity in which perceived similarity is determined by the individual matching features (both common and distinctive) between two objects or families of objects (e.g., an analogy). The extent to which psychological processes related to generalization are the same in the two situations (traditional vs. cognitive learning) is an empirical question that remains to be investigated. For instance, if there are generalization gradients for analogies similar to those that exist for simpler forms of learning (and this assumption is not unreasonable), then what are the relevant dimensions in analogies along which generalization can occur and the structures to which they apply?

A variety of other variables such as elaboration and advance organizers that have been investigated within the traditional framework of research on learning clearly involve mental activities and make assumptions similar to those discussed above for cognitive learning. In addition, Norman (1978) has suggested various ways in which interference and transfer (two very traditional factors in research on human learning) might be involved in various types of cognitive learning. Although a detailed discussion of the possible integration of these variables and phenomena with the types of concerns associated with cognitive learning is beyond the scope of the present article, a simple example may prove useful.

Contiguity (the proximity of two events) is well established as one of the fundamental variables affecting traditional types of learning (e.g., Shuell & Lee, 1976). In these simpler forms of learning, contiguity is nearly always defined in terms of time intervals (e.g., the time between the conditioned stimulus and unconditioned stimulus in classical conditioning, the time between response and reinforcement in operant conditioning), but other forms of contiguity (e.g., spatial, semantic) appear just as reasonable. Thus, in learning more complex material, contiguity between disparate pieces of information may determine the likelihood that the individual will induce a schema. In Sternberg's (1984a) list of five variables affecting the acquisition of concepts from text, one (location of cues) is a clear example of contiguity, and another (density of items) could involve contiguity, (e.g., the point at which cognitive overload occurs). In some cases, the learner may actively try to establish contiguity through the use of various learning strategies. Although contiguity may seem like an esoteric variable to some educators, it is a variable over which teachers and instructional designers (e.g., textbook authors) have considerable control; if more were known about the way contiguity affects meaningful learning, perhaps they could use it more effectively. In any case, a combination of concerns from traditional learning psychology and modern-day cognitive psychology should serve as a focal point of future research on cognitive learning.

Knowledge and Learning

Traditional conceptions and theories of learning are, for the most part, content free – that is, learning occurs in basically the same way, or follows the same principles, in all situations. Gradually, however, it has become increasingly clear that the amount of knowledge that one possesses has a substantial impact on the learning process (e.g., Chi, Glaser, & Rees, 1982). For example, adults normally are able to remember more (e.g., have considerably longer digit spans) than children, yet Chi (1978) found that 10-year-old chess experts remembered more about the placement of chess pieces on a board than adults who were only novice chess players (the traditional finding of adult superiority was obtained when the same subjects were asked to remember digits). In addition, individuals who know a great deal about something (experts) encode new material related to that knowledge in a different way than individuals who know little about the topic (novices) (see, e.g., Chi et al., 1982; Siegler, 1983). While these expert/novice differences demonstrate that cognitive learning involves qualitative and not merely quantitative changes, we need to know more than the nature of the differences; we need to know how the transition between novice and expert takes place, especially if education is to facilitate the process.

There is also evidence that learning is much more domain specific than earlier learning theorists believed (for a good discussion of this point, see Glaser, 1984). For example, Chase and Ericsson (1981) report on an average college student (SF) who over a period of 25 months of practice steadily increased his average digit span from seven to over 80 digits. This feat was accomplished by encoding the digits into running times (SF was an avid and proficient long-distance runner) and developing an elaborate, hierarchical retrieval structure. But the skills SF learned in acquiring the largest memory span ever reported in the literature are domain specific; SF's memory span is normal (about seven symbols) when recalling other types of stimuli such as random consonants. Apparently SF lacked the knowledge base relevant to consonants, for example, that would be necessary to demonstrate his proficiency with other types of stimuli.

Yet it seems unlikely that all learning is domain specific. If it were, then it would be difficult to explain how individuals deal with novel situations or learn material that is totally new to them. Obviously, learning involves both domain-specific and domain-independent processes. One challenge for future research to address is how these two aspects of learning interrelate with one another and with the skill and/or knowledge that is being acquired.

Another issue that is likely to be addressed by future research is the relationship between various types of knowledge. As already noted, cognitive psychologists frequently distinguish between declarative and procedural knowledge, and other types of knowledge have also been suggested (e.g., Gagné & White, 1978). But is one type more basic than other types? For example, Rumelhart and Norman (1981) propose that "...all knowledge is properly considered as *knowledge how* but...the system can sometimes interrogate this *knowledge how* to produce *knowledge that*" (p. 343). This emphasis on "learning by doing" (Anzai & Simon, 1979) – "...expertise comes about through the use of knowledge and not by analysis of knowledge" (Neves & Anderson, 1981, p. 83) – is reminiscent of themes heard in education, although the emphasis is somewhat different. In any case, these issues have important implications for educational practices, since different types of knowledge have different instructional requirements.

Phases of Learning

The notion that learning progresses in what might be thought of as phases or stages is not a new idea. Some 30 years ago, Fleishman and Hempel (1954, 1955) provided evidence that psychomotor learning proceeds in this manner with performance in the various stages drawing upon different abilities. Other researchers provided evidence for stages in both paired-associate (e.g., McGuire, 1961; Underwood, Runquist, & Schulz, 1959) and free-recall learning (Labouvie, Frohring, Baltes, & Goulet, 1973). In addition Brainerd (1985) and Brainerd, Howe, and Desrochers (1982) developed a sophisticated mathematical model of learning. Nearly all of this research, however, deals with relatively simple forms of learning. Very little empirical evidence is available on the phases that learners might go through in learning more complex, meaningful material.

In recent years, several cognitive theorists have suggested that stages are involved in cognitive learning. For example, Bransford and Franks (1976) have argued that learning that involves understanding moves from concrete to abstract representations, and J. R. Anderson's (1982) ACT theory postulates that learning proceeds from declarative knowledge to procedural knowledge. Other types of stages or phases of learning are possible, and it is reasonable to expect that different variables may be involved during the various phases.

For example, in school we typically expect students to acquire complex bodies of knowledge with some degree of understanding. When the individual begins this undertaking, he or she normally begins by acquiring a number of relatively disparate pieces of information (e.g., the "basic facts" stressed in most classrooms). During this early phase of learning, pictorial and verbal mnemonics (or various other learning strategies) may facilitate learning by providing the conceptual glue necessary to hold these disparate pieces in memory, and variables such as repetition may play a relatively important role. As learning progresses, however, and the individual begins to fit some of the pieces together, mnemonics may play a less important (or different) role and other types of factors (organizational strategies?)

may play an increasingly important role. Still later, as performance becomes well established, mnemonics may have little or no effect on learning since the underlying knowledge structure now holds the information together in some meaningful, integrated whole – to use an extremely elementary example, C - A - T has become CAT.

Thus, given variables may facilitate acquisition during one phase of learning and have little, if any, effect during other phases. Although retention is not really a phase of learning in the sense being discussed here, perhaps the relationship is similar enough to provide a useful analogy. Elaboration clearly has a facilitative effect on learning, but it has been found not to affect retention independent of learning (Olton, 1969); likewise, immediate feedback normally facilitates learning, but delayed feedback appears to facilitate retention (Surber & Anderson, 1975).[5] The more important forms of human learning that interest most cognitive scientists and educators involve what is fundamentally a long-term process involving weeks, months, and even years. The phases that we go through as we engage in long-term learning are unknown at present, but they undoubtedly exist and deserve our attention.

Implications for Education

Changes in the way we think about learning and what we know about the way learning occurs have important implications for those situations in which we want to facilitate changes in what people know and/or do. In education, for example, corresponding changes are occurring in the way we think about teaching. Since learning is an active process, the teacher's task necessarily involves more than the mere dissemination of information. Rather, if students are to learn desired outcomes in a reasonably effective manner, then the teacher's fundamental task is to get students to engage in learning activities that are likely to result in their achieving these outcomes, taking into account factors such as prior knowledge, the context in which the material is presented, and the realization that students' interpretation and understanding of new information depend on the availability of appropriate schemata. Without taking away from the important role played by the teacher, it is helpful to remember that what the student does is actually more important in determining what is learned than what the teacher does.

Although many educators have long advocated that teachers actively engage their students in the learning process, there has not been a great deal of scientific knowledge to support these contentions. "Open education" and "discovery learning" are just two examples of educational practices that failed to produce encouraging results due, at least in part, to the lack of a viable theory of cognitive learning. Many other educators, of course, have advocated "back to the basics" and other approaches stressing more behavioral forms of learning variables. With the advent of cognitive theories of learning and knowledge of how specific learning processes in the student are engaged by specific instructional variables, we may have the beginning of a viable body of scientific knowledge on how best to capitalize on the active nature of learning. Some of the cognitive research on learning discussed earlier may form the basis for this endeavor, although the nature of an instructional situation does have some unique characteristics. Theories of learning from instruction are somewhat different from regular theories of learning (Shuell, 1980), and important research on cognitive theories of learning from instruction (e.g., Leinhardt & Putnam, 1986; Snow & Lohman, 1984) is beginning to appear in the literature.

With regard to prior knowledge, we know that students often begin learning with substantial misconceptions about the material they are studying (e.g., Champagne, Klopfer, & Gunstone, 1982) and that remnants of these misconceptions even persist in students who receive high grades in the course (Champagne, Klopfer, & Anderson, 1980; Gunstoke & White, 1981). Students also make systematic errors (such as always subtracting the smallest digit from the largest digit, regardless of which one is on top) sometimes referred to as "buggy algorithms" (Brown & VanLehn, 1982; Resnick, 1982). There errors are not careless mistakes or even the result of faulty reasoning; rather, they represent what students reasonably consider to be appropriate ways of dealing with the problem on which they are working, given their current knowledge structure (i.e., prior knowledge). Analysis of these errors can provide the teacher (or textbook writer, etc.) with useful insights into the type of instruction that has the best chance of being successful; at the very least, it highlights the crucial role played by prior knowledge in any real-life learning situation.

What these concerns mean is that the teacher's role is different from the one frequently envisioned in traditional conceptions of teaching. What have changed are the focus and the realization that good teachers are not merely people who can articulate a large number of relevant facts and ideas (although a sound understanding of the subject matter they are teaching is certainly essential); effective teachers must know how to get students actively engaged in learning activities that are appropriate for the desired outcome(s). This task involves the appropriate selection of content, an awareness of the cognitive processes that must be used by the learner in order to learn the content, and understanding of how prior knowledge and existing knowledge structures determine what and if the student learns from the material presented (and hopefully being studied). Consequently, we need to know more about the way in which specific content and instructional procedures engage and/or elicit the psychological processes and knowledge structures appropriate for the desired learning outcome(s) to be achieved – fortunately, some advances are beginning to be made in this direction (e.g., Winne & Marx, 1983).

Summary

The cognitive sciences have begun to give serious consideration to research on human learning, and several different theories of cognitive learning have been suggested. Although the orientation of those interested in cognitive learning differs considerably from the more traditional, behavioral orientation toward learning, there are also similarities and common concerns between the two approaches. Learning is now viewed as being active, constructive, cumulative, and goal oriented. Yet, concerns for cognitive learning do not necessarily invalidate traditional concerns of learning psychology, and for investigators who look at learning in simpler terms, many of the traditional concerns of learning research remain viable. Individual learners go about learning in different ways (Bruner, 1985), and there are different types of learning outcomes (e.g., Gagné, 1965, 1984; Rumelhart & Norman, 1978). Thus, the more traditional principles of learning may be appropriate for certain types of learning while new principles need to be forged for other types of learning, especially those more complex forms of learning in which the desired outcome involves the understanding of relationships among many separate pieces of information. The possibility of identifying and integrating these multiple aspects of learning presents an important challenge to future research on learning and its application to a variety of applied problems, including classroom learning and instruction.

Notes

1. Most discussions of knowledge structures by cognitive psychologists go beyond the associative networks and habit-family hierarchies sometimes discussed by associationists.
2. The suggestion that there is more than one type of learning is not unique to current concerns for cognitive learning. For example, Kimble (1961) discussed differences between classical and operant conditioning, and Gagné (1965) postulated eight different types of learning ranging from classical conditioning to problem solving.
3. The process of carrying will be ignored for the sake of simplicity.
4. While individual productions may appear to some readers as being very similar to stimulus-response associations in which a particular response is under the control of a discriminating stimulus, production systems are different from S-R associations in the way individual productions are interrelated in an organized system under the control of various goals and subgoals. Note also how control of the system can be shifted from a goal to a subgoal, as in production P3 below.
5. For a more complete discussion of this point, see Shuell and Lee (1976).

References

Anderson, J. R. (1980). *Cognitive psychology and its implications.* San Francisco: Freeman.
Anderson, J. R. (1982). Acquisition of cognitive skill. *Psychological Review, 89,* 369–406.
Anderson, J. R. (1983). *The architecture of cognition.* Cambridge, MA: Harvard University Press.

Anderson, R. C. (1984). Some reflections on the acquisition of knowledge. *Educational Researcher, 13*(9), 5–10.

Anzai, Y., & Simon, H. A. (1979). The theory of learning by doing. *Psychological Review, 86*, 124–140.

Ausubel, D. P. (1962). A subsumption theory of meaningful verbal learning and retention. *Journal of General Psychology, 66*, 213–224.

Ausubel, D. P. (1963). *The psychology of meaningful verbal learning.* New York: Grune & Stratton.

Bartlett, F. C. (1932). *Remembering: A study in experimental and social psychology.* Cambridge, England: Cambridge University Press.

Bereiter, C. (1985). Toward a solution of the learning paradox. *Review of Educational Research, 55*, 201–226.

Block, R. A. (1985). Education and thinking skills reconsidered. *American Psychologist, 40*, 574–575.

Bower, G. H. (1970). Analysis of a mnemonic device. *American Scientist, 58*, 496–510.

Bower, G. H., & Hilgard, E. R. (1981) *Theories of learning* (5th ed.). Englewood Cliffs, NJ: Prentice-Hall.

Brainerd, C. J. (1985). Model-based approaches to storage and retrieval development. In C. J. Brainerd & M. Pressley (Eds.), *Basic processes in memory development: Progress in cognitive development research* (pp. 143–207). New York: Springer-Verlag.

Brainerd, C. J., Howe, M. L., & Desrochers, A. (1982). The general theory of two-stage learning: A mathematical review with illustrations from memory development. *Psychological Bulletin, 91*, 634–665.

Bransford, J. D., & Franks, J. J. (1976). Toward a framework for understanding learning. In G. H. Bower (Ed.), *Psychology of learning and motivation* (Vol. 10, pp. 93–127). New York: Academic Press.

Bransford, J. D., & Johnson, M. K. (1972). Contextual prerequisites for understanding: Some investigations of comprehension and recall. *Journal of Verbal Learning and Verbal Behavior, 11*, 717–726.

Bransford, J. D., & McCarrell, N. S. (1974). A sketch of a cognitive approach to comprehension: Some thoughts about understanding what it means to comprehend. In W. B. Weimer & D. S. Palermo (Eds.), *Cognition and the symbolic process* (pp. 189–229). Hillsdale, NJ: Lawrence Erlbaum Associates.

Brown, A. L. (1978). Knowing when, where, and how to remember: A problem of metacognition. In R. Glaser (Ed.), *Advances in instructional psychology* (Vol. 1, pp. 77–165). Hillsdale, NJ: Lawrence Erlbaum Associates.

Brown, A. L., Bransford, J. D., Ferrara, R. A., & Campione, J. C. (1983). Learning, remembering, and understanding. In P. H. Mussen (Ed.), *Handbook of child psychology: Vol. III. Cognitive development* (4th ed., pp. 77–166). New York: Wiley.

Brown, J. S., & VanLehn, K. (1982). Towards a generative theory of "bugs." In T. P. Carpenter, J. M. Moser, & T. A. Romberg (Eds.), *Addition and subtraction: A cognitive perspective* (pp. 117–135). Hillsdale, NJ: Lawrence Erlbaum Associates.

Bruner, J. S. (1957). Going beyond the information given. In J. S. Bruner, E. Brunswik, L. Festinger, F. Heider, K. Muenzinger, C. Osgood, & D. Rapaport, *Contemporary approaches to cognition* (pp. 41–69). Cambridge, MA: Harvard University Press.

Bruner, J. S. (1961). The act of discovery. *Harvard Educational Review, 31*, 21–32.

Bruner, J. (1985). Models of the learner. *Educational Researcher, 14*(6), 5–8.

Carpenter, T. P., Moser, J. M., & Romberg, T. A. (Eds.) (1982). *Addition and subtraction: A cognitive perspective.* Hillsdale, NJ: Lawrence Erlbaum Associates.

Carroll, J. B. (1976). Psychometric tests as cognitive tasks: A new "structure of intellect." In L. B. Resnick (Ed.), *The nature of intelligence* (pp. 27–56). Hillsdale, NJ: Lawrence Erlbaum Associates.

Champagne, A. B., Klopfer, L. E., & Anderson, J. H. (1980). Factors influencing the learning of classical mechanics. *American Journal of Physics, 48,* 1074–1079.

Champagne, A. B., Klopfer, L. E., & Gunstone, R. F. (1982). Cognitive research and the design of science instruction. *Educational Psychologist, 17,* 31–53.

Chase, W. G., & Ericsson, K. A. (1981). Skilled memory. In J. R. Anderson (Ed.), *Cognitive skills and their acquisition* (pp. 141–189). Hillsdale, NJ: Lawrence Erlbaum Associates.

Chi, M. T. H. (1978). Knowledge structures and memory development. In R. S. Siegler (Ed.), *Children's thinking: What develops?* (pp. 73–96). Hillsdale, NJ: Lawrence Erlbaum Associates.

Chi, M. T. H., Glaser, R., & Rees, E. (1982). Expertise in problem solving. In R. Sternberg (Ed.), *Advances in the psychology of human intelligence* (Vol. 1, pp. 7–75). Hillsdale, NJ: Lawrence Erlbaum Associates.

Cofer, C. N. (1973). Constructive processes in memory. *American Scientist, 61,* 537–543.

Dooling, D. J., & Lachman, R. (1971). Effects of comprehension on retention of prose. *Journal of Experimental Psychology, 88,* 216–222.

Ebbinghaus, H. (1913). *Memory.* (H. A. Ruger & C. E. Bussenius, Trans.). New York: Teachers College. (Original work published 1885)

Feigenbaum, E. A. (1959). *An information-processing theory of verbal learning* (Paper No. P-1817). Santa Monica, CA: RAND Corp.

Fitts, P. M. (1964). Perceptual-motor skill learning. In A. W. Melton (Ed.), *Categories of human learning* (pp. 243–285). New York: Academic Press.

Flavell, J. H. (1979). Metacognition and cognitive monitoring: A new area of cognitive-developmental inquiry. *American Psychologist, 34,* 906–911.

Flavell, J. H. (1981). Cognitive monitoring. In W. P. Dickson (Ed.), *Children's oral communication skills* (pp. 35–60). New York: Academic Press.

Flavell, J. H., & Wellman, H. M. (1977). Metamemory. In R. V. Kail, Jr. & J. W. Hagen (Eds.), *Perspectives on the development of memory and cognition* (pp. 3–33). Hillsdale, NJ: Lawrence Erlbaum Associates.

Fleishman, E. A., & Hempel, W. E., Jr. (1954). Change in factor structure of a complex psychomotor test as a function of practice. *Psychometrika, 19,* 239–252.

Fleishman, E. A., & Hempel, W. E., Jr. (1955). The relation between abilities and improvement with practice in a visual discrimination reaction task. *Journal of Experimental Psychology, 49,* 301–310.

Gagné, R. M. (1962). The acquisition of knowledge. *Psychological Review, 69,* 355–365.

Gagné, R. M. (1965). *The conditions of learning.* New York: Holt, Rinehart and Winston.

Gagné, R. M. (1984). Learning outcomes and their effects: Useful categories of human performance. *American Psychologist, 39,* 377–385.

Gagné, R. M., & White, R. T. (1978). Memory structures and learning outcomes. *Review of Educational Research, 48,* 187–222.

Glaser, R. (1984). Education and thinking: The role of knowledge. *American Psychologist, 39,* 93–104.

Glaser, R. (1985). All's well that begins and ends with both knowledge and process: A reply to Sternberg. *American Psychologist, 40,* 573–574.

Greeno, J. G. (1978). A study of problem solving. In R. Glaser (Ed.), *Advances in instructional psychology* (Vol. 1, pp. 13–75). Hillsdale, NJ: Lawrence Erlbaum Associates.

Greeno, J. G. (1980a). Psychology of learning, 1960–1980: One participant's observations. *American Psychologist, 35,* 713–728.

Greeno, J. G. (1980b). Some examples of cognitive task analysis with instructional implications. In R. E. Snow, P-A Federico, & W. E. Montague (Eds.), *Aptitude, learning, and instruction: Vol. 2. Cognitive process analyses of learning and problem solving* (pp. 1–21). Hillsdale, NJ: Lawrence Erlbaum Associates.

Gunstone, R. F., & White, R. T. (1981). Understanding of gravity. *Science Education, 65,* 291–300.

Heller, J. I., & Reif, F. (1984). Prescribing effective human problem-solving processes: Problem description in physics. *Cognition and Instruction, 1,* 177–216.

Jenkins, J. J. (1974). Remember that old theory of memory? Well, forget it! *American Psychologist, 29,* 785–795.

Johnson-Laird, P. N. (1985). Deductive reasoning ability. In R. J. Sternberg (Ed.), *Human abilities: An information-processing approach* (pp. 173–194). New York: Freeman.

Keil, F. C. (1984). Mechanisms of cognitive development and the structure of knowledge. In R. J. Sternberg (Ed.), *Mechanisms of cognitive development* (pp. 81–99). New York: W. H. Freeman.

Kendler, H. H., & Kendler, T. S. (1962). Vertical and horizontal processes in problem solving. *Psychological Review, 69,* 1–16.

Kimble, G. A. (1961). *Hilgard and Marquis' conditioning and learning* (2nd ed.). New York: Appleton-Century-Crofts.

Kimble, G. A. (1984, August). *The psychology of learning enters its second century.* Master lecture presented at the meeting of the American Psychological Association, Toronto.

Labouvie, G. V., Frohring, W. R., Baltes, P. B., & Goulet, L. R. (1973). Changing relationship between recall performance and abilities as a function of stage of learning and timing of recall. *Journal of Educational Psychology, 64,* 191–198.

Langley, P., & Simon, H. A. (1981). The central role of learning in cognition. In J. R. Anderson (Ed.), *Cognitive skills and their acquisition* (pp. 361–380). Hillsdale, NJ: Lawrence Erlbaum Associates.

Leinhardt, G., & Putnam, R. T. (1986, April). *The skill of learning from classroom lessons* Paper presented at the annual meeting of the American Educational Research Association, San Francisco.

Markman, E. M. (1981). Comprehension monitoring. In W. P. Dickson (Ed.), *Children's oral communication skills* (pp. 61–84). New York: Academic Press.

McGuire, W. J. (1961). A multiprocess model for paired-associate learning. *Journal of Experimental Psychology, 62,* 335–347.

Miller, G. A., Galanter, E., & Pribram, K. L. (1960). *Plans and the structure of behavior.* New York: Holt, Rinehart and Winston.

Moravcsik, J. (1979). Understanding. *Dialectica, 33,* 201–216.

Neves, D. M., & Anderson, J. R. (1981). Knowledge compilation: Mechanisms for the automatization of cognitive skills. In J. R. Anderson (Ed.), *Cognitive skills and their acquisition* (pp. 57–84). Hillsdale, NJ: Lawrence Erlbaum Associates.

Newell, A. (1980). Reasoning, problem solving, and decision processes: The problem space as a fundamental category. In R. S. Nickerson (Ed.), *Attention and performance VIII* (pp. 693–718). Hillsdale, NJ: Lawernce Erlbaum Associates.

Newell, A., & Simon, H. A. (1972). *Human problem solving.* Englewood Cliffs, NJ: Prentice-Hall.

Norman, D. A. (1978). Notes toward a theory of complex learning. In A. M. Lesgold, J. W. Pellegrino, S. D. Fokkema, & R. Glaser (Eds.), *Cognitive psychology and instruction* (pp. 39–48). New York: Plenum Press.

Norman, D. A., Rumelhart, D. E., & the LNR Research Group. (1975). *Explorations in cognition.* San Francisco, CA: Freeman.

Olton, R. M. (1969). The effect of a mnemonic upon the retention of paired-associate verbal material. *Journal of Verbal Learning and Verbal Behavior, 8,* 43–48.

Omanson, R. C., Beck, I. L., Voss, J. F., & McKeown, M. G. (1984). The effects of reading lessons on comprehension: A processing description. *Cognition and Instruction, 1,* 45–67.

Paivio, A. (1969). Mental imagery in associative learning and memory. *Psychological Review, 76,* 241–263.

Paivio, A. (1971). *Imagery and verbal processes.* New York: Holt, Rinehart and Winston.

Pellegrino, J. W., & Glaser, R. (1982). Analyzing aptitudes for learning: Inductive reasoning. In R. Glaser (Ed.), *Advances in instructional psychology* (Vol. 2, pp. 269–345). Hillsdale, NJ: Lawrence Erlbaum Associates.

Pressley, M., & Levin, J. R. (Eds.) (1983a). *Cognitive strategy research: Educational applications.* New York: Springer-Verlag.

Pressley, M., & Levin, J. R. (Eds.) (1983b). *Cognitive strategy research: Psychological foundations.* New York: Springer-Verlag.

Resnick, L. B. (1982). Syntax and semantics in learning to subtract. In T. P. Carpenter, J. M. Moser, & T. A. Romberg (Eds.), *Addition and subtraction: A cognitive perspective* (pp. 136–155). Hillsdale, NJ: Lawrence Erlbaum Associates.

Resnick, L. B. (1984). Comprehending and learning: Implications for a cognitive theory of instruction. In H. Mandl, N. L. Stein, & T. Trabasso (Eds.), *Learning and the comprehension of text* (pp. 431–443). Hillsdale, NJ: Lawrence Erlbaum Associates.

Rothkopf, E. Z. (1965). Some theoretical and experimental approaches to problems in written instruction. In J. D. Krumboltz (Ed.), *Learning and the educational process* (pp. 193–221). Chicago: Rand McNally.

Rothkopf, E. Z. (1970). The concept of mathemagenic activities. *Review of Educational Research, 40,* 325–336.

Rumelhart, D. E., & Norman, D. A. (1978). Accretion, tuning, and restructuring: Three modes of learning. In J. W. Cotton & R. L. Klatzky (Eds), *Semantic factors in cognition* (pp. 37–53). Hillsdale, NJ: Lawrence Erlbaum Associates.

Rumelhart, D. E., & Norman, D. A. (1981). Analogical processes in learning. In J. R. Anderson (Ed.), *Cognitive skills and their acquisition* (pp. 335–359). Hillsdale, NJ: Lawrence Erlbaum Associates.

Scandura, J. M. (1970). The role of rules in behavior: Toward an operational definition of what (rule) is learned. *Psychological Review, 77,* 516–533.

Scandura, J. M. (1977). *Problem solving: A structural/process approach with instructional implications.* New York: Academic Press.

Shuell, T. J. (1969). Clustering and organization in free recall. *Psychological Bulletin, 72,* 353–374.

Shuell, T. J. (1980). Learning theory, instructional theory, and adaptation. In R. E. Snow, P.-A. Federico, & W. E. Montague (Eds.), *Aptitude, learning, and instruction: Vol. 2, Cognitive process analyses of learning and problem solving* (pp. 277–302). Hillsdale, NJ: Lawrence Erlbaum Associates.

Shuell, T. J. (1985). Knowledge representation, cognitive structure, and school learning: A historical perspective. In L. H. T. West & A. L. Pines (Eds.), *Cognitive structure and conceptual change* (pp. 117–130). Orlando, FL: Academic Press.

Shuell, T. J., & Lee, C. Z. (1976). *Learning and instruction.* Monterey, CA: Brooks/Cole.

Siegler, R. S. (1983). Five generalizations about cognitive development. *American Psychologist, 38,* 263–277.

Siegler, R. S. & Klahr, D. (1982). When do children learn? The relationship between existing knowledge and the acquisition of new knowledge. In R. Glaser (Ed.), *Advances in instructional psychology* (Vol. 2, pp. 121–211). Hillsdale, NJ: Lawrence Erlbaum Associates.

Simon, H. A., & Feigenbaum, E. A. (1964). An information-processing theory of some effects of similarity, familiarization and meaning. *Journal of Verbal Learning and Verbal Behavior, 3,* 385–396.

Skinner, B. F. (1950). Are theories of learning necessary? *Psychological Review, 57,* 193–216.

Snow, R. E., & Lohman, D. F. (1984). Toward a theory of cognitive aptitude for learning from instruction. *Journal of Educational Psychology, 76,* 347–376.

Sternberg, R. J. (1977). *Intelligence, information processing, and analogical reasoning: The componential analysis of human abilities.* Hillsdale, NJ: Lawrence Erlbaum Associates.

Sternberg, R. J. (1979). The nature of mental abilities. *American Psychologist, 34*, 214–230.

Sternberg, R. J. (1984a). A theory of knowledge acquisition in the development of verbal concepts. *Developmental Review, 4*, 113–138.

Sternberg, R. J. (1984b). Mechanisms of cognitive development: A componential approach. In R. J. Sternberg (Ed.), *Mechanisms of cognitive development* (pp. 163–186). New York: W. H. Freeman.

Sternberg, R. J. (1985). All's well that ends well, but it's a sad tale that begins at the end: A reply to Glaser. *American Psychologist, 40*, 571–573.

Stevenson, H. (1983). How children learn – The quest for a theory. In P. H. Mussen (Ed.), *Handbook of child psychology: Vol. I. History, theory, and methods* (4th ed., pp. 213–236). New York: Wiley.

Surber, J. R., & Anderson, R. C. (1975). Delay-retention effect in natural classroom settings. *Journal of Educational Psychology, 67*, 170–173.

Tennyson, R. D., & Park, O. C. (1980). The teaching of concepts: A review of instructional design research literature. *Review of Educational Research, 50*, 55–70.

Thorndike, E. L. (1913). *Educational psychology: Vol. 2. The psychology of learning.* New York: Teachers College.

Tolman, E. C. (1932). *Purposive behavior in animals and men.* New York: Appleton-Century-Crofts.

Tulving, E. (1968). Theoretical issues in free recall. In T. R. Dixon & D. L. Horton (Eds.), *Verbal behavior and general behavior theory* (pp. 2–36). Englewood Cliffs, NJ: Prentice-Hall.

Tulving, E. (1985). How many memory systems are there? *American Psychologist, 40*, 385–398.

Tversky, A. (1977). Features of similarity. *Psychological Review, 84*, 327–352.

Underwood, B. J. (1963). Stimulus selection in verbal learning. In C. N. Cofer & B. S. Musgrave (Eds.), *Verbal behavior and learning: Problems and processes* (pp. 33–48). New York: McGraw-Hill.

Underwood, B. J. (1964). Laboratory studies of verbal learning. In E. R. Hilgard (Ed.), *Theories of learning and instruction* (The sixty-third yearbook of the National Society for the Study of Education, Part I, pp. 133–152). Chicago: University of Chicago Press.

Underwood, B. J., Runquist, W. N., & Schulz, R. W. (1959). Response learning in paired-associate lists as a function of intralist similarity. *Journal of Experimental Psychology, 58*, 70–78.

Underwood, B. J., & Schulz, R. W. (1960). *Meaningfulness and verbal learning.* Philadelphia: Lippincott.

Voss, J. F. (1978). Cognition and instruction: Toward a cognitive theory of learning. In A. M. Lesgold, J. W. Pellegrino, S. D. Fokkema, & R. Glaser (Eds.), *Cognitive psychology and instruction* (pp. 13–26). New York: Plenum Press.

Weinstein, C. E., & Mayer, R. E. (1986). The teaching of learning strategies. In M. C. Wittrock (Ed.), *Handbook of research on teaching* (3rd ed., pp. 315–327). New York: Macmillan.

White, S. H. (1970). The learning theory tradition and child psychology. In P. H. Mussen (Ed.), *Carmichael's manual of child psychology* (3rd ed., Vol. 1, pp. 657–701). New York: John Wiley.

Winne, P. H., & Marx, R. W. (1983). *Matching students' cognitive processes and teacher skills to enhance learning from teaching.* (Instructional Psychology Research Group, Final Report). Burnaby, B. C., Canada: Simon Fraser University.

Wittrock, M. C. (1974). Learning as a generative process. *Educational Psychologist, 11*, 87–95.

Wittrock, M. C. (1978). The cognitive movement in instruction. *Educational Psychologist, 13*, 15–29.

Wittrock, M. C. (1986). Student's thought processes. In M. C. Wittrock (Ed.), *Handbook of research on teaching* (3rd ed., pp. 297–314). New York: Macmillan.

39

Meaning in Complex Learning

Ronald E. Johnson

What role does meaningfulness play in the learning of complex verbal materials? If meaningfulness does facilitate learning, how is the facilitation accomplished? What are the means by which learning may be made meaningful? Answers to these questions depend upon a satisfactory definition of meaningfulness and valid measures of the construct. Unfortunately, a review of the literature shows that meaningfulness has been neglected both theoretically and empirically.

Perhaps the most important reason for neglect has been the intuitive certainty that meaningfulness does influence learning. In addition, investigators have had so much faith in intuition that meaningfulness levels typically have been decreed simply by personal judgment (e.g., English, Welborn, & Killian, 1934). When empirical assessments have been attempted, researchers have been stymied by excessive reliance upon the classical methods of assessing meaningfulness. Neglect also stems from the lack of agreement in defining meaningfulness (Alston, 1964; Creelman, 1966; Fries, 1954). Given the differences in theoretical viewpoints, it is not surprising to find Bousfield (1961) viewing meaning as "an unnecessary concept for verbal learning" (p. 81), while Osgood (1961) views meaning as "the single most important variable in human learning, verbal or otherwise" (p. 91).

A thesis of this critical review is that meaningfulness is potentially the most powerful variable for explaining the learning of complex verbal discourse. In the review, the possibility is examined that meaningfulness may be pivotal in explaining the effects of other variables. Next, it is argued that the classical methods of measuring meaningfulness are generally

Source: *Review of Educational Research*, 45(3) (1975): 425–459.

inappropriate for calibrating the meaningfulness of verbal discourse. Attention is drawn to variables that influence meaningfulness, and suggestions are made regarding requisite conditions for adequately measuring meaningfulness. Finally, the need for additional research is emphasized by sampling problem areas in which productive research could be conducted.

Meaning – A Theory of Associational Reference

Through experience, a person acquires knowledges about an object or idea. Such knowledges include associations about attributes, properties, functions, interrelationships, contextual correlates, and affect. The synthesis of these knowledges constitutes meaning. Although meaning may consist of a vast number of associations, the constituent knowledges are not just a random concatenation. Certain attributes, such as form, are more likely to be salient and to be entered into associational structure. Similarly, organization is derived from learners' tendencies to bias input data through reliance on preferred cognitive transformations such as grouping and contrast (Campbell, 1958; Deese, 1965). The associational acquisition may or may not include the name of the object or idea. Furthermore, the referential knowledges are not necessarily in conscious awareness, although the existence of such knowledges may be verified by various semantic analyses and experimental techniques.

As compared with previous theories in philosophy or linguistics, the present view of meaning is an extreme version of a referential or ideational theory (Alston, 1964).[1] Stated as an ideational theory, meaning is asserted to be nothing more nor less than a person's referential knowledge about a word, an object, or idea. Rephrased as a theory of reference, the referential object of a word or phrase is asserted to be a conceptual class designated by referential associations. Rather than restricting the term *referent* to an objective tangible object, the referent of a word is presumed to be a psychological entity. Each word in the subjective lexicon thus represents an entity of particular associations. Such referential associations are not assumed to be derived from a hypothetical construct called *meaning*; instead, the referential associations are the meaning. By thinking about a concept in relation to other concepts, however, the learner can expand or change existing meanings by acquiring new referential associations.

The adoption of an ideational-referential stance does provide heuristic advantages in examining the relationship of meaning and learning. Although objections have been raised to similar theories of meaning (Alston, 1964, pp. 10–31; Church, 1961, pp. 124–132; Fodor, Bever, & Garrett, 1974, pp. 141–170; Lyons, 1968, pp. 400–442; Miller, 1965, pp. 16–18), the objections are not disabling. Space does not permit analysis of all criticism, but the reassertion of an ideational-referential theory argues the necessity for reexamining the most common objections (see Table 1).

Table 1: Examination of criticisms of referential or ideational theories of meaning in relation to present view

Criticism	Example	Present theory
1) Two phrases may have identical referents and yet have different meanings (Miller, 1965).	"George Washington" vs. "first President of the United States."	Since each of the two phrases arouses different associations, the phrases do not have the same referents or meaning even though ostensibly referring to the same individual.
2) "Sentences are meaningful, but their meaning cannot be given by their referent, for they may have none." (Miller, 1965, p. 16).	Abstract words such as *rule* or *duty*. Also, combinations of words/concepts that have never been experienced directly.	The referent need not be a concrete tangible object – abstract words also arouse associations. For each sentence, referential associations are aroused by the individual words, the various combinations of words, earlier sentences, and the psychological situation in which the sentence is uttered.
3) Phrases may have identical meaning and yet have different referents (Alston, 1964; Black, 1968; Pollio, 1974).	Utterance "I" has similar meaning for each person, but referent of the phrase depends upon the speaker.	Objection unnecessarily assumes a single objective referent which is invariant for all users, and further assumes that meaning is invariant in all lexical contexts.
4) Sentences can express hypothetical events, assertions of nonexistence, untrue events, and nonsensical events (Black, 1968; Church, 1961, p. 124).	"The centaur is a strange creature." "It was nothing." "The cat began to bark." "The apple was calendar."	No claim is made that semantic propositions mirror reality or truth, or that referential associations are veridically congruent with reality, but verbal descriptions of hypothetical events do arouse associations or meaning.

(Continued)

Table 1: (*Continued*)

Criticism	Example	Present theory
5) Since proper names refer only to a particular person, object, or situation, this restriction allegedly eliminates the possibility of meaning (Fodor et al., 1974, p. 145; Terwilliger, 1968, pp. 149–150).	A particular name such as "Ralph Jones."	Referential associations (i.e., meaning) are established to the entity designated by the proper noun. Such associations may include memorial representations in the form of referential imagery (Paivio, 1971, pp. 50–77), either as a particular image, as one of a number of particular images, or as a schematized generic image.
6) Function words such as articles, conjunctions, and prepositions have no external or denotative reference (Fodor et al., 1974; Glanzer, 1962; Pollio, 1974), and some words in a sentence do not arouse a distinguishable idea (Alston, 1964, pp. 12, 24).	Words such as *in, on, with, despite.*	Function words do have denotative meaning (Carroll, 1964a) and do arouse associations (Kanungo, 1968; Palermo & Jenkins, 1964). Each word in discourse is a unique functional component of the total meaning which is engendered; any change in wording, including substitution of synonyms, usually alters meaning (Alston, 1964, pp. 44–49; Lyons, 1968; Quine, 1960).
7) Referential associations to a word may indicate the arousal of a meaning opposite to the usual meaning.	*In* arouses association of *out.* Similarly, *big* produces *little* or *small, man* results in associate of *woman,* and *buy* arouses *sell.*	Componential analyses of semantic features show that antonymous associations are closely related semantically to the stimulus word (Clark, 1970; Lyons, 1968). The single reversed semantic feature indicates as much focus on the critical defining dimension as occurs in the production of a synonymous associate.

Meaningfulness

Assuming meaning to be a synthesis of referential associations, meaningfulness may be defined literally as the extensiveness of the network of referential associations. However, the type, relevance, and organization of associations may be more important than quantity in determining the "fullness" of meaning. In any event, a differentiation between meaning and meaningfulness has important educational implications in that the "fullness" of meaning appears critical in learning.

Learning may be said to be meaningful to the extent that the new learning task can be related to the existing cognitive structure of the learner, i.e., to the residual of his earlier learnings. The presence of meaning, however, does not guarantee meaningfulness. A person's associations to a conceptual entity may include all of the associations that normatively define the concept. Yet, the sparseness of associations, or the quality of the associations, may make it difficult for the learner to establish useful associational linkages. Whether a concept is meaningful thus depends upon the associational background of the learner and also the semantic structure of the concept within the linguistic community.

Indirect Experimental Manipulations of Meaningfulness

If meaningfulness is a powerful variable in learning, its influence ought to be evident even in experimental comparisons designed to test the influence of other variables. To illustrate, the active learner learns better than the passive learner, and this superiority may result because the active learner is more successful in relating the new material to existing ideas. Bobrow and Bower (1969) compared the remembering of learners who generated their own linking sentences for a noun pair as opposed to merely reading an equivalent linking sentence. When learners generated their own associative links, recall was superior, and Bobrow and Bower concluded that recall was facilitated when learners comprehended the meaning of the sentence. In their words, "the mere act of searching for something in memory at the time of input of a noun pair is not the beneficial factor. Rather it appears that the memory search has to be relevant to constructing a relational bridge between the two nouns" (p. 457).

Similar conclusions were reached by R. C. Anderson and his associates (Anderson, Goldberg, & Hidde, 1971; Anderson & Kulhavy, 1972). In the 1971 experiment, learners who were required to fill in blanks at the end of sentences learned more than those who read whole sentences. As interpreted by Anderson et al., the completing of the sentence forced the learner to comprehend the other words in the sentence. Thus, the advantage was thought to result from "the process of giving meaningful representation to the words" (Anderson et al., 1971, p. 398).

In another experiment, Watts and Anderson (1971) inserted different types of questions into textual prose. A criterion test required learners to select correct examples of the learned concepts. Some learners received textual questions requiring them to identify the example used in the passage. Other learners received inserted questions requiring them to identify a new example. On the final criterion test, the group that applied their knowledge to new examples showed the best overall performance. As interpreted by Watts and Anderson (1971), the application questions induced the learners to process the text more thoroughly. In the present context, the "more thorough processing" suggests that the questions induced the learners to relate the new learning to old learnings, i.e., to learn meaningfully.

Associations that are aroused during learning usually are semantically related to the new content (Clark & Card, 1961; Fillenbaum, 1971; Sachs, 1967), but the insertion of questions into text also can influence meaningfulness by directing the learner to relevant associations or concepts (e.g., Frase, 1970; Rothkopf & Bisbicos, 1967). Questions appearing prior to the relevant content influenced the learning of that content, but relatively little incidental information was remembered. When the inserted questions occurred after the relevant segment of text, learners recalled incidental information as well as relevant information.

Questions also can influence the depth of processing (Rickards & Di Vesta, 1974). Interspersed post-questions directing attention to the learning of specific facts resulted in high levels of factual recall, but poor recall of superordinate generalizations. Querying the learner's knowledge of superordinate generalizations, however, resulted in high recall both of the superordinate statements and also the subordinate facts. When the questions requested the retrieval of subordinate facts to substantiate the superordinate statement, as opposed to simply requesting the recall of the superordinate idea, the patternings of later recall suggested a greater cognitive integration of the superordinate and subordinate facts. Consistent with the results of Rickards and Di Vesta (1974), the effects of questioning procedures may be viewed as a direct derivative of the extent to which the questions induce the retrieval and processing of a particular set of referential associations.

Orientation also may be provided by organizational subheadings. The title of a passage ordinarily orients the learner to the central theme, and the learner's apprehension of the theme presumably would increase the meaningfulness of relevant segments. In a test of this hypothesis, learners who were permitted to see a thematic title showed significantly greater recall of the passage (Dooling & Lachman, 1971). A second experiment indicated that superiorities in recognitive performance were limited to content words that were semantically related to the theme. Evidence that the locus of the effect is in the learning phase is shown by the finding that receiving the title after the passage has been learned does not influence recall (Bransford & Johnson, 1972; Dooling & Mullet, 1973).

Meaningfulness also may be increased by inducing appropriate learner strategies. Bower and Clark (1969) presented 12 successive serial lists consisting of 10 concrete nouns. One group of learners was told to construct a meaningful story woven around the words to be remembered. A yoked control group received the usual serial learning instructions. Immediate recall performances were virtually perfect, but on a delayed recall test, the average median recall of the narrative group was 93%, whereas the control group recalled only 13%. The difference in performance presumably resulted from the learners' differential success in relating the learning material to some central theme or organizational framework. In short, the narrative strategy allowed the learners to learn meaningfully. Consistent with this interpretation, Thieman's (1973) extension of Bower and Clark's (1969) experiment led to the conclusion that the differences in remembering corresponded directly with the degree of meaningful processing induced by the learning task.

Finally, the ubiquitous influence of meaningfulness also appears critical in the distinction between short-term and long-term memory. Since 1965 the verbal learning literature has been dominated by multistore theories of memory in which processing flows from a limited capacity short-term store to a larger capacity long-term store (Atkinson & Shiffrin, 1968; Waugh & Norman, 1965). Encoding in the short-term store is assumed to be mainly acoustical, and forgetting is assumed to be rapid unless the learner engages in repetitive rehearsal. Long-term memories, however, are relatively permanent, and the encodings are presumed to be semantic. Entry into the long-term store is assumed to be directly related to the amount of time spent in short-term storage.

At both the empirical and theoretical levels, the distinctions between short-term memory and long-term memory are fading rapidly (Craik, 1973; Craik & Lockhart, 1972; Wickelgren, 1973). As a theoretical replacement for multistore models, Craik (1973) suggests that differences in capacity, encoding, and rates of forgetting depend upon the learner's "depth of processing." A rehearsal process that simply holds or maintains the trace in short-term memory, for example, does not lead to long-term retention, whereas rehearsal that involves associative encoding does (Craik & Watkins, 1973; Gardiner, 1974; Jacoby, 1973; Woodward, Bjork & Jongeward, 1973). Thus, linguistic units that are encoded meaningfully are more likely to be remembered. The behavioral evidence that purportedly differentiates two types of memories actually may reflect differences in the extent to which linguistic units are encoded meaningfully.

To summarize, some variables appear to exert their influence by increasing or decreasing meaningfulness. Note, however, that the experimenters did not intentionally manipulate meaningfulness. Let us now examine direct attempts to measure meaning, and inquire into the validity of such techniques for complex learning materials.

Classical Methods of Measuring Meaning

Associational Frequency

The meaningfulness of verbal units in isolation has been assessed by the frequency of individuals reporting an association (Archer, 1960; Glaze, 1928; Noble, 1961), the mean production of associates (Noble, 1952), and categorical ratings of associational frequency (Noble, 1961). Such techniques have successfully measured variations in meaningfulness among nonsense syllables. Among words, however, differentiations in levels of meaningfulness are virtually nonexistent, and such measurements are not obviously applicable when the words occur in a prose context.

Word Frequency and Readability Indices

A classical measure of meaningfulness is the frequency of occurrence of words (Thorndike & Lorge, 1944). Over the entire frequency range, frequently occurring words are more likely to be meaningful. The degree of relationship, however, is not strong. If one considers recall to be a validating measure of meaningfulness, for example, the relationship between word frequency and recall is slight or nonexistent (Hall, 1971; Saltz, 1971; Underwood & Schulz, 1960).

Word frequency also has been an important component in readability formulas, along with variables such as word length, number of syllables, sentence length, number of personal words, and measures of grammatical complexity (e.g., Flesch, 1948). However, in eight validation studies comparing readability indices with independent measures of comprehension or retention, only three studies reported validity coefficients higher than .50, whereas four studies had coefficients below .50 (Klare, 1963, pp. 148–156). Aside from disappointing validity, readability indices can be computed only for large sections of prose, and the method cannot accurately gauge the meaningfulness of individual linguistic subunits.

Word Associations

The classical technique of free association also has been used to uncover the structure of meaning. In an examination of associative overlap, Deese (1959) demonstrated that the frequency with which words in a list elicited each other as associates was highly correlated ($r = .88$) with free recall. Such associative networks, derived from the cognitive operations of contrast and grouping, were presumed to be the essence of meaning (Deese, 1965). Deese's theorizing was based upon free-association responses given to single-word stimuli, but he concludes that the meaning of sentences also is derived from the associational structures of the individual words. The major difference, he assumes, is that associations to words in a sentence are influenced by syntactic and referential constraints.

As evidence, Deese (1965, pp. 168–170) cites Clark's (1966) study in which participants produced sentence-associations having the same grammatical format as the stimulus sentence. To the sentence *The lazy student failed the exam*, sentence associations included *The smart girl passed the test* and *The industrious pupil passed the course*. Individuality in producing sentence-associations was quite evident, but the sentence-associations did bear semantic similarities to the original sentences. Word replacements were similar in kind and in frequency to the distribution of associations given to the same stimulus words in the classical free association task (Deese, 1965, p. 169).

Are the meanings of sentences derived from the dominant associations aroused by the individual words? To the stimulus words of *working, good, from, comes*, and *health*, the corresponding primary associates are *hard, bad, to, goes*, and *sickness* (Palermo & Jenkins, 1964). Yet, if the words are arranged in the sentence *Good health comes from working*, an individual does not give as a sentence association the words *Bad sickness goes to hard*. Clearly, when words are placed into sentences, associations are aroused that are not predictable from the individual words (Barclay, Bransford, Franks, McCarrell, & Nitsch, 1974).

What, then, were the forces that resulted in sentential associations that were both semantically related and in the form of a sensible sentence? Perhaps the simplest explanation is that subjects were required to provide associational sentences in the same grammatical form as the original sentence. If grammatical congruence had not been required, the number of primary associates probably would have been substantially smaller. Equally important, Clark's subjects apparently were producing associational sentences in response to the overall meaning (Gestalten) of the stimulus sentence. Understanding and responding to a sentence requires not only knowledge of the individual words, but also an understanding of the relationships among the words (Anisfeld, 1970; Fillenbaum, 1974a; Olson, 1970). Individuals do retrieve and synthesize referential associations that link the individual words of a sentence.

Associative Communality

Howe (1972) has argued that the meaningfulness of sentences may be determined by the communality of word associations. According to Howe, meaningful words are more likely to produce the same associational response in each person. The occurrence of a variety of associates presumably reflects the greater possibilities of associative interference. This view is very similar to Martin's (1968) theory that units of low meaning are likely to be variably encoded; units of high meaning are likely to be encoded in the same way on each occasion. Ironically, a greater number of associates, when evoked from individuals, is one index of higher meaningfulness (m via Noble's (1952) production method), whereas the occurrence of a greater number of different associates in a group of individuals, as measured only for the first occurring associate, is said to signal the existence of lower meaningfulness.

As evidence that associative communality measures meaningfulness, Howe (1972) cites Clark's (1966) data relating the learning of individual sentences to the normative popularity of associations given in response to the stimulus-sentences. Recall of sentence parts was found to be best when the corresponding sentence associations showed less diversity.

Is associative communality a valid measure of meaningfulness? As would be expected, communality does predict recall. Furthermore, communality conceivably might signal the degree of accord with associational backgrounds. Common associates, however, also could hinder or be irrelevant to the required learning. Like Deese (1965), Howe's (1972) premise is that the meaningfulness of a sentence is derived from the word-associations given to the individual words. The theory thereby is subject to the same limitations noted for Deese's theory and Clark's (1966) data.

Cloze Procedure

In the cloze procedure, readers' success in guessing deleted words is said to measure readability or comprehensibility. Might cloze also be used to assess meaningfulness? A passage containing frequently used words, rather than uncommon words, ordinarily would be more meaningful. Meaningfulness also might be higher when verbal passages contained higher proportions of concrete referents and lower proportions of abstract referents. In agreement, Coleman (1971) found substantial correlations between cloze scores and the densities of either concrete or abstract nouns. Similarly, a passage containing some redundancies ordinarily would be easier to comprehend than prose without redundancy.

The extremely high correlations with measures of redundancy (Coleman, 1971; MacGinitie, 1971; Taylor, 1954), however, suggest that missing words often could be inserted without understanding the passage. Learning performances on high redundancy passages also may be misleadingly high. As evidenced in programmed instruction, learning may be hindered when the learner is provided with too many cues (Anderson, 1970). Research on reading also shows that excessive cues or redundancy may make the passage become less meaningful to the learner by reducing his attention and making him less active in his learning efforts (Samuels, 1970).

In sum, the cloze procedure does tap certain aspects of meaningfulness, although the extent to which these dimensional taps are contaminated remains to be seen (Bormuth, 1965; Weaver & Kingston, 1963). Second, the technique offers simplicity of measurement for comparisons of two or more passages. Disadvantages include the excessively heavy reliance on redundancy. Another disadvantage is that the method offers only gross comparisons among passages, and does not offer calibrations of smaller linguistic units such as the sentence or phrase.

Semantic Differential

A valid measure of semantic similarity conceivably could be an appropriate measure of the meaningfulness of complex verbal units. Osgood, Suci, and Tannenbaum (1957) have proposed that the connotative meaning of a word can be represented in a three-dimensional semantic space on the factorial dimensions of evaluation, activity, and potency. Words close to each other in semantic space are said to be similar in meaning.

An acknowledged limitation of Osgood's semantic differential, as a general measure of meaning, is that it mainly measures connotative meaning. The technique has not been successfully applied to the measurement of denotative meaning. The words *boat, income, bright,* and *eat* occupy virtually identical locations in semantic space, but it is obvious that the differences in meaning are great. Whether the semantic differential could be revised to include dimensions measuring denotation is not known, but the number of potentially independent dimensions appears insurmountably large. In addition, another limitation of the semantic differential is that its usefulness is restricted largely to isolated words rather than words in context.

Toward Adequate Measures of Meaningfulness

As noted, inadequacies are evident in existing methods of measuring meaningfulness in verbal discourse. Even when the classical methods reveal differences among words (Paivio, Yuille, & Madigan, 1968), the relationship to meaningfulness is not always obvious. To illustrate, in the Paivio et al. study, more associations supposedly signaled greater meaningfulness, but the following alignment of production values does not arouse faith in the scaling procedure: FATIGUE, 3.88; FACT, 4.29; SALUTATION, 5.24; PASSION, 5.68; SCIENCE, 6.56; PELT, 6.76; SOVEREIGN, 7.12; WHALE, 7.24; FIRE, 7.36; SEASON, 7.88; PRAIRIE, 8.16.

The classical methods of measuring meaningfulness (Archer, 1960; Noble, 1961) also have located almost all words at the extreme high end of the scale, and thus have been insensitive to actual differences in meaningfulness. One possible solution might be to use scaling procedures that force raters to make differentiations. Using an eliminative method analogous to the forced-choice technique, for example, Johnson's (1973) raters judged meaningfulness by eliminating prose units of lower meaningfulness until only a specified proportion of the content remained. Similar procedures could be fruitful in calibrating the meaningfulness of a sample of isolated words.

Another source of difficulty is that experimenters have focused on prose segments that were inappropriate in size. Some procedures are applicable only to gross comparisons between lengthy passages. Other methods have failed, in part, because the unit of analysis was the single word. If the previous assessment was correct, the associational linkages among words make it highly unlikely that the meaning of a sentence can be derived solely from an analysis of words studied in isolation.

A successful measure of meaningfulness, then, must be responsive to semantic relationships among words. Compare, for example, "the nail file was used to remove the small screw," with "the nail screw was used to remove the small file.·, The words in the two phrases are identical, as are the grammatical structures, but the exchange of *file* and *screw* has rendered the second phrase into a less meaningful assertion. In an analogous experiment, Rosenberg (1968) found that sentences containing words having strong associative relations with each other, such as *The old king ruled wisely*, were remembered better than poorly integrated sentences such as *The poor king dined gravely.*

Even with strongly integrated sentences, however, the arousal of particular referents depends upon the associational context provided by other words in the sentence (Barclay et al., 1974). For example, when nouns from different taxonomic categories were presented in a list, recall patterns showed evidence of categorical clustering (Bousfield, 1953). When such nouns were integral parts of sentences, however, Cofer (1968) found that clustering and recall were disrupted by sentential context. Similarly, the importance of context is evident from Harris and Brewer's (1973) experiments on the accuracy of recalling tenses of verbs. When sentences contained a temporal adverb such as "yesterday," as opposed to a nontemporal adverb such as "accidentally," memory for verb tense was more accurate. According to Harris and Brewer, the temporal context imparted greater meaning to verb tense, and hence resulted in better remembering. Similar outcomes were evident in the recall of other sentence elements in which full meaning depended upon a sentential context designating a particular time, place, or speaker (Brewer & Harris, 1974).

Grammatical structure also determines the particular associational linkages induced by words in a sentence. The grammatical usage of a word, e.g., *train* as either a noun or a verb, may determine meaning, and differences in meaningfulness are evident even when different grammatical usages lead to essentially the same semantic interpretations, e.g., *fill* as a verb or as a noun (Brown, 1958b, pp. 247–253; Carroll, 1970). Even when the object and subject of a sentence remain the same, as in active and passive transformations, different understandings are engendered (Anisfeld & Klenbort, 1973; Herriot, 1970; Offir, 1973). As a consequence, slight variations in syntax can lead to sizable differences in recall (Bock & Brewer, 1974). The recall of two temporally ordered events, for example, is best when the presentation order in the sentence corresponds to the actual ordering of events (Blount & Johnson, 1973; Clark & Clark, 1968). Thus, as evidence has increasingly shown (e.g., Fodor et al., 1974; Weisberg, 1971), sentence structure serves as one basis for sentence interpretation. Here again we have evidence for contextual influence in determining meaningfulness.

In sum, meaningfulness judgments are not likely to be valid unless the linguistic units are in their appropriate verbal contexts (Jenkins, 1974). Classical measures of the meaningfulness of individual words hinted at the possibility that such measures, in conjunction with a set of some unknown combinatorial rules, might predict the learning of any possible combination of words and phrases. That aim has not been achieved, and the contextual determinancy of meaningfulness makes it unlikely that adequate combinatorial rules will be devised.

Given the infinite number of possible word combinations, and the realization that contextual specificity does not allow prediction to other combinations of words, is it worthwhile to measure the meaningfulness of prose subunits? Although the generality of measurement is disappointing, the potential usefulness of such endeavors appears undeniable. One possible use might be pilot assessments of textual subunits prior to their use. Important segments rated low in meaningfulness could be revised to increase the probability of learning. At first glance, the task appears forbidding, but reliable ratings can be achieved with small numbers of raters (Johnson, 1973). Furthermore, when categorical ratings are made of phrase units in prose, the task requires relatively little time beyond that of normal reading, and the relative rankings are very similar to those produced by the eliminative method.

Equally important, measures of the meaningfulness of prose could be useful either as independent or dependent variables in research on learning. Experimental variations in semantic or syntactic variables, for example, presumably would influence the meaningfulness of linguistic subunits, and the ease with which the subunits were learned. Through such studies, generalizable relationships could be established.

A Sampler of Needed Research

Assessing Meaning

Empirical studies are needed to determine whether meaningfulness ratings are more valid when raters make global judgments in contrast to ratings made of dimensional indicants such as amount or quality of aroused imagery.

If raters are instructed to attend simultaneously to the various components of meaningfulness, the task may be too complex. Alternately, if raters are told simply to furnish an overall global rating, they may develop differing reliances on the various component dimensions. An empirical solution may be to collect global ratings and also ratings of the component dimensions, and then determine the degree of overlap and the extent to which the various ratings predict criterion performances.

The development of alternative methods of measuring meaning and meaningfulness also warrants research priority. Methods used in measuring comprehension (Carroll, 1972), for example, perhaps could be adapted for global measurements of meaningfulness. In developing analytical measures of particular aspects of meaning, researchers perhaps could improvise on techniques used with individual words. Fillenbaum and Rapoport (1971), for example, show much ingenuity in analyzing similarity judgments by techniques such as nonmetric multidimensional scaling, graph theoretic analysis, and hierarchical clustering analysis. Fillenbaum (1974a) probed other aspects of meaning through analyses of attempted paraphrases (also see Fillenbaum, 1974b; Gleitman & Gleitman, 1970), as well as raters' judgments of sentence equivalence, informativeness, and semantic plausibility. Using a method of componential paraphrasing, followed by empirical analyses of subjects' sortings of words according to "similarity of meaning," Miller's (1969, 1972) research provides additional directionality for developing alternative methods.

To appreciate the facilitation that could result from new methods of assessing meaning, consider the catalytic influence of Bransford and Franks' (1971) research in stimulating additional research (Barclay, 1973; Barclay & Reid, 1974; Bransford, Barclay, & Franks, 1972; Cofer, 1973; Franks & Bransford, 1972, 1974; Johnson, Bransford, & Solomon, 1973; Paris & Carter, 1973; Peterson & McIntyre, 1973; Potts, 1972; Singer & Rosenberg, 1973). Although Bransfors methodological procedures and conclusions have been criticized (Katz, 1973; Katz & Gruenewald, 1974; Reitman & Bower, 1973), the powerful impact of Bransford and his associates appears derived from the use of an explicit method for showing that learners have considerable recognitive difficulty in distinguishing between the semantic content of the message and their own implicitly generated semantic content. In agreement with Bartlett's (1932) reconstructive theory of remembering, the semantic content of a message appears to become fused with existing referential knowledges.

The adoption of a referential theory of meaning argues the importance of developing methods that assess the referential associations of discourse units. As noted earlier, word associations to individual stimulus words do not necessarily predict the associations that will be given when the stimulus words are embedded in discourse. Yet, free associations to prose units undoubtedly tap certain aspects of the structure of meaning. Typically, the bulk of the associations can be categorized as being either opposites;

synonyms; superordinates; subordinates; logical coordinates, e.g., *apple-pear*; or functional, e.g., *needle-thread* (Karwoski & Berthold, 1945; Moran, Mefferd, & Kimble, 1964). Is there a code that allows translation of such word associations into structural or theoretical representations of meaning?

In an important paper, Clark (1970) postulates the existence of associational rules that govern the production of word associations. Theorizing from the linguistic viewpoints of Katz and Fodor (1963) and of Chomsky (1965), Clark assumes a componential approach in which a word is comprehended as a set of syntactic and semantic features. The features of *man*, for example, might be characterized as: +Noun, +Det −, +Count, +Animate, +Human, +Adult, and +Male. In the free-association task, an "associating rule" is applied to the list of features, such as "change the sign of the last feature" (e.g., +Male to −Male), and an association is then produced which is congruent with the altered feature list, e.g., *woman*. "Changing the sign of the last feature" is also labeled the "minimal contrast rule" because the antonymous associations produced by the rule have the maximum number of features in common with the stimulus. Within the context of a referential theory of meaning, the "last" feature which is reversed appears centrally related to the semantic dimension on which the word is primarily defined. The word *short*, for example, leads to the association of *long* because length is the primary defining attribute of *short*. In experience, the psychological attribution of *short* is contrasted with the anchoring alternative of *long*.

The "marking rule" describes another associational transformation common in word associations (Clark, 1970). With antonymic words, one member of the pair is marked or positive with regard to the presence of a feature, whereas the opposite member is neutral or unmarked (Greenberg, 1966). For example, *dog* is unmarked with regard to the classification of sex, but *bitch* is marked. In association tasks, marked stimulus words show a greater tendency to produce their unmarked counterparts as associational responses (Clark, 1970). The marked stimulus of *better*, for example, produces the unmarked response *of good* more often than *good* produces *better*. In the recall of sentences, unmarked words are remembered better than marked, and qualitative changes in memory also tend to proceed from the marked to the unmarked form rather than in the reverse direction (Benjafield & Giesbrecht, 1973; Carpenter, 1974; Clark & Card, 1969). Significantly, however, memorial change toward the unmarked form tends to occur only when such change allows the preservation of the original meaning of the sentence (Brewer & Lichtenstein, 1974). Although linguistic criteria are used to differentiate marked from unmarked words (Greenberg, 1966), Deese (1973) notes that unmarked members of a pair occur more frequently in written language and that children learn to use unmarked words prior to marked words. Equally important, marked words tend to be rated negatively on evaluative scales of affect (Deese, 1973). Given such differential experiences, it is not surprising that unmarked words have priority in associational structures. For the marking rule, as well as other associational rules, regularities in associative responses may prove useful in delineating the structure of meaning.

Similar associational transformations presumably mediate the referents aroused to linguistic units in prose. With linguistic units larger than one word, however, verbal associations elicited in free association probably represent associational structure only indirectly. In analyses of verbs of motion, for example, Miller (1972, pp. 345, 369) suggests that some concepts have associational representations which are blends of existing concepts or words. Such associational blends, coupled with the person's ability to derive a fused representation of separate semantic knowledges, may play a determining role in the excellence of college students in judging the adequacy of their own paraphrases (Fillenbaum, 1974b). In any event, with passages of prose containing many ideational units, the associational blends sometimes become even more composite, until it is perhaps appropriate to speak of schemas (Bartlett, 1932), surrogate structures (Pompi & Lachman, 1967), themes (Dooling & Lachman, 1971), or conceptual macro-structures (Bower, 1974).

If schemas do mediate the recall of prose, research ought to be able to discover the basis of such mediation. The foggy notion of schema, unfortunately, has not been operationalized empirically (Oldfield, 1972), but ingenious experimenters should be capable of closing this empirical gap. Perhaps schemas can be inferred from various regularities in recall. Recall patternings in prose, for example, appear analogous to the clusterings observed in categorized lists (Bousfield, 1953), and such clusterings appear to represent the influence of organizational processes during learning (Mandler, 1967). If schemas do determine clustering in the recall of prose, it should be possible to infer the schemas from clustering. Similarly, patternings of errors also might signal the existence of schemas in remembering (Bartlett, 1932). Learners under the influence of preexisting schematic knowledge, for example, made recognitive errors which were thematically congruent with their schema (Sulin & Dooling, 1974).

Schemas also might be inferred from the effectiveness of linguistic segments in inducing the recall of other linguistic segments. The use of cuing to assess memory structures in prose learning has its counterpart in the cuing techniques used to induce the remembering of list members (e.g., Mandler, 1967; Tulving & Pearlstone, 1966; Slamecka, 1968). Just as with previous research, it may be assumed that the cuing taps existing superordinate categories that have not been remembered. With the development of such methods for measuring schemas, insight may be gained into the manner in which referential meanings are translated into recall.

Empirical Issues

The adoption of a referential theory of meaning bespeaks the importance of relating learning to the organizational structure of existing referential knowledges. The organization and availability of referential associations, for example, can be influenced by the input order of a sequence of sentences (Anderson, J., & Hastie, 1974). Furthermore, even subtle differences in the focus of a sentence can arouse different associational referents. The sentence "It was Mr. Smith who ordered the coffee," for example, presupposes that coffee was ordered by someone, whereas "It was the coffee that Mr. Smith ordered" presupposes that Mr. Smith ordered something. When recognitive paraphrases of such sentences violated presuppositional knowledges, changes in wording were more easily detected than when the alternative phrasings did not violate presuppositions (Offir, 1973).

Referential emphasis within a paragraph appears to be another factor influencing the associative representation of embedded sentences (Perfetti & Goldman, 1974). For a sentence such as *The serfs rebelled against the baron*, the extent to which the paragraph focused on either the subject or object of the sentence was related to the effectiveness of that subject or object as a retrieval cue in remembering the remaining portion of the sentence.

Additional evidence for the importance of referential availability may be found in the results of Haviland and Clark (1974) and Moesner and Bregman (1972). In the latter study, when learners attempted to acquire an artificial phrase-structure language without the aid of semantic referents, there was practically no learning of the syntactic rules even after hundreds of trials. With the referential availability of geometrical forms that portrayed the syntactic relations, the learners readily learned the grammatical rules.

An important area for empirical investigation is the determination of variables influencing the availability of referential knowledges. One determinant may be the structural organization of the learning material (Anderson, J., & Hastie, 1974). Material that possesses a logical or hierarchical structure may facilitate the arousal of subsuming associations (Ausubel, 1963; de Villiers, 1974). Meaningfulness also may be fostered by the adoption of a set to learn meaningfully rather than by rote (Ausubel, 1963). In turn, the major consequence of adopting a meaningful set may be the arousal of referential associations relating to the material to be learned. Similarly, gaining access to appropriate referential associations can be accomplished by redirection of the learner's set (e.g., Luchins, 1942).

The quality and organization of aroused referents also appears important in learning. Sentences containing pronouns as the subject are remembered better than sentences with nouns as the subject, even though the pronouns themselves are not remembered better (Martin & Walter, 1969). In contrast, the denotative specificity of nouns in prose, as gauged by superordinate-subordinate status, is positively related to remembering, even when the nouns are equivalent in concreteness-abstractness (August, Proctor, Hynes, & Johnson, Note 1). Similarly, memory is better for sentences having specific verbs than for sentences having general verbs (Thios, 1975). Increases in denotative specificity via the restriction of a noun modifier, however, do not influence remembering (August et al., Note 1). Are such differences in remembering due to differences in the parceling of referential associations? The partitioning of referents for superordinates and subordinates, and for verbs, occurs along the referential boundaries of existing concepts, whereas the denotative restriction enjoined by an adjectival modifier is an arbitrary parceling of a noun's referential class. As an alternate hypothesis, the effects of adjectival modification might be related to the extent to which the parceling induces the retrieval of concrete associates to the noun (Anderson, 1974).

What are the dimensional or functional attributes of referents that influence learning? Are referents more easily aroused to specific categories such as *diamond* than to general categories such as *gem*? Or, as suggested by Brown (1958a) and by Loftus and Bolton (1974), perhaps the retrievability of referents is partially determined by usage habits. Do subordinate nouns evoke referential associations that are qualitatively different from the referents of superordinate nouns? For example, are referents to subordinate nouns more likely to be concrete? Are the meanings of general words stored in the format of a specific exemplar (Anderson & McGaw, 1973)? If so, why are errors in recall more likely to be memorial changes from specificity to generality than from generality to specificity (August et al., Note 1)? Is there a quantitative difference in the number of referents evoked by superordinates and subordinates (Smith, Shoben, & Rips, 1974)? Does the storage node for a word contain only referential distinguishers, and not the referential attributes common to the superordinate of the word (Collins & Quillian, 1969)? The answers to questions like these will add to our knowledge regarding the processes by which meaningfulness influences learning and retention.

Studies of the component dimensions of meaningfulness could test Paivio's (1971) conclusion that meaningfulness is important only when a particular sequential ordering is required in recall. Under other conditions, says Paivio, imagery is a more important predictor than meaningfulness. As evidence, Paivio cites a widely quoted study by Paivio, Smythe, and Yuille (1968) in which imagery influenced learning even when differences in meaningfulness were equated. When meaningfulness was varied and imagery was constant, meaningfulness exerted no additional effect on learning. An examination of the words used in the Paivio et al. study, however, suggests the possibility of bias in the selectional procedure. As assessed by the production method, the mean number of associates to the high-*m* list averaged only two more than the low-*m* list. The high-*m* list was designed to be high in meaningfulness and low in imagery, and included words such as *abode, molecule, theologian*, and *whalebone*. Suppose, instead, that the high-*m* list was composed of words such as *answer, cost, idea, law*, and *duty*, and the low-*m* list was composed of words such as *labyrinth, rosin*, and *edifice*. In such a comparison, the outcome might be different.

Paivio's (1971) dual coding hypothesis has received considerable experimental support, but Goldfarb, Wirtz, and Anisfeld's (1973) evidence suggests that all verbal material is coded for referential meaning, and that differences in recognitive memory for abstract and concrete phrases are due to differences in denotative distinctiveness rather than imagibility. Since denotative distinctiveness was operationally defined by judgments of personal relevancy, the generality of the Goldfarb et al. conclusion is uncertain. Paivio and Olver (1964), however, found that stimulus imagery did not influence the learning of paired associates when specificity was held constant, whereas stimulus specificity was significantly correlated with recall ($r = .41$) even when imagery was held constant. Imagery and denotative specificity also show some independence in factor analyses (Paivio, 1968; Spreen & Schulz, 1966). Coupled with the conflicting research evidence on the longevity of learning mediated by imagery (Begg & Robertson, 1973; Postman & Burns, 1973), research clearly is still needed on the relationships among imagery, meaningfulness, denotative specificity, and learning.

Research also is needed to determine the influence of multiple referents on learning. Words such as *tripod* have quite limited sets of referential associations. Others, e.g., *triangle*, have extensive associations. For some concepts with multiple referents, such as *scare*, the referential associations are all related conceptually, whereas the multiple referents of words such as *light* are related to different denotative meanings. Based upon studies of verbal learning and retention, it might be predicted that ambiguous words and phrases would be more susceptible to negative transfer and interference. Complicating the prediction, however, is the fact that frequently occurring nouns, as measured in the Thorndike-Lorge (1944) count, are more likely to have a greater number of meanings (Saltz & Modigliani, 1967). Even with Thorndike-Lorge frequencies controlled, however, Saltz and Modigliani found superior learning of paired associates when the response terms were nouns having a greater number of meanings.

Contrary to expectations, Saltz and Modigliani (1967) found that the number of meanings was virtually unrelated to Noble's (1952) production measure of meaningfulness. If associative production is unrelated to the number of meanings, what associations are being tapped? Saltz (1971) suggests that the associations given to a stimulus word tend to exhaust a single meaning, and that words with high-*m* values differ from low-*m* words in the richness of their connotative meanings. Other explanations are possible, and it is clear that analytical investigations are needed to determine the relationships between the production of associations, the number and types of meanings associated with a linguistic unit, and learning.

Empirical studies also could delineate the conditions under which separate knowledges become fused. Unification tends to be enhanced by a correct temporal sequencing of events (Clark & Clark, 1968), perceived cause and effect relationships (Fillen-baum, 1971), pronominalization (Lesgold, 1972), and the use of the definite article (de Villiers, 1974). When a series of sentences were perceived as a unified story, rather than an unrelated set, de Villiers' (1974) learners recalled more sentences, recalled the sentences more often in their story order, and more often showed gist recall. Furthermore, ratings of thematic centrality were directly related to sentential recall, whereas ratings of imagery were unrelated to remembering. In contrast, when not viewed as a story, centrality ratings were unrelated to recall, and imagery ratings were directly related. The associative relatedness of the input units thus appears critical in determining semantic fusion. As further evidence, when semantically related sentences are presented, learners cannot later discriminate the input sentences from distractor sentences containing semantically compatible content (Bransford & Franks, 1971; Franks & Bransford, 1974; Peterson & McIntyre, 1973). If presented with a lengthy series of semantically unrelated sentences, however, learners are quite accurate in discriminating old from new sentences (Shepard, 1967).

A related empirical problem is that of understanding memory for gist. Semantic changes in recognitive foils are detected much more readily than syntactical changes (Sachs, 1967; Begg & Wickelgren, 1974), and the verbatim recall of prose is a rarity (Bartlett, 1932; Johnson, 1974). The learner's remembering of gist displays itself through the recall of verbal equivalences, the selective remembering of important content (Johnson, 1970), and the occurrence of meaning-preserving errors (Fillenbaum, 1966). Since judgments about the equivalence of meaning involve some subjectivity, experimenters have tended to study verbatim memory and to avoid studies of gist. As demonstrated by Fillenbaum (1966), however, gist can be studied objectively, and there is critical need for describing and understanding the transformational changes that occur from the original input of sentences to the display of gist.

Probes also are needed to ascertain the relationships between learning and the organizational complexity of the referential associations. Perhaps the major characteristic differentiating abstract from concrete units is the complexity of the referent package. Verbal units that are concrete, such as *chair*, have referential attributes that are organized conjunctively. To be a *chair*, an object must have a base, a seat, and a back. The referential dimensions of a concrete unit ordinarily can be specifically denoted, and a potential instance or example of the category can be identified by noting the co-occurrences of the criterial attributes. Such co-occurrences, e.g., size and weight, are so regular that children often have difficulty in disentangling the attributes on occasions in which the attributes are not correlative (Ervin & Foster, 1960; Piaget, 1947/1960).

The defining attributes of abstract categories are less obvious or distinct and are more highly interrelated with other concepts (Goldfarb et al., 1973). As shown by Carroll's (1964b) analyses of *immigrant* and *tort*, abstract concepts are more likely to have complex referential systems requiring knowledges of relationships and disjunctive combinations. From a research viewpoint, the descriptive classification of concepts needs to progress beyond Bruner, Goodnow, and Austin's (1956) categories of conjunctive, disjunctive, and relational.

Empirical information also is needed on the referential attributes that are salient to the learner. Deese (1973), for example, notes the pervasiveness of spatial information in our cognitive and affective categories. Apparently, then, spatiality is salient to the learner, and spatial information has a high probability of becoming incorporated into referential structures. In identifying other salient attributes, Rips, Shoben, and Smith (1973) had raters judge how typical each word (e.g., *chicken*) was of its superordinate category (e.g., *birds*). A multidimensional scaling procedure was then applied to the ratings to suggest salient dimensions (e.g., *size* and *predaciousness*). Using another method of identifying salient attributes, Bruner, Olver, and Greenfield (1966) had children judge how objects were alike and different. Developmental changes were found in the various modes by which equivalence judgments were made. Similarly, a mapping of salient semantic attributes might be obtained through the use of a set of structured questions to judges.

Scattered throughout the developmental literature, there are studies reporting developmental changes in children's understanding of different tasks and instructions (e.g., Luria, 1961; Piaget, 1947/1960; Piaget & Inhelder, 1968/1973). Data also exist on the ages at which particular words are acquired, developmental changes in word associations (Entwisle, 1966), and systematic progressions in the usage of different syntactical structures (Fodor, et al., 1974; McNeill, 1970; Menyuk, 1969). Surprisingly little research, however, has focused on semantic development (Anglin, 1970; McNeill, 1970; Palermo & Molfese, 1972). The discovery of developmental regularities in the acquisition of meanings could provide insights into both the cognitive functioning of children (Barclay & Reid, 1974) and also the structural representation of meaning in adults. For many of the research questions raised in the present review, counterpart questions exist regarding developmental regularities in semantic development. Although theoretical statements on the developmental acquisitions of meanings are virtually non-existent, recent speculations by E. V. Clark (1973) and by Nelson (1974) appear to have ended the drought. Recent theorizing on the acquisition of semantic meanings in adults, to be discussed in the next section, also may provide impetus for comparable theorizing on developmental regularities in the acquisition and use of referential knowledges.

Associative Network Models

The conceptual emphasis of the present review has much in congruence with the recent spate of associative network models of semantic memory (Anderson & Bower, 1973; Collins & Quillian, 1972; Kintsch, 1972; Quillian, 1968; and Rumelhart, Lindsay, & Norman, 1972). Quillian's (1968) view, for example, is that the full meaning of a concept consists of all the memory nodes that can be reached from the concept via an exhaustive tracing process. In these network models, the basic unit of analysis typically is the "proposition," consisting of a "relation" (usually verbs, adjectives, conjunctions) and one or more "arguments" (usually a noun or other proposition). Within a proposition, the semantic destiny of a lexical item is partially determined by case-grammar rules regarding acceptable parsings. If the word has been encountered previously, the existing storage node is used. Otherwise, a new node is formed automatically. Meanings of lexical items thus become defined through cumulative entries of propositional statements containing the unit. After entry into memory, words also can gain new meanings through the operation of various inferential and transformational rules.

Although the network models are couched in the familiar jargon of associationism, such speculations represent new vistas for psychologists and educators. In the empirical testing of the network models, one important consequence may be a shift in the dominant learning paradigm from serial lists and paired associates to studies of prose. With respect to theories of meaning, the network theories may become battlefields that will provide insights into the role of meaningfulness in learning. Since Anderson and Bower's (1973) associative model (HAM) is the most explicit formulation and has received considerable support, it is appropriate to sample some of their assumptions that deserve empirical testing.

Most basic, perhaps, is Anderson and Bower's (1973) assertion that propositional organization is required for the formation of associations. Although Rohwer (1966) has demonstrated that propositional formats often aid learning, words ostensibly can be associated without benefit of verb or other propositional connectives. Furthermore, even if propositional structure is required, the structural components of such propositions are not obvious. Anderson and Bower postulate the existence of a context subtree containing location and temporal information, and also a fact subtree representing a topic, predications about the topic, and adverbial or adjectival modifiers of the predications. The resultant associative structures may be represented graphically by sentence diagrams similar to the tree-like parsings rendered by grammarians and generations of schoolboys. Figure 1, for example, shows Anderson and Bower's (1973, p. 160) associative representation of "During the night in the park the hippie touched the debutante."

Note that other associative paths might be assumed, but Anderson and Bower (1973, p. 167) allow representation only of ideational combinations

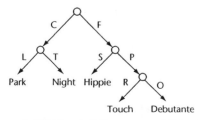

Figure 1: Anderson & Bower's (1973) associative representation of "During the night in the park the hippie touched the debutante"

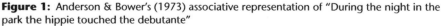

that represent direct predications. Might not a direct object (e.g., *debutante*), however, be directly associated with a location (e.g., *park*)? In what sense, psychologically, is location information (e.g., *park*) more closely associated with the subject (e.g., *hippie*) than with the object (e.g., *debutante*)? Is the verb concept (e.g., *touch*) semantically closer to the object (e.g., *debutante*) than to the subject (e.g., *hippie*)? Might the associational structure of a proposition be related to the syntactical structure in which the proposition is phrased? Anderson and Bower (pp. 295–314) examined the validity of their structural hierarchy by providing cues for stimulating the recall of previously unrecalled components. Their predictions of directional differences in recall received only marginal support from the data. Overall, then, the validity of HAM's associational structure is not obvious, and reaction-time probes and other techniques might provide evidence of different associational structures.

Anderson and Bower (1973, p. 284) assume that all associative links within a proposition are actually transformed into long-term memory associations. On the initial input, for example, the sentence in Figure 1 becomes parsed into 13 associational linkages that are equivalent in strength. With such an assumption, unfortunately, the problem of meaningfulness is skirted, and prior associational memories are assigned no role in determining whether an association will be formed. Differential recall of propositional components does occur (Anderson & Bower, 1973, pp. 295–329), and this fact suggests differential encodings during input. A successful model of associative memory needs to account for this fact, as well as evidence showing that the encoding and recall of linguistic units are related to dimensional characteristics such as abstractness-concreteness, semantic importance, and interest (Gomulicki, 1956; Johnson, 1974).

Another challenge to researchers and theorists is to develop a memory system sensitive to the fact that associative representations depend on learners' encoding strategies. The accuracy of remembering semantic content depends, in part, upon the learner's set for accurate remembering (Brockway, Chmielewski, & Cofer, 1974). Similarly, with certain types of encoding strategies, the learner shows a long-term remembering of the grammatical voice of input sentences (Anderson & Bower, 1973, pp. 224–228). An adequate theory of semantic memory also needs to account for persistent encoding biases such as preferences for recoding linguistic units into abbreviated forms, and for the remembering of gist rather than surface detail.

Additional structural components also may be required to adequately represent the full array of semantic information. Function words, for example, are given only token representation in HAM (pp. 139, 206), but our earlier analysis argued that each word carries elements of meaning. Furthermore, if a separate component is needed for storing temporal information, why is there not comparable representation for spatial information? As another example, informational predications regarding the meaning of verbs occur only infrequently in everyday discourse, and the operation of HAM appears to offer limited opportunity for establishing equivalences in the meanings of verbs (Anderson & Bower, 1973, pp. 193–196). Yet, contrary to what might be predicted from HAM, subsets of verbs, such as verbs of motion, appear to be organized in meaning by rather complex structures of shared semantic components (Miller, 1972). Finally, HAM appears deficient in representing semantic information regarding the structural importance of the various propositions within a message. Informational input in HAM is not categorized according to importance or saliency, and all propositional inputs have equal representation. According to Anderson and Bower (1973, pp. 383–386), the saliency of propositions is determined by input frequency and recency, but there is evidence that structural importance is related to remembering even when input frequency is equivalent for all propositions (Johnson, 1970). On this issue, and on other issues, theorists and researchers have ample opportunity for challenging Anderson and Bower's conception of associative meaning.

Concluding Comment

The present designation of meaningfulness as an area needing research is predicated on the assumption that meaningfulness is a critical variable in learning. Empirical support for this assumption is evident in a study relating the recall of textual prose to meaningfulness (Johnson, 1973). Textual subunits rated in the highest level of meaningfulness were recalled approximately three to eighteen times better than subunits ranked in the lowest level of meaningfulness. Further evidence of the importance of meaningfulness may be found in paraphrasing studies (Fillenbaum, 1974a, 1974b) in which subjects were explicitly instructed "not to improve the sentences or make them more sensible, but to *paraphrase* them, rewording each in a way that captures its meaning as accurately as possible." However, when the semantic content violated the paraphrasers' existing knowledge, they nevertheless paraphrased the content more meaningfully even though they were aware of differences between the original content and their own paraphrases. In the words of Fillenbaum (1974b), "even in the peculiar circumstances of the psychological laboratory Ss seem to be acting on the basic assumption that *what is described in discourse will be sensible*, that what is described will conform to the customary order of events and will satisfy normal qualitative and causal relations between events or actions" (p. 577).

As Bartlett (1932) said in his classical work on remembering, the person's learning may be characterized as "an effort after meaning." To quote Bartlett (1932), "there is a constant effort to get the maximum possible of meaning into the material presented" (p. 84). How may this be accomplished? Quoting Bartlett again, "such effort is simply the attempt to connect something that is given with something other than itself" (p. 227). Thus, when learning occurs, the learner inevitably attaches the new experience to the residual of previous experiences. In turn, the residual of past experiences, organized into schemas, determines the quality of remembering. Bartlett's research (1932), as well as others (e.g., Campbell, 1958; Johnson, 1962; Paul, 1959), have provided convincing evidence that qualitative distortions in remembering are related to the individual's cognitive structure. Furthermore, whether a particular verbal unit is remembered or not remembered is also determined by the organized residual of the learner's past experiences (Gomulicki, 1956; Johnson, 1974; Zangwill, 1972).

It has been more than 40 years since the publication of Bartlett's (1932) work. Since that time, there have been methodological advances which allow for a renewed attack on the problem of meaning. The time does seem ripe for theoretical and empirical reexaminations of the role of meaning in complex learning.

Note

1. Dixon's (1965, pp. 23–104) historical account of western thoughts about language, from Plato to Chomsky, documents the everpresent attempts to grapple with the concept of meaning. A review of earlier experimental attempts to assess meaning may be found in Creelman (1966). Modern philosophers and linguists continue to write copiously and polemically on the topic of meaning, and reference to this literature may be initiated through Alston (1964), Lehrer and Lehrer (1970), and Lyons (1968).

Reference Note

1. August, G. J., Proctor, D. L., Hynes, K. P., & Johnson, R. E. *Recall of prose as a function of denotative specificity.* Paper presented at the meeting of the American Psychological Association, New Orleans, September 1974.

References

Alston, W. P. *Philosophy of language.* Englewood Cliffs, N.J.: Prentice-Hall, 1964.

Anderson, J., & Hastie, R. Individuation and reference in memory: Proper names and definite descriptions. *Cognitive Psychology,* 1974, *6,* 495–514.

Anderson, J. R., & Bower, G. H. *Human associative memory.* Washington, D.C.: V. H. Winston, 1973.

Anderson, R. C. Control of student mediating processes during verbal learning and instruction. *Review of Educational Research,* 1970, *40,* 349–369.

Anderson, R. C. Concretization and sentence learning. *Journal of Educational Psychology,* 1974, *66,* 179–183.

Anderson, R. C., Goldberg, S. R., & Hidde, J. L. Meaningful processing of sentences. *Journal of Educational Psychology,* 1971, *62,* 395–399.

Anderson, R. C., & Kulhavy, R. W. Learning concepts from definitions. *American Educational Research Journal,* 1972, *9,* 385–390.

Anderson, R. C., & McGaw, B. On the representation of meanings of general terms. *Journal of Experimental Psychology,* 1973, *101,* 301–306.

Anglin, J. M. *The growth of word meaning.* Cambridge, Mass.: M.I.T. Press, 1970.

Anisfeld, M. False recognition of adjective-noun phrases. *Journal of Experimental Psychology*, 1970, *86*, 120–122.

Anisfeld, M., & Klenbort, I. On the functions of structural paraphrase: The view from the passive voice. *Psychological Bulletin*, 1973, *79*, 117–126.

Archer, E. J. A re-evaluation of meaningfulness of all possible CVC trigrams. *Psychological Monographs*, 1960, *74* (10, Whole No. 497).

Atkinson, R. C., & Shiffrin, R. M. Human memory: A proposed system and its control processes. In K. W. Spence & J. T. Spence (Eds.), *The psychology of learning and motivation: Advances in research and theory* (Vol. 2). New York: Academic Press, 1968.

Ausubel, D. P. *The psychology of meaningful verbal learning.* New York: Grune & Stratton, 1963.

Barclay, J. R. The role of comprehension in remembering sentences. *Cognitive Psychology*, 1973, *4*, 229–254.

Barclay, J. R., Bransford, J. D., Franks, J. J., McCarrell, N. S., & Nitsch, K. Comprehension and semantic flexibility. *Journal of Verbal Learning and Verbal Behavior*, 1974, *13*, 471–481.

Barclay, J. R., & Reid, M. Semantic integration in children's recall of discourse. *Developmental Psychology*, 1974, *10*, 277–281.

Bartlett, F. C. *Remembering.* London: Cambridge University Press, 1932.

Begg, I., & Robertson, R. Imagery and long-term retention. *Journal of Verbal Learning and Verbal Behavior*, 1973, *12*, 689–700.

Begg, I., & Wickelgren, W. A. Retention functions for syntactic and lexical vs. semantic information in sentence recognition memory. *Memory and Cognition*, 1974, *2*, 353–359.

Benjafield, J., & Giesbrecht, L. Context effects and the recall of comparative sentences. *Memory and Cognition*, 1973, *1*, 133–136.

Black, M. *The labyrinth of language.* New York: Praeger, 1968.

Blount, H. P., & Johnson, R. E. Grammatical structure and the recall of sentences in prose. *American Educational Research Journal*, 1973, *10*, 163–168.

Bobrow, S. A., & Bower, G. H. Comprehension and recall of sentences. *Journal of Experimental Psychology*, 1969, *80*, 455–461.

Bock, J. K., & Brewer, W. F. Reconstructive recall in sentences with alternative surface structures. *Journal of Experimental Psychology*, 1974, *103*, 837–843.

Bormuth, J. R. Cloze tests as a measure of ability to detect literary style. *International Reading Association Proceedings*, 1965, 287–290.

Bousfield, W. A. The occurrence of clustering in the recall of randomly arranged associates. *Journal of General Psychology*, 1953, *49*, 229–240.

Bousfield, W. A. The problem of meaning in verbal learning. In C. N. Cofer & B. S. Musgrave (Eds.), *Verbal learning and verbal behavior.* New York: McGraw-Hill, 1961.

Bower, G. H. Selective facilitation and interference in retention of prose. *Journal of Educational Psychology*, 1974, *66*, 1–8.

Bower, G. H., & Clark, M. C. Narrative stories as mediators for serial learning. *Psychonomic Science*, 1969, *14*, 181–182.

Bransford, J. D., Barclay, J. R., & Franks, J. J. Sentence memory: A constructive versus interpretative approach. *Cognitive Psychology*, 1972, *3*, 193–209.

Bransford, J. D., & Franks, J. J. The abstraction of linguistic ideas. *Cognitive Psychology*, 1971, *2*, 331–350.

Bransford, J. D., & Johnson, M. K. Contextual prerequisites for understanding: Some investigations of comprehension and recall. *Journal of Verbal Learning and Verbal Behavior*, 1972, *11*, 717–726.

Brewer, W. F., & Harris, R. J. Memory for deictic elements in sentences. *Journal of Verbal Learning and Verbal Behavior*, 1974, *13*, 321–327.

Brewer, W. F., & Lichtenstein, E. H. Memory for marked semantic features versus memory for meaning. *Journal of Verbal Learning and Verbal Behavior*, 1974, *13*, 172–180.

Brockway, J., Chmielewski, D., & Cofer, C. N. Remembering prose: Productivity and accuracy constraints in recognition memory. *Journal of Verbal Learning and Verbal Behavior*, 1974, *13*, 194–208.

Brown, R. How shall a thing be called? *Psychological Review*, 1958, *65*, 14–21. (a)

Brown, R. *Words and things.* New York: Free Press, 1958. (b)

Bruner, J. S., Goodnow, J. J., & Austin, G. A. *A study of thinking.* New York: Wiley, 1956.

Bruner, J. S., Olver, R. R., & Greenfield, P. M. *Studies in cognitive growth.* New York: Wiley, 1966.

Campbell, D. T. Systematic error on the part of human links in communication systems. *Information and Control*, 1958, *1*, 334–369.

Carpenter, P. A. On the comprehension, storage, and retrieval of comparative sentences. *Journal of Verbal Learning and Verbal Behavior*, 1974, *13*, 401–411.

Carroll, J. B. *Language and thought.* Englewood Cliffs, N.J.: Prentice-Hall, 1964. (a)

Carroll, J. B. Words, meanings, and concepts. *Harvard Educational Review*, 1964, *34*, 178–202. (b)

Carroll, J. B. *Comprehension by 3rd, 6th, and 9th graders of words having multiple grammatical functions* (Final Report, Project No. 0-0439, Grant No. OEG-2-9-400439-1059, U.S. Office of Education). Princeton, N.J.: Educational Testing Service, 1970. (ERIC Document Reproduction Service No. ED 048 311)

Carroll, J. B. Defining language comprehension: Some speculations. In J. B. Carroll & R. O. Freedle (Eds.), *Language comprehension and the acquisition of knowledge.* Washington, D.C.: V. H. Winston, 1972.

Chomsky, N. *Aspects of the theory of syntax.* Cambridge, Mass.: M.I.T. Press, 1965.

Church, J. *Language and the discovery of reality.* New York: Random House, 1961.

Clark, E. V. What's in a word? On the child's acquisition of semantics in his first language. In T. E. Moore (Ed.), *Cognitive development and the acquisition of language.* New York: Academic Press, 1973.

Clark, H. H. The prediction of recall patterns in simple active sentences. *Journal of Verbal Learning and Verbal Behavior*, 1966, *5*, 99–106.

Clark, H. H. Word associations and linguistic theory. In J. Lyons (Ed.), *New horizons in linguistics.* Baltimore: Penguin, 1970.

Clark, H. H., & Card, S. K. Role of semantics in remembering comparative sentences. *Journal of Experimental Psychology*, 1969, *82*, 545–553.

Clark, H. H., & Clark, E. V. Semantic distinctions and memory for complex sentences. *Quarterly Journal of Experimental Psychology*, 1968, *20*, 129–138.

Cofer, C. N. Free recall of nouns after presentation in sentences. *Journal of Experimental Psychology*, 1968, *78*, 145–152.

Cofer, C. N. Constructive processes in memory. *American Scientist*, 1973, *61*, 537–543.

Coleman, E. B. Developing a technology of written instruction: Some determiners of the complexity of prose. In E. Z. Rothkopf & P. E. Johnson (Eds.), *Verbal learning research and the technology of written instruction.* New York: Teachers College Press, 1971.

Collins, A. M., & Quillian, M. R. Retrieval time from semantic memory. *Journal of Verbal Learning and Verbal Behavior*, 1969, *8*, 240–247.

Collins, A. M., & Quillian, M. R. How to make a language user. In E. Tulving & W. Donaldson (Eds.), *Organization of memory.* New York: Academic Press, 1972.

Craik, F. I. M. A "levels of analysis" view of memory. In P. Pliner, L. Krames, & T. Alloway (Eds.), *Communication and affect.* New York: Academic Press, 1973.

Craik, F. I. M., & Lockhart, R. S. Levels of processing: A framework for memory research. *Journal of Verbal Learning and Verbal Behavior*, 1972, *11*, 671–684.

Craik, F. I. M., & Watkins, M. J. The role of rehearsal in short-term memory. *Journal of Verbal Learning and Verbal Behavior*, 1973, *12*, 599–607.

Creelman, M. B. *The experimental investigation of meaning*. New York: Springer, 1966.

Deese, J. Influence of inter-item associative strength upon immediate free recall. *Psychological Reports*, 1959, *5*, 305–312.

Deese, J. *The structure of associations in language and thought*. Baltimore: Johns Hopkins Press, 1965.

Deese, J. Cognitive structure and affect in language. In P. Pliner, L. Krames, & T. Alloway (Eds.), *Communication and affect*. New York: Academic Press, 1973.

de Villiers, P. A. Imagery and theme in recall of connected discourse. *Journal of Experimental Psychology*, 1974, *103*, 263–268.

Dixon, R. M. W. *What is language? A new approach to linguistic description*. London: Longmans, Green & Co., 1965.

Dooling, D. J., & Lachman, R. Effects of comprehension on retention of prose. *Journal of Experimental Psychology*, 1971, *88*, 216–222.

Dooling, D. J., & Mullet, R. L. Locus of thematic effects in retention of prose. *Journal of Experimental Psychology*, 1973, *97*, 404–406.

English, H. B., Welborn, E. L., & Killian, C. D. Studies in substance memorization. *Journal of General Psychology*, 1934, *11*, 233–260.

Entwisle, D. R. *The word associations of young children*. Baltimore: Johns Hopkins Press, 1966.

Ervin, S. M., & Foster, G. The development of meaning in children's descriptive terms. *Journal of Abnormal and Social Psychology*, 1960, *61*, 271–275.

Fillenbaum, S. Memory for gist: Some relevant variables. *Language and Speech*, 1966, *9*, 217–227.

Fillenbaum, S. On coping with ordered and unordered conjunctive sentences. *Journal of Experimental Psychology*, 1971, *87*, 93–98.

Fillenbaum, S. Or: Some uses. *Journal of Experimental Psychology*, 1974, *103*, 913–921. (a)

Fillenbaum, S. Pragmatic normalization: Further results for some conjunctive and disjunctive sentences. *Journal of Experimental Psychology*, 1974, *102*, 574–578. (b)

Fillenbaum, S., & Rapoport, A. *Structures in the subjective lexicon*. New York: Academic Press, 1971.

Flesch, R. F. A new readability yardstick. *Journal of Applied Psychology*, 1948, *32*, 221–233.

Fodor, J. A. A review of *Language and thought*, by J. B. Carroll. *The Modern Language Journal*, 1965, *49*, 384–386.

Fodor, J. A., Bever, T. G., & Garrett, M. F. *The psychology of language: An introduction to psycholinguistics and generative grammar*. New York: McGraw-Hill, 1974.

Franks, J. J., & Bransford, J. D. The acquisition of abstract ideas. *Journal of Verbal Learning and Verbal Behavior*, 1972, *11*, 311–315.

Franks, J. J., & Bransford, J. D. Memory for syntactic form as a function of semantic context. *Journal of Experimental Psychology*, 1974, *103*, 1037–1039.

Frase, L. T. Boundary conditions for mathemagenic behaviors. *Review of Educational Research*, 1970, *40*, 337–347.

Fries, C. C. Meaning and linguistic analysis. *Language*, 1954, *30*, 57–68.

Gardiner, J. M. Levels of processing in word recognition and subsequent free recall. *Journal of Experimental Psychology*, 1974, *102*, 101–105.

Glanzer, M. Grammatical category: A rote learning and word association analysis. *Journal of Verbal Learning and Verbal Behavior*, 1962, *1*, 31–41.

Glaze, J. A. The association value of nonsense syllables. *Journal of Genetic Psychology*, 1928, 35, 255–269.

Gleitman, L. R., & Gleitman, H. *Phrase and paraphrase*. New York: W. W. Norton, 1970.

Goldfarb, C., Wirtz, J., & Anisfeld, M. Abstract and concrete phrases in false recognition. *Journal of Experimental Psychology*, 1973, *98*, 25–30.

Gomulicki, B. R. Recall as an abstractive process. *Acta Psychologica*, 1956, *12*, 77–94.

Greenberg, J. H. *Language universals*. The Hague: Mouton, 1966.

Hall, J. F. *Verbal learning and retention*. Philadelphia: J. B. Lippincott, 1971.

Harris, R. J., & Brewer, W. F. Deixis in memory for verb tense. *Journal of Verbal Learning and Verbal Behavior*, 1973, *12*, 590–597.

Haviland, S. E., & Clark, H. H. What's new? Acquiring new information as a process in comprehension. *Journal of Verbal Learning and Verbal Behavior*, 1974, *13*, 512–521.

Herriot, P. *An introduction to the psychology of language*. London: Methuen & Co. Ltd, 1970.

Howe, E. S. Number of different free associates: A general measure of associative meaningfulness. *Journal of Verbal Learning and Verbal Behavior*, 1972, *11*, 18–28.

Jacoby, L. L. Encoding processes, rehearsal, and recall requirements. *Journal of Verbal Learning and Verbal Behavior*, 1973, *12*, 302–310.

Jenkins, J. J. Remember that old theory of memory? Well, forget it. *American Psychologist*, 1974, *29*, 785–795.

Johnson, M. K., Bransford, J. D., & Solomon, S. K. Memory for tacit implications of sentences. *Journal of Experimental Psychology*, 1973, *98*, 203–205.

Johnson, R. E. The retention of qualitative changes in learning. *Journal of Verbal Learning and Verbal Behavior*, 1962, *1*, 218–223.

Johnson, R. E. Recall of prose as a function of the structural importance of the linguistic units. *Journal of Verbal Learning and Verbal Behavior*, 1970, *9*, 12–20.

Johnson, R. E. Meaningfulness and the recall of textual prose. *American Educational Research Journal*, 1973, *10*, 49–58.

Johnson, R. E. Abstractive processes in the remembering of prose. *Journal of Educational Psychology*, 1974, *66*, 772–779.

Kanungo, R. Paired-associate learning of function words. *Psychonomic Science*, 1968, *10*, 47–48.

Karwoski, T. F., & Berthold, F., Jr. Psychological studies in semantics: II. Reliability of the free association tests. *Journal of Social Psychology*, 1945, *22*, 87–102.

Katz, J. J., & Fodor, J. A. The structure of a semantic theory. *Language*, 1963, *39*, 170–210.

Katz, S. Role of instructions in abstraction of linguistic ideas. *Journal of Experimental Psychology*, 1973, *98*, 79–84.

Katz, S., & Gruenewald, P. The abstraction of linguistic ideas in "meaningless" sentences. *Memory and Cognition*, 1974, *2*, 737–741.

Kintsch, W. Notes on the structure of semantic memory. In E. Tulving & W. Donaldson (Eds.), *Organization of memory*. New York: Academic Press, 1972.

Klare, G. R. *The measurement of readability*. Ames: Iowa State University Press, 1963.

Lehrer, A., & Lehrer, K. (Eds.), *Theory of meaning*. Englewood Cliffs, N.J.: Prentice Hall, 1970.

Lesgold, A. M. Pronominalization: A device for unifying sentences in memory. *Journal of Verbal Learning and Verbal Behavior*, 1972, *11*, 316–323.

Loftus, E. F., & Bolton, M. Retrieval of superordinates and subordinates. *Journal of Experimental Psychology*, 1974, *102*, 121–125.

Luchins, A. S. Mechanization in problem solving: The effect of Einstellung. *Psychological Monographs*, 1942, *54* (6, Whole No. 248).

Luria, A. R. *The role of speech in the regulation of normal and abnormal behavior*. New York: Liveright, 1961.

Lyons, J. *Introduction to theoretical linguistics*. Cambridge, England: Cambridge University Press, 1968.

MacGinitie, W. H. Discussion of Professor Coleman's paper. In E. Z. Rothkopf & P. E. Johnson (Eds.), *Verbal learning research and the technology of written instruction*. New York: Teachers College Press, 1971.

Mandler, G. Organization and memory. In K. W. Spence & J. T. Spence (Eds.), *The psychology of learning and motivation*. New York: Academic Press, 1967.

Martin, E. Stimulus meaningfulness and paired-associate transfer: An encoding variability hypothesis. *Psychological Review*, 1968, *75*, 421–441.

Martin, E., & Walter, D. A. Subject uncertainty and word-class effects in short-term memory for sentences. *Journal of Experimental Psychology*, 1969, *80*, 47–51.

McNeill, D. *The acquisition of language: The study of developmental psycholinguistics.* New York: Harper & Row, 1970.

Menyuk, P. *Sentences children use.* Cambridge, Mass.: M.I.T. Press, 1969.

Miller, G. A. Some preliminaries to psycholinguistics. *American Psychologist*, 1965, *20*, 15–20.

Miller, G. A. A psychological method to investigate verbal concepts. *Journal of Mathematical Psychology*, 1969, *6*, 169–191.

Miller, G. A. English verbs of motion: A case study in semantics and lexical memory. In A. W. Melton & E. Martin (Eds.), *Coding processes in human memory.* Washington, D.C.: V. H. Winston, 1972.

Moesner, S. D., & Bregman, A. S. The role of reference in the acquisition of a miniature artificial language. *Journal of Verbal Learning and Verbal Behavior*, 1972, *11*, 759–769.

Moran, L. J., Mefferd, R. B., & Kimble, J. P., Jr. Idiodynamic sets in word association. *Psychological Monographs*, 1964, *78* (2, Whole No. 579).

Nelson, K. Concept, word, and sentence: Interrelations in acquisition and development. *Psychological Review*, 1974, *81*, 267–285.

Noble, C. E. An analysis of meaning. *Psychological Review*, 1952, *59*, 421–430.

Noble, C. E. Measurements of association value (*a*), rated associations (*a'*), and scaled meaningfulness (*m'*) for the 2100 CVC combinations of the English alphabet. *Psychological Reports*, 1961, *8*, 487–521.

Offir, C. E. Recognition memory for presuppositions of relative clause sentences. *Journal of Verbal Learning and Verbal Behavior*, 1973, *12*, 636–643.

Oldfield, R. C. Frederick Charles Bartlett: 1886–1969. *American Journal of Psychology*, 1972, *85*, 133–140.

Olson, D. R. Language and thought: Aspects of a cognitive theory of semantics. *Psychological Review*, 1970, *77*, 257–273.

Osgood, C. E. Comments on Professor Bousfield's paper. In C. N. Cofer & B. S. Musgrave (Eds.), *Verbal learning and verbal behavior.* New York: McGraw-Hill, 1961.

Osgood, C. E., Suci, G. J., & Tannenbaum, P. *The measurement of meaning.* Urbana, Illinois: University of Illinois Press, 1957.

Paivio, A. A factor-analytic study of word attributes and verbal learning. *Journal of Verbal Learning and Verbal Behavior*, 1968, *7*, 41–49.

Paivio, A. *Imagery and verbal processes.* New York: Holt, Rinehart, and Winston, 1971.

Paivio, A., & Olver, M. Denotative-generality, imagery, and meaningfulness in paired-associate learning of nouns. *Psychonomic Science*, 1964, *1*, 183–184.

Paivio, A., Smythe, P. C., & Yuille, J. C. Imagery versus meaningfulness of nouns in paired-associate learning. *Canadian Journal of Psychology*, 1968, *22*, 427–441.

Paivio, A., Yuille, J. D., & Madigan, S. A. Concreteness, imagery, and meaningfulness values for 925 nouns. *Journal of Experimental Psychology Monograph*, 1968, *76* (1, Pt. 2).

Palermo, D. S., & Jenkins, J. J. *Word association norms.* Minneapolis: University of Minnesota Press, 1964.

Palermo, D. S., & Molfese, D. L. Language acquisition from age five onward. *Psychological Bulletin*, 1972, *78*, 409–428.

Paris, S. G., & Carter, A. Y. Semantic and constructive aspects of sentence memory in children. *Developmental Psychology*, 1973, *9*, 109–113.

Paul, I. H. Studies in remembering: The reproduction of connected and extended verbal material. *Psychological Issues*, 1959, *1*, No. 2.

Perfetti, C. A., & Goldman, S. R. Thematization and sentence retrieval. *Journal of Verbal Learning and Verbal Behavior*, 1974, *13*, 70–79.

Peterson, R. G., & McIntyre, C. W. The influence of semantic 'relatedness' on linguistic integration and retention. *American Journal of Psychology*, 1973, *86*, 697–706.

Piaget, J. *The psychology of intelligence*. Patterson, New Jersey: Littlefield, Adams, 1960. (English-version reprint of 1947 edition.)

Piaget, J., & Inhelder, B. *Memory and intelligence*. New York: Basic Books, 1973. (English-version reprint of 1968 edition.)

Pollio, H. R. *The psychology of symbolic activity*. Reading, Mass.: Addison-Wesley, 1974.

Pompi, K. F., & Lachman, R. Surrogate processes in the short-term retention of connected discourse. *Journal of Experimental Psychology*, 1967, *75*, 143–150.

Postman, L., & Burns, S. Experimental analysis of coding processes. *Memory and Cognition*, 1973, *1*, 503–507.

Potts, G. R. Information processing strategies used in the encoding of linear orderings. *Journal of Verbal Learning and Verbal Behavior*, 1972, *11*, 727–740.

Quillian, M. R. Semantic memory. In M. L. Minsky (Ed.), *Semantic information processing*. Cambridge, Mass.: M.I.T. Press, 1968.

Quine, W. V. O. *Word and object*. Cambridge, Mass.: M.I.T. Press, 1960.

Reitman, J. S., & Bower, G. H. Storage and later recognition of exemplars of concepts. *Cognitive Psychology*, 1973, *4*, 194–206.

Rickards, J. P., & Di Vesta, F. J. Type and frequency of questions in processing textual material. *Journal of Educational Psychology*, 1974, *66*, 354–362.

Rips, L. J., Shoben, E. J., & Smith, E. E. Semantic distance and the verification of semantic relations. *Journal of Verbal Learning and Verbal Behavior*, 1973, *12*, 1–20.

Rohwer, W. D., Jr. Constraint, syntax and meaning in paired-associate learning. *Journal of Verbal Learning and Verbal Behavior*, 1966, *5*, 541–547.

Rosenberg, S. Association and phrase structure in sentence recall. *Journal of Verbal Learning and Verbal Behavior*, 1968, *7*, 1077–1081.

Rothkopf, E. Z., & Bisbicos, E. Selective facilitative effects of interspersed questions on learning from written material. *Journal of Educational Psychology*, 1967, *58*, 56–61.

Rumelhart, D. E., Lindsay, P. H., & Norman, D. A. A process model for long-term memory. In E. Tulving & W. Donaldson (Eds.), *Organization of memory*. New York: Academic Press, 1972.

Sachs, J. S. Recognition memory for syntactic and semantic aspects of connected discourse. *Perception and Psychophysics*, 1967, *2*, 437–442.

Saltz, E. *The cognitive bases of human learning*. Homewood, Illinois: Dorsey, 1971.

Saltz, E., & Modigliani, V. Response meaningfulness in paired-associates: T-L frequency, *m*, and number of meanings (*dm*). *Journal of Experimental Psychology*, 1967, *75*, 313–320.

Samuels, S. J. Effects of pictures on learning to read, comprehension and attitudes. *Review of Educational Research*, 1970, *40*, 397–407.

Shepard, R. N. Recognition memory for words, sentences, and pictures. *Journal of Verbal Learning and Verbal Behavior*, 1967, *6*, 156–163.

Singer, M., & Rosenberg, S. T. The role of grammatical relations in the abstraction on linguistic ideas. *Journal of Verbal Learning and Verbal Behavior*, 1973, *12*, 273–284.

Slamecka, N.J. An examination of trace storage in free recall. *Journal of Experimental Psychology*, 1968, *76*, 504–513.

Smith, E. E., Shoben, E. J., & Rips, L. J. Structure and process in semantic memory: A featural model for semantic decisions. *Psychological Review*, 1974, *81*, 214–241.

Spreen, O., & Schulz, R. W. Parameters of abstraction, meaningfulness, and pronounceability for 329 nouns. *Journal of Verbal Learning and Verbal Behavior*, 1966, *5*, 459–468.

Sulin, R. A., & Dooling, D. J. Intrusion of a thematic idea in retention of prose. *Journal of Experimental Psychology*, 1974, *103*, 255–262.

Taylor, W. L. Application of 'cloze' and entropy measures to the study of contextual constraints in continuous prose. (Doctoral dissertation, University of Illinois, 1954). *Dissertation Abstracts*, 1955, *15*, 464–465. (University Microfilms No. MicA 55–592)

Terwilliger, R. F. *Meaning and mind.* New York: Oxford University Press, 1968.

Thieman, T. J. Levels of processing serial lists embedded in narratives. *Journal of Experimental Psychology*, 1973, *100*, 423–425.

Thios, S. J. Memory for general and specific sentences. *Memory and Cognition*, 1975, *3*, 75–77.

Thorndike, E. L., & Lorge, I. *The teacher's word book of 30,000 words.* New York: Teachers College Press, 1944.

Tulving, E., & Pearlstone, Z. Availability versus accessibility of information in memory for words. *Journal of Verbal Learning and Verbal Behavior*, 1966, *5*, 381–391.

Underwood, B. J., & Schulz, R. W. *Meaningfulness and verbal learning.* Chicago: Lippincott, 1960.

Watts, G. H., & Anderson, R. C. Effects of three types of inserted questions on learning from prose. *Journal of Educational Psychology*, 1971, *62*, 387–394.

Waugh, N. C, & Norman, D. A. Primary memory. *Psychological Review*, 1965, *72*, 89–104.

Weaver, W. W., & Kingston, A. J. A factor analysis of the cloze procedure and other measures of reading and language ability. *Journal of Communication*, 1963, *13*, 252–261.

Weisberg, R. W. On sentence storage: The influence of syntactic versus semantic factors on intrasentence word associations. *Journal of Verbal Learning and Verbal Behavior*, 1971, *10*, 631–644.

Wickelgren, W. A. The long and short of memory. *Psychological Bulletin*, 1973, *80*, 425–438.

Woodward, A. E., Jr., Bjork, R. A., & Jongeward, R. H., Jr. Recall and recognition as a function of primary rehearsal. *Journal of Verbal Learning and Verbal Behavior*, 1973, *12*, 608–617.

Zangwill, O. L. Remembering revisited. *Quarterly Journal of Experimental Psychology*, 1972, *24*, 123–138.

40

Phases of Meaningful Learning

Thomas J. Shuell

L earning is a much more complex and drawn out process than generally acknowledged. The type of complex, meaningful learning that occurs in school and throughout the life span occurs over a period of weeks, months, and years, and there is good reason to believe that the nature of the learning process changes as the task of mastering a complex body of knowledge unfolds. For example, there is good evidence that experts and novices in a field respond to tasks in fundamentally different ways (e.g., Chi, Glaser, & Rees, 1982). As one progresses from the initial encounter with a complex body of knowledge to the point where the expert is able to demonstrate understanding of that knowledge in ways that are more-or-less automatic, a task that once constituted a problem for the new learner (and elicited various problem-solving strategies) becomes little more than a simple recall task for the more experienced and sophisticated learner.

This article will explore the notion that distinct stages or phases can be identified along the journey from knowing virtually nothing about a complex body of knowledge to the demonstration of a highly proficient mastery of that knowledge. After a discussion of several issues related to a phase theory of learning, research relevant to phases in simpler types of learning will be presented, followed by a similar discussion of phases in more meaningful learning. Finally, implications of these reviews will be discussed with regard to both theories of learning and educational practices.

The idea of stages is certainly not new to psychology. There are the developmental stages of Piaget and Bruner and a long-standing concern for stages in problem solving (Andre, 1986; Mayer, 1983). Over the years, a variety of stage

Source: *Review of Educational Research*, 60(4) (1990): 531–547.

theories have been suggested for various types of learning (e.g., Anderson, 1982; Fleishman & Hempel, 1954, 1955; McGuire, 1961; Underwood, Runquist, & Schulz, 1959), and Brainerd (1985; Brainerd, Howe, & Desrochers, 1982) has developed a sophisticated mathematical two-stage model of learning. A concern for stages is clearly evident, at least implicitly, in the current literature on cognitive learning – for example, the growing body of literature on expert-novice differences (e.g., Chi, Glaser, & Rees, 1982).

A number of factors have contributed to this concern for stages, or phases, in meaningful, cognitive learning. Current theories of learning, for instance, emphasize that learning is an active, constructive, cumulative, and goal-oriented process that involves problem solving (e.g., Shuell, 1986a, 1990). This view of learning as a complex, drawn-out process (e.g., Norman, 1978) that depends on factors from many sources suggests that learning may change as it progresses. This possibility, coupled with evidence that performance is strongly influenced by one's prior knowledge (e.g., Bransford & Johnson, 1972; Chiesi, Spilich, & Voss, 1979), makes a concern for phases in meaningful learning an appropriate and timely pursuit.

Although many cognitive theorists seem to accept the notion of phases in meaningful learning, there have been few systematic attempts to explore the issue in depth. Most of the empirical evidence on stages of learning deals with simpler forms of learning. Although the evidence of phases in long-term meaningful learning is not as convincing at present as one would like, there is good reason to postulate their presence. The following review combines evidence from empirical studies and theoretical discussions of both simple and meaningful forms of learning in order to evaluate this possibility.

An Overview of the Problem

Imagine yourself about to embark on a long journey, a journey that involves learning a complex body of knowledge with which you currently are unfamiliar. At first, the new terrain appears strange, although certain similarities with familiar territory can be identified. During the first leg of this journey you find yourself primarily memorizing isolated facts (i.e., landmarks), for you do not yet possess a schema for interpreting and integrating the various pieces of information that are encountered. Initially, for example, you may find that mnemonics are helpful in remembering these more-or-less isolated facts. As learning progresses, however, and you begin to group and organize the facts and integrate them into higher order structures, you may find that mnemonics play a less beneficial role. In their place, various types of organizational aids (e.g., developing hierarchies and matrices) that were of little help initially may begin to play a more important role.

But the nature of the learning process is not the only thing that changes as learning progresses; the learning process also becomes more diverse. Initially, the learner must rely on experiences associated with a particular course or on a few books selected for self-study. As the learner becomes more familiar with the territory through which he or she is traveling, the learner is likely to encounter a variety of relevant books, to attend lectures, to discuss issues with other students (at the same and/or more advanced levels), to use his or her knowledge to interpret various situations (e.g., a play, a movie, the failure of something to work in the way it is supposed to, the behavior of other people), and so forth. In short, meaningful learning in any field is a much more complex process than often realized; different types of learning are involved, and – as this article will address – various phases or stages occur during which the nature of the learning process changes in systematic ways.

What Is a Phase of Learning?

Because special connotations are usually associated with the use of the term *stage* within psychology, it seems advisable to address at the onset the way in which *phase* will be used in this article. Generally speaking, the term *stage* is used to refer to distinct time periods. Each period is characterized by psychological functioning that is qualitatively different from that which occurs during other periods. The most notable examples, of course, are developmental stages such as those of Jean Piaget. Developmental stages of this type are structural in nature and apply across all domains. For example, most developmental stage theories consider it impossible for a child to be in the formal-operations stage in mathematics and in the concrete-operations stage in social studies, and thus developmental stages are considered to be independent of specific content domains.

There is a growing body of literature, however, that challenges the validity of developmental stages conceived in this way (e.g., Keil, 1986). There is increasing evidence that the qualitative changes that occur with age are the result of knowledge-based competencies within a particular content domain, although the possibility of general competencies arising from similarities among the various domains is not ruled out. An example of such knowledge-based competencies is demonstrated in a study by Chi (1978). There is a great deal of evidence, reviewed by Chi, that *memory span* (the number of items that can be recalled after a single presentation) increases in a linear manner with age, with adults remembering up to twice as much as children five- to seven-years old. Chi's study involved children in the third through eighth grade (mean age was 10.5 years) who were experts at playing chess and adults who were only novice chess players. The typical finding of adult superiority in memory span was obtained when the subjects were asked to remember digits (6.1 vs. 7.8). However, when the subjects were asked to remember the placement of pieces on a chess board, the performance of the 10-year-old experts far surpassed that of the adults (9.3 vs. 5.9).

This finding is often cited as evidence that knowledge differences may explain many of the developmental differences (and perhaps developmental stages as well) typically found in the literature.

Karmiloff-Smith (1984, 1986) makes a useful distinction among *stage, phase,* and *level Stage* is used to refer to periods of time that differ qualitatively from both the preceding and succeeding stages. These stages, by definition, cover performance in a variety of content domains, and, once a person achieves a particular stage, he or she cannot return to a preceding one. Although a *phase* may include behavior across several domains, phases are recurrent in that individuals can pass through the various phases in each of many different content domains. Phases are based on:

> ... the hypothesis that children (and adults, for that matter) attack any new problem by going through the same three phases, both within the various parts of particular domains and across different domains. The phase concept is focused on underlying *similarity of process* [italics added], whereas the stage concept usually refers to similarity of structure. (Karmiloff-Smith, 1984, p. 41)

Level refers to qualitative changes within a particular domain (e.g., the proper use of modifiers such as adjectives and adverbs) and accounts for specific changes within that domain. "Like stages, and unlike phases, levels are not recurrent. Once a child is at, say, level 3 in a specific domain, she does not return to level 1" (Karmiloff-Smith, 1984, pp. 41–42). Within this type of conceptual framework, it makes most sense to think in terms of learning phases rather than learning stages, and, consequently, that term is used in this article.

Do Phases Add Anything Worthwhile to Our Understanding of Human Learning?

If learning is a continuous process – and most of us would agree that it is – then one might reasonably ask what the notion of phases adds to our understanding of complex, meaningful learning. Both theoretical and practical implications exist if in fact the nature of the learning process changes in fundamental ways as learning progresses. Theoretically, it means that learning is a much more complex process than we had imagined. Not only must the type of learning be considered when conducting research but factors related to the length of time that the learning has been taking place must be considered, and prior knowledge will need to be considered in a much more explicit manner than is typically the case. In addition, concern for boundary conditions of various learning principles will need to include factors related to the phase of learning in which the learner is working.

On the more practical side, there are also implications for teaching. Just as one should not teach in the same way when different types of outcomes are sought (e.g., the acquisition of concepts vs. the acquisition of facts), one should teach differently when different phases of learning are involved. The teaching methods employed, as well as the content, should be appropriate for the phase of learning in which the students are engaged. For example, one would teach differently if a new topical area is just being introduced than if the students had already gained some proficiency in the domain. Thus, introductory courses should be taught differently from more advanced courses – at least in part – but, in more instances than not, introductory and advance courses in a particular content area are taught in basically the same way.

Procedures for Identifying Phases

In order to study phases of learning, objective and methodologically valid techniques must be used to distinguish among the various phases. Merely postulating their existence, defining them in terms of how much time has passed (how much practice/experience has occurred), and/or giving them plausible names are clearly insufficient methods of establishing their existence. The qualitative differences that presumably exist among the phases must be specified and verified in some objective way.

One, and perhaps the best, way to differentiate among phases is to identify variables that function differently and/or have different effects during the various phases. For example, the distinction between short-term and long-term memory has been validated in this manner, for the effects of acoustic similarity are much greater in short-term than in long-term memory, whereas the effects of semantic similarity are much greater in long-term than in short-term memory (e.g., Baddeley, 1966; Conrad, 1964; Kintsch & Buschke, 1969). Expanding on this approach, a matrix can be established to portray the way in which relevant factors/variables operate in the various phases. Such a matrix, from Dreyfus and Dreyfus (1986), is presented in Table 1. In developing a matrix of this type, the defining factors/variables should be specified in an objective manner, and there needs to be clear evidence that these variables/processes actually change in the systematic manner specified.

Various techniques have been used to identify the presence of stages or subproblems in problem solving. For example, Restle and Davis (1962) calculated the number of stages involved in solving a problem by dividing the square of the average time (across subjects) to solve a problem by the square of the standard deviation. Hayes (1965, 1966) and Thomas (1974) identified subproblems by comparing response times at each step of a well-defined problem. They assumed that response time is faster as a subject completes a subproblem and slower as he or she begins working on a new subproblem (presumably because time is required to think about a solution to the next subproblem).

Table 1: Stages of skill acquisition

Skill level	Components	Perspective	Decision	Commitment
Novice	Context-free	None	Analytical	Detached
Advanced beginner	Context-free and situational	None	Analytical	Detached
Competent	Context-free and situational	Chosen	Analytical	Detached understanding and deciding. Involved in outcome
Proficient	Context-free and situational	Experienced	Analytical	Involved understanding. Detached deciding
Expert	Context-free and situational	Experienced	Intuitive	Involved

Note: From *Mind Over Machine: The Power of Human Intuition and Expertise in the Era of the Computer* (p. 50) by Hubert L. Dreyfus and Stuart E. Dreyfus, 1986, New York: The Free Press. Copyright 1986 by Hubert L. Dreyfus and Stuart E. Dreyfus. Reprinted by permission of The Free Press, a Division of Macmillan, Inc.

All three techniques are based on questionable assumptions and serve merely to identify the number of stages involved. They provide little, if any, information on the nature of each stage or the variables that affect learning during that stage. In addition, they do not lend themselves to the more complex and meaningful forms of learning addressed in this article.

Phase Theories in Simpler Forms of Learning

Various forms of a phase theory of learning have existed since the earliest days of research on learning. For example, Bryan and Harter's (1897, 1899) well-known studies of telegraph operators learning Morse code provide evidence for a phase theory of learning. The beginner first learns the alphabet of dots and dashes and sends and receives words on a letter-by-letter basis. With practice, the operator begins to combine these individual letters into higher order units that correspond to words, and, with continued practice, he or she combines words into units comprised of several words (i.e., phrases and short sentences).

During the 1950s and 1960s, phase theories of paired-associated learning and skill learning were proposed. Later, John Anderson (1982) suggested a phase theory of procedural learning. These various theories of learning phases in complex forms of human learning will be discussed in the remainder of this section. Phase theories concerned with more meaningful forms of learning will be discussed in the subsequent section as well as expert-novice differences in processing meaningful material and the corresponding concern for the nature and development of intellectual competence that implies, at least implicitly, a phase theory of learning.

Paired-Associated Learning

During the early 1960s, several theorists proposed multiprocess theories of paired = associate (PA) learning. In their influential book, *Meaningfulness and Verbal Learning*, Underwood and Schulz (1960) suggested a two-stage analysis of PA learning consisting of a *response learning*, or *response recall*, stage (in which the subject learns the various responses that are used on the list) and an *associative*, or *hook up*, stage (in which the connection between each response and its corresponding stimulus is acquired). A number of other investigators, however, suggested two-process theories consisting of a stimulus differentiation phase and an associative phase in situations in which the responses were all well learned (see Battig, 1968, for a comprehensive discussion of multiprocess theories in PA learning). McGuire's 1961 report of his 1954 dissertation suggested the first three-stage theory consisting of (a) *stimulus encoding*, or *stimulus predifferentiation* (in which the subject learns to discriminate among the various stimuli on the list); (b) *mediation* (in which a link is found for associating each stimulus with the appropriate response); and (c) *response learning* (in which the subject must learn the various response items that are being used). For example, in learning the list DOG-TREE, CAT-TABLE, and MAN-CHAIR, the learner must first learn to differentiate among dog, cat, and man (the task would be more difficult, of course, if the stimuli were XJC, YJB, and XKB). Note that it is not necessary to learn the responses, because they are always presented. Then he or she must find a way of linking each member of the pair (the cat is on the table, etc.). In addition, the subject must learn that tree, table, and chair (but not house) are the various responses that are appropriate.

Evidence to support these stage theories of paired-associate learning are based on findings that response meaningfulness affects paired-associate learning to a greater extent than stimulus meaningfulness and that intralist response similarity (i.e., all of the responses in the list are more-or-less synonymous in meaning vs. being unrelated) has a facilitative effect on response learning but a detrimental effect on overall learning (that presumably includes both the response-learning and associative phases; Underwood, Runquist, & Schulz, 1959). In addition, McGuire (1961) presented support for his three-stage theory in a detailed analysis of correct responses and intrusion errors in the learning of pairs in which the stimuli were solid black circles of varying diameters and the responses were numbers.

In a related study involving free-recall learning, Labouvie, Frohring, Baltes, and Goulet (1973) compared the correlation patterns between free-recall performance of pictorial stimuli (with recall commencing either immediately after presentation or after a 30-second delay) and a battery of eight intelligence and memory-ability tests. Although the same acquisition curves were obtained under immediate and delayed recall, there were systematic differences in the patterns of correlations obtained for the two conditions. Intelligence variables correlated to a fairly high extent (.53 to .77) with recall during the later stages of acquisition under conditions of delayed recall, but the correlations were considerably less (.29 to .45) during the early stages of delayed recall and during all stages of immediate recall. Memory variables, on the other hand, were significantly correlated (.55 to .56) with performance during early stages of acquisition under conditions of immediate recall but not under the other conditions. Thus, it appears that the task demands involved in learning may change systemically as learning progresses.

Skill Learning

More research has been done on phases in skill learning than in any other type of research on learning, beginning with Bryan and Harter's (1897, 1899) classic studies on learning Morse code. During the mid-1950s, a series of factor analytic studies by Fleishman and Hempel (1954, 1955) revealed systematic changes in the particular combination of psychomotor abilities (e.g., reaction time, manual dexterity, rate of movement, spatial relations) most important for performance as learning progressed. For example, nonmotor abilities such as verbal ability and spatial relations play an important role early in learning, but their importance decreases progressively with practice. Motor abilities (e.g., reaction time, rate of movement), on the other hand, play an increasingly important role as learning progresses, as does a factor specific to the task itself.

Later, Fitts (1962; 1964) suggested that skill learning consists of three phases: (a) *cognitive*, (b) *associative*, and (c) *autonomous* (although the labels applied to the three phases differ somewhat in his various writings). The initial phase can be relatively short, depending on the complexity of the task and consisting of "the time required to understand instructions, to complete a few preliminary trials, and to establish the proper cognitive set for the task" (Fitts, 1964, p. 262). The intermediate phase involves mediation and learning to associate various responses to specific cues as well as cognitive set learning. During the late phase, highly skilled performance continues to improve indefinitely. It should be noted that Fitts (1964) emphasizes that skill learning is a continuous process, without distinct stages as such.

> Instead, we should think of gradual shifts in the factor structure of skills, or in the nature of the processes (strategies and tactics; executive routines and subroutines) employed, as learning progresses. The evolving process is revealed by the organization of behavior into larger and larger units ... and toward hierarchical organization. (pp. 261–262)

Dreyfus and Dreyfus (1986) have also suggested a phase theory of skill learning. Based on their observations of skill acquisition in airplane pilots, chess players, automobile drivers, and adults learning a second language, they suggest that five stages are involved in learning a complex skill: (a) *novice*, (b) *advanced beginner*, (c) *competent*, (d) *proficient*, and (e) *expert*. The phases are defined largely by the manner in which four factors (components, perspective, decision, and commitment) operate in the respective phases (see Table 1). Each stage is described in considerable detail, but the data on which their theory is based are never presented. Consequently, it is difficult to determine the validity of the various stages or whether five stages (e.g., rather than three) are really needed to explain the data. Benner (1984), starting with the five stages as a given, attempted to validate the Dreyfus model in an interview study of expert and novice nurses. The nurses were asked for their perceptions of what was important in a series of case studies and how they would seek a solution to the problem involved in the case. Unfortunately, the study does not provide a clear test of the theory.

Procedural Learning

In some ways, Anderson's (1982, 1987) research could be included in the section on meaningful learning, for it deals with intellectual skills, such as solving mathematics problems, and Anderson argues that the model applies to all complex learning. It is represented in this section, however, because it has been presented consistently as a model of skill learning. Anderson proposes three phases of procedural learning very similar to Fitts' (1964) three phases of skill learning; Anderson refers to them as the (a) *declarative*, (b) *knowledge-compilation*, and (c) *procedural* phases.

Anderson (1982, 1987) makes the common distinction between *declarative*, or *propositional* knowledge (knowledge about something), and *procedural* knowledge (knowledge of how to do something), and he argues that we begin learning a new domain by encoding a set of facts in largely unanalyzed form that we subsequently can interpret without allowing it to control our behavior. That is, we can withhold judgment about the behavioral implications of such declarative knowledge until we see examples of and reflect upon ways in which it can be used. With additional experience, we begin to combine some of this declarative knowledge into procedures that allow us to apply it on a limited basis that still does not demand explicit control of our behavior. Ultimately, procedures evolve that do control our behavior without a great deal of conscious thought and effort – that is, the behavior comes automatic.

Phase Theories in Meaningful Learning

Phase theories have also been discussed with regard to more meaningful forms of learning, although usually on a more implicit and less well-developed basis than the phase theories discussed in the preceding section. Although there is considerable agreement among various investigators on the viability of phases in long-term meaningful learning, the empirical evidence to support their presence is not overwhelming at present. Thus, the following review of the literature is based more on theoretical arguments than on empirical evidence, although the latter will be discussed whenever possible.

Perhaps the earliest discussion of stages in meaningful learning was Wallas' (1926) suggestion that problem solving involves four stages: preparation, incubation, illumination, and verification. Unfortunately, Wallas' stages, as well as similar ones suggested by other investigators, are based more on introspection than on sound scientific investigations of any kind. A good critique of this literature is contained in Mayer (1983).

Within the context of a schema-based theory of long-term memory, Rumelhart and Norman (1978) have suggested three qualitatively different types of learning: (a) *accretion*, or the encoding of new information in terms of existing schemata; (b) *tuning*, or schema evolution, the slow modification and refinement of a schema as a result of using it in different situations; and (c) *restructuring*, or schema creation, the process by which new schemata are created. Rumelhart and Norman imply that these three kinds of learning occur sequentially, but, whereas there is consistency in listing accretion as the first phase, they interchange the order of tuning and restructuring in their discussion.

Spiro, Coulson, Feltovich, and Anderson's (1988) cognitive flexibility theory focuses on advanced knowledge acquisition. This phase of learning occurs between one's initial attempts to study a subject area and the high levels of expertise that come with massive amounts of experience. According to Spiro et al.:

> This often neglected intermediate stage is important because the aims and means of advanced knowledge acquisition are different from those of introductory learning. In introductory learning the goal is often mere exposure to content and the establishment of a general orientation to a field; objectives of assessment are likewise confined to the simple effects of exposure (e.g., recognition and recall). At some point in learning about a knowledge domain the goal must change; at some point students must 'get it right.' This is the stage of advanced knowledge acquisition. (p. 1)

Although the phase aspect of the Spiro et al. theory is based more on their experience than on sound empirical evidence that the various phases actually exist, it does provide an example of current thinking among cognitive psychologists on the topic. Probably the best developed and most empirically based phase theory of meaningful learning is Karmiloff-Smith's (1984, 1986) theory of cognitive development, discussed in the following section. The subsequent section will explore the implications of research on expert-novice differences (and the corresponding concern for the development of competence) for a phase theory of learning.

Developmental Learning

Based on evidence from several studies, Karmiloff-Smith (1984, 1986) has developed a knowledge-based theory of cognitive development. She believes that the theory is relevant to individuals of all ages who are learning a new content area. Phases and levels are distinguished from stages (as described earlier in this article), and she postulates the involvement of three phases/levels referred to as: (a) procedural, (b) metaprocedural, and (c) conceptual.[1]

During the procedural phase/level, the individual's responses are generated primarily by data-driven processes generated by the individual's adapting to external stimuli. The person's behavior is controlled predominantly by the environment. During this initial phase/level, one observes behavioral change with no attempt to develop an overall organization capable of linking the isolated behavioral units into a consistent whole.

During the second (or metaprocedural) phase, the individual beings to work in a "top-down" manner on the mental representations formed during the first phase – that is, the person begins to reflect or think about these representations as entities in their own right. During this phase, external stimuli become secondary to an internal representation that the person imposes on the environment. The person's external behavior may actually deteriorate somewhat from what was observed during the preceding phase, for external stimuli are ignored as he or she experiments with the internal representation.

The third (or conceptual) phase is governed by a subtle control mechanism that modulates the interaction between the data-driven processes characteristic of the first phase and the top-down processes characteristic of the second phase. The person is now in control of both environmental stimuli and the internal representations that guide his or her behavior. During this phase, the individual is able to consider environmental feedback without jeopardizing the structure of the internal representations.

Expert-Novice Differences

Research on expert-novice differences grew out of a concern for the nature of intellectual competence and the way it develops. Because experts and novices are presumed to differ primarily, if not exclusively, in terms of the experience they have had in a particular subject-matter domain, we are dealing once again with a knowledge-based approach to learning. Although there is general agreement that a continuum exists as the individual moves from novice to expert in a particular field, most of the research to date has been concerned with describing differences in the way the two groups solve problems. It should be noted that in this research *novice* typically refers to someone who has had limited experience with the field or material being investigated, not someone with no experience. For example, in research on physics problem solving, a novice might have had one undergraduate course in physics, whereas an expert might be a professor of physics or someone with comparable experience. Such minimal experience for the novice is necessary in order to have a reasonable basis for comparison, for data on how novices solve a problem could not be obtained if the subjects could not solve the problem at all.

A number of qualitative differences between experts and novices have been identified (for a brief review, see Glaser & Chi, 1988; Shuell, 1986b). For example, in solving physics problems, experts tend to perform a qualitative analysis of the problem prior to deciding which equations to use, whereas novices tend to focus on equations from the onset and engage in a direct syntactic translation (e.g., identifying variables and then plugging them into an equation) rather than generating a physical representation of the problem situation. Likewise, novices tend to focus on literal objects and/or key terms explicitly mentioned in the problem, whereas experts tend to identify features that reflect the states and conditions of the physical situation described in the problem (Chi et al., 1982). Thus, novices might respond to (identify or classify) a problem in terms of "friction" or "gravity," whereas experts might refer to it in terms of "given initial conditions" or "no external force" (p. 64).

Few attempts have been made to identify stages or phases that might exist between the two states, although Voss, Greene, Post, and Penner (1983) discuss differences among undergraduates (novices), graduate students, and experts. Chi (1978) distinguishes among novice, advanced novice, and expert. Champagne, Klopfer, and Gunstone (1982) differentiate between uninstructed, or preinstructional students (i.e., those who have no experience studying the topic); novice (those with minimal experience in the field – i.e., the typical novice in expert-novice studies); and experts in their discussion of research relevant to the teaching of physics.

Not only do Champagne et al. (1982) provide a detailed description of differences between the schemata of students in these three phases of learning based on their analysis of various empirical studies, they also discuss ways in which these differences are related to teaching students in each phase. Uninstructed students, for example, use principles that are little more than generalized rules derived from their everyday experiences. Consequently, these principles tend to be imprecise due to the students' vague understanding of concepts, errors of magnitude, and inappropriate formulations of general rules. For novices, however, principles involve relationships between physical variables in the form of equations or rules. Although the major laws of physics are expressed in equation form, there is no indication that these equations serve an organizing function (e.g., as schemata). For experts, principles represent major laws of physics in a highly abstract form that expresses relationships with great generality. Each principle includes the conditions under which the principle applies and has an associated schema that serves to organize the relevant material.

Conclusions

Meaningful cognitive learning is an active, constructive, and cumulative process that occurs gradually over a period of time (Shuell, 1986a). It is a goal oriented process best characterized in terms of problem solving (Anderson, 1987; Bereiter, 1989; Shuell, 1990). Learning is not merely an additive process – qualitative, as well as quantitative, changes occur, and qualitative differences are evident in both the substance of what is being learned and in the learning processes most appropriate for acquiring additional knowledge.

The preceding review of the literature reveals reasonable agreement among investigators that a learner passes through a series of phases as his or her knowledge about something evolves. During these phases, the learning process and the variables influencing it change in systematic ways. The exact number of phases that might be involved is not clear (although most theories have postulated three), and the characteristics of each phase have not been worked out in any detail. Needless to say, the number of phases and the defining characteristics of each one must be established on the basis of sound methodology, as discussed earlier in this article. Merely postulating their existence is not enough. Nevertheless, it may prove useful to attempt an initial description of what the various phases might be like as well as some speculative comments about the transition from one phase to another.

Initial Phase

During the initial phase of learning, the individual encounters a large array of facts and pieces of information that are more-or-less isolated conceptually. Merely because someone familiar with the topic (teacher, expert, etc.) may see an organizing structure with many interrelationships among the various facts does not mean that the novice learner can make sense out of them. Initially, there appears to be little more than a wasteland with few landmarks to guide the traveler on his or her journey toward understanding and mastery.

Under the circumstances, the learner does the only thing that is reasonable: memorizes facts and uses preexisting schemata to interpret the isolated pieces of data. Some of this new information is added to existing knowledge structures – for example, Rumelhart and Norman's (1978) notion of accretion – and these preexisting knowledge structures are used for interpreting the new information and giving it meaning. If no meaning can be found, the information remains as isolated facts.

Because the learner has little specific knowledge of the domain, the initial processing is global in nature (Sternberg, 1984). The learner must rely on general, domain-independent problem solving strategies and knowledge from other domains to interpret the new information, to make comparisons and contrasts, and to find analogies that appear relevant to the learner (Anderson, 1987; Brown, Bransford, Ferrara, & Campione, 1983). The information acquired during this initial phase is concrete rather than abstract and bound to the specific context in which it occurs (Bransford & Franks, 1976). Thus, the encounter with a new domain of knowledge involves the rote learning of more-or-less isolated facts (we memorize new terms or what appear to be key facts – if we are learning a structured body of knowledge such as history, literature, or psychology – or we identify and try to remember key landmarks if we are learning to navigate around a large city.[2]

Gradually, the learner begins to form an overview of what the new domain is all about. In pursuing this task, our prior knowledge provides some help (or in certain cases hindrance) by suggesting initial possibilities and by establishing boundary constraints that assist in identifying both the sameness and the uniqueness of the new information (Bransford & Franks, 1976). Analogies from other domains may be used to represent the new domain, although these initial analogies must be modified as learning progresses (Anderson, 1987). The sophisticated learner may make assumptions, based on previous learning experiences, such as (a) "the knowledge [I am learning] has a structure that is more complex than [presently evident]," (b) "[I am] going to have trouble judging the importance of information and [it is] better to err on the side of overestimating importance," and (c) "familiar words may have special meanings in the [new] domain" (Bereiter, 1989, p. 4). The fog that has shrouded the terrain is beginning to lift, but it is still difficult to see things clearly.

During the initial phase, relatively simple forms of learning (e.g., operant conditioning, verbal learning) account for a large part of the learning that occurs. Classical conditioning may also be relevant with regard to establishing an emotional/affective predisposition to learning within that domain. Early stages of concept learning (e.g., grouping) may also occur, but the learner has acquired insufficient information for more complex forms of propositional and procedural learning to occur – such as Rumelhart and Norman's (1978) tuning and restructuring. Thus, one might reasonably expect *mnemonic strategies* (a form of elaborative encoding) to have a greater affect on learning than *chunking* (a form of reductive encoding).[3]

Intermediate Phase

Gradually, the learner begins to see similarities and relationships among these conceptually isolated pieces of information. The fog continues to lift but still has not burnt off completely. As these relationships become better developed, they are formed into higher order structures and networks. New schemata that provide the learner with more conceptual power are formed, but these new structures and schemata do not yet allow the learner to function on a fully autonomous, or automatic, basis.

More meaningful forms of propositional and procedural learning predominate – what Spiro et al. (1988) refer to as *advanced knowledge acquisition* – and the student must now "'get it right' ... attain a deeper understanding of content material, reason with it, and apply it flexibly in diverse contexts" (Spiro et al., 1988, p. 1). We extend our knowledge by applying it to new situations and by learning by doing – that is, the information acquired during the initial phase is now applied to the solution of various problems that the learner encounters, including understanding and explaining various situations such as might be involved in answering an essay question.

An important advantage of this phase is that we can try out new knowledge in various ways and receive feedback on its appropriateness without its having autonomous control over our behavior (Anderson, 1982). Thus, there is the opportunity for reflection. As our knowledge becomes more abstract and more capable of being generalized to a variety of situations, it becomes less dependent on the specific context in which it was originally acquired (Karmiloff-Smith, 1984, 1986). During this phase, there may be a temporary deterioration in performance as all of these competing factors are sorted out (Karmiloff-Smith, 1984, 1986; Lesgold et al., 1988).

Does learning automatically progress to this intermediate phase? Not necessarily. To insure that the transition occurs from the initial to the intermediate phase, certain things need to occur. Unfortunately, these things often are missing from an educational system that emphasizes the accumulation of more and more factual information – that is, an additive model of learning. In order for information to become more abstract, or decontextualized, Bransford and Franks (1976) suggest that concepts and knowledge should be used to clarify different situations, and they stress the importance of encountering relevant examples, a recommendation that is similar to Spiro et al.'s (1988) emphasis on learning by cases. The teacher and/or the learner can additionally employ various organizational strategies such as outlining and cognitive mapping (that can help the learner to identify and develop higher order relationships in the information being learned) and use the information to solve problems of various types (learning by doing). Variables such as mnemonics, for example, that had substantial affects on learning during the initial phase may have little, if any, affect on learning during the intermediate phase.

Terminal Phase

During the last phase of learning, the knowledge structures and schemata formed during the intermediate phase become better integrated and function more autonomously. In most situations, performance will be automatic, unconscious, and effortless, because relevant knowledge structures now control behavior in a more direct manner (Anderson, 1982). The individual relies heavily, if not exclusively, on domain-specific strategies for solving problems, answering questions, and so forth. The emphasis in this phase is on performance rather than learning, because any change in performance is most likely the result of different task requirements rather than changes in one's cognitive structure or potential for performing in a particular manner.

In fact, performance (e.g., solving a mathematics problem) that may have involved learning during an earlier phase may involve little, if any, learning during the terminal phase. The ability to perform a task (including answering certain questions about a complex body of knowledge) that is accomplished in a straightforward, automatic manner (i.e., one merely utilizes preexisting procedures) involves neither learning nor problem solving. The learning that does occur during this phase most likely consists of either: (a) the addition of new facts to preexisting schemata (i.e., accretion), or (b) increasingly higher levels of interrelationships (e.g., where the schemata consist of other schemata rather than facts). In one sense, learning in a particular domain never ends, but a point is reached when the expert (not necessarily defined in the traditional sense) functions autonomously on automatic pilot, giving little thought and/or exerting little mental effort to the control of what he or she is doing.

Transition Between Phases

The most problematic part of any phase theory concerns the transition between phases. What, for example, is the nature of the change that occurs as one moves from one phase to the next? And what factors lead to the changes that are purported to occur? To many people, phases suggest the presence of separate and distinct entities with clear-cut boundaries between adjoining stages. But it seems unlikely that such is the case. It probably is best to think of learning as a continuous process; the boundaries between phases are most likely fuzzy, and the transitions between phases gradual rather than dichotomous (see Fitts' [1964] quote cited earlier).

The truth of the matter is that we currently have a very poor understanding of how these transitions occur and what factors precipitate them. But this type of problem is not unique to psychology; the physical sciences have similar problems – for example, understanding the changes and precipitating factors when a steady stream of water turns into a series of discrete drops. In both instances, the separate states (phases) can be documented, but the transition escapes current understanding. It may be the case, at least with phases of learning, that during the transition characteristics of both phases are operating in an overlapping manner. Thus, the learner might continue to rely on mnemonics even though their usefulness has diminished and the need for organization has become paramount. Such duplication could even serve a functional purpose in that new behavior is often unstable and the involvement of more than one factor could minimize the potentially negative effect of phenomena such as regression and forgetting.

Finally, it is reasonable in an educational context to raise the issue as to whether the transitions between phases can be stimulated or encouraged. Given our lack of understanding of how these transitions operate, little can be said that might be helpful in this regard. Nevertheless, it does not seem unreasonable (neither is it anything new) to speculate that transitions can be facilitated by encouraging learners to utilize strategies consistent with the phase they are about to enter. However, the good teacher, as well as the good learner, will be aware that premature involvement of facts may be counter-productive. Let them be available in working memory, but let them enter into the learning process in their own due time. One final possibility is worth considering – namely, that phases and the transitions between them may be by-products of the learning process rather than an integral part. If such is the case, attempts to facilitate transitions per se will accomplish little.

Other Considerations

There appears to be sufficient rationale to support the notion that learning a complex body of knowledge – whether it be the type we learn in school, the compilation of life experiences, or the mastering of the skills inherent in a craft, trade, or profession – involves a series of phases during which the learning process is fundamentally different. It is usually assumed that these phases are organized in a linear manner, but it is possible that they may be organized in a hierarchical, spiral, and/or concentric manner as well (Wade, 1989). Earlier phases may be subsumed into subsequent phases (in much the same way as the developmental stages of Piaget), or new phases may exist side-by-side (as in the developmental stages of Jerome Bruner).[4]

The present analysis and review has focused on cognitive aspects of learning, but learning, especially the type of long-term learning being discussed, involves emotional, affective, and social aspects as well. The extent to which these various aspects of learning interrelate in a manner conducive or detrimental to learning may also vary as a function of the phase of learning. For example, an individual may begin studying a domain of knowledge with considerable enthusiasm and interest only to discover later that the domain was not what he or she originally expected, and the converse can exist as well (e.g., begin with low expectations and a dislike that becomes more positive as learning progresses).

In closing, it must be cautioned that, although a phase analysis of learning is appealing in many ways, much more evidence is needed if the existence of phases is to be established in a scientifically valid manner. Some of the methodological concerns have been discussed in this article, but delineation of the phases (with regard to both the number of phases that might be involved and the characteristics of each phase) must await future research. In the meantime, the realization that phases most likely exist in the learning of complex and potentially meaningful knowledge provides useful insights into the learning process (including a basis for explaining why certain variables affect learning in some situations but not in others). In teaching such knowledge, it also suggests that we should pay attention to the way the teaching/learning process changes as learning progresses.

Notes

1. Phases and levels are similar in that both involve equivalency of process across either various domains or within a specific domain, respectively. They differ in that an individual progresses through the same three phases whenever he or she acquires a new body of knowledge (e.g., physics vs. literature), but, once he or she moves from Level 1 to Level 2 in a particular domain (e.g., the American novel), returning to Level 1 in that domain is not possible.
2. Too frequently, rote learning and meaningful learning are pitted against one another in a good/bad or either/or manner. In reality, both play an important role in learning from instruction, for at times it is intelligent to memorize something by rote, especially in the present context where rote learning is a means to an end rather than necessarily being an end in itself.
3. See Norman (1978) for a detailed discussion of learning strategies, general characteristics, modes of testing, and transfer relevant to accretion, restructuring, and tuning.
4. The distinctions that Karmiloff-Smith (1984, 1986) makes among stages, phases, and levels are also relevant here.

References

Anderson, J. R. (1982). Acquisition of cognitive skill. *Psychological Review, 89*, 369–406.

Anderson, J. R. (1987). Skill acquisition: Compilation of weak-method problem solutions. *Psychological Review, 94*, 192–210.

Andre, T. (1986). Problem solving and education. In G. D. Phye & T. Andre (Ed.), *Cognitive classroom learning: Understanding, thinking, and problem solving* (pp. 169–204). Orlando, FL: Academic Press.

Baddeley, A. D. (1966). The influence of acoustic and semantic similarity on long-term memory for word-sequences. *Quarterly Journal of Experimental Psychology, 18*, 302–309.

Battig, W. F. (1968). Paired-associate learning. In T. R. Dixon & D. L. Horton (Eds.), *Verbal behavior and general behavior theory* (pp. 149–171). Englewood Cliffs, NJ: Prentice-Hall.

Benner, P. (1984). *From novice to expert: Excellence and power in clinical nursing practice.* New York: Addison-Wesley.

Bereiter, C. (1989, March). The role of an educational learning theory: Explaining difficult learning. In W. J. McKeachie (Chair), *Toward a unified approach to learning as a multi-source phenomenon.* Symposium conducted at the meeting of the American Educational Research Association, San Francisco.

Brainerd, C. J. (1985). Model-based approaches to storage and retrieval development. In C. J. Brainerd & M. Pressley (Eds.), *Basic processes in memory development: Progress in cognitive development research* (pp. 143–207). New York: Springer-Verlag.

Brainerd, C. J., Howe, M. L., & Desrochers, A. (1982). The general theory of two-stage learning: A mathematical review with illustrations from memory development. *Psychological Bulletin, 91*, 634–665.

Bransford, J. D., & Franks, J. J. (1976). Toward a frame wok for understanding learning. In G. H. Bower (Ed.), *Psychology of learning and motivation* (Vol. 10, pp. 93–127). New York: Academic Press.

Bransford, J. D., & Johnson, M. K. (1972). Contextual prerequisites for understanding: Some investigations of comprehension and recall. *Journal of Verbal Learning and Verbal Behavior, 11*, 717–726.

Brown, A. L., Bransford, J. D., Ferrara, R. A., & Campione, J. C. (1983). Learning, remembering, and understanding. In P. H. Mussen (Ed.), *Handbook of child psychology: Vol. III. Cognitive development* (J. H. Flavell & E. M. Markman, Vol. Eds.) (4th ed., pp. 77–166). New York: John Wiley & Sons.

Bryan, W. L., & Harter, N. (1897). Studies in the physiology and psychology of the telegraphic language. *Psychological Review, 4*, 27–53.

Bryan, W. L., & Harter, N. (1899). Studies on the telegraphic language: The acquisition of a hierarchy of habits. *Psychological Review, 6*, 345–375.

Champagne, A. B., Klopfer, L. E., & Gunstone, R. F. (1982). Cognitive research and the design of science instruction. *Educational Psychologist, 17*, 31–53.

Chi, M. T. H. (1978). Knowledge structures and memory development. In R. S. Siegler (Ed.), *Children's thinking: What develops?* (pp. 73–96). Hillsdale, NJ: Lawrence Erlbaum Associates.

Chi, M. T. H., Glaser, R., & Rees, E. (1982). Expertise in problem solving. In R. Sternberg (Ed.), *Advances in the psychology of human intelligence* (Vol. 1, pp. 7–75). Hillsdale, NJ: Lawrence Erlbaum Associates.

Chiesi, H. L., Spilich, G. J., & Voss, J. F. (1979). Acquisition of domain-related information in relation to high and low domain knowledge. *Journal of Verbal Learning and Verbal Behavior, 18*, 251–273.

Conrad, R. (1964). Acoustic confusions in immediate memory. *British Journal of Psychology, 55*, 75–83.

Dreyfus, H. L., & Dreyfus, S. E. (1986). *Mind over machine: The power of human intuition and expertise in the era of the computer*. New York: Free Press.

Fitts, P. M. (1962). Factors in complex skill training. In R. Glaser (Ed.), *Training research and education* (pp. 177–197). Pittsburgh: University of Pittsburgh Press.

Fitts, P. M. (1964). Perceptual-motor skill learning. In A. W. Melton (Ed.), *Categories of human learning* (pp. 243–285). New York: Academic Press.

Fleishman, E. A., & Hempel, W. E., Jr. (1954). Changes in factor structure of a complex psychomotor test as a function of practice. *Psychometrika, 19*, 239–252.

Fleishman, E. A., & Hempel, W. E., Jr. (1955). The relation between abilities and improvement with practice in a visual discrimination reaction task. *Journal of Experimental Psychology, 49*, 301–310.

Glaser, R., & Chi, M. T. H. (1988). Overview. In M. T. H. Chi, R. Glaser, & M. J. Farr (Eds.). *The nature of expertise* (pp. xv–xxviii). Hillsdale, NJ: Lawrence Erlbaum Associates.

Hayes, J. R. (1965). Problem topology and the solution process. *Journal of Verbal Learning and Verbal Behavior, 4*, 371–379.

Hayes, J. R. (1966). Memory, goals, and problem solving. In B. Klenmuntz (Ed.), *Problem solving: Research, method, and theory*. New York: John Wiley & Sons.

Karmiloff-Smith, A. (1984). Children's problem solving. In M. E. Lamb, A. L. Brown, & B. Rogoff (Eds.), *Advances in developmental psychology* (Vol. 3, pp. 39–90). Hillsdale, NJ: Lawrence Erlbaum Associates.

Karmiloff-Smith, A. (1986). Stage/structure versus phase/process in modelling linguistic and cognitive development. In I. Levin (Ed.), *Stage and structure: Reopening the debate* (pp. 164–190). Norwood, NJ: Ablex.

Keil, F. C. (1986). On the structure-dependent nature of stages of cognitive development. In I. Levin (Ed.), *Stage and structure: Reopening the debate* (pp. 144–163). Norwood, NJ: Ablex.

Kintsch, W., & Buschke, H. (1969). Homophones and synonyms in short-term memory. *Journal of Experimental Psychology, 80*, 403–407.

Labouvie, G. V., Frohring, W. R., Baltes, P. B., & Goulet, L. R. (1973). Changing relationship between recall performance and abilities as a function of stage of learning and timing of recall. *Journal of Educational Psychology, 64*, 191–198.

Lesgold, A., Rubinson, H., Feltovich, P., Glaser, R., Klopfer, D., & Wang, Y. (1988). Expertise in a complex skill: Diagnosing x-ray pictures. In M. T. H. Chi, R. Glaser, & M. J. Farr (Eds.), *The nature of expertise* (pp. 311–342). Hillsdale, NJ: Lawrence Erlbaum Associates.

Mayer, R. E. (1983). *Thinking, problem solving, cognition.* New York: W. H. Freeman.

McGuire, W. J. (1961). A multiprocess model for paired-associate learning. *Journal of Experimental Psychology, 62*, 335–347.

Norman, D. A. (1978). Notes toward a theory of complex learning. In A. M. Lesgold, J. W. Pellegrino, S. D. Fokkema, & R. Glaser (Eds.), *Cognitive psychology and instruction* (pp. 39–48). New York: Plenum Press.

Restle, T., & Davis, J. H. (1962). Success and speed of problem solving by individuals and groups. *Psychological Review, 69*, 520–536.

Rumelhart, D. E., & Norman, D. A. (1978). Accretion, tuning, and restructuring: Three modes of learning. In J. W. Cotton & R. L. Klatzky (Eds.), *Semantic factors in cognition* (pp. 37–53). Hillsdale, NJ: Lawrence Erlbaum Associates.

Shuell, T. J. (1986a). Cognitive conceptions of learning. *Review of Educational Research, 56*, 411–436.

Shuell, T. J. (1986b). Individual differences: Changing concepts in research and practice. *American Journal of Education, 94*, 356–377.

Shuell, T. J. (1990). Teaching and learning as problem solving. *Theory into Practice, 29*, 102–108.

Spiro, R. J., Coulson, R. L., Feltovich, P. J., & Anderson, D. K. (1988). *Cognitive flexibility theory: Advanced knowledge acquisition in ill-structured domains* (Tech. Rep. No. 5). Springfield, IL: Southern Illinois University School of Medicine, Conceptual Knowledge Research Project.

Sternberg, R. J. (1984). Mechanisms of cognitive development: A componential approach. In R. J. Sternberg (Ed.), *Mechanisms of cognitive development* (pp. 163–186). New York: W. H. Freeman.

Thomas, J. C. (1974). An analysis of behavior in the hobbits-orcs problem. *Cognitive Psychology, 6*, 257–269.

Underwood, B. J., Runquist, W. N., & Schulz, R. W. (1959). Response learning in paired-associate lists as a function of intralist similarity. *Journal of Experimental Psychology, 58*, 70–78.

Underwood, B. J., & Schulz, R. W. (1960). *Meaningfulness and verbal learning.* Philadelphia: Lippincott.

Voss, J. F., Greene, T. R., Post, T. A., & Penner, B. C. (1983). Problem-solving skill in the social sciences. In G. H. Bower (Ed.), *The psychology of learning and motivation: Advances in research and theory* (Vol. 17, pp. 165–213). New York: Academic Press.

Wade, L. (1989). *General and domain-specific elements related to stages of learning.* Unpublished manuscript, State University of New York at Buffalo.

Wallas, G. (1926). *The art of thought.* New York: Harcourt Brace Jovanovich.

41

Growth, Development, Learning, and Maturation as Factors in Curriculum and Teaching

William C. Trow

In bringing together the diverse aspects of educational psychology indicated by the title of this chapter, and in focusing them on instructional practice, it would seem appropriate first to look for the hypotheses that lie behind both research and practice. The ideas embodied in these hypotheses can then be noted in the implications of the research that has been done. The treatment of this chapter will therefore concentrate on learning and the curriculum since growth and development are reviewed in a separate issue of this journal.

Hypotheses for Research and for School Practice Affecting Teaching and the Curriculum

The basic idea that underlies all the others in modern education is to be found in John Dewey's recurrent emphasis on the experience of the child as of central concern. Regard for his all-round development has shifted the emphasis from forcing him to acquire knowledge, to making provision for an inner living motivation (22). We cannot know what to teach, how to teach, or when to teach until we know whom we are teaching, and from what homes, groups, and cultures our students come, and until we can identify

---

Source: *Review of Educational Research*, XXI(3) (1951): 186–195.

and project their current needs against the future needs of a dynamic society (55). If these things are to be done, man in general, and the pupil in particular, must be viewed not as a free soul, a capricious creature, but as a dynamic, lawful system interacting with the energy systems of the environment. Anderson (3) contrasted the effects on one's view of pupil capacity, motivation, practice, and transfer when man is viewed (a) as a "free soul" and (b) as a "dynamic lawful system." American psychology supports the latter under which there have been identified two basic systems of behavior and of learning, the association system and the field system.

If man is viewed as a dynamic lawful system, it means, first, that the individuals in a learning group must be perceived as a group of dynamically interactive personalities (27). Included in this perception will be what Snygg and Combs (69) called the "phenomenological" approach, which seeks to explain behavior on the basis of the behaver's perception of himself and of the world, and deal with it accordingly.

It means, second, that the objectives of education will include the development of attitudes toward other individuals and groups (50), but they must be "right" attitudes. Research is therefore needed on value concepts and their role and influence in social behavior (87). Modern education is actually reoriented toward human values (14), yet probably few teachers realize they are applying axiology when they try to answer a child's, "Why do we have to?" If axiology is viewed as the science of preferential behavior (53), the way is open for the coalescence of value concepts with those derived from the study of personality and referred to as needs.

The third implication of the view of man as a dynamic lawful system, then, is that the educator, in working out a curriculum to promote pupil learning, will be a student of the dynamics of normal personality. As expounded by Dollard and Miller (29) and others, knowledge of personality is derived from psychoanalysis, social psychology, and anthropology, from which areas light is being thrown on the nature of social motivation and drive, of fear and conflict, and on the cultural conditions of learning. Harsh and Shrickel (41) traced successive developmental stages which produce changes in motivation, ability, and learned adjustment patterns and which must be more adequately reflected in the school program. For example, Miller (56) found that rats learned to get relief from an electric shock by striking each other, and when alone they struck a celluloid doll. The rats, like the child in play who beats the "mamma doll," revealed the Freudian mechanism of displayed aggression, as would the child restricted by too narrow curriculum demands.

Kluckhohn and Murray (51) in one of the chapters in *Personality: In Nature, Society and Culture*, to which a number of authors have contributed, outlined their dynamic, organismic concept of personality. They see it as a continuity of functional forces and forms manifested thru sequences of organized integrative processes. Its functions, among others, are self-expression and the reduction of tensions and conflicts thru social conformity, identification, and the creation of a design for living that permits periodic and harmonious appeasement of most of the needs, and gradual progression toward distant goals.

If education is to profit from the empirical approach here indicated, as Bode (15) pointed out, it will have to accept Dewey's view (28) and abandon its hope for truth as conformity to an alleged immutable cosmic order. Money (57) suggested a kind of compromise in view of the fact that the difference between private delusions, widely accepted beliefs, and scientific facts, is one of actual or possible validation. Since some beliefs, referred to as absolutes, have eased psychosomatic existence, may they not be considered as axioms that might be changed in content by common agreement; thus satisfying the philosophical need for stability and also the scientific need for change? In any case, scientific method has a long way to go in the social realm before it will be able to keep the thinking even of trained minds out of the mental channels of the child, the primitive, and the psychotic. These channels of thinking were mapped in detail by Werner (85) as follows, each with its scientific opposite: the syncretic to the discrete, the diffuse to the articulated; the indefinite to the definite, the rigid to the flexible, and the labile to the stable.

Learning and the Curriculum

Since the relation of mental hygiene and guidance to the curriculum and teaching is not included in this issue of the Review, suffice it to say with Wright (88) that two kinds of childhood needs should be differentiated: the normative as they are appreciated by the adult, and the psychological as felt by children. But since the child responds not to generalities but to specifics, it is important, if his basic needs are to provide effective motivation, that curriculum activities be cognitively well-structured so that the activities lead clearly to the goals sought.

Blair (11) indicated the nature of the psychologically effective curriculum as one which makes provision for varying maturity and experience levels, gears learning activities to pupil needs and goals, provides units of experience that have structure and meaning for the pupil, and selects and appraises projected pupil activities in terms of their transfer value to life situations. Brownell (19), however, pointed to the discrepancy between learning experiments and improvement in teaching, and called for long-term studies of the learning process in the classroom. He contended (18) that less emphasis in initial learning should be placed on speed and accuracy in the product, and more on improvement of the process and the establishment of principles transferable to new procedures.

Detailed applications of educational psychology to the processes of learning and instruction are to be found in the Forty-Ninth Yearbook of the

National Society for the Study of Education (58). In this volume, a number of authors who themselves have long been conducting research in this field interpreted their findings and those of their colleagues. Following chapters on the nature of learning and of motivation, a second section describes the ways children learn motor types of activities, concepts and generalizations, interests and attitudes, personal and social adjustments, esthetic responses, and the technics of problem solving. Implications of learning principles are then pointed out for the different school levels and for teaching procedures.

English (31) presented a brief discussion of the nature of learning and a history of learning theory, while the most intensive and extensive treatment was given by Hilgard (45), who critically reviewed the current theories. Tolman (78) sought to explain the divergencies in theory by asserting that there is more than one kind of learning and listed six kinds including field expectancies, field cognition modes, drive discriminations and motor patterns. A detailed report of the psychological studies from which the theories are derived is to be found in the *Annual Review of Psychology* (70), the first issue of which appeared last year. In it there is a critical review of learning theory, with a 101-item bibliography by Melton, an analysis of problem-solving processes by Johnson, a report of growth and age changes especially in motor functions and mental abilities by Jones and Bayley, and a review of studies of assorted items from the field of educational psychology by Cronbach.

Piaget (62) continuing his long series of studies on the genetics of mental functions traced four stages in the development of what he called the moral judgment of the child by analyzing children's acceptance of the rules in the game of marbles. Gebhard (37) found that the attractiveness of an activity is determined not only by past experience of success but by the expectation of future success. Grace (39) concluded that verbal approval was more effective with the well-adjusted and emotionally stable. Postman (63), drawing from a 332-item bibliography, summarized the history and present status of the law of effect. In this connection, mention should be made of Thorndike's *Selected Writings from a Connectionist's Psychology* (76), in which studies published from 1913 to 1947 were chosen and arranged by the author himself including seven on learning.

Postman (65) is the senior author of one study in which it was found that forgetting in the form of retroactive inhibition is smaller when a change of set (e.g., direction of association or type of logical relationship) is used. In another study (64) he concluded that the subject's readiness for a particular type of test is a factor influencing set.

A 136-item bibliography accompanies an article (36) on the measurementof transfer of training which concluded that various methods of measurement suggest that different functions are being measured. Not only is it time that some of these functions are isolated, but the conditions under which what is learned in school will be used when needed require still further study.

School experimentation is bedeviled by the almost insuperable difficulty of the control of innumerable variables. Some, however, have faced up to the task. Anderson (2) found little difference in the result when pupils were taught arithmetic by a "drill method" (connectionist) and a "meaning method" (gestalt), altho the latter proved superior, for pupils scoring high on ability but low on initial achievement, in improving transfer to different kinds of materials.

A study of pupil interests (47) revealed that variations are determined largely by opportunities and incentives of the environment, which means that the learning factor is important; and since elementary pupils revealed more interest in school than high-school pupils, it was concluded that the schools can use their influence to create more satisfactory learning situations.

Studies of learning when learner differences are extreme have important implications for the wide range of abilities in the schools. Cruickshank (25) found that mentally retarded boys were less competent than normal boys of the same mental age in solving arithmetic problems. Strauss and Lehtinen (72) summarized 20 years of outstanding research on brain-injured children, reviewing especially-devised test situations, the characteristic behavior found, and applications to learning situations. Gesell (38) added a collection of papers reporting significant aspects of his work at the Yale Clinic previous to his retirement. And Terman and Oden (74) published the fourth volume of the *Genetic Studies of Genius – The Gifted Child Grows Up*, a 25-year follow-up of the original superior group, with educational and other implications, among which is the conclusion that in spite of the environmentalist's efforts, the hereditary hypothesis seems to stand up.

General Sources Based on Research Studies with Implications for the Curriculum and Teaching

Brickman (17) reviewed 16 texts and reference works in the field of educational psychology which were published during the years 1945–1948, and since then other texts have appeared including those by Beaumont and Macomber (8), Simpson (67), and Trow (79). Specific relationships of educational measurements and of a knowledge of individual differences to the curriculum were pointed out by Freeman (35) and Cook (24) respectively. Williams (86), after a survey of 223 titles, analyzed the approaches directed toward reducing and controlling intergroup tensions to which curriculum activities can make an important contribution.

Growth factors influencing the curriculum have received detailed standard treatment by a number of authors including Breckenridge and Vincent (16) and Hurlock (48, 49). Rasey (66) brought out a unique volume which develops the implications of the whole-child concept and includes reports from the autobiographies of 1600 students with critic-teacher comments.

Olson (60) is the author of a significant report of research which has been continuing over a period of 20 years. The results of longitudinal studies are presented with important implications for elementary-school activities. Remedial reading, self-selection, and promotional policies, among other problems, receive attention. Beck in *Human Growth* (9) described the physiological changes accompanying adolescence as was done in the film by the same name. Havighurst (42) defined an interesting concept, the "developmental task," as one which, if successfully accomplished, leads to happiness and success with later tasks, but if not results in unhappiness, disapproval by society, and difficulty with later tasks.

At the elementary-school level, Averill (5) prepared a textbook for the whole period, and Forest (33) for students of early childhood education. Lee and Lee (52) emphasized the "integrative approach" in handling the elementary-school subjects, and Hildreth (44) developed the principles of organized and unified learning in harmony with behavioral development, interpreting them in terms of realistic life experiences.

At the high-school level two rather unique documents have appeared. One of them (73) presents in pamphlet form discussions of a hypothetical workshop group relating learning to diverse viewpoints and to curriculum experiences. The other (43), the "Prairie City" studies of the development of personality, is full of implications for programs of character education. Mention should also be made of a selected list of 72 references on gifted children (82), and of the Yearbook of the National Society for the Study of Education on *The Education of Exceptional Children* (59).

Curriculum and Co-curriculum – What Shall Students Learn?

While curriculum revisions are predominantly in the field of social learning, among the others that might be selected for special mention is Cureton's (26) work on physical fitness appraisal and guidance, which, along with other influences is likely to have the effect of improving the physical education program.

Luchins and Luchins (54) carried forward the structural approach to the comprehension of spatial relationships, supplementing Wertheimer's chapter on the area of a parallelogram which appeared in his *Productive Thinking*. Geometry teachers will find here suggestions for improving pupil comprehension. Meaning in arithmetic was studied by Van Engen (83) who favored what he called the concept of operational arithmetic, in which meanings are derived from acts or operations, in contrast with the social-meaning theory, the structural-meaning theory, and the nihilistic theory of numbers as meaningless symbols, which latter is perhaps far too prevalent.

A number of papers at the college level deal with the place of educational psychology in the training of teachers. Anderson (1, 4) defined the field of educational psychology, enumerating the contributions it can make to the education of teachers and indicated suggestions for content. Trow (80) carried the analysis further enunciating the objective as effective pupil participation, this to be attained in proportion to the extent to which the teacher can learn to structure the school environment, organize activities (curriculum), recognize proper objectives in terms of needs and values, and teach appropriate behavior (knowledge, skills, and attitudes). Details were elaborated by others: Blair analyzed the content of various texts (12) and pointed out what teachers should know about adolescence (13). Bruce indicated relationships with general psychology (21) and the importance of a knowledge of child development (20). Freeman (34) and Cook (23) emphasized the importance of a study of individual differences and of educational measurement (24) for the curriculum and for the education of teachers.

The direct approach has been made to the high-school pupil in order to facilitate his social learning thru the medium of the textbook. Thorpe (77) discussed understanding ourselves and others, maintaining personal and social integrity, character and religion, and personality and the welfare of society. Smart and Smart (68) were primarily concerned with the feelings and attitudes of children and their parents, and Duvall (30) prepared a text for family living which includes chapters on personality development, family interrelationships, boy-girl relationships, and preparation for marriage.

Weiner (84) reported on the prolonged preacademic curriculum of the Wayne County Training School and furnished a guide for the objective observation of preacademic achievements, a program designed for high-grade feeble-minded children, but which should be taken to heart by elementary teachers in regular schools. The important implications of play therapy for general educational activities were elaborated by Axline (6) and helpful hints for an elementary-school council were provided by O'Toole (62).

The lush growth of group dynamics at Bethel and elsewhere forces the question of its place in the regular school situation where the teacher perforce has the roles both of leader and of resource person, as well as others. After doing background reading on group dynamics (10) and the psychodrama technic (40) developed by Moreno, the reader may wish to consider some of the implications of considering the class as a group (75, 81).

From the social-work angle, group work has been going on for some time, and Strang (71) showed its relevance to schools and institutions of higher learning. Such efforts would seem appropriate since Bath (7) in a follow-up study found little to distinguish the winners from the non-winners of a junior high-school efficiency certificate in a good citizenship program of 20 years ago. Perhaps the most promising program for the future was initiated by the Horace Mann-Lincoln Institute of School experimentation. If effective improvements are to be made in the curriculum they will be made not so much as a consequence of what is done to teachers as of what they themselves do. This involves (46) research on the educational program thru cooperative teacher research and planning. More schoolwork than in the past will probably be carried on thru problem-centered group activities (32). This term designates an educational process by which teachers and students work cooperatively to solve problems related to the experiences, interests, and concerns of young people, in the process of which attitudes are structured and self-evaluation is encouraged.

Bibliography

1. Anderson, George Lester. "Educational Psychology and Teacher Education." *Journal of Educational Psychology* 40: 275–84; May 1949.
2. Anderson, George Lester. "Quantitative Thinking as Developed Under Connectionist and Field Theories of Learning." In Swenson, Esther; Anderson, G. Lester; and Stacey, Chalmers L. *Learning Theory in School Situations.* Minneapolis: University of Minnesota Press, 1949. 103 p.
3. Anderson, George Lester. "Theories of Behavior and Some Curriculum Issues." *Journal of Educational Psychology* 39: 133–40; March 1948.
4. Anderson, George Lester. "What the Psychology of Learning Has To Contribute to the Education of the Teacher." *Journal of Educational Psychology* 41: 362–65; October 1950.
5. Averill, Lawrence A. *The Psychology of the Elementary School Child.* New York: Longmans, Green and Co., 1949. 459 p.
6. Axline, Virginia Mae. *Play Therapy: The Inner Dynamics of Childhood.* Boston: Houghton Mifflin Co., 1947, 379 p.
7. Bath, John A. "A Study of Selected Participants and Non-Participants in a Program Directed Toward the Development of Initiative and Good Citizenship." *Journal of Experimental Education* 16: 161–75; March 1948.
8. Beaumont, Henry, and Macomber, Freeman G. *Psychological Factors in Education.* New York: McGraw-Hill Book Co., 1949. 318 p.
9. Beck, Lester F. *Human Growth.* New York: Harcourt, Brace and Co., 1949. 124 p.
10. Benne, Kenneth D.; Bradford, Leland P.; and Lippitt, Ronald. *Group Dynamics and Social Action.* New York: Anti-Defamation League of B'nai B'rith, 1950. 62 p.
11. Blair, Glenn M. "How Learning Theory Is Related to Curriculum Organization." *Journal of Educational Psychology* 39: 161–66, March 1948.
12. Blair, Glenn M. "The Content of Educational Psychology." *Journal of Educational Psychology* 40: 267–74; May 1949.
13. Blair, Glenn M. "What Teachers Should Know About the Psychology of Adolescence." *Journal of Educational Psychology* 41: 356–61; October 1950.
14. Bode, Boyd H., and others. *Modern Education and Human Values.* Pittsburgh: University of Pittsburgh Press, 1947. 165 p.
15. Bode, Boyd H. "John Dewey's Philosophy of Education." *New Republic* 121: 10–39, October 1949.
16. Breckenridge, Marian E., and Vincent, Elizabeth Lee. *Child Development.* Revised edition. Philadelphia: Saunders Co., 1943. 1949. 622 p.
17. Brickman, William W. "Educational Psychology: A Review." *School and Society* 68: 218–23; September 1948.
18. Brownell, William A. "Criteria of Learning in Educational Research." *Journal of Educational Psychology* 39: 170–82; March 1948.

19. Brownell, William A. "Learning Theory and Educational Practice." *Journal of Educational Research* 41: 481–97; March 1948.
20. Bruce, William F. "How Can the Psychology of Development in Infancy and Childhood Help Teachers?" *Journal of Educational Psychology* 41: 348–55; October 1950.
21. Bruce, William F. "The Relations of Educational Psychology with General Psychology." *Journal of Educational Psychology* 40: 261–66; May 1949.
22. Caswell, Hollis L. "Influence of John Dewey on the Curriculum of American Schools." *Teachers College Record* 51: 144–46; December 1949.
23. Cook, Walter W. "Individual Differences and Curriculum Practice." *Journal of Educational Psychology* 39: 141–418; March 1948.
24. Cook, Walter W. "What Educational Measurement in the Education of Teachers?" *Journal of Educational Psychology* 41: 339–47; October 1950.
25. Cruickshank, William M. "Arithmetic Ability of Mentally Retarded Children." *Journal of Educational Research* 42: 161–70, 279–88; November–December 1948.
26. Cureton, Thomas K. *Physical Fitness Appraisal and Guidance.* St. Louis: C. V. Mosby Co., 1947. 566 p.
27. Dennis, Wayne, editor. *Current Trends in Social Psychology.* Pittsburgh: University of Pittsburgh Press, l948. 299 p.
28. Dewey, John. *Reconstruction in Philosophy.* Enlarged edition. Boston: Houghton Mifflin Co., 1948. 224 p.
29. Dollard, John, and Miller, Neal E. *Personality and Psychotherapy.* New York: McGraw-Hill Book Co., 1950. 488 p.
30. Duvall, Evelyn Millis. *Family Living.* New York: Macmillan Co., 1950. 410 p.
31. English, Horace B. *Learning as Psychotechnology.* Columbus: Ohio State University, 1949. 81 p.
32. Evans, Hubert M., editor. "The Problem-Centered Group and Personal-Social Problems of Young People." *Teachers College Record* 51: 438–59; April 1950.
33. Forest, Ilse. *Early Years at School.* New York: McGraw-Hill Book Co., 1949. 381 p.
34. Freeman, Frank S. "The Study of Individual Differences in the Education of Teachers." *Journal of Educational Psychology* 41: 366–72; October 1950.
35. Freeman, Frank S. "How the Curriculum Is Evaluated and Modified Through Educational Measurement." *Journal of Educational Psychology* 39: 167–69; March 1948.
36. Gagne, Robert M.; Foster, Harriet; and Crowley, Miriam E. "The Measurement of Transfer of Training." *Psychological Bulletin* 45: 97–130; March 1948.
37. Gebhard, Mildred E. "The Effect of Success and Failure upon the Attractiveness of Activities as a Function of Experience, Expectation, and Need." *Journal of Experimental Psychology* 38: 371–88; August 1948.
38. Gesell, Arnold. *Studies in Child Development.* New York: Harper and Brothers, 1948. 224 p.
39. Grace, Gloria Lauer. "The Relation of Personality Characteristics and Responses to Verbal Approval in a Learning Task." *Genetic Psychology Monographs* 37: 73–99; 1948.
40. Grambs, Jean E. "Dynamics of Psychodrama in the Teaching Situation." *Sociatry* 1: 383–99; March 1948.
41. Harsh, Charles M., and Schrickel, H. G. *Personality, Development and Assessment.* New York: The Ronald Press Co., 1950. 518 p.
42. Havighurst, Robert J. *Developmental Tasks and Education.* Chicago: University of Chicago Press, 1948. 86 p.
43. Havighurst, Robert J., and Taba, Hilda. *Adolescent Character and Personality.* New York: John Wiley and Sons, 1949. 315 p.
44. Hildreth, Gertrude. *Child Growth Through Education.* New York: The Ronald Press Co., 1948. 437 p.
45. Hilgard, Ernest R. *Theories of Learning.* New York: Appleton-Century-Crofts, 1948. 409 p.

46. Horace Mann-Lincoln Institute of School Experimentation. "The Social-Cultural Context of the School Program." *Teachers College Record* 49: 325–29; February 1948.
47. Horace Mann-Lincoln Institute of School Experimentation. "Child Development and the Curriculum." *Teachers College Record* 49: 314–24; February 1948.
48. Hurlock, Elizabeth B. *Adolescent Development.* New York: McGraw-Hill Book Co., 1949. 566 p.
49. Hurlock, Elizabeth B. *Child Development.* Second edition. New York: McGraw-Hill Book Co., 1950. 669 p.
50. John Dewey Society. *Intercultural Attitudes in the Making.* Ninth Yearbook. New York: Harper and Brothers, 1947. 246 p.
51. Kluckhohn, Clyde, and Murray, Henry A., editors. *Personality: In Nature, Society, and Culture.* New York: Alfred A. Knopf, 1948. 561 p.
52. Lee, Jonathan Murray, and Lee, Doris May. *The Child and His Curriculum.* Second edition. New York: Appleton-Century-Crofts, 1950. 710 p.
53. Lepley, Ray, editor. *Value: A Cooperative Inquiry.* New York: Columbia University Press, 1949. 487 p.
54. Luchins, Abraham S., and Luchins, Edith H. "A Structural Approach to the Teaching of the Concept of Area in Intuitive Geometry." *Journal of Educational Research* 40: 528–33; March 1947.
55. MacLean, Malcolm S. "Adolescent Needs and Building the Curriculum." *Trends in Student Personnel Work.* (Edited by E. G. Williamson.) Minneapolis: University of Minnesota Press, 1949. p. 27–39.
56. Miller, Neal E. "Theory and Experiment Relating Psychoanalytic Displacement to Stimulus-Response Generalization." *Journal of Abnormal and Social Psychology* 43: 155–78; April 1948.
57. Money, John. "Delusion, Belief, and Fact." *Psychiatry* 11: 33–38, February 1948.
58. National Society for the Study of Education. *Learning and Instruction.* Forty-Ninth Yearbook, Part I. Chicago: University of Chicago Press, 1950. 352 p.
59. National Society for the Study of Education. *The Education of Exceptional Children.* Forty-Ninth Yearbook. Part II. Chicago: University of Chicago Press, 1950. 350 p.
60. Olson, Willard C. *Child Development.* Boston: D. C. Heath and Co., 1949. 417 p.
61. O'Toole, John F., Jr. "A Study of the Elementary School Student Council." *Elementary School Journal* 50: 259–67; January, 1950.
62. Piaget, Jean. *The Moral Judgment of the Child.* Glencoe, Ill.: Free Press, 1948. 418 p.
63. Postman, Leo J. "The History and Present Status of the Law of Effect." *Psychological Bulletin* 44: 489–563; November 1947.
64. Postman, Leo J., and Jenkins, William O. "An Experimental Analysis of Set in Rote Learning." *Journal of Experimental Psychology* 38: 683–89; December 1948.
65. Postman, Leo J., and Postman, Dorothy L. "Change in Set as a Determinant of Retroactive Inhibition." *American Journal of Psychology* 61: 236–42; April 1948.
66. Rasey, Marie I. *Toward Maturity.* New York: Hinds, Hayden, and Eldredge, 1947. 242 p.
67. Simpson, Robert G. *Fundamentals of Educational Psychology.* New York: J. B. Lippincott Co., 1949. 380 p.
68. Smart, Mollie S., and Smart, Russel C. *Living and Learning with Children.* Boston: Houghton Mifflin Co., 1949. 271 p.
69. Snygg, Donald, and Combs, Arthur W. *Individual Behavior, A New Frame of Reference.* New York: Harper and Brothers, 1948. 386 p.
70. Stone, Calvin P., editor. *Annual Review of Psychology.* Stanford, Calif.: Annual Reviews, 1950. 330 p.
71. Strang, Ruth. "Group Work in Schools and Institutions of Higher Learning." *A Decade of Group Work.* (Edited by Charles E. Hendry.) New York: Association Press, 1948. p. 95–104.

72. Strauss, Alfred A., and Lehtinen, Laura E. *Psychopathology and Education of the Brain-Injured Child.* New York: Grune and Stratton, 1947. 220 p.
73. Sugarman, Myrtle F., editor. *Effective Learning for Use in Junior High School.* Denver Public Schools, 1949. 72 p.
74. Terman, Lewis M., and Oden, Melita H. *The Gifted Child Grows Up.* Stanford, Calif.: Stanford University Press, 1947. 448 p.
75. Thelen, Herbert A. "Human Dynamics in the Classroom." *Journal of Social Issues* 6: 30–55; 1950.
76. Thorndike, Edward L. *Selected Writings from a Connectionist's Psychology.* New York: Appleton-Century-Crofts, 1949. 370 p.
77. Thorpe, Louis P. *Personality and Youth.* Dubuque, Iowa: William C. Brown Co., 1949. 378 p.
78. Tolman, Edward C. "There Is More than One Kind of Learning." *Psychological Review* 56: 144–55; May 1949.
79. Trow, William Clark. *Educational Psychology.* Revised edition. Boston: Houghton Mifflin Co., 1950. 761 p.
80. Trow, William Clark. "Educational Psychology Charts a Course." *Journal of Educational Psychology* 40: 285–94; May 1949.
81. Trow, William Clark, and others. "Psychology of Group Behavior." *Journal of Educational Psychology* 41: 322–38; October 1950.
82. U.S. Office of Education. "Selected References on Gifted Children." *Understanding the Child* 17: 56–64; April 1948.
83. Van Engen, Henry. "An Analysis of Meaning in Arithmetic." *Elementary School Journal* 49: 321–29, 395–400; February-March 1949.
84. Weiner, Bluma Beryl. "The Use of Systematic Classroom Observation To Aid in Curriculum Planning and Guidance for Young Mentally Retarded Boys." *American Journal of Mental Deficiency* 52: 331–36, April 1948.
85. Werner, Heinz. *Comparative Psychology of Mental Development.* Revised edition. Chicago: Follett Publishing Co., 1948. 564 p.
86. Williams, Robin M., Jr. *The Reduction of Intergroup Tensions: A Survey of Research on Problems of Ethnic, Racial, and Religious Group Relations.* Social Science Research Council Bulletin No. 57, 1947. 153 p.
87. Woodruff, Asahel D. "Motivation Theory and Educational Practice." *Journal of Educational Psychology* 40: 33–40; January 1949.
88. Wright, Herbert F. "How the Psychology of Motivation Is Related to Curriculum Development." *Journal of Educational Psychology* 39: 149–56; March 1948.

Section III: Motivation

42

Maslow, Monkeys and Motivation Theory

Dallas Cullen

T he influence of Abraham Maslow's (1943) hierarchy of needs is ubiquitous in management education and theory. Despite the common belief that Maslow's theory is outdated and ignored (see, for example, Greiner, 1992: 61), current textbooks present the theory in approving terms. It is described as the 'most widely recognized theory of motivation' (Hellriegel et al., 1995: 174), the 'most well-known need theory' (Moorhead and Griffin, 1995: 83) and a 'classic paper' (Luthans, 1995:150). At the level of theory, Maslow's hierarchy is so pervasive that it has almost become invisible, in that its basic framework and concepts are accepted without question. Managerial practices that permit or encourage employee autonomy and personal growth are justified on the grounds that such practices will enable employees to satisfy the esteem and self-actualization needs in Maslow's hierarchy. Some of the recent literature on employee empowerment, for example, suggests that only those employees who value higher order needs such as personal growth will respond positively to being given greater autonomy in their work (Lawler, 1992: 83). This argument both follows from and incorporates the concept of 'growth need strength' in Hackman and Oldham's (1980) theory of job design. In turn, the theory of job design draws on expectancy theory, which itself incorporates the needs in Maslow's hierarchy (Porter and Lawler, 1968: 131).

These links are not in any way hidden, but the question arises of why there is this acceptance of Maslow's theory as the starting point, given that this acceptance coexists with the recognition that there is, at best, limited empirical evidence for the hierarchy (see, for example, Mitchell and Moudgill, 1976; Wahba

Source: *Organization*, 4(3) (1997): 355–373.

and Bridwell, 1976). Indeed, Maslow himself wrote in his journal in 1962 that 'My motivation theory was published 20 years ago, and in all that time nobody repeated it, or tested it, or really analyzed it or criticized it. They just used it, swallowed it whole with only the most minor modifications' (Lowry, 1982: 63).

In terms of research, the usual explanation is that the theory has not been disconfirmed; rather, research has not yet supported it, because of methodological problems in interpreting, operationalizing and measuring its concepts (Wahba and Bridwell, 1976: 235). The textbook explanations for including the needs hierarchy are that it 'implicitly states the goals people value' (Hellriegel et al., 1995: 176), makes managers 'aware of the diverse needs of employees at work' (Luthans, 1995: 152) and 'makes a certain amount of intuitive sense' (Moorhead and Griffin, 1995: 85). Because the hierarchy seems to describe what the average employee seeks, it gives management a simple and quick means of understanding differences or changes in employee motivation (Huczynski, 1993: 24). These explanations, however, beg the question. Why are there problems in interpreting the hierarchy's central concepts? Why does it make intuitive sense?

One answer to these questions lies in recognizing that Maslow's humanistic psychology contains both a 'democratic' premise, which emphasizes authenticity, self-fulfillment and respect for the choices, preferences and values of each individual, and an 'aristocratic' premise, which emphasizes vocational competence, self-criticism and deference to the choices, preferences and values of the self-actualizing elite (Aron, 1977). The presence of these contradictory premises might then lead to difficulties in measuring or implementing the hierarchy's concepts.

But why does Maslow's theory contain these contradictory premises? One explanation has focussed on the hierarchy's links to liberal democratic theory. For example, Buss (1979) argues that Maslow's humanistic psychology was a liberal reaction to the conservatism embodied in both the positivistic methodology of behaviorist psychology and the pessimistic determinism of Freudian psychoanalysis. The democratic premise of individual autonomy and self-fulfillment in Maslow's hierarchy is the psychological counterpart of liberal democratic theory's stress on individual rights. However, in modern liberal democratic societies control belongs to a small and powerful elite rather than the masses, and the aristocratic premise reflects this reality. Consequently, Buss believes, the contradictions in Maslow's theory are real rather than conceptual, since the theory is grounded in the historical and social realities of the growth of democratic elitism.

Shaw and Colimore (1988) take this analysis one step further. Given the close link between politics and economics, they argue, Maslow's theory is best understood as an affirmation of capitalist ideology. Since growth comes through vocational achievement, Maslow's theory glorifies individual initiative for personal gain. At the same time, its hierarchical structure justifies the class system found in capitalistic societies, treating this system as both inescapable and beneficial.

While Buss believed that the needs hierarchy was a reflection of Maslow's own liberal values, Shaw and Colimore (1988: 69) were 'stunned' by the 'non-liberating quality' of Maslow's contributions to the management literature. However, they, like Buss, conclude that Maslow's contradictions are unintentional and unconscious reflections of the society of which he was a part. This rather benign assessment suggests that Maslow was unaware of the implications of his theory, an assessment that I believe reflects an incomplete understanding of the framework in which he developed the hierarchy.

That framework was his own earlier empirical research on the importance of dominance in explaining non-human primate (that is, monkey and ape) and human behavior. Maslow's dominance studies were a significant contribution to the primatology research of the 1930s and references to them occur throughout a variety of more recent literature in that field (see, for example, de Waal, 1996; Fedigan, 1992; Haraway, 1989; Rowell, 1974). Whereas writers on primatology who mention Maslow's dominance research often note that he is most known for the needs hierarchy (Haraway, 1989: 409, who describes this fact as 'ironic'; de Waal, 1996: 99), other writers' assessments of Maslow's work slight or ignore this connection. Neither Aron's nor Buss's discussions refer to the dominance research, while Shaw and Colimore (1988: 63), in noting Maslow's 'lifelong fascination with individual superiority and social dominance', cite but do not discuss it. My focus in this paper is an analysis of the ways in which the dominance research was the foundation of self-actualization theory and the implications of the link between the dominance studies and the needs hierarchy. Such an analysis, I believe, suggests why the hierarchy is intuitively appealing and, consequently, why it remains so influential.

As I will demonstrate, Maslow explained dominance in terms of the characteristics of the individuals involved, not in terms of the attributes of either the interaction between them or the setting in which this interaction occurred. Instead, group organization or behavior was due to individual psychology. A given individual's ability to be dominant over others was due to that individual's acknowledged natural superiority, and differences in human or monkey groups and cultures occurred because of differences in the exercise of dominance by the individuals in those groups and cultures. As I will also demonstrate, the incorporation of these ideas into the needs hierarchy means that Maslow's theory justifies managerial power, and enables managers to adopt motivational practices that appear to be responsive to employee needs while at the same time absolving them of accountability for the ineffectiveness of those practices.

To set the context for this analysis, I begin with a description of Maslow's career up to the point at which the needs hierarchy was published. I then discuss Maslow's primate research and his study of dominance in humans and demonstrate how the findings from these studies form the basis for the needs hierarchy. I next move to the implications of the dominance research for motivation theory, and finish with a discussion of the implications of a reexamination of Maslow's monkey research in light of current primatological research.

Maslow's Early Career

Maslow was the first doctoral student of Harry Harlow (Suomi and LeRoy, 1982: 341), who later gained fame for his work on monkeys raised by surrogate mothers (see, for example, Harlow, 1974). In 'an effort to see who was more correct, Freud or Adler, sex or dominance' (Lowry, 1982: 55), Maslow focussed his doctoral research on the relationship between sexual behavior and dominance behavior in monkeys. He completed his doctorate in 1934 and became a research assistant to Edward Thorndike in the Institute for Educational Research at Columbia University the following year. Thorndike had his assistants complete a variety of intellectual and scholastic aptitude tests; Maslow's tested IQ was an 'astounding' 195 (Hoffman, 1988: 74). For Maslow, this was evidence of his 'factual superiority', which meant that ultimately he was correct in his observations, intuitions and conclusions (see, for example, Lowry, 1982: 122–3). For his part, Thorndike was so impressed that he permitted Maslow to study whatever he wanted, which allowed Maslow to extend his studies of dominance and sexuality to humans (Wilson, 1972: 141).

Maslow collected most of these data during 1936 (Hoffman, 1988: 75, 80), the same year that his studies of dominance in monkeys were published. Between this time and the publication of the needs hierarchy in 1943, his intellectual interests and activities also included other disciplines. In 1937, he began teaching at Brooklyn College, where he co-authored a textbook on abnormal psychology (Maslow and Mittelmann, 1941) and, relying primarily on his intuition, provided informal therapy to students (Hoffman, 1988: 142). He wrote a book chapter on the influence of culture on personality (Maslow, 1937c), and, in the summer of 1938, following anthropologist Ruth Benedict's suggestion, undertook fieldwork among the Blackfoot in southern Alberta (Hoffman, 1988: 114). During this general time period, he also studied with the German psychoanalysts and Gestalt psychologists who had left Nazi Germany to work at the New School of Social Research (Hoffman, 1988: 87), including Kurt Goldstein, who had initially coined the term 'self-actualization' (Maslow, 1943: 382). He also continued to publish other papers based on his monkey studies (Maslow, 1937a; 1940a).

While the studies of human dominance and sexuality were critical to the development of the needs hierarchy (Cullen, 1994; Lowry, 1973), for Maslow, 'My primate research is the foundation upon which everything rests' (Hoffman, 1988: 49). His confidence in the insights he gained from 'my monkeys' was in part due to his belief that this research involved a form of 'loving perception'; it was 'more "true", more "accurate", in a certain sense, more *objectively* true' because he was both 'fond of' and 'fascinated' by the monkeys (Maslow, 1971: 17, emphasis in original). We turn now to what he learned from his monkeys.

Dominance in Monkeys

While the study of animal behavior is of value and interest in and of itself, its greater appeal for many people is its potential for teaching us about human behavior. This is particularly true of the study of non-human primates, especially the great apes (orangutans, chimpanzees and gorillas) and the Old World (Asian and African) monkeys such as macaques and baboons.

One reason for this importance is that studies of non-human primates can give us insights into the behavior of our own earliest ancestors. How has human behavior evolved? What behaviors have led to, or ensured, our survival as a species? A second, but clearly related, reason is that non-human primate behavior can give us insights into behaviors that present-day humans share regardless of culture. In other words, monkeys and apes can tell us something about 'true' human nature, or, as Haraway (1986: 77) has observed, 'what is "beneath", "at the heart of", or "outside", our own behavior.

Maslow himself clearly believed that this was the case. As noted earlier, his dissertation research was an attempt to compare the relative importance of sex and dominance in explaining behavior. He reported, however, that his initial attempt to study this relationship was a 'failure', both because of the 'complexity of the problem' and because his 'own personality and social norms acted like a sieve or a filter' (Maslow, 1937a: 488). In order to achieve 'impartiality and objectivity' he turned to animal studies, which allowed him to develop 'a specific objective criterion or scale by which to judge human behavior' and to see relationships among dominance, sexuality and social behavior that were 'less confused by repression, inhibition, social norms and social values' (Maslow, 1937a: 489). Comparative research of this type, Maslow argued, was a means of developing insights into 'general humanness' (1937a: 487).

Given this potential significance, it is not surprising that primatology is a field of conflicting and contested data and interpretations, a field which is 'politics by other means' (Haraway, 1986). Conscious and unconscious social and political considerations influence what is observed about primate behavior; in turn, what is observed about primate behavior has social and political meaning. Consequently, each era of primatological research reflects the wider concerns of its time period (Haraway, 1989). Primatology in the 1930s, a time of political, social and economic turmoil, concentrated on the general themes of aggression and its control, cooperation and competition, and the means by which social order was maintained. Primatology researchers identified the dominance hierarchy, which is, quite literally, the 'pecking order' among the members of a group, as that means of social control.

To the researchers of the era, the dominance hierarchy was the 'foundation of cooperation', ensuring that the social order did not collapse into destructive competition (Haraway, 1978a: 33). Moreover, dominance was inextricably linked with sexuality: the potentially destructive competition amongst males was for access to sexually receptive females, who accepted a subordinate status in order to gain access to desired items (such as food) which the males' greater size enabled them to control. This difference in size and subsequent subordination of females, it was argued, influenced or led to the creation of a patriarchal family unit (see, for example, Yerkes, 1939: 131). In other words, dominance was necessary and male dominance was natural.

For those working within this paradigm, the issue was not the presence or absence of dominance, but rather its manifestations and underlying sources. In 1929, Yerkes and Yerkes emphasized that 'Dominance and subordination are evident in every group of primates ... Dominance may be by either sex, but dominance there must be' (p. 250). Ten years later, in a review of the 'social psychology' of vertebrates, Crawford (1939: 418) observed that 'exploration of the significance of the concept of dominance has hardly begun', since knowledge of the connection between dominance relations and other social relations, as well as the factors that determined which animal was dominant, were still not fully clear. However, some answers were emerging. In his discussion of dominance in primates, Crawford focussed on two main studies: Maslow's four papers and Zuckerman's (1932) study of dominance in baboons.

Zuckerman had argued that, because female primates (unlike other animals) are continually sexually receptive, and hence continually sexually active, male and female primates live in permanent groupings. The fighting and aggression inherent in this continual association is regulated through a dominance hierarchy in the form of a harem, in which a male 'overlord' controls access to as many females as he can, thus ensuring his own reproductive success.

Zuckerman's theory of females' continual sexual receptivity is now considered to be an oversimplification (Fedigan, 1992: 158), but, at the time, it was enormously influential, helping to establish dominance as a fact rather than as a concept (Haraway, 1978b: 47). Maslow's own papers refer to Zuckerman's 'excellent study' which gives 'a clear indication of the importance of the dominance principle in primate sociology' (1936a: 261). At the same time, however, Maslow contended Zuckerman had 'missed the full significance' and 'grossly underestimated the importance' of dominance as a cause of social behavior (1936a: 262, 275). The constant sexual activity in monkeys, Maslow believed, occurred because of both the hormonal cycle and a dominance drive (1936b: 330), a conclusion that was based on his own observational and experimental studies.

During most of 1932 and the first few months of 1933, Maslow had made observations of small groups of monkeys housed at the Vilas Park Zoo in Madison, Wisconsin (Maslow, 1936a). An 'experienced observer' like Maslow was easily able to determine which monkey was dominant in a group: it 'struts' rather than 'slinks', has a 'cocky, aggressive and confident air', and 'stares fixedly and ferociously' at the other monkeys (Maslow, 1936a: 266). Maslow later labelled this stare 'the 'Gaze': it was a 'look of command' that is 'level, unwavering, unyielding, even unself-conscious & spontaneous', with which 'the overlord just looked, & the other dropped his [sic] eyes as if he'd been mastered & admitted it' (Lowry, 1982: 89, 30).

From his observations, Maslow concluded (as had Zuckerman) that each group had a dominance hierarchy with one monkey who was the overlord. Dominance was related to size and age, but was not related to gender. Females could be dominant over both males and other females, and the behavior of dominant females was the same as that of dominant males. However, dominant females seemed to lose their dominance when they came into heat.

These observations were followed in 1933–4 by the study of experimental pairings of macaque (rhesus) monkeys at the Primate Laboratory at the University of Wisconsin (Maslow, 1936b, 1936c; Maslow and Flanzbaum, 1936). In the pairings, monkeys which had been caged separately were brought together in another chamber for a varying number of brief experimental periods, during which all their behavior was recorded. Based on his analysis of these behaviors, Maslow (1936c: 183) decided that the best indicators of dominance were mounting (taking the male role in sexual behavior) and bullying, while the best indicators of subordinance were cringing and flight. It was on this basis that he argued that there was a continuum of sexual behavior, with one end being sexual behavior motivated by 'sexual drive' and the other end being sexual behavior motivated by 'dominance drive', with the latter type being used as a 'power weapon' (Maslow, 1936b: 319, 336).

Maslow also concluded that all monkeys have this dominance drive; a subordinate monkey is one 'whose dominance has been overshadowed by greater dominance' (1936a: 264). What, then, causes a given monkey's ability to overshadow another? According to Maslow, dominance is 'determined by or actually is a composite of social attitudes, attitudes of aggressiveness, confidence or cockiness that are at times challenged, and which must then, of course, be backed up by physical prowess' (Maslow and Flanzbaum, 1936: 305). In the experimental pairings, dominance was usually established quite rapidly since 'one animal seemed, in most cases, to assume at once that he [sic] was dominant, and that the other animal seemed, just as naturally, to admit that he was subordinate' (Maslow and Flanzbaum, 1936: 303–4). The superiority of one was accepted by both.

The Nature of Dominance

The picture of dominance that emerges in Maslow's monkey studies is an unpleasant one. In Zuckerman's baboons and Maslow's macaques, dominance was 'rough, brutal and aggressive; it is of the nature of a powerful, persistent, selfish urge' that resulted in bullying and fighting (Maslow, 1940a: 316). Furthermore, dominance status (that is, a given monkey's position in the dominance hierarchy) was 'jealously guarded and affirmed' (Maslow, 1940a: 319). However, not all non-human primates expressed dominance in such a brutal manner. Among chimpanzees, who were considered to be the most sociable of the great apes (Yerkes and Yerkes, 1929: 557), dominance was 'mostly of a friendly kind' (Maslow, 1940a: 314). One dominant male exercised his dominance in a teasing and playful, rather than a vicious, way (Maslow, 1935: 57). Another dominant chimpanzee tolerated, or was even apparently amused by, displays of anger or aggression by a subordinate (Maslow, 1940a: 315–16).

Maslow was the first researcher to call attention to these genuine differences in the exercise of dominance (de Waal, 1996: 126); what is important to the development of the needs hierarchy is the conclusion he drew about them. He made what he called the 'far-reaching and important' suggestion that differences in group behavior were based on differences in individual personality (Maslow, 1940a: 322). The manner in which dominant chimpanzees behaved, as compared to the manner in which dominant baboons and macaques behaved, led to differences in chimpanzee society as compared to baboon and macaque society.

As a result, Maslow hypothesized that cultural (or sub-cultural) differences among humans might be based on differences in the manner in which dominant individuals in those cultures behaved. What, then, would lead a dominant human to behave like a benevolent chimpanzee rather than a despotic baboon? The answer, according to Maslow, was the individual's sense of emotional security. We turn now to the reasoning that led him to this conclusion.

Maslow's discussions of his human data reveal the same intermingling of dominance, sexuality and superiority as do his discussions of his monkey data. However, observing and measuring dominance in humans was more complicated than observing and measuring dominance in monkeys. For example, whereas a woman might dominate her husband, treating him with condescension, pity or aloofness, she might also be dominated by other people, an outcome which would not be apparent if one observed her only with her husband (Maslow, 1937b: 405–7). Consequently, Maslow focussed on people's feeling of dominance, that is, the attitude which was analogous to the feeling of confidence he had observed in his dominant monkeys. He initially labelled this human attitude 'dominance-feeling' (Maslow, 1937b), but over time renamed it 'ego-level' (Maslow, 1939) and finally 'self-esteem' (Maslow, 1940b, 1942b), although he used the terms interchangeably.

This renaming was intended to avoid the power-seeking connotation of 'dominance-feeling' (Maslow, 1942b: 269). Whatever its name, the attitude was difficult to define, so he provided a list of 'near-synonyms' that dominant people used to describe their own feelings about themselves, including self-confidence, self-respect, forcefulness of personality, feelings that others do and ought to admire and respect one, and a consciousness of superiority in a general sense (Maslow, 1937b: 407). This feeling of superiority that high-dominance people experienced was a 'calm, objective recognition of facts that exist'; when factual inferiority was recognized, however, it did not lead to feelings of inferiority (Maslow, 1937b: 420).

The data on the relationship between self-esteem and sexual behavior was collected in intensive, unstructured interviews totalling, on average, about 15 hours with each subject (Maslow, 1940b: 257). Initially, Maslow interviewed both men and women, but he found that 'the men were far more evasive and tended to lie, exaggerate, or distort their sexual experiences', whereas women, once they had agreed to participate, were more open (Hoffman, 1988: 77). In addition, Maslow found that interviewing women 'was more fun – illuminating for me, the nature of women, who were certainly, to a shy boy, still mysterious' (Wilson, 1972: 157), or, as his biographer describes it, the 28-year-old Maslow 'got a thrill of excitement interviewing the women' (Hoffman, 1988: 77). Consequently, the study was limited to women.

In all, Maslow interviewed about 140 women, practically all of whom were middle-class college women between the ages of 20 and 28 (Maslow, 1942b: 270). Initially, he recruited subjects through word of mouth, but found that most of these volunteers were moderate to high in self-esteem (Maslow, 1937b: 418). In order to find more low self-esteem women, he developed a test of self-esteem (Maslow, 1940b) which he used to identify potential subjects; he then persuaded these women to 'decide to submit to interview' (Maslow, 1942b: 266).

Based on the information Maslow elicited in the interviews, he assigned each woman a score on a scale of self-esteem. He also scored both her attitude toward sex and her sex drive, with the latter rating based on such factors as the ease, intensity and frequency of climax in hetero=sexual acts and the number of everyday stimuli which were sexually arousing (Maslow, 1942b: 264). Although he calculated correlations among these scores, Maslow relied more on the qualitative relationships, the 'relationships as they impressed the experimenter' (Maslow, 1942b: 272), to draw his conclusion that a woman's sexual attitudes and behavior were more closely related to her self-esteem than to her sex drive.

Judging from the items in the self-esteem scale (Maslow, 1940b: 267–70), high self-esteem women are also male-identified. They prefer men for company in sports, intellectual activities and conversation, and consider most other women catty and petty. Not surprisingly, they dominate most of the women of their own age that they know; they also dominate most of the men of their own age that they know. In more general terms, high self-esteem women are more independent, socially poised, extroverted, relaxed and unconventional than low self-esteem women, who are timid, shy, modest, neat and retiring (Maslow, 1942b: 261).

Low self-esteem women, however, were more honest than high self-esteem women (Maslow, 1942b: 261). Maslow does not seem to have fully realized the implications of this difference. He clearly believed that, since he had established good rapport and stressed the importance of telling the truth, his subjects were completely frank (Maslow, 1939: 5) and, as a result, his ratings were valid. Consequently, the possibility that his rating of self-esteem was simply a measure of a woman's willingness to discuss sex with him, or that high self-esteem, male-identified women might have lied, exaggerated and distorted their sexual experiences (as did men) does not appear to have seriously influenced his interpretation of his results. Instead, he concluded that high self-esteem women were psychologically free and more natural, whereas low self-esteem women were inhibited and over-socialized (Maslow, 1939: 32).[1]

Maslow also concluded that among humans, and women in particular, dominance behavior is affected and inhibited by local and general cultural pressures and socialization as well as the specific situation (Maslow, 1939: 4); as a result, high self-esteem people might not always demonstrate their dominance. At the same time, however, being dominant is not always a sign of high self-esteem, since some people compensate for their low self-esteem by acting in a dominant way. Thus, Maslow had to differentiate between 'true' and 'compensatory' dominance behavior. Compensatory dominance behavior gives the impression of being 'strained and unnatural ... aggressive and louder than seems to be appropriate to the situation' (Maslow, 1937b: 418), and occurs in people who have a 'great craving' for dominance, people who 'feel weak but wish to appear strong' (Maslow, 1937b: 422, 417). This craving occurs because of emotional or psychological insecurity. While insecure people feel isolated and rejected, are suspicious of others and crave power and status, secure people feel liked or loved, trust others and have a feeling of strength (Maslow, 1942a: 334–5).

Maslow's sense of the significance of emotional security had been reinforced by his experiences among the Blackfoot in 1938. Whereas the average person in North American society in general tended to be insecure (Maslow, 1942b: 269), Maslow saw the Blackfoot as very emotionally secure, a condition that he believed was due to the adults' emphasis on instilling a sense of personal responsibility in children (Hoffman, 1988: 125). In addition, there was an almost perfect correlation between wealth and ability among 'my Blackfoot Indians' (Maslow, 1965: 137). Because of their emotional security, wealthy people were generous, giving away the goods that their ability had enabled them to acquire, and, as a result, they were admired and loved by others (Maslow, 1971: 204). Consequently, in Maslow's perception (which may or may not have been accurate), dominance in Blackfoot society had positive connotations: capable people, appropriately rewarded for their capability, benefitted their society as a whole. Much as the less dominant in chimpanzee society had no reason to fear the more dominant, the less dominant in Blackfoot society had no reason to fear the more dominant. Indeed, they had every reason to praise and support them.

The Blackfoot were also important for another reason. Maslow was originally a cultural relativist, arguing that 'we must treat the individual first as a member of a particular cultural group, and only after this can we attempt to treat him [sic] as a member of the general human species' (Maslow, 1937c: 409). However, he came to feel that 'my Indians were first human beings and *secondly* Blackfoot Indians' (Hoffman, 1988: 128, emphasis in the original). It was this feeling that led him to the concept of a 'fundamental' or 'natural' personality structure (Hoffman, 1988: 128), in other words, the universal theory of human motivation found in the needs hierarchy.

In that hierarchy, emotional security is achieved through satisfaction of the love or belongingness needs. Satisfaction of the esteem needs comes through a willing and genuine acceptance of a given individual's factual superiorities by both that individual and others. Hence, only the emotionally secure superior individual will develop the need to self-actualize. Self-actualization means taking one's place among the elite who 'enjoy responsibility' and who are 'parental or fatherly ... stern as well as loving' (Maslow, 1965: 131). A self-actualizer, because of his or her 'deep feeling of identification, sympathy and affection' for humanity in general, has a 'genuine desire to help' those 'creatures whom he [sic] must regard with, if not condescension, at least the knowledge that he can do many things better than they can, that he can see things that they cannot see' (Maslow, 1954: 217). The self-actualizing elite are able to provide this help through their clearer perception of reality, which makes their judgments a 'partial basis for a true science of values, and consequently of ethics, social relations, politics, religion, etc.' (Maslow, 1954: 204). Most important, only self-actualizers are 'fully human' (see, for example, Hoffman, 1996: 70).

Dominance and Motivation Theory

Haraway (1978a: 21) has observed that the primatology of the 1930s represented a union between the political and the physiological (see also Sperling, 1991); Maslow's needs hierarchy is the psychological outcome of that union. The psychological is based not just on the political but also on the physiological. This is explicit in the lowest of the needs in the hierarchy, the physiological needs, but also in the concept that the hierarchy itself is innate, and hence physiological or biological.

The assumption that the needs hierarchy is innate leads to both the democratic and aristocratic premises in Maslow's theory. An innate hierarchy of needs means that all people possess or have these needs: they are universal, ahistorical and not linked to gender, class or culture. At the same time, however, the biological basis of the needs hierarchy leads to its aristocratic premise. Just as only some people have the biological potential to become extremely tall while others do not, only some people have the biological potential to self-actualize while others do not. Whether or not the individual is able to develop this potential to self-actualize depends on the type of environment in which she or he lives. For Maslow, the 'good' society is one in which the 'biological elite' are given the opportunity to develop their superiority, but are protected from the 'almost inevitable malice of the biologically nongifted' (Hoffman, 1996: 71), who cannot accept the reality that their inferiority is a matter of biological chance.

This opportunity for the elite to develop their potential is particularly crucial in organizations, because of the commitment to work in self-actualizing people's lives: 'These highly evolved individuals assimilate their work into the identity, into the self, i.e., work actually becomes part of the self, part of the individual's definition of himself [sic]' (Maslow, 1965: 1). Self-actualizers are the living embodiment of the Protestant work ethic, in that '*Salvation Is a By-Product of Self-Actualizing Work and Self-Actualizing Duty*' (Maslow, 1965: 6, capitals and emphasis in the original).

Salvation is also available to the masses since proper management of the ways in which people work and earn their living 'can improve them and improve the world and in this sense be a utopian or revolutionary technique' (Maslow, 1965: 1). There are, however, limits to what proper management can achieve, in that it will be successful, and is appropriate, only when employees are already developed (Maslow, 1965: 15–33). In other words, there are limits to what even enlightened management can achieve if employees are incapable of growth.

One reason for the intuitive appeal of Maslow's theory is now apparent. In a 'good' organization, the truly superior will be able to rise to the upper levels of that organization, while the inferior will properly remain in the lower levels. Managers are entitled to their positions since they deserve them, just as subordinates deserve their positions. If managers have achieved their positions because of their recognized genuine superiority, then their dominance can be assumed to be 'of the "chimpanzee" sort, older-brotherly, responsible, affectionate, etc.' (Maslow, 1965: 18). By responsibly and affectionately directing the activities of subordinates, managers are enabling those subordinates to grow and develop. At the same time, however, a subordinate's level of growth and development is ultimately dependent not on the manager's behavior but on the limited potential that that subordinate was born with. Thus, Maslow's hierarchy justifies managerial power in organizations while minimizing managerial accountability for what occurs in those organizations.[2]

The incorporation of Maslow's needs hierarchy into other motivational theories extends these effects, while at the same time reinforcing the apparent validity of Maslow's theory. Many textbooks (see, for example, Hellriegel et al., 1995: 187, and Luthans, 1995: 154) explicitly equate the lower and higher needs in Maslow's hierarchy with, respectively, the hygiene factors and motivators in Herzberg's (1966) two-factor theory. While Herzberg (1982: 292–3) considered this comparison an act of 'creativity' on the part of textbook writers (who, according to Herzberg, are compelled to provide personal input when they write about other people's theories), the comparison gives credence to both Maslow and Herzberg.

Similarly, Porter and Lawler's (1968) expectancy theory uses a modification of Maslow's theory to specify the needs that determine which rewards for effective performance will be satisfying, valued and hence lead to greater future effort. Expectancy theory is an application of cognitive psychology, in that it explains behavior in terms of the individual's perception of environmental events (that is, in terms of whether or not an environmental event is felt to satisfy a need) rather than in terms of the environment itself. However, cognitive psychology, like Maslow's theory itself, is psychology as ideology. Focussing on the individual's subjective reactions to external events deflects an examination of those external events and thus serves to perpetuate the status quo and the interests of the powerful (Sampson, 1981), in much the same way as does attributing differences in power to biological inevitability.

The commonality between the biological and cognitive approaches is perhaps best illustrated by the moderating variable of growth need strength in Hackman and Oldham's (1980) job design application of expectancy theory. Some people, they observe, have a strong need for self-development, while others do not. The latter 'may not recognize the existence of such opportunities [for self-development], or may not value them, or may even find them threatening and balk at being "pushed" or stretched too far by their work' (Hackman and Oldham, 1980: 85). Similarly, Lawler (1992: 83) cautions that employees who do not value the higher-order needs of achievement, competence and personal growth will be frustrated rather than motivated by the work structure of involvement-oriented organizations. Again, those who cannot or will not grow will resist enlightened management's attempts to enable them to do so.

Primatology and Motivation Theory

The fundamental problem with motivation theory's use of Maslow's hierarchy is not necessarily the concept of dominance as such since, in both human and monkey societies, some individuals are able to dominate other individuals. Indeed, the study of the maintenance of patterns of dominance and subordination is an essential feature of the analysis of organizations.

Nor is the problem necessarily the hierarchy's basis in primatology data, since management theory has relied on insights drawn from other animal studies, as the example of organizational behavior modification illustrates. Skinner (see, for example, 1953) developed the principles of reinforcement theory in studies of rats and pigeons, and then applied these principles to understanding human behavior.

Rather, the issue is the nature of the animal data on which Maslow based his understanding of dominance. His assumption that it was women's self-esteem that enabled them to dominate others was based on his earlier conclusion that his monkeys' confidence had enabled them to dominate others. However, his monkeys were both caged and isolated from one another except for the brief experimental periods they spent together. The methodology of Maslow's monkey research led him to an individualistic conception of dominance, a conception which minimizes, if not ignores, the impact of the social setting and environment on the relationship between the more dominant and the less dominant.

If we rely on a theory based on animal data that was collected more than 60 years ago, we are obligated to consider the accuracy and validity of that data. While Maslow assumed that 'the behavior of caged animals differs in no *fundamental* way' from that of uncaged animals, and that the behavior of animals in the zoo or laboratory was not 'abnormal or perverted' (1936a: 268, emphasis in original), we need to consider whether or not this is the case.

In recent years, a major source of primatological data has been extended observations of free-living monkeys and apes in their natural habitats (for example, Goodall, 1990; Strum, 1987); as a consequence, primatologists' understanding of dominance, aggression and competition has been significantly revised. The focus has shifted from explanations based on a given monkey's size and physical strength to explanations based on that individual's social skills. Concurrently, there has been growing attention to the means by which monkeys use cooperation as a means of maintaining the social systems in which they live (Fedigan, 1992: xix–xx).

Most baboons and macaques, for example, live in multi-male, multi-female groups in which there are separate dominance hierarchies for each sex. Baboon and macaque societies are essentially female-bonded groups, since mothers and daughters form the permanent basis of the troop; at puberty, the males leave their original group and move to a new one (Napier and Napier, 1985: 71). Female hierarchies are relatively stable and primarily based on kinship, with the status of the mother being transferred to her daughters. While females rely on family members to maintain their position, they also form alliances with non-relatives (see, for example, Chapais, 1992; Datta, 1992).

In the adult male hierarchy, while rank is determined by age and fighting ability, it is also determined by the length of time a male has been in the group and by his ability to form and maintain alliances with other members of the group. Dominant males are not isolated superiors, but rather are enmeshed in the 'systems of social reciprocity they can actively construct' (Strum, 1987: 152) through the exchange of social favors such as grooming or assistance in times of conflict. The formation of alliances or enduring cooperative relationships is a purposive act, involving complex social skills. Each individual monkey must recognize all of the others, be aware of and take into account its own relationship with each of those others, plus be aware of and take into account the relationships among the others (de Waal, 1982: 182) before it can begin to use those relationships for its own purposes.

The experimental methods Maslow used did not permit him to see the social skills involved in establishing and maintaining dominance in non-human primate societies. As a result, he overestimated the autonomy of the dominant individual, and instead saw this individual as able to function independently and separately from others in the social setting. Concurrently, he underestimated the extent to which the dominant individual needed to pay attention to social links with others and use interpersonal skills in order to develop and maintain those links.

His focus on the characteristics of the dominant individual in turn led to his belief that differences in the way those individuals behaved caused the differences in the nature of dominance in primate societies. However, the tendency of free-living monkeys and apes to form alliances, combined with the extent to which individuals are able to leave one group and enter another, provides an alternative explanation for these differences. The dominant individual in a group in which the less dominant are constrained from leaving can intimidate and oppress those subordinates, whereas the dominant individual whose subordinates can escape must behave more considerately (de Waal, 1996: 127). This environmental interpretation of differences in dominance style would seem to have more relevance for complex social settings such as organizations than does Maslow's individualistic interpretation.

Indeed, this new interpretation suggests another reason for both the initial and continuing intuitive appeal of Maslow's theory. In times of economic growth and plentiful jobs, when employees are easily able to leave one organization for another, managers must treat those employees considerately, in order to ensure that they remain in the organization. These are precisely the conditions that existed in the 1960s, when Maslow's theory entered the management literature. Organizations were able to recruit and retain employees by appearing to allow those employees the opportunity to develop their innate potential. In times of economic downturn, when jobs are not plentiful, managers can treat employees less considerately, threatening to discard them, or actually doing so through downsizing, restructuring, reengineering and rightsizing. However, these oppressive uses of control can be disguised by the contention that the remaining employees are 'empowered', and thus still apparently allowed to develop their innate potential.

Perhaps a more intriguing aspect of current primatology's understanding of dominance, however, is the possibility that it provides for another perspective from which to view and develop theories of motivation. What would be the form of a motivation theory in which people's prime goal is to create and strengthen social bonds in order that they can survive individually and collectively? What would be the form of a motivation theory that is based on cooperation as a fundamental construct? What would be the form of a motivation theory that stresses the influence of the social and environmental setting rather than the needs and reactions of the individual? What implications would such theories have for managerial practices?

Applying insights from a discipline as contentious and contested as primatology is not without danger. If we make use of such a field, we cannot ignore its debates and changes. The point is not that it is inappropriate to rely on principles drawn from animal studies, but rather that we need to recognize the source of these principles, and the ways in which they may reflect and reproduce values and assumptions under the guise of objective science. We cannot achieve this recognition when we adopt these principles and then repeat them, mantra-like, without critical analysis. How many more examples of Maslow and his monkeys does management theory contain?

Notes

I especially want to thank Linda Fedigan for encouraging my exploration of the primatology literature. I appreciate the always valuable comments of Barbara Townley, and the supportive advice of the editors and reviewers of *Organization*. I also want to thank Karen Farkas for her careful reading of an earlier version of this paper, A.D. (Tony) Fisher for his advice about Blackfoot culture, and Hope Olson for her material support.

1. See Cullen (1994) for a more detailed critique of these studies and a discussion of their implications for the women in management literature.
2. Another reason for the intuitive appeal of Maslow's theory may lie in the ways in which it reflects and reinforces the sexuality of organizations (Hearn and Parkin, 1987) through its conflation of self-actualization with masculinity, dominance and sexuality. However, this aspect of its appeal, and the implications for the analysis of gender in organizations, will not be developed in this paper.

References

Aron, A. (1977) 'Maslow's Other Child', *Journal of Humanistic Psychology* 17(2): 9–24.
Buss, A.R. (1979) 'Humanistic Psychology as Liberal Ideology: The Socio-Historical Roots of Maslow's Theory of Self-Actualization', *Journal of Humanistic Psychology* 19(3): 43–55.
Chapais, B. (1992) 'The Role of Alliances in Social Inheritance of Rank among Female Primates', in A.H. Harcourt and F.B.M. de Waal (eds) *Coalitions and Alliances in Humans and Other Animals*, pp. 29–59. New York: Oxford University Press.
Crawford, M.P. (1939) 'The Social Psychology of the Vertebrates', *Psychological Bulletin* 36: 407–46.

Cullen, D. (1994) 'Feminism, Management and Self-Actualization', *Gender, Work and Organization* 1: 127–37.

Datta, S.B. (1992) 'Effects of Availability of Allies on Female Dominance Structure', in A.H. Harcourt and F.B.M. de Waal (eds) *Coalitions and Alliances in Humans and Other Animals*, pp. 61–82. New York: Oxford University Press.

Fedigan, L.M. (1992) *Primate Paradigms: Sex Roles and Social Bonds.* Chicago: University of Chicago Press.

Goodall, J. (1990) *Through a Window: My Thirty Years with the Chimpanzees of Gombe.* Boston, MA: Houghton Mifflin.

Greiner, L.E. (1992) 'Resistance to Change During Restructuring', *Journal of Management Inquiry* 1: 61–5.

Hackman, J.R. and Oldham, G.R. (1980) *Work Redesign.* Reading, MA: Addison-Wesley.

Haraway, D. (1978a) 'Animal Sociology and a Natural Economy of the Body Politic, Part I: A Political Physiology of Dominance', *Signs: Journal of Women in Culture and Society* 4: 21–36.

Haraway, D. (1978b) 'Animal Sociology and a Natural Economy of the Body Politic, Part II: The Past is the Contested Zone: Human Nature and Theories of Production and Reproduction in Primate Behavior Studies', *Signs: Journal of Women in Culture and Society* 4: 37–60.

Haraway, D. (1986) 'Primatology is Politics by Other Means', in R. Bleier (ed.) *Feminist Approaches to Science*, pp. 77–118. New York: Pergamon.

Haraway, D. (1989) *Primate Visions: Gender, Race, and Nature in the World of Modern Science.* New York: Routledge.

Harlow, H.F. (1974) *Learning to Love.* New York: Jason Aronson.

Hearn, J. and Parkin, W. (1987) *'Sex' at 'Work': The Power and Paradox of Organization Sexuality.* New York: St Martin's Press.

Hellriegel, D., Slocum, J.W. Jr and Woodman, R.W. (1995) *Organizational Behavior*, 7th edn. Minneapolis/St Paul: West.

Herzberg, F. (1966) *Work and the Nature of Man.* New York: New American Library.

Herzberg, F. (1982) *The Managerial Choice: To be Efficient and to be Human.* Salt Lake City, UT: Olympus Publishing Co.

Hoffman, E. (1988) *The Right to be Human.* Los Angeles: Jeremy P. Tarcher.

Hoffman, E., ed. (1996) *Future Visions: The Unpublished Papers of Abraham Maslow.* Thousand Oaks, CA: Sage.

Huczynski, A.A. (1993) *Management Gurus: What Makes Them and How to Become One.* London: Routledge.

Lawler, E.E. III (1992) *The Ultimate Advantage: Creating the High-Involvement Organization.* San Francisco, CA: Jossey-Bass.

Lowry, R.J., ed. (1973) *Dominance, Self-esteem, Self-actualization: Germinal Papers of A. H. Maslow.* Monterey, CA: Brooks/Cole.

Lowry, R.J., ed. (1982) The *Journals of Abraham Maslow.* Lexington, MA: Lewis.

Luthans, F. (1995) *Organizational Behavior*, 7th edn. New York: McGraw-Hill.

Maslow, A.H. (1935) 'Individual Psychology and the Social Behavior of Monkeys and Apes', *International Journal of Individual Psychology* 1: 47–59.

Maslow, A.H. (1936a) 'The Role of Dominance in the Social and Sexual Behavior of Infra-Human Primates: I. Observations at Vilas Park Zoo', *Journal of Genetic Psychology* 48: 261–77.

Maslow, A.H. (1936b) 'The Role of Dominance in the Social and Sexual Behavior of Infra-Human Primates: III. A Theory of Sexual Behavior of Infra-Human Primates', *Journal of Genetic Psychology* 48: 310–38.

Maslow, A.H. (1936c) 'The Role of Dominance in the Social and Sexual Behavior of Infra-Human Primates: IV. The Determination of Hierarchy in Pairs and in a Group', *Journal of Genetic Psychology* 49: 161–98.

Maslow, A.H. (1937a) 'The Comparative Approach to Social Behavior', *Social Forces* 15: 487–90.

Maslow, A.H. (1937b) 'Dominance-Feeling, Behavior, and Status', *Psychological Review* 44: 404–29.

Maslow, A.H. (1937c) 'Personality and Patterns of Culture', in R. Stagner *Psychology of Personality*, pp. 408–28. New York: McGraw-Hill.

Maslow, A.H. (1939) 'Dominance-Feeling, Personality and Social Behavior in Women', *Journal of Social Psychology* 10: 3–39.

Maslow, A.H. (1940a) 'Dominance-Quality and Social Behavior in Infra-Human Primates', *Journal of Social Psychology* 11: 313–24.

Maslow, A.H. (1940b) 'A Test for Dominance-Feeling (Self-Esteem) in College Women', *Journal of Social Psychology* 12: 255–70.

Maslow, A.H. (1942a) 'The Dynamics of Psychological Security–Insecurity', *Character and Personality* 10: 331–44.

Maslow, A.H. (1942b) 'Self-Esteem (Dominance-Feeling) and Sexuality in Women', *Journal of Social Psychology* 16: 259–94.

Maslow, A.H. (1943) 'A Theory of Human Motivation', *Psychological Review* 50: 370–96.

Maslow, A.H. (1954) *Motivation and Personality*. New York: Harper.

Maslow, A.H. (1965) *Eupsychian Management*. Homewood, IL: Irwin.

Maslow, A.H. (1971) *The Farther Reaches of Human Nature*. New York: Viking.

Maslow, A.H. and Flanzbaum, S. (1936) 'The Role of Dominance in the Social and Sexual Behavior of Infra-Human Primates: II. An Experimental Determination of the Behavior Syndrome of Dominance', *Journal of Genetic Psychology* 48: 278–309.

Maslow, A.H. and Mittelmann, B. (1941) *Principles of Abnormal Psychology: The Dynamics of Psychic Illness*. New York: Harper.

Mitchell, V.F. and Moudgill, P. (1976) 'Measurement of Maslow's Need Hierarchy', *Organizational Behavior and Human Performance* 16: 334–49.

Moorhead, G. and Griffin, R.W. (1995) *Organizational Behavior*, 4th edn. Boston, MA: Houghton Mifflin.

Napier, J.R. and Napier, P.H. (1985) *The Natural History of the Primates*. Cambridge, MA: MIT Press.

Porter, L.W. and Lawler, E.E. III (1968) *Managerial Attitudes and Performance*. Homewood, IL: Irwin.

Rowell, T.E. (1974) 'The Concept of Social Dominance', *Behavioral Biology* 11: 131–54.

Sampson, E.E. (1981) 'Cognitive Psychology as Ideology', *American Psychologist* 36: 730–43.

Shaw, R. and Colimore, K. (1988) 'Humanistic Psychology as Ideology: An Analysis of Maslow's Contradictions', *Journal of Humanistic Psychology* 28(3): 51–74.

Skinner, B.F. (1953) *Science and Human Behavior*. New York: Macmillan.

Sperling, S. (1991) 'Baboons with Briefcases vs. Langurs in Lipstick: Feminism and Functionalism in Primate Studies', in M. di Leonardo (ed.) *Gender at the Crossroads of Knowledge: Feminist Anthropology in the Postmodern Era*, pp. 204–34. Berkeley: University of California Press.

Strum, S.C. (1987) *Almost Human: A Journey into the World of Baboons*. New York: Random House.

Suomi, S.J. and LeRoy, H.A. (1982) 'In Memoriam: Harry Harlow (1905–1981)', *American Journal of Primatology* 2: 319–42.

de Waal, F. (1982) *Chimpanzee Politics: Power and Sex among Apes*. New York: Harper & Row.

de Waal, F. (1996) *Good Natured: The Origins of Right and Wrong in Humans and Other Animals*. Cambridge, MA: Harvard University Press.

Wahba, M.A. and Bridwell, L.G. (1976) 'Maslow Reconsidered: A Review of Research on the Need Hierarchy Theory', *Organizational Behavior and Human Performance* 15: 212–40.

Wilson, C. (1972) New *Pathways in Psychology: Maslow and the Post-Freudian Revolution.* London: Victor Gollancz.

Yerkes, R.M. (1939) 'Social Dominance and Sexual Status in the Chimpanzee', *The Quarterly Review of Biology* 14: 115–36.

Yerkes, R.M. and Yerkes, A.W. (1929) *The Great Apes: A Study of Anthropoid Life.* New Haven, CT: Yale University Press.

Zuckerman, S. (1932) *The Social Life of Monkeys and Apes.* London: Kegan.

43

Maslow's Theory of Motivation: A Critique

Andrew Neher

This critique will evaluate Abraham Maslow's theory of motivation, including each of its basic propositions. Although other critics have addressed various aspects of Maslow's theory, no one, as far as I know, has taken on Maslow's basic theory *in toto*.

Two decades after his death, Maslow is still revered as one of the founders and guiding lights of humanistic psychology. Unfortunately, humanistic psychologists have yet to probe the flaws in Maslow's theory in any concerted or thorough fashion. Why is this? Maybe it stems from motivations such as loyalty to the cause, but it may also relate to the tendency of humanistic psychologists to be "accepting" rather than "critical."

Of course, Maslow is known outside of humanistic psychology circles. Maslow himself sought to apply his theory to fields in the borderlands of psychology, where it still wields influence in some quarters – for example in the fields of management (Maslow, 1967), religion (Maslow, 1964), and science (Maslow, 1969). In addition, Maslow is routinely cited when general psychology texts discuss humanistic psychology. Texts in "adjustment" courses, in particular, tend to pay him much attention, sometimes to the extent of recommending that students evaluate their own lives to see how well they conform to Maslow's ideas concerning the "good life."

On the other hand – the field of management excepted (e.g., Huizinga, 1970) – Maslow is seldom cited in the research literature on motivation, which means that his theory, to a significant extent, lies outside the mainstream of testing and critical evaluation that is the lifeblood of any vital theory.

Source: *Journal of Humanistic Psychology*, 31(3) (1991): 89–112.

Thus there are many reasons to take a close look at Maslow's theory and bring its flaws into the light of day. This article is a contribution to that effort.

Maslow's Theory Outlined

Most of Maslow's basic theory is found in the 1970 edition of his book, *Motivation and Personality*, although I will draw from some of his other works from time to time. According to his theory

1. Each of us is endowed at birth with a full and, to an important extent, unique complement of needs that, allowed expression by our environment, will guide our growth in a healthy direction.
2. These needs function in a hierarchical manner. The bottom step of Maslow's 5-step hierarchy, or pyramid, includes physiological needs (for food, water, and so on). Then come safety needs; next, needs for love and intimacy; then self-esteem needs; and, finally, at the apex of the pyramid, self-actualization (e.g., intellectual and esthetic) needs. By *hierarchy* is meant that needs lower on the pyramid must generally be satisfied before needs at higher levels are "activated." For example, starving people (deprived on level one) will find it difficult to be very concerned about their relationships with others (needs on level three) until they are fed.
3. Needs on the first four levels are called deficiency-needs (or D-needs) because they drive us to gratify the need, at which point the need lapses in its importance to us until deprivation again motivates us to take action to satisfy the need. Self-actualization needs (on the fifth and highest level), on the other hand, are called being-needs (or B-needs) because, among other unique features, they sustain our interest without our being driven by feelings of deprivation.
4. The level of self-actualization, the end-point of the process outlined above, constitutes the highest level of human experience.

To illustrate his theory, Maslow described a number of people he considered self-actualizers, including such well-known figures as Abraham Lincoln and Eleanor Roosevelt. All of these people, according to Maslow, share various personality traits (which Maslow subsumed under rubrics such as being-cognition and being-values). These include being relatively creative, spontaneous, able to see the "large picture," nonjudgmental, and rich in emotional life; in particular, self-actualizers are more apt to experience euphoric heights of emotion that Maslow labeled peak experience.

To summarize, we are born with certain needs, some of which, such as hunger, are prepotent in that they occupy our attention until they are satisfied. But such motivations are not what make us fully human. Only by living a life in which these lower needs are satisfied can we rise to our full human potential, becoming self-actualized, as we free ourselves to become involved in higher pursuits such as art, literature, and science, and to experience the finer human qualities of broad understanding, tolerance, and the sublime emotions.

Stated in rough outline, Maslow's theory finds ready acceptance with many people. The theory seems reasonable and fits many of our preconceptions: For example, of course hungry people are concerned with little else besides finding food. But as we take a closer look we will see that almost every aspect of Maslow's theory is burdened with a multitude of problems.

We will see that many of these problems stem from the extreme stands that his theory, as a close examination will show, tends to take. The problem of overstatement is not unique, of course, to Maslow. It is a common trait of theorists who attempt, as Maslow did, to develop a perspective in opposition to prevailing theories. In Maslow's case, the prevailing theories of motivation stemmed from psychoanalysis on the one hand and behaviorism on the other. Thus we should not be surprised that Maslow overstated his case in an attempt to make his theory distinctive when compared with competing theories.

Other problems involve some of Maslow's more peripheral statements that contradict many of the assumptions of his own theory. To some extent, Maslow seemed to have second thoughts about his theory, but these modifications never filtered down to his general theoretical statements. This might have been intentional, in part, because these qualifications to his theory have the effect, as we shall see, of "watering it down" and making it less distinctive. But perhaps the most significant basis of these inconsistencies was Maslow's tendency, which he himself recognized, to be impressionistic, rather than conceptually rigorous, in his thinking and writing (Daniels, 1982, pp. 62, 70–71).

Finally, still other problems concern the internal logic of his theory.

Maslow's Theory Critiqued

Let us evaluate the various components of Maslow's theory in the order that they were presented earlier.

1. *Each of us is endowed at birth with a complete, and, to some extent, unique complement of needs that, allowed expression by our environment, will foster our growth in a healthy direction* (Maslow, 1970, pp. 77–104). Few psychologists would disagree that our lower needs in general (hunger, need for intimacy, and so on) are innate. But many would question whether, in general, the higher needs (intellectual, esthetic) are innate as Maslow claimed (1970, pp. 100–101). Although there is good evidence for the innate nature of some of the higher needs (e.g., the curiosity drive; Eisenberger, 1972), others, such as esthetic motivations, are probably largely shaped by cultural experience. Maslow's tendency to downgrade the role of the environment in

forming the human psyche has been noted by several critics (e.g., Aron, 1977; Daniels, 1982; Geller, 1982; Smith, 1973) and seems to be related to his rejection of the behaviorist perspective, which traditionally committed the opposite error of viewing environmental influence as all-important (Maslow, 1970, pp. 88–89). According to Maslow,

> once [lower needs are met] each person proceeds to develop in his own style, uniquely, using these necessities for his own private purposes. In a very meaningful sense, development then becomes determined from within rather than from without.... The role of the environment is ultimately to permit him or help him to actualize *his own* potentialities [because] *he* "knows" better than anyone else what is good for him. (1968, pp. 34, 160, 198)

To sum up, Maslow believed that, given basic support and nurturance from the environment, our inborn needs are sufficient to foster our psychological growth in a healthy direction.

Thus it is clear that Maslow is squarely in the camp of the nativists, who stress the role of hereditary influences in human experience. In this regard, he is in accord with many other humanistic psychologists (e.g., Carl Rogers) and, as a consequence, suffers along with them from a number of difficulties.

If the most culture can do, or should do, is provide for basic needs and freedom of expression, then most of the structure of cultures around the world must be viewed as potentially disruptive. In particular, child-rearing practices may conflict with innate needs of children to develop in directions other than those sanctioned by the culture. As Maslow said, "Our human instincts [including our needs] are so weak that they need protection against culture, against learning – in a word, against being overwhelmed by the environment" (1970, p. 103). Of course, as Maslow admitted (1970, p. 278), our culture is relatively tolerant, but he believed that we still need to tip "the balance [even more] in favor of spontaneity, the ability to be expressive... creative, etc." (1968, p. 198).

Let us take Maslow at his word, and let us take language as our example. According to the widely accepted Sapir-Whorf hypothesis, the particular language we speak determines to some extent the way in which we are able to think about the world (Whorf, 1956). If this is so, then teaching our own language to our children has the effect, in part, of putting their thoughts in an intellectual straitjacket – perhaps, unfortunately, in ways that conflict with their innate needs to conceptualize the world in their own unique fashion. So perhaps we should "protect" our children from hearing our language so that they can create their own. But, of course, we know that, although children inherit a genetic ability to learn language that they hear in their environment (Piattelli-Palmarini, 1980), they do not inherit the ability to create, from scratch, their own language (Malson, 1972). And, if they could, can you imagine the problem of attempting to communicate with one another, each of us in a different language? Much the same could be said, of course, of a multitude of other cultural traits that serve as a common basis for human relations in any culture.

One way to understand our need to learn the folkways of our culture is to remember that the trend in human evolution has been away from strong genetic programming. Instead, we develop our "humaness," to a significant extent, through being socialized into the norms of our particular culture. In fact, our genetic heritage seems to consist, to a large degree, of a potential to adapt to any of the wide variety of cultures that have ever existed; that is, our genetic endowment seems very flexible in this regard. And, although we each inherit a unique mix of needs and potentials, these require for their development a context of cultural inputs (language, and so on) that are, at least initially, imposed upon us. This is because, as young children, our nervous systems are not sufficiently developed to allow us to choose from among these inputs. Of course, parents should be sensitive to their childrens' unique individual needs, but it is hardly possible to tailor basic cultural inputs (language is a good example) to the individual. Naturally, as we mature most of us are increasingly able to choose the life experiences that best "fit" us, but these choices are a product of the unique mix of genes and culture that each of us embodies by the time we are old enough to make these choices.

In sum, Maslow's list of needs ignores considerations such as these. It does not include the need to learn language or any of the other cultural traits that create our humanness and bind us socially. To repeat, his theory implies that the imposition of cultural norms is unnecessary at best, and, at worst, destructive of our unique potential as individuals. In this regard, he and many other humanistic psychologists are in the mainstream of Western values that tend to glorify the individual.

Maslow's failure to acknowledge the need to learn cultural norms may have stemmed from more than one source. On the one hand, he may have assumed that, with the advent of pluralistic societies such as ours, we all need to pick and choose our own path, and that the best basis for this is the unique mix of needs we each inherit. But, as has already been pointed out, this assumption is undermined by the fact that we are helpless as children to "pick and choose" until we have already been socialized into the language patterns and other basic norms of our particular culture. Of course, if Maslow's theory does apply only to pluralistic societies, then it is culture specific rather than universal in application. On the other hand, Maslow may have been reacting against the obvious failures of our own society, his solution being to base human development on the "wisdom" of the unique biological makeup of each of us rather than on bankrupt cultural priorities. However, a good argument can be made that extreme individualism, whether or not it is founded on the notions of individual biological uniqueness that Maslow favored, in fact, fosters much of the social alienation and dehumanization that plagues our society. One critic noted the "irony that those as deeply concerned about the human condition as ... Maslow ... should have developed a theory the practical recommendations of which sustain and strengthen the very dehumanization against which in part they are reacting" (Geller, 1982, p. 72).

Thus the nativist position is more than just a theoretical issue. For example, we have all known parents who have hesitated to "put their own trip" on their child, for fear of violating their child's unique nature, to the point where they became ineffective as parents. And we have all known children who have, in conformance with pop-psych beliefs, agonized over who the "real me" is as distinct from the "me whom my parents created." But these hesitancies and agonies, of course, are predicated on the notion that there is a more or less complete, original "me" waiting to blossom given only a nurturing and accepting, but otherwise neutral environment. So whether or not the assumptions of Maslow – and other nativists such as Carl Rogers – are valid is a very significant question, with very real ramifications.

Another difficulty with the nativist position concerns its internal logic. If all that we require to become self-actualized is that our culture provide for our basic needs and freedom of expression, then our genetic potential is indeed potent. As Maslow said, our "inner nature ... tends strongly to persist" (1968, p. 190). But, if this is so, then why was Maslow, in agreement with many other humanistic psychologists, so fearful that our culture will misdirect us in ways that violate this potential? Elsewhere Maslow said that "this inner nature ... is weak and delicate ... and easily overcome by ... cultural pressure" (1968, p. 4). Maslow seemed to want it both ways – a *strong* innate tendency to self-actualize on the one hand, but also a disturbing *weakness* in the face of cultural dictates on the other. But, of course, he cannot have it both ways. At least one assumption must be wrong – or, more likely, less extreme versions of both might be correct.

A final issue related to Maslow's nativist position concerns values rather than logic. Along with other nativists, Maslow maintained, in essence, that we have to live with whatever the genetic roll of the dice provides us, because environmental influences (other than providing for our needs) are viewed either as relatively insignificant or as potentially insensitive to our innate tendencies (Daniels, 1988, p. 25). Where behaviorists have traditionally said "You can become whatever you want, and we'll show you how," Maslow, and other nativist theorists, have said, "You can become what your native potential allows you to become, and nothing else." Although the behaviorists are undoubtedly overly optimistic in their view, Maslow seems overly pessimistic. In this case, Maslow goes *against* the grain of Western values, which maintain that practically unlimited possibilities are open to any of us.

To summarize, Maslow's tendency to emphasize the role of our innate needs in directing the course of healthy psychological development, and his tendency to downgrade the importance of cultural input in this process, leads to a view of human development that is one-sided and consequently very difficult to support. Thus we start to see some of the problems that stem from Maslow's tendency to take extreme stands.

Now let us move ahead and examine the second component of Maslow's theory.

2. *Our needs function in a hierarchical fashion, so that our basic needs (for food, etc.) are prepotent, in that generally they must be satisfied before we can feel "free" of them and move on to satisfy our higher needs* (Maslow, 1970, pp. 35–51). Actually, in advanced societies our physiological and safety needs (the first two steps on Maslow's need-pyramid) are often satisfied, whereas the next two steps – needs for love and for self-esteem – constitute stumbling blocks for many people. In simpler societies, on the other hand, the situation is often the reverse. In such societies, people may periodically go hungry and suffer from life-threatening illnesses, but nevertheless, unless these problems are severe (Turnbull, 1974), people in these societies typically exhibit strong social ties and a strong sense of self. In fact, it appears that a certain degree of hardship in meeting basic needs can bring people together and give them a sense of purpose as they cooperate to overcome adversity. Most of us can probably recall experiences of our own that illustrate this process. For example, many couples say that struggling together to make ends meet when they were young fostered strong bonds between them, compared with their later years when they had finally achieved a life of ease and comfort. If these examples are valid, they stand Maslow's need-hierarchy on its head: In these instances, deprivation at lower-need levels (survival needs) seems to facilitate need satisfaction at higher levels (e.g., the achievement of intimacy) rather than hinder it as Maslow would predict.

Aside from such anecdotal evidence, some researchers, particularly in the field of management, have attempted to test Maslow's hierarchy in a more systematic fashion. In general, these researchers have wanted to determine if Maslow's theory can clarify the factors involved in job choice and job satisfaction. Here is a sampling of these studies, many of which are summarized in Wahba and Bridwell (1979).

Some of these studies have been designed to test Maslow's particular ordering of needs in his hierarchy. Briefly, the results of these studies are equivocal; results range from some support (Graham & Balloun, 1973; Mathes, 1981; Wuthnow, 1978), to no support (Miner & Dachler, 1973), to outright refutation (Wofford, 1971).

Other studies have attempted to test Maslow's assertion that need satisfaction leads to a diminution of that need in the future. These studies show a similar spread, from some support (Alderfer, 1969; Graham & Balloun, 1973), to no support (Lawler & Suttle, 1972), to results that indicate that need-satisfaction leads to *heightened* salience of the need (Hall & Norigaim, 1968)!

Obviously the research picture is rather equivocal. However, research of this nature seldom yields definitive answers and should not be considered, in and of itself, the last word. Thus let us take a closer look at Maslow's assertion that "need gratification diminishes the strength of the need," because, in spite of its quality of seeming obvious, I believe it is highly questionable.

First of all, no one denies that need satisfaction leads to a temporary decrease in the strength of a need. But most needs are cyclical, in that they are satisfied for a time, only to resurface later. Hunger and sex are obvious examples. What Maslow meant is that, over the long term, the strength of a need that is readily and easily satisfied will decline. For example: "If a mother kisses her child often, the drive itself disappears and the child learns *not* to crave kisses" (Maslow, 1970, p. 63). As with much of Maslow's theory, this statement seems reasonable at first glance. It certainly ties in with much of our experience, as well as with other theories, such as psychoanalysis, that are widely accepted: When we express our needs, we are less "bothered" by them. But there is another possibility. Behaviorists would probably maintain that kissing, for example, is usually *more* valued by adults than by children, partly because of the pleasures that have been associated with it on so many different occasions. And, strangely enough, we can probably all think of examples from our own experience that support this alternative perspective. So which is it? Over the long term, do needs "dry up" or "well up" when they are satisfied? Unfortunately, there is no ready answer to this question, and psychologists remain divided on the issue. If Maslow meant that we should oversatiate our needs (e.g., eat until we are sick of eating) then we would probably agree that needs would tend to "dry up," but there is no indication that he had this in mind. The point is that Maslow's assumption – that satisfying needs reduces their strength in the long run, which is so crucial to his theory as a whole – is much more tenuous than he indicated. It is important to keep in mind that Maslow put himself in such a tenuous position because he was intent on eliminating the lower needs, in this process, as a motivational force in our lives; this was his prescription for moving up the needs hierarchy to the level of self-actualization.

At this point, we need to examine another of Maslow's assumptions that is not obvious on first inspection – namely, that the highest level in his need hierarchy, self-actualization, is, ideally, autonomous. It is obvious that our motivations to engage in creative, intellectual, or esthetic pursuits (pursuits on the highest level of the hierarchy) may, in fact, stem from lower needs – such as needs to gain social recognition, enhance our self-esteem, or even, perhaps, to satisfy physiological survival drives. In general, both psychoanalysts and behaviorists would agree with this view, citing mechanisms such as sublimation on the one hand and conditioned associations on the other. Maslow himself made the point that "the cognitive capacities ... are a set of adjustive tools, which have, among other functions, that of satisfaction of our basic needs. ... Acquiring knowledge and systematizing the universe [are], in part, techniques for the achievement of basic safety in the world" (1970, pp. 47–48). But, of course, it is central to Maslow's theory that these lower motivations, when they are present, detract from the true essence of self-actualization. In Maslow's theory, remember, the road to self-actualization requires having already satisfied these basic needs. This means that Maslow must, as he said, "distinguish the artistic and intellectual products of basically satisfied people from those of basically unsatisfied people" (1970, p. 46), to make sure their accomplishments are not contaminated by lower needs. Not an easy task.

If the self-actualization needs are, ideally, autonomous, how then did Maslow explain the mechanism through which this occurs? His main theme, of course, was that the self-actualization needs evolved biologically (Maslow, 1970, pp. 100–101). The problem was that he was not clear how this came about. Now, our higher needs might have evolved to serve lower needs, and/or they might have evolved because they are adaptive in their own right. If they evolved to meet our lower needs, then we must somehow explain how, on a biological level, they have become autonomous. If they evolved because they are adaptive in their own right, we must postulate that creative, intellectual, and artistic endeavors facilitate survival in and of themselves and thus have been incorporated into the gene pool. As far as I know, Maslow never discussed these possibilities. Maslow's chief explanation for the autonomous nature of the self-actualization needs invoked Gordon Allport's (1937) notion of "functional autonomy [in which the higher need] develops only on the basis of the lower, but eventually, when well established, may become *relatively* independent of the lower" (Maslow, 1970, pp. 103–104). For example, consider the following scenario: Let us imagine that you have a natural talent for music for which you are praised (which satisfies social recognition and self-esteem needs) in your younger years. As you grow up, your interest in music itself is enhanced because of its association with social rewards, and thus you develop your musical skills more and more "for their own sake." Also, behaviorists would predict this increasingly autonomous interest in music on the basis that the "schedule" of social reinforcement becomes intermittent and unpredictable. But, as reasonable as this scenario is, it is a poor fit with the rest of Maslow's theory. It requires some initial degree of lower-need deprivation, which violates his conception of the self-actualizing process, and, because it derives from an environmentalist perspective, it goes against the grain of his biological bias. Actually, it is questionable whether Maslow truly understood the implications of the functional autonomy theory. In sum, Maslow never adequately accounted, as far as I can determine, for the autonomous nature that he postulated for the self-actualization needs.

Now let us address in greater detail Maslow's belief that satiation of lower needs leads to self-actualization. This is such an important assertion that we need to be clear concerning what Maslow said about it: "Gratification of any basic need ... is a move in the healthy direction" (1970, pp. 61–62), and "a man who is thwarted in any of his basic needs may fairly be envisioned simply as ... less than fully human" (1970, p. 57). Seems pretty clear. Then what can we make of a statement such as "the *complete absence* of frustration, pain or danger is dangerous. To be strong, a person must acquire frustration-tolerance" (1968, p. 200). Obviously there is a contradiction here: Maslow said that thwarting of basic needs is unhealthy, but also that lack of frustration is unhealthy. Despite such contradictions, it is clear that Maslow's theory favors a high level of need satisfaction. So let us go back to his basic theoretical position and see why, in fact, it does present great difficulties. Let us imagine what kind of circumstances would produce consistent gratification, remembering that partial gratification will produce less movement toward self-actualization. Using the hunger drive as an example, perhaps the only way that consistent gratification could be achieved is through eating small amounts of food almost continuously (although intravenous feeding would achieve a similar result). We can imagine similar conditions for other needs – for example, sexual gratification should be available just as soon as the urge arises. Do not make the mistake of dismissing this as farfetched. To the extent we allow ourselves to be hungry, or sexually unsatisfied, our efforts will be directed towards satisfying our lower needs rather than towards self-actualization. Following this logic, then, parents who want to raise self-actualized children should strive to meet their basic needs as soon as they arise, ideally before the children begin to feel much deprivation or motivation to make efforts to satisfy these needs. Now, if you are beginning to think that this approach might lead to problems, you are not alone. Researchers have found, not surprisingly, that parents who "pamper, indulge, and fawn over the youngster in such ways as to teach him that his every wish is a command to others" (Millon, 1969, p. 263) tend to raise children who are narcissistic, are exploitive of others, have little self-control, and lack competency skills (Millon, 1969, pp. 261–266). In fact, there are many threads of research and theory in psychology that postulate, contrary to Maslow, that some frustration and deprivation is necessary for healthy psychological development. Among these are (a) Robert White's competence theory (1959), (b) Yerkes-Dodson's law (Yerkes & Dodson, 1908), (c) Hans Selye's eustress theory (1974), and (d) Alfred Adler's compensation theory (Ansbacher & Ansbacher, 1959).

In fact, these perspectives are far from esoteric; their essence can be found in any number of self-help books written for the general public (e.g., Bloomfield & Felder, 1985; Brown, 1983; Houston, 1981).

In spite of their differences, all of these perspectives agree on one or more of the following points: (a) that a moderate amount of deprivation stimulates our creative potential; (b) that this keeps us motivated and interested in life; and (c) that this leads to a sense of competence that helps us deal with the vicissitudes of living. Nietzsche said it in a particularly pithy (and extreme) fashion: "What does not kill me makes me stronger."

In addition, research indicates that some degree of deprivation, and thus challenge, are necessary to keep us from feeling bored. In particular, this research indicates a connection between low levels of deprivation and psychosomatic illness (Goldberg, 1978). Note that this finding also conflicts with the widely noted position of Holmes and Rahe (1967), who, along with Maslow, believe that the less deprivation and stress (in their theory, stress that arises from having to adjust to change) the better. George Bernard Shaw's memorable comment on the matter is certainly an overstatement, but it clearly states the alternative view to Maslow's: "The only thing worse than not getting what you want is getting what you want."

Finally, it might be said that conditions that allow for consistent gratification of needs are probably only possible in advanced affluent societies such as ours. In fact, Maslow's theory could be considered elitist in this regard (Smith, 1973, p. 29). This also makes it difficult to image the evolutionary conditions that would give rise to a self-actualization potential which could be realized only in a society that didn't come into being until recently.

So where did Maslow go wrong? His error, I think, lies in overstating his position. We can all agree that extreme need deprivation is ordinarily psychologically damaging. But this doesn't mean that the opposite condition, extreme ease of need gratification, is psychologically healthy. As with many issues, a moderate position is the most defensible.

Of course, as we have seen, Maslow did vacillate on this issue. This is understandable when we realize, on the one hand, how important his absolutist stand is to his theory as a whole. After all, if some deprivation is psychologically healthy, then not only does his theory lose much of its distinctiveness, but its chain of reasoning loses one of its crucial links: if we are deprived at lower-need levels, how then, in Maslow's way of thinking, are we able to move up the need hierarchy and become fully self-actualized? On the other hand, as we have also seen, Maslow experienced great difficulty maintaining his absolutist stand in the face of so much opposing theory and research.

Now we are ready to discuss the third component of Maslow's theory.

3. *The self-actualization needs differ qualitatively from the lower (or "deficiency") needs in that they motivate us in the absence of a sense of deficiency – hence they are called "being" needs* (Maslow, 1968, pp. 29–37). As Maslow said, being motivation involves a state "of desirelessness, purposelessness, [and] lack of D-need (deficiency-need)" (1971, p. 128). If Maslow were referring to the psychological state that often persists for a period following the gratification of a need, this would be an obvious statement. However, it is clear that he was describing a more or less ongoing level of functioning. Now we can grant that, for example, compared with eating a meal, there is a different feeling associated with creating art, writing literature, or getting involved in a favorite building project. Our involvement with these activities seems self-sustaining, persistent, and intrinsically rewarding, and this is certainly the quality that Maslow tried to capture in his theory. But we have seen that, when it comes to Maslow's theory, initial impressions are often misleading. So let us take a closer look at this aspect of his theory.

Let us begin by examining the logic of Maslow's assumption that we can be motivated in the absence of a sense of deficiency. Another way to state this is that we can be motivated to gain or achieve something *even though we don't lack it* in the first place. Not very logical. As Salvatore Maddi says, "In order to define a motive, you must specify a goal state that is to be achieved. ... And once you define a goal, you are of necessity assuring that the person having the motive is in a deprived state until he reaches the goal" (1968, p. 83). Think about your own experiences with higher-level needs. Don't you find yourself setting goals, perhaps very long-range goals, but goals that consist of something you lack at present? If you achieve your goals, don't you typically set new goals for yourself, and the cycle repeats itself? Certainly this has a different quality than eating a meal, but the difference doesn't seem to have to do with deficiency, as Maslow maintained. Rather, the difference seems to involve such matters as experiencing greater freedom to *choose* higher-level motivations, or challenges – deprivations if you will – that are practically unlimited in their potential scope. These characteristics of higher-order motivations might arise because a wide variety of such motivations can meet a multitude of lower-level needs or because these motivations have truly become functionally autonomous or both. In any case, the basis of the distinctiveness of the self-actualization needs seems not to hinge on the absence of a sense of deprivation.

Maslow's discontent with motivation based on deprivation stemmed from his rejection of the traditional behaviorist position, which postulated tension or drive reduction – that is, overcoming deprivation, especially with respect to basic needs – as the sole basis of motivation (Maslow, 1968, p. 38). Behaviorists traditionally ignored higher drives such as curiosity and exploration, which seem to involve pursuing challenges and thus heightened drive states (Berlyne, 1960). However, it now appears that these higher drives are capable of being satiated, at least in some species (Eisenberger, 1972). Because satiation implies a prior state of deprivation, these findings call into question Maslow's assumption that these higher motives operate in the absence of feelings of deprivation.

To sum up, what appears to be unique about higher-order needs is not the absence of feelings of deprivation, but rather a number of other characteristics, including the purposeful choosing of challenges, and thus deprivations, which can provide almost limitless motivation and satisfaction.

Now we come to the final component of Maslow's theory of motivation.

4. *The level of self-actualization, which is the end-point of the process outlined above, constitutes the highest level of human experience* (Maslow, 1970, pp. 149–180; Maslow, 1971). Let us start with a quotation from Maslow: "Western civilization has generally believed that the animal in us was a bad animal" (1970, pp. 82–83). So, to some extent, does Eastern civilization, and most important, so, to some extent, did Maslow. Where Maslow differed from both Western and Eastern traditions is in the route he favored to overcome

our animal nature, by which he meant our basic needs that we share with other animals – needs for food, sex, and so on. You will remember that Maslow's prescription runs as follows: 'The easiest technique for releasing the organism from the bondage of the lower ... needs is to gratify them" (1970, p. 61). Of course, we have already seen that it is questionable whether this approach is effective, but how does it compare with more traditional approaches? Now, traditionally in both East and West, the most common way to overcome lower needs is to deny and to suppress them. Of course, Maslow's approach probably fits our modern-day affluent society much better, which often seems to believe that the best way to overcome temptation is to give in to it. But Maslow's value judgment is the same as the traditional one – that a part of our basic biological makeup is sufficiently unworthy that it should be eliminated as an important concern in our lives (Daniels, 1988, p. 23). You may agree or disagree with Maslow's value judgment (it makes little sense to me), but, for a theorist such as Maslow, who claimed to be taking his lead from basic biological characteristics, it seems strangely nonbiological.

Why are these lower needs seen as unworthy (the term *lower* itself reinforces this assumption)? Maslow, in particular, considered them lower partly because he believed that they are basically selfish in nature (Maslow, 1968, p. 202). However, research in sociobiology has demonstrated that many lower drives, including the traditional archvillain, sex, are, biologically speaking, largely altruistic in nature. For example, animals will sometimes risk their own lives to conceive, or later to protect, their offspring (Wilson, 1980).

Moving on to the characteristics of people who have attained self-actualization, Maslow once more had difficulty being consistent. We already know that 'The perfectly healthy [self-actualized] man has no sex needs or hunger needs, or needs for safety, or for love, or for prestige, or self-esteem" (Maslow, 1970, p. 57). But elsewhere Maslow maintained that self-actualized people "tend to be good animals, hearty in their appetites and enjoying themselves without regret or shame or apology" (1970, p. 156). Of course, it makes no sense to say that people with no hunger needs are hearty in their appetites. This is yet another instance of Maslow contradicting Maslow.

Maslow also granted that need satisfaction is not the only route to self-actualization: 'There are apparently innately creative people in whom the drive to creativeness seems to be more important than any other counter-determinant" (1970, p. 52). By this, Maslow meant that some people are chiefly motivated by higher-level needs even though they have failed to satisfy needs lower in the hierarchy. Examples would include artists or scientists who are so wrapped up in their work that they forgo eating, or sex, or meaningful relationships of any kind, for lengthy periods.

Finally, Maslow admitted that his formula – satisfying lower needs is the way to achieve self-actualization – does not always work: "I have individual subjects in whom apparent basic-need-gratification is compatible with 'existential neurosis,' meaninglessness, valuelessness, or the like" (1971, pp. 300–301). Maslow suggested that, to deal with this difficulty, he needed to modify his basic theory: "It is now more clear to me that gratification of the basic needs is not a sufficient condition for self-actualization" (1971, p. 300). And this is indeed a drastic modification. What, then, did Maslow propose as a sufficient condition for achieving self-actualization? Although he was far from clear on this point (Maslow, 1971, pp. 39, 301), he seems to have concluded that, because the potential for self-actualization is genetically based, some people will inherit it and some people won't (Frick, 1982, pp. 32–40). To expand on his reasoning, according to the principle of genetic variation, inherited needs are likely to be distributed more or less according to a normal curve, with some individuals demonstrating a high level of the need, others a low level, but most people a moderate level. This principle should apply as well to self-actualization needs, if they are indeed genetic in character. Thus some individuals would be expected to inherit a very low self-actualization potential. In the extreme case, for example, seeking to specify a process by which retarded individuals could function consistently at the level of higher motivations would probably be a futile endeavor. For such people to satisfy completely their lower needs might indeed be a misguided effort, because other motivations may not be available to sustain them. Thus Maslow recognized that a low genetic potential for self-actualization might account for the feelings of "meaninglessness" he said he observed in some people who were gratified in their basic needs. The problem is that this view clashes with other statements of his regarding self-actualization – for example, "What a man *can* be, he *must* be. He must be true to his own nature. This need we may call self-actualization" (1970, p. 46). This statement, of course, conveys quite a different conception of self-actualization; according to it, we would conclude that anyone can potentially become self-actualized. But, as we have just seen, Maslow elsewhere realized that his genetic theory in fact limits self-actualization to a favored proportion of the population. But, of course, Maslow cannot have it both ways. One of these positions must be wrong.

Let us conclude this section on self-actualization with a look at the people Maslow cited as self-actualized. Remember, they include such well-known personalities as Abraham Lincoln and Eleanor Roosevelt. Now, according to Maslow, to be self-actualized, individuals should "have been satisfied in their basic needs throughout their lives, particularly in their earlier years" (Maslow, 1970, p. 53). Thus, achieving a high level of need satisfaction late in life won't do; this situation fits the alternative "deprivation followed by fulfillment" model of human well-being, rather than Maslow's "constant-fulfillment" model. Now, if you are familiar with the early lives of Abraham Lincoln and Eleanor Roosevelt, you know that they both had extraordinary challenges and deprivations to overcome. In other words, they fail to qualify as exemplars of Maslow's theory. Why did Maslow include such individuals in his attempts to support his theory? The answer seems to be that Maslow chose his sample of self-actualizers on the basis of their *adult* traits, not their past life experiences (Maslow, 1970, pp. 149–180). Thus, unfortunately, instead of serving as a test of his theory (Does a consistently high level of need gratification produce self-actualized individuals?), his sample chiefly shows that if you look for people who meet any particular criteria of psychological health, you can probably find people who meet those criteria. For this reason, his demonstration of the traits of self-actualizers is "circular" and has little bearing on his theory.

On the other hand, Maslow's sample does demonstrate that some adults seem able to function much of the time at higher-need levels. However, most of the possible mechanisms for achieving self-actualization – we have discussed these in previous sections – are not encompassed by Maslow's theory. In any particular instance, of course, it is difficult to know which of these mechanisms might be involved: for example, (a) gratification of lower needs in later life, (b) repression of lower needs, (c) a particularly strong genetic self-actualization potential, (d) a linkage between the two levels by which the pursuit of higher needs helps to meet lower needs, or (e) the achievement of functional autonomy of higher needs. Most likely, different combinations of these mechanisms operate in different people at different times.

With respect to the traits of self-actualizers, you will remember that such people are said to be exceptionally creative, spontaneous, and nonjudgmental. However, in spite of the value Maslow seemed to attach to being nonjudgmental, Maslow's theory is *very* judgmental – about what produces and what constitutes a self-actualized individual. In this, he is allied with other nativist theorists such as Carl Rogers. That is, because they postulate a more or less predetermined and unchanging human nature, they have a framework for judging whether or not people are pursuing the "correct path" to self-actualization. In contrast, behaviorists, for example, traditionally make no judgments about what an ideal human is like, because our human potential, in their view, is not fixed, but rather is infinitely malleable. Of course, either of these extreme positions is difficult to support.

A final characteristic of self-actualizers deserves comment, and that is their ability to experience heights of emotion – what Maslow called peak experience, or what is more commonly referred to as mystical experience. Remember that, according to Maslow, people become self-actualized, and thus more likely to have peak experiences, when their lower needs have been met. However, as we have already said, both Eastern and Western traditions favor deprivation and suppression as a means of curtailing the lower needs, and this same approach, carried to an extreme, constitutes perhaps the most common path to mystical experience (Neher, 1990, pp. 107–121). At one point, and contrary to his theory, Maslow admitted that "higher needs may occasionally emerge, not after gratification, but rather after forced or voluntary deprivation, renunciation, or suppression of lower basic needs [as is] reported to be common in Eastern cultures" (1970, pp. 59–60). Probably all of us have experienced the ecstasy that can follow fulfillment after a long period of deprivation – for example, reunion with a loved one after a lengthy separation. But how do we make sense of deprivation practices of mystics, East and West, whose fulfillment, when it comes, seems to be in the form of transcendental feelings or visions of achieving oneness with a higher essence? St. Teresa's accounts of ecstatic union with spiritual beings is probably the best-known example. Perhaps, as with much of experience, fulfillment is more a matter of expectation and perception than of external reality (Neher, 1990, pp. 122–130).

Short of such extremes, most of us can remember when we have purposefully deprived ourselves of basic needs; going camping is a good example. Having to concern ourselves with providing shelter, keeping warm, and catching and preparing fish to eat may only prove what Cicero said: "Hunger is the best seasoning for meat." But such experiences also seem to provide a connection with our primal roots (i.e., our basic needs) that can be very meaningful and invigorating.

All these examples of purposeful need deprivation in the service of achieving apparently higher states of being tend, of course, to undermine further Maslow's belief that satiating lower needs constitutes the most reasonable path to self-actualization and peak experience.

To summarize, the problem here is not that the level of self-actualization is not worth attaining. The problems are that, first, there is a serious question whether its attainment is a consequence of the process Maslow advocated. In particular, the requirement that lower-level motivations must first be eliminated, through satiating them, is highly questionable on a number of grounds. And, second, there is good reason to believe that lower motivations are not always burdensome. In fact, they can make their own unique and significant contribution to our lives.

Conclusion

With respect to the main outlines of his theory, Maslow certainly deserves credit for his general thesis: Undoubtedly, we do have a difficult time reaching the heights of experience if we are preoccupied with attaining the base essentials of life. However, many of the details of his theory need modification. In particular, the four components of the theory need some reworking.

1. We do inherit needs, but among these are needs that Maslow failed to acknowledge as necessary for developing as fully functioning humans. These needs involve the necessity for a great deal of cultural input, more than just what is necessary to gratify our lower needs. In particular, many

higher needs undoubtedly require encouragement from the environment for their development.

2. There probably is some sort of need hierarchy, in that our basic needs are ordinarily more urgent in their demands than are higher-level needs. However, it is not clear that, in the long run, satisfying our lower needs diminishes their urgency, which Maslow felt was necessary for higher needs to emerge. In fact, for many reasons, a moderate level of need gratification seems to be more growth enhancing than the high levels of need gratification that Maslow favored. In addition, there is probably more linkage between various need levels than Maslow proposed. In particular, the higher needs may not be as autonomous as Maslow's theory suggests. For example, if we could, we might often trace them to their origin, either in evolutionary or individual experience, in helping us meet lower needs.

3. Higher-level needs seem not to operate apart from a sense of deficiency, as Maslow proposed. However, higher needs certainly are distinctive in that, unlike lower needs, we are able to choose our higher motivations (or challenges, and thus deprivations) they are farthest because removed from essential survival needs.

4. The level of self-actualization, as Maslow described it, is unique to humans and is worthy of attainment. However, his widely cited sample of self-actualized individuals does not support his theory that a history of high-levels of satiation of basic needs, which is intended to eliminate them as motivations, is required for the attainment of self-actualization. In fact, there are many reasons to believe that "lower" motivations, far from always being a burden, can provide important fulfillments and satisfactions of their own. Nevertheless, there are a number of possible mechanisms, most of which Maslow's theory fails to encompass, that may be involved in the achievement of self-actualization.

In the face of these many problems, humanistic psychologists have a choice. They can ignore the difficulties, preserve Maslow's teachings intact, and consequently run the risk of ideological atrophy as has happened, to some extent, in psychoanalysis. Or they can view Maslow's theory as a serious scientific contribution that therefore deserves scrutiny and modification in the light of new insights and new information.

The particulars of his theory aside, Maslow certainly deserves credit for a number of accomplishments. He attacked behaviorism, as well as psychoanalysis, at some of their most vulnerable points, and encouraged us to think about alternative ways of viewing motivation. And he encouraged us to devote more attention to the example of psychologically healthy individuals and what they can teach us about the positive aspects of living. There is little question that these are worthy accomplishments.

References

Alderfer, C. P. (1969). An empirical test of a new theory of human needs. *Organizational Behavior and Human Performance, 4*, 142–175.

Allport, G. W. (1937). The functional autonomy of motives. *American Journal of Psychology, 50*, 141–156.

Ansbacher, H., & Ansbacher, R. (1959). *The individual psychology of Alfred Adler*. New York: Basic Books.

Aron, A. (1977). Maslow's other child. *Journal of Humanistic Psychology, 17*(2), 9–24.

Berlyne, D. E. (1960). *Conflict, arousal, and curiosity*. New York: McGraw-Hill.

Bloomfield, H., & Felder, L. (1985). *The Achilles syndrome: Transforming your weaknesses into strengths*. New York: Random House.

Brown, W. (1983). *Welcome stress*. Minneapolis, MN: Compcare.

Daniels, M. (1982). The development of the concept of self-actualization in the writings of Abraham Maslow. *Current Psychological Reviews, 2*, 61–76.

Daniels, M. (1988). The myth of self-actualization. *Journal of Humanistic Psychology, 28*(1), 7–38

Eisenberger, R. (1972). Explanation of rewards that do not reduce tissue needs. *Psychological Bulletin, 77*, 319–339.

Frick, W. (1982). Conceptual foundations of self-actualization. *Journal of Humanistic Psychology, 22*(4), 33–52.

Geller, L. (1982). The failure of self-actualization theory. *Journal of Humanistic Psychology, 22*(2), 56–73.

Goldberg, P. (1978). *Executive health*. New York: McGraw-Hill.

Graham, W., & Balloun, J. (1973). An empirical test of Maslow's need hierarchy. *Journal of Humanistic Psychology, 13*(1), 97–108.

Hall, D. T., & Norigaim, K. E. (1968). An examination of Maslow's need hierarchy in an organizational setting. *Organizational Behavior and Human Performance, 3*,12–35.

Holmes, T. H., & Rahe, R. H. (1967). The social readjustment rating. *Journal of Psychosomatic Research, 11*, 213–218.

Houston, J. (1981). *The pursuit of happiness*. Glenview, IL: Scott, Foresman.

Huizinga, G. (1970). *Maslow's need hierarchy in the work situation*. Groningen, Netherlands: Wolters-Noordhoff.

Lawler, E., & Suttle, J. L. (1972). A causal correlational test of the need hierarchy concept. *Organizational Behavior and Human Performance, 7*, 265–287.

Maddi, S. (1968). *Personality theories*. Belmont, CA: Dorsey.

Malson, L. (1972). *Wolf children and the problem of human nature*. New York: Monthly Review Press.

Maslow, A. (1964). *Religions, values, and peak experiences*. Columbus, OH: Ohio State University.

Maslow, A. (1967). *Eupsychian management: A journal*. Homewood, IL: Irwin-Dorsey.

Maslow, A. (1968). *Toward a psychology of being* (2nd ed.). New York: Van Nostrand.

Maslow, A. (1969). *The psychology of science: A reconnaissance*. New York: Harper & Row.

Maslow, A. (1970). *Motivation and personality* (2nd ed.). New York: Harper & Row.

Maslow, A. (1971). *The farther reaches of human nature*. New York: Viking.

Mathes, E. (1981). Maslow's hierarchy of needs as a guide for living. *Journal of Humanistic Psychology, 21*(4), 69–72.

Millon, T. (1969). *Modern psychopathology*. Philadelphia: W. B. Saunders.

Miner, J. B., & Dachler, H. P. (1973). Personal attitudes and motivation. *Annual Review of Psychology, 24*, 379–402.

Neher, A. (1990). *The psychology of transcendence* (2nd ed.). New York: Dover.

Piattelli-Palmarini, M. (1980). *Language and learning.* Cambridge, MA: Harvard University Press.

Selye, H. (1974). *Stress without distress.* Philadelphia: Lippincott.

Smith, M. B. (1973). On self-actualization: A transambivalent examination of a focal theme in Maslow's psychology. *Journal of Humanistic Psychology, 13*(2), 17–33.

Turnbull, C. M. (1974). *The mountain people.* New York: Simon & Schuster.

Wahba, M. A., & Bridwell, L. G. (1979). Maslow reconsidered: A review of research on the need hierarchy theory. In R. M. Steers & L. W. Porter (Eds.), *Motivation and work behavior* (pp. 47–55). New York: McGraw-Hill.

White, R. (1959). Motivation reconsidered: The concept of competence. *Psychological Review, 66,* 297–333.

Whorf, B. (1956). *Language, thought, and reality.* Cambridge, MA: MIT Press.

Wilson, E. O. (1980). *Sociobiology.* Cambridge, MA: Harvard University Press.

Wofford, J. C. (1971). The motivational bases of job satisfaction and job performance. *Personnel Psychology, 24,* 501–518.

Wuthnow, R. (1978). An empirical test of Maslow's theory of motivation. *Journal of Humanistic Psychology, 18*(3), 75–77.

Yerkes, R., & Dodson, J. D. (1908). The relation of strength of stimulus to rapidity of habit formation. *Journal of Comparative Neurology and Psychology, 18,* 459–482.

44

Caught on Fire: Motivation and Giftedness

Ann Robinson

I do not mean zeal without capacity, nor capacity without zeal.
—*Sir Francis Galton (1869)*

A few years ago, a film based on real events surrounding a British team of Olympic runners found favor with movie goers. The film, Chariots of Fire, traced the development of two great athletes as they prepared for the 1924 Olympic games after the First World War. One long distance runner, Eric Liddell, was a devout missionary from Scotland; the other was Harold Abrahams, a young Jewish runner utterly absorbed by his sport. Despite early difficulties and experiences with ethnic prejudice, Abrahams went on to become an institution in British athletics. Liddell pursued a life in the church. The film is a revealing examination of zeal, or the eagerness to work. In the film, each of the two leading actors communicates the joy, the desire and the powerful identification with one's talents that we have come to understand as integral to giftedness.

Indeed, as a construct, motivation permeates our field (Feldhusen, 1986). We can trace its modern roots to the Victorian Sir Francis Galton who believed that great achievements called for both intellect and enthusiasm. Moving into the 1940's, 1950's and 1960's, motivation was a focal point for researchers like White (1959) and McClelland (1961). Researchers began to refine their understanding of intrinsic and extrinsic motivation. Students who worked for personal feelings of satisfaction were intrinsically motivated and thought to be more likely to continue learning for its own sake than those

---

Source: *Gifted Child Quarterly*, 40(4) (1996): 177–178.

who achieved in school because of extrinsic rewards. Later achievement motivation researchers discriminated between task versus ego involvement. A student with task involvement learned because he or she was "carried away" with the activity itself. Ego-involved students were more likely to work in order to best others.

Prominent figures in gifted education like E. Paul Torrance recognized the importance of "falling in love with an idea." Here, motivation became an emotional state rather than a behavior or an action. More recently, Csikzentmihalyi conceptualized such feelings as flow – an optimal experience which transports the person beyond themselves.

As classroom teachers, we have embraced Renzulli's use of task commitment to describe the persistence necessary to the development of talent. The widespread use of task commitment by schools to define giftedness and to identify gifted students is testimony to the consensus that motivation counts in the real world.

And count, it does. There can be no more valuable outcome for education than the love of learning. Unfortunately, in an attempt to categorize and to create handy taxonomies, educators have too often compartmentalized intellect and feeling. We speak or cognitive and affective domains as if they do not meet in the same individual. By artificially divorcing our cogitations from our passions, we have committed Descartes' error – the belief that heart and mind are quite separate organs or entities. A thoughtful teacher observing a child happily, passionately, and zealously engaged in learning knows quite the contrary.

In This Issue

First, Gottfried and Gottfried trace the development of academic intrinsic motivation from childhood through early adolescence. In their longitudinal study, gifted children were more likely than a comparison group to report higher motivation across all subject areas. The authors conclude that the enjoyment of learning is greater for gifted students and that motivation is important for the development of giftedness. Their contribution to our knowledge base includes the developmental finding that motivation in gifted children remains stable over time.

Next, Chan examines the motivational orientations and metacognitive abilities of gifted children and their average achieving peers. Using the framework of attribution theory, she notes that gifted children have greater confidence in their feelings of control over success and failure in school than do their agemates. Gifted children are more likely to report that they can control the amount of effort they put into a school task and the strategies they use to learn them.

In "Gifted and Non-Selected Children's Perceptions of Academic Achievement, Academic Effort, and Athleticism," Udvari and Rubin extend the landmark study by Tannenbaum (1962). They studied younger children and they introduced gender as a variable. Their results indicate that gifted children are more tolerant of "brilliant" peers than average children are, that neither group actively disparaged effort nor did they particularly reward it, and that athleticism continued to be the most important contributor to social acceptability.

In the next article, Kurt Heller of Germany summarizes the considerable literature on gender differences in mathematics and the natural sciences from a motivational perspective. This important contribution to the knowledge base distills a vast literature with significant implications for the development of gifts and talents in girls and women. He examines the hypothesis that the lowered performance of girls and women may be due to their attributions about their abilities in these subject areas. To support his conjecture, he reviews empirical research which indicates that girls and women hold unrealistically low expectations of their abilities in mathematics and science. Then, Heller reports two studies of his own on attribution retraining programs which successfully modify attributions of high school and college women and which subsequently raise their level of achievement. Neither study reviewed has been accessible to English speaking scholars until now.

What happens when motivation is diverted from a healthy course? How frequently is that likely to happen among gifted students? Is it truly unhealthy? In "The Incidence of Perfectionism in Gifted Students," Parker and Mills explore these questions and conclude that gifted students and a comparison group of age peers do not differ significantly in the incidence of perfectionism. They also suggest that the anecdotal reportage of perfectionism among gifted youth may be the result of differential labeling. What is viewed as healthy effort among the general cohort may be viewed by others as unhealthy overachievement among gifted students. Finally, they urge the field to develop a more precise distinction between striving which stimulates excellence and striving which inhibits it.

Our "In the Public Interest" shares the reflections of Pamela Clinkenbeard on what the literature on motivation and giftedness has to offer us as we set about developing the talents of our students in the schools. She notes that the studies which conceptualize motivation as a trait or state lead us to include measures or markers of motivation in the identification of gifted students. Leading us further, she points out that the field will benefit from viewing the motivation to learn as the outcome as well as an identification "input" of our programs and services.

Finally, we close with two book reviews which contribute to our understanding of giftedness and motivation. First, Pat Haensly reviews Karen Arnold's study of high school valedictorians. Her thoughtful review of Arnold's thoughtful text poses an important question. To what extent does the traditional avenue of recognition for school achievement – class standing – divert talented young people from a life happily lived and creatively expressed? The review leads us to the fitting, final piece in this special issue on giftedness and motivation, Gary Davis' review of a biography of E. Paul Torrance by Garnet Miller. Working through document analysis, interviews and extensive converations with Dr. Torrance himself, Millar has produced a portrait of a man who fell in love with an idea and made it a way of life.

References

Csikzentmihalyi, M. (1991). *Flow: The psychology of optimal experience*. New York: Harper Perennial.

Feldhusen, J. F. (1986). A conception of giftedness. In R. J. Sternberg & J. F. Davidson (Eds.), *Conceptions of giftedness*. Cambridge, England: Cambridge University Press.

Galton, E. (1869). *Hereditary genius: An inquiry into its laws and consequences*. London: Macmillan & Co.

McClelland, D. (1961). *The achieving society.* New York: The Pree Press.

Renzulli, J. S. (1978). What makes giftedness? Re-examining a definition. *Phi Delta Kappan, 60*, 180–184, 261.

Tannenbaum, A. (1962). *Adolescents attitudes toward academic brilliance*. New York: Teachers College Press.

White, R. (1959). Motivation reconsidered: The concept of competence. *Psychological Review, 66*, 297–333.

45

An Empirical Test of Maslow's Theory of Motivation

Eugene W. Mathes and Linda L. Edwards

M aslow's (1970) theory of motivation suggests that there are five basic classes of needs and that they are hierarchically organized as follows: physiological, security, belongingness, esteem, and self-actualization. Each need level is prepotent to the next higher need level. This means that an individual initially attempts to satisfy his or her physiological needs, and only when they are satisfied does the individual attempt to satisfy security needs. Once security needs are satisfied the individual attempts to satisfy belongingness needs and so on. Although a number of studies have shown that satisfaction of physiological (Cofer & Appley, 1964), security (Maslow, Birsh, Honigmann, McGrath, Plason, & Stein, 1952), belongingness (Rogers & Dymond, 1954), and esteem needs (Maslow, 1939; 1940; 1942) facilitates self-actualization, there is no evidence demonstrating that these lower needs form the hierarchy specified by Maslow. The purpose of the study reported below was to test the hierarchical aspect of Maslow's theory of motivation.

To accomplish this end, student subjects (36 males, 76 females) were given self-report inventories: the Security-Insecurity Scale of Maslow et al. (1952); a belongingness scale devised by the authors; Rosenberg's (1965) Self-Esteem Scale; and Shostrom's (1965) measure of self-actualization, the Personal Orientation Inventory (POI). Physiological need satisfaction was not measured because it was assumed that the subjects' physiological needs were satisfied.

It was hypothesized that subjects scoring above the median on one of these measure of need satisfaction would obtain significantly higher *average*

Source: *Journal of Humanistic Psychology,* 18(1) (1978): 75–77.

scores on all of the measures of need satisfaction further up the hierarchy than subjects scoring below the median. Specifically, three hypotheses were made:

Hypothesis 1. Subjects scoring above the median on the measure of security need satisfaction would obtain significantly higher average belongingness satisfaction, esteem satisfaction, and self-actualization scores than subjects scoring below the median on the security measure.

Hypothesis 2. Subjects scoring above the median on the measure of belongingness need satisfaction would obtain significantly higher average scores on the measures of esteem need satisfaction and self-actualization than subjects scoring below the median on the belongingness measure.

Hypothesis 3. Subjects scoring above the median on the measure of esteem need satisfaction would obtain a significantly higher average score on the measure of self-actualization than subjects scoring below the median on the esteem measure.

To test the first hypothesis, subjects were split into secure and insecure groups by means of a median split of Security-Insecurity Scale scores. The average scores of these two groups on the Belongingness, Self-Esteem, and POI scales were then compared by means of *t* tests. As Table 1 shows, Hypothesis 1 was entirely supported by the women's data but only partially supported by the men's. Although the secure men scored significantly higher on the POI than the insecure men, significant differences were not found for the other two scales.

To test the second hypothesis, subjects were split into belonging and nonbelonging groups by means of a median split of Belongingness Scale scores. The average scores of these two groups on the Self-Esteem and POI scales were then compared by means of *t* tests. As Table 1 shows, Hypothesis 2 was not supported.

Table 1: Mean satisfaction scores of subjects scoring above and below the median on lower level need satisfaction measures

	Women			Men		
	Insecure ss	*Secure ss*	p	*Insecure ss*	*Secure ss*	p
Belonging	18.58	21.16	.0013	19.28	21.11	n.s.
Self-Esteem	48.37	60.47	.0011	53.89	55.22	n.s.
POI	96.52	106.00	.0054	92.61	107.50	.0006
	Unloved ss	*Loved ss*	p	*Unloved ss*	*Loved ss*	p
Self-Esteem	52.74	56.11	n.s.	53.50	57.11	n.s.
POI	98.42	104.11	n.s.	99.50	102.50	n.s.
	Low Self-Esteem	*High Self-Esteem*	p	*Low Self-Esteem*	*High Self-Esteem*	p
POI	98.08	104.45	n.s.	101.44	98.22	n.s.

To test the third hypothesis, subjects were split into high and low self-esteem groups by means of a median split of Self-Esteem scale scores. The average scores of these two groups on the POI were then compared by means of a *t* test. Table 1 shows that Hypothesis 3 was not supported.

The results of this study suggest that Maslow's hierarchical theory of motivation should be modified to include only two or three levels. Security was shown to be a prerequisite to self-actualization, while belongingness and esteem were shown not to be essential prerequisites.

References

Cofer C. N., & Appley, M. H. *Motivation: Theory and research.* New York: Wiley, 1964.

Maslow, A. H. Dominance-feeling, personality and social behavior in women. *Journal of Social Psychology*, 1939, **10**, 3–39.

Maslow, A. H. A test for dominance-feeling (self-esteem) in women. *Journal of Social Psychology*, 1940, **12**, 255–270.

Maslow, A. H. Self-esteem (dominance feeling) and sexuality in women. *Journal of Social Psychology*, 1942, **16**, 259–294.

Maslow, A. H. *Motivation and personality* (Revised ed.). New York: Harper and Row, 1970.

Maslow, A. H., Birsh, E., Honigmann, I., McGrath, F., Plason, F., & Stein, M. *Manual for the security-insecurity inventory.* Palo Alto, Calif.: Consulting Psychologists Press, 1952.

Rogers, C. R., & Dymond, R. F. (Eds.). *Psychotherapy and personality change.* Chicago: University of Chicago Press, 1954.

Rosenberg, M. *Society and the adolescent self-image.* Princeton, N.J.: Princeton University Press, 1965.

Shostrom, E. L. A test for the measurement of self-actualization. *Educational and Psychological Measurement*, 1965, **24**, 207–218.

46

Meaningfulness, Commitment, and Engagement: The Intersection of a Deeper Level of Intrinsic Motivation

Neal Chalofsky and Vijay Krishna

The managerial and popular literature has been increasingly referring to the "baby boomers" in America (the disproportionately large generation born just after World War II) nearing retirement age and questioning the meaning and purpose of their work and their lives. At the same time, their children, Generations X and Y, have started their careers asking the same questions.

The classic motivation theorists and humanistic psychologists clearly supported the notion that individuals have an inherent need for a work life that they believe is meaningful (Alderfer, 1972; Herzberg, Mausner, & Snyderman, 1959; Maslow, 1943, 1954, 1971; McClelland, 1965; McGregor, 1960; Rogers, 1959, 1961). Maslow (1971) wrote that individuals who do not perceive the workplace as meaningful and purposeful will not work up to their professional capacity. There is a long history of research and discourse about what motivates employees and the relationship between job satisfaction and performance/productivity. The need or content theories of the 1960s and 1970s and their emphasis on the individual gave way to the reinforcement and person–environment interaction theories of the 1970s through the 1990s and their emphasis on performance, organizational systems, and productivity. Most of the research, therefore, has been in relation to these theories. The resurgence of interest of intrinsic factors such as meaning, purpose, spirituality, and commitment

Source: *Advances in Developing Human Resources*, 11(2) (2009): 189–203.

and the recent introduction of engagement has resulted in an increase in both the popular and scholarly literature concerning the role of work as a motivator in the organization (Csikszentmihalyi, 1990; Fox, 1994; Lockwood, 2007; Meyer & Herscovitch, 2001).

Employee commitment and engagement have emerged as very important constructs in organizational research on account of their favorable relationship with employee behaviors that promote organizational retention and performance. According to Porter (1968), commitment involves the willingness of employees to exert higher efforts on behalf of the organization, a strong desire to stay in the organization, and accept major goals and values of the organization (as cited in Porters, Steers, Mowday, & Boulin, 1974). A number of studies have shown a positive correlation between employee commitment and job performance (Hunter & Thatcher, 2007; Pool & Pool, 2007). Angle and Perry (1981) showed in their research that organizational commitment correlates positively with employees' and organization's ability to adapt to unforeseeable events.

Studies also suggest that organizational commitment supports organizational citizenship behaviors that are central to flatter organizations, effective teams, and empowerment (Dessler, 1999). Kanter (1968) in her study of the 19th century American utopian societies, such as the Shakers, showed that the commitment-producing strategies distinguished successful from unsuccessful societies: "commitment is central to the understanding of both human motivation and system maintenance" (p. 499). According to Senge (1993), personnel commitment is one of the key requirements to become a learning organization. Be it a utopian society or a learning organization, commitment is seen as one of the key factors for organizational survival and growth. Despite the tremendous interest that organizational commitment research generates (Beck & Wilson, 2000), questions about the process and determinants of organizational commitment remain unanswered (Cohen, 2003; Meyer & Herscovitch, 2001).

One of the possible reasons for this lack of a clear understanding of the motivational processes is because of the separation of the intrinsic aspects of motivation from the organizational and contextual factors that affect its development. Although there has been some research that suggests that employee engagement is related to workforce efficiency and productivity, very little empirical research exists that explains the processes through which engagement develops. Engagement has been defined as "the extent to which employees commit to something or someone in their organization, [and] how hard they work and how long they stay as a result of that commitment" (Corporate Leadership Council, 2004).

The purpose of this article is to explore a deeper level of intrinsic motivation, *meaningfulness*, and to discuss the connections between meaning *of work* and meaning *at* work, represented by the concepts of employee commitment and engagement as organizational and contextual factors. A holistic approach to workplace motivation that combines the intrinsic aspects of work motivation with the contextual and organizational factors has not been developed in the literature. This approach is important because although motivation is an individual and personal process, it is also significantly influenced and shaped by the contextual and organizational factors. Hence, while studying motivational factors, it is necessary to consider both the individual and the organizational factors that affect its development.

This article attempts to fill this gap by generating a conceptual frame of a deeper level of motivation, namely, meaningfulness or meaningful work, and outlines the connection between meaning *of* work and meaning *at* work that is expressed in terms of employee commitment and engagement. This article seeks to contribute to the organizational behavior field by linking these streams of research and conceptual development that have not been connected previously. The integrative approach adopted in this article provides a new perspective on the connections between workplace motivation, employee commitment, and employee engagement.

Conceptual Background

In preindustrial society, work was performed in the same community setting where people lived. Consequently, people knew one another closely and saw the connection between their work and how that work benefited the rest of the community. The work of an individual was intricately tied to the well-being of the self and the community. There was no separation of work from self, community, and life. The twin forces of reduction in agricultural work and rise of mechanical work meant more people becoming wage earners who were working for others (Brisken, 1996). In 1860, half the working population was self-employed; by 1900, two thirds were wage earners. Work became governed by the clock, by uniform standards, and by supervisors. "Reason demanded that workers subordinate their own experience of natural rhythms to the logic of efficiency" (Brisken, 1996, p. 100).

The industrial era separated work from the community and created the bureaucracy to house, organize, and control work. There was little or no contact between the organization where employees worked and the community where they lived. Work was no longer an integral part of community life; it was detached, separated, and contained within specific buildings and times. In bureaucracies, hierarchies separated executives from workers, and internal competition forced workers against workers as they fought to move up the increasingly narrow upper levels of the organization. Wall Street further separated the owners from the employees.

Now there are people who commute from New York or Boston to Washington and beyond, as well as people all over the globe who work in virtual teams and even virtual organizations. Consequently, people are not only moving work further away but are further away from the rest of their lives. As work has become separated from the community and life, it has lost its original sense of meaning as an integral aspect of human existence. One hypothesis is that motivation only became an issue because meaning disappeared when the work became separated from the rest of life and community. "As a consequence motivation theories have become surrogates for the search for meaning" (Sievers, 1984, p. 3). There is very little research based on the premise that meaningful work is lost when work becomes separated from being a natural and integral part of the community.

In the 1960s and 1970s, the classic motivation theorists and humanistic psychologists clearly supported the notion that individuals have an inherent need for a work life that they believe is meaningful (Alderfer, 1972; Herzberg et al., 1959; Maslow, 1943, 1971; McGregor, 1960; Rogers, 1959, 1961). Maslow (1971) wrote that individuals who do not perceive the workplace as meaningful and purposeful will not work up to their professional capacity. They theorized that individuals are motivated to take certain actions based on fulfilling needs believed to be inherent in all humans. These theorists all proposed that as these needs move from the basic survival needs to higher-order needs, they become more intrinsic and reflective in nature. The higher-order needs reflect life values: working toward a higher cause, meaningfulness, and life purpose. Maslow (1971) expressed these values as *being* values, referred to as *B-values*. B-values included truth, transcendence, goodness, uniqueness, aliveness, justice, richness, and meaningfulness. Maslow believed that individuals have the potential to reach what he called self-actualization, which is the process of developing one's potential, of expressing oneself to the fullest possible extent in a manner that is personally fulfilling. It is not an end-state but an ongoing process of becoming. Near the end of his life, Maslow wrote of people who seemed to transcend self-actualization. He labeled this phenomenon "Theory Z" after McGregor's (1960) "Theories X and Y." In this state, people are devoted to a task, vocation, or calling that transcends the dichotomies of work and play. Maslow (1971) viewed this as a dynamic process of expanding the capabilities of the self to virtually unlimited potential. Also noteworthy were the thoughtful concepts from Rogers (1961), Locke (1975), and Ackoff (1981). Rogers believed that people find purpose when they experience freedom to be exactly who they are in a fluid and changing manner. Locke (1975) wrote that people strive to attain goals to satisfy their emotions and desires. Ackoff (1981) described purpose and meaning as progress toward an ideal that converts mere existence into significant living by making choice meaningful.

Meaning *of* Work

In the late 1990s and early 2000s, spirituality and meaning at work emerged as a reaction to the loss of job security, as well as other factors (Darling & Chalofsky, 2004). One set of events was the environmental disasters of Chernobyl, the chemical pollution at Bhopal, and the big oil spills off the coasts of Canada and Europe. These sparked an increase in the collective conscious about corporate social responsibility. The second set of events was the ethics scandals by Enron, Worldcom, and others. There have been a host of books, articles, and other media questioning our misuse of this planet, the role of work in capitalist societies, and our moral, ethical, and spiritual stance around life's meaning and purpose (Holbecke & Springnett, 2004).

In the past several years, organizations had been attempting to attract and retain highly qualified workers in advance of a projected labor shortage and amid increasing global competition. More recently, the economic downturn that began in 2007/2008 has been causing tremendous turmoil in employment. Yet new young professionals are still expressing a preference to work for socially responsible, ethically driven organizations that allow the "whole self" to be brought to work. And the "baby boomers" in America have been going through midlife and early retirement questioning the meaning and purpose of work in their lives, especially those who went through the downsizings of the 1990s (both the ones who lost their jobs and the survivors). When you ask these people about how they feel about work, according to one consulting group, they talk about a sense of loss; a lack of purpose, trust, and commitment; a loosening of emotional ties to the workplace; and a questioning of whether their work is worthwhile (Holbecke & Springnett, 2004).

According to the Society for Human Resource Management's (2008b) workplace forecast report, 4 of the 10 key themes identified were the following:

- The implications of increased global competitiveness, *especially the need for an educated and skilled workforce*
- Demographic changes, especially the aging of the workforce, the impending retirement of the baby boom generation, and *the greater demand for work/life balance*
- Growing need to develop *retention strategies* for current and future workforce
- Demographic shifts leading to a *shortage of high-skill* workers
- Other findings from their survey that were relevant include the following:
- Growth in the number of *employees with caring responsibilities* (elder care, child care, and both elder care and child care at the same time)
- Generational issues – recognizing and *catering to groups such as Generation Y* (born 1980–2000), Generation X (born 1965–1980), and so on

As mentioned earlier, the United States and the rest of the world were going through a chaotic economic decline, and even before the economic turmoil fully emerged, employees identified job security as their top concern (Society for Human Resource Management, 2008a). The Society for Human Resource

Management study identified contributors to employee job satisfaction, and the rest of the top four were the following: benefits, compensation, and feeling safe in the work environment. The top four contributors to job satisfaction were actually *not satisfiers*, based on Herzburg, but basic hygiene factors, or lower-order Maslow's hierarchy levels. And they were rated high, at least in part, because of the dismal economic situation. So to call them contributors to satisfaction, or motivational factors, is a misnomer.

But five out of the top 10 contributors to job satisfaction are motivational:

- Opportunities to use skills and abilities
- Relationship with immediate supervisor
- The work itself
- Meaningfulness of job
- Flexibility to balance life and work issues

What all these findings point to is the American workforce's desire to be part of an organization that is going to take care of them and help them take care of their families, support their growth through skill and knowledge development, understand their need to have some work–life balance, and use their skills and abilities in a way that is meaningful.

Motivation and Meaning

The literature refers to values as intrinsic motivators to performing a task and deriving satisfaction from the accomplishment of that task (or job). Although the emphasis may be on the congruence of the task with our beliefs, objectives, and anticipated rewards, motivation is seen as focused on the accomplishment of the task. The common assumption is that we are motivated by values based on result or outcome. Meaning, on the other hand, is more deeply intrinsic than values, suggesting three levels of satisfaction: extrinsic, intrinsic, and something even deeper. This level of intrinsic motivation is about the meaning *of* the work itself to the individual.

Csikszentmihalyi (1990), in his attempt to define meaning, readily acknowledged the difficulty the task presents by suggesting that any definition of the term would undoubtedly be circular. However, he pointed to three ways in which the word may be defined, two of which are (a) having a purpose or the significance of something and (b) the intentions one holds. Similarly, Dirkx (1995) subscribed to the theory that work is one of the ways that a mature adult cares for oneself and others. This was expressed by respondents in the Schaefer and Darling (1996) study, who defined work as an opportunity for service to others and not distinct from the rest of life. The term may also be definitive of one's uniqueness and a way of expressing one's self in the world.

The significance of Csikszentmihalyi's research was how intrinsically motivated people are driven by the work itself rather than by the accomplishment of the task. He included people in a wide range of occupations and activities and discovered a particular kind of experience where people's performance seemed effortless. They described the feeling of being able to continue forever in their task and wanting to learn additional skills to master more demanding challenges. The fun, sense of mastery, and the potential for growth of self was what he labeled *flow*. In addition, they were disappointed when the work was finished because they were no longer in the flow state. This flow state was very similar to Maslow's peak experiences at the self-actualization level.

The work itself is but one aspect of Chalofsky's (2003) construct of meaningful work. Chalofsky identified three themes: *sense of self, the work itself*, and *the sense of balance*. These themes represent a deeper level of motivation than the traditional intrinsic values of a sense of accomplishment, pride, satisfaction of finishing a task, and praise from a supervisor. This emerging new paradigm links back to some of the work of the content theorists but takes their thinking and the concept of intrinsic motivation to a deeper evolutionary level.

Sense of Self

The idea of people needing to bring their whole selves (mind, body, emotion, and spirit) to their work is critical to finding meaning in work. People often fail to bring their whole selves to work out of fear of rejection, prejudice, or misunderstanding. "We work hard to create physical safety in our workplaces. Can we also create mental, emotional, and spiritual safety – safety for the whole person?" (Richards, 1995, p. 87). Mitroff and Denton (1999), in their groundbreaking study of spirituality in the workplace, found that the word that best described what people were feeling was a loss of interconnectedness, and what upset them the most was not being able to bring their complete selves into the workplace. For those people who felt adrift spiritually, their work and the workplace ceased to be a source to find deeper meaning, satisfaction, and connection.

Helping individuals integrate their work and spiritual lives might mean that the time people spend working in their lifetime are more joyful, balanced, and meaningful and spiritually nourishing (Gibbons, 2007). These more fulfilled individuals might then return to their families, friends, and communities contented, refreshed, and ready to contribute. Because of this integration, one might expect that these people might be more ethical and more productive workers – which would benefit their employers. Moreover, a values-based organization culture might help businesses to become humane, socially active, and environmentally responsible.

Before one can bring the whole self to work, one has to first be aware of one's own values, beliefs, and purpose in life. The sense of self also includes constantly striving to reach one's potential and believing in one's ability to reach that potential. And it includes an alignment between one's purpose in life and the purpose for the work. Fulfillment, in part, comes from feeling that what we do on this earth makes a difference to other people. In fact, Maslow's (1971) views expressed in the *Farther Reaches of Human Nature* would warrant the term *selfless*-actualization rather than self-actualization (Greene & Burke, 2007). His last work espoused human development beyond the self in self-actualization. Maslow's (1971) message was that people must ultimately move from a focus on self to a focus and concern for other people to achieve the highest level of human nature. People who move beyond self-actualization "are, without a single exception, involved in a cause outside of their skin: in something outside of themselves, some calling or vocation" (p. 42). Meeting the self-actualization needs focuses on achieving a personal identity and complete acceptance of self and then moving beyond to a higher connection with others.

The Work Itself

In the not-so-distant past, managers made decisions about the structure and process of work activities, in the name of efficiency (Thomas, 2000). Jobs were broken down into tasks, which involved certain competencies, and specific and measurable objectives. But work has now changed dramatically. Organizations have realized that they need to rely more and more on workers to make decisions about how the work should get accomplished. This requires more worker autonomy, flexibility, empowerment, continuous learning, risk taking, and creativity. Thomas captures what the research has demonstrated with his list of the four most critical intrinsic rewards: sense of meaning and purpose, sense of choice, sense of competence, and sense of progress. Although the work itself relates back to both Maslow's self-actualization and Alderfer's growth levels, and to an extent Herzberg's motivators, the focus is on carrying out one's life purpose through the work itself. "This is what I was meant to do." It is not about productivity or other end state. It is about working and growing as a never-ending process.

Professionalism is a related concept about taking pride in your work, a commitment to quality, a dedication to the interests of the client (be they internal or external), and a sincere desire to help. The premise of *Good Work* (Gardner, Csikszentmihalyi, & Damon, 2001) also speaks to professionalism but expands the concept to include ethics and social responsibility. They define good work as "work of expert quality that benefits the broader society" (p. ix). And people know that they are doing good work because it feels good. This may sound too simple, but people know when the work they are doing is good and meaningful. It is about trusting both one's judgment and one's intuition. The more we know ourselves, the more we can evaluate and change our professional behavior, our moral and ethical judgment, and how our performance affects those around us.

Sense of Balance

To paraphrase a Zen Buddhist saying, work and pleasure should be so aligned that it is impossible to distinguish one from the other. The sense of balance at its ideal is that life is so integrated that it does not matter whether what one is doing so long as it is meaningful. But given that most of us do not live in an ideal world, a sense of balance concerns the choices we make between the time spent at paid work, unpaid work (work at home, with family, as a volunteer), and at pleasurable pursuits, such that no one area of our lives is so dominant that we cease to value the other areas. All work and no play is stressful, overwhelming, and usually results in our health, family, and social lives suffering – even when the work is meaningful. All play and no work quickly becomes boring and meaningless.

We also need to balance the nourishing of our different selves (mental, physical, emotional, and spiritual) because, in the less than ideal world, we do not have the luxury of meeting all our needs through one major activity. So we need to take the time to learn, to keep fit, to reflect, to meditate or pray, and to give to others. Again, because we usually worry most about doing our paid work, we do not take the time to care for ourselves. And when we do not take care of ourselves, we usually cannot be there for others. So we end up running on the proverbial treadmill until we finally realize we are not meeting our own or anyone else's needs. The statistics we read in the media on work-related stress, people being overweight and less than physically fit, depression, divorce, and even workplace violence speak for themselves.

Employees today are defining success on their own terms and some are opting out of the corporate rat race. Instead of living to work, people are working to live. They are tired of the inflexibility of standard work hours and the lack of concern for work–family balance and are leaving corporate positions in favor of more flexible career options.

Meaningful work is not just about the meaning of the paid work we perform; it is about the way we live our lives. It is the alignment of purpose, values, and the relationships and activities we pursue in life. It is about living our lives and performing our work with integrity. It is about integrated wholeness.

Meaning *at* Work

Meaning *at* work implies a relationship between the person and the organization or the workplace, in terms of commitment and engagement. Richards (1995) talked about the situation that when there is meaning at work, "[only then] will our work become more joyful [and] our organizations will flourish with commitment, passion, imagination, spirit, and soul" (p. 94). As noted earlier, commitment involves the willingness of employees to exert higher efforts on behalf of the organization, a strong desire to stay in the organization, and accept major goals and values of the organization (as cited in Porters et al., 1974).

Commitment

The primary drivers of commitment are identification with the organization's goals and values, congruence between individual and organizational goals, and internalization of organizational values and mission. The term *work commitment* refers to a broader concept than organizational commitment and includes the different forms commitment can take in the workplace. According to Morrow (1993), there are five universal forms of work commitment, namely, (a) work ethic endorsement, (b) career commitment, (c) affective organizational commitment, (d) continuance organizational commitment, and (e) job involvement. The third form refers to an affective or psychological bonding that binds an employee to his/her organization. The primary drivers of this form of commitment are *identification* with the organizations goals and values, *congruence* between individual and organizational goals, and *internalization* of organizational values and mission. Of all the forms of commitment, affective commitment has been found to have the strongest positive relationship with desirable outcomes (Eisenberger, Huntington, Hutchison, & Sowa, 1986). Organizations that want to foster affective commitment must in turn show their commitment to the employees by providing supportive work environments. The research that has examined the relationship between perception of organizational support and organizational commitment has found a consistent positive relationship between them. Perception of organizational support states that "employees form a global belief concerning the extent to which the organization cares about them and values their contribution to the organization" (Aselage & Eisenberger, 2003, p. 492). Employees will be loyal to their organization if their organization values and appreciates them (Tyler, 1999, as cited in Fuller, Barnett, Hester, & Relyea, 2003). Organizations that are committed to employee development, their well being, and their need for actualization tend to have employees with high commitment (Dessler, 1999). Paul and Anantharaman (2004), in their research study, found that of all the human resource management variables that correlate with commitment, the human resource development variables of (a) career development, (b) development-oriented appraisal, (c) comprehensive training, and (4) employee-friendly work environment have the strongest correlation.

In a study on culture and employee-friendly/humane organizations, Chalofsky (2008) found that there was an interdependent relationship based on the values of the organizational culture. Although no organization can be all things to all people, the organizations that were studied work hard to recognize and support employees' work, family, leisure, personal, and community needs. They knew that if work–life balance is provided, then more of the whole employee will be able to focus (and wants to focus) on their work. Employees of the organizations are not there just because they have great benefits. The benefits are a result of the culture, because the culture values employees. In turn, employees have an overwhelming commitment to their organizations. It is all intertwined and synergistic. This was evident by the overwhelming alignment between the organizations' missions and their commitment to their employees, customers, suppliers, and community. The organization supports the whole person, and the whole person is engaged in the organization.

Engagement

Employee engagement has emerged as the most recent "business driver" of organizational success (Lockwood, 2007). A number of consulting companies (e.g., Gallup, Blessing-White) have surveyed their clients and have found a concern that the majority of employees are not engaged in their work and their organizations. One survey (Blessing-White, Inc., 2005) found that some of those employees who are not engaged may care about the organization and their work, but did not feel there is a good fit between their capabilities and their tasks. Others were not dissatisfied enough to leave the organization but were biding their time and not committed to either their work or the organization. The rest are actively looking to leave the organization.

Engaged employees, on the other hand, work harder, are more committed, and are more likely to go "above and beyond" the requirements and expectations of their work (Lockwood, 2007). Engaged employees tend to feel that their work actually positively affects their physical health and their psychological well-being (Crabtree, 2005). The findings of Blessing-White, Inc. (2006) were similar: Engaged employees were proud to work in their organizations and trusted their immediate managers. Overall, their emotional connections were positive. Emotionally based commitment to the work and the organization results in higher levels of engagement and commitment based on developmental, financial, or professional rewards (Corporate Leadership Council, 2004).

Conclusion: Meaningfulness, Commitment, and Engagement

One of the primary challenges organizations are facing today concerns motivating employees to carry out broader and more proactive roles. The current workforce is becoming more emergent and less traditional. An emergent workforce is driven by opportunity as against a traditional work force that believes that tenure dictates growth (Campbell, 2002). Hence, organizations will need to develop novel approaches to motivation to retain an emergent workforce. Given the current state of the economy, it may seem that hiring and retention are not as important as they were thought to be several years ago. But organizations that want to be sustainable and successful over the long term need to still consider how to attract and grow high performing and committed employees.

In view of the ineffectiveness of extrinsic motivational factors in fostering employee commitment and engagement, and the limited impact of traditional intrinsic factors in isolation, this article develops a conceptual framework of the relationship between commitment and engagement and a deeper level of intrinsic motivation, namely, meaningful work. This article builds on the premise that people with the highest levels of productivity and fulfillment view themselves as inseparable from their work (Mohrman & Cohen, 1995), are intrinsically motivated by the work itself (Csikszentmihalyi, 1990), and are professionally committed to and engaged with the organization. This approach combines the individual aspect of motivation emanating from a psychological perspective to a contextual dimension of motivation that highlights the importance of workplace environment and culture. Although the commitment construct has been researched for more than four decades, the research pertaining to engagement is of recent origin. Most of the engagement literature at this time is primarily based on survey results generated by consulting companies rather than empirical research. More research needs to be conducted concerning engagement as a viable construct and the relationship between engagement, commitment, and meaningfulness.

The connections of the concepts of meaningful work, employee commitment, and engagement can give human resource development practitioners and managers powerful tools to develop workplace strategies that can greatly improve employee satisfaction, fulfillment, and loyalty. Organizational productivity, retention, and sustainability will be enhanced, and individuals will feel good about their work and how it affects the rest of their lives.

References

Ackoff, R. L. (1981). *Creating the corporate future: Be planned or be planned for*. New York: Wiley.

Alderfer, C. P. (1972). *Existence, relatedness and growth: Human needs in organizational settings*. New York: Free Press.

Angle, H. L., & Perry, J. L. (1981). An empirical assessment of organizational commitment and organizational effectiveness. *Administrative Science Quarterly, 26*, 1–13.

Aselage, J., & Eisenberger, R. (2003). Perceived organizational support and psychological contracts: A theoretical integration. *Journal of Organizational Behavior, 24*, 491–509.

Beck, K., & Wilson, C. (2000). Development of affective organizational commitment: A cross-sequential examination of change with tenure. *Journal of Vocational Behavior, 56,* 114–136.

Blessing-White, Inc. (2005). *Employee engagement report 2005.* Princeton, NJ: Author.

Blessing-White, Inc. (2006). *Employee engagement report 2006.* Princeton, NJ: Author.

Brisken, A. (1996). *The stirring of the soul in the workplace.* San Francisco: Jossey-Bass.

Campbell, B. (2002). The high cost of turnover: Why holding on to your employees can improve your bottom line. *Black Enterprise, 33*(5), 61.

Chalofsky, N. (2003). An emerging construct for meaningful work. *Human Resource Development International, 6,* 69–83.

Chalofsky, N. (2008). Work-life programs and organizational culture: The essence of workplace community. *Organization Development Journal, 26,* 11–18.

Cohen, A. (2003). *Multiple commitments at work: An integrative approach.* Hillsdale, NJ: Lawrence Erlbaum.

Corporate Leadership Council. (2004). *Driving performance and retention through employee engagement.* Washington, DC: Author.

Crabtree, S. (2005). Engagement keeps the doctor away. *Gallup Management Journal.* Retrieved November 12, 2007, from http://gmj.gallup.com/content/14500/Engagement-Keeps-Doctor-Away.aspx

Csikszentmihalyi, M. (1990). *Flow: The psychology of optimal experience.* New York: Harper Perennial.

Darling, J., & Chalofsky, N. (2004). Spirituality in the workplace. In M. Marquardt (Ed.), *Encyclopedia of life support systems (EOLSS).* Oxford, UK: EOLSS. Retrieved February 5, 2009, from http://www.eolss.nct/outlinecomponents/Human-Resources-Management.aspx

Dessler, G. (1999). How to earn your employees' commitment. *Academy of Management Executive, 13,* 58–67.

Dirkx, J. (1995). *Earning a living or building a life? Reinterpreting the meaning of work in the practice of workplace education.* Paper presented at the Academy of Human Resource Development Conference, San Antonio, TX.

Eisenberger, R., Huntington, R., Hutchison, S., & Sowa, D. (1986). Perceived organizational support. *Journal of Applied Psychology, 71,* 500–507.

Fox, M. (1994). *The reinvention of work: A new vision of livelihood for our time.* New York: Harper Collins.

Fuller, J. B., Barnett, T., Hester, K., & Relyea, C. (2003). A social identity perspective on the relationship between perceived organizational support and organizational commitment. *Journal of Social Psychology, 143,* 789–791.

Gardner, H., Csikszentmihalyi, M., & Damon, W. (2001). *Good work: When excellence and ethics meet.* New York: Basic Books.

Gibbons, P. (2007). *Spirituality at work: A pre-theoretical overview.* Retrieved September 8, 2008, from http://www.paulgibbons.net

Greene, L., & Burke, G. (2007). *Beyond self-actualization.* Texas State University, School of Health Administration. Retrieved September 22, 2008, from http://ecommons.txstate.edu/cgi/viewcontent.cgi?article=1001&context=sohafacp

Herzberg, F., Mausner, B., & Snyderman, B. B. (1959). *The motivation to work.* New York: Wiley.

Holbecke, L., & Springnett, N. (2004). *In search of meaning in the workplace.* Unpublished report, Roffey Park Institute, London.

Hunter, L. W., & Thatcher, S. M. (2007). Feeling the heat: Effects of stress, commitment, and job experience on job performance. *Academy of Management Journal, 50,* 953–968.

Kanter, R. M. (1968). Commitment and social organization: A study of commitment mechanisms in utopian communities. *American Sociological Review, 33,* 499–517.

Locke, E. A. (1975). Personnel attitudes and motivation. *Annual Review of Psychology, 26,* 457–498.

Lockwood, N. R. (2007). *Leveraging employee engagement for competitive advantage: HR's strategic role* (SHRM Research Quarterly Report). Alexandria, VA: Society for Human Resource Management.

Maslow, A. H. (1943). A theory of human motivation. *Psychological Review, 50,* 370–396.

Maslow, A. H. (1954). *Motivation and personality.* New York: Harper.

Maslow, A. H. (1971). *The farther reaches of human nature.* New York: Penguin.

McClelland, D. C. (1965, November/December). Achievement motivation can be developed. *Harvard Business Review, 43,* 7–16.

McGregor, D. (1960). *The human side of enterprise.* New York: McGraw-Hill.

Meyer, J. P., & Herscovitch, L. (2001). Commitment in the workplace: Toward a general model. *Human Resources Management Review, 11,* 299–326.

Mitroff, I., & Denton, E. (1999). A study of spirituality in the workplace. *Sloan Management Review, 40,* 83–92.

Mohrman, S. A., & Cohen, S. G. (1995). When people get out of the box: New relationships, new systems. In A. Howard (Ed.), *The changing nature of work* (pp. 365–410). San Francisco: Jossey-Bass.

Morrow, P. (1993). *The theory and measurement of work commitment.* Greenwich: CT: JAI Press.

Paul, A. K., & Anantharaman, R. N. (2004). Influence of HRM practices on organizational commitment: A study among software professionals in India. *Human Resource Development Quarterly, 15,* 77–88.

Pool, S., & Pool, B. (2007). A management development model: Measuring organizational commitment its impact on job satisfaction among executives in a learning organization. *Journal of Management Development, 26,* 353–369.

Porters, L. W., Steers, R. M., Mowday, R. T., & Boulin, P. V. (1974). Organizational commitment, job satisfaction, and turnover among psychiatric technicians. *Journal of Applied Psychology, 59,* 603–609.

Richards, R. (1995). *Artful work: Awakening joy, meaning, and commitment in the workplace.* San Francisco: Berrett-Koehler.

Rogers, C. (1959). A theory of therapy, personality, and interpersonal relationships as developed in the client-centered framework. In S. Koch (Ed.), *Psychology: A study of science* (Vol. 3, pp. 184–256). New York: McGraw-Hill.

Rogers, C. (1961). *On becoming a person.* Boston: Houghton Mifflin.

Schaefer, C. & Darling, J. Contemplative Disciplines in Work and Organizational Life," High Tor Alliance, Spring Valley, NY, 1996.

Senge, P. (1993). *The fifth discipline: The art and practice of the learning organization.* New York: Doubleday.

Sievers, B. (1984). *Motivation as a surrogate for meaning* (Arbeitspapiere des Frachbereichs). Wupprtal, Germany: Bergische Universitat.

Society for Human Resource Management. (2008a). *Job satisfaction survey report.* Alexandria, VA: Author.

Society for Human Resource Management. (2008b). *Workplace forecast.* Alexandria, VA: Author.

Thomas, K. (2000). Unlocking the mysteries of intrinsic motivation. *OD Practitioner, 32*(4), 27–30.

47

Motivation and Human Growth: A Developmental Perspective

M.S. Srinivasin

Introduction

Motivation is a subject of perennial interest in management, psychology and leadership. However, most modern motivational theories suffer from two inadequacies – a lack of sufficient attention to the higher motives of the mental, moral and spiritual being in humans; and a too-heavy insistence on performance rather than on growth. What is not recognized fully is that motivation can be a means or lever of human development in the organization. A human being is not merely a knowledge, skill and productivity engine created solely for filling the coffers of an organization or meeting its bottom line and deadlines. It is a complex living entity with a sacred essence, created for a higher purpose. Most wisdom-traditions of the world agree that this higher purpose is a progressive unfolding of the human potential, culminating in fully blossomed flowers of humanity.

This article provides a conceptual framework for understanding the process of motivation from an evolutionary and developmental perspective.

Hierarchy of Motives

Equality of humans may be a spiritual truth, but is not yet an actual fact of life because individuals are at various levels of development. Needs, values and attitudes of individuals depend on their nature and the level of their inner

Source: *Journal of Human Values*, 14(1) (2008): 63–71.

development. The task or challenge of corporate leadership is, therefore, to understand intuitively this inner spirit of an employee and provide him with an individualized motivational programme that matches his unique needs. But how is this motivational level of each individual employee to be determined? This is where the importance of the well known 'need hierarchy of motives' model of Abraham Maslow comes in.

This model identifies five basic human needs and arranges them in an ascending order. They are: first, biological ones for sex, survival and other physical needs; second, those for material and emotional security; third, social needs for affection, autonomy, achievement, status, recognition and attention; and, finally, the highest need of all, self-actualization. According to Maslow, as each of these needs become substantially satisfied, the next needs become dominant. So the right motivation requires a clear understanding of these motivational needs of each individual and focus on satisfying them (Robins 1997: 214).

This need hierarchy model of Maslow, after a powerful initial impact on management thinkers and professionals, later went out of favour for supposedly better theories. Maslow's idea was criticized on many points. For example, it was accused of ignoring the cultural factor; of lacking empirical validity; and that the needs are parallel rather than hierarchical. All these criticisms can be valid, for no concept or theory can hope to explain or encompass the incredible complexity of human nature and its motives. But Maslow's need hierarchy model has two plus points over other modern motivational theories. First, it recognizes the process of evolution, viewing the human being as an evolving entity, moving progressively towards higher and higher levels of motivation; second, its intuition or idea is broader and more comprehensive than other modern theories.

However, from the viewpoint of Indian spiritual vision, Maslow's model has two flaws. First, it ignores or fails to articulate clearly the higher intellectual, moral and spiritual motives in man; and, second, from a holistic perspective, it needs to be integrated with a comprehensive vision of human development. This is where the Indian vision of human development can rectify and complement Maslow's model.

Evolution and Motivation: The Indian Paradigm

According to Indian thought, there are four stages in the evolution of humans that takes them towards their spiritual goal. Every human being begins the evolutionary journey as a physical entity driven by biological and security needs. He progresses to becoming a vital being with emotional and vital needs.[1] There are two sub-stages in the evolution of the vital human. First, he becomes someone who lives predominantly in his emotional and pragmatic mind with its need for mutuality, harmonious relationship, enjoyment and pragmatic adaptation to life. In the need hierarchy of Maslow these social needs constitute only one part of our emotional needs. At the next stage, the vital human becomes a person of strong will and abundant vital energy, the leader or the warrior type, with needs for power, achievement, conquest, expansion, name and fame. These 'esteem' needs, are again, one part of the needs of the human type of will and power in Maslow 's theory. Alexander and Napoleon are archetypal vital men of power, while in the corporate world, great and successful entrepreneurs and executives like Carnegie and Ford of the old economy, and Gates and Grove of the new economy, are predominantly vital men.

As the person progresses further, he becomes the intellectual, moral and artistic type of personality with intellectual, ethical and aesthetic needs for knowledge, values, ideals and vision; in other words, the mental human.[2] He looks beyond physical and vital needs, seeking to understand higher aims, values and laws of life, and trying to organize it according to these higher verities. Socrates and Plato, Tagore and Leonardo da Vinci, Einstein, Confucius and Gandhi are different types of mental men who have reached the higher plateaus of the human mind. One of the major aims of the social philosophy and practices of ancient Indian and Chinese civilization is to create a society governed by the mental and moral motives of *dharma*. As the mental human reaches the highest peak of intellectual, ethical and aesthetic development, he becomes aware of a spiritual reality beyond the mind and awakens to this highest spiritual need for self-realization, truth and God. He begins to become the spiritual human. The Vedic and Upanishadic sages, St Francis of Asisi, Meister Eckhart, and modern age sages like Sri Aurobindo, Vivekananda and Ramana Maharishi are different types of accomplished spiritual men.

We must note here that the stages of an individual's evolution depend mainly on the dominant temperament and motives that shape and drive his life, and not on academic status or mental development. In the process of evolution, mind and vital need develop simultaneously, although some vital persons may be at a transitional stage from the vital to the mental phase of development. Take for example someone like Andy Grove of Intel, the microchip giant. He started his career as a brilliant research engineer with a doctorate in chemical engineering, did some outstanding research work in fluid mechanics and semiconductor physics, and wrote six books. But when we look at his later life as CEO of Intel, we can see his dominant temperament and motives are that of the vital human, with an aggressive push for power, dominance, achievement, name and fame.

There four types or stages in human evolution can be placed in a corresponding four-fold motivational spectrum. At the lower end of the spectrum are the outwardly motivated who need the stimulus of external reward or punishment to remain active. At the higher end first come the self-motivated who feel an intrinsic joy in work and, therefore, need no external stimulus to remain motivated. Next come the ethically motivated who feel the need to contribute or serve a higher moral or social cause. The ethically awakened individual seeks not only joy in work, but a higher meaning as well. The last and the highest is spiritual motivation, which develops when the individual is awakened to his spiritual self beyond his body and mind. Let us now try to relate these four stages of evolution to their motivation spectrum.

The physical human who is bound to the needs and instincts of the body is at the lowest level of the motivation spectrum. For his higher evolution and development, his vital and emotional being have to be awakened by external motivators like the need for wealth, power, enjoyment and success. The vital man is capable of self-motivation and self-dedication to a higher moral or spiritual cause. When he awakens to these higher motives and dedicates himself to a higher ideal, he not only accelerates his own higher evolution, but also becomes a dynamic instrument for the higher evolution of the collectivity. The vital being, inspired by higher values, can be a very effective and heroic leader and crusader for manifesting these higher values in the outer life. Some of the Indian kings like Ashoka, Shivaji and Akbar, and statesmen of the West like Winston Churchill and Abraham Lincoln belong to this category. However, if there is a lack of sufficient mental or spiritual illumination in the mind, the vital man can become an aggressive and intolerant tyrant, forcefully championing a narrow dogmatic idea.

Similarly, when the mental human awakens to the spiritual realm may blossom into a high thinker, sage or a saint sowing luminous, kindly or inspiring ideals in the consciousness of people. But if there is a lack of strength in the will or vital force, the mental or moral individual will be ineffective as a leader. So, to fully realize moral and spiritual potentialities, both vital and mental humans must pursue a mental, moral and spiritual education and discipline, leading to a deepening, widening and refinement of mind and heart, linking their consciousness and will to a spiritual inspiration and energy. One such discipline is the *karma yoga* or *yoga* of action of the Indian scripture, the Bhagavad Gita. A main principle of this discipline, which has direct relevance for the corporate world, is to renounce the eager and anxious seeking of rewards of action and concentrate all our energies on the present, on the work to be done. If we have faith in God, we may add to this a consecration of all our activities to the divine power. The *karma yoga* path of the Gita leads to motiveless action, driven not by human motives – vital, mental or moral – but by a universal spiritual force, transcending the individual and collective ego.

Thus, Indian spiritual vision links motivation with human development in an integrated perspective. This scheme provides a broad and general framework for understanding and identifying the process of motivation in an evolutionary perspective. However, as mentioned earlier, human evolution is a complex process that cannot be rammed into any mental formula. We are at once a physical, vital, mental and a spiritual being. The motives and impulses of all these parts exist simultaneously within us although some of them may be dormant, weak or unmanifest.[3] The stage of our inner development depends on the most dominant, conscious or manifest part of our personality. For example, if the dominant part is vital we are in the second, vital stage of development. We also admit that this Indian scheme of human evolution is only one among many other possible formulas. Other schemes with different systems of classification are also possible and equally valid, but the Indian concept is preferable because we find it integral, embracing all the fundamental elements constituting the human organism.

Beyond Job Satisfaction

This brings us to one of the major objectives of modern motivational strategies – job satisfaction. Job satisfaction happens when the nature of work and the rewards received for this work match the motivational needs of an employee. But mere job satisfaction cannot be the highest ideal for an evolving human being.

In an evolving world, growth and progress is an eternal law and a higher need. Anything that does not grow disintegrates and perishes. So we have to create a work culture that consciously promotes and accelerates the progressive evolution of the individual by awakening in him the dormant higher needs. So the aim of motivational strategy has to be not only to satisfy the employee's present needs, but also to awaken higher needs. This means the physical being has to be awakened to his vital and mental needs, and helped to become the vital and mental being; the vital human to his mental, moral and aesthetic needs to bring the light of a higher culture to his life of raw desire and ambition; and the mental or moral individual to his highest spiritual goal.

The need for this evolutionary transition to higher needs is indicated by a lack of interest in the needs and activities of the present stage of development, and a growing interest in the needs and activities of higher stages. Here is an example from the *Harvard Business Review* illustrating this transition.

Mark was a star at the large West Coast Bank where he had worked for three years. He had an MBA from a leading business school and he had distinguished himself as a skilled lending officer. He excelled in every work task the bank gave him. He was smart and knew no other way to approach than to give it his all. The bank paid Mark well and senior managers had every intention of promoting him. But over time Mark grew more and more unhappy. He was seriously considering leaving the organization. Fortunately for both Mark and the bank, after consulting a counsellor, he was able to identify the cause of his unhappiness: he was no longer interested in his present job, which involved number crunching and interaction with customers. He wanted a more intellectually stimulating job. Using this insight, he was able to find a new assignment that required conceptual and analytical thinking, making him happy and satisfied (Butler and Waldrop 1999).

It is very difficult to say with precision or certainty what the psychological factors behind Mark's motivational problem were. One could be a shift in his life-motives from the vital to the mental level. However, sometimes this awakening to higher motives may express itself not in the professional life of the person, but in his hobbies and extra-professional interests. For example, it was reported in a leading business journal that a top executive from a big business house was very much interested in the field of unified theory in physics and in his spare time read every available book on the subject.

The Corporate World in the Motivation Map

We are now in a better position to relate the motivational process sketched so far to the present state of the corporate world.

Our modern age represents a rapid and increasing 'vitalization' and 'mentalization' (terms coined by Sri Aurobindo) of the human mass. So the pure physical type of personality satisfied with basic minimum needs are becoming fewer and fewer, for in the hyper-competitive and charged atmosphere of the corporate world, with its new thrust towards empowerment, knowledge, innovation and relentless chasing of deadlines, there is not much scope for the physical human. However, most of the shop floor and clerical workforce in the corporate world may perhaps live predominantly in their physical consciousness, but with a growing awakening to vital and mental needs.

Moving up to the managerial cadre, we have some interesting insights on executive motivation from two psychologists, Timothy Butler and James Waldrop, as elaborated in their article in the *Harvard Business Review*. According to these two Harvard psychologists, most executives in business are driven by seven basic 'business core functions' related to their deeply embedded life-interests or needs. They are: application of technology; enterprise control; managing people and relationships; quantitative analysis; counselling and mentoring; theory development and conceptual thinking; and influencing through language and ideas (ibid. 1999.) The first four factors are predominantly needs of the vital and pragmatic mind, while the last three are needs of the thinking and communicating mind. But this classification is based on the expression of life needs of people in their professional life. For a better understanding of the motivational level of people, we have to take into consideration the nature of their extra-professional activities.

Moreover, there are probably a considerable number of people in the corporate world who are seeking a moral and spiritual fulfilment or meaning in and through work. For example, the US Academy of Management recently launched a new magazine, *Journal of Management, Spirituality and Religion*, focusing on these higher needs and broader issues emerging in the management community.

However, motivation is not only individual, but also collective. Just as an individual, the collectivity can also move up the motivational ladder in the course of its natural evolution. Contemporary business is perhaps in such a state of evolutionary transition towards some higher mental and moral needs.

The first major change is what we may call the people-knowledge factor, a shift in the strategic motive of business from reliance on a mechanical and mass application of technology to the living knowledge or creativity of people or individual employees. As Michael Burns, chairman and CEO of Mercer Human Resource Consulting points out: 'The last decade has been technology fuelled productivity. Now is the turn of the knowledge-economy' (Burns 2007). And knowledge economy is people-centric. Christopher Barret of the Harvard Business School explains:

> We can't just manage by systems which are invariably defined in financial terms, we need to focus on people and on developing, managing and building our capacities through them.... Because they are the ones with the expertise and that is replacing capital as the scarce strategic resource. The new model, of the Individualized Corporation that we have evolved requires companies to leverage individual competencies, capacities, knowledge and skills. This is going to be the source of competitive advantage. (1999: 61)

Barret gives the following example of ISS, a Denmark-based firm which is in the cleaning business:

> It is a business with minute margins, so they have to focus on costs. They could have regarded their employees as labourers who were asked to go and do their job, directed in the classical hierarchal form. But what they did instead was to create individual teams that worked together on cleaning contracts.... Then they engaged in education ... where they took the front-line people through a series of training sets. The first obviously was teaching them how to clean properly. The second was to work together in a team. Third, they started focusing on quality. Fourth they got their teams to focus on customer service and listening to customers. Fifth, the teams were taught to read financials. Eventually the teams became interested in what the customer wanted and became capable of interpreting data. This is innovation. You get costs down by driving responsibility down the organization, creating entrepreneurial initiative and leveraging ideas across the organization – it's a different philosophy. (ibid.)

The second factor is the growing interest in ethics. There are two important features in the emerging ethical debate in business. First is the recognition of the motivational power of ethics. As former CEO of Johnson & Johnson, James Burke, says:

> Here we believe strongly in three things, decentralization, managing for the long-term, and the ethical principles embodied in our Credo. Credo is the sort of thing that inspires the best in people. I think that all of us have

a basic moral imperative hidden somewhere in us. In some people it is more central to their being, but it's always there. To tap that well-spring creates energy that you can't get elsewhere. (1986: 19)

The second feature is the growing demand for fairness and transparency. As founder of Infosys N.R. Narayana Murthy states: 'Investors, customers, employees and vendors have all become more discerning and are demanding greater transparency and fairness in all dealings' (Skaria 1999: 25). This shows that the corporate world as a whole is becoming more sensitive to ethical issues. The third factor is the concept of corporate social responsibility (CSR), which is spreading fast in the business community. CSR seems to be the new fad in business and management. As a columnist in the business section of a leading Indian daily points out:

> Call it guilt cleansing or genuine concern for the downtrodden; the fact is that from single-minded devotion to bottom line till a few years ago, corporations are increasingly putting their mind and money to the bottom of social pyramid. Philanthropy indeed is fast becoming an integral part of corporate culture. Today nearly every major corporate house is supporting some cause or social initiative. And they are no longer taking it as charity but as a responsibility. In today's world being a good and responsible corporate citizen is as important as increasing your business. (Vishwajeet 2006)

For example, in India most of the major players in the new economy like Satyam, Wipro, Infosys, and Dr Reddy's Laboratory have their charitable trusts working on social causes. In the US, two icons of the new economy, Bill Gates and Andy Grove, have their own foundations.

The Path Ahead

These mental and moral needs emerging in the corporate mind hold great promise for the future evolution of business, but these needs have to be explored to their highest potential. This requires a deep insight into the psychological and spiritual sources of knowledge and ethics, and which must be harnessed for the higher evolution of business. If businesses can do this, it will give a quantum thrust to their future evolution. This higher evolution is not a matter of idealism, but a crucial choice that will determine the future status of individuals and collectivities. Tex Gunning (2007), a vice-president of the Unilever Group, in his valedictory address to the CII national summit on corporate social responsibility, said:

> Many companies did not exist more than 60 to 70 years because they do not evolve.... Earning money was essential but it was not the essence of life. Companies have to create social capital, economic capital, spiritual capital and intellectual capital. Companies that don't create this kind of

wealth would be dissolved or swept away. We have to act now out of choice or have change forced on us.

These prophetic words from the mind of a top business executive display an instinctive recognition of what Sri Aurobindo perceived with a more conscious, enlightened and far-seeing vision in the beginning of the twentieth century. 'In the next stage of human progress,' said Sri Aurobindo, 'it is not a material but a spiritual, moral and psychological progress that has to be made ... [and] whatever race or whatever country that seizes on the lines of these evolution and fulfills it will be the leader of humanity' (Sri Aurobindo 1972a, 1972b).

In the scheme of nature, whatever that does not evolve either becomes extinct or has to play second fiddle to the leaders who surge ahead. However, there is one more important factor related to this higher evolution, which we would like to briefly touch upon before concluding our discussion. Human motivation or action has an inner intent as well as an outer content. The word 'motive' is normally used to describe mainly the inner intent. For example, if I become moral out of fear of hell in the life after death or because of karmic consequences, then my motivation is ethical only in the outer content and not in the inner intent, which is still the vital motive of fear. In this sense, the mental and moral needs emerging in business are very much mixed. There is a change only in the outer content, but not much in the inner intent of still vital needs like productivity, competitive advantage, and the pressure of outer circumstances.

However, our human organism is 'psychosomatic'. Our body and mind, thoughts, feelings and actions have a mutual interaction and influence. An outer action, when it is done with sincerity, persistence and conviction, has corresponding inner results. For example, someone who becomes moral out of vital or material needs may one day become conscious of the inherent joy of virtue and as a result the lower needs may drop away. Or else, as he grows mentally, he may awaken to the fact that ethics is an integral part of the higher laws of life, and as a result, a corresponding change may occur in the inner motives of action. For instance, the modern environmental movement is the result of such a mental awakening to the laws of physical nature. When there is a similar awakening to the psychological and spiritual ecology of universal nature, and when these higher laws of life are implemented and institutionalized in the corporate life, then it will give a decisive thrust to the higher evolution of the collective life of humanity. The corporate mind in business has to consciously strive for this higher awakening.

Notes

1. We use the term 'vital' to denote that part of our consciousness that is the source of our emotions, passions, enthusiasm, energy, and the dynamic will for action and execution.

2. We use the word 'mental' for that part of our consciousness that houses our intellectual, ethical and aesthetic intelligence. A human being can achieve his full development, or in other words, become the true mental human, only when he develops fully all the potentialities of his higher mental nature made of the rational, ethical and aesthetic being, and govern the rest of his nature with this higher element in him. This is the reason why in our scheme of human development we have placed the mental above the vital in the evolutionary ladder. Beyond the perfection of 'humanhood' there is what we may call the perfection of 'soulhood', which can be achieved only by realizing our spiritual nature beyond mind.

3. Even when we are fully awakened to the higher needs and try to organize our life around them, lower needs are still present – perhaps very much suppressed and held down, but not mastered. Therefore, they can cast their overt or covert influence over our actions. So the intellectual, the artist and the saint can still be swayed by vital motives like name and fame and power and wealth. This is the reason why the path of yoga in which the seeker makes a conscious effort to rise beyond the mind into the spiritual consciousness is so difficult. Even after we have kindled the fire of aspiration and kept it burning, our lower nature may still throw its smoke and dust and filth into the sacred flame and disturb the inner sacrifice, or even extinguish the flame. This fact of the inner life is symbolically conveyed in Indian mythology in the image of titanic beings disturbing the fire-sacrifice rituals of the *rishis*.

References

Barret, Christopher (1999), 'Interview: Create a Purpose to Engage People', *Business Today*, 7 May, 61–69.

Burke, James (1986), Interview, in Thomas R. Horton, ed., *What Works For Me*, pp. 16–25 (New York: Random House).

Burns, Michael (2007), 'Interview: Now it is the Turn of the Knowledge Economy', *Business Today*, 15 June.

Butler, Timothy and James Waldrop (1999), 'Job Sculpting: The Art of Retaining Your Best People', *Harvard Business Review*, September–October, 41–63.

Robins, Stephen (1997), *Organizational Behavior* (New Delhi: Prentice-Hall).

Gunning, Tex (2007), 'Corporates Should have a Conscience', *Hindu*, 16 June.

Skaria, George (1999) 'The Well-governed Corporation', *Business Today*, 21 November, 25–31.

Sri Aurobindo (1972a), *Collected Works: Bande Matharam* (Pondicherry: Sri Aurobindo Ashram).

———. (1972b). *Collected Works: Supplement* (Pondicherry: Sri Aurobindo Ashram).

48

Evolutionary Perspectives on Human Motivation

Jutta Heckhausen

B efore Charles Darwin's theory gained influence in the social and behavioral sciences, the traditional philosophical and theological views distinguished human motivation from animal motivation as something governed by the "free will," as opposed to by instinct. The growing acceptance of Darwinian ideas resulted in three major innovations in psychology, which led to a segregation rather than integration of approaches.

First, McDougall (1908) argued that a set of basic instincts and drives guides not only animal but also human behavior. His approach is reflected in modern ethological approaches to fundamental behavioral systems, such as aggression (Bischof, 1985; Lorenz, 1966), parenting (Bischof, 1985; Bowlby, 1969), and foraging (L. Tinbergen, 1960; N. Tinbergen, 1951).

Second, simultaneously with McDougall's (1908) ideas about human motivational drives, Sigmund Freud developed his psychodynamic theory, which conceptualizes behavior and cognition as influenced by latent and unconscious drives of the individual. This approach found its continuation in personality conceptions of motivation and their specific diagnostic instruments, namely, projective tests (McClelland, 1971; Murray, 1938).

Third, the ability to adjust instinctual behavior to changing environmental conditions is a key feature of human behavior, which should be precedented by early forms of intelligent behavior in related animal species. The pioneer of comparative research in learning (i.e., associative) capacity was Thorndike (1898). His groundbreaking work, together with James's (1890) conception

Source: *American Behavioral Scientist,* 43(6) (2000): 1015–1029.

of "habit," laid the foundation for behaviorism, which unfortunately dominated psychology at the expense of all other approaches for nearly three decades.

In consequence of the excessive and prolonged domination of psychology by behaviorism, human motivation appeared to be an unworthy domain of psychological research. Nevertheless, the field made important advances in terms of adopting models of instrumentality of behavior (Vroom, 1964) and of decision rationality by way of combining the expectations about outcomes with perceived outcome value as determinants of human motivation and thus behavioral investment. Atkinson (1957) combined this expectancy-value approach with an interindividual-difference construct of motive strength, thus creating a predictive model of motivated behavior. However, the model became ever more cognitive and thus segregated from ethological and comparative approaches to motivation. The human-animal gap widened even more with the rise of attributional theory in motivation (Kelley, 1967; Weiner, 1972), which may have been, in part, a reaction to the overdominance of behaviorism.

The modern revival of human motivation in psychology (e.g., see J. Heck-hausen & Dweck, 1998) was largely associated with the cognitive paradigm and its integration with an interindividual-difference approach to motives (H. Heck-hausen, 1991). This course of scientific evolution has largely bypassed the issue of evolutionary precursors of motivated human behavior. At the same time, comparative psychology has focused on cognitive phenomena to the exclusion of phenomena of motivational engagement and disengagement.

Why Should Evolutionary Psychology Be Interested in Motivation?

Evolutionary psychology has thus far paid little attention to phenomena of motivation and emotion (see review in Schneider & Dittrich, 1990), and has mostly focused on the cognitive functioning involved in social exchange (e.g., Cosmides & Tooby, 1992), risk perception (e.g., Gigerenzer, Todd, & the ABC Research Group, in press; Rode & Wang, 2000 [this issue]), foraging and food preferences (Stephens & Krebs, 1986; Rozin, 2000 [this issue]), mate choice (Buss, 1994; Todd, 2000 [this issue]), and parenting (e.g., Keller, 2000 [this issue]; Mann, 1992).

An evolutionary approach to motivation and emotion must first ask the question of how the organism can direct its behavior to seek favorable and avoid harmful environments and outcomes (Schneider & Dittrich, 1990). Hypothetically, one might postulate either of two extreme types of mechanisms: The first is fixed stimulus-response patterns, which are preadapted by genetically transferred programs of behavior, what Mayr (1974) referred to as "closed behavior programs." The alternative mechanisms would be one that directly guides the organism's behavior in view of the requirements of maximizing inclusive fitness (Hamilton, 1964; Wilson, 1975), a view promoted by radical sociobiologists. Both these extreme alternative mechanisms seem unlikely to play a key role in human behavioral regulation. Fixed or "closed behavior programs" (Mayr, 1974) are not flexible enough to effectively guide the behavior of a species living in a highly complex material and social environment. Intentional pursuit of ultimate goals of reproductive fitness would exceed the capacity of a central regulating mechanism, in terms of both the complexity and coordination of subsystems.

Instead of such extreme models, an approach that integrates the operation of "open behavioral programs" (Mayr, 1974) or behavioral modules (Cosmides & Tooby, 1994; Rozin, 1976) and more general processes of behavior direction associated with emotional states and motivational tendencies (Hamburg, 1963; Plutchik, 1980; Scherer, 1984) is more promising. Evolutionary psychology has furnished an impressive range of research programs in various domain-specific modules preadapted to solve specific tasks involved in the optimization of inclusive fitness (Cosmides & Tooby, 1994; Fodor, 1983; Rozin, 1976; Tooby & Cosmides, 1992). However, little attention has been invested and consequently no consensus has been achieved with respect to the regulation of behavior across domains. In complex situational settings that afford more than one module of behavior (e.g., foraging and mate selection), the organism needs to manage cross-domain trade-offs. Moreover, in a mobile species capable of highly varied and flexible behavior, the attainment of proximate goals may require prolonged effort even in the absence of immediate situational affordances. This constellation of challenges for behavioral regulation requires mediational mechanisms, which help the organism select the most appropriate behavior given a certain combination of need state, environmental opportunity, and expected control.

Emotional mediation between situational affordances and the organism's responses provides an overall directionality to behavior, and thus enables the organism to activate behavior that tightly fits its specific needs and the environmental opportunities. An example is sexual excitement in rhesus monkeys that facilitates a variety of behavior patterns ranging from mounting to grooming or even masturbating, depending on the presence and behavior of a potential mate. Emotional mediating also allows the organism to put learning experiences acquired within its own ontogenesis to use, rather than having to rely on phylogenetically evolved preadapted and fixed stimulus-response connections. Learning the relation between a certain behavior and a certain desired (or feared) outcome makes it possible to bring behavior under the control of anticipated consequences. In sum, motivational and emotional mechanisms might provide the missing link to the environment-need fit in the activation and deactivation of behavioral and cognitive modules. In this way, behavioral regulation by motivation may be part of a multilevel architecture of the mammal and, indeed, the human mind.

How Could Motivational Psychology Profit
from an Evolutionary Perspective?

Motivational psychology has started out with the great complexity involved in adult human action. The first motivational research was focused around the concepts of volition and the free will (Ach, 1910; James, 1890; Wundt, 1896). What could be more cerebral, and thus discrepant, from the regulation of behavior in animals? However, phenomena of volition in human motivation did not suddenly occur with modern man. Motivational mechanisms, including those of volition and the free will had evolutionary precursors.

Evolution can not invent solutions to environmental or regulative challenges because it is not teleologically guided. Therefore, nature needs to work with what evolution has already brought about in previously evolved species. This is as true for behavioral programs as it is for older brain structures and for basic body plans of anatomy (Rumbaugh, Savage-Rumbaugh, & Washburn, 1994). It is known from comparative psychological research that various complex psychological mechanisms can be traced to simpler, more basic processes in nonhuman species (e.g., Leger, 1992; Roitblad, 1987). To be sure, the evolutionary heritage is not necessarily the best solution for present problems but merely the best solution selected in the phylogenetic past, given the constraints of already existing canalizations of phylogeny at the time.

Although evolutionary psychology, with its present emphasis on specific cognitive modules involved in foraging, decision making, and risk-related behavior focuses on those modules believed to be a product of hunter-gatherer evolution (Barkow, Cosmides, & Tooby, 1992), I would argue that key modules involved in the motivational regulation of human behavior go back as far as early mammal or even vertebrate evolution.

To arrive at a model of the origins and evolution of motivational processes, I should start with a task analysis of survival and reproductive fitness in terms of its motivational implications. The basic survival functions involve the internal regulation of body metabolism by way of breathing, cardiovascular functioning, and balancing of substances, as well as regulatory challenges involving control of the immediate environment to attain food, liquid, and shelter; avoid predators; seek a mate; reproduce; and (in some species) care for offspring. It can probably be said that for most invertebrates, these challenges of inclusive fitness are mastered by way of closed-behavior programs (Mayr, 1974), which comprise genetically fixed stimulus-response connections (e.g., hunger triggers species-typical foraging behavior, followed by consummatory activity).

However, even in some invertebrates and lower vertebrates, these stimulus-response connections are modifiable by need states in the sense that higher need lowers the threshold for the stimulus-typical response (Ewert, 1976; Kravitz, 1988). Thus the animal may, for example, react with sexual behavior even to objects that are remotely similar in appearance to conspecifics. This modification of response threshold may be the very earliest form of flexibilization of the fixed stimulus-response connections in closed behavior programs (Mayr, 1974). However, these closed connections between need states, behavior, need-relevant stimulus, and responses provide no degree of freedom for multiple behavioral options and the adaptation of behavioral means to variations in the environment. In vertebrate – and especially mammal – evolution, open behavior programs evolved that provide greater degrees of freedom to flexibly adapt behavior to environmental conditions for foraging, predator avoidance, reproduction, and other challenges. An example is adaptively varied insect foraging patterns in birds across an array of food patches with varying food availability, familiarity, and under conditions of high (with hatchlings) versus low need states (e.g., Krebs, 1980; McFarland, 1977; L. Tinbergen, 1960).

The evolutionary precursors of emotional processes probably evolved hand in hand with the transition from vertrebrates, which fed by filtering nutritious particles out of water, to those actively searching for larger individual pieces of nutrients. The latter need to regulate their movement patterns, whereas the former had no choice. Recent work on the first steps in the evolution of neo-cortical structures at the transition between invertebrate and vertebrate strata (e.g., *Appendicularia*) shows that extrapyramidal neocortical structures resemble those dedicated to visual orientation in more complex species and occur strictly contingent with the ability to move in the water, rather than being fixed to a certain place. A transition species even showed an ontogenetic contingent with the juvenile form moving about and endowed with a minute and basic neocortical structure, which the stationary adult form loses.

Emotional states may have come about with the emergence of neocortical structures, which allowed the secondary projection and integration of sensory input and motor programs with the vegetative and endocrinological systems that had evolved even earlier for the maintenance of internal bodily equilibrium. The types of species that are associated with this milestone in the evolution of motivational regulation are reptiles. It has been shown with contemporary caimans (Keating, Kormann, & Horel, 1970) that artificial stimulation of certain central cortical areas elicited directed-flight behavior, including the circumvention of obstacles and involving heavy breathing and vocalizations. Thus, these reptiles exhibited all the constitutional aspects of motivated behavior and both vegetative and motoric behavioral patterns of emotional responses.

Comparative research in learning patterns provides strikingly convergent evidence for the transition from fixed to emotionally mediated (in the broadest sense) connections between behavior and environmental events. Species differences in the response to changes in reinforcement incentives (food pellets) reflect probably the earliest step in this evolutionary advance. Bitterman's (1975) classical comparative study of learning revealed that whereas fish and certain turtle species exhibit a direct relation between resistance to extinction and magnitude of reinforcement (i.e., resistance to extinction increases with magnitude of reinforcement), mammals such as rats show an inverse relation between extinction and reinforcement (resistance to extinction decreases with magnitude of reinforcement). These findings may be interpreted as an impressive illustration of the mediating effects of emotional states. In species with more sophisticated neuronal systems, behavior changes do not simply mirror changes in reinforcement. Higher developed species instead react to the change in incentives by disproportionately decreasing the operant behavior after decreases in incentives and disproportionately increasing it after increases in incentives. It is an intriguing question whether this phylogenetic transition may be associated with the evolution of reptiles and thus converge with the transition to earliest forms of behavior motivated by emotional states (for findings on caiman behavior, see Keating et al., 1970).

In mammals, emotional reactions are found that mediate between stimulus and reaction and provide a general directionality of behavior, for example, in terms of appetence with regard to favored and needed food or avoidance with regard to predators or superior rivals. This general directionality of behavior then allows the specific behavioral means to be adjusted in accordance to the specific affordances of the environment. Such emotional mediators can become effective incentives of behavior, not only via conscious expectations but also by way of Pavlovian conditioning of emotional responses to stimulus constellations. This way, certain situations and behavioral patterns become marked emotionally, and are thus incorporated into internal mental representations and modifiable by learning (Schneider & Dittrich, 1990). Hence, even without any insight into the ultimate goals of behavior in terms of reproductive fitness, the organism is steered toward maximizing inclusive fitness in the various domains of survival and reproduction.

The major motivational systems of prosocial (altruistic) behavior, aggression, affiliation, power, and achievement lend directionality and dynamics to behavior by way of need (push) and incentives (pull) and involve motive-specific emotions (H. Heckhausen, 1991). Although the completeness of this list may be debated and various longer lists have been proposed, the systems mentioned play a key role in regulating behavior by way of a hidden agenda that maximizes reproductive fitness while being experienced by the organism as highly need- and situation-specific motivators of behavior. A telling case in point is altruistic behavior, which is costly to the individual, yet holds benefits for inclusive fitness, and thus is an ultimate goal for adaptation (Hoffman, 1981). The mediation between proximate incentives and this ultimate goal is provided by empathic affective experiences, which motivate the individual to invest altruistic behavior in ameliorating distress in others. As altruism researcher Hoffman (1981) notes,

> Empathy may be uniquely suited for bridging the gap between egoism and altruism, since it has the property of transforming another person's misfortune into one's own feeling of distress.... an aversive state that may often best be alleviated by helping the victim, (p. 133)

Basic Motivational Modules as Domain-General Regulators of Human Behavior

A common feature of all motivated behavior is that the organism attempts to achieve outcomes in the environment by its own activity. In activities such as trying to find food, winning a mate, or struggling with a rival, the organism strives for control in terms of bringing about desired outcomes and preventing unde-sired ones. I therefore argue that the most fundamental and universal of motivational modules should relate to this basic endeavor to control the environment (J. Heckhausen & Schulz, 1995, in press). The strive for control should also be shared with the broadest range of species and go back the furthest into the phylogenetic past; at least as far back as to those species that first acquired a notable flexibility in their behavior programs (Gallistel, 1990; Rumbaugh & Sterritt, 1986).

From a functionalistic perspective, one would hypothesize a set of basic motivational modules that would together favor an overall preference for controlling the environment and maximizing one's resources and capacities for control (J. Heckhausen & Schulz, in press; Schulz & Heckhausen, 1997). Because of the dearth of comparative psychological research into motivational processes, one has to rely on reasoning about functional requirements of behavior regulation in active, complex, and resource-needy organisms such as mammals.

First, one might expect a selectively enhanced attentional readiness and sensitivity to detect contingencies between behavior and external stimuli. Such a module for detecting behavior-event contingencies would help the organism to generally learn about its effectiveness to bring about events in the environment and identify specific behavioral patterns as causes for certain desired or dreaded outcomes.

Second, control striving is promoted by an inherent preference for behavior-event contingencies. By inherent, it is meant that the preference holds even when there is no reinforcement with regard to a specific need, such as hunger, thirst, and so on. There is ample evidence for this assumption both with regard to humans and to other mammals (see review in Rumbaugh et al., 1994; White, 1959). Animals of various mammal species have been shown to become listless and depressed when experiencing uncontrollable negative events (Overmier & Seligman, 1967). Operant conditioning studies with mammals show that behavior-event contingencies are preferred to event-event contingencies even in the absence of consummatory behavior (see review in White, 1959). Chimpanzees favor objects that can be moved, changed, or made to emit sounds and light (Welker, 1956); monkeys spend hours solving mechanical puzzles (Harlow, 1953); and both children and rats prefer response-elicited rewards to receiving the same rewards without having to respond (Singh, 1970; see also aversion of freeloading phenomenon, Osborne, 1977). These preferences for behavior-event contingencies are already in place at the very beginning of life. Even human neonates are able to detect behavior-event contingencies (Janos & Papousek, 1977; Papousek, 1967). Papousek (1967) found, for example, that very young infants learned head movements contingent on acoustic signals and milk reinforcement. Even after complete satiation, when the milk had lost its reinforcing potential, signals elicited prompt head movements and pleasure on the occurrence of the expected contingent presentation of the milk bottle.[1]

The third motivational module, which would favor control behavior, is a tendency to repeat responses when they have led to desirable consequences. This is the classical behaviorist notion of the "law of effect" (Thorndike, 1898) and operant conditioning (Skinner, 1938), which has been shown to hold for an extensive variety of vertebrate species, ranging from fish to birds, rats, monkeys, and humans. However, as discussed above, there appear to be interesting interspecies differences in the response to changes in reinforcers, so that species with elaborated neocortex structures exhibit enhanced reactions to shifts in incentives.

The fourth motivational module is an asymmetric pattern of affect reactions to negative and positive changes in the environment. This asymmetry in affective responses is closely related to the basic forms of affective transformations discussed in the previous paragraph. Frijda (1988) has proposed "the laws of emotion" that humans affectively respond to negative change more strongly than to positive change. After a change for the worse, the negative emotions are stronger and typically last much longer than the positive emotions that follow a change for the better. In terms of control behavior, an interesting fact is that positive emotions of pride, feeling satisfied with the environment, and so on would hardly motivate the individual to become active to change the environment. In contrast, a negative emotion after a negative change motivates the individual to do something to change the environment to get rid of the noxious situation. Thus, the asymmetry in responding emotionally to positive and negative changes leads to a selective promotion of control behavior directed at changing the environment. Bitterman's (1975) findings on interspecies differences may suggest the transition in phylogeny when this asymmetry evolved.

The fifth motivational module involved in promoting control behavior is curiosity and exploration. Those species that operate based on open-behavior programs (Mayr, 1974) rely heavily on the acquisition of experience and knowledge during each organism's ontogenesis. Experience and knowledge acquisition is, of course, most promoted when the organism exposes itself to novel situations. It is striking how similar and almost stereotypical mammal species with more complex neocortices are with regard to their typical exploratory behavior; they gaze at, walk around, sniff, touch, and manipulate an unknown object or animal (Schneider, 1996). It would seem likely that curiosity and exploration is a universal motivational system in higher mammals. An organism can only profit from the experiences of exploration when they are stored in some kind of mental representation, as expectancies, schemata, and so on. With greater neocortical capacity came the ability to store more complex schemata about object relations and causal connections. Violations of expectancies can then become instigators of curiosity and elicit exploratory behavior. This phenomenon of a preference for moderate discrepancy has been widely researched in the wake of Helson's (1964) adaptation-level theory (McClelland, 1953).

As a sixth component of motivational regulation, humans exhibit a perception of personal control, mastery, and self-efficacy (Bandura, 1982; Harter, 1974; Watson, 1966; White, 1959). The developmental origin of this mastery perception is a generalized awareness of behavior-event contingency (Watson, 1966) that emerges during the first 2 or 3 years of life and provides a motivational resource for active control attempts (J. Heckhausen, 1989; see also review in J. Heckhausen & Schulz, 1995). Such a generalized conception of one's own competence, efficacy, and control enables the organism to view activities directed at attaining outcomes in the environment as opportunities to experience and test competence, thus creating a motivational resource for overcoming difficulties and pursuing effortful activities, even in the face of obstacles or long-term delays of gratification. Anticipated self-reinforcement then, is the missing link to adult human achievement motivation (H. Heckhausen, 1991). Unfortunately, very little is known about the potential nonhuman primate or even mammal precursors of such generalized concepts. Rumbaugh and Sterritt (1986) suggested that perceptions of control may have had both proximate reinforcement value as a buffer against anxiety with overwhelmingly novel stimulation and ultimate reproductive advantage by facilitating the development of new activities and experiences. With regard to the phylogenetic availability of the phenomenon of perceived control, it should be taken into account that perceived control most likely requires an awareness of self, which phylogentically did not evolve before the higher primates. In the great apes, however, self-recognition seems to be present (Gallup, 1970, 1979), and thus a notion of one's own competence may play a role as a motivating factor of control activities, as well.

In addition to these modules that would steer an organism toward selecting activities directed at achieving goals in the environment, there are probably other facilitative processes that help to focus attention and behavior on a chosen goal of control. Among these should be mechanisms of intention-based priming, which enhance the salience of goal-relevant cues and benefits while degrading irrelevant and particularly conflicting goals and their respective cues. Modern approaches to human motivation (Gollwitzer, 1990; H. Heckhausen & Gollwitzer, 1986; H. Heckhausen, 1991; Kuhl, 1984) have put such long-forgotten volitional processes back into the larger field of motivational psychology. Moreover, recent models of control behavior and developmental regulation have addressed self-regulatory processes as part of motivational engagement and disengagement (J. Heckhausen, 1999; J. Heckhausen &Schulz, 1993,1998; Schulz & Heckhausen, 1996).

The motivational modules discussed so far all are directed at engaging the organism with goals of controlling the external world. However, control when striving for a particular goal may become dysfunctional when the goal turns out to be unattainable or the costs for striving become excessive and harm other, more important goal pursuits. Under such presumably not uncommon circumstances, the organism needs to disengage from a control goal so as to avoid wasting behavioral and motivational resources in futile goal pursuits, or become frustrated (a consequence of emotional-laden goal commitment) or even depleted in self-esteem and hopefulness (for those species that can construct a conception of their own competence).

Deactivating behavior programs is not a challenge uniquely encountered by humans. All behavior that is to some extent flexible and involves choosing among options can go awry and should be susceptible to deactivation. Activities such as searching for food on a particular patch, chasing prey, courting a potential mate, or fighting a rival can turn out futile and thus wasteful or even directly destructive. Thus, mechanisms that promote engagement in goal pursuits need to be balanced by those allowing disengagement. Such mechanisms seem to be in place. Animals do not follow a prey until they collapse from exhaustion, they do not exploit a patch until collecting the last grain of food, or fight a superior rival until they are killed. Instead, there seem to be discontinuous mechanisms of goal deactivation that allow the animal to switch from complete engagement to disengagement in a sudden, discrete manner.

The mechanisms involved in such deactivation of goal pursuit can be seen as the building blocks for human self-regulation of goal pursuit and coping with failure and losses. They enable the individual to switch behavioral and motivational resources over to comparatively more promising goal pursuits, and to avoid frustration with blocked goals. In addition to these two important functions of goal disengagement, humans also have to compensate for the negative consequences of failure experiences on self-esteem and general self-related conceptions of competence. Self-protective processes of reinterpreting failure or loss (e.g., by self-serving causal attributions; Snyder, Stephan, & Rosenfield, 1978) are probably unique to humans, although they do not rely on conscious processing of information. In fact, they may be all the more effective the less intentional they are (Brandtstädter & Renner, 1992; Brandtstädter, Wentura, & Greve, 1993).

Summary and Conclusion

The history of psychology has disconnected motivational and comparative perspectives that had once inspired each other. After the prolonged reign of behaviorism, both comparative and motivational psychology have become dominated by a strong emphasis on cognitive processes at the expense, and to the exclusion of, affect-related processes. This has made it difficult to formulate and pursue an evolutionary approach to human motivation. However, evolutionary psychology should be keenly interested in motivational issues, given that problems of behavior and self-regulation are not resolved by merely addressing cognitive skills and modules. Instead, organisms with a substantial neocortex and behavioral flexibility require mechanisms that mediate between environmental challenges and behavior and allow adjustment of behavioral means in accordance with a complex and changing environment.

From the point of view of motivational psychology, the paradigm of evolutionary psychology can provide a good approximation to the likely phylogenetic origins of specific motivational processes in other primates, mammals, and vertebrates. The problems of behavior regulation share common features across an impressive range of different species, and may have led to the selection of a few basic modules involved in affecting change in the environment. The set of potential motivational modules discussed promotes control behavior directed at the environment and is broadly applicable across domains of functioning and tasks involved in reproductive fitness.

Note

1. A related but functionally distinct issue is the preference for self-determination or self-controlled selection of goals for behavior. For example, Washburn and Rumbaugh (1991) report that rhesus monkeys perform better on tasks that they had selected themselves than on tasks assigned to them. A similar argument is made by Deci and Ryan (1985; Ryan, Kuhl, & Deci, 1997) with regard to basic psychological needs in humans. This preference for autonomy is a most interesting phenomenon with regard to those species that live in hierarchical social structures. Choosing one's own behavioral goals is counteracting the dominance of high-status individuals. It may have benefits for the individual, but certainly not for group stability.

References

Ach, N. (1910). *Über den Willensakt und das Temperament* [On acts of will and temperament]. Leipzig, Germany: Quelle & Meyer.
Atkinson, J. W. (1957). Motivational determinants of risk-taking behavior. *Psychological Review, 64,* 359–372.
Bandura, A. (1982). Self-efficacy mechanisms in human agency. *American Psychologist, 37,* 122–147.
Barkow, J. H., Cosmides, L., & Tooby, J. (Eds.). (1992). *The adapted mind: Evolutionary psychology and the generation of culture.* New York: Oxford University Press.
Bischof, N. (1985). *Das Rätsel Ödipus* [The Oedipus mystery]. München, Germany: Piper.
Bitterman, M. E. (1975). The comparative analysis of learning. *Science, 188,* 699–709.
Bowlby, J. (1969). *Attachment and loss: Attachment* (Vol. 1). New York: Basic Books.
Brandtstädter, J., & Renner, G. (1992). Coping with discrepancies between aspirations and achievements in adult development: A dual-process model. In L. Montada, S.-H. Filipp, & M. R. Lerner (Eds.), *Life crises and experiences of loss in adulthood* (pp. 301–319). Hillsdale, NJ: Lawrence Erlbaum.

Brandtstädter, J., Wentura, D., & Greve, W. (1993). Adaptive resources of the aging self: Outlines of an emergent perspective. *International Journal of Behavioral Development, 16,* 323–349.

Buss, D. M. (1994). *The evolution of desire: Strategies of human mating.* New York: Basic Books.

Cosmides, L., & Tooby, J. (1992). Cognitive adaptations for social exchange. In J. H. Barkow, L. Cosmides, & J. Tooby (Eds.), *The adapted mind: Evolutionary psychology and the generation of culture* (pp. 163–228). New York: Oxford University Press.

Cosmides, L., & Tooby, J. (1994). Origins of domain-specificity: The evolution of functional organization. In L. A. Hirschfeld & S. A. Gelman (Eds.), *Mapping the mind: Domain specificity in cognition and culture* (pp. 85–116). Cambridge, UK: Cambridge University Press.

Deci, E. L., & Ryan, R. M. (1985). *Intrinsic motivation and self-determination in human behavior.* New York: Plenum.

Ewert, J.-P. (1976). *Neuro-Ethologie. Einführung in die neurophysiologischen Grundlagen des Verhaltens* [Neuro-ethology: Introduction to the neurophysiological foundations of behavior]. Berlin: Springer.

Fodor, J. (1983). *The modularity of mind.* Cambridge, MA: MIT Press.

Frijda, N. H. (1988). The laws of emotion. *American Psychologist, 43,* 349–358.

Gallistel, C. R. (1990). *The organization of learning.* Cambridge: MIT Press.

Gallup, G. G., Jr. (1970). Chimpanzees: Self-recognition. *Science, 167,* 86–87.

Gallup, G. G., Jr. (1979). Self-recognition in chimpanzees and man: A developmental and comparative perspective. In M. Lewis & L. Rosenblum (Eds.), *The child and its family: The genesis of behavior* (Vol. 2, 107–126). New York: Plenum.

Gigerenzer, G., Todd, P. M., & ABC Research Group, (in press). *Simple heuristics that make us smart.* New York: Oxford University Press.

Gollwitzer, P. M. (1990). Action phases and mind-sets. In E. T. Higgins & R. M. Sorrentino (Eds.), *Handbook of motivation and cognition: Foundations of social behavior* (Vol. 2, pp. 53–92). New York: Guilford.

Hamburg, D. A. (1963). Emotions in the perspective of human evolution. In P. H. Knapp (Ed.), *Expression of emotions in man* (pp. 300–317). New York: International University Press.

Hamilton, W. D. (1964). The genetical evolution of social behavior. *Journal of Theoretical Biology, 7,* 1–52.

Harlow, H. F. (1953). Mice, monkeys, men, and motives. *Psychological Review, 60,* 23–32.

Harter, S. (1974). Pleasure derived from cognitive challenge and mastery. *Child Development, 45,* 661–669.

Heckhausen, H. (1991). *Motivation and action.* New York: Springer.

Heckhausen, H., & Gollwitzer, P. M. (1986). Information processing before and after the formation of an intent. In F. Klix & H. Hagendorf (Eds.), *In memoriam Hermann Ebbinghaus: Symposium on the structure and function of human memory* (pp. 1071–1082). Amsterdam: Elsevier.

Heckhausen, J. (1989). Normatives Entwicklungswissen als Bezugsrahmen zur (Re)Konstruktion der eigenen Biographie [Normative conceptions about development as a frame of reference for (re)constructing one's own biography]. In P. Alheit & E. Hoerning (Eds.), *Biographisches Wissen: Beiträge zu einer Theorie lebensgeschichtlicher Erfahrung,* (pp. 202–282). Frankfurt, Germany: Campus.

Heckhausen, J. (1999). *Developmental regulation in adulthood: Age-normative and sociostructural constraints as adaptive challenges.* New York: Cambridge University Press.

Heckhausen, J., & Dweck, C. S. (Eds.). (1998). *Motivation and self-regulation across the life span.* New York: Cambridge University Press.

Heckhausen, J., & Schulz, R. (1993). Optimisation by selection and compensation: Balancing primary and secondary control in life-span development. *International Journal of Behavioral Development, 16*, 287–303.

Heckhausen, J., & Schulz, R. (1995). A life-span theory of control. *Psychological Review, 102*, 284–304.

Heckhausen, J., & Schulz, R. (1998). Developmental regulation in adulthood: Selection and compensation via primary and secondary control. In J. Heckhausen & C. S. Dweck (Eds.), *Motivation and self-regulation across the life span* (pp. 50–77). New York: Cambridge University Press.

Heckhausen, J. & Schulz, R. (in press). The primacy of primary control is a human universal: A reply to Gould's critique of the life-span theory of control. *Psychological Review.*

Helson, H. (1964). *Adaptation-level theory.* New York: Harper and Row.

Hoffman, M. L. (1981). Is altruism a part of human nature? *Journal of Personality and Social Psychology, 40*, 121–137.

James, W. (1890). *The principles of psychology* (Vol. 2). New York: Holt, Rinehart & Winston.

Janos, O., & Papousek, H. (1977). Acquisition of appetition and palpebral conditioned reflexes by the same infants. *Early Human Development, 1*, 91–97.

Keating, E. G., Kormann, L. A., & Horel, J. A. (1970). The behavioral effects of stimulating and ablating the reptilian amygdala (Caiman sklerops). *Physiology and Behavior, 5*, 55–59.

Keller, H. (2000). Human parent-child relationships from an evolutionary perspective. *American Behavioral Scientist, 43*, [957–969].

Kelley, H. H. (1967). Attribution theory in social psychology. In D. Levine (Ed.), *Nebraska symposium on motivation* (pp. 192–238). Lincoln: Nebraska University Press.

Kravitz, E. A. (1988). Hormonal control of behavior: Amines and the biasing of behavioral output in lobsters. *Science, 241*, 1775–1781.

Krebs, J. R. (1980). Optimal foraging, predation risk and territory defense. *Area, 68*, 83–90.

Kuhl, J. (1984). Motivational aspects of achievement motivation and learned helplessness: Toward a comprehensive theory of action control. In B. A. Maher & W. B. Maher (Eds.), *Progress in experimental personality research* (Vol. 13, pp. 99–171). New York: Academic Press.

Leger, D. W. (1992). *Biological foundations of behavior: An integrative approach.* New York: HarperCollins.

Lorenz, K. (1966). Ethologie, die Biologie des Verhaltens [Ethology, the biology of behavior]. In F. Gessner & L. V. Bertalanffy (Eds.), *Handbuch der Biologie* (Vol. 2, pp. 341–559). Frankfurt, Germany: Athenäum.

Mann, J. (1992). Nurturance or negligence: Maternal psychology and behavioral preference among preterm twins. In J. H. Barkow, L. Cosmides, & J. Tooby (Eds.), *The adapted mind: Evolutionary psychology and the generation of culture* (pp. 367–390). New York: Oxford University Press.

Mayr, E. (1974). Behavior programs and evolutionary strategies. *American Scientist, 62*, 650–659.

McClelland, D. C. (1953). *The achievement motive.* New York: Appleton-Century-Crofts.

McClelland, D. C. (1971). *Assessing human motivation.* New York: General Learning Press.

McDougall, W. (1908). *An introduction to social psychology.* London: Methuen.

McFarland, D. J. (1977). Decision making in animals. *Nature, 269*, 15–21.

Murray, H. A. (1938). *Explorations in personality.* New York: Oxford University Press.

Osborne, S. R. (1977). The free food (contrafreeloading) phenomenon: A review and analysis. *Animal Learning and Behavior, 5*, 221–235.

Overmier, J. B., & Seligman, M.E.P. (1967). Effects of inescapable shock upon subsequent escape and avoidance responding. *Journal of Comparative and Physiological Psychology, 63*, 28–33.

Papousek, H. (1967). Experimental studies of appetitional behavior in human newborns and infants. In H. W. Stevenson, E. H. Hess, & H. L. Rheingold (Eds.), *Early behavior: Comparative developmental approaches* (pp. 249–277). New York: John Wiley.

Plutchik, R. (1980). *Emotion. A psychoevolutionary synthesis.* New York: Harper and Row.

Rode, C., & Wang, X. T. (2000). Risk-sensitive decision-making examined within an evolutionary framework. *American Behavioral Scientist, 43*, 926–939.

Roitblad, H. L. (1987). *Introduction to comparative cognition.* New York: Freeman.

Rozin, P. (1976). The evolution of intelligence and access to the cognitive unconscious. In J. M. Sprague & A. N. Epstein (Eds.), *Progress in psychobiology and physiological psychology* (pp. 245–277). New York: Academic Press.

Rozin, P. (2000). Evolution and adaptation in the the understanding of behavior, culture, and mind. *American Behavioral Scientist, 43*, 970–986.

Rumbaugh, D. M., Savage-Rumbaugh, E. S., & Washburn, D. A. (1994). Learning, prediction, and control with an eye to the future. In M. M. Haith, J. B. Benson, R. J. Roberts, Jr., & B. F. Penning-ton (Eds.), *The development of future-oriented processes* (pp. 119–138). Chicago: University of Chicago Press.

Rumbaugh, D. M., & Sterritt, G. M. (1986). Intelligence: From genes to genius in the quest for control. In W. Bechtel (Ed.), *Integrating scientific disciplines.* Dordrecht: Martinus Nijhoff.

Ryan, R. M., Kuhl, J., & Deci, E. L. (1997). Nature and autonomy: An organizational view of social and neurobiological aspects of self-regulation in behavior and development. *Development and Psychopathology, 9*, 701–728.

Scherer, K. R. (1984). On the nature and function of emotion: A component process approach. In K. R. Scherer & P. Ekman (Eds.), *Approaches to emotion* (pp. 293–317). Hillsdale, NJ: Lawrence Erlbaum.

Schneider, K. (1996). Intrinsisch (autotelisch) motiviertes Verhalten – dargestellt an den Beispielen des Neugierverhaltens sowie verwandter Verhaltenssysteme (Spielen und leistungsmotiviertes Handeln) [Intrinsic (autotelic) behavior – discussed on examples of curious behavior and related behavioral systems]. In J. Kuhl & H. Heckhausen (Eds.), *Enzyklopädie der Psychologie: Motivation, Volition und Handlung* (pp. 119–152). Göttingen, Germany: Hogrefe.

Schneider, K., & Dittrich, W. (1990). Evolution und Funktion von Emotionen [Evolution and function of emotions]. In K. R. Scherer (Ed.), *Enzyklopädie der Psychologie: Psychologie der Emotion* (pp. 41–114). Göttingen, Germany: Hogrefe.

Schulz, R., & Heckhausen, J. (1996). A life-span model of successful aging. *American Psychologist, 51*, 702–714.

Schulz, R., & Heckhausen, J. (1997). Emotions and control: A life-span perspective. In K. W. Schaie & M. P. Lawton (Eds.), *Annual review of gerontology and geriatrics* (Vol. 17, pp. 185–205). New York: Springer.

Singh, D. (1970). Preference for bar-pressing to obtain reward over freeloading in rats and children. *Journal of Comparative and Physiological Psychology, 73*, 320–327.

Skinner, B. F. (1938). *The behavior of organisms: An experimental approach.* New York: Appleton-Century-Crofts.

Snyder, M. L., Stephan, W. G., & Rosenfield, D. (1978). Attributional egotism. In J. H. Harvey, W. Ickes, & R. F. Kidd (Eds.), *New directions in attribution research* (Vol. 2, pp. 91–117). Hills-dale, NJ: Lawrence Erlbaum.

Stephens, D. W. E., & Krebs, J. R. (1986). *Foraging theory.* Princeton, NJ: Princeton University Press.

Thorndike, E. L. (1898). Animal intelligence: An experimental study of the associative pro-cesses in animals. *The Psychological Review Monograph Supplements, 2* (Whole No. 8).

Tinbergen, L. (1960). The natural control of insects in pinewoods. Factors influencing the intensity of predation in songbirds. *Archives Neerlandaiscs de Zoologie, 13,* 265–343.

Tinbergen, N. (1951). *The study of instinct.* London: Oxford University Press.

Todd, P. M. (2000). The ecological rationality of mechanisms evolved to make up minds. *American Behavioral Scientist, 43,* 940–956.

Tooby, J., & Cosmides, L. (1992). The psychological foundation of culture. In J. H. Barkow, L. Cosmides, & J. Tooby (Eds.), *The adapted mind: Evolutionary psychology and the generation of culture* (pp. 19–136). New York: Oxford University Press.

Vroom, V. H. (1964). *Work and motivation.* New York: John Wiley.

Washburn, D. A., & Rumbaugh, D. M. (1991). Ordinal judgments of numerical symbols by macaques (Macaca mulatta). *Psychological Science, 2,* 190–193.

Watson, J. S. (1966). The development and generalization of 'contingency awareness' in early infancy: Some hypotheses. *Merrill-Palmer Quarterly, 12,* 123–135.

Weiner, B. (1972). *Theories of motivation,* Chicago: Markham.

Welker, W. L. (1956). Some determinants of play and exploration in chimpanzees. *Journal of Comparative Physiological Psychology, 49,* 84–89.

White, R. W. (1959). Motivation reconsidered: The concept of competence. *Psychological Review, 66,* 297–333.

Wilson, E. O. (1975). *Sociobiology: The new synthesis.* Cambridge, MA: Harvard University Press.

Wundt, W. (1896). *Grundriß der Psychologie* [Foundations of psychology]. Leipzig: Engelmann.

49

The Debate about Rewards and Intrinsic Motivation: Protests and Accusations Do Not Alter the Results

Judy Cameron and W. David Pierce

Our research (Cameron & Pierce, 1994) has clearly touched a nerve. The results of our meta-analysis indicate that rewards can be used effectively to enhance or maintain an individual's intrinsic interest in activities. These findings are challenging to those who espouse the view that rewards and reinforcement are generally detrimental to a person's intrinsic motivation. Our article has drawn criticism because the data from approximately 100 experiments show that there is only one small negative effect of reward, an effect that is highly circumscribed and easily avoided. This finding is disconcerting to those who contend that the negative effects of reward are substantial, generalized and occur across many conditions.

Our analysis of 20 years of research is the most extensive review of the literature on rewards and intrinsic motivation to date. Because of its thoroughness, the data, analysis, and conclusions must be taken seriously. Faced with the evidence, researchers who have argued that rewards produce harmful effects under a wide range of conditions are put in a difficult position. One option they can take is to reanalyze the data in an attempt to show that rewards have strong negative effects on intrinsic motivation. Our data are readily available for additional analyses, and our procedures are clearly outlined in the original article. Failing this option, a second strategy is to suggest that the findings are invalid due to intentional bias,

Source: *Review of Educational Research*, 66(1) (1996): 39–51.

deliberate misrepresentation, and inept analysis. Our critics have chosen the second strategy.

Lepper, Keavney, and Drake (1996); Ryan and Deci (1996); and Kohn (1996) have responded to the results of our meta-analysis by accusing us of asking inappropriate questions, omitting important moderator variables, excluding critical experiments, and contradicting other reviews on the topic. In addition, they criticize our meta-analytic procedures and decisions as flawed.

In response to these criticisms, we show that all relevant studies were included in our analyses and that the questions and reward conditions we assessed expand on previous reviews to provide a more comprehensive picture of the effects of rewards on intrinsic motivation. We answer the statistical concerns of our critics and show that our analysis is appropriate, accurate, and robust. Most importantly, we show that none of the objections raised by our critics negates our findings.

The results and conclusions of our meta-analysis remain important, especially for those involved in education and other applied settings. An issue of prime concern to educators is how to use rewards effectively to promote learning without disrupting students' intrinsic interest. Contrary to Ryan and Deci's (1996) claim that our "theoretical position acknowledged no conditions under which one should expect negative effects" (p. 33), our results provide important clarifications about the conditions under which rewards produce positive or negative effects on intrinsic motivation. Of primary importance in classroom situations is the finding that rewards can be used to maintain or enhance students' intrinsic interest in schoolwork. Verbal praise and performance feedback increase the value of an activity. When tangible rewards are offered contingent on level of performance or are given unexpectedly, students remain motivated in the subject area. A slight negative effect can be expected when a teacher offers a tangible reward without regard to the students' level of performance. Under this condition, when the rewards are withdrawn, students will continue to like their schoolwork as much as others, but they may spend slightly less time on it in a free period. This negative effect can be easily prevented by offering students rewards for successful solution of problems, completion of work, or for attaining specified levels of performance on particular tasks. The point is that teachers can reward the level and quality of students' work without disrupting motivation and interest in learning. These conclusions are not altered by the comments of Kohn, Ryan and Deci, and Lepper et al.

In the following commentary we address our critics' concerns. Our response is organized in two sections; the first deals with the general issues that have been raised by our critics, and in the second we focus on specific statistical criticisms.

General Issues

The Overall Question

One issue of contention involves our decision to begin our meta-analysis by investigating the overall effect of reward on intrinsic motivation (overall effect hypothesis). Lepper and his colleagues state that "to ask about the 'overall' or 'in general' effects of rewards or reinforcers is to pose a fundamentally meaningless question" (p. 7). They argue that the question is senseless and misleading, a view echoed by Kohn and by Ryan and Deci.

We maintain that the overall effect hypothesis is central to an understanding of this area of research. One reason is practical. Many educators, parents, and administrators have adopted Kohn's (1993) position that overall, rewards and incentive systems are harmful. In the present context, this stance means that rewards negatively affect students' intrinsic interest, a question of overall effect. Others involved in education are still open to the possibility that rewards may be beneficial. A classroom teacher who wishes to implement an incentive system is first of all interested in whether rewards disrupt intrinsic interest in the subject matter. Of course, it may be advantageous to target particular subgroups or implement additional measures, but the question of the overall effect of reward is crucial to one's teaching strategy.

Another reason to address the main effect hypothesis is that academic journals, introductory textbooks, newspapers, and some of our critics continue to point to the overall negative or harmful effects of reward and reinforcement. In a prominent scientific journal, *Nature*, we learn that "it has been repeatedly shown that if people are rewarded for performing a task they find intrinsically pleasurable, they do it less, not more" (Sutherland, 1993, p. 767). A major introductory psychology textbook informs us that

> when an extrinsic reward is given, the motivation becomes extrinsic and the task itself is enjoyed less. When the extrinsic rewards are withdrawn, the activity loses its material value. . . . The moral is: *A reward a day makes work out of play.* (Zimbardo, 1992, p. 454, italics in the original)

Even in this issue of *Review of Educational Research*, Kohn asserts that "there is more than adequate justification for avoiding the use of incentives to control people's behavior, particularly in a school setting" (p. 3).

These examples are but a small sample of the claims made about the overall effects of reward. Many university students, educators, and parents have been exposed to this negative main effect assumption and base their own understanding and use of rewards on it. Social policy in our schools and other institutions reflects these beliefs. Because of this, an analysis of the general effects of reward is warranted.

In their critiques of our meta-analysis, Lepper et al. and Ryan and Deci indicate that they and others have long recognized that the negative overall effect hypothesis is incorrect. Nonetheless, numerous writers interpret the research findings as indicative of an overall negative effect and decry the use of rewards in educational and work settings (e.g., see Kohn, 1993). As a result, many parents, teachers, and others are reluctant to use rewards – any rewards – under any circumstances! Lepper and his colleagues suggest that reversing this incorrect conclusion will be harmful. They imply that we are trying to propagate our own myth – that rewards have no negative effects. We do not want to add any more myths to this research area. So let us be clear in stating that our research demonstrates that rewards have either positive or negative effects depending on the way they are administered. Importantly, the only negative effect of reward on intrinsic motivation occurs under a circumscribed set of conditions, namely, when rewards are tangible and promised to individuals without regard to any level of performance.

The Role of Moderator Variables

A major focus of our meta-analysis was to assess the effects of various moderator variables. The moderators we included (type of reward, reward expectancy, and reward contingency) were chosen because of their theoretical and practical importance in the literature on intrinsic motivation as well as replication over a number of experiments. Our results indicate that the detrimental effects of reward are limited and depend on multiple moderators. All of our critics, Lepper et al., Ryan and Deci, and Kohn, are concerned that we failed to assess the impact of additional important moderators. The implication of their comments is that decremental effects of reward occur under numerous conditions and are far more widespread than our analysis suggests. Interestingly, however, as we describe below, an analysis of additional moderators would, in fact, show the opposite.

Lepper et al. point to studies that assessed the impact of initial task interest and reward salience on intrinsic motivation. Other moderator variables hypothesized to influence intrinsic motivation include reward attractiveness, presence or absence of the experimenter, task difficulty, reward magnitude, and so on. It is critical to point out that the few studies designed to investigate the impact of these moderators typically begin with the one condition that produces a negative effect. Furthermore, such moderators have been shown to enhance, mitigate, or reverse the negative effects of expected, tangible, noncontingent reward. For example, Ross (1975) found that salient rewards make the negative effect of tangible, expected, noncontingent reward greater. McLoyd (1979), on the other hand, demonstrated that individuals offered a noncontingent, tangible reward experienced an increase in intrinsic motivation when the task was less interesting, while Williams's (1980) research indicated that the negative effects of tangible, expected, noncontingent reward could be offset by offering attractive rewards. In other words, the variables we have not assessed are moderators that have typically been added to the conditions that produce the single negative effect of reward found in our meta-analysis. Thus, an analysis of studies that included moderators that increase the negative effects of expected, tangible, noncontingent reward would serve to place further restrictions on the circumstances under which rewards undermine intrinsic motivation. That is, the negative effect phenomenon may be even more circumscribed than our data indicate, a finding contrary to the implications hinted at by our critics.

Presently, however, there is no way to assess the theoretical or applied importance of these moderator variables. This is because only one or two studies have replicated the same moderator procedures on a common dependent measure of intrinsic motivation. If the effects of moderators such as reward salience, reward attractiveness, and so on were systematically replicated, a subsequent meta-analysis could be conducted to determine the conditions that moderate the negative effect on intrinsic motivation of tangible, expected, noncontingent rewards when they are removed. Of course, such an analysis would simply extend our findings and show that tangible, expected, noncontingent rewards produce negative effects on intrinsic motivation only when other conditions are present. For example, in terms of reward attractiveness, Williams's (1980) research shows that when tangible, expected, noncontingent, *unattractive* rewards are given, intrinsic motivation decreases; the same reward condition with *attractive* rewards does not produce a decrement. Although present theoretical accounts (e.g., cognitive evaluation theory, the overjustification hypothesis) may be able to organize such circumscribed effects, the theories would become less and less generalizable. In applied settings, negative effects of reward on intrinsic motivation would depend on so many conditions that there would be little need for concern.

Both Kohn (1996) and Ryan and Deci (1996) raise the question of moderators in the context of our finding that verbal praise produces positive effects both on the free time students spend on tasks and on attitude measures of intrinsic motivation. Specifically, they claim that verbal praise directed at controlling student behavior has negative effects on intrinsic motivation, whereas informational praise does not. We did not conduct an analysis on the control-informational dimension of verbal reward because these variables appear in only one or two studies. In addition, most research on this topic has been conducted without adequate no-feedback control groups (e.g., Ryan, 1982). Until a sufficient number of experiments with control groups are conducted, a meta-analysis of conditions that have few replications would not be reliable or beneficial to our understanding of reward and intrinsic motivation. We note, however, that although there are so few studies on this topic, the effects of controlling and informational verbal reward were analyzed in a recent meta-analysis by Tang & Hall (1995). They found no significant effects on either of these dimensions.

In sum, although our meta-analysis was designed to assess the effects of several moderators on reward and intrinsic motivation, Lepper et al., Ryan and Deci, and Kohn have suggested that many additional important moderators were omitted. As we have shown, an analysis of additional moderators would not alter our conclusions or change any of the results of our meta-analysis. That is, negative effects of reward on intrinsic motivation are highly conditional and occur solely in the presence of multiple moderators. In educational settings, negative effects can be avoided by praising students for their work and making tangible rewards contingent on performance.

Our Findings in Context

Both Ryan and Deci and Lepper et al. argue that our findings contradict previous narrative reviews and other meta-analyses of reward and intrinsic motivation. Lepper et al. are not consistent on this point, and in a later section of their critique they concede that "other recent meta-analyses, ... as well as numerous previous narrative reviews, have reached exactly [our] conclusion" (p. 7). In this section, we show that our results are in accord with other summaries of reward and intrinsic motivation and that our review advances the knowledge in this area. We briefly comment on three other meta-analyses on this topic (Rummel & Feinberg, 1988; Tang & Hall, 1995; Wiersma, 1992).

The most recent meta-analysis on rewards and intrinsic motivation, conducted by Tang and Hall (1995), was designed to test several theoretical propositions about the overjustification effect. Fifty studies were included, largely a subset of the experiments examined in our review. One analysis concerned assessing the effects of expected, tangible, task-contingent (noncontingent) reward on the free time measure of intrinsic motivation. Tang and Hall found a negative effect, as did we. Also, in accord with our findings, they found no detrimental effect with unexpected, tangible reward. It is difficult to compare our findings on the effects of verbal reward on free time with their study, because their analysis included only two effect sizes (their result was not significant).

Tang and Hall (1995) reported a negative effect on the free time measure for performance-contingent reward, whereas we found no significant effect. This difference in findings is due to Tang and Hall's classification of performance-contingent reward as well as to their omission of several relevant studies. Of the seven studies that Tang and Hall analyzed as performance contingent, six are actually task-contingent reward procedures, as defined by Deci and Ryan (1985). We used Deci and Ryan's definitions and identified 10 studies of performance-contingent reward; overall, there was no evidence of a negative effect. Additional measures of intrinsic motivation (e.g., attitude toward task) that we examined were not reported by Tang and Hall.[1]

The meta-analyses by Wiersma (1992) and Rummel and Feinberg (1988) were discussed in our original article (Cameron & Pierce, 1994). Wiersma analyzed 20 studies, and Rummel and Feinberg analyzed 45 studies. We cannot compare our findings with those of Rummel and Feinberg, because they averaged over different dependent measures of intrinsic motivation. Our meta-analysis shows that this is inappropriate, because the free time and attitude measures do not necessarily covary with the same experimental treatment. In addition, in both Rummel and Feinberg's and Wiersma's analyses, many of the effect sizes reported came from studies where one reward condition was compared to another reward condition. The lack of a no-reward group makes a comparison of findings problematic. Wiersma does, however, report effect size estimates for six experiments on free time that compared a no-reward condition to an expected, tangible, noncontingent reward condition. Though we have not conducted a meta-analysis on his results, we computed the average of the six independent effects sizes and found a negative effect, a finding compatible with our original conclusions.

All in all, our findings for rewards that are tangible, expected, and noncontingent are consistent with other meta-analyses. Our research, however, went beyond an analysis of the one negative reward procedure and assessed the effects of reward under a variety of conditions. In terms of other reward procedures (e.g., verbal reward, performance-contingent reward) and other measures of intrinsic motivation (e.g., attitude toward a task), we failed to find any detrimental effects on intrinsic motivation. That is, our study showed that most reward procedures can be used to maintain or enhance intrinsic motivation; the negative effect other reviews have detected is only a small part of a larger picture. Thus, our meta-analysis provides a more complete account of the effects of rewards on intrinsic motivation.

The Completeness of Our Review

A criticism put forward by Kohn, as well as by Ryan and Deci, is that we failed to include several critical experiments in our meta-analysis. The implication is that had such studies been included, our results would have been different.

Kohn cites a number of studies that he believes we have overlooked. Most of these studies were located in our original search and were not included in our meta-analysis because of the lack of an adequate no-reward control condition. In addition, as we reported in our original article, our meta-analysis included studies published up to and including 1991. The studies from the period 1992–1994 cited by Kohn (Boggiano et al., 1992; Freedman, Cunningham, & Krismer, 1992; Gottfried, Fleming, & Gottfried, 1994) were, of course, not included. Of these, Freedman et al. varied the amount of reward but had no nonreward control group. The article by Boggiano et al. reported past research in order to develop a theory or model of students' achievement patterns. Gottfried et al. examined parental motivational practices; their study did not include any of the reward conditions or dependent measures that we analyzed in our meta-analysis. Earlier studies by Birch, Marlin, and Rotter (1984) and Fabes, Fultz, Eisenberg, May-Plumlee, and Christopher (1989) concerned food preferences and prosocial behavior, respectively. Clearly, all these studies are off topic. Other papers that Kohn cites as missing are, in fact, included in our analyses (a list of all studies is presented in Cameron & Pierce, 1994, pp. 399–403).

In contrast to Kohn, Lepper et al. charge us with including too many "bad" studies. An essential criterion of a reliable meta-analysis, however, is that all the studies done in a field are examined, independently of one's own theoretical position and the degree to which the results of any particular study may be promising. We have met this criterion. In fact, our meta-analysis on the effects of rewards on intrinsic motivation is the most comprehensive review of this literature to date. The results are based on a large number of studies, and, to our knowledge, no relevant published studies were omitted. Due to the large sample of studies included in our analyses, any single study that may have been overlooked would not alter the conclusions. Overall, our results were based on all the available evidence, and the findings are central to an understanding of the effects of rewards on intrinsic motivation.

Meta-Analytic Issues

In addition to the general criticisms discussed above, Lepper and his associates object to our use of meta-analysis for assessing the research on the effects of rewards on intrinsic motivation. In particular, they contend that the distributions of effect sizes in our article indicate that meta-analytic tests should not have been conducted. In accord with Ryan and Deci (1996) and Kohn (1996), they further suggest that the statistical procedures used in our meta-analyses must be flawed. Specifically, they criticize the technique of aggregating effect sizes within a single study when moderator variables are present. In this section, we respond to our critics' meta-analytic and statistical concerns. We show that our analyses are appropriate, that the data are approximately normal and homogeneous, that inclusion or exclusion of outliers does not alter the results, and that our procedures yield correct estimates for the effects of rewards on intrinsic motivation at each level of analysis.

The Appropriateness of Meta-Analysis

There are two main issues that concern Lepper et al. with regard to our use of meta-analytic techniques for assessing the effects of rewards on intrinsic motivation. First, they suggest that the apparent normality of our distributions for the critical measures of intrinsic motivation (free time, attitude) is deceptive. Their second concern is that the data are not homogeneous (equal spread of effect sizes) and that meta-analytic tests should therefore not have been performed.

As Lepper et al. acknowledge (p. 13–14), our distributions of effect sizes approximate a normal shape. However, they attribute the normality of these distributions to the inclusion of "pure zero cases" and random estimates. They argue that our inclusion of "pure zero cases" in our graphic portrayal of effect sizes (Cameron & Pierce, 1994, Figures 1 and 2) guarantees a normal distribution around the value of zero. Pure zero cases refer to studies that did not provide sufficient information to calculate effect sizes or random estimates (4 cases for free time and 17 cases for attitude). The truth is that we did not include pure zero cases in these figures. This is clearly stated on pages 379 and 384 of our original article. The normality of the distributions centering around zero is not due to pure zero cases. Thus, Lepper and his associates need not be concerned.

In terms of our use of random estimates of effect sizes, our procedure is innovative and may be more appropriate than merely assigning a zero effect to the experiment or omitting the study itself. The procedure depended on the information available in each study. When t or F values were nonsignificant and were reported as less than some value (e.g., <1), a random number between 0.01 and that value was selected; and an effect size was then calculated. In other cases, t or F values were not available, but means or directions of means were reported. In these situations, a random number between 0.01 and the critical value of t or F at $p = .05$ was drawn, and an effect size was then calculated. (For more information, see Cameron & Pierce, 1994, p. 376).

With regard to the normality of our distributions, it is important to note that the direction of effect for random estimates was always known. If more studies had had negative effects, the distribution would have been pulled in that direction. The actual shape of the distribution shows that positive and negative effect sizes occurred with similar frequency. This is based not on our use of random estimates but on the actual direction of effects reported in such studies. In other words, the use of random estimates in no way biases the results toward an average zero effect size. The normality of the distributions centering around zero is not due to this, and, again, there is no need for concern. The point is that the effect size distributions approximated a normal shape, and meta-analytic tests could be used with confidence.

Although Lepper et al. agree that our distributions are normal, they argue that our data are heterogeneous (lacking equal spread) and therefore inappropriate for meta-analysis. Our decision to use meta-analytic procedures involved a consideration of several issues. Initially, we were concerned with the normality of the distribution of effect sizes. We showed that the distributions were approximately normal and reported the degree of kurtosis and skewness of the free time distribution in the original article (p. 381). Next we considered the results of the Q test for homogeneity. It is well known that this test is liberal in the sense that the null hypothesis (homogeneity) is too often rejected (Hunter, Schmidt, & Jackson, 1982). Because of this problem, we set the critical value of Q farther out on the chi-square distribution, just below the value at the .01 level (that is, $p > .01$).

Homogeneity was achieved by excluding extreme effect sizes. The exclusion of outliers is not unusual and is recommended by Hedges (1987) as a method for obtaining more equal spread of the effect sizes. To assess any biases due to the removal of outliers, we reported all analyses with extreme values included and excluded. In addition, we identified the studies with extreme values and discussed the conditions that may have led to these atypical results. Inspection of our original article shows that the results do not change to any extent by excluding outliers.

The validity of our meta-analysis is also increased by the use of the CL statistic (McGraw & Wong, 1992). CL is another way to express effect size. Importantly, McGraw and Wong conducted 118 tests (simulations) to show that the CL statistic is robust with respect to violations of normality and homogeneity. Because of this, we used CL in all our analyses and reported results identical to those of the other meta-analytic tests.

In sum, the distribution of effect sizes for the critical measures of intrinsic motivation approximated a normal shape. The normality was not due to the inclusion of "pure zero cases" or random estimates as Lepper and his associates have suggested. Homogeneity of effect sizes was achieved by excluding outliers. All results were reported with outliers included and excluded; our findings were not altered to any extent by the exclusion of outliers. In addition, given our use of the CL statistic, we are confident that our analyses are appropriate and that the results are accurate and valid.

Aggregation of Effect Sizes in Meta-Analysis

Lepper et al., Ryan and Deci, and Kohn are critical of the method of aggregating effect sizes within a study to yield a single estimate for each meta-analytic test. They contend that such procedures yield inaccurate estimates of the effects of reward on intrinsic motivation. Underlying this criticism is the supposition that the effects of important moderators and interactions were not detected in our analyses. Again, the implication of these comments is that negative effects of reward are more prevalent than our results communicate.

In response to this concern, we first note that aggregation of effect sizes within a study is a common procedure in meta-analysis that avoids violation of the assumption of independence (Cooper, 1989; Hedges & Olkin, 1985). The procedures for aggregation are clearly described in our original article (pp. 376–377). It is important to point out that a serious statistical violation occurs when more than one effect size from an individual experiment is entered into a single meta-analysis. Typically, in such cases, a control group is compared with more than one experimental treatment within a study, several effect sizes are calculated, and each is entered into a single meta-analytic test. The major problem is that the effect sizes are not independent (errors among observations are correlated). If the dependencies in such data were properly accounted for, the error term would become larger and mean effect sizes would become smaller. Another problem is that a particular study will contribute more weight to the overall meta-analytic outcome than a study yielding only one effect size. Other meta-analyses on reward and intrinsic motivation favored by Lepper et al. (p. 5) have violated the assumption of independence by entering several (sometimes over 10) effect sizes from one study into a single meta-analytic test (e.g., Rummel & Feinberg, 1988; Tang & Hall, 1995). The implication is that conclusions based on these meta-analyses could be incorrect.

The way to achieve independence and at the same time retain effect sizes for an analysis of the impact of various moderators is to (a) aggregate them into a single estimate for an overall analysis of the effects of rewards on intrinsic motivation and (b) conduct further analyses of the effects of various moderator variables. For factorial designs, the main effect of reward is entered into an analysis of the overall effects of reward; interaction effects that have been replicated in a sufficient number of experiments are then analyzed separately. These are the procedures we used in our meta-analyses. As we indicated previously, the moderators we analyzed (reward type, reward expectancy, and reward contingency) were chosen because of their theoretical and applied importance as well as replication.

Lepper et al. are concerned that aggregation of the moderators (rather than separate analyses) yields inaccurate estimates of the effects of reward on intrinsic motivation (p. 11–13). As mentioned earlier, the moderators not assessed in our analyses (e.g., presence of experimenter, reward attractiveness, salience, distraction, etc.) have appeared in only one or two studies, and in these studies they have been added to the tangible, expected, noncontingent reward condition to decrease, mitigate, or increase the negative effect. In terms of such studies, it is possible to obtain an unbiased estimate of the effect size of tangible, expected, noncontingent reward. When the results are pooled across all studies, the effects of any additional moderators are averaged out. That is, although any one of these manipulations may push intrinsic interest up (e.g., reward attractiveness) or down (e.g., surveillance, reward salience) in a given study, their effects are expected to cancel out across many studies. In other words, the best estimate of the effect size of tangible, expected, noncontingent reward when additional moderators are present is the average of all the comparisons of the rewarded conditions with nonrewarded control groups.

Of course, additional meta-analyses could be conducted on the effects of these moderators if they were sufficiently replicated. As we pointed out, however, because they are added to the one reward procedure that produces a reliable negative effect, the results would show that decremental effects of reward on intrinsic motivation depend on even stricter conditions than our analysis indicates. This is demonstrated in Lepper et al.'s analysis of three factorial experiments (Calder & Staw, 1975; Loveland & Olley, 1979; McLoyd, 1979) that crossed initial task interest (high, low) with reward (reward, no reward). Lepper et al. (p. 10) show that in these three studies, rewarding activities with high intrinsic interest yields a large negative effect size. In contrast, rewarding a task with low initial interest produces a positive effect size. In each of these studies, the reward procedure involved tangible, expected, noncontingent (or task-contingent) rewards – the one procedure that produces a negative effect on the free time measure of intrinsic motivation.

Thus, if Lepper et al.'s analysis is reliable, the results indicate that tangible, expected, noncontingent rewards are harmful only when delivered for more interesting tasks. It is worth mentioning here, however, that a study excluded in Lepper et al.'s analysis (Mynatt et al., 1978) also crossed task interest with tangible, expected, noncontingent reward but found positive effects of reward for both low- and high-interest tasks. Given that there are so few studies of the interest variable, the results from this one study could substantially alter Lepper et al.'s conclusions about the importance of level of task interest when rewards are tangible, expected, and noncontingent.

In summary, the procedures used in our meta-analysis yield correct estimates for the effects of reward on intrinsic motivation at each level of analysis. Our critics have implied that analyses of additional moderators and interactions would yield more general negative effects of reward on intrinsic motivation. However, as we have shown, further analyses would actually reveal that positive effects of reward are more general and that decremental effects of reward occur under even more restricted circumstances than our results indicate.

Conclusion

A prominent view in education and social psychology is that rewards decrease a person's intrinsic motivation. Our meta-analysis of 20 years of research suggests that this view is incorrect. The findings from approximately 100 studies indicate that rewards can be used effectively to enhance or maintain intrinsic interest in activities. The only negative effect of reward occurs under a highly specific set of conditions, circumstances that are easily avoided. Not surprisingly, these results have not been well received by those who argue that rewards produce negative effects on intrinsic motivation under a wide range of conditions.

In response to the findings, Lepper, Keavney, and Drake (1996), Ryan and Deci (1996), and Kohn (1996) have suggested that the questions asked in our meta-analysis were inappropriate, that critical studies were excluded, that important negative effects were not detected, and that the techniques used in our meta-analysis were unsuitable. In this response, we have shown that the questions asked are fundamental to an understanding of the relationship between rewards and intrinsic motivation and that our meta-analytic techniques are appropriate, robust, and statistically correct. Our meta-analysis includes all relevant studies on the topic, and the results clearly show that negative effects of rewards occur under limited conditions. All told, the results and conclusions of our meta-analysis are not altered by our critics' protests and accusations.

Our findings have important practical implications. In applied settings, the results indicate that verbal rewards (praise and positive feedback) can be used to enhance intrinsic motivation. When tangible rewards (e.g., gold stars, money) are offered contingent on performance on a task or are delivered unexpectedly, intrinsic motivation is maintained. A slight negative effect of reward can be expected when tangible rewards are offered without regard to level of performance. Under this condition, when the rewards are withdrawn, individuals report as much interest in the activity as those in a nonrewarded group, but they may spend slightly less time on it in a free period.[2] This negative effect can be prevented by rewarding people for completing work, solving problems successfully, or attaining a specified level of performance. In other words, rewards can be used effectively in educational and other applied settings without undermining intrinsic motivation.

Notes

1. Tang and Hall (1995) reported effect sizes for questionnaire measures of intrinsic motivation. The studies they analyzed used questionnaire items to index attributions of causality; moral obligation; attitude toward the task; perceptions of luck, ability, effort, and difficulty; feelings of competence; negative affect; self-esteem; and so on. Tang and Hall combined the effect sizes of all these measures and reported meta-analyses based on this composite index. They did not examine attitude toward the task separately, as we did. Thus, we cannot compare our findings on the attitude measure of intrinsic motivation.

2. It may be informative to consider how serious the negative effect of expected, tangible, noncontingent reward on free time really is. How much less time would students spend on academic subjects if a teacher implemented this reward procedure and then removed it? Results from our meta-analysis indicate that the average effect size for a comparison between people who receive an expected, tangible, noncontingent reward and nonrewarded individuals on time on task following withdrawal of reward is -0.26.

   In the original experiments, time on task was typically measured over an 8-minute period. In order to convert the effect size of -0.26 to real time, one needs to know the pooled standard deviation of rewarded and nonrewarded groups. Because many researchers reported only t or F statistics, we will use a well-designed study by Pretty and Seligman (1984) to estimate a pooled standard deviation. Their study reported two experiments with large sample sizes and readily available statistical information. Both experiments compared a condition of expected, tangible, noncontingent reward ($N = 30$) with a nonrewarded control group ($N = 30$) on 8 minutes of free time. The pooled standard deviation was 2.6 minutes.

Using this estimate of error, we are able to convert the negative effect size from the meta-analysis into real time. An effect size of -0.26 would mean that in an 8-minute period, the average individual who is promised a noncontingent, tangible reward will spend about 41 seconds less time on the task when the reward procedure is withdrawn than the average nonrewarded individual. Given this result, what would happen if a teacher implemented this incentive procedure in a reading program and then removed it? According to the estimate, students who are offered gold stars for reading would spend about 3 minutes, 25 seconds less time reading in a 40-minute free-choice period than students not given the incentive. Of course, this is a hypothetical example, but it does illustrate the magnitude of this negative effect size in terms of real time.

References

Birch, L. L., Marlin, D. W., & Rotter, J. (1984). Eating as the "means" activity in a contingency: Effects on young children's food preference. *Child Development, 55*, 431–439.

Boggiano, A. K., Shields, A., Barrett, M., Kellam, T., Thompson, E., Simons, J., & Katz, P. (1992). Helplessness deficits in students: The role of motivational orientation. *Motivation and Emotion, 16*, 271–296.

Calder, B. J., & Staw, B. M. (1975). Self-perception of intrinsic and extrinsic motivation. *Journal of Personality and Social Psychology, 31*, 599–605.

Cameron, J., & Pierce, W. D. (1994). Reinforcement, reward, and intrinsic motivation: A meta-analysis. *Review of Educational Research, 64*, 363–423.

Cooper, H. M. (1989). *Integrating research: A guide for literature reviews* (2nd ed.). Beverly Hills, CA: Sage.

Deci, E. L., & Ryan, R. M. (1985). *Intrinsic motivation and self-determination in human behavior.* New York: Plenum.

Fabes, R. A., Fultz, J., Eisenberg, N., May-Plumlee, T., & Christopher, F. S. (1989). Effects of rewards on children's prosocial motivation: A socialization study. *Developmental Psychology, 25*, 509–515.

Freedman, J. L., Cunningham, J. A., & Krismer, K. (1992). Inferred values and the reverse-incentive effect in induced compliance. *Journal of Personality and Social Psychology, 62*, 357–368.

Gottfried, A. E., Fleming, J. S., & Gottfried, A. W. (1994). Role of parental motivation practices in children's academic intrinsic motivation and achievement. *Journal of Educational Psychology, 86*, 104–113.

Hedges, L. (1987). How hard is hard science, how soft is soft science? The empirical cumulativeness of research. *American Psychologist, 42*, 443–55.

Hedges, L., & Olkin, I. (1985). *Statistical methods for meta-analysis.* Orlando, FL: Academic.

Hunter, J. E., Schmidt, F. L., & Jackson, G. B. (1982). *Meta-analysis: Cumulating research findings across studies.* Beverly Hills, CA: Sage.

Kohn, A. (1993). *Punished by rewards.* Boston: Houghton Mifflin.

Kohn, A. (1996). By all available means: Cameron and Pierce's defense of extrinsic motivators. *Review of Educational Research, 66*, 1–4.

Lepper, M. R., Keavney, M., & Drake, M. (1996). Intrinsic motivation and extrinsic rewards: A commentary on Cameron and Pierce's meta-analysis. *Review of Educational Research, 66*, 5–32.

Loveland, K. K., & Olley, J. G. (1979). The effect of external reward on interest and quality of task performance in children of high and low intrinsic motivation. *Child Development, 50*, 1207–1210.

McGraw, K. O., & Wong, S. P. (1992). A common language effect size statistic. *Psychological Bulletin, 111*, 361–365.

McLoyd, V. C. (1979). The effects of extrinsic rewards of differential value on high and low intrinsic interest. *Child Development, 50*, 1010–1019.

Mynatt, C., Oakley, D., Arkkelin, D., Piccione, A., Margolis, R., & Arkkelin, J. (1978). An examination of overjustification under conditions of extended observation and multiple reinforcement: Overjustification or boredom? *Cognitive Therapy and Research, 2*, 171–177.

Pretty, G. H., & Seligman, C. (1984). Affect and the overjustification effect. *Journal of Personality and Social Psychology, 46*, 1241–1253.

Ross, M. (1975). Salience of reward and intrinsic motivation. *Journal of Personality and Social Psychology, 32*, 245–254.

Rummel, A., & Feinberg, R. (1988). Cognitive evaluation theory: A meta-analytic review of the literature. *Social Behavior and Personality, 16*, 147–164.

Ryan, R. M. (1982). Control and information in the intrapersonal sphere: An extension of cognitive evaluation theory. *Journal of Personality and Social Psychology, 43*, 450–461.

Ryan, R. M., & Deci, E. L. (1996). When paradigms clash: Comments on Cameron and Pierce's claim that rewards do not undermine intrinsic motivation. *Review of Educational Research, 66*, 33–38.

Sutherland, S. (1993). Impoverished minds. *Nature, 364*, 767.

Tang, S., & Hall, V. (1995). The overjustification effect: A meta-analysis. *Applied Cognitive Psychology, 9*, 365–404.

Wiersma, U. J. (1992). The effects of extrinsic rewards in intrinsic motivation: A meta-analysis. *Journal of Occupational and Organizational Psychology, 65*, 101–114.

Williams, B. W. (1980). Reinforcement, behavior constraint, and the overjustification effect. *Journal of Personality and Social Psychology, 39*, 599–614.

Zimbardo, P. G. (1992). *Psychology and life* (13th ed.). New York: Harper Collins.

50

A Comprehensive Expectancy Motivation Model: Implications for Adult Education and Training

Kenneth W. Howard

M otivating adult learners has always been a critical concern of adult education theorists and practitioners. Motivation has been defined as a hypothetical mechanism which controls goal-directed behavior (Reykowski, 1965). Various theoretical frameworks have been used to explain motivation in the context of adult education. Of these various frameworks, perhaps Maslow's (1943) five-stage self-actualization model has been the most prominent (Gilmore, 1974).

In recent years, expectancy theory has begun to gain popularity as a model for understanding educational motivation. Derived from social learning theory generally and cognitive or field theory specifically, it views people as purposeful beings who interact proactively with their environments based on their expectancies about the likelihood that their efforts will result in outcomes that they value. In other words, they choose to perform in ways that they believe are likely to benefit them (McMillan, 1980). Such a model has relevance to adult education and training, not only as a means of increasing learner motivation and performance in the learning situation, but also for refining enrollment strategies, reducing dropout rates, and insuring that learning has a practical application for the learner.

Source: *Adult Education Quarterly*, 39(4) (1989): 199–210.

The Development of Expectancy Theory

Expectancy theory has its origins in the theories of Lewin (1938) and Tolman (1932), who postulated that human behavior was a result of the interaction of the individual and the environment, in the context of a specific situation, and that individuals develop beliefs about the probability of various possible outcomes of their behaviors, preferring some outcomes over others. Julian Rotter (1954, 1971), a social learning theorist, expanded on Lewin's ideas regarding expectancy and motivation by adding elements of stimulus-response theory, suggesting that behaviors are motivated by the interaction of three factors: expectancy, reinforcement value, and the specific psychological situation. Some outcomes hold greater reinforcement value than others because they satisfy stronger needs. Specific situational cues (e.g., novelty of the situation, other people present) may alter expectancy or reinforcement values.

Building on the work of Lewin, Tolman, and others, Vroom (1964a) developed valence-instrumentality-expectancy (VIE) theory in its classical form. He postulated that the force of motivation behind any behavior was a product of valence, instrumentality, and expectancy. He defined expectancy as the individual's subjective estimation of the likelihood of successfully performing a particular behavior, instrumentality as the individual's subjective estimation of the likelihood that the behavior would be rewarded, and valence as the positive or negative value that the individual placed on the reward. Vroom (1964b) spelled out three basic assumptions underlying VIE theory: (a) that anticipation of reward energizes individual behavior, (b) that perceived value of various outcomes gives direction to individual behavior, and (c) that learned connections develop between behavior and outcome expectancy.

Expectancy theory originated as a theory of work motivation and job satisfaction (Vroom, 1964a). Hence, most early applications of the theory were focused on business and industry, as were most early expectancy research studies. Yet despite the fact that expectancy theory had become the dominant motivation model in industry, it had been largely ignored by educators and educational administrators (Wright, 1985). However, in recent years adult education theorists have begun to recognize that expectancy theory has significant implications for adult education, particularly in accounting for the importance of barriers (internal or external) in predicting dropout (Darkenwald, 1981). Swedish theorists Rubenson and Hoghielm (1976, 1978) adapted Vroom's VIE theory to explain and predict dropout from adult education. This was later refined by Borgstrom (1980). Their model described Force (Vroom's force of motivation), the strength of which determines if the individual completes or drops a course, as resulting from valence (the extent to which the individual regards a course as a fruitful means of satisfying perceived needs) and expectancy (the extent to which the individual feels capable of completing or coping with a course).

Results of Expectancy Research

Researchers have tested aspects and variations of expectancy theory with a variety of adult populations involved in both traditional and non-traditional educational settings, including: undergraduate university students (Arvey & Dunnette, 1980; Butler & Womer, 1985; Constantinople, 1967; Henson, 1976; Mitchell & Knudson, 1971; Mitchell & Nebeker, 1973; Polczynski & Shirland, 1976; Schmitt, 1975); adult GED students (Darkenwald, 1987; Moore & Davies, 1984); community college students (Malloch & Michael, 1981; Pritchard & DeLeo, 1973); graduate students (Miskel, DeFrain, & Wilcox, 1980), and public school teachers (Miskel, DeFrain, & Wilcox, 1980; Wright, 1985). Expectancy theory has also undergone extensive research in business and industry settings, in addition to the limited research in educational settings described above. Excellent comparative analyses of these studies and their results have been compiled by Heneman and Schwab (1972) and House, Shapiro, and Wahba (1974).

Results of expectancy research have been mixed: the expectancy basis for motivation is supported but the individual elements of the theory are not consistently supported. Certainly, a simple, multiplicative model as proposed by Vroom cannot be supported. For example, while some studies support a multiplicative relationship between the VIE process variables (Lawler, 1968), others support an additive relationship (Feldman, 1974), others support both under different conditions (Butler & Womer, 1985), and others support neither an additive nor a multiplicative relationship (Hackman & Porter, 1968; Pritchard & Sanders, 1973). Some have found significant effects for all of the VIE process variables; others have found significant effects for some of the variables but not others (Arvey & Dunnette, 1980; House, Shapiro, & Wahba, 1974; Malloch & Michael, 1981; Moore & Davies, 1984; Pritchard & DeLeo, 1973). Although most studies agree that some combination of the VIE process variables is predictive of effort, a large number of studies have demonstrated that the VIE process variables alone are not predictive of performance (House, Shapiro, & Wahba, 1974). These studies have identified various other variables (e.g., ability, self-esteem, various personality traits) which either intervene between motivation and performance or influence the VIE process variables (Arvey & Dunnette, 1980; Butler & Womer, 1985; Darkenwald, 1987; House, Shapiro, & Wahba, 1974; Henson, 1976; Malloch & Michael, 1981; Mitchell & Knudson, 1971; Mitchell & Nebeker, 1973; Moore & Davies, 1984).

These mixed results can be traced to two major areas: problems with research methodology and the lack of a sufficiently comprehensive model that better describes the complex relation between both the expectancy process variables and the other variables. Because several researchers have cogently and thoroughly addressed methodological problems in expectancy research (Butler & Womer, 1985; House, Shapiro, & Wahba, 1974), these are not discussed in detail in this paper. A few theorists (Graen, 1969; Lawler, 1973) have either commented on the need for a more complex model of expectancy motivation or have suggested specific additions or changes to existing models. While these have been positive contributions, none have proved sufficiently comprehensive. Therefore, this paper addresses the need for a comprehensive model of expectancy motivation.

A Comprehensive Expectancy Motivation Model

A comprehensive expectancy motivation model must meet three criteria. First, it must accurately describe the dynamics of the fundamental process variables. Second, it must place expectancy motivation in the context of a cycle that explains not only the influence of expectancy motivation on the actual behavior of individuals but also the influence of actual performance, reward, and need satisfaction on expectancy motivation. Third, it must describe the influence of other variables on the motivation process. This paper proposes such a model.

The Primary Expectancy Motivation Variables

In this model, motivation is seen as the product of four primary process variables (see Figure 1): effort-performance (E-P) expectancy, performance-reward (P-R) expectancy, reward-need satisfaction (R-N) expectancy, and valence (V). E-P expectancy is defined as an individual's perception of the likelihood that his or her effort will lead to successful performance of a specific behavior(s) in a specific situation. P-R expectancy is defined as the perception of the likelihood of being rewarded for successful performance. R-N expectancy is defined as the perception of the likelihood that those rewards will meet important personal needs. Valence (V) is defined as the value the individual places on the object (e.g., performance, reward, or need satisfaction) of any of the above expectancies.

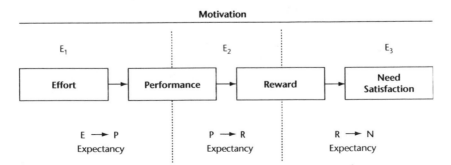

Figure 1: The primary expectancy motivation variables

For example, an individual's motivation in a learning situation would be high if that person: (a) perceived a high likelihood of performing successfully in the classroom and transferring those behaviors to the job (E-P), (b) perceived that improved job performance was likely to be rewarded by recognition from co-workers and supervisor (P-R), (c) perceived a high likelihood that recognition would meet basic acceptance needs (R-N), and (d) placed a high value (V) on each of the above.

How a situation is viewed varies among individuals who will have different expectancies and valences. For example, a learner with internal perceived locus of control would be more likely to value (and expend effort towards) intrinsic (i.e., built-in, learner-centered) than extrinsic (i.e., educator-administered) rewards.

Expectancy Motivation as a Dynamic Process

Figure 2 illustrates the dynamic nature of the expectancy motivation process variables. The model is a cyclical one: The outcomes of motivation (i.e., effort, performance, reward, and need satisfaction) affect the individual's level of motivation on a continuous basis. Initial motivation is based on an individual's subjective prediction of the probability of performance, reward, and need satisfaction. However, initial motivation results in actual effort, which in turn may result in actual performance, reward, and need satisfaction. Based on these observed results, the individual tests the accuracy of initial predictions (i.e., expectancies) and revises current E-P, P-R, and R-N expectancies.

In any given situation, motivation directly influences only the amount of effort a person will expend towards performing required behaviors (e.g., learning tasks). Actual effort is the only variable directly related to motivation; the rest are indirectly related.

Actual effort may or may not result in successful performance. Initial success (or progress) may increase a person's E-P expectancy and, thereby, motivation to continue efforts toward performing subsequent tasks. Similarly, initial lack of success results in lower E-P expectancy. Successful performance of

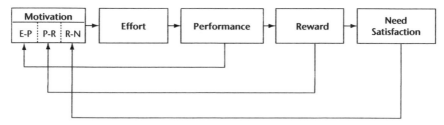

Figure 2: Expectancy motivation as a dynamic process

initial learning tasks motivates the learner to work toward subsequent learning tasks. Conversely, poor performance of initial learning tasks may lead to lower motivation on subsequent learning tasks. Continued poor performance may lower E-P expectancy to the point that the learner may decide that continued effort is wasted and drop out of the learning activity.

Actual performance may or may not result in rewards. In a given situation, consistent reward for successful performance improves an individual's P-R expectancy. Similarly, lack of reward (or inconsistent or inequitable rewards) results in lowered P-R expectancy. Reinforcement of newly learned behavior improves the learner's P-R expectancy and therefore increases that person's motivation to continue in the activity. If learned behavior is not reinforced, P-R expectancy and resultant motivation are decreased.

Actual rewards may or may not meet the individual's needs. If rewards satisfy the individual's needs, that person's R-N expectancy – and resulting motivation – will be increased. Learning programs tailored to unique learner needs result in higher motivation.

This model implies that performance would have a stronger impact on satisfaction than satisfaction would have on performance. In other words, successful performance in a learning situation results in increased learner satisfaction (performance-reward-need satisfaction), setting up a cycle of reinforcement which becomes stronger over time.

The Influence of Other Variables on Expectancy Motivation

As Figure 3 illustrates, expectancies are not only modified by ongoing feedback in the current situation but also by the individual's past experience. Personal experience in similar situations provides the individual with a basis for determining E-P, P-R, and R-N expectancies. Observed experience (e.g., knowledge obtained by directly observing others' experiences in similar situations) and communicated experience (e.g., shared information from others about their experiences in similar situations) are other sources.

Repeated exposure to similar situations develops an individual's knowledge, skills, and abilities (KSAs). An individual with moderate motivation and a high skill level will probably perform better than one with moderate motivation but a lower skill level. An individual whose effort frequently results in successful performance will have higher self-esteem than one who experiences frequent failures. Lower self-esteem translates as lower E-P expectancy and, therefore, lower motivation. P-R and R-N expectancies are similarly influenced by the individual's past experience in similar situations. Personality variables also influence expectancy motivation. Finally, uncontrollable environmental forces sometimes interfere with actual performance and reward. A turbulent environment decreases E-P and P-R expectancies.

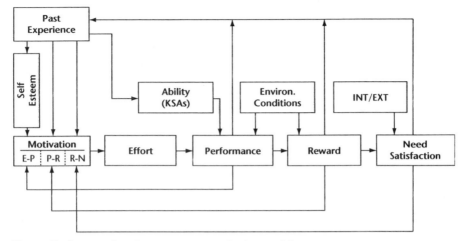

Figure 3: A comprehensive expectancy motivation model

Implications for Adult Education and Training

Increasing and maintaining learner motivation is a fundamental concern of adult educators. One might broadly conceptualize learning situations as having three stages, each with a different motivational focus: Pre-Learning (i.e., the period immediately prior to the learning situation), Learning (i.e., the actual learning situation), and Post-Learning (i.e., the period immediately following the learning situation). In the Pre-Learning stage, prospective learners must be motivated to become initially involved in learning. In the Learning stage, learners must be motivated to continue and take an active part in learning activities. In the Post-Learning stage, learners must be motivated to apply what they have learned. In each stage the same internal process variables – E-P, P-R, and R-N expectancies, and Valence – determine the level of motivation.

The implications of this model are clearest for planned, structured adult education programs with specific learning objectives. Increased planning and structure provide the adult educator with more opportunities to manipulate the expectancy variables. Similarly, increased structure and specific learning objectives increase the ability of the learner to formulate clear expectancies regarding the learning situation. However, even in less structured learning situations or learning situations with broader goals (e.g., liberal education programs, self-directed learning projects) the same principles still apply: Learners that believe the learning goals are achievable and will result in personal rewards that meet their individual needs will be more motivated than those who do not. Similarly, learners involved in self-directed learning activities can plan and structure their learning according to the principles of the Comprehensive Expectancy Motivation Model in order to maximize their motivation in the context of their learning projects.

Pre-Learning: Motivating Initial Involvement

To motivate learners to become involved in a specific learning project, the adult educator must persuade them that: (a) the learning tasks are within their ability to perform, given reasonable effort (increased E-P expectancy); (b) successful performance of these tasks will be rewarded, both in the learning situation and in practical application, (increased P-R expectancy); and (c) the reward will satisfy their needs (increased R-N expectancy). The individual's perception of the situation – not the objective reality – influences motivation at this stage, since the person has no direct experience to go on. This means that the learners will formulate expectancies based on past experience in similar learning programs, and particularly on what others have said about the learning program in question.

Marketing can be a key factor in maximizing motivation. Brochures should clearly describe learning objectives and demonstrate how they translate into improved performance (E-P). They should clearly state the minimum experience and the KSA levels for which a program is designed (E-P). In the case of industry-based programs, they should describe organizational sanctions or incentives in support of programs (P-R); supervisors should be made aware of programs so that they can encourage appropriate employees to attend (E-P and P-R). Word-of-mouth marketing from employees currently or previously involved in similar programs can also be motivating (E-P, P-R, and R-N).

This assumes that program objectives are, in fact, based on assessed needs related to typical tasks, and that the learning program is designed in such a way that successful performance in the learning program is analogous and transferable to practical performance. It also suggests that in-house trainers should actively work with management to build support for job-related education, as well as for specific learning programs. One way of maximizing job relevance, organizational support, and effective word-of-mouth marketing would be to involve representatives of targeted groups in the design of programs. Another option would be to include a representative cross-section of staff on an advisory committee.

Learning: Motivating Continued Involvement

During this stage learner motivation is much more fluid and may be influenced by actual experience in the learning situation. Learners' initial motivation may decrease if their experience in the learning situation leads them to believe: (a) that they cannot perform the learning tasks (E-P), (b) that learning task performance will not translate to performance on the job (E-P), (c) that performance will not be rewarded in either the learning situation or in the practical settings (P-R), or (d) that the rewards will not satisfy their needs (R-N). If motivation drops significantly, they may become uninvolved or may drop out altogether. The learner's perception is still the only thing that counts. However, now we are dealing with the learner's perception of his or her own actual learning experience.

Adult educators should attempt to build success into learning designs. The curriculum should build on skills that learners already possess. Learning should be in steps that are challenging, yet achievable, and the tasks related to the practical setting. A variety of opportunities for performing should be offered, allowing for different learning styles and incorporating both intrinsic and extrinsic rewards. Successful performance builds learner motivation directly, through experience in the learning situation, and indirectly, by building self-esteem.

The adult educator should attempt early in the program to engage the individual learners in explicit goal setting, focusing on clarifying expectancies regarding the learning situation. Specifically, the focus should be on whether the program will accomplish the learner's goals (R-N) and whether the learner can – with reasonable effort – achieve the learning objectives (E-P). Learning contracts are ideal for use in such goal-setting activities. Learning contracts, though strongly validated by field practice, have been criticized for their lack of a theoretical base (Polczynski & Shirland, 1976). Expectancy theory would appear to provide a strong theoretic basis for contract learning. The adult educator should be alert at this stage for adaptations necessary to bring the learning activities in line with overall learner expectancies.

On the other hand, adult educators should not devote excessive time to unrelated warm-up exercises, ice breakers, and strategies aimed at making learners feel good about themselves, since the model presented here does not support the assumption that such strategies will improve motivation to learn. Rather, it suggests that learner practice be encouraged as early in the program as possible.

Learner practice should be followed with immediate, constructive feedback from the adult educator and other learners. Clear ground rules for feedback, set early in the program, allow for reinforcement of learner expectancies that effort will in fact result in successful performance on learning tasks. Such feedback can also help shape performance in the learning situation into performance that can be more easily transferred to real-life situations which are more likely to reward learners in ways that satisfy their needs. Effective problem-solving methods, imparted early in the program, can help maintain learner motivation by providing the learner with the tools to improve performance, which, in turn, will both directly and indirectly raise expectancy levels.

Post-Learning: Motivating Application of Learning

In the Post-Learning stage, the learners must be motivated to apply the skills learned. Learners' motivation may decrease if they develop the perception that: (a) learning task performance will not translate to actual performance (E-P), (b) actual performance will not be rewarded (P-R), or (c) that the rewards will not satisfy their needs (R-N)- These issues need to be addressed toward the end of the program. Learners' problem-solving strategies should also be refined and action and contingency plans developed for implementing their new skills. Conscious planning is helpful in maintaining motivation.

The problem of maintaining motivation can also be dealt with by breaking up the program into a series of sessions, interspersed with opportunities for practical application. This gives the learner the opportunity to "phase in" actual performance in small, achievable steps, thus undergirding self-esteem and building an objective, experiential foundation on which to base expectancies. Finally, the adult educator should encourage learners to form support groups during the Post-Learning period. In job-related training, the adult educator should attempt to educate learners' supervisors to the need to reinforce successful performance during this period through constructive feedback and by suggesting opportunities to use the new skills.

Testing the Comprehensive Expectancy Motivation Model

The Comprehensive Expectancy Motivation Model presented in this paper suggests a number of hypotheses regarding motivation that can be tested empirically:

1. The learner's expectancies would change and become more accurate and consistent with continuing experience in any situation.
2. The expectancies of individuals with prior experience in similar situations would be more accurate and consistent than those of others who had not.
3. Successful performance in a learning situation would increase the learner's E-P expectancy; failure to perform would decrease it.
4. Consistent reward in a learning situation would increase the learner's P-R expectancy; lack of rewards or inconsistent rewards would decrease it.
5. Lack of fit between rewards and the learner's perceived needs would decrease the learner's R-N expectancy.
6. Successful performance would have a greater impact on learner satisfaction than learner satisfaction would have on performance.
7. Expectancy and ability combined would be a better predictor of successful performance than either would separately. At the start of any learning situation, expectancy motivation would predict effort, while ability would be more strongly correlated with performance. However, with increased experience in any given situation the correlation between expectancy motivation and performance would become stronger.

8. Learner practice should be encouraged as early in the program as possible since the model does not support the assumption that warm-up exercises, ice breakers, and other strategies aimed at making the learners feel good about themselves improve motivation to learn.

The Comprehensive Expectancy Motivation Model provides a framework that encompasses and explains the dynamic relationships among most of the commonly observed adult learning principles. Adult educators have long observed that adults are more motivated to learn when involved in setting their own learning goals, when given opportunities for relevant practice, when the "payoff" of learning is immediate, and so forth. This paper has described how these principles can be integrated into a single, predictive model that can be tested empirically.

References

Arvey, R, & Dunnette, M. (1980). *Task performance as a function of perceived effort-performance and performance-reward contingencies* (Technical Report No. 4003). Washington, DC: Office of Naval Research.

Borgstrom, L. (1980). Drop-out in municipal adult schools in the context of allocation policy. In R. Hoghielm and K. Rubenson (Eds.), *Adult education for social change* (pp. 105–130). Stockholm: Stockholm Institute of Education.

Butler, Jr., J., & Womer, N. (1985). Hierarchical vs. non-nested tests for contrasting expectancy-valence models: Some effects of cognitive characteristics. *Multivariate Behavioral Research, 20,* 335–352.

Constantinople, A. (1967). Perceived instrumentality of the college as a measure of attitudes toward college. *Journal of Personality and Social Psychology,* 5(2), 196–201.

Darkenwald, G. (1981). *Retaining adult students.* Columbus, OH: National Center for Research in Vocational Education.

Darkenwald, G. (1987). Dropout as a function of discrepancies between expectations and actual experiences of the classroom social environment. *Adult Education Quarterly, 37,* 152–163.

Gilmore, R. (1974). Expectancy beliefs, ability, and personality in predicting academic performance. *Journal of Educational Research, 156*(4), 28–37.

Graen, G. (1969). Instrumentality theory of work motivation: Some experimental results and suggested modification. *Journal of Applied Psychology, 53,* 2.

Feldman, J. (1974). Note on the utility of certain weights in expectancy theory. *Journal of Applied Psychology, 59*(6), 727–730.

Hackman, J., & Porter, L. (1968). Expectancy theory predictions of work effectiveness. *Organizational Behavior and Human Performance, 3,* 417–426.

Heneman, H., & Schwab, D. (1972). Evaluation of research on expectancy theory predictions of employee performance. *Psychological Bulletin, 78*(1), 1–9.

Henson, R (1976). Expectancy beliefs, ability, and personality in predicting academic performance. *Journal of Educational Research, 70,* 41–44.

House, R., Shapiro, H., & Wahba, A. (1974). Expectancy theory as a predictor of work behavior and attitude: A re-evaluation of empirical evidence. *Decision Sciences, 5,* 481–506.

Lawler, E. (1968). A correlation-causal analysis of the relationship between expectancy attitudes and job performance. *Journal of Applied Psychology, 52*, 462–468.

Lawler, E. (1973). *Motivation in work organizations.* Monterey, CA: Brooks-Cole.

Lewin, K. (1938). *The conceptual representation and the measurement of psychological forces.* Durham, NC: Duke University Press.

Maslow, A. (1943). A theory of human motivation. *Psychological Review, 50*, 370–396.

Malloch, D., & Michael, W. (1981). Predicting student grade point average at a community college from scholastic aptitude tests and from measures representing three constructs in Vroom's expectancy theory model of motivation. *Educational and Psychological Measurement, 41*, 1127–1135.

McMillan, J. (1980). Social psychology and learning. In J. H. McMillan (Ed.), *The social psychology of school learning.* New York: Academic Press.

Miskel, C, DeFrain, J., & Wilcox, K. (1980). A test of expectancy work motivation in educational organizations. *Educational Administration Quarterly, 16*(1), 70–92.

Mitchell, T, & Knudson, B. (1971). Instrumentality theory predictions of students attitudes towards business and their choice of business as an occupation. *Journal of Applied Psychology, 57*, 61–67.

Mitchell, T., & Nebeker, D. (1973). Expectancy theory predictions of academic effort and performance. *Journal of Applied Psychology, 57*, 61–67.

Moore, R., & Davies, J. (1984). Predicting GED scores on the bases of expectancy, valence, intelligence, and pretest skill levels with the disadvantages. *Educational and Psychological Measurement, 44*, 483–490.

Polczynski, J., & Shirland, L. (1976). Expectancy theory and contract grading combined as an effective motivational force for college students. *Journal of Educational Research, 70*, 238–241.

Pritchard, R., & DeLeo, R. (1973). Experimental test of the valence-instrumentality relationship in job performance. *Journal of Applied Psychology, 57*, 264–270.

Pritchard, R., & Sanders, M. (1973). The influence of valence, instrumentality, and expectancy on effort and performance. *Journal of Applied Psychology, 57*, 55–60.

Reykowski, J. (1965). Motivation as a component of the regulatory system of behavior. In M. Jones (Ed.), *Human Motivation* (pp. 71–85). Lincoln, NE: University of Nebraska Press.

Rotter, J. (1954). *Social learning and clinical psychology.* Englewood Cliffs, NJ: Prentice-Hall.

Rotter, J. (1971). *Clinical psychology.* Englewood Cliffs, NJ: Prentice-Hall.

Rubenson, K. (1976). *Recruitment in adult education: A research strategy.* Stockholm: Stockholm Institute of Education.

Rubenson, K, & Hoghielm, R. (1978). *The teaching process and study dropouts in adult education.* Stockholm: Stockholm Institute of Education.

Schmitt, N. (1975). A causal-correlational analysis of expectancy theory hypotheses. *Psychological Reports, 37*, 427–431.

Tolman E. (1932). *Purposeful behavior in animals and men.* New York: Appelton-Century-Crofts.

Vroom, V. (1964a). *Work and motivation.* New York: John Wiley.

Vroom, V. (1964b). Some psychological aspects of organizational control. In W. W. Cooper (Ed.), *New perspectives in organizational research* (pp. 72–86). New York: John Wiley.

Wright, R. (1985). Motivating teacher involvement in professional growth activities. *The Canadian Administrator, 24*(5), 1–6.

51

The Academic Motivation Scale: A Measure of Intrinsic, Extrinsic, and Amotivation in Education

Robert J. Vallerand, Luc G. Pelletier, Marc R. Blais, Nathalie M. Brière, Caroline Senécal and Evelyne F. Vallières

One of the most important psychological concepts in education is certainly that of motivation. Indeed, much research has shown that motivation is related to various outcomes such as curiosity, persistence, learning, and performance (for a review of the literature see Deci and Ryan, 1985). In light of the importance of these consequences for education, one can easily understand the interest of researchers for motivation in educational settings.

Several conceptual perspectives have been proposed in order to better understand academic motivation (see *The Educational Psychologist*, 1991, Issue 4, for a complete number devoted to academic motivation). One useful perspective posits that behavior can be intrinsically motivated, extrinsically motivated, or amotivated (Deci and Ryan, 1985, 1991). This theoretical approach has generated a considerable amount of research and appears rather pertinent for the field of education (see Deci and Ryan, 1985; Deci, Vallerand, Pelletier, and Ryan, 1991). This approach is detailed below.

Intrinsic Motivation

In general, intrinsic motivation (IM) refers to the fact of doing an activity for itself, and the pleasure and satisfaction derived from participation (Deci,

Source: *Educational and Psychological Measurement,* 52 (1992): 1003–1017.

1975; Deci and Ryan, 1985). An example of IM is the student that goes to class because he or she finds it interesting and satisfying to learn more about certain subjects. Deci and Ryan posit that IM stems from the innate psychological needs of competence and self-determination. Thus, activities that allow individuals to experience such feelings will be engaged in again freely out of IM.

While most researchers posit the presence of a global IM construct, certain theorists (Deci, 1975) have proposed that IM might be differentiated into more specific motives. Unfortunately, these authors have not indicated which types of IM follow from the more general IM construct. More recently, a tripartite taxonomy of intrinsic motivation has been postulated (Vallerand, Blais, Brière, and Pelletier, 1989). This taxonomy is based on the IM literature which reveals the presence of three types of IM that have been researched on an independent basis. These three types of IM can be identified as IM to know, to accomplish things, and to experience stimulation. These types of IM are described more fully below.

Intrinsic motivation to know (IM-to know). This type of IM has a vast tradition in educational research. It relates to several constructs such as exploration, curiosity, learning goals, intrinsic intellectuality, and finally the IM to learn (e.g., Gottfried, 1985; Harter, 1981). To the above perspectives which are more specific to the realm of education, may be added others that are more global such as that of the epistemic need to know and understand, and that of the search for meaning (see Vallerand et al., 1989). Thus, IM-to know can be defined as the fact of performing an activity for the pleasure and the satisfaction that one experiences while learning, exploring, or trying to understand something new. For instance, students are intrinsically motivated to know when they read a book for the sheer pleasure that they experience while learning something new.

Intrinsic motivation toward accomplishments (IM-to accomplish things). This second type of IM has been studied in developmental psychology as well as in educational research under concepts such as mastery motivation (Harter, 1981). In addition, other authors have postulated that individuals interact with the environment in order to feel competent, and to create unique accomplishments (Deci, 1975; Deci and Ryan, 1985, 1991). Finally, to the extent that individuals focus on the process of achieving rather than on the outcome, achievement motivation can be seen as being subsumed under the umbrella of IM-to accomplish things. Thus, IM-to accomplish things can be defined as the fact of engaging in an activity for the pleasure and satisfaction experienced when one attempts to accomplish or create something. Students who extend their work beyond the requirements of a term paper in order to experience pleasure and satisfaction while attempting to surpass themselves display IM toward accomplishments.

Intrinsic motivation to experience stimulation (IM-to experience stimulation). Finally, IM-to experience stimulation is operative when someone engages in an activity in order to experience stimulating sensations (e.g., sensory pleasure, aesthetic experiences, as well as fun and excitement) derived from one's engagement in the activity. Research on the dynamic and holistic sensation of flow, on feelings of excitement in IM, on aesthetic stimulating experiences, and peak experiences is representative of this form of IM (e.g., Csikszentmihalyi, 1975). Students who go to class in order to experience the excitement of a stimulating class discussion, or who read a book for the intense feelings of cognitive pleasure derived from passionate and exciting passages represent examples of individuals who are intrinsically motivated to experience stimulation in education.

Extrinsic Motivation

Contrary to IM, extrinsic motivation (EM) pertains to a wide variety of behaviors which are engaged in as a means to an end and not for their own sake (Deci, 1975). Recently, Deci, Ryan and their colleagues (Deci and Ryan, 1985, 1991) have proposed that three types of EM can be ordered along a self-determination continuum. From lower to higher levels of self-determination, they are: external regulation, introjection, and identification[1].

External regulation corresponds to EM as it generally appears in the literature. That is, behavior is regulated through external means such as rewards and constraints. For instance, a student might say: "I study the night before exams because my parents force me to." With *introjected regulation*, the individual begins to internalize the reasons for his or her actions. However, this form of internalization, while internal to the person, is not truly self-determined since it is limited to the internalization of past external contingencies. Thus, the individual might say: "I study the night before exams because that's what good students are supposed to do." To the extent that the behavior becomes valued and judged important for the individual, and especially that it is perceived as chosen by oneself, then the internalization of extrinsic motives becomes regulated through *identification*. The individual might say, for instance: "I've chosen to study tonight because it is something important for me."

Amotivation

In addition to intrinsic and extrinsic motivation, Deci and Ryan (1985) have recently posited that a third type of motivational construct is important to consider in order to fully understand human behavior. This concept is termed amotivation. Individuals are amotivated when they do not perceive contingencies between outcomes and their own actions. They are neither intrinsically nor extrinsically motivated. When amotivated individuals experience feelings of incompetence and expectancies of uncontrollability. They perceive their behaviors as caused by forces out of their own control. They feel undeceived, and start asking themselves why in the world they go to school. Eventually they may stop participating in academic activities.

Although scales assessing motivation toward education do exist, no scale currently allows to assess all constructs discussed above. Harter's (1981) Intrinsic vs Extrinsic Orientation Scale pits IM against EM on the same continuum and thus prevents an independent assessment of these two constructs. In addition, it does not measure the different types of EM and amotivation. Gottfried's (1985) Children Academic Intrinsic Motivation Inventory assesses only intrinsic interest toward learning in various subjects (e.g., reading, social sciences) as well as toward school in general. Thus, it does not measure the different types of IM, EM, or amotivation. Furthermore, while Ryan and Connell (1989) have recently developed a scale that does assess IM, identification, introjection, and external regulation, the psychometric properties of this scale have not been fully presented. In addition, this scale does not include the different types of IM or amotivation. Finally, it should be noted that all of the above scales are aimed at elementary and beginning high-school students. No existing scale seems to assess motivation toward post-secondary studies within the present theoretical framework.

In light of the importance of conducting research on academic motivation with an instrument based on a valid theoretical conceptualization, and the fact that no scale to date seems to assess IM, EM, and amotivation toward post-secondary studies, Vallerand et al. (1989) developed and validated in French the Echelle de Motivation en Education (EME). This scale is made up of seven subscales of four items each assessing the three types of IM (IM to know, to accomplish things, and to experience stimulation), three types of EM (external, introjected, and identified regulation), and amotivation. In the EME, motivation is operationalized as the underlying "why" of behavior (Deci and Ryan, 1985) and focus on the perceived reasons for engaging in the activity. Thus, the scale asks the question "Why do you go to college?" and items represent possible answers to that question, thus reflecting the different types of motivation. Here are some sample items from the scale: Amotivation subscale, "Honestly I don't know; I really feel that I'm wasting my time in college"; External Regulation, "In order to get a more prestigious job later on"; Introjected Regulation, "To prove to myself that I can do better than just a high-school degree"; Identified Regulation, "Because eventually it will allow me to enter the job market in a field that I like"; IM-to know, "Because I experience pleasure and satisfaction while learning new things"; IM-Accomplishment, "For the pleasure I experience while surpassing myself in my studies"; IM-Stimulation, "For the high feeling that I experience while reading on various interesting subjects."

Preliminary (Daoust, Vallerand, and Blais, 1988; Vallerand and Bissonnette, in press) and validation studies (Vallerand et al., 1989), which involved more than 3,000 students, revealed that the EME has satisfactory internal consistency levels (a mean alpha score of .80), as well as high indices of temporal stability (a mean test-retest correlation of .75) over a one-month period. Results of a confirmatory factor analysis (with LISREL) also confirmed the seven-factor structure of the EME. Finally, the construct validity of the scale was supported by a series of correlational analyses among the seven subscales, as well as between these scales and other psychological constructs relevant to education, such as interest toward school, time spent in academic activities, being distracted in class, academic satisfaction, positive emotions in the classroom, and nihilism toward education. These findings replicated the results reported earlier on the role of the different IM, EM, and amotivation in various educational outcomes. In addition, earlier versions as well as the current version of the EME were able to predict dropout behavior in high school and junior college (see Vallerand et al., 1989). The French version of the EME therefore appears to represent a reliable and valid measure of IM, EM, and amotivation in education.

Because the EME was initially validated in French, it was thus not available to researchers conducting research with English-speaking students. In light of the psychometric qualities of the EME, the findings it has yielded, and the importance of assessing motivation from a sound theoretical perspective, it was decided to cross-culturally validate the EME in English. To validate a scale into another language involves much more than translation (Brislin, 1986; Vallerand, 1989). In addition to appropriate translation, one must conduct research in order to show that this new version of the scale shares the same psychometric properties as the original scale. Thus, the overall purpose of the present study was to translate the scale in English and to conduct initial assessment of its psychometric properties.

The Current Investigation

Purpose

A four-fold purpose guided this investigation: (a) to translate the EME in English using appropriate cross-cultural procedures, (b) to replicate the seven-factor structure of the AMS through confirmatory factor analysis (with LISREL), (c) to assess the reliability (internal consistency and temporal stability) of the seven subscales, and (d) to assess whether the results from the Vallerand et al. (1989) study which revealed that females reported higher levels of IM to know, IM to experience stimulation, identification, and introjection, but lower levels of amotivation than males, would be replicated with a population of English-speaking students.

Method

Translation of the EME in English

In line with recent approaches to cross-cultural scale translation (Brislin, 1986; Vallerand, 1989), three steps were taken. First, the scale was translated from French to English. This was done with the parallel back-translation procedure (Brislin, 1986). Back translation first involves translating the scale from the original to the target language by a bilingual individual. This translation is then translated back to the original language by another bilingual individual without the use of the original scale. To the extent that the original scale is appropriately retranslated, this method provides an initial assessment of the adequacy of the translated version of the scale. The parallel back-translation procedure necessitates the use of two independent back translation sequences. This approach is preferred to the single back-translation method because it prevents the occurrence of certain biases that could result from the two specific bilingual individuals used in the back translation. In this study, four bilingual individuals (two social psychologists and two graduate students in social psychology) well cognizant of Deci and Ryan's (1985) motivation theory conducted the parallel back-translation procedure. This led to two preliminary English versions of the AMS that were evaluated in the next phase.

In the second phase, the items produced by the two back-translations were thoroughly assessed by a committee. The committee was formed of the individuals who participated in the back translation procedures and the authors of the original version of the scale (the EME). The committee selected the items that had been retranslated appropriately, that is which had retained the original meaning, and that had been conveyed in acceptable English. Once the 28 English items were selected the committee prepared the scale format and instructions so that they be identical to the ones used with the original French-Canadian version. Thus, the experimental version of the English AMS lists 28 items that may represent reasons why students go to college. These reasons are scored on a 7-point scale anchored by the end point "Not at all" (1) to "Exactly" (7) with a midpoint at 4 ("Moderately").

Third and final, a pretest was conducted with 10 junior-college students in order to determine whether the AMS was clear and formulated in a language to which post-secondary studies students can relate (Vallerand, 1989). Students were asked to read the AMS and to verbalize any questions they may have with the items or instructions. This led to some minor modifications with the instructions.

Procedures

The AMS was completed by 745 university students from the province of Ontario. This sample was composed of 484 females and 261 males with a mean age of 21.0 years. In order to assess the temporal stability of the AMS, a second sample of 57 university students (27 males and 30 females) with a mean age of 19.3 years also completed the AMS twice over a one-month period. Students were informed that we were interested in better understanding the reasons why they go to the university. To this end, we asked students to complete the AMS. Students were told that they did not have to complete the questionnaire but that their collaboration would be very much appreciated. Subjects completed the AMS in class at the beginning of the period.

Statistical Analyses

The various statistical analyses conducted dealt with the confirmatory factor analysis (with LISREL), the internal consistency (Cronbach alphas), test-retest correlations of the seven subscales, and the analysis of variance on the means of the subscales in order to test for sex differences.

Results and Discussion

Confirmatory Factor Analysis

The data were subjected to a confirmatory factor analysis with LISREL VI (Jöreskog and Sörbom, 1984). This analysis tests the extent to which the theoretical model, in this case the seven-factor model corresponding to the seven subscales, adequately represents the covariance matrix of the data. The fitting function estimated by the procedure was assessed through several indices, namely a chi-square statistic, the Goodness of Fit Index (GFI), the Adjusted Goodness of Fit Index (AGFI), and the Normed Fit Index (NFI) being the most widely used. These indices vary from 0 to 1 where 1 indicates a perfect fit for the model.

In the initial model, seven factors were postulated. These factors corresponded to the seven subscales and were made up of the four corresponding items. No cross-loadings were postulated. Although the confirmatory factor analysis of the initial measurement model yielded fit values of .89 for the NFI, .87 for the AGFI, and .89 for the GFI, the model did not reach statistical nonsignificance ($\chi^2 = 1228.27$, df $= 329, p < .001$). Correlations between pairs of measured-variable residuals were added to the model on the basis of the inspection of the modification indices. This resulted in 26 correlated residuals added to the model. With these additions the fit indices for the final measurement model showed that the model fits the data reasonably well, NFI $= .93$, AGFI $= .91$, GFI $= .94$, although the model did not reach statistical nonsignificance ($\chi^2 = 748.64$, df $= 303, p \leq .001$).

This improvement in fit was highly significant, difference in $\chi^2 = 479.63$, $df = 26, p < .001$.

In order to assess whether the inclusion of these theta delta values in the model could bias the interpretation of the model, the initial parameter estimates from the initial model were correlated with those from the final model. Results from the correlations involving the lambda x parameters yielded a .99 correlation value, while those including the lambda x and phi parameters indicated a .98 correlation value. These results underscore the fact that including the additional parameters in the model did not bias interpretation of the model.

In sum, results from the confirmatory factor analysis replicated the findings obtained with the original French-Canadian version (the EME), and confirmed the seven-factor structure of the AMS. Loadings from the final model, which were all significant, are presented in Table 1.

Reliability

The internal consistency of the subscales was assessed with the use of the Cronbach alpha. Values appear in the first column of Table 2. It can be seen that values varied from .83 to .86, except for the Identification subscale which had an alpha value of .62. These findings are remarkably similar to those obtained with the original version of the scale (EME) where values varied from .76 to .86, except for the Identification subscale which had a value of .62. Overall, considering the fact that these subscales are made up of 4 items, they appear to display adequate levels of internal consistency equivalent to that obtained with the original scale.

In order to assess the temporal stability of the AMS, a second sample of 57 university students completed the AMS twice over a one-month period. Results from the test-retest correlations appear in the last column of Table 2. It can be seen that correlations are fairly high ranging from .71 to .83, with a mean test-retest correlations of .79. These results are once again very similar to those obtained with the French-Canadian version (the EME), and support the temporal stability of the English version of the scale. In addition, the alpha values for the pretest and posttest appear in Table 2. It can be seen that these values are quite acceptable varying from .72 to .91 at the pretest, and from .78 to .90 at the posttest. The alpha values for the identification subscale were of .72 and .78 at the pretest and posttest, respectively thereby further supporting the reliability of that subscale. In sum, overall these results provide support for the internal consistency and the temporal stability of the AMS.

Analyses of Variance on the Subscale Means

Means of the seven subscales as a function of sex appear in Table 3. A sex X scale repeated measure analysis of variance, with repeated measures on the

Table 1: Standardized loadings from the confirmatory factor analysis (LISREL)

	Amotivation	External regulation	Introjected regulation	Identified regulation	Intr.Mot. knowledge	Intr.Mot. accomplishment	Intr.Mot. stimulation
Amotivation 1	1.059						
Amotivation 2	0.750						
Amotivation 3	1.025						
Amotivation 4	0.940						
External Regulation 1		1.143					
External Regulation 2		1.024					
External Regulation 3		1.139					
External Regulation 4		1.262					
Introjected Regulation 1			1.384				
Introjected Regulation 2			1.321				
Introjected Regulation 3			1.398				
Introjected Regulation 4			1.225				
Identified Regulation 1				0.582			
Identified Regulation 2				0.808			
Identified Regulation 3				0.749			
Identified Regulation 4				0.783			
Intrinsic Motivation-Knowledge 1					0.953		
Intrinsic Motivation-Knowledge 2					0.918		
Intrinsic Motivation-Knowledge 3					1.223		
Intrinsic Motivation-Knowledge 4					1.226		
Intrinsic Motivation-Accomplishment 1						1.198	
Intrinsic Motivation-Accomplishment 2						1.174	
Intrinsic Motivation-Accomplishment 3						1.261	
Intrinsic Motivation-Accomplishment 4						1.292	
Intrinsic Motivation-Stimulation 1							0.878
Intrinsic Motivation-Stimulation 2							1.424
Intrinsic Motivation-Stimulation 3							1.449
Intrinsic Motivation-Stimulation 4							1.445

Table 2: Internal consistency values (Cronbach alpha) and test-retest correlations of the AMS 7 subscales: Samples 1 and 2

	Alpha sample 1 (n = 745)	Alpha pretest sample 2 (n = 57)	Alpha posttest sample 2 (n = 57)	Test-retest correlations sample 2 (n = 57)
Amotivation	.85	.91	.88	.83
External Regulation	.83	.85	.89	.83
Introjected Regulation	.84	.76	.83	.73
Identified Regulation	.62	.72	.78	.71
IM-to Know	.84	.85	.90	.79
IM-Accomplishment	.85	.90	.87	.83
IM-Stimulation	.86	.88	.84	.80

Table 3: Means (and standard deviations) for males and females on the AMS: Sample 1

Subscales	Males (n = 261)	Females (n = 484)
Amotivation	6.74 (3.96)	6.51 (4.14)
External Regulation	21.78 (4.79)	21.80 (5.27)
Introjected Regulation*	16.0 (5.82)	17.80 (5.81)
Identified Regulation*	21.60 (3.57)	22.19 (3.98)
Intrinsic Motivation – Knowledge*	18.89 (4.22)	20.46 (4.74)
Intrinsic Motivation – Accomplishment*	15.93 (5.03)	17.52 (5.39)
Intrinsic Motivation – Stimulation*	12.21 (5.33)	13.83 (5.75)

* Females scored significantly higher ($p < .01$) than males.

scale factor, revealed the presence of main effects for sex, $F(1, 743) = 21.10$, $p < .001$, and scale, $F(6, 738) = 1035.18$, $p < .001$. The latter main effect revealed that all subscales differed from each other except for the Introjection and IM to Accomplish subscales, and the identification and external regulation subscales, respectively. The most important forms of motivation for the students in this sample were, in decreasing order: identification, external regulation, IM to know, introjection, IM toward accomplishments, IM to experience stimulation, and amotivation. However, these main effects must be interpreted in light of the significant sex X scale interaction, $F(6, 738) = 3.87, p < .001$. Results from the simple main effects revealed that female students scored higher than males on the 3 IM subscales (knowledge, accomplishment, and stimulation), as well as on the Identification and Introjection subscales. However, no sex differences were found on the other subscales (all $Fs > 4.03, ps > .05$).

General Discussion

The purpose of the present study was to cross-culturally validate the English version of the EME. Results revealed that the AMS has adequate levels of reliability and factorial validity, very much in line with those of the original French-Canadian version. With respect to the reliability of the scale, results from this study revealed that the internal consistency of all subscales was adequate, typically ranging in the .80s, with the exception of the Identification subscale which yielded values of .62 in the large sample, and .72 and .78 with the second sample used to assess the temporal stability of the scale. Finally, it should be reiterated that all AMS subscales displayed acceptable levels of temporal stability with a mean test-retest correlation value of .79 over a one-month period. These last results support the contention that the AMS measures students' rather stable motivational orientations toward education.

With respect to the validity of the AMS, the present results are also very encouraging on at least three accounts. First, results from the confirmatory factor analysis confirmed the seven-factor structure of the AMS and thus provided some support for the factorial validity of the scale. Second, results from the confirmatory factor analysis and the pattern of means of the IM subscales yielded preliminary support for the discriminant validity of the three IM subscales. Finally, gender differences on the various subscale means generally reproduced findings from the original study (Vallerand et al., 1989). The only difference between these two studies is that in the Vallerand et al. study (1989) females were also less amotivated than males and there was no sex differences on the IM Accomplishment subscale (although the means were in the predicted direction). These differences between the results from the Vallerand et al. and this study could be due to several factors including distinctions between the French and English-Canadian cultures, the motivation of university students (this study) and junior-college students (the Vallerand et al., 1989 study), as well as specificities (e.g., age, socio-economic background) of the samples used in the present and Vallerand et al. (1989) studies. Future research is needed in order to more fully understand these sex differences. However, one thing seems rather clear: In line with past research in education (e.g., Daoust et al., 1988; Vallerand and Bissonnette, in press; Vallerand et al., 1989) it appears that female students display a more self-determined motivational profile than male students.

Overall, the findings from the series of studies replicated the results obtained with the French-Canadian version (EME). It now appears that preliminary support exists for the reliability and some elements of validity of the AMS. Although these findings are indeed very encouraging, they must nevertheless be perceived as being only preliminary in nature. A complete assessment of the psychometric properties of the scale will necessitate additional research. In that perspective, recent research of ours (Vallerand, Pelletier, Blais, Brière, Senécal, and Vallieres, in press) has shown that the AMS has elements of concurrent and construct validity. Specifically, it was found that the scale was correlated as hypothesized with other motivational scales such as that of Gottfried (1985). In addition, the AMS correlated as predicted from cognitive evaluation theory (Deci and Ryan, 1985) with motivational antecedents and consequences. Future research in that direction would therefore appear fruitful.

In addition, it seems appropriate to reiterate that the operational definition of the AMS directly reflects the conceptual definition of intrinsic/extrinsic motivation which refers to one's perceived reasons for engaging in a given activity (the "why" of behavior), be they for the activity itself or for reasons lying outside the activity. Such an equivalence between the conceptual and operational definition of motivation should lead to more meaningful research. Furthermore, it should also be noted that contrary to other unidimensional instruments (e.g., Gottfried, 1985), the AMS assesses several types of motivation in a multidimensional fashion. These types of motivation go beyond the usual IM/EM distinction and allow a finer analysis of the motivational forces in education, thereby opening the door to innovative research.

In sum, even though the AMS represents a recent scale whose evaluation should be pursued in future research, results from the present study provide support for the adequacy of its psychomometric properties. Not only does the AMS represent an adequate cross-cultural adaptation of the original French-Canadian version (the EME), but it represents a reliable and valid scale in its own right. The psychometric properties of the AMS, as well as the flexibility allowed through its multidimensional structure, should make it a useful tool in motivation research in educational settings.

Note

1. Deci and Ryan (1985) also include integrated regulation as one type of extrinsic motivation. However, integrated regulation was not initially included in the Echelle de Motivation en Education (EME) and therefore is not assessed in the Academic Motivation Scale (AMS). Two major reasons supported this initial decision. First, pilot data revealed that integrated regulation did not come out as a perceived reason for participating in educational activities. Second, factor analyses on experimental forms of the EME revealed that integrated regulation did not distinguish itself from identified regulation. The above findings may have been due to a host of potential factors including the fact that young adults may be too young to have achieved a sense of integration with respect to school activities. Future research would appear necessary on this issue.

References

Brislin, R. W. (1986). The wording and translation of research instruments. In W. Lonner and J. Berry (Eds.), *Field methods in cross-cultural research* (pp. 137–164). Beverly Hills, CA: Sage.

Csikszentmihalyi, M. (1975). *Beyond boredom and anxiety*. San Francisco: Jossey-Bass.

Daoust, H., Vallerand, R. J., and Blais, M. R. (1988). Motivation and education: A look at some important consequences. *Canadian Psychology*, 29 (2a), 172. (abstract).

Deci, E. L. (1975). *Intrinsic motivation*. New York: Plenum Press.

Deci, E. L. and Ryan, R. M. (1985). *Intrinsic motivation and self-determination in human behavior*. New York: Plenum Press.

Deci, E. L. and Ryan, R. M. (1991). A motivational approach to self: Integration in personality. In R. Dienstbier (Ed.), *Nebraska Symposium on motivation: Vol. 38. Perspectives on motivation* (pp. 237–288) Lincoln, NE: University of Nebraska Press.

Deci, E. L., Vallerand, R. J., Pelletier, L. G., and Ryan, R. M. (1991). Motivation in education: The self-determination perspective. *The Educational Psychologist*, 26, 325–346.

Gottfried, A. E. (1985). Academic intrinsic motivation in elementary and junior high school students. *Journal of Educational Psychology*, 77, 631–645.

Harter, S. (1981). A new self-report scale on intrinsic versus extrinsic orientation in the classroom: Motivational and informational components. *Developmental Psychology*, 17, 300–312.

Jöreskog, K. G. and Sörbom, D. (1984). *LISREL VI*. Chicago, IL: National Educational Resources.

Ryan, R. M. and Connell, J. P. (1989). Perceived locus of causality and internalization: Examining reasons for acting in two domains. *Journal of Personality and Social Psychology*, 57, 450–461.

Vallerand, R. J. (1989). Vers une méthodologie de validation trans-culturelle de questionnaires psychologiques: Implications pour la recherche en langue française (Toward a cross-cultural validation methodology for psychological scales: Implications for research conducted in the French language). *Canadian Psychology*, 30, 662–680.

Vallerand, R. J. and Bissonnette, R. (in press). Intrinsic, extrinsic, and amotivational styles as predictors of behavior: A prospective study. Journal of Personality.

Vallerand, R. J., Blais, M. R., Brière, N. M., and Pelletier, L. G. (1989). Construction et validation de l'Echelle de Motivation en Education (EME) [Construction and validation of the Echelle de Motivation en Education (EME)]. *Canadian Journal of Behavioral Sciences*, 21, 323–349.

Vallerand, R. J., Pelletier, L. G., Blais, M. R., Brière, N. M., Senécal, C., and Vallières, E. F. (in press). On the assessment of intrinsic, extrinsic, and amotivation in education: Evidence on the concurrent and construct validity of the Academic Motivation Scale. EDUCATIONAL AND PSYCHOLOGICAL MEASUREMENT.

52

Extrinsic Rewards and Intrinsic Motivation in Education: Reconsidered Once Again

Edward L. Deci, Richard Koestner and Richard M. Ryan

Gold stars, best-student awards, honor roles, pizzas for reading, and other reward-focused incentive systems have long been part of the currency of schools. Typically intended to motivate or reinforce student learning, such techniques have been widely advocated by some educators, although, in recent years, a few commentators have questioned their widespread use. The controversy has been prompted in part by psychological research that has demonstrated negative effects of extrinsic rewards on students' intrinsic motivation to learn. Some studies have suggested that, rather than always being positive motivators, rewards can at times undermine rather than enhance self-motivation, curiosity, interest, and persistence at learning tasks. Because of the widespread use of rewards in schools, a careful summary of reward effects on intrinsic motivation would seem to be of considerable importance for educators.

Accordingly, in the Fall 1994 issue of *Review of Educational Research*, Cameron and Pierce (1994) presented a meta-analysis of extrinsic reward effects on intrinsic motivation, concluding that, overall, rewards do not decrease intrinsic motivation. Implicitly acknowledging that intrinsic motivation is important for learning and adjustment in educational settings (see, e.g., Ryan & La Guardia, 1999), Cameron and Pierce nonetheless stated that "teachers have no reason to resist implementing incentive systems in the classroom" (p. 397). They also advocated abandoning Deci and Ryan's (1980) cognitive

Source: *Review of Educational Research*, 71(1) (2001): 1–27.

evaluation theory (CET), which had initially been formulated to explain both positive and negative reward effects on intrinsic motivation.

In the Spring 1996 issue of *RER,* three commentaries were published (Kohn, 1996; Lepper, Keavney, & Drake, 1996; Ryan & Deci, 1996) arguing that Cameron and Pierce's meta-analysis was flawed and that its conclusions were unwarranted. In that same issue, Cameron and Pierce (1996) responded to the commentaries by claiming that, rather than reanalyzing the data, the authors of the three commentaries had suggested "that the findings are invalid due to intentional bias, deliberate misrepresentation, and inept analysis" (p. 39). Subtitling their response "Protests and Accusations Do Not Alter the Results," Cameron and Pierce stated that any meaningful criticism of their article would have to include a reanalysis of the data. Subsequent to that interchange, Eisenberger and Cameron (1996) published an article in the *American Psychologist* summarizing the Cameron and Pierce (1994) meta-analysis and claiming that the so-called undermining of intrinsic motivation by extrinsic rewards, which they said had become accepted as reality, was in fact largely a myth.

We do not claim that there was "intentional bias" or "deliberate misrepresentation" in either the Cameron and Pierce (1994) meta-analysis or the Eisenberger and Cameron (1996) article, but we do believe, as Ryan and Deci argued in 1996, that Cameron and Pierce used some inappropriate procedures and made numerous errors in their meta-analysis. Therefore, because we believe the problems with their meta-analysis made their conclusions invalid, because we agree that a useful critique of their article must involve reanalysis of the data, and because the issue of reward effects on intrinsic motivation is extremely important for educators, we performed a new meta-analysis of reward effects on intrinsic motivation (Deci, Koestner, & Ryan, 1999). Our meta-analysis included 128 experiments, organized so as to provide a test of CET, much as Cameron and Pierce had done. The new meta-analysis, which we summarize in this article, showed that, in fact, tangible rewards do significantly and substantially undermine intrinsic motivation. The meta-analysis provided strong support for CET and made clear that there is indeed reason for teachers to exercise great care when using reward-based incentive systems.

The new meta-analysis was published in *Psychological Bulletin* (Deci et al., 1999). Included in that article was an appendix table (here reproduced with permission as Table 1a) listing every study in the meta-analysis and explaining exactly where errors were made by Cameron and Pierce, how our meta-analysis corrected their errors, and what studies were included in ours that had been overlooked or omitted by them. The table allows interested readers to see for themselves exactly how it is that Cameron and Pierce's meta-analysis and our meta-analysis arrived at such different conclusions.

In the seven years since the publication of Cameron and Pierce's (1994) article, academics, school administrators, and classroom teachers from many countries have spoken to us about the article, making it clear that the conclusions of the article had been widely disseminated and that the issue of reward effects is of considerable interest to educators around the world. Given the great importance of this issue for education, then, the current article is intended to set the record straight for the many readers of *RER*. In this article, we provide a brief description of CET, because it has guided much of the research in the field. This is followed by a summary of the methods and results of our meta-analysis and, finally, a discussion of the relevance of the results for education.

Cognitive Evaluation Theory

CET proposes that underlying intrinsic motivation are the innate psychological needs for competence and self-determination. According to the theory, the effects on intrinsic motivation of external events such as the offering of rewards, the delivery of evaluations, the setting of deadlines, and other motivational inputs are a function of how these events influence a person's perceptions of competence and self-determination. Events that decrease perceived self-determination (i.e., that lead to a more external perceived locus of causality) will undermine intrinsic motivation, whereas those that increase perceived self-determination (i.e., that lead to a more internal perceived locus of causality) will enhance intrinsic motivation. Furthermore, events that increase perceived competence will enhance intrinsic motivation so long as they are accompanied by perceived self-determination (e.g., Ryan, 1982), and those that decrease perceived competence will diminish intrinsic motivation. Finally, rewards (and other external events) have two aspects. The *informational* aspect conveys self-determined competence and thus enhances intrinsic motivation. In contrast, the *controlling* aspect prompts an external perceived locus of causality (i.e., low perceived self-determination) and thus undermines intrinsic motivation.

As noted, CET applies not only to reward effects but to the effects of various other external factors such as evaluations (Smith, 1975), deadlines (Amabile, DeJong, & Lepper, 1976), competition (Deci, Betley, Kahle, Abrams, & Porac, 1981), and externally imposed goals (Mossholder, 1980), as well as to the general climate of classrooms, schools, and other interpersonal settings (e.g., Deci, Connell, & Ryan, 1989; Deci, Schwartz, Sheinman, & Ryan, 1981). In this article, however, we focus only on CET as an explanation for reward effects.

In making predictions about reward effects on intrinsic motivation, CET analyzes the type of reward and the type of reward contingency to determine whether the reward is likely to be experienced as informational or controlling. The theory acknowledges that in some cases both the informational and controlling aspects will be somewhat salient, so, in those situations, additional factors are taken into account in making predictions. We begin our discussion of CET's reward-effect predictions by distinguishing between verbal rewards and tangible rewards, considering verbal rewards first and then moving on to tangible rewards.

Verbal Rewards

Although we do not usually use the term *verbal rewards,* preferring instead to speak of "positive feedback," we do use that term here in order to include the positive-feedback studies within the general category of reward effects. Verbal rewards typically contain explicit positive performance feedback, so CET predicts that they are likely to enhance perceived competence and thus enhance intrinsic motivation. In the meta-analysis, we tested the hypothesis that verbal rewards would enhance intrinsic motivation.

Nonetheless, verbal rewards can have a significant controlling aspect leading people to engage in behaviors specifically to gain praise, so verbal rewards have the potential to undermine intrinsic motivation. The theory therefore suggests that the interpersonal context within which positive feedback is administered can influence whether it will be interpreted as informational or controlling. As used here, the term *interpersonal context* refers to the social ambience of settings, such as classrooms, as they influence people's experience of self-determination (Deci & Ryan, 1991). When studied in laboratory experiments, the interpersonal climate is usually manipulated in terms of the interpersonal style used by the experimenter when providing the feedback (e.g., Ryan, 1982; Ryan, Mims, & Koestner, 1983). An interpersonal context is considered controlling to the extent that people feel pressured by it to think, feel, or behave in particular ways. Verbal rewards administered within such a context are thus more likely to be experienced as controlling rather than informational. For example, CET suggests that if a teacher uses an interpersonal style intended to make students do what he or she wants them to, verbal rewards administered by that teacher are likely to be experienced as controlling. In a supplemental meta-analysis involving five studies, we tested the prediction that controlling positive feedback would lead to less intrinsic motivation than informational positive feedback.

Tangible Rewards

Unlike verbal rewards, tangible rewards are frequently offered to people as an inducement to engage in a behavior in which they might not otherwise engage. Thus, according to CET, tangible rewards will tend to be experienced as controlling, and as a result they will tend to decrease intrinsic motivation.

The meta-analysis tested the hypothesis that, overall, tangible rewards would decrease intrinsic motivation.

In order for tangible rewards to be experienced as controlling, however, people would need to be engaging in the behavior for the rewards; that is, they would need to expect that the behavior would lead to the rewards. If tangible rewards are given unexpectedly to people after they have finished a task, the rewards are less likely to be experienced as the reason for doing the task and are thus less likely to be detrimental to intrinsic motivation. The meta-analysis tested the hypothesis that unexpected tangible rewards would not undermine intrinsic motivation, whereas expected tangible rewards would.

Expected tangible rewards can be administered through various contingencies; that is, they can be made contingent upon different aspects of task-related behavior. In making more refined predictions about the effects of expected tangible rewards on intrinsic motivation, CET takes account of task contingency. Ryan et al. (1983) specified three types of reward contingencies: *task-noncontingent* rewards, which do not require engaging in the activity per se but are instead given for some other reason such as simply participating in the experiment; *task-contingent* rewards, which require doing or completing the target activity; and *performance-contingent* rewards, which require performing the activity well, matching a standard of excellence, or surpassing a specified criterion (e.g., doing better than half of the other participants).

A further distinction has been made between task-contingent rewards that specifically require completing the target task (herein referred to as *completion-contingent* rewards) and those that require engaging in the activity but do not require completing it (herein referred to as *engagement-contingent* rewards). We (e.g., Deci & Ryan, 1985) have considered the completion-contingent and engagement-contingent rewards to constitute the single category of task-contingent rewards because the effects of these two reward contingencies have seemed to be remarkably similar; however, we separated them for this meta-analysis in order to evaluate whether the effects of completion-contingent and engagement-contingent rewards are, in fact, the same.

Because task-noncontingent rewards do not require doing, completing, or doing well at the target task, there is no reason to expect these rewards to be experienced as either informational or controlling with respect to the task. Accordingly, the meta-analysis tested the hypothesis that intrinsic motivation would not be affected by these rewards.

Engagement-contingent rewards specifically require that people work on the task, so the rewards are likely to be experienced as controlling the task behavior. Because these rewards carry little or no competence affirmation, they are unlikely to increase perceived competence, and thus there will be nothing to counteract the negative effects of the control. Thus, the meta-analysis tested the hypothesis that engagement-contingent rewards would undermine intrinsic motivation.

Completion-contingent rewards require that people complete the task to obtain the rewards, so the rewards are likely to be experienced as even more controlling than engagement-contingent rewards. However, with completion-contingent rewards, receipt of the rewards conveys competence if the task required skill and the person had a normative sense of what constitutes good performance on the task. To the extent that the rewards do represent competence affirmation, this implicit positive feedback could offset some of the control. Still, averaged across different types of tasks, the competence-affirming aspect of completion-contingent rewards is not expected to be strong relative to the controlling aspect, so we tested the hypothesis that completion-contingent rewards would undermine intrinsic motivation at a level roughly comparable to that of engagement-contingent rewards. Parenthetically, because the category of task-contingent rewards is composed of engagement-contingent and completion-contingent rewards, we also expected this larger category to yield significant undermining of intrinsic motivation.

Finally, performance-contingent rewards are linked to people's perfor-mance, so there is even stronger control. People have to meet a standard to maximize rewards, and thus there is a strong tendency for these rewards to undermine intrinsic motivation. However, performance-contingent rewards can also convey substantial positive competence information when a person receives a level of reward that signifies excellent performance. In those cases, there would be a tendency for performance-contingent rewards to affirm competence and, thus, to offset some of the negative effects of control. In the meta-analysis, we tested the hypothesis that performance-contingent rewards would undermine intrinsic motivation, but we also expected that other fac-tors would influence the effects of these rewards on intrinsic motivation. One such factor is whether or not the level of reward implies excellent perfor-mance. Thus, we examined the hypothesis that performance-contingent rewards would be more undermining of intrinsic motivation if the rewards did not convey high-quality performance.

Another factor that is expected to influence the effects of performance-contingent rewards is the interpersonal context (as was the case with verbal rewards). If the interpersonal climate within which these rewards are admin-istered is demanding and controlling, the rewards are expected to be more undermining of intrinsic motivation.

Although few studies have manipulated the interpersonal context of performance-contingent rewards, Ryan et al. (1983) compared a performance-contingent rewards group in which the rewards were administered in a rela-tively controlling manner and one in which they were administered in a relatively non-controlling manner. As predicted, the controlling administra-tion of performance-contingent rewards led to undermining of intrinsic motivation relative to the noncontrolling administration. In terms of educa-tion, this is a particularly important finding because it suggests that when rewards are used in the classroom, it is important that the climate of the classroom be supportive rather than controlling so that the students will be less likely to experience the rewards as controlling.

Method

Our meta-analytic strategy (Deci et al., 1999) involved a hierarchical approach in which the results of 128 experiments were examined in two separate meta-analyses. The first involved 101 of the studies that had used a free-choice behavioral measure of intrinsic motivation, and the second involved 84 of the studies that had used self-reported interest as a dependent variable. In a hierarchical meta-analysis, one begins with the most general category and reports the composite effect size. If the set of effects is heterogeneous, then one proceeds to differentiate the overall category into meaningful subcategories in an attempt to achieve homogeneity of effects within the subcategories. Thus, in both meta-analyses (i.e., with the two dependent measures), we began by calculating the effects of all rewards on intrinsic motivation and then systematically differentiated the reward conditions. Only after we had exhausted all possible moderator variables did we discard outliers to create homogeneity within subcategories. Using this approach, we ended up discarding only about 4% of the effects as outliers, whereas Cameron and Pierce (1994) had discarded approximately 20% of the effects as outliers.

In the differentiation, studies were first separated into those that examined verbal rewards versus those that examined tangible rewards. Then tangible rewards, which have been extensively studied, were analyzed as follows. The effects of rewards that were unexpected versus expected were examined separately. Studies of expected tangible rewards were then separated into four groups, depending on what the rewards were contingent upon. The groups were as follows: task noncontingent (rewards that did not explicitly require working on a task), engagement contingent (rewards that did require working on the task), completion contingent (rewards that required finishing a task), and performance contingent (rewards contingent upon a specified level of performance at a task). As described subsequently, because the performance-contingent reward effects on the free-choice measure were heterogeneous, that category was further differentiated. Finally, in categories in which the effect sizes were heterogeneous after all theoretically based differentiations had been completed, we compared the effects of the reward types on schoolchildren versus college students, an issue that had not been considered previously but emerged from an inspection of the data and seemed very important in terms of the educational relevance of the results.

Inclusion criteria for studies that spanned the period 1971 to 1996 were the following. First, because intrinsic motivation is pertinent to tasks that people experience as interesting and because the field of inquiry has always been defined in terms of reward effects on intrinsic motivation for interesting tasks, we included only studies or conditions within studies if the target task was at least moderately interesting (i.e., if it either was not defined a priori as a boring task by the experimenter or did not have a prereward interest rating below the midpoint of the scale). In contrast, Cameron and Pierce (1994) had aggregated across boring and interesting tasks without even addressing the issue in their article. Second, the analyses included only studies that assessed intrinsic motivation after the rewards had been clearly terminated, because while the reward is in effect participants' behavior reflects a mix of intrinsic and extrinsic motivation. Cameron and Pierce, however, included assessments which they called intrinsic motivation but which had been taken while the reward contingency was still in effect. Third, studies were included only if they had an appropriate no-reward control group. Cameron and Pierce had made numerous comparisons based on questionable selections of control groups, at times even using inappropriate control groups when appropriate ones were available.

In conducting the meta-analyses, we used Cohen's d as the measure of effect size. It reflects the difference between the means of two groups divided by the pooled within-group standard deviations, adjusted for sample size (Hedges & Olkin, 1985). The mean of the control group was subtracted from the mean of the rewards group, so a negative d reflects an "undermining effect," whereas a positive d reflects an "enhancement effect."

Means, standard deviations, t tests, F tests, and sample sizes were used to calculate d values. For any study in which insufficient data were provided to calculate an effect size, we assigned an effect of $d = 0.00$, and we included those imputed values in all analyses. All effect-size computations and summary analyses were done with DSTAT (Johnson, 1993), a meta-analytic software program. Each calculation of a composite effect size is accompanied by a 95% confidence interval (CI) (for additional methodological details, see Deci et al., 1999).

Results

Effects of All Rewards

Although the early discussions of extrinsic reward effects on intrinsic motivation (e.g., deCharms, 1968) tended to consider extrinsic rewards as a unitary concept, even the very first investigations of this issue differentiated the concept. Deci (1971, 1972b) distinguished between tangible rewards and verbal rewards (i.e., positive feedback), reporting that tangible rewards decreased intrinsic motivation, while verbal rewards increased it. Furthermore, Deci (1972a) differentiated task-contingent rewards from task-noncontingent rewards, finding that task-contingent rewards decreased intrinsic motivation but task-noncontingent rewards did not, and Lepper, Greene, and Nisbett (1973) distinguished between rewards that were expected and those that were unexpected, finding that expected rewards decreased intrinsic motivation but unexpected rewards did not.

Accordingly, given that different rewards and different reward contingencies seem to have different effects on intrinsic motivation, aggregating across all types of rewards meta-analytically is, in a sense, a meaningless endeavor, because the outcome will depend primarily on how many studies of each type of reward or reward contingency are included in the meta-analysis (Ryan & Deci, 1996). Nonetheless, because Cameron and Pierce (1994) calculated the effect of all rewards on intrinsic motivation in their meta-analysis, we also calculated it for comparative purposes. The effect of all types of rewards across all relevant studies revealed significant undermining for the free-choice behavioral measure of intrinsic motivation ($k = 101$; $d = -0.24$; $CI = -0.29, -0.19$),[1] although the overall effect for the self-report measure was not significant. These and other major results are summarized in Table 1.

Table 1: Major results of the meta-analysis of the effects of extrinsic rewards on free-choice intrinsic motivation and self-reported interest, shown as Cohen's composite d, with k effects included

	Free-choice behavior		Self-reported interest	
	d	k	d	k
All rewards	−0.24*	101	0.04	84
Verbal rewards	0.33*	21	0.31*	21[a]
College	0.43*	14[a]		
Children	0.11	7[a]		
Tangible rewards	−0.34*	92	−0.07*	70
Unexpected	0.01	9[a]	0.05	5[a]
Expected	−0.36*	92	−0.07*	69
Task noncontingent	−0.14	7[a]	0.21	5[a]
Engagement contingent	−0.40*	55	−0.15*	35[a]
College	−0.21*	12[a]		
Children	−0.43*	39[a]		
Completion contingent	−0.44*	19[a]	−0.17*	13[a]
Performance contingent	−0.28*	32	−0.01	29[a]
Maximal reward	−0.15*	18[a]		
Not maximum reward	−0.88*	6[a]		
Positive feedback control	−0.20*	10[a]		
Negative feedback control	−0.03	3[a]		

[a] These categories were not further differentiated and are homogeneous. Some of the studies used to determine the overall composite effect size (i.e., for all rewards) in each meta-analysis had multiple reward conditions, so the sums of the numbers of effect sizes in the most differentiated categories of each meta-analysis are greater than the numbers in the all-rewards category. There were 150 effect sizes in the most differentiated categories for the free-choice analyses, of which 6 were removed as outliers, and there were 114 effect sizes in the most differentiated categories of the self-report analyses, of which 6 were removed as outliers.

* Significant at $p < .05$ or greater.

As already mentioned, we expected that all rewards would not affect intrinsic motivation in a uniform way, and thus we both expected and found that the set of effects for the all-rewards category was heterogeneous. Consequently, we proceeded with more differentiated analyses of specific types of rewards, based on both theoretical and empirical considerations. We first separated studies of verbal rewards from those of tangible rewards.

Verbal Rewards (Positive Feedback)

We first tested the CET prediction that, on average, verbal rewards would enhance intrinsic motivation. Twenty-one studies examined the effects of verbal rewards on free-choice intrinsic motivation, and 21 examined its effects on self-reports of interest. Results indicated that verbal rewards enhanced intrinsic motivation: for the behavioral measure, $d = 0.33$ (CI $= 0.18, 0.43$), and for self-reports, $d = 0.31$ (CI $= 0.19, 0.44$).

However, there are two important caveats to this general finding. First, because the set of effect sizes for verbal-reward effects on free-choice behavior was heterogeneous, we inspected the studies to determine whether there was any obvious pattern in the results. We noticed that the effects of verbal rewards on schoolchildren appeared to be different from the effects on college students, so we conducted separate analyses for schoolchildren and college students. It turned out that verbal rewards enhanced free-choice intrinsic motivation for college students ($k = 14$; $d = 0.43$; CI $= 0.27, 0.58$) but not for children ($k = 7$; $d = 0.11$; CI $= 0.11$, 0.34), a point that is very important when thinking about educational practices.

Second, CET has emphasized that although positive feedback can enhance intrinsic motivation, it can actually undermine intrinsic motivation if it is administered with a controlling interpersonal style. Five studies examined the administration of verbal rewards with an informational versus controlling interpersonal style, so we did a supplemental analysis of these studies. The results indicated, as hypothesized, that although informationally administered verbal rewards enhanced intrinsic motivation ($d = 0.66$; CI $= 0.28, 1.03$), controllingly administered verbal rewards undermined intrinsic motivation ($d = -0.44$; CI $= -0.82, -0.07$).

To summarize, research indicates that verbal rewards (i.e., positive feedback) tend to have an enhancing effect on intrinsic motivation; however, verbal rewards are less likely to have a positive effect for children than for older individuals. Furthermore, verbal rewards can even have a negative effect on intrinsic motivation if the interpersonal context within which they are administered is controlling rather than informational.

Tangible Rewards

Next, we tested the CET prediction that, overall, tangible rewards (including material rewards, such as money and prizes, and symbolic rewards, such as trophies and good player awards) would decrease intrinsic motivation, because tangible rewards are frequently used to persuade people to do things they would not otherwise do, that is, to control their behavior. The meta-analysis included 92 tangible reward studies with a free-choice measure and 70 with a self-report measure. As predicted by CET, results indicated that, on average, tangible rewards significantly undermined both free-choice intrinsic motivation ($d = -.34$; CI $= -0.39, -0.28$) and self-reported interest ($d = -0.07$; CI $= -0.13, -0.01$). Of course, we have regularly argued that a full understanding of the effects of tangible rewards requires a consideration of additional factors such as reward contingency and interpersonal context, but these results do highlight the general risks associated with the use of tangible rewards as a motivator.

Because age effects had emerged for verbal rewards, we also compared the effects of tangible rewards in studies of children versus college students. This revealed that even though tangible rewards significantly undermined intrinsic motivation for both groups, the undermining effect was significantly greater for children than for college students on both behavioral and self-report measures of intrinsic motivation. The real-world implications of this pattern of results are extremely important. There is great concern about children's motivation for school work, as well as for other behaviors such as sports, art, and prosocial activities, and a study conducted by Boggiano, Barrett, Weiher, McClelland, and Lusk (1987) indicated that adults tend to view salient extrinsic rewards as an effective motivational strategy for promoting these behaviors in children. However, the age-effect analyses indicate that, although tangible rewards may control immediate behaviors, they have negative consequences for subsequent interest, persistence, and preference for challenge, especially for children. In summary, the age effects that emerged from our meta-analysis indicate that tangible rewards have a more negative effect on children than on college students and that verbal rewards have a less positive effect on children than on college students.

Unexpected Rewards and Task-Noncontingent Rewards

We next tested the CET prediction that unexpected rewards would not be detrimental to intrinsic motivation, whereas expected rewards would. The reasoning was that if people are not doing a task in order to get a reward, they are not likely to experience their task behavior as being controlled by the reward. The meta-analysis supported the hypothesis. Nine studies of free-choice behavior revealed no undermining ($d = 0.01$; CI $= -0.20, 0.22$), and five studies of self-reported interest revealed similar results ($d = 0.05$; CI $= -0.19, 0.29$).

In contrast, analyses of expected rewards did yield undermining for both free-choice behavior ($k = 92$; $d = -0.36$; CI $= -0.42, -0.30$) and self-reported interest ($k = 69$; $d = -0.07$; CI $= -0.13, -0.01$). It is interesting in this regard to note that verbal rewards are generally unexpected, and that may be one of the reasons they do not typically have a negative effect on intrinsic motivation.

According to CET, rewards not requiring task engagement should be unlikely to affect intrinsic motivation for the task because the rewards are not given for doing the task. Although relatively few studies of task-noncontingent rewards have been done, the meta-analysis revealed no evidence that these rewards significantly affected either measure of intrinsic motivation ($k = 7$; $d = -0.14$; CI $= -0.39, 0.11$, for free-choice behavior and $k = 5$; $d = 0.21$; CI $= -0.08, 0.50$, for self-reported interest).

Engagement-Contingent Rewards

Engagement-contingent rewards are offered explicitly for engaging in an activity. When children were told they would get a good player award for working on an art activity (Lepper et al., 1973), the reward was engagement contingent. Similarly, when college students were told they would receive a reward if they performed a hidden-figures activity, the reward was engagement contingent (Ryan et al., 1983). In neither case was there a performance requirement: Participants did not have to finish the task or do well on it; they simply had to work on it. More studies have used engagement-contingent rewards than any other reward contingency, and that is particularly true for studies of children. Results of the meta-analyses confirmed that engagement-contingent rewards significantly diminished intrinsic motivation measured in both ways ($k = 55$; $d = -0.40$; CI $= -0.48, -0.32$, for free-choice and $k = 35$; $d = -0.15$; CI $= -0.25, -0.06$, for self-reports). Furthermore, the undermining on the free-choice measure, while significant for both children and college students, was significantly stronger for children than for college students. The strength of the undermining on self-reports did not differ for the two groups.

Completion-Contingent Rewards

The first study of reward effects on intrinsic motivation in humans (Deci, 1971) employed completion-contingent rewards. In it, participants were offered $1 for each of four puzzles they completed within a specified amount of time. As already mentioned, the pressure associated with the completion-contingent rewards was greater than that associated with engagement-contingent rewards, but we expected this to be offset somewhat by the implicit competence affirmation provided by the reward. Overall, we predicted an undermining effect for this category of rewards comparable to that for engagement-contingent rewards (Ryan et al., 1983).

Twenty studies examined completion-contingent reward effects on free-choice behavior, and 15 examined effects on self-reports. Analyses revealed that completion-contingent rewards significantly undermined intrinsic motivation for both dependent measures. Because the effects for these rewards on free-choice behavior were heterogeneous and there were no age effects, we had to remove one outlier to achieve homogeneity. With the outlier removed, the results were as follows: $k = 19$; $d = -0.44$; CI $= -0.59, -0.30$. For self-reports, the effects were also heterogeneous, and again there were no age effects; thus, we had to remove two outliers. With these outliers removed, we also found significant undermining by the completion-contingent rewards ($k = 13$; $d = -0.17$; CI $= -0.33, -0.00$, for self-reports).[2] As expected, the effects of engagement-contingent and completion-contingent rewards were virtually identical.

Task-Contingent Rewards

In the first taxonomy of reward contingencies, Ryan et al. (1983) included task-contingent rewards, and Cameron and Pierce included the category in their meta-analysis. Because the task-contingent reward category is simply the aggregate of engagement-contingent rewards and completion-contingent rewards, this category is redundant. However, for comparative purposes, we mention it here. Task-contingent rewards undermined intrinsic motivation assessed with both measures ($k = 74$; $d = -0.39$; CI $= -0.46, -0.32$, for free choice and $k = 48$; $d - -0.12$; CI $- -0.20, -0.04$, for self-reports). Again, the undermining tended to be worse for children.

Performance-Contingent Rewards

From the standpoint of CET, performance-contingent rewards are the most interesting type of tangible rewards. Performance-contingent rewards were defined by Ryan et al. (1983) as rewards given explicitly for doing well at a task or for performing up to a specified standard. Examples of performance-contingency studies include the Ryan et al. study, in which all participants in the performance-contingent-rewards condition received $3 for "having done well at the activity," and the Harackiewicz, Manderlink, and Sansone (1984) study, in which participants received a reward because they were said to have performed better than 80% of other participants.

According to CET, performance-contingent rewards have the potential to affect intrinsic motivation in two ways, one quite positive and one quite negative. Performance-contingent rewards can maintain or enhance intrinsic motivation if the receiver of the reward interprets it informationally, as an affirmation of competence. Yet, because performance-contingent rewards are often used as a vehicle to control not only what the person does but how well he or she does it, such rewards can easily be experienced as very controlling, thus undermining intrinsic motivation. According to CET, it is the relative salience of the informational versus controlling aspects of performance-contingent rewards which determines their ultimate effect on intrinsic motivation.

In most experiments examining performance-contingent rewards, all participants receive rewards as if they had done very well (which, of course, does not happen in the real world). Therefore, these studies do not address the effects of receiving only partial rewards or no rewards under performance contingencies, a circumstance that is more common in the real world and would undoubtedly diminish both perceived competence and perceived self-determination and accordingly have a very negative effect on intrinsic motivation. There can thus be little doubt that research on the effects of performance-contingent rewards markedly underestimates the negative effects of this type of reward, since it has focused largely on people who succeed at the contingency. In contrast, a real-world contingency in which only those achieving above the 80th percentile receive a reward, if veridically applied, would mean that 80% of participants would end up getting no reward and, implicitly, receiving negative competence feedback.

The meta-analyses for the overall effects of performance-contingent rewards included 32 studies with a free-choice measure and 30 with a self-report measure. Performance-contingent rewards significantly undermined free-choice behavior ($d = -0.28$, CI $= -0.38, -0.18$), whereas results for the self-report studies were not significant. We did not do further analyses of studies with the self-report measure because the set of effects was homogeneous with only one outlier removed. However, the effects for the free-choice measure were quite heterogeneous. Consequently, we separated the effects into four categories based on the following two considerations.

First, different studies of performance-contingent rewards have used different control groups; specifically, some have used control groups in which participants received neither rewards nor feedback, whereas others have used control groups in which participants received no rewards but did receive the same feedback conveyed by the rewards to the participants who received rewards. In this latter instance, for example, if the rewards were given for doing better than 80% of the participants, participants in a no-reward control group that received feedback would have been told that they did better than 80% of the participants.

To examine the *combined* effects of performance-contingent rewards and the feedback inherent within them, one would compare the rewards condition with a no-rewards, no-feedback condition. On the other hand, to examine the effects of the rewards per se, independent of the feedback conveyed by them, one would compare the rewards group with a no-rewards group that received comparable feedback.

Second, although the definition of performance-contingent rewards used in the majority of studies involves giving rewards to all participants as if they had performed well, some studies gave rewards in a way that conveyed to some or all of the participants that they had not performed well. These participants got less than the maximum available rewards, thus indicating that their competence was not optimal. For example, in a study conducted by Rosenfield, Folger, and Adelman (1980) that involved a feedback control group, rewarded participants got a small reward for performing in the bottom 15% of all participants, and the corresponding control group received the comparable "negative" feedback without the reward. Clearly, this and other such studies are quite different from the more typical studies of performance-contingent rewards in which all participants receive the same maximum reward for having done well.

Studies involving different types of control groups and different levels of performance were aggregated without comment by Cameron and Pierce (1994). In our meta-analysis, however, because performance-contingent reward effects were not homogeneous, we examined four categories of performance-contingent rewards rather than simply discarding outliers as Cameron and Pierce had done. The four categories were as follows: effects involving no-feedback control groups in which everyone received the maximum possible rewards, effects involving no-feedback control groups in which all participants did not receive the maximum possible rewards, effects involving comparable-feedback control groups in which all participants received positive feedback, and effects involving comparable-feedback control groups in which all participants received negative feedback.

With the free-choice measure, for studies that compared no-feedback control groups and participants who received the maximum possible rewards, there was significant undermining ($k = 18$; $d = -0.15$; CI $= -0.31, -0.00$).[2] For studies with no-feedback control groups in which all participants did not receive the maximum possible rewards, there was also significant undermining ($k = 6$; d $= -0.88$; CI $= -1.12, -0.65$). The same was true for studies with comparable-feedback control groups in which everyone received positive feedback ($k = 10$; $d = -0.20$; CI $= -0.37, -0.03$). However, for the three studies with comparable-feedback control groups in which participants received negative feedback, there was not a significant effect for reward versus no reward.

The group in which at least some participants got less than the maximum possible rewards and the control group received no feedback stands out and deserves special mention. This represents the type of performance-contingent rewards that one would typically find in the real world, in that here rewards are a direct function of performance. Those who perform best get the largest rewards, and those who perform less well get smaller rewards or no rewards. The analysis showed that this type of reward had the largest undermining effect of any category used in the entire meta-analysis ($d = -0.88$), indicating clearly that rewarding people as a direct function of performance runs a very serious risk of negatively affecting their intrinsic motivation.

Summary of the Primary Analyses

To summarize the primary findings from the meta-analyses, when free-choice behavior was used as the dependent measure, all rewards, all tangible rewards, all expected rewards, engagement-contingent rewards, completion-contingent rewards, task-contingent rewards, and performance-contingent rewards significantly undermined intrinsic motivation. Only verbal rewards enhanced intrinsic motivation in general, but verbal rewards did undermine intrinsic motivation if they were given with a controlling interpersonal style. The undermining of intrinsic motivation by tangible rewards was worse for children than for college students, and the enhancement by verbal rewards was weaker for children than for college students. The most damaging reward contingency was the commonly used one of performance-contingent rewards in which not all participants receive maximum rewards.

When self-reported interest served as the dependent measure, all tangible rewards, all expected rewards, engagement-contingent rewards, completion-contingent rewards, and task-contingent rewards significantly undermined intrinsic motivation. Verbal rewards enhanced self-reported interest.

Supplemental Analyses

To further clarify the limiting conditions and moderator effects of rewards, we performed two supplemental analyses. First, to determine whether the undermining of intrinsic motivation is simply a transitory phenomenon, we examined the effects of tangible rewards on the free-choice behavior of children, dividing the studies into three groups: those for which intrinsic motivation was assessed immediately after the reward was terminated, those for which it was assessed a few days later, and those for which it was assessed at least a week later. Analyses indicated that timing of the dependent measure did not affect the results. For all three groups, the composite effect sizes were between −0.40 and −0.53, all statistically significant. If anything, the undermining was strongest in the studies in which the measure was taken at least a week after the rewards were given.

Second, although our primary meta-analyses included only studies for which the target activity was initially interesting, whereas Cameron and Pierce collapsed across interesting and dull tasks without analyzing task effects, we conducted a set of analyses to consider this issue empirically. In our first analysis, we included data from the dull-task conditions and repeated the overall meta-analysis. For the free-choice analyses, every undermining effect that had appeared when only initially interesting tasks were included also appeared after the dull-task conditions were added in; for the self-report analyses, all except one of the effects that had indicated significant undermining when only interesting tasks were used were again significant when the dull-task conditions were included. The one exception for self-report studies was that the inclusion of the dull-task data led the undermining of self-reported interest in the completion-contingent condition to drop to nonsignificance.

In our second analysis, we examined the 13 studies that had included both interesting and dull tasks, assessing the effects of tangible rewards separately for interesting and dull tasks. For the 11 studies with a free-choice measure, results indicated a large undermining by rewards in the interesting-task conditions ($d = -0.68$; CI $= -0.89, -0.47$) but not in the dull-task conditions ($d = 0.18$; CI $= -0.03, 0.39$). For 5 studies with self-reports, there was also significant undermining with the interesting task ($d = -0.37$; CI $= -0.67$, -0.07) but not the dull task ($d = 0.10$; CI $= -0.09, 0.40$).

In summary, it is clear that rewards do not undermine people's intrinsic motivation for dull tasks because there is little or no intrinsic motivation to be undermined. But neither do rewards enhance intrinsic motivation for such tasks. From our perspective (see, e.g., Ryan & Deci, 2000; Ryan & Stiller, 1991), the issue of promoting self-regulation of uninteresting activities is addressed with the concept of internalization rather than reward effects on intrinsic motivation. In other words, if a task is dull and boring, the issue is not whether the rewards will lead people to find the task intrinsically interesting because rewards do not add interest value to the task itself. Rather, the issue is how to facilitate people's understanding the importance of the activity to themselves and thus internalizing its regulation so they will be self-motivated to perform it.

Summary and Conclusions

To summarize, results of the meta-analysis make clear that the undermining of intrinsic motivation by tangible rewards is indeed a significant issue. Whereas verbal rewards tended to enhance intrinsic motivation (although not for children and not when the rewards were given controllingly) and neither unexpected tangible rewards nor task-noncontingent tangible rewards affected intrinsic motivation, expected tangible rewards did significantly and substantially undermine intrinsic motivation, and this effect was quite robust. Furthermore, the undermining was especially strong for children. Tangible rewards – both material rewards, such as pizza parties for reading books, and symbolic rewards, such as good student awards – are widely advocated by many educators and are used in many classrooms, yet the evidence suggests that these rewards tend to undermine intrinsic motivation for the rewarded activity. Because the undermining of intrinsic motivation by tangible rewards was especially strong for school-aged children, and because studies have linked intrinsic motivation to high-quality learning and adjustment (e.g., Benware & Deci, 1984; Ryan & Grolnick, 1986), the findings from this meta-analysis are of particular import for primary and secondary school educators.

Specifically, the results indicate that, rather than focusing on rewards for motivating students' learning, it is important to focus more on how to facilitate intrinsic motivation, for example, by beginning from the students' perspective to develop more interesting learning activities, to provide more choice, and to ensure that tasks are optimally challenging (e.g., Cordova & Lepper, 1996; Deci, Schwartz, et al., 1981; Harter, 1974; Reeve, Bolt, & Cai, 1999; Ryan & Grolnick, 1986; Zuckerman, Porac, Lathin, Smith, & Deci, 1978). In these ways, we will be more able to facilitate the type of motivation that has been found to promote creative task engagement (Amabile, 1982), cognitive flexibility (McGraw & McCullers, 1979), and conceptual understanding of learning activities (Benware & Deci, 1984; Grolnick & Ryan, 1987).

The results of the meta-analysis also provided strong support for CET. Specifically, the predictions made by CET, based on an analysis of whether reward types and reward contingencies are likely to be experienced as informational or controlling, were uniformly supported and were particularly strong for the behavioral measure. Thus, although Cameron and Pierce argued that CET should be abandoned and stated that there is no reason for teachers to resist using rewards in the classroom, it is clear that CET provides an excellent account of reward effects and that there is, in fact, good reason for teachers to think carefully about when and how to use rewards in the classroom.

Appendix

A list of each study used in our meta-analyses. A (D) indicates an unpublished dissertation. The second column indicates types of rewards and/or reward contingencies, followed by whether participants were children or undergraduates, followed by whether the dependent measure was free-choice behavior or self reported interest. (Codes appear in Notes to the Appendix.) Finally, we explain whether our treatment of the study and results differed from Cameron and Pierce's. If a study was coded the same, the same control groups were used in the comparisons, and the effect sizes we reported did not differ from the effect sizes Cameron and Pierce reported by more than 0.10 in either direction, we noted that the study was the same in the two meta-analyses. If there was a difference, we explained what it was.

Table 1a: Studies used in our meta-analyses compared with Cameron and Pierce (1994)

Study	Variables	Comparison with Cameron & Pierce's (1994) analysis
Amabile et al., 1986, Exp. 1	E, 1, F, S	Same.[1]
Amabile et al., 1986, Exp. 3	E, 2, S	Same.
Anderson et al., 1976	V, E, 1, F	This had multiple no-reward control groups. We selected the one recommended as appropriate by the study's authors and comparable to ones used for other studies in this meta-analysis. C. & P.[2] used a control group that the authors said was inappropriate, in which the experimenter avoided eye contact with the young children and ignored their attempts to interact, even though there were just the two people in the room. The study's authors said that this condition was uncomfortable, even painful, for both the children and experimenter. Not surprisingly, that group showed free-choice intrinsic motivation that was considerably lower than any other group.
Anderson & Rodin, 1989	V, 2, S	Nearly the same.[3] Both meta-analyses treated the composite dependent variable as self-report.
Arkes, 1979	C, 2, F, S	Same.
Arnold, 1976	E, 2, S	Same.
Arnold, 1985	E, C, 2, S	Same.
Bartelme, 1983 (D)	P, 2, S	Excluded, type I.[4]
Blanck et al., 1984, Exp. 1	V, 2, F, S	Same for free-choice; nearly the same for self-report.
Blanck et al., 1984, Exp. 2	V, 2, F, S	Excluded, type II.[5]
Boggiano & Ruble, 1979	E, P, 1, F	Excluded, type II.
Boggiano et al., 1982	E, 1, F	Same.
Boggiano et al., 1985	E, C, P, 1, F	The study's authors crossed reward contingency with salience of reward. They referred to the two reward contingencies as task contingent and performance contingent, and C. & P. coded them that way, treating the task-contingent conditions as engagement contingent.[6] However, the salience manipulation in the task-contingent condition changed the contingency. In the low-salience group, rewards were given for simply working on the puzzles, which makes them engagement contingent, but in the high salience group, rewards were given for each puzzle "completed," which makes them completion contingent.
Brennan & Glover, 1980	E, 2, F	This was engagement contingent because participants got rewards if they "work with the Soma puzzle for at least 8 minutes," but C. & P. coded it task noncontingent. Further, C. & P. combine two control groups, including one that had not worked on the task for the same amount of time as the rewards group during the experimental period, but we used only the control group that had worked on the task for the same amount of time.

(Continued)

Table 1a: (Continued)

Study	Variables	Comparison with Cameron & Pierce's (1994) analysis
Brewer, 1980 (D)	E, P, 1, F, S	Excluded, type I.
Brockner & Vasta, 1981	C, 2, F, S	Same.
Butler, 1987	V, 1, S	Nearly the same.
Calder & Staw, 1975	C, D, 2, S	This study provided monetary rewards for completing a set of puzzles, thus making it completion contingent, but C. & P. coded it engagement contingent. Also, C. & P. collapsed across interesting and dull tasks.[7]
Chung, 1995	E, P, D, 1, F	Excluded, type III.[8]
Cohen, 1974 (D)	V, P, 2, F, S	Excluded, type I.
Crino & White, 1982	V, 2, F, S	Same.
Dafoe, 1985 (D)	N, P, 1, F, S	Excluded, type I.
Daniel & Esser, 1980	P, D, 2, F, S	In this study, participants were told "they could win up to $2 depending on how quickly they correctly assembled the puzzles." This conveyed that the rewards depended on doing well relative to a standard and not just on finishing the puzzles. Thus, we coded it performance contingent, but C. & P. coded it completion contingent. Also, C. & P. collapsed across interesting and dull tasks.
Danner & Lonky, 1981, Exp. 2	V, E, 1, F, S	Nearly the same.
Deci, 1971, Exp. 1	C, 2, F, S	Same.
Deci, 1971, Exp. 3	V, 2, F, S	Same.
Deci, 1972a	N, 2, F	Same.
Deci, 1972b	V, C, 2, F	Same.
Deci et al., 1975	V, 2, F	Same.
DeLoach et al., 1983	E, 1, F	Excluded, type II.
Dimitroff, 1984 (D)	E, 1, F, S	Same.
Dollinger & Thelen, 1978	V, P, 1, F, S	Excluded, type I.
Earn, 1982	N, 2, F, S	This had three tangible rewards groups, a verbal rewards group, and a control group. C. & P. inappropriately collapsed across verbal and tangible rewards, and they did not use the free-choice data.
Efron, 1976 (D)	V, E, P, 2, S	Rewards were given "simply for participating in the study" which makes it task noncontingent, but C. & P. coded it engagement contingent.
Eisenstein, 1985	U, C, D, 1, F	Excluded, type I.
Enzle et al., 1991	P, 2, F	Excluded, type II.
Fabes, 1987, Exp. 1	C, P, 1, F	Excluded, type II.
Fabes, 1987, Exp. 2	C, 1, F	Same for the performance-contingent condition. For the other condition, participants were given rewards "when they finished" a block construction, making it completion contingent, but C. & P. coded it engagement contingent. This study used the same procedure as the completion-contingent condition in Fabes (1987, Exp. 1), making it completion contingent, but C. & P. coded it engagement completion.

Study	Codes	Notes
Fabes et al., 1986	E, 1, F, S	Excluded, type II.
Fabes et al., 1988	E, 1, F, S	Same for free-choice, but C. & P. did not include the self-report. In this study, children selected a face ranging from frown to smile to reflect how much they enjoyed the task, a procedure that is common for obtaining self-report data from young children.
Fabes et al., 1989	E, 1, F	Excluded, type II.
Feehan & Enzle, 1991, Exp. 2	C, 2, F	Excluded, type II.
Goldstein, 1977 (D)	V, C, P, 1, F, S	Excluded, type I.
Goldstein, 1980 (D)	C, 2, F	Excluded, type I. This included competition conditions but we did not use those because competition has a complex effect on intrinsic motivation (Reeve & Deci, 1996).
Greene & Lepper, 1974	U, E, P, 1, F	Same for the two unexpected groups and the engagement-contingent group, but C. & P. exclude the performance-contingent group.
Griffith, 1984 (D)	E, D, 1, F	Excluded, type I. To be comparable to most other studies in this meta-analysis, we included only participants who worked in the individual context.
Griffith et al., 1984	C, 1, F	Children were rewarded for finishing reading a passage up to the bookmark, which makes it completion contingent, but C. & P. coded it engagement contingent. (The McCloyd, 1979 study used the same instructions and C. & P. did code it completion contingent.)
Hamner & Foster, 1975	E, C, D, 2, S	Same coding for completion contingent. In engagement contingent, participants were paid "75 cents for the 20 minute task," but C. & P. coded it as task noncontingent. Also, C. & P. collapsed across interesting and dull tasks.
Harackiewicz, 1979	V, E, P, 1, S	Same for verbal rewards. Nearly the same for engagement contingent. C. & P. excluded the two performance-contingent rewards groups.
Harackiewicz & Manderlink, 1984	P, 1, S	Same.
Harackiewicz et al., 1984, Exp. 1	P, 2, F, S	Same.
Harackiewicz et al., 1984, Exp. 2	U, P, 2, F, S	Same coding, but C. & P. made an error in the self report effect size for performance contingent, showing it as enhancement when in fact it was undermining with a $d = -0.16$.
Harackiewicz et al., 1984, Exp. 3	P, 2, F, S	Same.
Harackiewicz et al., 1987	P, 1, S	Same.
Hitt et al., 1992	E, D, 2, F, S	Excluded, type III.
Hyman, 1985 (D)	E, P, 1, F	Excluded, type I.
Karniol & Ross, 1977	E, P, 1, F	Same except we coded the performance-contingent conditions for whether participants got the maximum rewards with implicit positive feedback or less than maximum rewards with implicit negative feedback.
Kast & Connor, 1988	V, IC, 1, S	Excluded, type II.
Koestner et al., 1987	V, 2, F, S	Same.

(Continued)

Table 1a: (Continued)

Study	Variables	Comparison with Cameron & Pierce's (1994) analysis
Kruglanski et al., 1971	N, 1, S	Rewards were given "because you have volunteered for this study ..." so they were task noncontingent, but C. & P. coded them engagement contingent.
Kruglanski et al., 1972	U, 1, S	Same.
Kruglanski et al., 1975, Exp. 1	C, 1, S	Participants were rewarded either for the number of coin flips they guessed correctly or for the number of block constructions they completed correctly, making it completion contingent, but C. & P. coded it performance contingent. It explored moderation by endogenous versus exogenous rewards.
Kruglanski et al., 1975, Exp. 2	P, 1, S	There were two reward groups and two control groups. In one pair, people worked on a stock market game and earned cash after each trial for good investments. The control group was the same as the experimental group except they were told they had to give back their earnings, so it was not a reasonable no-reward control group. In the other pair of conditions, money was not mentioned to the no-reward control group. We excluded the pair of conditions without a proper control group, but C. & P. collapsed across the two pairs of conditions.
Lee, 1982 (D)	P, 2, F, S	Excluded, type I.
Lepper et al., 1973	U, E, 1, F	Same coding. Same effect sizes for engagement contingent. C. & P. made an error in calculating the effect size for unexpected rewards.
Lepper et al., 1982, Exp. 3	E, 1, F	Excluded, type II.
Liberty, 1986, Exp. 1 (D)	C, 2, F, S	Excluded, type I.
Liberty, 1986, Exp. 2 (D)	C, 2, F, S	Excluded, type I.
Loveland & Olley, 1979	E, D, 1, F	Same coding, but C. & P. collapsed across interesting and dull tasks.
Luyten & Lens, 1981	C, P, 2, F, S	Same for performance contingent. In the other rewards condition participants were paid after each of three puzzles they solved, so it was completion contingent, but C. & P. coded it as engagement contingent.
McGraw & McCullers, 1979	C, 2, S	Same.
McLoyd, 1979	C, D, 1, F	Coded the same, but C. & P. collapsed across interesting and dull tasks.
Morgan, 1981, Exp. 1	E, 1, F, S	Same on free-choice; nearly the same on self-report.
Morgan, 1981, Exp. 2	E, 1, F, S	Same.
Morgan, 1983, Exp. 1	E, 1, F, S	Same on free-choice; nearly the same on self-report.
Morgan, 1983, Exp. 2	E, 1, F, S	Same.
Mynatt et al., 1978	E, D, 1, F	Coded the same, but C. & P. collapsed across interesting and dull tasks.
Newman & Layton, 1984	E, D, 1, F	Excluded, type II.
Ogilvie & Prior, 1982	E, 1, F	Same.
Okano, 1981, Exp. 1	E, 1, F, S	Excluded, type II.
Okano, 1981, Exp. 2	N, E, 1, F, S	Excluded, type II.

Study	Codes	Comment
Orlick & Mosher, 1978	V, U, P, 1, F	Same coding for verbal and unexpected. In performance contingent, children got rewards "if you do a good job today and tomorrow on the balance board," but C. & P. coded it as completion contingent. There were discrepancies in the effect sizes.
Pallak et al., 1982	V, U, P, 1, F	Same for verbal and unexpected. C. & P. did not report how they coded the tangible expected rewards condition, which was performance contingent.
Patrick, 1985 (D)	E, P, 1, F, S	Excluded, type I.
Perry, et al., 1977	E, 1, F, S	Excluded, type II.
Picek, 1976 (D)	E, P, 2, F, S	Excluded, type I.
Pittman et al., 1977	P, 2, F, S	Same coding, but C. & P. used only self-report. We also used free-choice persistence, calculated as the number of trials.
Pittman et al., 1980	V, IC, 2, F	Same except that C. & P. did not do an analysis of informational versus controlling positive feedback.
Pittman et al., 1982, Exp. 1	N, E, 1, F	Same codings and nearly the same free-choice effects. C. & P. imputed a self-report value of 0.00, but participants were not asked how interesting or enjoyable they found the activity.
Pittman et al., 1982, Exp. 2	E, 1, F	Nearly the same.
Porac & Meindl, 1982	C, 2, F	C. & P. coded this engagement contingent, but participants received $1.50 for each puzzle solved. C. & P. reported a comparison for 40 experimental and 20 control participants, but there were only 50 participants in the study. We calculated the reward effect size based on a comparison of the rewarded groups with neutral and extrinsic mind sets versus the non-rewarded groups with neutral and extrinsic mind sets, because that comparison provided corresponding reward versus no-reward conditions.
Pretty & Seligman, 1984, Exp. 1	V, U, E, 2, F, S	Same for unexpected and engagement contingent. Nearly the same for verbal on free-choice.
Pretty & Seligman, 1984, Exp. 2	U, E, 2, F, S	Same.
Reiss & Sushinsky, 1975, Exp. 1	E, 1, F	Same.
Rosenfield et al., 1980	P, 2, F, S	This study had performance-contingent, completion-contingent, and task-noncontingent groups, and a control group with feedback comparable to that in performance contingent. There was no appropriate control group for completion contingent or task noncontingent. It also crossed tangible rewards with positive versus negative feedback. C. & P. reported a verbal effect for positive versus negative feedback, and then they collapsed across feedback to examine tangible-reward effects. We did a moderator analysis of rewards signifying positive versus negative feedback. C. & P. listed a performance-contingent self report $d = 2.80$, but the correct d was 0.22. For free-choice, there was a modest discrepancy.
Ross, 1975, Exp. 1	E, 1, F, S	Same for free-choice; they did not include self-report.
Ross, 1975, Exp. 2	E, 1, F, S	Nearly the same for free-choice; they did not include self-report.
Ross et al., 1976	N, E, 1, F	Same for engagement contingent. In the other group, children were rewarded "for waiting," which is task noncontingent, but C. & P. coded it engagement contingent.
Ryan, 1982	IC, 2, F	We included this study only in the supplemental meta-analysis of Informational versus Controlling verbal rewards. C. & P. excluded it.

(Continued)

Table 1a: (Continued)

Study	Variables	Comparison with Cameron & Pierce's (1994) analysis
Ryan et al., 1983	V, E, P, IC, 2, F, S	Same on verbal and engagement contingent. There were two performance-contingent groups, one informational and one controlling. There were three no-reward control groups, one with informational positive feedback, one with controlling positive feedback, and one with no-feedback. We compared performance-contingent both to comparable-feedback controls and no-feedback controls in the moderator analyses. C. & P. did only the comparable-feedback comparisons. Also, C. & P. did not do an informational-controlling comparison.
Salancik, 1975	P, 2, F, S	Same coding. C. & P. collapsed across positive and negative feedback conditions, but we did a moderator analysis for positive versus negative.
Sansone, 1986	V, 2, S	Same.
Sansone, 1989	V, 2, S	Same.
Sansone et al., 1989	V, 2, S	Same.
Sarafino, 1984	E, 1, F, S	Same.
Shanab, 1981	V, 2, F, S	Same.
Shiffman-Kaufman, 1990 (D)	E, P, 1, F, S	Excluded, type I. For comparability with other studies, we used only data from the 10-day assessments.
Smith, 1975 (D)	V, U, P, 2, F, S	Excluded, type I.
Smith, 1980 (D)	E, D, 1, F	Excluded, type I. In this study, there was also a condition called positive feedback, but the statements were not competence feedback.
Smith & Pittman, 1978	P, 2, F, S	Same for self-report. C. & P. imputed a score of 0.00 for free-choice performance, even though means and significance tests were reported.
Sorensen & Maehr, 1976	C, 1, F	Excluded, type II.
Staw et al., 1980	C, 2, S	Participants got a $1 reward for completing 15 puzzles, making it completion contingent, but C. & P. coded it engagement contingent.
Swann & Pittman, 1977, Exp. 1	N, E, 1, F	Same.
Swann & Pittman, 1977, Exp. 2	E, 1, F	There were two engagement-contingent groups, an engagement-contingent plus verbal-rewards group, and two no-reward control groups. There was not a control group for the engagement plus verbal group. We compared the two engagement to the two control groups, but C. & P. used all three reward groups.
Taub & Dollinger, 1975	P, 2, S	Same.
Thompson et al., 1993	E, 2, F	Excluded, type III.
Tripathi & Agarwal, 1985	V, E, 2, F, S	Nearly the same.
Tripathi & Agarwal, 1988	E, P, 2, F, S	Same for engagement contingent on free-choice. For performance contingent, there were two tasks, with free-choice data reported for only one. Both we and C. & P. used the data for the one task and assigned $d = 0.00$ for the other, but C. & P. averaged the effects whereas we combined them meta-analytically. In the self-report data, C. & P. combined the engagement and performance conditions so it is unclear which analysis they were used in.

Vallerand, 1983	V, 1, S	Same.
Vallerand & Reid, 1984	V, 2, S	Same.
Vasta & Stirpe, 1979	C, 1, F	This study had pre-post data for a rewards group and a control group. We compared the rewards group and ignored the control group. C. & P. did pre-post analyses for the rewards group with pre-post analyses. We coded it completion contingent, but C. & P. did not code it.
Weinberg & Jackson, 1979	P, 2, S	Same.
Weiner, 1980	C, 2, F, S	Participants received $.25 for each anagram completed, which makes it completion contingent, but C. & P. coded it performance contingent.
Weiner & Mander, 1978	E, P, 2, F, S	Same.
Williams, 1980	E, 1, F, S	Same.
Wilson, 1978 (D)	E, D, 2, F, S	Excluded, type I.
Wimperis & Farr, 1979	N, C, 2, S	In one group, participants received $1.75 for being in the study, making it task noncontingent, but C. & P. coded it engagement contingent. In the other, participants "were paid for each model or subunit completed," making it completion contingent, but C. & P. coded it performance contingent.
Yuen, 1984 (D)	E, 2, F, S	Excluded, type I.
Zinser, 1982	V, 1, F	Same.

Note: (D) = Unpublished Dissertation; V = Verbal Rewards; U = Unexpected Tangible Rewards; N = Task-Noncontingent Rewards; E = Engagement-Contingent Rewards; C = Completion-Contingent Rewards; P = Performance-Contingent Rewards; D = Dull-Task condition included in study and used in supplemental meta-analysis; IC = Informational versus Controlling comparison was made in supplemental meta-analysis. The code of 1 means the participants were children and the code of 2 means they were undergraduates. Finally, F means that the free-choice dependent measure was used and S means that the self-report measure was used.

[1] Same means that Cameron and Pierce and we coded the study the same, used the same control groups, and found effects sizes that did not differ from each other by more than 0.10 in either direction.

[2] C. & P. refers to Cameron and Pierce.

[3] Nearly the same means the studies were coded the same and the same control groups were used, but that the effect sizes were different by more than 0.10, probably due to differences in estimation of standard deviations. If the discrepancy is large, we make note of that.

[4] "Excluded, type I" refers to dissertations, and Cameron and Pierce excluded all dissertations.

[5] "Excluded, type II" refers to studies that Cameron and Pierce excluded for no apparent reason.

[6] Cameron and Pierce (1994) did not use the term "engagement-contingent." When we say they coded a reward engagement-contingent, it means that they coded it as both "task-contingent" and what they referred to as "not contingent using a behavioral definition." Because the intersection of those two codes is equivalent to our engagement-contingent code, we say that they coded it as engagement-contingent to minimize confusion for the reader. Similarly, they did not use the term completion-contingent, but what they coded as both "task-contingent" and "contingent using a behavioral definition" is equivalent to what we call completion-contingent.

[7] These studies used both interesting and uninteresting tasks. We excluded the uninteresting tasks from the primary meta-analyses and included them in the supplemental meta-analysis concerned with initial task interest. Cameron and Pierce collapsed across the interesting and dull tasks even though it has been firmly established in the literature that initial task interest interacts with reward effects.

[8] "Excluded, type III" refers to studies that Cameron and Pierce excluded because they were published after Cameron and Pierce's cut-off date.

Notes

1. The value k represents the number of effects considered in calculating a composite effect size. Because, for any given calculation, the data were aggregated across all relevant conditions within a study in order to ensure independence of effect sizes, k also represents the number of studies that were included in the calculation of a composite effect size. The value d represents the composite effect size corrected for reliability (Hedges & Olkin, 1985). In regard to CIs, if both endpoints are on the same side of 0.00, it indicates that the mean for the reward groups is significantly different from the mean for the no-reward groups.
2. Although one end of the CI appears to be 0.00, it was actually slightly negative and was rounded to 0.00. A significance test indicated that the composite effect size was significant.

References

Amabile, T. M. (1982). Social psychology of creativity: A consensual assessment technique. *Journal of Personality and Social Psychology, 43*, 997–1013.

Amabile, T. M., DeJong, W., & Lepper, M. R. (1976). Effects of externally imposed deadlines on subsequent intrinsic motivation. *Journal of Personality and Social Psychology, 34*, 92–98.

Benware, C., & Deci, E. L. (1984). Quality of learning with an active versus passive motivational set. *American Educational Research Journal, 21*, 755–765.

Boggiano, A. K., Barrett, M., Weiher, A. W., McClelland, G. H., & Lusk, C. M. (1987). Use of the maximal-operant principle to motivate children's intrinsic interest. *Journal of Personality and Social Psychology, 53*, 866–879.

Cameron, J., & Pierce, W. D. (1994). Reinforcement, reward, and intrinsic motivation: A meta-analysis. *Review of Educational Research, 64*, 363–423.

Cameron, J., & Pierce, W. D. (1996). The debate about rewards and intrinsic motivation: Protests and accusations do not alter the results. *Review of Educational Research, 66*, 39–52.

Cordova, D. I., & Lepper, M. R. (1996). Intrinsic motivation and the process of learning: Beneficial effects of contextualization, personalization, and choice. *Journal of Educational Psychology, 88*, 715–730.

deCharms, R. (1968). *Personal causation*. New York: Academic Press.

Deci, E. L. (1971). Effects of externally mediated rewards on intrinsic motivation. *Journal of Personality and Social Psychology, 18*, 105–115.

Deci, E. L. (1972a). Effects of contingent and non-contingent rewards and controls on intrinsic motivation. *Organizational Behavior and Human Performance, 8*, 217–229.

Deci, E. L. (1972b). Intrinsic motivation, extrinsic reinforcement, and inequity. *Journal of Personality and Social Psychology, 22*, 113–120.

Deci, E. L., Betley, G., Kahle, J., Abrams, L., & Porac, J. (1981). When trying to win: Competition and intrinsic motivation. *Personality and Social Psychology Bulletin, 7*, 79–83.

Deci, E. L., Connell, J. P., & Ryan, R. M. (1989). Self-determination in a work organization. *Journal of Applied Psychology, 74*, 580–590.

Deci, E. L., Koestner, R., & Ryan, R. M. (1999). A meta-analytic review of experiments examining the effects of extrinsic rewards on intrinsic motivation. *Psychological Bulletin, 125*, 627–668.

Deci, E. L., & Ryan, R. M. (1980). The empirical exploration of intrinsic motivational processes. In L. Berkowitz (Ed.), *Advances in experimental social psychology* (Vol. 13, pp. 39–80). New York: Academic Press.

Deci, E. L., & Ryan, R. M. (1985). *Intrinsic motivation and self-determination in human behavior.* New York: Plenum.

Deci, E. L., & Ryan, R. M. (1991). A motivational approach to self: Integration in personality. In R. Dienstbier (Ed.), *Nebraska Symposium on Motivation: Vol. 38. Perspectives on motivation* (pp. 237–288). Lincoln: University of Nebraska Press.

Deci, E. L., Schwartz, A. J., Sheinman, L., & Ryan, R. M. (1981). An instrument to assess adults' orientations toward control versus autonomy with children: Reflections on intrinsic motivation and perceived competence. *Journal of Educational Psychology, 73,* 642–650.

Eisenberger, R., & Cameron, J. (1996). Detrimental effects of reward: Reality or myth? *American Psychologist, 51,* 1153–1166.

Grolnick, W. S., & Ryan, R. M. (1987). Autonomy in children's learning: An experimental and individual difference investigation. *Journal of Personality and Social Psychology, 52,* 890–898.

Harackiewicz, J. M., Manderlink, G., & Sansone, C. (1984). Rewarding pinball wizardry: The effects of evaluation on intrinsic interest. *Journal of Personality and Social Psychology, 47,* 287–300.

Harter, S. (1974). Pleasure derived by children from cognitive challenge and mastery. *Child Development, 45,* 661–669.

Hedges, L. V., & Olkin, I. (1985). *Statistical methods for meta-analysis.* New York: Academic Press.

Johnson, B. T. (1993). *DSTAT 1.10: Software for the meta-analytic review of literatures* [Software and manual]. Hillsdale, NJ: Erlbaum.

Kohn, A. (1996). By all available means: Cameron and Pierce's defense of extrinsic motivators. *Review of Educational Research, 66,* 1–4.

Lepper, M. R., Greene, D., & Nisbett, R. E. (1973). Undermining children's intrinsic interest with extrinsic rewards: A test of the "overjustification" hypothesis. *Journal of Personality and Social Psychology, 28,* 129–137.

Lepper, M. R., Keavney, M., & Drake, M. (1996). Intrinsic motivation and extrinsic rewards: A commentary on Cameron and Pierce's meta-analysis. *Review of Educational Research, 66,* 5–32.

McGraw, K. O., & McCullers, J. C. (1979). Evidence of a detrimental effect of extrinsic incentives on breaking a mental set. *Journal of Experimental Social Psychology, 15,* 285–294.

Mossholder, K. W. (1980). Effects of externally mediated goal setting on intrinsic motivation: A laboratory experiment. *Journal of Applied Psychology, 65,* 202–210.

Reeve, J., Bolt, E., & Cai, Y. (1999). Autonomy-supportive teachers: How they teach and motivate students. *Journal of Educational Psychology, 91,* 537–548.

Rosenfield, D., Folger, R., & Adelman, H. (1980). When rewards reflect competence: A qualification of the overjustification effect. *Journal of Personality and Social Psychology, 39,* 368–376.

Ryan, R. M. (1982). Control and information in the intrapersonal sphere: An extension of cognitive evaluation theory. *Journal of Personality and Social Psychology, 43,* 450–461.

Ryan, R. M., & Deci, E. L. (1996). When paradigms clash: Comments on Cameron and Pierce's claim that rewards do not undermine intrinsic motivation. *Review of Educational Research, 66,* 33–38.

Ryan, R. M., & Deci, E. L. (2000). Self-determination theory and the facilitation of intrinsic motivation, social development, and well-being. *American Psychologist, 55,* 68–78.

Ryan, R. M., & Grolnick, W. S. (1986). Origins and pawns in the classroom: Self-report and projective assessments of individual differences in children's perceptions. *Journal of Personality and Social Psychology, 50,* 550–558.

Ryan, R. M., & La Guardia, J. G. (1999). Achievement motivation within a pressured society: Intrinsic and extrinsic motivations to learn and the politics of school reform. In T. C. Urdan (Ed.), *Advances in motivation and achievement: The role of context* (Vol. 11, pp. 45–85). Greenwich, CT: JAI Press.

Ryan, R. M., Mims, V., & Koestner, R. (1983). Relation of reward contingency and interpersonal context to intrinsic motivation: A review and test using cognitive evaluation theory. *Journal of Personality and Social Psychology, 45*, 736–750.

Ryan, R. M., & Stiller, J. (1991). The social contexts of internalization: Parent and teacher influences on autonomy, motivation and learning. In M. L. Maehr & P. R. Pintrich (Eds.), *Advances in motivation and achievement* (Vol. 7, pp. 115–150). Greenwich, CT: JAI Press.

Smith, W. E. (1975). *The effect of anticipated vs. unanticipated social reward on subsequent intrinsic motivation*. Unpublished doctoral dissertation, Cornell University, Ithaca, NY.

Zuckerman, M., Porac, J., Lathin, D., Smith, R., & Deci, E. L. (1978). On the importance of self-determination for intrinsically motivated behavior. *Personality and Social Psychology Bulletin, 4*, 443–446.

53

Beyond the Rhetoric: Understanding Achievement and Motivation in Catholic School Students

Janine Bempechat, Beth A. Boulay,
Stephanie C. Piergross and Kenzie A. Wenk

In the early 1980s, James Coleman's work on the academic advantage associated with Catholic school membership generated a variety of research studies that examined the nature and extent of these early findings (Coleman, Hoffer, & Kilgore, 1982). Since then, a growing literature has documented that low-income students of color in Catholic high schools tend to outperform their peers in public schools in virtually every measure of pre- and post-secondary achievement, including GPA, SAT scores, enrollment in higher-track coursework, and high school completion (Bryk, Lee, & Holland, 1993; Carbonaro, 2003; Ellison & Hallinan, 2004; Morgan, 2001; Sander & Krautman, 1995). More recently, research on college acceptance has found that, on average and relative to their public school peers, students who graduate from Catholic high schools are more likely to attend college and be admitted to more selective colleges (Altonji, Elder, & Taber, 2005; Eide, Goldhaber, & Showalter, 2004).

The research on what has come to be called the "Catholic school advantage" cannot be taken lightly. It is known that urban Catholic schools advance their students' achievement with far fewer resources and curricula and pedagogy that are not necessarily on the cutting edge of educational research (Bempechat, Drago-Severson, & Boulay, 2002; Cattaro, 2002a).

Source: *Education and Urban Society*, 40(2) (2008): 167–178.

Furthermore, inner-city Catholic schools achieve the greatest success with students who are the most disadvantaged and at risk for school failure, for both demographic and public policy reasons (Ilg, Massucci, & Cattaro, 2004; Peterson & Walberg, 2002). In other words, students at risk – those who are poor, whose first language is not English, who are members of an ethnic minority, and whose own parents have limited educations – are the most likely to suffer the negative consequences of the resurgence of school segregation and the increasing use of school promotion examinations (Heubert, 2002; Orfield, Frankenberg, & Lee, 2002).

Yet enduring concerns about self-selection, although not inappropriate, have made it commonplace to attribute the higher achievement of Catholic school students to factors having nothing to do with pedagogy. Because Catholic school are schools of choice, students who enroll may be smarter, be better off materially, and have parents who are themselves better educated and therefore more motivated to ensure academic excellence in their children (Chubb, 2005; Goldberger & Cain, 1982). It could also be the case that administrators select the most well-behaved students and expel the most disruptive from their midst, making teachers' jobs that much more manageable (Hoxby, 2003; Salganik & Karweit, 1982). Despite increased evidence of *negative* selection (i.e., that Catholic schools educate under- rather than over-achieving students; Sander, 2001), the positive outcomes associated with Catholic school enrollment are seemingly routinely dismissed.

This is regrettable because something impressive is going on in urban Catholic schools, something from which we can and should want to learn (Cattaro, 2002b). As educators and students of educational reform, our goal is to look beyond outcome variables to probe the underlying factors that motivate students to achieve. The purpose of this article is to suggest new directions for research that go beyond an enumeration of outcome scores. Specifically, we present a program of research that we designed to build grounded theory on achievement and motivation in urban Catholic high school students. We first provide the reader with a brief background on the research context in which our work has evolved.

The Motivational Underpinnings of Success

Research in achievement motivation has demonstrated that students' beliefs about what it takes to do well in school are better predictors of their performance than even achievement test scores (Grant & Dweck, 2003). Beliefs about reasons for success and failure are particularly powerful because they predict the extent to which students will persist in the face of difficulty (Weiner, 2005). For example, students who tend to attribute poor performance to internal factors within their control, such as lack of effort, are more likely to feel ashamed and work harder for the next assignment or test.

In contrast, students who tend to implicate external factors over which they have little or no control, such as a difficult test or a teacher who does not like them, are more likely to believe that investing more effort for the next test will be of little consequence for their ultimate performance (Weiner, 1994). To the extent that urban Catholic school students are outperforming their public school peers *academically,* is it possible that they adhere to beliefs that place them at an advantage *motivationally?* We asked more than 1,000 public and Catholic school fifth and sixth graders to read short scenarios that described success or failure experiences and to indicate the extent to which effort (e.g., "I'm careful in my work"), ability (e.g., "Everyone knows I do math badly"), or external factors (e.g., "The teacher likes me") could explain the outcomes, if *they themselves* had actually lived through these experiences. Overall, we found that, relative to their public school peers, African American and Latino Catholic school students attributed success and failure to causes that were helpful for learning (Bempechat et al., 2002). For example, these students were much less likely than their public school peers to believe that success could be because of external factors, such as luck or an easy test. Relative to their public school peers, the Catholic school African American students were much less likely to believe that failure could be because of external factors, such as being disliked by the teacher or having studied the wrong material. Again, this is a helpful belief because it implies that failure is controllable and potentially avoidable.

This first phase of our work provided evidence that, at the elementary school level, Catholic school students seem to hold more adaptive beliefs about learning than do their public school peers. However, these findings were limited by the very method we chose to employ. Because we used a questionnaire, the particular learning beliefs that students responded to and the way in which they responded (a 5-point scale) were dictated by us from the outside (an *etic* perspective). However, what we as researchers feel are important constructs may not match what students believe to be important (an *emic* perspective; Strauss, 1987). We thus launched a 4-year, longitudinal investigation of the ways in which adolescents in Catholic high schools conceptualize and speak about learning, achievement, and motivation in the context of their educational experiences. Our goal is to build a grounded theory by focusing on the issues that students raise in response to open-ended and semistructured interviews (Bempechat, 2003).

Developing Grounded Theory: A Longitudinal Investigation

We designed our study to address the following research question: How do low-income adolescents of color construct meaning about learning, achievement, and motivation? More specifically, how do these students conceptualize the role that education plays in their lives, present and future? How do they perceive and interpret teachers' goals for them? What are the ways in which family and peers foster or inhibit their school progress?

At each of two urban Catholic high schools, we have been following a group of 20 students, half females and half males, all of whom come from low-income families. These students are not exemplary pupils. Many are struggling to stay in good academic standing. When we began this study, half of the students were 9th graders and half were 10th graders. At Sienna High, the students are African American. At Norman High, the students are of Dominican descent. With the schools' and parents' permission, we conducted two individual interviews with each student in the spring of 2000. With few exceptions, each student was interviewed by the same member of our research team. Each interview lasted about 45 minutes, or one school period. We audiotaped all the interviews for later transcription, and all students were assured that their comments and opinions would remain anonymous. They also understood that they were free to refuse to answer any question and knew that they had the option of withdrawing from the study at any time.

We designed the first interview to elicit open-ended descriptions of students' learning experiences. Our goal was to let the students dictate the topics of discussion. We were very concerned about not putting words into the students' mouths. We probed their responses by asking them to say more or give examples to illustrate the points they were making. After an initial reading of these interview transcripts, we developed the second interview as a semistructured questionnaire designed to examine perceived parent and peer support for learning and to ask students to speak about the meanings of academic-related words such as learning, motivation, success, failure, ability, and effort. After we reviewed the material from both interviews, we raised common themes in a focus group interview at the end of the school year. During a breakfast meeting at Norman High and a pizza lunch at Sienna High, the research team members asked the students to comment on issues that emerged in many of the interviews.

Following conventions of qualitative analyses, we first read each interview to get a sense of what each individual student was expressing – his or her own beliefs, concerns, and questions. We then read "across" the interviews, paying particular attention to words and phrases that the students used frequently and spontaneously. The themes that emerged – culture of caring, personal responsibility, and adaptive achievement beliefs – provide distinct categories, but the reader will see that they are very much interrelated.

"You Need to Work Up": The Culture of Caring

The students we interviewed described their school as a caring environment, where teachers take a deep interest in both their academic and psychosocial well-being. Many students described the Sienna and Norman High Schools' "family," even though Norman High has an enrollment of 1,100 students. Enrique described his perceptions in terms of his adjustment to the school:

> I thought it was going to be a lot harder for me, and it's like, everybody here at the school is just like one big family, they try to help out a lot. But the teachers, they help any time they can, like if they see you falling off, like, in the beginning, I was doing, I was like doing pretty good. But once the basketball season started, I kinda fell off a little bit. The teachers were like, "I see your grades dropping a little, you need to work up." So I started staying after, started to keep working.... It's like they care for you so much at this school, they make sure they don't want nobody, you know, to fall down in their grades and fail and not be able to, you know, reach their goals in life.

The students described their teachers variously, as "nice," "mean," "cool," boring," and "strict." Regardless of the characterization, students' overall comments describe a faculty who deeply care about and believe in their ability to learn. Abel experienced this as being pushed to higher levels, whereas for Darnell, in particular, this realization came through the fact that many teachers know who he is:

> Umm, the teachers here are like really cool. They, they're not narrow minded about just one thing. They're for everybody, they help everybody. If you're, you're doing bad or something, or you need help. They are there, like, to put you up to the other level that you should be in. (Abel)
>
> There's more people like, that know your name, like teachers, some teachers ... they might like know, like know the kids that really want to succeed in life. And they won't really know the kids, um, that really like, have low grades—they won't know their name, and they really wouldn't care about cuz it's only the people that have to care about. (Darnell)

"It Shows If You Don't Have Effort": Personal Responsibility in Learning

The theme of personal responsibility emerged in the many comments that students made about the importance of effort and the necessity of setting goals. For many students, effort can be a double-edged sword that leaves them unsure about how much and when they should invest effort in their learning (Covington & Dray, 2002). Most students recognize that effort will enhance their academic performance. Yet they also realize that if they have to try hard, this implies that they probably are not smart. We did not hear this view from any of the students we interviewed. Quite to the contrary, the students spoke about the importance of persistence, as in Juana's comments:

> Like, because I mostly think that effort is something that you put in, and it shows if you have effort, it shows if you doesn't have effort, don't have

effort. Because, umm, if you ... let's say you learn something but you don't get it and you give up. You know, there's no effort there. It's learning something that you don't get because you don't get it automatically. Umm, it really plays a part in school because ... also, umm, if you don't have effort ... in school you're not going to get everything, you're not like a genius, you know. Albert Einstein didn't get everything, you know. Umm, but like if you have effort and you want to do something so bad, like, it often turns into ability. Because if you have ability and you have effort, to do something bad you're going to eventually.... Well, it depends on how much time it takes, but you're going to eventually make a difference in your school, work, and whatever you do.

The notion that effort – an unstable quality – can be eventually trans-formed into ability – a more enduring trait – is notable because it is more common among very young children (Nicholls, 1978; Nicholls, Nolen, & Thorkildsen, 1995). As early as the second grade, most students begin to view the relationship between effort and ability as *compensatory*. In other words, they begin to endorse the view that the harder they *have* to try, the *"dumber"* they must be. A great deal of research attention has been paid to classroom factors that can promote the mature view that Juana articulates (Cheung & Rudowicz, 2003; Eccles, Roeser, Vida, Fredricks, & Wigfield, 2006; Schunk & Pajares, 2002).

Nadia talked about her desire to make it on the honor roll, noting that her failure thus far is her own doing:

> [It's a challenge] being on the honor role. [laughing] I can't get grades good enough to get on the honor role.... I ain't studying hard. I want it, just to be on it, cause like, ever since I was like in sixth grade and up I've never been on the honor role. But, like, in elementary school I was on the honor role a lot. And now no more.

Indeed, the students who conveyed some dissatisfaction with their perfor-mance blamed only themselves, mirroring findings from our questionnaire study of elementary school students.

"Failure Is Not Really Something Bad": Adaptive Achievement Beliefs

For many students, the experience of failure can be debilitating and lead to learned helplessness and feelings of inability. Educators have found that many students can be helped by reorienting their perception of failure toward the belief that mistakes and setbacks are a natural part of learning (Lepper, Corpus, & Iyengar, 2005). In this context, Margarita's comments about failure demonstrate that she values seeing the positive in what many consider a negative experience:

What [failure] means, umm ... it's not really something bad. It something that you need to try again. Umm, even if you fail at something that you want to do, don't, don't give up. Never, never give up. Umm, it's something that probably takes motivation away from you. But, at the same time it wants you ... umm, brings you new ideas to your head to break the obstacles. Like can I try this again, can I do something else. Umm, want me to move on our something. Like, it's not really a bad term because we people are like saying failure, they are like, oh! you're a failure. It's not really bad because you have so many chances in this life and you can always try again. And, umm, I think, like let's say I was to fail at something. I would try my hardest to do it again. To ... like ... make sure that something that I did wrong is fixed. Or because failure is the best way of learning, because when you fail something you learn, you learn more, because you want to succeed. And if you fail again, you even learn more. But like, and then at the same time when you fail and then you succeed it brings like ... if you just succeed it's just like I succeed, but if you fail and then you succeed, like, you learn more because you're like, I failed at something but then I didn't give up.... And then I got it right. That's what I think [failure] means for me.

We found that, even when speaking about academic challenges, many students fell back on effort as a means of strategizing their way out of difficulty. Notably, Hector can articulate a strategy for coping with challenge even when he dislikes the work in question:

Chemistry class, umm, that's the toughest class for any first year. To be honest with you, that's a tough class. And, and you know, I'm not going to lie to you but I can't stand that class. I hate, I hate that class. [laughing] And, umm, it's tough man. You have to memorize the periodic tables, the atoms. You know, stoichiometry, this and that, it's tough man. I mean, but like I said you got to show perseverance and never say never. And, go for it. And that's what I try to do.

Learning from Catholic Schools

The most interesting finding of this research is that, when given the opportunity to express their views, these Catholic school students focused on their teachers' commitment to them as learners and articulated mature and sophisticated views about their learning. The level of support and care that these students expressed has been reported in previous research on Catholic schools (Nelson & Bauch, 1997). Importantly, this finding dovetails not only with Noddings's (2005) work on the positive psychosocial influence of caring adults in students' lives but also with Wentzel's (2002) recent research on social motivation. Her research has revealed that students who feel cared for and who have supportive teachers who mentor them tend to do better in school, both academically and socially. Furthermore, they tend to be supportive of their peers and more prosocial in and out of the classroom (Wentzel, 2004).

However, we are struck by the degree to which educational goals and expectations were clearly communicated and understood by all students, an observation that has been made in previous work on Catholic school pedagogy (Hill, Foster, & Gendler, 1990). This is even more compelling when we consider that many of the students we interviewed fit the literature's definition of those who are at risk for school failure (RAND, 2005). The students we interviewed perceived that their teachers not only hold them to high standards but also offer the support they need to *meet* these standards. For these students, the standards are not mysterious – they are clear, are unambiguous, and apply to everyone. In setting such goals, teachers are communicating the belief that *all* students have what it takes to achieve at the level expected of them. It is certainly the case that in Catholic schools, as in public schools, children become increasingly aware of who learns faster or who is "smarter" (Marsh, Hau, & Craven, 2004). Nonetheless, the message that *all* teachers can promote is that despite differences in rates of learning, everyone can and will learn.

As all of us who study education reform know, higher standards in and of themselves do not guarantee higher achievement – they must be accompanied by ongoing support (Heubert, 2002). This support, according to the students we interviewed, was both emotional and academic. Teachers provided age-appropriate, pragmatic suggestions that helped them focus their efforts in ways that were likely to improve their performance. From the perspective of achievement motivation theory, the suggestions themselves can help to foster a sense of control over how well they do in school. Furthermore, to the extent that the teachers are offering up strategies for dealing with difficulty, they may be modeling persistence, a component of motivation that is critical for school success (Eccles et al., 2006).

Finally, the students in our study perceived the standards and support they received to be ongoing, ebbing and flowing with variations in their performance. In other words, these students understood that their teachers would not tolerate performance that did not meet their definition of an acceptable standard. These students knew that they could not rest on previous laurels without being taken to task, should the quality of their work deteriorate. According to these students, their teachers appeared to be relentless in their pursuit of high-quality work from their pupils. As Nicholls (1978; Nicholls et al., 1995) and others have shown, this insistence serves to communicate an unwavering belief in students' ability to master the required work, a conviction that is a powerful motivator for *all* students (EdSource, 2006; Rosenthal, 2002). We cannot know the extent to which the adaptive beliefs about learning, endorsed by Margarita, Hector, and their peers, were fostered by the teachers' pedagogical styles or were the result of factors having nothing to do with the school. Our goal remains the identification of influences that the students *themselves* perceive as influential. In this regard, it appears that these students appreciate teachers who believe in them, who closely monitor their progress, and who provide a variety of emotional and academic supports to help them excel in school. In our view, the more we understand about how students think about and interpret their educational experiences, the better equipped we are to develop models of intervention that promise success for all students. Our hope is that the important lessons that we can glean from the success of Catholic schools will not be lost in the ongoing debate over self-selection.

Authors' Note

The authors gratefully acknowledge the ongoing support of Sr. Kathleen Carr, CSJ, superintendent of schools, Archdiocese of Boston; Robert J. McCarthy, president, David Paskind, associate principal, Sister Ellen Powers, CSJ, former president/principal, and the faculty and students of North Cambridge Catholic High School; and David M. DeFillippo, principal, Christopher Sullivan, assistant principal, and the faculty and students of Central Catholic High School, Lawrence. This work was supported in part by a Spencer Foundation Small Grants Award.

References

Altonji, J. G., Elder, T. E., & Taber, C. R. (2005). Selection on observed and unobserved variables: Assessing the effectiveness of Catholic schools. *Journal of Political Economy, 113*(1), 151–184.

Bempechat, J. (2003). *Meeting the psychological and emotional needs of young adolescents: Exploring achievement and motivation in Catholic high school students.* Washington, DC: National Catholic Education Association.

Bempechat, J., Drago-Severson, E., & Boulay, B. A. (2002). Attributions for success and failure in mathematics: A comparative study of Catholic and public school students. *Catholic Education: A Journal of Inquiry and Practice, 5*, 357–372.

Bryk, A., Lee, V., & Holland, P. (1993). *Catholic schools and the common good.* Cambridge, MA: Harvard University Press.

Carbonaro, W. J. (2003). Sector differences in student learning: Differences in achievement gains across school years and during the summer. *Catholic Education: A Journal of Inquiry and Practice, 7*(2), 219–245.

Cattaro, G. M. (2002a). Catholic schools: Enduring presence in urban America. *Education and Urban Society, 35*(1), 100–110.

Cattaro, G. M. (2002b). Immigration and pluralism in urban Catholic schools. *Education and Urban Society, 34*(2), 199–211.

Cheung, C., & Rudowicz, E. (2003). Underachievement and attributions among students attending schools stratified by student ability. *Social Psychology of Education, 6*(4), 303–323.

Chubb, J. E. (2005). *Within our reach: How America can educate every child.* Lanham, MD: Rowman & Littlefield.

Coleman, J., Hoffer, T., & Kilgore, S. (1982). Cognitive outcomes in public and private schools. *Sociology of Education, 55*, 65–76.

Covington, M. V., & Dray, E. (2002). The developmental course of achievement motivation: A need-based approach. In A. Wigfield & J. S. Eccles (Eds.), *Development of achievement motivation* (pp. 33–56). San Diego, CA: Academic Press.

Eccles, J. S., Roeser, R., Vida, M., Fredricks, J., & Wigfield, A. (2006). Motivational and achievement pathways through middle childhood. In L. Balter & C. S. Tamis-LeMonda (Eds.), *Child psychology: A handbook of contemporary issues* (2nd ed., pp. 325–355). New York: Psychology Press.

EdSource. (2006). *Similar students, different results: Why do some schools do better?* Palo Alto, CA: Author.

Eide, E. R., Goldhaber, D. D., & Showalter, M. H. (2004). Does Catholic high school attendance lead to attendance at a more selective college? *Social Science Quarterly, 85*(5), 1335–1352.

Ellison, B. J., & Hallinan, M. T. (2004). Ability grouping in Catholic and public schools. *Catholic Education: A Journal of Inquiry and Practice, 8*(1), 107–129.

Goldberger, A., & Cain, G. (1982). The causal analysis of cognitive outcomes in the Coleman, Hoffer, and Kilgore report. *Sociology of Education, 55*, 103–122.

Grant, H., & Dweck, C. S. (2003). Clarifying achievement goals and their impact. *Journal of Personality and Social Psychology, 85*(3), 541–553.

Heubert, J. (2002). First, do no harm. *Educational Leadership, 60*(4), 26–30.

Hill, P. T., Foster, G. E., & Gendler, T. (1990). *High schools with character.* Santa Monica, CA: RAND.

Hoxby, C. (2003). *The economics of school choice.* Cambridge, MA: National Bureau of Economic Research Conference Report.

Ilg, T. J., Massucci, J. D., & Cattaro, G. M. (2004). Brown at 50: The dream is still alive in urban Catholic schools. *Education and Urban Society, 36*(3), 355–367.

Lepper, M. R., Corpus, J. H., & Iyengar, S. S. (2005). Intrinsic and extrinsic motivational orientation in the classroom: Age differences and academic correlates. *Journal of Educational Psychology, 97*(2), 184–196.

Marsh, H. W., Hau, K., & Craven, R. (2004). The big-fish-little-pond effect stands up to scrutiny. *American Psychologist, 59*(4), 269–271.

Morgan, S. L. (2001). Counterfactuals, causal effect heterogeneity, and the Catholic school effect on learning. *Sociology of Education, 74*, 341–374.

Nelson, M. D., & Bauch, P. A. (1997, March). *African American students' perceptions of caring teacher behaviors at Catholic and public schools of choice.* Paper presented at the American Educational Research Association, Chicago.

Nicholls, J. G. (1978). The development of the concepts of effort and ability, perception of own attainment, and the understanding that difficult tasks require more ability. *Child Development, 49*, 800–814.

Nicholls, J. G., Nolen, S. B., & Thorkildsen, T. A. (1995). Big science, little teachers: Knowledge and motives concerning student motivation. In J. G. Nicholls & T. A. Thorkildsen (Eds.), *Reasons for learning: Expanding the conversation on student-teacher collaboration* (pp. 5–20). New York: Teachers College Press.

Noddings, N. (2005). Care and moral education. In H. S. Shapiro & D. E. Purpel (Eds.), *Critical social issues in American education: Democracy and meaning in a globalizing world* (pp. 297–308). Mahwah, NJ: Lawrence Erlbaum.

Orfield, G., Frankenberg, E. D., & Lee, C. (2002). The resurgence of school segregation. *Educational Leadership, 60*(4), 16–20.

Peterson, P. E., & Walberg, H. J. (2002). *Countering the negative effect of poverty on learning.* Chicago: Heartland Institute.

RAND. (2005). *Children at risk: Consequences for school readiness and beyond.* Santa Monica, CA: Author.

Rosenthal, R. (2002). The Pygmalion effect and its mediating mechanisms. In J. Aronson (Ed.), *Improving academic achievement: Impact of psychological factors on education* (pp. 25–36). San Diego, CA: Academic Press.

Salganik, L., & Karweit, N. (1982). Voluntarism and governance in education. *Sociology of Education, 55*, 152–161.

Sander, W. (2001). *The effects of Catholic schools on religiosity, education, and competition* (Occasional Paper NCSPE-OP-32). New York: Teachers College.

Sander, W., & Krautman, A. C. (1995). Catholic schools, dropout rates and educational attainment. *Economic Inquiry, 33*(2), 217–233.

Schunk, D. H., & Pajares, F. (2002). The development of academic self-efficacy. In A. Wigfield & J. S. Eccles (Eds.), *Development of achievement motivation* (pp. 15–31). New York: Academic Press.

Strauss, A. (1987). *Qualitative analysis for social scientists.* Cambridge, UK: Cambridge University Press.

Weiner, B. (1994). Integrating social and personal theories of achievement strivings. *Review of Educational Research, 64*(4), 557–573.

Weiner, B. (2005). Motivation from an attributional perspective and the social psychology of perceived competence. In A. J. Elliot & C. S. Dweck (Eds.), *Handbook of competence and motivation* (pp. 73–84). New York: Guilford.

Wentzel, K. R. (2002). Are effective teachers like good parents: Teaching styles and student adjustment in early adolescence. *Child Development, 73*(1), 287–301.

Wentzel, K. R. (2004). Understanding classroom competence: The role of social-motivational and self-processes. In R. V. Kail (Ed.), *Advances in child development and behavior* (Vol. 32, pp. 231–241). San Diego, CA: Elsevier.

54

Dimensions of School Motivation: A Cross-cultural Validation Study

Dennis M. McInerney and Kenneth E. Sinclair

In a multicultural society such as Australia, educators are concerned with the school performance of children from various minority groups. Within the context of Australian education, aboriginal children appear particularly disadvantaged with regard to academic achievement and school retention, whereas the children of certain migrant minority groups appear, in the latter part of the century, to be performing particularly well. In recent studies, McInerney (1989, 1990, 1991a, 1991b; McInerney & Sinclair, 1991) has examined a range of factors that are considered influential in determining the success or otherwise of particular groups within school settings, and in particular the studies have focused on key variables that predict school retention for these groups.

In a study of aboriginal, migrant, and Anglo-Australian students (McInerney, 1988, 1989), a hypothesized set of influential background variables was examined using the Facilitating Conditions Questionnaire (FCQ). Parental influence emerged as the major discriminating variable for those aboriginal children who continued with school. It was also apparent that the child's feelings toward school and the perceived support the child received from teachers and friends to continue with school, were also critical variables distinguishing the aboriginal school-leaver and nonleaver. Other variables such as negative peer influence and perceived value of school appeared to be not important as discriminant variables. Although parental influence emerged as the most important discriminant variable for the nonaboriginal groups, affect to school and the positive influence of teachers and peers on the child's decision

Source: *Journal of Cross-Cultural Psychology*, 23(3) (1992): 389–406.

making appeared less important. For these groups the perceived value of school and negative peer influence appeared relatively more important. Convergent evidence for the importance of parental influence on the child's decision to continue with school was obtained in a further study with the same sample using the Behavioural Intentions Questionnaire (McInerney, 1990).

In addition to external factors such as parental encouragement and peer influence, factors intrinsic to the person, such as desire for achievement, competitiveness, and self-reliance also play an important role in influencing a student's application to learning and schooling. In the international literature a key construct used to examine differential school performance across cultural groups has been achievement motivation. However, the methodological and conceptual difficulties involved in measuring and defining achievement motivation for cross-cultural use have been discussed in a large number of publications (see Davidson & Thomson, 1980; De Vos, 1968, 1973; De Vos & Caudill, 1973; Draguns, 1979; Maehr, 1974; Maehr & Nicholls, 1980; Pedersen, 1979). A theoretical model with clear and significant implications for methodological improvements in cross-cultural research on achievement motivation is Maehr's Personal Investment Model (Braskamp & Maehr, 1983; Maehr, 1984; Maehr & Braskamp, 1986), which provides the framework for the present study.

Three critical components are designated by this model in determining an individual's personal investment (or motivation) in a specific situation. The first is *Sense of Self*, which refers to the more or less organized collections of perceptions, beliefs, and feelings related to who one is. Sense of Self is presumed to be composed of a number of components such as sense of competence, sense of autonomy, and sense of purpose, each contributing to the motivational orientation of the individual. The second component, *Personal Incentives*, refers to the motivational focus of activity, especially what the person defines as "success" and "failure" in a particular situation. Among possible personal incentives are task goals (e.g., experiencing adventure, novelty, or working to understand something), ego goals (e.g., doing better than others), social-solidarity goals (e.g., pleasing others and making others happy), and extrinsic-reward goals (e.g., working for a prize or reward of some kind). Each of these components is subdivided into two facets described in Figure 1. The third component, *Perceived Alternatives*, refers to the behavioral alternatives that a person perceives to be available and appropriate (in terms of the individual's sociocultural norms) in a given situation. Each of these components may be influenced by the design of the task, the personal experience and access to information of the individual, and the sociocultural context. In summary, personal investment or motivation in a particular task or behavior is a function of the sense of self, the feelings toward the behavior or task, the personal incentives operating, and the perceived options available.

Each of the dimensions, Maehr maintains, is significant in any individual or situation interaction and has been considered, at some time, important in explaining and interpreting the differential performances and motivation of

Personal Investment	=	Sense of Self	+	Affect	+	Personal Incentives

SR (self-reliance)	Ego	– Competitiveness (co)
SE (self-esteem)		– Power (pw)
GD (goal directed)	Extrinsic	– Recognition (rc)
		– Token rewards (tn)
	Social Solidarity	– Social concern (sc)
		– Affiliation (af)
	Task Rewards	– Task involvement (ta)
		– Striving for excellence (ex)

└──────────── ACTION POSSIBILITIES ────────────┘

Figure 1: Dimensions of Maehr's personal investment model

various cultural groups in school settings. The purpose of the present article is to describe the construction and validation of an instrument entitled the Inventory of School Motivation (ISM), which is based on the Personal Investment Model. The scale was developed (a) to test the "sense of self" and "personal incentives" dimensions of the Maehr model, (b) to test the applicability of the model and instrument in cross-cultural settings, and (c) to provide an instrument for measuring dimensions of motivation in classroom settings.

Method

Subjects

In total, 2,152 subjects were surveyed comprising 492 aboriginal students, 487 migrant-background students, and 1,173 Anglo students drawn from Year 7 to Year 10 in 12 NSW high schools. There were approximately equal numbers of males and females.

Materials

Inventory of School Motivation (ISM)

A presurvey of adult community members of the three groups was undertaken to ensure the cultural relevance of the items. An instrument was devised to evaluate the nature of school motivation for aboriginal-, Anglo-, and migrant-background children. For the ISM, questions were written to measure the following 11 dimensions of the Maehr model: self-reliance (e.g., I can do things as well as most people at school), self-esteem (e.g., at times I feel that I'm no good at anything at school), goal directed (e.g., it is good to plan ahead to complete my schooling), competitiveness (e.g., winning is important to me), power (e.g., I often try to be the leader of a group), recognition (e.g., having other people tell me that I did well is important to me), token rewards (e.g., getting merit certificates would make me work harder at school), social concern (e.g., it is very important for students to help each other at school), affiliation (e.g., I try to work with friends as much as possible at school), task involvement (e.g., the more interesting the school-work the harder I try), and striving for excellence (e.g., I try hard to make sure that I am good at my schoolwork). Items were measured by a Likert-type scale, from *strongly agree* (1) to *strongly disagree* (5).

There were 100 questions in the final pool of items in the Inventory of School Motivation. There were approximately 9 questions targeted on each dimension of the model. The questions were randomly assigned throughout the form and contained 24 negative items to guard against response bias. Items comprising the questionnaire are found in the appendix.

Procedure

Administration of the Survey

Each survey session began with a standardized explanation of the purpose of the survey and a request for the support of the students in completing the survey accurately. To ensure that procedures adopted for the survey were standardized from school to school, to avoid any difficulties students might have completing the survey due to poor reading skills, and to ensure that the majority of students completed the questionnaire in the available time, the chief researcher read the questionnaire (including the standardized directions) aloud while students filled in their responses. Students who experienced difficulties in answering questions or who required other assistance simply raised their hand and one of the research assistants went to their aid. In this way the procedure of the survey was not interrupted.

Statistical Analyses

Preliminary Data Reduction and Statistical Analysis

Factorial Study 1. Preliminary analysis consisted of determining whether the designed instrument had construct validity for the full group as well as for each of the separate groups, aboriginal, Anglo, and migrant. As the Maehr model hypothesizes, 11 dimensions relating to sense of self and personal incentives, a principal axis factor analysis with orthogonal (varimax) rotation setting the NFACTORS parameter at 11 was performed on the data for the full group and each separate group. Pairwise deletion of missing data was used to maximize the amount of data available for each analysis.

Factor analysis of the set of 100 items for the full group ($N = 2,152$, $M = 1,042$, $F = 1,110$) resulted in 10 theoretically interpretable factors accounting for 98.2% of the variance in these items (although the last three factors consisted of doublets). Factors were named based on the content of the items with factor loadings that exceed .30.

From this analysis it was apparent that for the full group of subjects the Inventory of School Motivation gave broad support for the existence of several discrete parameters that may influence student motivation in school settings, even though this analysis failed to find all of the 11 separate dimensions hypothesized in the Maehr model. The following dimensions were demonstrated: Self-Esteem, Self-Reliance, Affiliation, Social Concern, and Power (defined by group leadership). To a lesser extent, the existence of the dimensions Token Rewards and Competition was supported. The items designed by Maehr to measure ego and extrinsic rewards (viz., competitiveness, power, recognition, and token rewards) formed one general factor that we termed *Extrinsic Motivation*. Task rewards (viz., task involvement and striving for excellence) formed one factor that we called *Intrinsic Motivation*. It also included items written to measure Goal-Directed behavior.

In order to assess the cross-cultural validity of the model and its reliability, a further series of principal axis factor analyses were performed on the three groups in the sample, aboriginal, Anglo, and migrant. In each case a varimax solution was chosen and the NFACTOR parameter was set to 11. Key dimensions of the Maehr model, Intrinsic Motivation, Extrinsic Motivation, Self-Esteem, Self-Reliance, Affiliation, Social Concern, and Power (group leadership), emerged again as major factors. The consistency of the findings across the four groups argues very strongly for the reliability of the ISM as well as for its construct validity. It gives strong support to the theoretical model from which it is derived. The ability of the model to illustrate characteristics of specific relevance to each group indicates its validity for use in a cross-cultural context.

Discussion

The similarity of the factor pattern matrices across the three groups argues strongly for the etic validity of the constructs, whereas the differences that emerged in the composition of factors in the several groups support the emic validity of the scales derived from the constructs. It remains to demonstrate the relative importance of these dimensions for each group in determining performance level in educational settings.

All scales were analyzed by means of the reliability subprogram of the SPSS package (Nie & Hull, 1981) for each group. Cronbach's alphas were calculated for each scale. In general there was a high degree of reliability for each of the scales analyzed (with the majority being in excess of .70). Factor score variables were produced to represent the factors for each of the groups in later analyses. Reliability estimates are presented in Table 2.

The Significant Predictors

Multiple Regression and Intention to Complete Schooling

A series of stepwise multiple-regression analyses (based on listwise deletion of missing data) were conducted to ascertain which variables were of most significance for each of three groups in predicting school performance (in particular motivation to continue with school beyond the minimum school-leaving age). The criterion variable was the expressed intention of the subject to continue with school and complete the Higher School Certificate (the final year of study in NSW schools). The predictor variables included were scales derived from the factor analyses (earlier described). Table 2 presents the list of predictor variables for each of the three groups in the study. Because results from multiple-regression analyses can be severely affected by intercorrelations among the predictor variables, each of the predictor variables was correlated with each other using the Pearson correlation program from SPSS (Nie, Hull, Jenkins, Steinbrenner, & Bent, 1975). The pattern of correlations among the factor score scales indicated very low levels of intercorrelation ($\tau < .14$).

Further Model Testing and Data Reduction

Factorial Study 2. To test the model further and to reduce the number of items comprising the ISM (it was intended to develop a set of [composite] scales that might be used to assess the motivational characteristics of students within school settings), the data were subjected to a further set of principal axis factor analyses with varimax rotation. It was felt that limiting the NFACTOR parameter to 11 may have prevented a number of other salient dimensions of the Maehr model from emerging in earlier analyses. Consequently, for each group (Anglo, aboriginal, and migrant), a further factor analysis was performed without any limitation on the number of factors to be obtained.

These factor analyses of the ISM clearly identified important dimensions of the Maehr model, with the pattern of factor loadings providing support for the scales that the ISM was designed to measure. However, the unrestricted factor analyses generated more factors supportive of the Maehr model than the analyses based on an a priori restriction of the NFACTOR to 11 and they also generated a large number of trivial and poorly defined factors. In an attempt to remove them and to reduce the item set from the 100 original variables to a set more manageable for general classroom purposes, each factor analysis was scrutinized carefully in order to isolate those items that did not factor out for a particular group on any factor (there were only a small number of these), and those items that loaded on poorly defined or trivial factors. Through this procedure it was possible to select, for further analysis, items of greatest relevance to each particular group.

The reduced set of items for each group was subjected to a principal axis factor analysis using varimax rotation. Pairwise deletion of missing data was utilized. Table 1 presents a comparison of the factor structure for the three groups. Items defining each factor are included.

Table 2 presents the multiple regression results for the three groups on the ISM for the intention to complete the Higher School Certificate. These

Table 1: Factor patterns for the ISM across three groups and items defining each factor for each group

Aboriginal	Migrant	Anglo
Intrinsic rewards (f1)[a]	Intrinsic rewards (f1)	Intrinsic rewards (f1)
Extrinsic rewards (f2)	Extrinsic rewards (f2)	Extrinsic rewards (f2)
Self-reliance (f3)	Self-reliance (f11)	Self-reliance (f5)
Affiliation (f4)	Affiliation (f5)	Affiliation (f6)
Competition (f5)	Competition (f7)	Competition (f7)
Recognition (f6)	Recognition (f3)	Recognition (f3)
Social concern (f7)	Social concern (f6)	Social concern (f8)
Self-esteem (f8)	Self-esteem (f4)	Self-esteem (f4)
Goal directed (f10)	Goal directed (f10)	Goal directed (f10)
Power (f11)	Power (f9)	Power (f9)
Confidence (aboriginal) (f9)	–	–
–	Token reward (f8)	–
–	–	Success (f11)

	Defining Items		
Scale[b]	Anglo	Aboriginal	Migrant
Intrinsic	7, 13, 16, 22, 30, 33 34, 40, 44, 56, 63, 66 68, 70, 79, 89	4, 7, 9, 11, 12, 13,16, 22 28, 30, 33, 34, 38, 39, 40 48, 54, 56, 57, 63, 69, 75 79, 83, 89, 96	7, 13, 40, 56, 59, 60 63, 66, 69, 74, 75, 79 83, 84, 89, 93
Extrinsic	3, 15, 18, 27, 32, 52, 53 65, 88	8, 14, 15, 23, 24, 27, 32, 41 44, 53, 65, 72, 73, 78, 91	3, 6, 15, 18, 27, 32 53, 65, 88, 94
Recognition	12, 17, 20, 23, 24, 28 41, 73, 91	3, 6, 17	8, 12, 20, 23, 28, 41 24, 50, 73, 91
Self-esteem	45, 55, 67, 77, 80, 81 82, 95, 98	45, 77, 81, 100	45, 55, 57, 67, 70, 82
Self-reliance	31, 59, 60, 69, 75, 83, 97	18, 60, 61, 66, 74, 90	31, 97
Affiliation	35, 36, 37, 42, 47	35, 36, 37, 42, 47	35, 36, 37, 42, 47, 61
Competition	1, 2, 14, 43, 76	1, 2, 76	1, 2, 14, 43, 76, 99
Social concern	10, 29, 46, 61, 74, 85	10, 21, 29, 46	10, 21, 29, 46, 85
Power	62, 71, 86, 94	86, 88	62, 71, 86
Goal directed	54, 84, 87	59, 87, 84	22, 38, 39, 48
Success	90, 93	–	–
Token	–	–	72, 78, 80, 90, 95, 98
Confidence	–	80, 95, 98	–

[a.] Order of factor.
[b.] Items are listed if they loaded 0.3 or greater on the factor.

Table 2: Sets of beta weights and multiple-correlation coefficients for each group (aboriginal, migrant, anglo) on predictor variables drawn from the inventory of school motivation (ISM) and intention to complete the higher school certificate

Factor score scale	Groups											
	Aboriginal (n = 492)				Migrant (n = 487)				Anglo (n = 1,173)			
Predictor variables	alpha[1]	fnum[2]	beta[3]	ord[4]	alpha	fnum	beta	ord	alpha	fnum	beta	ord
Intrinsic rewards	93[5]	1	419**	1	88	1	423**	1	89	1	241**	3
Extrinsic rewards	90	2	-002		91	2	-036		87	2	-052*	8
Self-reliance	44	3	102*	4	60	11	053		81	5	262**	2
Affiliation	67	4	-060		72	5	-095*	5	71	6	-070**	7
Competition	72	5	-039		82	7	223**	2	80	7	032	
Recognition	75	6	-047		85	3	084*	8	84	3	051*	9
Social concern	68	7	-014		63	6	121**	4	63	8	125**	5
Self-esteem	54	8	014		72	4	091*	6	79	4	152**	4
Goal directed	71	10	372**	2	74	10	185***	3	76	10	429***	1
Power	***	11	-036		75	9	026		66	9	-046	
Confidence (ab)	54	9	162**	3	–	–	–	–	–	–	–	–
Token reward (mig)	–	–	–	–	***	8	-087*	7	–	–	–	–
Success (Anglo)	–	–	–	–	–	–	–	–	***	11	-105*	6
Multiple R	627				591				665			

Note: 1. Reliability coefficients (Cronbach's alpha); 2. Order of factor; 3. Standardized beta weights; 4. Order of importance of the significant predictor variables; 5. All coefficients are presented without decimal points.

*p < .05.

**p < .01.

***Reliability not available due to limitation of the Reliability program (Nie & Hull, 1981). A minimum of three items is required to constitute a scale.

results indicate the usefulness of the ISM in determining the salient predictors of intentional behavior for the three groups studied. For each group (aboriginal, migrant, and Anglo), the combined set of culturally determined predictor variables developed from the personal investment theoretical framework was significantly related to the criterion variable. The multiple-regression analyses therefore indicate the usefulness of the ISM in explaining and describing the nature of motivation for students from different cultural backgrounds in school settings, given the adequacy of the ISM for the three groups in the first place.

In essence, the major correlates of intention for the nontraditional aboriginal students in this study were level of intrinsic motivation, desire to complete schooling, or lack of it, and level of confidence and self-reliance. Factors often alleged to be important determinants of aboriginal motivation in the school setting such as affiliation, social concern, self-esteem, and recognition did not emerge as important predictors in this study.

A greater number of predictors was important for the migrant group, with eight scales significantly related to the criterion. Intrinsic Motivation, Competition, Goal Directed (to have a better future), and Social Concern accounted for most of the explained variance in the criterion variable. After Intrinsic Motivation, Goal Directed (to have a better future) and Competition emerged as the two most significant factors. This interesting finding supports the notion that many migrant children do well in Australian schools because of encouragement by their parents to work hard for a better future, and therefore to compete. Other variables that were expected to be significant for the aboriginal group but were not (viz., affiliation, social concern, recognition, and self-esteem) attained significance for the migrant group.

For the Anglo group, all variables were found to be significantly related to the intention to complete schooling except for Competition. The most important predictor variable was Goal Directed (to complete schooling), followed by Self-Reliance and Intrinsic Motivation. Extrinsic Motivation was found to be significantly and negatively related to the intention to complete schooling. To the extent that the Anglo student is reward dependent, the less likely he or she is to hold the intention to finish school.

Summary

Although direct numerical comparisons across the groups are not possible as each regression equation is based on a different set of predictor variables, some generalizations can be made. For all groups, Intrinsic Motivation appears to be a major predictor. It was the single most important predictor for the aboriginal and migrant group, whereas for the Anglo group Goal Directed (to complete schooling) emerged as the single most important predictor followed by Intrinsic Motivation. For all groups, Goal-Directed motivation was a significant predictor but the nature of the goal direction varied across groups. The goal was school completion for the Anglo and aboriginal groups, and it was pinpointed as the student's desire to complete schooling and to do better than his or her parents for the migrant group.

A narrower range of predictors was significant for the aboriginal group. Apart from the two intrinsically oriented scales, aboriginal motivation to continue schooling is largely determined by feelings of self-reliance within the school setting. An attributional model of motivation thus appears particularly salient to this group of students. Attribution theory (Weiner, 1974) maintains that children who perceive that they lack ability (internal stable and uncontrollable factor) or perceive that the situation is beyond them (external, stable, uncontrollable factor) will withdraw from the task. These feelings of inadequacy may become intractable and lead to learned helplessness in school situations (Dweck & Goetz, 1978).

Extrinsic Motivation emerged as a low level predictor for the Anglo group, being negatively related to the intention of completing school. There was a negative, though nonsignificant, relationship between extrinsic motivation and intention to complete school for the other two groups. Clearly, to the extent students say they intend to complete schooling, they are less dependent on external rewards. Conversely, those children who perceive little value in schooling and/or dislike it are likely to be reward dependent to keep them at the task of learning.

Competition was not an important predictor for either the aboriginal or the Anglo groups; however, it was the second most important predictor for the migrant group. Power Motivation (indicated through a desire to be group leader) was not an important predictor for any group.

Motivational characteristics such as Affiliation and Social Concern often claimed to be important for the aboriginal group, emerged as more important predictors for the migrant and Anglo groups throwing into stark relief the cluster of variables that was found to be significant for the aboriginal group.

Prediction and Behavior: Are They Related?

Discriminant Analyses and Returning to School

As a final test of the validity of the Inventory of School Motivation, a series of discriminant analyses (with stepwise variable selection and minimization of Wilks's lambda) using the significant predictors from the initial analyses was performed with a subset of the data on those subjects who had continued with school or left it before completing the Higher School Certificate. In other words, we set out to examine the value of the predictor variables identified and discussed earlier in distinguishing between those who remained at school and those who left after Year 10. Subjects consisted of 658 Anglo students ($M = 313, F = 345$), 283 migrant students ($M = 154, F = 129$), and 85 aboriginal students ($M = 42, F = 43$).

Analyses with the Anglo group indicated that all of the predictor variables except Affiliation were retained in the analysis. The most important of these variables (based on standardized canonical discriminant coefficients) were Goal-Directed (school), Self-Reliance, and Success Motivation. Using this discriminant analysis, 72% of the sample were correctly classified as being at school or having left school ($p < .001$). Analyses with the migrant group indicated that the best set of predictors was Intrinsic Motivation, Recognition, Self-Esteem, Affiliation, Competition, Token Reward, and Power. This combination of variables correctly classified 63% of the sample as being at school or having left ($p < .001$).

Aboriginal analyses indicated that the best set of predictor variables was Goal Directed (school), Self-Reliance, and Confidence. Using this combination of variables, 70% of the sample were correctly classified ($p = .002$). Table 3 presents the comparison of the major discriminant variables for each group studied.

Table 3: A comparison of the discriminant variables drawn from the inventory of school motivation across three groups (aboriginal, anglo, and migrant) on continuing with school or leaving school after year 10

	Standard canonical discriminant coefficients		
Discriminant variables	Aboriginal	Anglo	Migrant
Goal directed	.962*	.697	
Self-reliance	.449	.485	
Confidence	.405	.379	
Competition		.403	.579
Intrinsic		.173	.551
Power		.207	.331
Token			.305
Self-esteem		.232	.216
Recognition		.121	.189
Social concern		.199	
Extrinsic		.096	
Affiliation			.267
% of group correctly classified	70%**	72%**	63%**

*Standardized canonical discriminant function coefficients indicate the relative importance of the variable to the discriminant equation. The higher the number the more important the variable.
**Significant at the .001 level.

Discussion

The pattern of discriminant variables for each group bears comparison. The major discriminant variables for the Year 10 aboriginal and Anglo groups are strikingly similar and stand in marked contrast to the pattern established for the migrant group. In the former case a self-efficacy model explains behavior; that is, an aboriginal or Anglo child who feels confident, is self-assured, and has a sense of purpose in schooling continues with schooling. An interesting difference between these two profiles should be highlighted, however. First, the range of variables relevant to the Anglo group is much greater, suggesting a more complex interplay of factors in the Anglo child's decision to continue with school. In the case of the aboriginal children there is clear evidence that the explanatory base for their decision making is much narrower and relates very much to feelings of confidence and assurance within the school setting; this finding is of great importance.

Contrary to expectations, competition was not found to be an important discriminant variable for the Anglo group. The pattern of discriminant variables for the aboriginal group appears even more telling when compared with the migrant group. In this latter case, the significant variables are rewards and competition. This pattern gives clear support to the hypothesis that the children of migrants are more competitive, independent, and desirous of proving their capacity to obtain rewards, both through self-satisfaction and extrinsic modes (such as recognition, marks, and power through group leadership), than Anglo or aboriginal children. The success rate of migrant children at school and their retention levels increasingly appears better than norms established for the nonmigrant groups. It should be noted that Goal Directed (to improve one's life-style), which was an important predictor variable for this group, was not a discriminant variable. It is possible that those migrant children who leave school hope to obtain an occupation that will enable them to do better than their parents, even though they may lack the competitive drive and intrinsic motivation that characterizes their non-leaving confreres.

Variables, which according to generally held beliefs about aboriginal students should have been discriminant variables, such as Affiliation, Social Concern, Competition, and Self-Esteem, did not emerge as such. Given the adequacy of the dimensions in the first place there seems little justification for emphasizing these variables in any analysis of aboriginal student performance at school. Greater attention should be given to investigating the development of school confidence and self-reliance in aboriginal students as well as the development of a positive sense of the value of schooling.

Appendix: Items Comprising the Inventory of School Motivation

Predicted factors:
- (ta) working for the inherent interest
- (ex) striving for excellence
- (co) competitiveness
- (pw) power
- (afi) affiliation
- (sc) social concern
- (re) recognition
- (tn) token rewards
- (gd) goal directed
- (sr) self-reliance
- (se) self-esteem

1. I want to do well at school to be better than my classmates.
2. Winning is important to me.
3. I try to do well at school to please my teachers.
4. I like being given the chance to do something again to make it better.
5. I often try new things on my own.
6. I work hard it. school for rewards from the teacher.
7. I want to do well at school to show that I can do it.
8. I work best in class when I can get some kind of reward.
9. The more interesting the schoolwork the harder I try.
10. It is very important for students to help each other at school.
11. I don't mind working a long time at schoolwork that I find interesting.
12. Having other people tell me that I did well is important to me.
13. I try hard to make sure that I am good at my schoolwork.
14. I am happy only when I am one of the best in class.
15. I work hard at school for presents from my parents.
16. I try to do well at school to please my parents.
17. Praise from my teachers for my good schoolwork is important to me.
18. I don't often make mistakes at school.
19. I am always getting into trouble at school.
20. Getting a reward for my good schoolwork is not very important to me.
21. I like to help other students do well at school.
22. I want to do well at school so that I can have a good future.
23. Praise from my friends for good schoolwork is important to me.
24. Getting merit certificates would make me work harder at school.
25. Students shouldn't depend on their friends for help with schoolwork.
26. I usually do the wrong things at school.
27. I like my teacher to show my work to the rest of the class.
28. I like to be encouraged for my schoolwork.
29. I care about other people at school.

30. When I get good marks I work harder at school.
31. I can do things as well as most people at school.
32. I work hard because I want the teacher to take notice of what I say.
33. I like to see that I am improving in my schoolwork.
34. I need to know that I am getting somewhere with my schoolwork.
35. I do not like working with other people at school.
36. I can do my best work at school when I am working with others.
37. I try to work with friends as much as possible at school.
38. I aim my schooling toward getting a good job.
39. I want to do well at school so that I have something better to look forward to than my parents.
40. I work hard to try to understand something new at school.
41. At school I work best when I am praised.
42. I do better work by myself at school.
43. Coming first is very important to me.
44. Getting good marks is everything for me at school.
45. At times I feel that I'm not good at anything at school.
46. I enjoy helping others with their schoolwork even if I don't do so well myself.
47. When I work in groups at school I don't do my best.
48. I try hard to do well at school so I can get a good job when I leave.
49. Not doing better than my friends in class is important to me.
50. Having people notice my good schoolwork is not really important to me.
51. I just do my schoolwork day by day without thinking about the future.
52. I try to do well at school to please my friends.
53. I like my schoolwork to be compared with others.
54. It is good for me to plan ahead so I can do well at school.
55. I feel I always need help with difficult schoolwork.
56. When I am improving in my schoolwork I try even harder.
57. Marks are the best way to know that you've done well at school.
58. No one pays much attention to me at school.
59. I am bright enough to continue my schooling to the Higher School Certificate.
60. I like to think things out for myself at school.
61. I don't worry about other students, I just do my own work.
62. I often try to be the leader of a group.
63. Most of the time I feel that I can do my schoolwork.
64. Kids usually pick on me at school.
65. I work hard because I want to feel important in front of my school friends.
66. I don't need anyone to tell me to work hard at school; I do it myself.
67. I often think that there are things I can't do at school.
68. The harder the problem the harder I try.
69. On the whole I am pleased with myself at school.
70. How I get on with other students is more important than how I get on with my schoolwork.
71. At school I don't like being in charge of a group.
72. Getting rewards of money would make me work harder at school.

73. I want to be praised for my good schoolwork.
74. As long as I am doing my own work well other students don't matter much.
75. I am very confident at school.
76. I work harder if I'm trying to be better than others.
77. I wish I had a little more confidence in my schoolwork.
78. Praise for good work is not enough, I like a reward.
79. I try hard at school because I am interested in my work.
80. Trying hard at school is not much fun if the competition is too strong.
81. I often worry that I am not very good at school.
82. Other students have to help me a lot with my work.
83. I think that I can do quite well at school.
84. I work hard at school so that I can go on to Year 12.
85. It makes me unhappy if my friends aren't doing well at school.
86. It is very important for me to be a group leader.
87. It is good to plan ahead to complete my schooling.
88. I work hard at school because I want the class to take notice of me.
89. I am always trying to do better in my school work.
90. Things hardly ever bother me at school.
91. Praise from my parents for good schoolwork is important to me.
92. If I'm working alone, difficult schoolwork doesn't bother me.
93. I succeed at whatever I do at school.
94. I work hard at school so that I will be put in charge of things.
95. I only like to do things at school that I feel confident at.
96. I often forget the time when I'm working on something interesting at school.
97. I think I'm as good as everybody else at school.
98. I always choose easy work for myself to do at school so that I don't have too much trouble.
99. I don't like trying to be better than someone else.
100. I don't like being told my marks.

Authors' Note

This research was supported, in part, by two grants from the Australian Institute of Aboriginal Studies. We would like to thank Don Apearritt and Jenny Tjugiarto for their invaluable assistance. Requests for reprints should be sent to Dennis McInerney, School of Education and Language Studies, University of Western Sydney, Macarthur, P.O. Box 555, Campbelltown, NSW 2560, Australia.

References

Braskamp, L. A., & Maehr, M. L. (1983). *Personal investment: Theory, assessment and application*. Revision of a paper present at AERA, Montreal, Canada.

Davidson, A. R., & Thomson, E. (1980). Cross-cultural studies on attitudes and beliefs. In H. C. Triandis & R. Brislin (Eds.), *Handbook of cross-cultural psychology* (Vol. 5). Boston: Allyn & Bacon.

De Vos, G. A. (1968). Achievement and innovation in culture and personality. In E. Norbeck, D. Price-Williams, & W. M. McCord (Eds.), *The study of personality. An interdisciplinary appraisal*. New York: Holt, Rinehart & Winston.

De Vos, G. A. (Ed.). (1973). *Socialisation for achievement: Essays on the cultural psychology of the Japanese*. Berkeley: University of California Press.

De Vos, G. A., & Caudill, W. (1973). Achievement, culture and personality: the case of Japanese-Americans. In G. DeVos (Ed.), *Socialisation for achievement. Essays on the cultural psychology of the Japanese*. Berkeley: University of California Press.

Draguns, J. G. (1979). Culture and personality. In A. J. Marsella, R. G. Tharp & T. J. Ciborowski (Eds.), *Perspectives on cross-cultural psychology*. New York: Academic Press.

Dweck, C. S., & Goetz, T. (1978). Attributions and learned helplessness. In J. H. Harvey, W. J. Ickles, & R. F. Kidd (Eds.), *New directions in attribution research* (Vol. 2). Hillsdale, NJ: Lawrence Erlbaum.

Maehr, M. L. (1974). Culture and achievement motivation. *American Psychologist, 29*, 887–896.

Maehr, M. L. (1984). Meaning and motivation. Toward a theory of personal investment. In R. Ames & C. Ames (Eds.), *Research on motivation in education: Vol. 2. Student motivation*. Orlando, FL: Academic Press.

Maehr, M. L., & Braskamp, L. A. (1986). *The motivation factor: A theory of personal investment*. Lexington, MA: Lexington.

Maehr, M. L., & Nicholls, J. C. (1980). Culture and achievement motivation: A second look. In N. Warren (Ed.), *Studies in cross-cultural psychology* (Vol. 2). London: Academic Press.

McInerney, D. M. (1988). *The psychological determinants of motivation of urban and rural non-traditional Aboriginal students in school settings: A cross-cultural study*. Unpublished doctoral dissertation presented to the University of Sydney, Australia.

McInerney, D. M. (1989). A cross-cultural analysis of students' motivation. In D. M. Keats, D. Munro, & L. Mann (Eds.), *Heterogeneity in cross-cultural psychology*. Lisse: Zwets & Zeitlinger.

McInerney, D. M. (1990). The determinants of motivation for urban Aboriginal students: A cross-cultural analysis. *Journal of Cross-Cultural Psychology, 21*, 474–495.

McInerney, D. M. (1991a). The key determinants of motivation of urban and rural non-traditional Aboriginal students in school settings: Recommendations for educational change. *Australian Journal of Education, 35*, 154–174.

McInerney, D. M. (1991b). The behavioural intentions questionnaire. An examination of face and etic validity in an educational setting. *Journal of Cross Cultural Psychology, 22*, 293–306.

McInerney, D. M., & Sinclair, K. E. (1991). Cross-cultural model testing: Inventory of School Motivation. *Educational and Psychological Measurement, 51*, 123–133.

Nie, N., & Hull, C. (1981). *SPSS update*. New York: McGraw-Hill.

Nie, N., Hull, C., Jenkins, J., Steinbrenner, K., & Bent, D. (1975). *SPSS: Statistical package for the social sciences* (2nd ed.). New York: McGraw-Hill.

Pedersen, P. (1979). Non-western psychology; the search for alternatives. In A. J. Marsella, R. G. Tharp and T. J. Ciborowski (Eds.), *Perspectives on cross-cultural psychology*. New York: Academic Press.

Weiner, B. (1974). *Achievement motivation and attribution theory*. Morristown, NJ: General Learning Press.

55

Achievement Motivation in Children of Three Ethnic Groups in the United States

Manuel Ramirez III and Douglass R. Price-Williams

In a recent article on achievement motivation, Maehr (1974) points out that McClelland's well-known work in this area (1961) has given minimal attention to the fact that motives to achieve may be actualized in different ways in different cultures. He states:

> The important principle is that achievement and achievement motivation must be understood in terms of the sociocultural context in which they are found, as well as in terms of generalized descriptions of achieving norms or abstract constructions of psychological processes (p. 894).

In addition, Maehr points out that:

> Much of the research that attempts to understand the motivational patterns of ethnic and cultural groups involves placing children in a 'middle-class-biased' performance setting and then observing behavior (p. 894).

Maehr suggests that we would do well to pursue an ethnographic approach to the study of achievement motivation in cross-cultural research. He argues for an experimental anthropology of motivation. Gallimore, Weiss, and Finney (1974) agree with this point of view.

Source: *Journal of Cross-Cultural Psychology,* 7(1) (1976): 49–60.

In reviewing research on delay of gratification, they note:

A methodological problem common to many cross-cultural, cross-ethnic investigations is the use of behavior observation classifications irrelevant or inappropriate to one or more groups about which comparative statements are made (p. 78).

De Vos (1968) has indicated that McClelland's definition of achievement motivation is based on a Western view of psychodynamics – that it is dependent on a conception of human behavior as individualistically motivated. To support his argument, De Vos cites the importance of affiliation in motivation among "successful" Japanese, indicating that in Japan, striving for success is more often motivated by a concern for the reaction of others than by the pursuit of what in the West is considered self-satisfaction. A similar orientation toward achievement was also observed among Japanese Americans (Caudill and De Vos, 1956).

Gallimore, Weiss, and Finney (1974) have noted that affiliation is critical to achievement among Hawaians. These investigators observed that Hawaiian parents socialized their children to be attentive to the concerns and expectations of others, and that this type of training makes children more responsive to affiliation and social rewards. In particular, Gallimore, Boggs, and Jordan (1974) found that young Hawaiians regard contributions to and continuing affiliation with the family system as more important goals than personal achievement and independence as these are represented by McClelland's conceptualization of achievement motivation.

The fact that Hawaiian culture and socialization emphasize identification with the family may be the critical variable in understanding why McClelland's measures for n Achievement may not be appropriate for them. McClelland's definition of n Achievement is consonant with socialization that encourages children to view themselves as individuals separate from their families. It is not likely that measures based on his definition would be appropriate for assessment of achievement motivation in most Mexican-American and Black children. We hypothesize that many Mexican-American and Black children, like Hawaiians and Japanese, are socialized to identify themselves with their family and ethnic group, and to cooperate for attainment of mutual goals: socialization in Mexican-American and Black cultures has strong affiliation components.

Recent research by Gray (1975) supports this hypothesis for Mexican-American children. Using a questionnaire, she found that Mexican-American children expressed a greater tendency to want to achieve for others than did Anglo children.

The research reported below studied achievement motivation in children of three ethnic groups in Houston, Texas: Mexican-American, Black, and Anglo. It was predicted that Mexican-American and Black children would score higher in family achievement – oriented toward achievement goals which would benefit the family or achievement for recognition from family members. It was also predicted that the Anglo children in the study would score higher on n Achievement.

Method

The subjects were 180 fourth grade children (mean age, 10.4) from Catholic parochial schools in Houston, Texas.[1, 2] Sixty children were Mexican-American, 60 Black, and 60 Anglo. Half of the subjects in each group were male, half were female. There were also equal numbers of children of the lower and middle socioeconomic classes in each sex and ethnic group. Father's occupation was used as an indicator of SES (Moore and Holtzman, 1965).

A research team administered a short questionnaire in English to all fourth-grade children at the schools from which subjects were drawn. The questionnaire contained items concerning the language(s) spoken by the child and the parents, family activities, number of persons residing in the child's home and their relationship to the child, and the size of the home. The children were also asked to draw a human figure. Those who had difficulty answering the questions or drawing the human figure were eliminated; the others were placed in a pool from which the subjects for the study were selected on the basis of ethnicity, sex, and SES.

Mexican-Americans

The majority of Mexican Americans selected for this study are bilingual. These people are well identified with the traditional Mexican-American system of values, that is, they have close ties to members of their extended families, they are familiar with both Mexican and Mexican-American history, and their interpersonal relationships are characterized by warmth and a commitment to mutual help. Child-rearing practices emphasize respect for adults, family, and religious authority, and there is strong identification with Mexican Catholic ideology. The majority of the children selected to participate in this study were second- and third-generation Americans.

Blacks

The Black residents of the areas of Houston from which our subjects were selected differ in many respects from Black populations in most urban settings in the United States. Most of these people are bilingual (French/English) and most of the adults were reared in rural areas of Louisiana. Observations of these subjects indicated an emphasis on strong ties to the extended family, respect for adults, respect for family and religious authority, and identification with the teachings of the Catholic Church.

Anglo-Americans

The majority of Anglos from which we chose our subjects were Caucasians who made no indication that they identified with their original ethnic groups. None of the children were bilingual.

Observations of the Anglo families indicated that there was a strong emphasis on encouraging children to develop identities separate from those of the family group. Children were also encouraged to be individually competitive.

Procedure

The subjects were asked to tell a story to each of seven line drawings depicting a person(s) in a setting related to education. The tester asked each child to tell the most interesting story he could think of. In composing the story, each child was asked to answer three questions: (1) What is happening? (2) What happened before? (3) How will the story end? The content of each of the seven cards in the set is as follows: (1) student and teacher, (2) student and mother, (3) student and father, (4) two students of the same ethnic group, (5) two students, one of darker complexion than the other, (6) student, parents, and principal, and (7) student studying alone. Different male and female sets of cards were constructed for each of the ethnic groups.

The subjects were tested individually in two separate sessions. Three cards were administered during the first sessions and four during the second. The subjects were tested by a member of their ethnic group. To score for n Achievement, a version of the McClelland scoring system devised by Riccuiti and Clark (1957) was abbreviated. A maximum of four points could be given for each story. One point was given for each of the following categories:[3] (1) imagery – reference made to achievement or to a goal related to achievement (competition with a standard of excellence); (2) instrumental activity – any activity independent of the original statement indicating that the character in the story is doing something to attain an achievement goal; (3) positive outcome of instrumental activity – activity leads to attainment of the achievement goal; and (4) thema – the plot of the story revolves around achievement.

The scoring categories for family achievement[4] are as follows: (1) imagery – reference made to achievement or attainment of an achievement goal (competition with a standard of excellence) from which the family would benefit or that would gain recognition from family members; (2) instrumental activity – any activity independent of the original statement that helps the character achieve for his family; (3) positive outcome of instrumental activity – activity leads to attainment of the achievement goal; and (4) thema – achievement is the central plot or theme of the story.

Those who scored the stories were trained with the manual by McClelland, Atkinson, Clark, and Lowell (Atkinson, 1958). All stories were scored blind, without knowledge of the sex or ethnic group membership of the subject.

Results

The findings listed in Table 1 show that Mexican-American and Black subjects scored higher on family achievement than did Anglo children, while Anglo children scored higher than Mexican Americans and Blacks on n Achievement.

A $3 \times 2 \times 2$ ANOVA revealed significant ethnic effects for both the family achievement ($F = 5.79$, $p < .01$) and the n Achievement data ($F = 5.73$, $p < .01$). Sex and SES effects were insignificant for both the n Achievement and family achievement data. A separate ANOVA on the n Achievement data from the three parent cards of the SSPST yielded a significant ethnic effect ($F = 6.87$, $p < .01$). Mean scores for each subgroup on these three cards are contained in Table 2.

A close examination of the data revealed that the highest scores on n Achievement were those of Mexican-American males; Mexican Americans scored lower than Anglos as a group because of the lower scores of Mexican-American females. Black and Anglo females also scored lower on n Achievement than the males of their respective groups. Females in all three ethnic groups scored higher than males on family achievement.

Results of post hoc comparisons (Tukey) showed that Mexican Americans scored significantly higher than Black Americans on n Achievement ($X_{MA} - X_{BA} = 2.39$, $p < .05$) and significantly higher than Anglos on family achievement ($X_{MA} - X_{AA} = 1.81$, $p < .05$). There was no significant difference between Anglos and Mexican Americans on n Achievement.

Table 1: Ethnic group means and standard deviations of scores on family achievement and need achievement

	Ethnic group											
	Black-American				Mexican-American				Anglo-American			
	Family achievement		Need achievement		Family achievement		Need achievement		Family achievement		Need achievement	
Sex	$\bar{X}$	S.D.	$\bar{X}$	S.D.	$\bar{X}$	S.D.	$\bar{X}$	S.D.	$\bar{X}$	S.D.	$\bar{X}$	S.D.
Male	3.11	3.75	3.13	4.22	3.51	3.29	5.77	4.62	1.65	2.27	5.65	6.72
Female	3.19	2.54	2.50	3.16	3.54	2.97	4.66	4.25	1.77	3.14	5.39	5.01

N = 30 for each group.

Table 2: Ethnic group means and standard deviations on need achievement scores on the three parent cards of the SSPST

| | Ethnic group | | | | | | | | |
| | Black-American | | | Mexican-American | | | Anglo-American | | |
Sex	N	$\bar{X}$	S.D.	N	$\bar{X}$	S.D.	N	$\bar{X}$	S.D.
Male	30	2.80	1.16	30	2.80	1.63	30	2.17	1.44
Female	30	2.23	1.17	30	3.23	1.81	30	1.83	1.41

Also, Anglo subjects scored significantly higher than Blacks on n Achievement ($X_{AA} - X_{BA} = 2.68$, p < .01), but Blacks scored significantly higher than Anglos on family achievement ($X_{BA} - X_{AA} = 1.44$, p < .05).

Discussion

The results obtained here support the contention by Maehr (1974) that contextual conditions are important in expressions of achievement motivation and that the particular form in which achievement is expressed is determined by the definition which culture gives to it. The importance of contextual conditions for eliciting achievement responses is most evident in our finding that Mexican-American and Black children tended to score higher on n Achievement than Anglo children on those cards with parental figures, but scored lower than Anglos overall.[5]

These findings seem to be in line with those obtained by Schwartz (1969) with Mexican-American children in Los Angeles. Schwartz found that Mexican Americans, in contrast to Anglo-Americans, were more concerned about adult than about peer approval of their actions.

Since the Mexican-American and Black subjects in the current study expressed achievement motivation in the form of family achievement, then, it seems likely that if more cards in the test set had contained scenes with parent figures the overall n Achievement scores of these subjects would have been higher.

The most important cultural determinant of achievement motivation, at least for the members of the three groups studied here, may be the degree to which identification with the family is encouraged in socialization. The Mexican-American and Black groups seemed to encourage children to identify with the family early in life and to remain so identified, while the Anglo group seemed to encourage children to consider themselves as separate individuals early in life.

The finding that females in all three cultural groups scored higher than males on family achievement and lower on n Achievement may indicate that the females were socialized to identify with the family more than were the males.

The discovery that Mexican-American males scored higher on n Achievement than the other subgroups and were exceeded on family achievement only by Mexican-American females may indicate that Mexican-American males have been socialized both to achieve for the self and for the family. This may be a result of the separation of the sex roles in Mexican-American culture (Madsen, 1964; Ramirez and Castaneda, 1974; also Tuddenham, Brooks, and Melkovich, 1974) and Mexican culture (Diaz-Guerrero, 1955). Researchers have indicated that Mexican and Mexican-American males are not subjected to as much pressure as females to adhere to convention and that as they get older they interact less with family members and more with persons outside the extended family. Tuddenham et al. (1974) found that Mexican-American mothers reported more sex differences in behaviors of their ten-year-old children than Black, Anglo, or Oriental mothers.

The results of this study apply only to motivation attributed to like-sexed pictures. Future research should counterbalance sex of the main character in the pictures to ensure that data are not affected by the fact that achievement in most cultures is frequently associated with the male role.

In the past, it has been all too readily concluded that Mexican Americans and Blacks have little motivation to achieve, and it has been assumed that somehow their cultures interfere with the development of this motivation. The results of the current study, however, show that the aforementioned conclusions are unjustified. That is, members of certain cultural groups may have appeared to exhibit little achievement motivation because the particular methodology used did not tap achievement motivation as interpreted by that cultural group and/or because the achievement motivation expressed was not recognized as such due to the narrow definition of achievement used.

Authors' Note

The work described in this paper was supported by a grant from the center for Research in Social Change and Economic Development, Rice University, Houston, Texas, financed under ARPA order 738. Subsequent analysis of results was supported in part by Research Grant HD 04612, NICHD, Mental Retardation Research Center, UCLA; by the California Department of Mental Hygiene; and by the University of California.

Notes

1. The authors would like to thank the Diocese of Houston for making subjects available for this study.
2. All of the schools were in neighborhoods which were ethnically homogenous and most of the instructional and administrative personnel in the schools were of the same ethnic group as the community and children.
3. The four scoring categories given above are those found by Riccuiti and Clark (1957) to have the greatest validity in scoring for n Achievement.

4. Family achievement should not be confused with s Power, as defined by McClelland et al. (1972).
5. The card that elicited most stories with family achievement themes from Mexican-American and Black children showed a child, parent, and a school principal in the principal's office. A common story to this card was the following: The child is experiencing difficulty in school or has no interest in his(her) studies; the parents are asked to go to school to confer with the principal; after the conference, the parents take an interest in the child's progress in school and ask the child to study more; this motivates the child to work hard and he(she) succeeds in school making his(her) parents proud of him(her).

References

Atkinson, J. W. [ed.] (1958) Motives in Fantasy, Action and Society. Princeton, N.J.: Van Nostrand.

Caudill, W. and G. A. De Vos (1956) "Achievement culture and personality: the case of the Japanese Americans." Amer. Anthropologist 58: 1102–1126.

De Vos, G. A. (1968) "Achievement and innovation in culture and personality," in E. Norbeck, D. Price-Williams, and W. M. McCord (eds.) Personality: An Interdisciplinary Approach. New York: Holt, Rinehart & Winston.

Diaz-Guerrero, R. (1955) "Neurosis and the Mexican family structure." Amer. J. of Psychiatry 112: 411–417.

Gallimore, R., J. W. Boggs, and C. Jordan (1974) Culture, Behavior, and Education: A Study of Hawaiian-Americans. Beverly Hills: Sage.

Gallimore, R., L. B. Weiss, and R. Finney (1974) "Cultural differences in delay of gratification: a problem of behavior classification." J. of Personality and Social Psychology 30, 1: 72–80.

Gray, T. (1975) "A bicultural approach to the issue of achievement motivation." Ph.D. Dissertation: Stanford University, School of Education.

Madsen, W. (1964) Mexican Americans of South Texas. New York: Holt, Rinehart & Winston.

Maehr, M. L. (1974) "Culture and achievement motivation." Amer. Psychologist 29: 887–895.

McClelland, D. C. (1961) The Achieving Society. New York: Free Press.

———, W. N. Davis, R. Kalin, and E. Wanner (1972) The Drinking Man. New York: Free Press.

Moore, B. M. and W. Holtzman (1965) Tomorrow's Parents: A Study of Youth and Their Families. Austin: Univ. of Texas Press.

Ramirez, M. and A. Castaneda (1974) Cultural Democracy, Bicognitive Development and Education. New York: Academic Press.

Riccuiti, H. N. and R. A. Clark (1957) A Comparison of Need-Achievement Stories Written by Experimentally "Relaxed" and "Achievement Oriented" Subjects: Effects Obtained with New Pictures and Revised Scoring Categories. Princeton, N.J.: Educational Testing Service.

Schwartz, A. J. (1969) "Comparative values and achievement of Mexican-American and Anglo pupils." Center for the Study of Evaluation, UCLA Graduate School of Education, Report No. 37.

Tuddenham, R. D., J. Brooks, and L. Melkovich (1974) "Mothers' reports of behavior of ten-year-olds: relationship with sex, ethnicity and mother's education." Developmental Psychology 10, 6: 959–995.

56

Motivation and Learning Environment Differences between Resilient and Nonresilient Latino Middle School Students

Hersholt C. Waxman, Shwu-yong L. Huang and
Yolanda N. Padrón

Although many programs and school-based interventions have been found to be effective for some types of students at risk of failure, these programs and interventions have not necessarily been effective for Latino students because programs need to specifically address many of the concerns of these students. Furthermore, even within the general Latino population, it cannot be assumed that all Latino students have similar backgrounds, motivation, and perceptions toward school (Reyes & Valencia, 1993). Some Latino students, for example, have been very successful academically in school, whereas other Latino students have experienced failure and despair in school. Consequently, it may be necessary to first look at Latino students who have done well in school and then see how they differ from less successful Latino students. One area of research that has important implications for the educational improvement of Latino students is that of examining *resilient* students, or students who succeed in school despite the presence of adverse conditions (Gordon & Song, 1994; Matsen, 1994; McMillan & Reed, 1994; Wang & Gordon, 1994; Winfield, 1991). Although the resilience construct has been widely used in areas like developmental psychopathology (Garmezy, 1991; Matsen, 1994; Matsen, Best, & Garmezy, 1990;

Source: *Hispanic Journal of Behavioral Sciences*, 19(2) (1997): 137–155.

Rutter, 1987, 1990), its application to educational phenomena has been fairly recent. Wang, Haertel, and Walberg (1994) defined *educational resilience* as "the heightened likelihood of success in school and other life accomplishments despite environmental adversities brought about by early traits, conditions, and experiences" (p. 46). Alva (1991) used the term *academic invulnerability* to describe students who "sustain high levels of achievement motivation and performance, despite the presence of stressful events and conditions that place them at risk of doing poorly in school and ultimately dropping out of school" (p. 19).

Some Latino students do well in school despite coming from at-risk environments, and it is important to know why these resilient students succeed, whereas other Latino students (i.e., nonresilient students) from equally stressful environments do not. This approach is important because it focuses on the predictors of academic success rather than on academic failure. This focus may also help us design more effective educational interventions because it enables us to specifically identify those alterable factors that distinguish resilient and nonresilient students. The research thrust in this area is to extend previous studies that merely identified and categorized students at risk and to shift to studies that focus on identifying potential individual and school processes that lead to and foster success (Winfield, 1991). In other words, the construct of educational resilience is not viewed as a fixed attribute of some students but, rather, as alterable processes or mechanisms that can be developed and fostered for all students. Fixed attributes of individuals such as students' ability have not been found to be characteristic of resilient students (Bernard, 1993; Gordon & Song, 1994; Matsen et al., 1990). On the other hand, there are several alterable processes or characteristics that have been found to be associated with resilient children. Bernard (1993), for example, maintained that there are four attributes or personal characteristics that resilient children have: (a) social competence like responsiveness, (b) problem-solving skills, (c) autonomy, and (d) a sense of purpose. McMillan and Reed (1994) described four factors that appear to be related to resiliency: (a) individual attributes, (b) positive use of time, (c) family, and (d) school. There have been very few studies, however, that have actually compared resilient and nonresilient Latino students on these characteristics. Furthermore, the research in this area has not typically used the resilience construct. Instead, it has generally focused on characteristics that have differentiated more successful and less successful students.

In one such study, Alva (1991) examined the characteristics of a cohort of 10th-grade Mexican American students and found that successful or invulnerable students reported higher levels of educational support from their teachers and friends and were more likely to "(a) feel encouraged and prepared to attend college, (b) enjoy coming to school and being involved in high school activities, (c) experience fewer conflicts and difficulties in their intergroup relations with other students, and (d) experience fewer family conflicts and difficulties" (p. 31). She also supported the view that research on students at risk needs to focus on aspects of school success rather than school failure. She also maintained that educational policies need to focus on expanding both the protective resources and students' subjective appraisals (e.g., perceptions or attitudes toward their classroom environment).

In a study designed to understand successful high school students, Reyes and Jason (1993) examined factors that distinguished the success and failure of Latino students from an inner-city high school. Based on their 9th-grade attendance rate and academic achievement, they identified 24 10th-grade students as being at high risk for dropping out of school and 24 students as at low risk. They individually interviewed each participant on a number of topics that covered four areas: (a) family background, (b) family support, (c) overall school satisfaction, and (d) gang pressures. They found that there were no differences between the two groups on (a) socioeconomic status, (b) parent-student involvement, and (c) parental supervision. Low-risk students, however, reported significantly more satisfaction with their school than did high-risk students. On the other hand, high-risk students were more likely to respond that they had (a) been invited to join a gang and (b) brought a weapon to school.

The two studies previously described are examples of the growing body of research trying to address the issue of why some Latino students do well in school and succeed in school, whereas others have not been successful. One concern with these studies, however, is that they typically use only one indicator of success (e.g., grades or achievement data for 1 year) rather than measures that more accurately reflect the construct of educational resilience or being successful over time despite attending at-risk school environments. Furthermore, these studies do not examine important psychosocial behaviors that have been found to significantly influence students' cognitive and affective outcomes and several key motivational variables, like achievement motivation and academic self-concept.

Purpose of the Present Study

Although basic skills deficiencies are often cited as the most critical educational problem for Latino students and other students at risk of failure (Slavin, 1989), fostering or maintaining an effective classroom learning environment has been suggested as a means of enabling them to be successful in school (Chavez, 1988; Padrón, 1992; Pierce, 1994). There have been a few studies that have looked at the classroom learning environment of students at risk of academic failure (Duncan & Newby, 1993; Pierce, 1994; Waxman 1989; Waxman, Huang, Knight, & Owens, 1992), but those studies have not specifically compared resilient and nonresilient students' perceptions of their classroom learning environment and instructional learning environment in inner-city schools. Similarly, there have been very few studies that have examined the classroom learning environment of Latino students (Padrón, 1992). It is especially important to examine the learning environment of Latino students because there is some preliminary evidence that they perceive their learning environments very differently from English-monolingual students (Padrón, 1989) and African American students (Waxman, 1989). Furthermore, several studies have found that students perceive that there are differences in the ways high and low achievers are treated in the classroom (Babad, 1990; Weinstein, 1983, 1989; Weinstein & Middlestadt, 1979).

Another concern with the prior research in the field is that most of the studies on learning environments have not included measures of students' motivation and aspirations. It is important to include students' motivation and aspirations as important aspects of the learning environment because they have been found to be highly related to both students' academic achievement and the classroom learning environment (Cheng, 1994; Knight & Waxman, 1990, 1991; Uguroglu & Walberg, 1986). Furthermore, the variables of student motivation and classroom learning environments have often been researched and discussed separately, but they are so closely related conceptually that they need to be empirically examined together (Knight & Waxman, 1990). Only a limited number of studies, however, have investigated both the classroom learning environment and students' motivation.

The purpose of the present study is to compare resilient and nonresilient Latino students' motivation and classroom learning environment in mathematics. In addition, other important background characteristics such as academic aspirations, attendance record, and student' personal time allocation are examined between the two student groups because they have previously been found to be important variables that are related to students' academic achievement (Dossey, Mullis, Lindquist, & Chambers, 1988). Furthermore, grade-and sex-related differences are examined in the present study because they have been previously found to affect at-risk students' attitudes of their classroom environment (Duncan & Newby, 1993; Waxman & Eash, 1983).

This study specifically addresses the following research questions:

1. Are there significant differences between resilient and nonresilient Latino students on background characteristics, academic aspirations, attendance records, and time allocation?
2. Are there significant differences between resilient and nonresilient Latino students on the dimensions of academic self-concept, achievement motivation, involvement, affiliation, satisfaction, and parent involvement?
3. Are there significant differences in the dimensions of academic self-concept, achievement motivation, involvement, affiliation, satisfaction, and parent involvement by students' sex and grade level?
4. To what extent do students' background characteristics, classroom and instructional learning environment, and motivation discriminate resilient from nonresilient students?

Methods

Participants

The present study was conducted in the five middle schools of a multicultural school district located in a major metropolitan city in the south central region of the United States. The school district was selected because it had relatively equal representations of Latino, African American, Asian Americans, and White students in each school and classroom. About 25% of the students enrolled in the district were Latinos, 30% were Whites (i.e., White, non-Latino), 25% were African Americans, and 20% were Asian Americans. In addition, this district was selected because Latino students represented an unsuccessful minority group. Latino middle school students in this district scored significantly lower than all other ethnic groups on statewide standardized achievement tests in mathematics and on the district-administered Four-Step Problem Solving Test (Hofmann, 1986). Furthermore, Latino students in this district had a significantly higher drop-out rate than all the other ethnic groups. Finally, we selected this school district because there is no tracking and students are heterogeneously grouped for mathematics. In other words, each mathematics class would generally include both resilient and nonresilient students.

The majority of these middle school Latino students are foreign born, and the second largest number of these students were born in the United States but entered elementary school speaking a primary language other than English. Both groups of students typically received limited primary language instruction and were generally placed in submersion classroom environments with little special assistance. Most of the Latino students in the district came from working-class families. Most of these Latino parents do not have high school degrees, but they do have stable jobs in this urban community that has a large number of thriving businesses located within it.

Despite the fact that school district is classified by the state as below average in property wealth, only 15% of the students come from low-income families. There is a very strong academic orientation in this district, as evidenced by the facts that nearly two thirds of the students in the district attend college, and only 6% of the students drop out of school. Furthermore, the composite standardized achievement test scores for middle school students in the district show students scoring at around the 70th percentile.

Instruments

The following three standardized instruments were adapted and incorporated for use in the present study: (a) the Multidimensional Motivational Instrument (MMI; Uguroglu, Schiller, & Walberg, 1981; Uguroglu & Walberg, 1986),

(b) the Classroom Environment Scale (CES; Fraser, 1982, 1986), and (c) the Instructional Learning Environment Questionnaire (ILEQ; Knight & Waxman, 1989, 1990). All of the items on these instruments were modified to a personal form in the present study, which elicits an individual student's responses to his or her role in their mathematics class, rather than a student's perception of the class as a whole (Fraser, 1991).

The Achievement Motivation and Academic Self-Concept scales from the MMI were used in the present study. The instrument has been found to have test-retest reliability and construct and predictive validity (Uguroglu et al., 1981; Uguroglu & Walberg, 1986). The Achievement Motivation scale measures the extent to which students feel the intrinsic desire to succeed and earn good grades in mathematics, and the Academic Self-Concept scale measures the extent to which students exhibit pride in their classwork and expect to do well in mathematics.

The CES is a questionnaire that has been widely used in a variety of different educational settings to measure students' perceptions of their relationships with students and teachers as well as the organizational structure of the classroom. The content and concurrent validities of the CES have been established through correlational studies and classroom observation (Fisher & Fraser, 1983; Fraser, 1982, 1986; Moos, 1979). Adequate internal consistency reliability coefficients were also obtained in previous studies (Fisher & Fraser, 1983; Fraser, 1982, 1986; Moos, 1979). For the present study, the two scales that were used were (a) the Involvement scale, which measures the extent to which students participate actively and attentively in their mathematics class, and (b) the Affiliation scale, which measures the extent to which students know, help, and are friendly toward each other in their mathematics class.

The ILEQ measures students' perceptions of several aspects of their instructional learning environment. It has been found to have adequate internal consistency reliability coefficients and test-retest reliability coefficients (Knight & Waxman, 1989, 1990; Waxman et al., 1992). For the present study, the two scales that were used were (a) the Satisfaction scale, which measures the extent of students' enjoyment of their mathematics class and school work in mathematics, and (b) the Parent Involvement scale, which measures the extent to which parents are interested and involved in what their children are doing in mathematics.

Each scale from the three instruments includes four items, and all of the items were measured on a 4-point, Likert-type scale ranging from 1 (*not at all true*) to 2 (*not very true*) to 3 (*sort of true*) to 4 (*very true*). Student responses to each item within the same scale were added and averaged. Consequently, a mean value of 4 indicates that the student responded favorably with the scale, whereas a mean value of 1 indicates that the student responded unfavorably to the scale.

Several background items selected from the National Educational Longitudinal Study of 1988 (NELS:88) were also included in the final study survey (Hafner, Ingels, Schneider, & Stevenson, 1990). These items included questions about students' (a) background characteristics (e.g., mathematics grades), (b) academic aspirations (e.g., how far they will go in school), (c) attendance (e.g., number of days missed), and (e) time allocation (e.g., time spent on homework).

Students' mathematics achievement was measured using the Four-Step Problem Solving Test (Hofmann, 1986). This test consists of 10 nonroutine mathematics problems, each with four related questions: (a) reading to understand the problem, (b) selecting a strategy, (c) solving the problem, and (d) reviewing and extending the problem. It is a multiple-choice, paper-and-pencil test designed to measure problem-solving mathematics skills of middle school students. The range for the total test is 0 to 40. The school district in the present study annually administers the Four-Step Problem Solving Test to all middle school students to assess their problem-solving achievement in mathematics, which is the district's top priority in mathematics.

Procedures

The scales from the three instruments and the background items from the NELS:88 survey were combined into one survey and were administered concurrently by trained researchers near the end of the school year during students' regular mathematics class. We selected two scales from each of the three instruments because the school district only allowed us about 45 minutes to administer the combined survey instrument. Students were informed by the researchers that they were not tests and that completed questionnaires would not be seen by their teachers or other school personnel. All middle school students in the district were asked to complete the questionnaire as part of an ongoing evaluation of the mathematics curriculum. The response rate for the student questionnaire was about 97%, and it took students approximately 40 minutes to complete.

From the entire population of Latino students in the district who completed the questionnaire, a stratified sample of 60 resilient and 60 nonresilient Latino students were randomly selected to be included in the present study. Students identified as *gifted or talented, special education*, or *developmental* were excluded from the population to avoid potential effects related to ability differences. Students were classified as resilient if they (a) scored on or above the 75th percentile on the district-administered, standardized Four-Step Problem Solving Test over a 2-year period and (b) reported receiving A's or B's in mathematics over a 2-year period. Students were classified as nonresilient if they (a) scored on or below the 25th percentile on the Four-Step Problem Solving Test for a 2-year period, (b) reported receiving C's, D's, or F's for mathematics this year, and (c) reported receiving B's, C's, D's, or F's in mathematics the previous year. A stratified sampling technique was used to obtain an equal number of students by sex and grade within each student group (i.e., resilient or nonresilient).

Chi-square tests were used to compare the frequencies of responses between resilient and nonresilient students on the background items from the NELS:88 survey. A three-way multivariate analysis of variance (MANOVA) was used to determine (a) whether there are motivational and perceptional differences by students' sex, grade, and student classification (resilient or nonresilient) and (b) whether there are any interaction effects by sex, student classification, and/or grade level. As a follow-up procedure, univariate analysis of variance (ANOVA) and post hoc multiple comparison tests were also performed to determine where the significant differences were. Finally, descriptive discriminant analysis was used to determine the extent to which the two groups differ with respect to their classroom learning environment, instructional learning environment, motivation, and background characteristics.

To ensure adequate reliability and validity of the six scales used in this study, internal consistency (Cronbach alpha) reliability and discriminant validity (correlations between scales) were conducted. These coefficients were calculated using the individual student as unit of statistical analysis. The results indicated that the mean alpha coefficient of these scales was .60, and the individual coefficients ranged from .42 to .73, indicating that the survey instrument has adequate reliability given the few number of items per scale. The mean correlation between the scales was .29, and the individual correlations between scales ranged from .11 to .59, indicating that the survey instrument has adequate discriminant validity. We also examined the reliability and validity coefficients separately for resilient and nonresilient students but did not find any substantial differences between the two groups of students.

Results

The descriptive and chi-square results for the two student groups revealed that there were no significant differences between the two groups on whether they spoke a non-English language before they started school, $\chi^2(1) = 1.35$, $p = .256$. About 76% of the resilient students indicated that they spoke a language other than English before they started school, whereas about 67% of the nonresilient students responded that they also spoke a language other than English before starting school. There were, however, statistically significant differences between the two groups on the extent to which students were held back a grade in school, $\chi^2(1) = 23.48, p = .000$. About 53% of the nonresilient students indicated that they were held back a grade in school, compared with only 13% of resilient students.

There were significant differences between the two student groups on their academic aspirations. Resilient students were significantly more likely to indicate that they were sure that they would graduate from high school,

$\chi^2(2) = 17.01, p = .000$, and they were significantly more likely to respond that they would graduate college and attend graduate schools, $\chi^2(4) = 29.00$, $p = .000$. About 78% of the resilient students indicated that they would graduate from high school, compared with only 43% of the nonresilient students. Similarly, over 90% of the resilient students indicated that they would graduate college or attend graduate school, compared with only about 46% of the nonresilient students. There were also significant differences between the two groups on attendance records. Resilient students were less likely to report cutting or skipping classes, $\chi^2(3) = 10.53, p = .015$, and being late for school than nonresilient students, $\chi^2(4) = 21.87, p = .000$. There were statistically significant differences between the two groups on two of the time allocation items. Resilient students reported that they spent significantly more time doing mathematics homework each week than nonresilient students, $\chi^2(4) = 11.71, p = .020$. Resilient students also indicated that they spent more time on additional reading than nonresilient students, $\chi^2(4) = 21.81, p = .000$. There were no significant differences between the two groups on the amount of time they spent watching television on weekends, $\chi^2(4) = 4.03, p = .402$, or during the weekdays, $\chi^2(4) = 4.89, p = .298$, and on the amount of time spent listening to CDs, tapes, or the radio, $\chi^2(4) = 7.54, p = .110$.

The three-way MANOVA results indicated that there are significant main effects of group and grade on middle school students' motivation and perceptions of their learning environment. Resilient students' overall motivation and perceptions of their mathematics classroom learning environment were significantly different from those of less resilient students, $F(6, 103) = 7.36, p = .0001$. Students' overall motivation and perceptions of their learning environment also differed by grade, $F(12, 206) = 1.97, p = .0280$. There were, however, no significant main effects for sex, or interaction effects of (a) group by sex, (b) group by grade, (c) sex by grade, or (d) group by sex and grade.

The descriptive and univariate ANOVA results for students' motivation and perceptions by group and grade revealed that resilient students had significantly higher perceptions of involvement, $F(1, 108) = 33.52, p = .000$, satisfaction, $F(1, 108) = 15.48, p = .000$, academic self-concept, $F(1, 108) = 28.10, p = .000$, and achievement motivation, $F(1, 108) = 13.15, p = .000$, than nonresilient students. There were no significant differences between the two groups of students on the Affiliation, $F(1, 108) = 3.18, p = .077$, and Parent Involvement, $F(1, 108) = 0.13, p = .718$, scales. With the exception of parent involvement, the mean values for the resilient students were over 3.0, which indicates a highly positive attitude and motivation. With the exception of affiliation, the mean values on the scales for the nonresilient students ranged from 2.6 to 2.9. These values are slightly higher than 2.5 median value, which indicates that nonresilient students had slightly higher than average perceptions and motivation. The standard deviations were similar for the two groups, with the exception of achievement motivation for which nonresilient students had greater variation among their responses.

In regard to the grade-related differences, sixth-grade students reported significantly higher involvement than seventh-grade students, $F(2, 108) = 5.20$, $p = .007$. Eighth-grade students also reported significantly higher achievement motivation than seventh-grade students, $F(2, 108) = 3.40$, $p = .037$. There were no significant differences on the Affiliation, $F(2, 108) = 2.48$, $p = .088$, Satisfaction, $F(2, 108) = 2.35$, $p = .100$, Parent Involvement, $F(2, 108) = 0.91$, $p = .405$, and Academic Self-Concept scales, $F(2, 108) = 0.77$, $p = .464$, among the three grade levels. The standard deviations were generally similar across the three grade levels.

A discriminant function analysis was performed to determine the extent to which the two groups differ with respect to their classroom learning environment, instructional learning environment, motivation, and background characteristics. To reduce the large number of variables examined in this study to a more parsimonious model, only those variables that were previously found to differ significantly between the two groups were entered directly into a discriminant model to see how well they were able to discriminate between the two groups of students. Descriptive discriminant analysis was used instead of predictive discriminant analysis because the purpose of the analysis was to describe the MANOVA results (Huberty & Barton, 1989).

The direct entry model examines the independent contribution of each of the variables in determining group membership. The model produced a Wilks's lambda of .501, $F(12,107) = 8.87$, which was statistically significant at the $p < .0001$ level. The discriminant function had a canonical correlation of .71, indicating a moderately strong relationship between the groups and the discriminant function. The squared canonical correlation coefficient for the model was .50, indicating that about 50% of the variance between the two groups can be explained by the 12 variables in this model. A classification matrix revealed that overall, 86% of the cases were correctly classified, with 90% of the resilient student cases correctly classified and 83% of the nonresilient student cases correctly classified.

The standardized discriminant function coefficients describe the impact or independent contribution of a given variable on the grouping variable, holding constant the impact of all the other discriminating variables. The results indicated that the variables of not held back in school, academic aspirations, and expectations for high school graduation were found to have the greatest impact, after adjusting for all the other variables in the analysis. The variables time spent on homework and academic self-concept were found to have the least impact on the grouping variable.

The canonical structure coefficients for each variable provide an indication of the relative contribution of each variable to the overall discriminant function. It describes how closely a variable and the discriminant function are related. The results indicated that 10 of the 12 independent variables included in the discriminant analysis were found to have structure coefficient values of .40 or greater and have the greatest practical significance for distinguishing between resilient and nonresilient students. These variables are academic aspirations, involvement, academic self-concept, expectations for high school graduation, not held back in school, satisfaction, late for school, time spent reading additional material, achievement motivation, and time spent on homework. Only the variables of days missed in school and cut or skipped class do not appear to be highly related to the discriminant function.

Discussion

In the present study, we specifically focused on Latino middle school students from a multicultural, metropolitan school district and found that their motivation and psychosocial processes significantly differed between resilient and nonresilient students. Despite coming from the same school environment and similar home environments, some Latino students have done exceptionally well in their mathematics classes, whereas others have done quite poorly. As expected, we also found that resilient students are much more motivated than their nonresilient classmates and that they are much more satisfied and involved with their mathematics classes. These findings are similar to other studies that have found that student satisfaction differentiates resilient and nonresilient students (Alva, 1991; Reyes & Jason, 1993).

Another interesting finding of the present study was that there was not a statistically significant difference between resilient and nonresilient students on the extent to which they spoke a language other than English before arriving at school. About 76% of the resilient students and 67% of the nonresilient students spoke a non-English language before they started going to school. This finding lends supports to other studies that have similarly found that language factors are not significant predictors and do not hinder Latino secondary students' academic achievement (Adams, Astone, Nunez-Wormack, & Smodlaka, 1994; Buriel & Cardoza, 1988).

Unlike previous studies, the findings from the present investigation did not reveal any sex-related differences. The grade-related differences found in this study revealed that sixth-grade students were more involved than seventh-grade students and that eighth-grade students had higher achievement motivation than seventh-grade students. Although not statistically significant, seventh-grade students were also found to be less satisfied with their mathematics class than sixth- and eighth-grade students. Additional studies may want to specifically investigate why seventh-grade Latino students have lower perceptions than other middle school students. Curriculum factors and/or instructional processes may need to be explored.

Another important finding from this study related to the high academic aspirations held by resilient Latino students. Although the findings for the nonresilient Latino students are very similar to the overall national results for Hispanic students from the NELS:88 (Peng, Wright, & Hill, 1995), the results for resilient students are much higher. Although there were no significant differences found between resilient and nonresilient students on their perceptions of parental involvement, which measures aspects of (a) parental interest (e.g., "My parents are often interested in what I do in mathematics") and (b) parent expectations (e.g., "My parents expect me to do well in mathematics"), it is still possible that there might be differences in parents' aspirations for their children. Another possible explanation for resilient Latino students' high aspirations stems from the overall high academic press and expectations for students in the district.

After all the quantitative data were collected, we informally asked two of the middle school mathematics teachers to help us explain why resilient students do significantly better in mathematics and have higher academic aspirations. They cited several personality traits like persistence and positive work habits that they thought distinguished resilient from nonresilient students. We specifically asked them about family characteristics that might distinguish the two groups of students, but they could not identify any family demographics that they thought were different. Further studies, however, may need to explicitly focus on students' home and family characteristics.

Students can be exposed to inappropriate educational experiences in either the family, school, or community (Pallas, Natriello, & McDill, 1989). Community demographics and family conditions, however, cannot be greatly changed by educators, whereas educational policy and practice can be modified to improve the education of students at risk (Comer, 1987; Waxman, 1992). Policymakers, administrators, teachers, and parents need to know why some students are successful and do well in school, whereas other students (a) from identical socioeconomic backgrounds, (b) from similar home environments, (c) with similar ability, and (d) from the same schools and classrooms do not do well academically. Examining these factors will allow us to investigate the circumstances that place these students at risk as well as those processes or factors that foster success. One of the major advantages of the approach of studying educational resilience is that it shifts us away from the educational research and policy perspective that has primarily focused on school failure and predictors of school failure to one that now focuses on the academic success of students who come from disadvantaged circumstances.

In the present study, we examined indicators of at least four important factors that McMillan and Reed (1994) identified as being related to resiliency: (a) individual attributes, such as students' motivation; (b) school and classroom factors, like satisfaction, involvement, and affiliation; (c) family factors, like parent involvement; and (d) positive use of time, like doing homework. Future studies should investigate other indicators of these four factors as well as examine other variables or factors that differentiate resilient and nonresilient Latino students. Nelson-LeGall and Jones (1991), for example, argue that classroom help-seeking behavior is a strategy or skill that allows learners to cope with academic difficulties and thus become a protective mechanism in the classroom learning context. Clark (1991) similarly suggests that social identity and support networks are resilient behaviors that need to be fostered and developed by students, and Barbarin (1993) maintains that we need to focus on the coping processes students use to mediate risk factors. These variables and others, like peer-group support, problem-solving skills, and students' cognitive learning strategies, need to be explored in future studies.

Although the present study specifically focused on examining motivational and psychosocial differences between resilient and nonresilient Latino students, other theoretical and conceptual work in the area has focused on the processes and mechanisms that can be developed and altered to facilitate students' resilient behaviors. Rutter (1987, 1990), for example, has identified four processes that can be developed to facilitate resiliency: (a) reducing the risk impact and changing students' exposure to the risk, (b) reducing the negative chain reactions that often follow exposure to risks, (c) improving students' self-efficacy or self-esteem, and (d) opening up or creating new opportunities for students. Matsen (1994) has similarly described four strategies for fostering resiliency: (a) reducing vulnerability and risk, (b) reducing stressors, (c) increasing available resources, and (d) mobilizing protective processes. Swanson and Spencer (1991) provide some specific suggestions for enhancing most of these resiliency processes. They maintain that to reduce the risk impact, we should (a) increase access to academically challenging programs for disadvantaged students, (b) forge alliances between schools, churches, organizations, and businesses, and (c) increase funding for early childhood programs. To reduce negative chain reactions, Swanson and Spencer argue that teacher training, teacher recruitment, and teacher retention need to be addressed and altered, and parent involvement in schools also needs to be increased. To improve students' self-efficacy, they argue that schools should recognize and demand academic performance and also redesign classrooms into heterogeneous ability groups rather than track by ability level. Finally, to open up opportunities, they maintain that there should be increased funding for compensatory education, student financial aid, pilot programs, and updated technological equipment. They also call for integrating resources from schools, businesses, and communities to help students make a smooth transition from the school to work environment. Although the results of the present causal-comparative study do not allow us to lend support to Rutter's (1987, 1990), Matsen's (1994), and Swanson and Spencer's (1991) research, the findings from this study suggest that future experimental studies examining areas such as improving students' motivation and self-efficacy may be warranted.

An important methodological consideration that needs to be examined in other studies is the criteria chosen to define educationally resilient and nonresilient Latino students. Several specific criteria were chosen for the present study. First, standardized achievement test scores for a 2-year period were used. Because the construct of educational resilience suggests sustained success or success over time, it is important that at least two measures of achievement over time are used. Standardized test scores are admittedly a narrow measure of students' achievement, but they do represent one of the primary outcomes that school districts use to assess their educational accomplishments. The addition of student grades as a criterion helps support the success criteria. Again, we used grades from a 2-year period to examine the resilient criteria. Resilient students received A's or B's for a 2-year period, whereas nonresilient students typically received C's or less for the 2-year period.

Finally, the selection of only mathematics test scores suggests that a student may be educationally resilient in one content or subject area but not resilient in another. Given the large body of research that has found that there are content-specific attitudinal, instructional, curricular, and achievement differences for students (Needels & Gage, 1991; Stodolsky, 1988; Stodolsky & Grossman, 1995), it may be important to conduct content-specific research on resilience before we determine whether or not educational resilience is a content-specific or generic phenomenon. In other words, additional studies should examine if educational resilience is content specific (i.e., different according to the content area examined) or generic (i.e., similar across all content areas).

Although the findings from the present study have some important educational implications, further descriptive, correlational, and especially experimental research is needed to verify these results. Longitudinal studies are also essential to adequately study the educational resilience phenomena. It is important to investigate at what point resilience develops, and it is also necessary to look at the long-term stability of the construct. Further studies also need to specifically examine how aspects of the classroom learning environment and instructional learning environment can be changed so that they can serve as protective mechanisms for students in at-risk school environments (Waxman, 1992). In addition, affective or motivational training programs may need to be developed and implemented to see if they improve Latino students' affective and cognitive outcomes. These and similar issues should be examined so that we can continue to understand why some Latino students are resilient and how we can help other students develop resiliency and become more successful.

References

Adams, D., Astone, B., Nunez-Wormack, E., & Smodlaka, I. (1994). Predicting the academic achievement of Puerto Rican and Mexican-American ninth-grade students. *Urban Review, 26*, 1–14.

Alva, S. A. (1991). Academic invulnerability among Mexican-American students: The importance of protective and resources and appraisals. *Hispanic Journal of Behavioral Sciences, 13*, 18–34.

Babad, E. (1990). Measuring and changing teachers' differential behavior as perceived by students and teachers. *Journal of Educational Psychology, 82*, 683–690.

Barbarin, O. A. (1993). Coping and resilience: Exploring the inner lives of African American children. *Journal of Black Psychology, 19*, 478–492.

Bernard, B. (1993). Fostering resiliency in kids. *Educational Leadership, 51*(3), 44–48.

Buriel, R., & Cardoza, D. (1988). Sociocultural correlates of achievement among three generations of Mexican American high school students. *American Educational Research Journal, 25*, 177–192.

Chavez, R. C. (1988). Theoretical issues relevant to bilingual multicultural climate research. *Educational Issues of Language Minority Students, 3*, 5–14.

Cheng, Y. C. (1994). Classroom environment and student affective performance: An effective profile. *Journal of Experimental Education, 62*, 221–239.

Clark, M. L. (1991). Social identity, peer relations, and academic competence of African-American adolescents. *Education and Urban Society, 24*, 41–52.

Comer, J. P. (1987). New Haven's school community connection. *Educational Leadership, 44*(6), 13–16.

Dossey, J. A., Mullis, I. V. S., Lindquist, M. M., & Chambers, D. L. (1988). *The mathematics report card: Trends and achievement based on the 1986 national assessment* (Rep. No. 17-M-01). Princeton, NJ: National Assessment of Educational Progress.

Duncan, L., & Newby, R. (1993). Attitudes of at-risk students toward their school environment. *Texas Researcher, 4*, 39–46.

Fisher, D. L., & Fraser, B. J. (1983). Validity and use of Classroom Environment Scale. *Educational Evaluation and Policy Analysis, 5*, 261–271.

Fraser, B. J. (1982). Development of short forms of several classroom environment scales. *Journal of Educational Measurement, 19*, 221–227.

Fraser, B. J. (1986). *Classroom environment*. London: Croom Helm.

Fraser, B. J. (1991). Validity and use of classroom environment instruments. *Journal of Classroom Interaction, 26*(2), 5–11.

Garmezy, N. (1991). Resilience and vulnerability to adverse developmental outcomes associated with poverty. *American Behavioral Scientist, 34*, 416–430.

Gordon, E. W., & Song, L. D. (1994). Variations in the experience of resilience. In M. C. Wang & E. W. Gordon (Eds.), *Educational resilience in inner-city America: Challenges and prospects* (pp. 27–43). Hillsdale, NJ: Lawrence Erlbaum.

Hafner, A., Ingels, S., Schneider, B., & Stevenson, D. (1990). *A profile of the American eighth grader: NELS:88 Student descriptive summary*. Washington, DC: U.S. Department of Education, National Center for Educational Statistics.

Hofmann, P. S. (1986). *Construction and validation of a testing instrument to measure problem-solving skills of students*. Unpublished doctoral dissertation, Temple University, Philadelphia.

Huberty, C. J., & Barton, R. M. (1989). An introduction to discriminant analysis. *Measurement and Evaluation in Counseling and Development, 2*, 158–168.

Knight, S. L., & Waxman, H. C. (1989, January). *Development and validation of the instructional learning environment questionnaire*. Paper presented at the annual meeting of the Southwest Educational Research Association, Houston, TX.

Knight, S. L., & Waxman, H. C. (1990). Investigating the effects of the classroom learning environment on students' motivation in social studies. *Journal of Social Studies Research, 14*, 1–12.

Knight, S. L., & Waxman, H. C. (1991). Students' cognition and classroom instruction. In H. C. Waxman & H. J. Walberg (Eds.), *Effective teaching: Current research* (pp. 239–255). Berkeley, CA: McCutchan.

Matsen, A. S. (1994). Resilience in individual development: Successful adaptation despite risk and adversity. In M. C. Wang & E. W. Gordon (Eds.), *Educational resilience in inner-city America: Challenges and prospects* (pp. 3–25). Hillsdale, NJ: Lawrence Erlbaum.

Matsen, A. S., Best, K. M., & Garmezy, N. (1990). Resilience and development: Contributions from the study of children who overcome adversity. *Development and Psychopathology, 2*, 425–444.

McMillan, J. H., & Reed, D. F. (1994). At-risk students and resiliency: Factors contributing to academic success. *The Clearing House, 67*, 137–140.

Moos, R. H. (1979). *Evaluating educational environments: Procedures, measures, findings, and policy implications.* San Francisco: Jossey-Bass.

Needels, M., & Gage, N. L. (1991). Essence and accident in process-product research on teaching. In H. C. Waxman & H. J. Walberg (Eds.), *Effective teaching: Current research* (pp. 3–31). Berkeley, CA: McCutchan.

Nelson-LeGall, S., & Jones, E. (1991). Classroom help-seeking behavior of African-American children. *Education and Urban Society, 24*, 27–40.

Padrón, Y. N. (1989, April). *A comparison of bilingual and English-monolingual students' perceptions of their classroom learning environment in reading.* Paper presented at the annual meeting of the American Educational Research Association, San Francisco.

Padrón, Y. N. (1992). Comparing bilingual and monolingual students' perceptions of their classroom learning environment. In H. C. Waxman & C. D. Ellett (Eds.), *The study of learning environments* (Vol. 5, pp. 108–113). Houston: University of Houston.

Pallas, A. M., Natriello, G., & McDill, E. L. (1989). The changing nature of the disadvantaged: Current dimensions and future trends. *Educational Researcher, 18*(5), 16–22.

Peng, S. S., Wright, D., & Hill, S. T. (1995). *Understanding racial-ethnic differences in secondary school science and mathematics.* Washington, DC: National Center for Education Statistics.

Pierce, C. (1994). Importance of classroom climate for at-risk learners. *Journal of Educational Research, 88*, 37–42.

Reyes, O., & Jason, L. A. (1993). Pilot study examining factors associated with academic success for Hispanic high school students. *Journal of Youth and Adolescence, 22*, 57–71.

Reyes, P., & Valencia, R. R. (1993). Educational policy and the growing Latino student population: Problems and prospects. *Hispanic Journal of Behavioral Sciences, 15*, 258–283.

Rutter, M. (1987). Psychosocial resilience and protective mechanisms. *American Journal of Orthopsychiatry, 37*, 317–331.

Rutter, M. (1990). Psychosocial resilience and protective mechanisms. In J. Rolf, A. Masten, D. Cichetti, K. Nuechterlein, & S. Weintraub (Eds.), *Risk and protective factors in the development of psychopathology* (pp. 181–214). New York: Cambridge University Press.

Slavin, R. E. (1989). Students at risk of school failure: The problem and its dimensions. In R. E. Slavin, N. L. Karweit, & N. A. Madden (Eds.), *Effective programs for students at risk* (pp. 3–19). Boston: Allyn & Bacon.

Stodolsky, S. S. (1988). *The subject matters: Classroom activity in math and social studies.* Chicago: University of Chicago.

Stodolsky, S. S., & Grossman, P. L. (1995). The impact of subject matter on curricular activity: An analysis of five academic subjects. *American Educational Research Journal, 32*, 227–249.

Swanson, D. P., & Spencer, M. B. (1991). Youth policy, poverty, and African-Americans: Implications for resilience. *Education and Urban Society, 24*, 148–161.

Uguroglu, M. E., Schiller, D. P., & Walberg, H. J. (1981). A multidimensional motivational instrument. *Psychology in the Schools, 18*, 279–285.

Uguroglu, M. E., & Walberg, H. J. (1986). Predicting achievement and motivation. *Journal of Research and Development in Education, 19*, 1–12.

Wang, M. C., & Gordon, E. W. (Eds.). (1994). *Educational resilience in inner-city America: Challenges and prospects.* Hillsdale, NJ: Lawrence Erlbaum.

Wang, M. C., Haertel, G. D., & Walberg, H. J. (1994). Educational resilience in inner cities. In M. C. Wang & E. W. Gordon (Eds.), *Educational resilience in inner-city America: Challenges and prospects* (pp. 45–72). Hillsdale, NJ: Lawrence Erlbaum.

Waxman, H. C. (1989). Urban Black and Hispanic elementary school students' perceptions of classroom instruction. *Journal of Research and Development in Education, 22,* 57–61.

Waxman, H. C. (1992). Reversing the cycle of educational failure for students in at-risk school environments. In H. C. Waxman, J. Walker de Felix, J. Anderson, & H. P. Baptiste (Eds.), *Students at risk in at-risk schools: Improving environments for learning* (pp. 1–9). Newbury Park, CA: Corwin.

Waxman, H. C., & Eash, M. J. (1983). Utilizing students' perception and context variables to analyze effective teaching: A process-product investigation. *Journal of Educational Research, 76,* 322–325.

Waxman, H. C., Huang, S. L., Knight, S. L., & Owens, E. W. (1992). Investigating the effects of the classroom learning environment on the academic achievement of at-risk students. In H. C. Waxman & C. D. Ellett (Eds.), *The study of learning environment* (Vol. 5, pp. 92–100). Houston: University of Houston.

Weinstein, R. S. (1983). Student perceptions of schooling. *Elementary School Journal, 83,* 287–312.

Weinstein, R. S. (1989). Perceptions of classroom processes and student motivation: Children's views of self-fulfilling prophecies. In C. Ames & R. Ames (Eds.), *Research on motivation in education: Goals and cognitions* (Vol. 3, pp. 187–221). San Diego, CA: Academic Press.

Weinstein, R. S., & Middlestadt, S. E. (1979). Students' perceptions of teacher interactions with male high and low achievers. *Journal of Educational Psychology, 71,* 421–431.

Winfield, L. F. (1991). Resilience, schooling, and development in African-American youth: A conceptual framework. *Education and Urban Society, 24,* 5–14.

57

Attracting and Retaining Teachers: A Question of Motivation

Karin Müller, Roberta Alliata and Fabienne Benninghoff

Introduction

Matching vacant teaching posts with qualified candidates is a key issue for the organization and running of schools. Given the cyclical patterns of teacher supply and demand, this matching operation is not an easy one. In a bid to overcome its short-term, annual recruitment horizon and to take early political action in order to avoid a shortage or surplus of teachers, the Canton of Geneva's Education Department put in place a human resources planning system (*Gestion prévisionnelle des enseignants* [GPE]) which allows the Department to forecast demand for teachers up to five years in advance. All in all, the Education Department employs 7300 teachers at primary and secondary school level, teaching students from age 4 to age 19. However, forecasting the number of teachers needed is not enough for purposes of directing policy responses. What are the most significant measures for attracting and retaining competent teachers within the profession? The Canton of Geneva's human resources planning system for teachers consists of complementary tools (i.e. a database, a dashboard of indicators, a prospective system and also surveys) to deliver information that will enable decision makers to identify areas where action might be particularly effective. The two surveys are aimed at a better understanding of the key stages in teaching careers: the motivation for entering teaching and the reasons for leaving the profession and taking early retirement.

Source: *Educational Management Administration & Leadership*, 37(5) (2009): 574–598.

The objective of our present article is to define to what extent an understanding of these different types of teacher motivation can provide a decision framework for defining teacher policies that will make it possible to attract, retain and develop effective teachers.

Education System in Switzerland

Swiss Institutional Background

Switzerland has a federalist system where responsibility for education is divided between the Confederation (e.g. vocational training and tertiary education) and the cantons (e.g. compulsory schooling). However, responsibilities are not distributed in a simple, dichotomic way between the Confederation and the cantons. The Confederation and the cantons cooperate and provide mutual support for each other, in a spirit of 'co-operative federalism'.

The new Federal Constitution of 18 April 1999 confirms the historical sovereignty of the 26 cantons: 'the cantons are sovereign insofar as their sovereignty is not limited by the Federal Constitution; they shall exercise all rights which are not transferred to the Confederation' (Article 3). In concrete terms, this means that the cantons have the right to legislate in certain domains. This is also the case for the education sector, and, according to the Federal Constitution:

> 1) Education is a cantonal matter. 2) The cantons are to ensure sufficient primary education, open to all children. This education shall be compulsory, and shall be placed under state direction or supervision. It shall be free in all public schools. The school year shall begin between mid-August and mid-September. (Article 62)

Since the Swiss system of education is essentially the responsibility of the cantons, it is not correct to talk about *a* Swiss education system, since Switzerland does not have a single 'Ministry of Education' but rather 26 independent and distinct systems. Within the cantons, educational responsibilities are administered by the cantonal departments of education.

Teacher Policy on the Current Political Agenda

The Teacher's Key Role in a Changing Environment

Interest in teacher policy research has intensified over the last few years for a number of reasons. First of all, key correlations exist between teacher quality and working conditions, on the one hand, and student learning, on the other. These correlations offer extensive political leverage for improving school performance (e.g. Rivkin et al., 1998; Gustafsson, 2003; SECTQ, 2004). Second, given the size of the teacher workforce, policies that address issues like working conditions or curriculum reforms have a major impact on the organization and coordination of schools. Recent research projects have thus focused particularly on understanding the teacher's role in respect of changes in society, the economy and schools in order to define effective teacher policies. The high level of international involvement (a total of 25 countries) in a recent study conducted by the Organisation for Economic Co-operation and Development (OECD), focusing on 'attracting, developing and retaining effective teachers', illustrates the scale of global interest (OECD, 2005). In Switzerland, worries about attracting, recruiting and retaining teachers have also been addressed by the Swiss Conference of Cantonal Ministers of Education (CDIP) that has drawn up guidelines for a recruiting strategy for teachers (Müller et al., 2003).

Geneva's Human Resources Planning System for Teachers

Education being primarily the responsibility of cantons, Geneva's Department of Education is also in charge of the planning and management of teaching personnel. In 2001, the Education Department decided to set up GPE – making it possible to anticipate recruitment needs and define policy options over a mid-term horizon of four to five years. The planning system sets out to capture the most relevant factors influencing the supply and demand of teachers and to provide valuable assistance to policymakers for the recruitment of competent teachers.

The GPE management tool is made up of four instruments: (1) the *database*, which constitutes the central database for teaching personnel; (2) the *dashboard*, with indicators that make it possible to track the evolution of the education system; (3) the *prospective system*, which is used as a tool to estimate quantitative needs for teaching personnel; and (4) the *surveys*, which permit the identification of key factors that are likely to influence the movements of teaching personnel (motivation for entering the profession and motivation for taking early retirement).

Theoretical Framework and Analysis of the Literature

Work Motivation Theories

When it comes to work motivation, many theoretical strands have been put forward to explain the relationship between individual motivation, job satisfaction and performance at work. The underlying hypothesis is that, with given individual capacities (intellectual, physical, know-how) and the organization put in place by a firm or administration (technical, human resources, administrative), motivation can directly influence the individual performance of each employee – and ultimately influence the success of an organization. Although there are multiple definitions of motivation, a certain consensus has evolved on the main dimension that characterizes motivation. In fact, since motivation is difficult to observe directly, it has been defined by the behaviour that individuals are supposed to develop (Roussel, 2000). Vallerand and Thill (1993: 18) summarize the concept of motivation as a 'hypothetical construct that is used to describe internal and/or external forces that generate the kick-off, the direction, the intensity, and the persistence of behaviour'. As a result, motivation can be defined as 'a process that activates, orients, reinforces and maintains the behaviour of individuals towards the achievement of intended objectives' (Roussel, 2000: 5). Ryan and Deci's (2000a: 54) definition of motivation underlines this process-oriented concept: 'to be motivated means to be moved to do something. A person who feels no impetus or inspiration to act is thus characterized as unmotivated, whereas someone who is energized or activated toward an end is considered motivated'.

Based on Kanfer's (1990) taxonomy of theories of motivation, there are three main paradigms that regroup current theoretical approaches: the first paradigm regroups need-motive-value approaches: according to these motivation theories, what leads an individual to start a type of behaviour, to direct it towards specific objectives and to support it both intensely and persistently is explained by needs, values and motives that have to be satisfied (e.g. Maslow's need hierarchy theory, Alderfer's ERG theory, Herzberg's dual-factor theory, McClelland's achievement motivation theory, Adams' equity theory).

The second paradigm regroups cognitive-choice theories: this paradigm rests on the guiding principle that 'behaviour is determined by the subjective value of the objectives towards which the individual is working, but also by their expectancy to see their behaviour producing the required results' (Oubraye-Rossel and Roussel, 2001) (e.g. Vroom's expectancy theory, Weiner's attribution theory).

The third paradigm regroups self-regulation/metacognition theories: these theories try to explain how goals can have an effect on individual work motivation and to understand the processes that determine the objectives chosen by the worker. These theories include Carver and Scheier's control theory, Locke's goal-setting theory and the social learning theory of Bandura). Self-regulation is a fairly new construct of motivation, and recent research on strategies for enhancing motivation, have focussed on its promotion. The term self-regulated can be used to describe performance guided by three key processes: self-observation (monitoring one's activities), self-judgement (self-evaluation of one's performance) and self-reaction (reactions to performance outcomes) (Zimmermann and Schunk, 2001).

We place our study within the theoretical framework of the first paradigm, which aims to identify the internal and external forces that have an impact on an individual's motivations. More specifically, we make reference to the cognitive evaluation theory (Deci, 1971; Deci, 1975; Amabile et al., 1976;

Zuckermann et al., 1978) that has been extended into the self-determination theory (Ryan et al., 1985; Gagné and Deci, 2005). These theories draw a distinction between two fundamental types of motivation. According to Ryan and Deci (2000a: 55) 'the most basic distinction is between intrinsic motivation, which refers to doing something because it is inherently interesting or enjoyable, and extrinsic motivation, which refers to doing something because it leads to a separable outcome'. Intrinsic motivation is also described as an 'inherent tendency to seek out novelty and challenges, to extend and exercise one's capacities, to explore, and to learn' (Ryan and Deci, 2000b: 70), while extrinsic motivation regulates behaviour 'in order to attain a separable outcome' (Ryan and Deci, 2000b: 71).

Self-determination theory considers extrinsic motivation from the angle of autonomy and control. It states that extrinsic motivation varies greatly with regard to its degree of autonomy: from external regulation (controlled motivation) right through to integrated regulation (autonomous motivation). The latter results from external values and behavioural regulations that tend to be internalized through socialization, thus leading to self-regulated behaviour (goal internalization). This means that 'a behavioural regulation and the value associated with it have been internalized. Internalization is defined as people taking in values, attitudes or regulatory structures, such that the external regulation of a behaviour is transformed into an internal regulation and thus no longer requires the presence of an external contingency' (Gagné and Deci, 2005: 334). To sum up, research findings on work motivation generally identify three sources of work motivation: intrinsic motivation, extrinsic motivation, and goal internalization as a subgroup of extrinsic motivation.

Studies (e.g. Deci, 1971; Lepper et al., 1973; Deci, 1975) that analysed the relationship between intrinsic and extrinsic motivations showed that they are not necessarily independent of each other and that they can interact positively or negatively. These studies revealed, for example, that extrinsic rewards, such as pay, can have a detrimental effect on intrinsic interest and task persistence. However, these undermining effects of extrinsic rewards do not occur automatically. According to Kanfer (1990: 88): 'Fisher (1978), for example, showed that financial rewards did not affect intrinsic motivation in situations consistent with societal norms about the role of pay for time and effort in real jobs'.

Motivation in Organization Theory and Human Resources Management

Employee motivation is regarded as a critical factor by organization and human resource management theories, since organizations that can create work environments that attract, motivate and retain effective individuals will be better positioned to succeed in a competitive environment. As a consequence, these theories set out to define organizational designs and human resource strategies that ensure high employee motivation.

Motivation-based organization theories that adopt a behavioural view emphasize the difference between intrinsic and extrinsic motivations (Argyris, 1964; McGregor, 1960; Osterloh et al., 2001). Drawing on the findings of psychological approaches, such as the cognitive evaluation theory (Deci, 1975) and the observed relationship between extrinsic and intrinsic motivations, organization theories aim to develop strategies to manage the potential trade-off between the two types of motivation. Osterloh and Frey (2000) state that there are three aspects that should be taken into account when considering the integration into an organization of market elements, such as profit centres or variable pay for performance: increased control, reduced personal relationships and also performance-based rewards have potentially negative effects on intrinsic motivations.

Qualified and motivated employees are considered to be a key factor for organizational success, according to resource-based human resource management theory (Wright and McMahan, 1992). Human resource management strategies are used to develop policies to select, develop, motivate and retain employees. Among these workforce management approaches, motivational inducement systems are applied in order to energize, direct, or sustain behaviour within organizations. Leonard et al. (1999) distinguish four commonly employed inducement systems applied in organizations: reward systems, managerial systems, task systems and social systems.

Findings Regarding Teacher Motivation

In line with the theoretical framework of work motivation cited above, both Kyriacou and Coulthard's (2000) and Obin's (2002) findings on the motivational choices that prompt people to enter teaching lead to three distinct categories: (1) intrinsic reasons related to the teaching activity itself, such as the transmission of subject knowledge and expertise; (2) extrinsic reasons, such as working conditions, autonomy, pay level, job security and status; and (3) altruistic reasons, such as the desire to help children to succeed and the consideration of teaching as a socially valuable profession. Within the self-determination theory, this latter category may be considered as internalized extrinsic motivation, since it represents values associated with the teaching profession.

Surveys carried out in the UK (Sturman, 2004), Australia (MCEETYA, 2003) and France (Esquieu, 2003; Esquieu, 2005) reveal a remarkable stability of motivational hierarchy: extrinsic aspects of a teacher's job play an important role in respect of job security, flexibility to organize work and autonomy in pedagogic choices. Salary and financial benefits, though, are less important for those considering teaching. Some research findings suggest that pay incentives are unsuccessful in increasing teacher motivation, since teachers are mainly motivated by gratification derived from higher-order needs, such as social relations and esteem (Sylvia and Hutchinson, 1985).

Barmby and Coe (2004) conclude from their literature survey that working conditions are nevertheless important considerations for teachers: stress, long hours and relatively low remuneration are decisive factors that discourage potential candidates from choosing teaching as a career.

Moreover, research into teacher motivation has revealed that key correlations exist between a student's motivation and the teacher's motivation. Pelletier et al. (2002: 193) found that 'by the same way students could become less self-determined when exposed to controlling teachers, our results indicate that, when teachers are pressured by the school's administration or by colleagues to behave in a specific manner, they also indicate that they are less self-determined toward their work'. Furthermore, the less teachers are self-determined towards teaching, the more controlling they become with students, which has a negative effect on the student's intrinsic motivation and self-determination (Reeve et al., 1999). However, existing research does not establish a clear consensus regarding the benefits of teacher motivation for increased levels of student achievement (Bishay, 1996).

In addition, a recent study conducted in the UK (Day et al., 2006) performed a quantitative analysis of the variations in a teacher's lifecycle on their motivation. The authors identified six professional life phases related to a teacher's experience and their relationship with specific motivational or demotivational factors. The first phase (0–3 years of experience) was thus associated with a crucial motivational factor, namely the support of the school and department leaders. Conversely, declining pupil behaviour had a negative impact on the motivation of this population of 'novice' teachers. As far as the second phase was concerned (4–7 years), the study identified the management of heavy workloads as being the most demotivating factor. In phase 3 (8–15 years), holding positions of responsibility, with the possibility of progression in their career, had a positive impact on the motivation of this teacher group. In phase 4 (16–23 years), further career advancement and good results had a positive impact on teacher motivation. Phase 4 was also associated with a large number of negative motivational factors, however, such as managing heavy workloads, facing additional responsibilities in school or demands outside of school, achieving a work-life balance, a feeling of career stagnation, lack of support in school and poor pupil behaviour. As for phase 5 (24–30 years), the most important reasons for teacher demotivation were a lack of support in school and bad pupil behaviour. Finally, in phase 6 (31 years and above), teachers generally considered they were having positive teacher-pupil relations and appreciated pupils' progress. In contrast, however, health issues were beginning to surface, and teachers were demotivated by government policies and pupil behaviour.

Research into teacher motivation is also often related to research into job satisfaction. According to Scholl (2002a: 2) these are 'related but distinct behavioural forces with different determinants and different outcomes'. While motivation is generally 'future directed' and has previously been defined as a process that activates, orients, and maintains the behaviour of individuals towards the achievement of intended objectives, job satisfaction is defined as the 'extent to which expectations are met resulting in positive feelings' (Scholl, 2002b: 3) and is therefore more 'present directed'. Scholl (2001: 1) states that 'dissatisfaction generally manifests itself in low membership motivation (absenteeism, turnover), and may result in the reduction of Extra Role Behaviour originally motivated by one of the inducement systems'. Research focusing on teachers and retention shows that teachers are more satisfied with their job, (1) if they feel supported by the school administration and by parents, (2) if they benefit from a certain autonomy in carrying out their job, and (3) if student behaviour and the school atmosphere are pleasant (NCES, 1997; Forneck et al., 2000; Gonik et al., 2000). Conversely, the physical and psychological fatigue of teachers increases, (1) if they face difficult relations with students and parents, (2) if they are subject to numerous reforms (pedagogic, organizational, technological, etc.), (3) if administrative tasks are increased, and (4) if they believe that teaching has lost its positive image (Spear et al., 2000; Basaglia and D'Oria, 2003; Cros and Obin, 2003; Papart, 2003). Studies that investigated specific reasons given by teachers for leaving their job mention the following factors as being particularly decisive: too heavy a workload, numerous government initiatives and reforms, the desire to take up a new challenge, a discouraging school situation (student behaviour, school management, etc.), stress, and personal circumstances (Smithers and Robinson, 2003; Luekens et al., 2004).

Towards a Decision Framework for an Effective Teacher Policy

Our present study is setting out to develop a decision framework for an effective teacher policy based on teacher motivation. First of all, taking work motivation theory as a basis, we single out those motivations that are particularly significant for explaining decisions to enter or leave the teaching profession. Having identified these main sources of teacher motivation, we then focus on those that are potentially accessible to human resource policy measures, in a bid to identify a teacher workforce policy that will make it possible to attract, develop and retain effective teachers.

Method and Data Sources

Method

The GPE has been conducting an annual survey since 2002, in a bid to better understand teachers' motivation for entering and also for leaving the teaching profession. In this article, we present the results of the most recent surveys (candidates: 2004/5 academic year; teachers taking early retirement: 2003/4 academic year). We saw that the results were homogenous over the years, indicating the potential transferability of the findings. Anonymous questionnaires were sent by post to all the candidates who fulfilled all the recruitment requirements (population 1) and to all the teachers taking early retirement (population 2).

Participants and Instruments

Survey of Motivations for Entering Teaching

The most recent survey among potential future teachers was distributed to 590 candidates who fulfilled all the recruitment requirements. The participation rate was 52% (306 questionnaires returned).[2] Women constitute the majority in the candidate survey (66%). They apply more for jobs as primary teachers (82%) than as secondary-level teachers (53%). Even though most candidates are aged between 20 and 29 (48%), a large proportion are between 30 and 39 years of age (32%) or even aged 40 or more (20%). In general, women candidates are younger than male candidates. This tendency is more marked for those applying for posts as primary teachers. Candidates took the decision to enter teaching at very different times: 36% decided to take up teaching 5 or more years ago, 42% between 1 and 5 years ago and 24% less than a year ago. Recent decisions are more common among candidates applying to be secondary teachers. It should also be noted that a quarter of candidates decided to enter the teaching profession after initial professional experience in another field.

The questionnaire drawn up for carrying out the candidates' survey included 43 questions on the motivation for entering teaching and 12 questions for measuring the teachers' socio-demographic characteristics. In order to structure the analysis, 35 items were grouped in seven motivation categories: (1) humanistic values; (2) professional vocation; (3) working conditions; (4) personal experience; (5) social status; (6) mobility; and (7) choice by default.

Survey of Motivations for Leaving Teaching

The questionnaire for teachers taking early retirement was sent to 204 teachers, 121 of whom (59%) replied. Somewhat more than 50 percent of the teachers decided to take early retirement less than one year prior to reaching retirement age, and slightly more than one third took this choice less than three years prior to retirement age.[3] The average age of teachers taking advantage of the early retirement plan (*Plan d'encouragement au départ anticipé, Plend*[4]) is 59 years. Teachers in primary education – the majority of whom are women – are generally younger when they leave the profession – at an average age of 57 years. In terms of the geographical location of the last school in which they worked, we saw that two-thirds of the teachers came from urban areas, one teacher in five from rural areas and 11% from suburban areas.

For the purpose of this second survey, the questionnaire was structured in three sections. In the first section, the teacher was invited to draw up an assessment of their career and to reflect on the positive features and weaknesses of the teaching profession. The second section was the longest in the questionnaire, since it included a question made up of 38 items, each of which constituted a reason for leaving teaching. These items were grouped in eight categories related to: (1) work conditions; (2) workload; (3) quality of relationships with principals; (4) fatigue and health; (5) private life (a wish to spend more time with the *family*); (6) school policy; (7) Plend characteristics; and (8) private life (a wish to spend more time on *leisure* activities). This last section measured five socio-demographic characteristics of participants.

Data Analysis

Data analysis was carried out in four stages: (1) a descriptive data analysis (frequencies) was used to draw up profiles of teachers according to their socio-demographic characteristics together with their motivation for entering or leaving the teaching profession; (2) a bivariate analysis (chi-squared tests) was applied, taking into account motivation for entering or leaving teaching together with socio-demographic variables, such as gender and the educational level being taught; (3) a multivariate analysis (factor analysis, cluster analysis) made it possible to identify different groups on the basis of the teacher's motivational profile with regard to their decision to enter or leave teaching. The objective of the factor analysis is to reduce the large number of variables to fewer dimensions and to achieve a two-dimensional representation of the essential information. This reduction is possible on account of the correlations that exist between the variables and is achieved by constructing synthetic variables, through a linear combination of the initial variables (Benzécri, 1973; Lebart et al., 1995). As far as cluster analysis is concerned, this consists in grouping the closest elements together in order to produce homogenous classes of individuals (Gordon, 1981; Lebart et al., 1995). Then (4), in order to map the motivations in more detail, we depicted the reasons for entering or leaving teaching on two matrixes. The x-axis represents the respective percentage of teachers who agreed with the entry or exit motivations suggested in the questionnaire (scale 1 to 10). On the y-axis, we classified each motivation on a scale according to its accessibility and responsiveness to policy measures in order to identify potential leverage (scale 1 to 10). The upper right quadrant of the two resulting matrixes thus sets out the critical motivations that are highly responsive to political actions taken by educational decision makers. Finally, by comparing these two matrixes, we set out to identify transversal teacher policy priorities.

Results

In the following, we highlight four groups of results that are organized on the basis of the data analysis stages set out above. The first three analyses are grouped according to survey.

Analysis of Motivations for Entering Teaching

Descriptive Analysis of Entry/Exit Motivations

The main motivations for teaching are grouped into three categories. *Humanistic values* are those which motivate candidates the most – for example, the wish to work in contact with children and young people (91 %), to help them succeed (95%), or the desire to transmit knowledge to them (88%), and the desire to give all students an equal chance (86%). Motivations associated with *professional vocation* – for example, identification with the teaching profession (76%), the possibility of exercising a profession they feel passionately about (93%) – and *work conditions* linked to the characteristics of the profession – for example, the possibility to work in a spirit of cooperation (91%) and to carry out an evolutionary and demanding job (91%) – also constitute key motivation categories for entering the profession (Table 1).

Differences in Motivational Orientation with Respect to Education Level and Gender

The global results presented above obviously mask certain disparities. It is clear, for example, that significant differences (chi-squared tests, $p < 0.05$) exist among the motivations as a function of *education level* and *gender.* As far as *education level* is concerned, candidates applying to be primary teachers have a tendency to place more importance on the humanistic values and psychological aspects of teaching, as well as on the social role and the evolutionary and demanding aspect of the job, whereas candidates applying to be secondary teachers are more attracted by work conditions, and mainly by the flexibility of the schedule and the holidays. With regard to *gender*, we find that female candidates are more motivated by the relational and psychological aspects of the teaching profession. Furthermore, their job applications have more frequently been stimulated by previous professional experience in teaching.

Table 1: Entry motivations by education level (classified by categories) (in %)

Entry motivations	Total (n = 306)	Primary level (n = 129)	Secondary level (n = 165)
Category 1: Humanistic values			
Wish to help children and young people to succeed	95	98	92
Opportunity to put key values into practice	91	95	86
Wish to work in contact with children and young people	91	98	85
Interest in work where human relations are important	89	95	84
Wish to transmit knowledge to children and young people	88	85	90
Interest in didactic and pedagogical aspects	86	92	81
Opportunity to give all students an equal chance	86	85	87
Interest in psychological aspects	83	91	76
Wish to contribute to improving society	82	86	78
Category 2: Professional vocation			
Profession that can be exercised with passion	93	94	92
Identification with the teaching profession	76	78	73
Teaching is still a useful profession	76	74	78
An opportunity to avoid routine	72	80	66
A vocation	68	67	69
A profession for life	56	56	56
A profession to be exercised for a few years only	15	15	15
Category 3: Work conditions			
Category 3a: Characteristics of the profession			
Wish to work in a spirit of cooperation and sharing experience	91	95	86
Motivated by an evolutionary and demanding job	91	96	86
Appreciation of the autonomy and independence of teaching	80	76	82
Interest in the possibilities for continuous training/professional development	78	85	74
Motivated by on-the-job teacher training	71	71	70
An opportunity to take on interesting responsibilities	47	50	45
Category 3b: Extrinsic conditions			
Opportunity to reconcile private and professional life	71	70	72
Appreciation of flexibility in schedule and activity rate	68	59	72
Appreciation of a stable and secure job	62	54	67
An opportunity to grant importance to family life	61	62	59
Wish for sufficient holidays and leisure time	48	41	52
Motivation of social security benefits and salary	42	33	49
Constitutes an interesting complementary activity	26	24	27
Category 4: Personal experience			
Currently the most appropriate choice	72	71	73
Motivated by previous teaching experience	70	64	72
Education pursued confirms this choice	61	68	56

Entry motivations	Total (n = 306)	Primary level (n = 129)	Secondary level (n = 165)
Category 5: Social status			
Finds it meaningful to exercise a profession of general interest	65	64	66
Wishes to practice a profession that has an important social role	58	68	50
Teaching is a profession valued by society	22	24	21
Aspires to attain the social status associated with the profession	19	13	23
Category 6: Mobility			
Interest in working in different sectors	57	56	57
Opportunity to work in different schools and locations within the canton	37	44	33
Permits a professional change	34	31	37
Permits work in different cantons and countries	29	32	27
Category 7: Choice by default			
Main objective of studies	38	45	33
Gave up an academic or research career	23	19	26
Difficulty in finding another job	14	9	18

Note: The percentages refer to the respondents who stated that their choice to enter teaching was influenced 'quite a lot' or 'very much' by each motivation.

Motivational Typologies of Teachers

A multiple correspondence analysis (Benzécri, 1973; Lebart et al., 1995) summarized the various response categories for the entry motivation variables in factors whose values were estimated for each individual. A hierarchical cluster analysis was performed on the resulting factor values, using Ward's (1963) algorithm, in order to establish groups of teachers who were as homogeneous and as distinct from other groups as possible. This analysis of the motivational profiles of teacher candidates provided four groups.

The 'passionate' group takes in 37% of all candidates. They identify strongly with the motivations related to the social dimension of teaching and the evolutionary nature of the job (e.g. an interest in professional development). They are also strongly motivated by the prospect of transferring their subject knowledge to students.

The 'engaged' group accounts for another 37% of all candidates. Their motivational profile corresponds largely to that of the previous group. Their degree of agreement is less strong, however.

Finally, candidates with 'mitigated' (9%) and 'disillusioned' (17%) motivations represent the last two groups. Even though they are somewhat motivated by the working conditions and humanistic values, they acknowledge that teaching is not their preferred professional choice.

Analysis of Motivations for Leaving Teaching

Descriptive Analysis of Entry/Exit Motivations

The eight types of motivation defined above can be grouped into two categories of factors: (1) motivational factors *internal* to the profession, or negative private motivations, which influence leaving decisions (*pushing factors*); and (2) motivational factors *external* to the profession, or positive private motivations, which attract teachers towards the choice of departure (*pulling factors*).

Five types of motivation correspond to the pushing factors category: these motivations are related to *changes in work conditions, workload, fatigue and health, relationships with principals* and *school policies.* Three types of motivations are pulling factors: these motivations are associated with private life – for *family* or *leisure* related reasons – or with the *Plend characteristics.*

According to the results of our study, two pushing factors have a key influence on early retirement decision: *changes in work conditions* (e.g. the manner of implementing institutional changes (50%), the effort put into disciplining rather than into teaching students [44%]), and *workload*, such as the evolution of work contents (55%) and an increasing workload (50%).

Two pulling factors also made a considerable contribution to the choice of those opting for early retirement: *the Plend characteristics* – especially with regard to the advantageous conditions involved (e.g. the attractiveness of the retirement package [63%]) – and the desire to spend more time on *leisure* activities (to profit from their remaining energy (84%) and to devote time to their hobbies [69%]) (Table 2).

Differences in Motivational Orientation with Respect to Education Level and Gender

As with the survey on entry motivations, the global results for the motivational factors behind early retirement also mask a number of disparities. For example, there are significant differences (chi-squared tests, $p < 0.05$) between *education levels.* Aspects related to changes in workload content were mentioned much more frequently by teachers in primary education than by secondary teachers. In the same way, work conditions – and more particularly the feeling of lack of freedom or autonomy – also pushed primary education teachers to leave the profession prematurely more than secondary teachers. Other factors, such as advantageous Plend conditions, also motivated primary education teachers more than secondary teachers.

As far as the *gender* variable is concerned, we found that women were over-represented among the teachers who were motivated by the wish to spend time on non-professional activities. Men, however, were overrepresented among teachers motivated by social changes and, more particularly, by the perception of a decline in pupils' competencies.

Table 2: Motivation for leaving teaching by education level (classified by categories) (in %)

Exit motivations	Total (n = 121)	Primary level (n = 40)	Secondary level (n = 81)
Category 1: Work conditions			
Manner of implementing institutional changes	50	58	46
Too much effort going into disciplining rather than into teaching students	44	50	40
Deterioration of profession's image	44	43	44
Student behaviour	33	33	33
Students' competence level	25	15	30
Feeling out of touch with students	13	8	15
Category 2: Workload			
Evolution of work contents	55	70	47
Increasing work load	50	58	46
Contents of institutional changes	44	45	44
Feeling of lack of freedom, autonomy	19	35	10
Category 3: Relationships with principals			
Relations with education department (administration)	22	18	24
Lacking support of school management	19	18	19
Category 4: Fatigue and health			
Lacking the energy required to teach	26	26	26
Health reasons	16	29	25
Category 5: Private life (family)			
To devote time to family	34	46	27
To take up non-professional activities (volunteering, etc.)	28	40	22
Spouse is already retired	26	41	18
Category 6: School policy			
Relations with school leaders	15	8	20
Unsatisfactory professional development	15	23	10
Category 7: Characteristics of early retirement conditions (Plend)			
Attractiveness of retirement package	63	82	53
Likely disappearance of retirement package	47	51	44
Category 8: Private life (leisure)			
To profit from remaining energy	84	90	81
To devote time to hobbies	69	79	65
To travel	41	39	42
Others			
Tired of teaching a specific school subject	13	8	1
Feeling unable to keep up with teaching content	11	21	6

Note: The percentages refer to the respondents who stated that their early retirement choice was influenced 'quite a lot' or 'very much' by each motivation.

Motivational Typologies of Teachers

In this second survey, the combined method of multiple correspondence analysis and hierarchical cluster analysis set out above was similarly employed.

When the profiles of teachers taking early retirement are analysed below, this shows that a teacher's overall assessment of his or her career correlates with his or her attitude towards institutional, pedagogic and social changes.

The largest portion of teachers (49%) taking early retirement have a 'positive assessment of their career' in overall terms. They do not mention 'changes' as being a decisive factor in their decision to leave. They succeeded in adapting their professional commitment to an evolving environment.

Thirty-two per cent of teachers finish their career with a fairly 'mixed assessment'. Their decision to leave has been influenced by pedagogical and institutional changes and an increasing workload. Also, they feel that the image of the teaching profession has lost a lot of its appeal.

There are 19% of teachers with an overall 'negative assessment of their career'. Their decision to leave has been largely influenced by institutional and pedagogic changes and increasing workload. They also mention insufficient support from their professional environment (school leaders and administration).

Evaluation by Matrix Analysis

The matrix for candidates (Figure 1) shows that altruistic motivations and intrinsic motivations rank high on the scale of motivation for becoming a teacher (x-axis) but low in respect of their accessibility and responsiveness to political action (y-axis) (lower right quadrant). Certain extrinsic motivations are highly ranked by teachers and are also susceptible to potential policy measures: i.e. possibilities for professional development, image of the profession, the evolving nature of the job and autonomy. However, there are a number of extrinsic factors, such as salary and job mobility, that score high with regard to their accessibility to political action but are of relatively low importance on the motivational scale (upper-left quadrant). This might be explained by the fact that Swiss teachers have a high salary level compared with other countries in Europe (OECD, 2005).

Looking at the reasons for taking early retirement from teaching (Figure 2), private motivations, such as spending more time with the family, and on hobbies and travelling, rank high on the motivational scale. However, these private motivations offer little scope for potential policy intervention (lower-right quadrant). Factors that are highly responsive to political measures and have a key influence on a teacher's decision to take early retirement are the way that institutional changes are carried out, the content of reforms, an increasing workload and advantageous pre-retirement benefits.

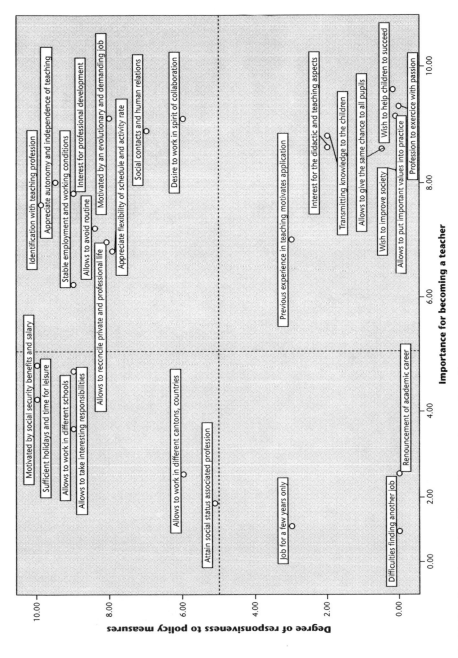

Figure 1: Motives for entering teaching and responsiveness to policy measures

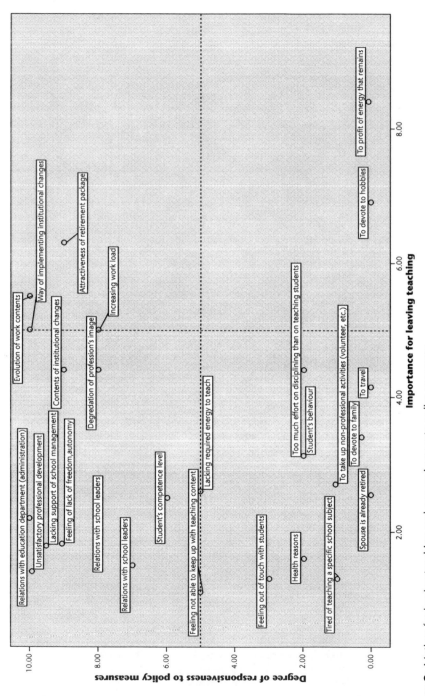

Figure 2: Motives for leaving teaching and responsiveness to policy measures

A Decision Framework for Defining Teacher Policies

How can the results of our previous analysis of teachers' motivation for entering and leaving the profession be of assistance in defining teacher policies aimed at attracting and retaining teachers in their profession? We have identified three issues that have been shortlisted from our previous matrix analysis that might be of particular interest, since they also have an impact on attracting new candidates as well as on retaining experienced teachers. Their transversal character holds scope for promising leverages for anchoring teacher policies over the full length of teachers' careers. More specifically, these three transversal issues relate to (1) job characteristics (e.g. activities), (2) working conditions, and (3) the image of the teaching profession (see Table 3). They all show similar patterns in

Table 3: Transversal issues to attract, develop and retain teachers

Transversal issues	Motivations for entering teaching	Motivations for leaving teaching	Motivational inducement systems involved
Job characteristics	Little job routine Working in a social network providing various human contacts (students, colleagues, parents)	Increasing work load (e.g. increasing diversity of tasks, more administrative work) Increasing number of meetings	Task system (e.g. job definition, job description)
	An evolving and demanding job	Dissatisfaction with content and the way that institutional reforms have been implemented	Leadership system (e.g. change implementation) Professional development system (e.g. enhancement of teacher's competencies)
	Transmission of knowledge to young people	Too much effort going into disciplining rather than into teaching students Student behaviour	Task system (e.g. evolution of teacher's responsibilities and professional activities) Social system (e.g. perception of teacher's role in society)
Working conditions	Autonomy in pedagogical choices and activities	Lack of autonomy and flexibility	Task system (e.g. structures and processes to carry out professional activities) Professional development system (e.g. opportunities to acquire skills and knowledge)
	Autonomy in performing teaching activities	Lack of hierarchical support Lack of flexibility	Leadership system (e.g. guidance and support to carry out professional activities) Social system (e.g. teamwork and feedback procedures) Reward system (e.g. pay and working conditions)
Professional image	Identification with teaching profession	Degradation of teaching profession's image	Task system (e.g. vision creation and mission development) Social system (e.g. shared vision and set of norms)

respect of teacher motivation: initially they have a positive impact but, over the years, they develop into the main reasons for leaving teaching.

With regard to job characteristics, one key factor is the way teachers face change in the course of their career. Table 3 shows that the fact that there is very little job routine is something that attracts teacher candidates to the profession. However, frequent changes in the activities involved in their job and their professional environment, due to school reforms for example, can become a key argument for losing one's motivation to teach. Furthermore, Table 3 shows that there is a similar pattern for working conditions, especially with regard to autonomy. It is important for teachers at the start of their career to have sufficient autonomy to implement their pedagogical choices and their professional activities. However, the reality for an experienced teacher is somewhat different. They regret having too little autonomy and flexibility with regard to pedagogical choices and feel there is a lack of hierarchical support for specific measures – leading to major frustration and teacher losses. Finally, strong identification with the teaching profession fades over time. It seems that the initial enthusiasm for teaching cannot, unfortunately, be maintained over the years. More experienced teachers regret, on a systematic basis, that the professional image of teaching has deteriorated over the course of their career and that they do not identify themselves with the current profession any more.

These changes highlight a key question for school principals and other practitioners: how can the initial motivational factors be maintained as teachers progress in their career? Our research is able to offer a number of answers to this fundamental question. Teaching-policy levers ought, in fact, to prevent the development of the gaps between entry and leaving motivations. Taking the motivational inducement system of Leonard et al. (1999), we can identify five determinants for leveraging the motivation of teachers: (1) task system; (2) leadership system; (3) reward system; (4) social system; and (5) professional development system. The last columns of Table 3 indicates what leverage could be used on a general basis to address issues related to job characteristics, work conditions and professional image.

More specifically: what kind of measures can be put in place by school authorities to prevent a loss in teacher motivation from coming about? Table 4 summarizes potential measures for keeping the initial motivational factors alive over a teacher's career. It is evident that several inducement systems are required in parallel in order to tackle motivational issues. Teacher policies can only be successful if they address motivational determinants in a complementary manner. Research on educational leadership shows that effective education leadership has a positive impact on teaching and learning. Leithwood et al. (2004) identify three sets of practices that make up the basic core of successful leadership: setting directions, developing people, and redesigning the organization. Developing people by providing teachers with necessary support and training to succeed is therefore a key task for those in leadership roles.

Table 4: Policy measures derived from motivational inducement systems

Transversal issues	Task system	Leadership system	Reward system	Professional development system	Social system
Characteristics of job activities	Determine teacher's job definitions and job descriptions Communicate expected competencies, organizational goals and the role which teachers are expected to play: e.g. subject matter and pedagogical knowledge, organizational and communication skills	Provide a professional network (e.g. school leaders, mentors) to provide a framework for and support teachers' activities at their workplace Build strong leadership systems in order to lead und support institutional and pedagogic changes	Provide a professional network and feedback (e.g. school leaders, mentors) to provide a framework for and support teachers' activities at their workplace Let teachers express their preferences in respect of their activities (choice of degree, of school, of branch)	Conceive of teacher's professional development as a continuing activity over the teacher's career Identify individual training needs and adapt specific professional development possibilities Complement teaching reforms with training opportunities that facilitate implementation of changes in a positive way	Clarify expectations with regard to the teacher's function, role and profile with key stakeholders (e.g. policymakers, parents, teachers) Prepare (future) teachers adequately for the reality of the job: confront expectations and reality early on in initial teacher education through practical experience and field training
Working conditions	Provide organizational structures and processes that allow flexibility and autonomy in carrying out teaching activities Offer possibilities to diversify teacher's activities (e.g. project involvement, professional experience in other domains)	Build adequate leadership to guide and support teachers in order to achieve common objectives (e.g. supervision, feedback) Offer possibilities for taking on new responsibilities (e.g. school leadership, mentoring, training)	Competitive salary Emphasize flexible working conditions and job autonomy, e.g. flexible working hours, possibility of working part time, job sharing, etc. Possibility of reducing workload towards the end of the career	Provide a work environment and resources that allow teachers to carry out their professional activities Provide opportunities for self-development and self-realization at the workplace	Encourage team building and peer recognition among teachers
Professional image	Create visions of current and future evolution of the teaching profession Evaluate missions with regard to social, institutional changes	Integrate teachers as responsible actors of change and job evolution	Provide attractive working conditions to improve image	Maintain high standards for professional development in order to retain highly qualified staff	Share and develop visions of the teaching profession in cooperation with key stakeholders Develop strategies to maintain and promote the image of teaching

First of all, change management emerges as one of the key elements with regard to evolving job characteristics. A clear understanding of the job definition and its evolution as a result of changing roles and modified expectations is crucial (task system). Furthermore, a strong leadership system is required in order to implement change and reforms. Professional development systems should provide additional support all along a teacher's career and, finally, interactions with key stakeholders, such as parents, administrative authorities, political organizations and business associations, are necessary in order to clarify and share the teacher's function, roles and profiles (social system).

Working conditions provide an important additional lever of teacher policy, since they touch on all five motivational inducement systems. In general, working conditions should be conducive to a teacher's motivation to carry out their professional work in a flexible and autonomous manner by providing the opportunity to work in a professional network and offering hierarchical support. Moreover, working conditions should provide an opportunity for teachers to keep up with evolving teaching contents and materials.

Finally, it is important to develop and enhance the professional image of teachers both inside and outside the school system. The task system, for example, allows visions regarding the current and future evolution of the teaching profession to be updated. It would appear, in fact, that some of the perceived loss of a teacher's image can be explained by the evolution of the job, which is perceived in a negative way by older teachers who fail to see their initial role confirmed. Furthermore, attractive working conditions and stringent requirements on the continuing education of teachers are measures that help maintain a positive professional image outside of the school system too.

From our previous analyses based on theories of work motivation and organizational behaviour, we see that employee motivation is a critical element in terms of its influence on individual performance and on the capacity of organizations to attain their objectives. Set in the context of schools, teacher motivation plays an essential role with regard to student learning as well as to a school's capacity to achieve its objectives as an organization. As a result, teacher motivation plays a key role in defining policies to attract, maintain and develop teachers, as has been illustrated by the measures identified above. Our suggested policy measures have been prioritized in respect of their potential impact on teacher motivation. Additional criteria, however, such as their political and economic feasibility, are to be considered for deciding on their final implementation.

Notes

1. In Switzerland, a distinction is drawn between pre-schools (*Kindergarten, école enfantine* or *scuola dell'infanzia*) and childcare outside the family (day nurseries, day-care mothers, play groups). Children of all cantons are entitled to have access to pre-school education before they enter compulsory education. Cantons and/or communes are responsible for organising and funding pre-school education.

2. Currently we do not have any information on non-respondents but we intend to collect data on the whole populations in forthcoming surveys so that we can compare the basic characteristics of respondents and non-respondents.
3. In Switzerland, the official retirement age for men is 65 years and, for women, 63 years.
4. The *Plend* early retirement plan (Plan d'encouragement au départ anticipé) was introduced in 1994 as a permanent measure, forming part of the Canton of Geneva's human resources policy for its public administration. A certain number of conditions must be fulfilled in order to benefit from this retirement plan; these relate to age, for instance (women: a minimum of 57 years old; men: a minimum of 58 years old) and seniority (a minimum 10 years' service as an employee with the canton of Geneva).

References

Amabile, T.M., DeJong, W. and Lepper, M.R. (1976) 'Effects of Externally Imposed Deadlines on Subsequent Intrinsic motivation', *Journal of Personality and Social Psychology* 34: 92–8.

Argyris, C. (1964) *Integrating the Individual and the Organization*. New York: Wiley.

Basaglia, G. and D'Oria V.L. (2003) 'Image and Health of Teachers in Italy: Framework, Problems and Proposals', Appendix 4. In: OCDE (2003). *Attracting, Developing and Retaining Effective Teachers. Country Background Report for Italy. OCDE Activity.* Available at: http://www.oecd.org/els/education/teacherpolicy. Accessed 14 May 2005.

Barmby, P. and Coe, R. (2004) Recruiting and Retaining Teachers: Findings from Recent Studies. Paper presented at the British Educational Research Association Conference, Manchester 14–18 September, Curriculum, Evaluation and Management Centre, University of Durham.

Benzécri, J.P. (1973) *L'analyse Des Données. Tome 1: La Taxinomie. Tome 2: L'analyse Des Correspondences*, 2nd edn. 1976. Paris: Dunod.

Bishay, A. (1996) 'Teacher Motivation and Job Satisfaction: A Study Employing the Experience Sampling Method', *Journal of Undergraduate Sciences* 3: 147–54.

Cros, F. and Obin, J.P. (2003) *Attirer, Former et Retenir Des Enseignants de Qualité*, Rapport de base nationale de la France dans le cadre de l'activité de l'OCDE. Available at: http://www.oecd.org/els/education/teacherpolicy. Accessed 14 May 2005.

Day, C. Stobart, G., Sammons, P., Kington, A., Gu, Q., Smees, R. and Mujtaba, T. (2006) *Variations in Teachers' Work, Lives and Effectiveness: Final report for the VITAE Project.* London: Department for Education and Skills.

Deci, E.L. (1971) 'Effects of Externally Mediated Rewards on Intrinsic Motivation', *Journal of Personality and Social Psychology* 18: 105–15.

Deci, E.L. (1975) *Instrinsic Motivation*. New York: Plenum.

Esquieu, N. (2003) *Être Professeur en Lycée et Collège en 2002*. Note d'information 03.37. Paris: Ministère de l'éducation nationale, de l'enseignement supérieur et de la recherché. Available at: http://www.education.gouv.fr/stateval. Accessed 23 May 2005.

Esquieu, N. (2005) *Portrait des Enseignants de Collèges et Lycées Interrogation de 1000 Enseignants du Second Degré en mai-juin 2004*. Note d'information 05.07. Paris: Ministère de l'éducation nationale, de l'enseignement supérieur et de la recherché. Available at: http://www.education.gouv.fr/stateval. Accessed 23 May 2005.

Federal Constitution of the Swiss Confederation of 18 April 1999, RS 101.

Fisher, C.D. (1978) 'The Effects of Personal Control, Competence, and Extrinsic Reward Systems on Intrinsic Motivation', *Organizational Behavior and Human Performance* 21: 273–88.

Forneck, H.J. and Schriever, F. (2000) *Die Individualisierte Profession. Untersuchung der Lehrerinnen und Lehrerarbeitszeit und -Belastung im Kanton Zürich*. Bildungsdirektion des Kantons Zürich. Available at: http://www.bildungsdirektion.zh.ch/internet/bi/de/publikationen/studien/evaluationen.html. Accessed 25 May 2005.

Gagné, M., and Deci, L.E. (2005) 'Self-Determination Theory and Work Motivation', *Journal of Organizational Behavior* 26: 33–362.

Gonik, V., Kurth, S. and Boillat, M.A. (2000) *Analyse du Questionnaire Sur L'état de Santé Physique et Mentale des Enseignants Vaudois. Rapport Final*. Lausanne: Institut universitaire romand de la Santé au Travail.

Gordon, A.D. (1981) *Classification: Methods for the Exploratory Analysis of Multivariate Data*. London: Chapman and Hall.

Gustafsson, J.E. (2003) 'What Do We Know About Effects of School Resources on Student Achievement', *Review of Educational Research* 66: 77–110.

Kanfer, R. (1990) 'Motivation Theory and Industrial and Organizational Psychology', in M.D. Dunnette and L.M. Hough (eds) *Handbook of Industrial and Organizational Psychology*, vol. 1, pp. 75–170. Palo Alto, CA: Consulting Psychologists Press.

Kyriacou, C. and Coulthard, M. (2000) 'Undergraduates Views of Teaching as a Career Choice', *Journal of Education for Teaching* 26(2): 117–26.

Lebart, L., Morineau, A. and Piron, M. (1995) *Statistiques Exploratoires Multidimensionnelles*. Paris: Dunod.

Leithwood, K. et al. (2004) *How Leadership Influences Student Learning. Learning from Leadership Project*. Minnesota: University of Minnesota, Center for Applied Research and Educational Improvement and Toronto: University of Toronto, Ontario Institute for Studies in Education.

Leonard, N.H., Beauvais, L.L. and Scholl, R.W. (1999) 'Work Motivation: The Incorporation of Self-Concept-Based Processes', *Human Relations* 52: 969–98.

Lepper, J.R., Greene, D. and Nisbett, R.E. (1973) 'Undermining Children's Intrinsic Interest with Extrinsic Rewards: A Test of the "Overjustification" Hypothesis', *Journal of Personality and Social Psychology* 28: 129–37.

Luekens, M., Lyter, D. and Fox, E. (2004) *Teacher Attrition and Mobility: Results from the Teacher Follow-Up Survey, 2000–01*. NCES 2004–301. Washington, DC: National Center for Education Statistics (NCES).

MCEETYA (Ministerial Council on Education, Employment, Training and Youth Affairs (2003) *Demand and Supply of Primary and Secondary School Teachers in Australia*. Melbourne: MCEETYA.

McGregor, D. (1960) *The Human Side of Enterprise*. New York: McGraw-Hill.

Müller, K., Bortolotti, R. and Bottani, N. (2003) *Stratégie de Recrutement des Enseignantes et Enseignants*. Etudes et rapports 17A. Berne: Conférence Suisse des directeurs cantonaux de l'instruction publique (CDIP).

NCES (National Center of Education Statistics) (1997) *Job Satisfaction among America's Teachers: Effects of Workplace Conditions, Background Characteristics, and Teacher Compensation. Statistical Analysis Report, July 1997*. Washington, DC: US Department of Education, Office of Educational Research and Improvement. Available at: http://www.nces.ed.gov/pubs97/97471.html. Accessed 12 June 2005.

Obin, J.P. (2002) *Enseigner, un Métier pour Demain*. Rapport au minister de l'éducation natonale. Mission de réflexion sur le métier d'enseignant. Available at: http://www.education.gouv.fr/rapport/obin.pdf. Accessed 12 June 2005.

OECD (Organization of Economic Cooperation and Development) (2003) *Le Rôle des Systèmes Nationaux de Certification Pour Promouvoir l'Apprentissage Tout au Long de la vie*. Rapport de base de la Suisse. Paris: OECD.

OECD (Organization of Economic Cooperation and Development) (2005) 'Teachers Matter: Attracting, Developing and Retaining Effective Teachers', *Education and Training Policy*. Paris: OECD.

Osterloh, M. and Frey, B.S. (2000) 'Motivation, Knowledge Transfer, and Organizational Forms', *Organization Science* 11: 538–50.

Osterloh, M., Frey, B. and Frost, J. (2001) 'Managing Motivation, Organization and Governance', *Journal of Management and Governance* 5: 231–39.

Oubraye-Rossel, N. et Roussel, P. (2001) *Le Soi et la Motivation*. Notes du Laboratoire Interdisciplinaire de recherche sur les Ressources Humaines et l'Emploi (LIRHE), Note No. 345. Toulouse: LIRHE.

Papart, J.P. (2003) *La Santé des Enseignants et des Éducateurs de L'enseignement Primaire, Rapport à L'organisation du Travail*. Versoix: Actions en santé publique. Available at: http://www.geneve.ch/primaire/corps_enseignant.html. Accessed 12 June 2005.

Pelletier, L.G., Legault, L. and Séguin-Lévesque, C. (2002) 'Pressure from Above and Pressure from Below as Determinants of Teachers' Motivation and Teaching Behaviors', *Journal of Educational Psychology* 94: 186–96.

Reeve, J., Bolt, E. and Cai, Y. (1999) 'Autonomy-Supportive Teachers: How they Teach and Motivate Students', *Journal of Educational Psychology* 9: 537–48.

Rivkin, S., Hanushek, E. and Kain, J. (1998) *Teachers, Schools, and Academic Achievement: Working Paper 6691*. Cambridge, MA: National Bureau of Economic Research (NBER).

Roussel, P. (2000) *La Motivation au Travail – Concept et Theories*. Notes du Laboratoire Interdisciplinaire de recherché sur les Ressources Humaines et l'Emploi (LIRHE), Note No. 326. Toulouse: LIRHE.

Ryan, R.M., Connell, J.P. and Deci, E.L. (1985) 'A Motivational Analysis of Self-Determination and Self-Regulation in Education', in C. Ames and R.E. Ames (eds) *Research on Motivation in Education: The Classroom Milieu*, pp. 13–51. New York: Academic Press.

Ryan, R.M. and Deci, E.L. (2000a) 'Intrinsic and Extrinsic Motivations: Classic Definitions and New Directions', *Contemporary Educational Psychology* 25: 54–67.

Ryan, R.M. and Deci, E.L (2000b) 'Self-Determination Theory and the Facilitation of Intrinsic Motivation, Social Development, and Well-Being', *American Psychologist* 55: 68–78.

Scholl, R.W. (2001) 'Motivation Diagnostic Framework using Sources of Motivation Framework'. Availableat:http://www.cba.uri.edu/scholl/Notes/Motivation_Diagnosis2.html. Accessed 7 March 2006.

Scholl, R.W. (2002a) 'Motivation'. Available at: http://www.cba.uri.edu/scholl/Notes/Motivation.html. Accessed 7 March 2006.

Scholl, R.W. (2002b) 'Analysis and Diagnosis of Behavioral Problems'. Available at: http://www.cba.uri.edu/scholl/Notes/Behavioral_Diagnosis.html. Accessed 7 March 2006.

SECTQ (The Southeast Center of Teaching Quality) (2004) *Teacher Working Conditions are Student Learning Conditions: A report to Governor Mike Easley on the 2004 North Carolina Teacher Working Conditions Survey*. Chapel Hill, NC: The Southeast Center of Teaching Quality. Available at: http://www.teachingquality.org/TWC.htm. Accessed 31 May 2005.

Smithers, A. and Robinson, P. (2003) *Factors Affecting Teachers' Decision to Leave the Profession*. Nottingham: Department for Education and Skills (DfES).

Spear, M., Gould, K. and Lee, B. (2000) *Who Would be a Teacher? A Review of Factors Motivating and Demotivating Prospective and Practicing Teachers*. Slough: National Foundation for educational research (NFER).

Sturman, L. (2004) *Contented and Committed? A Survey of Quality of Working Life Amongst Teachers*. Slough: National Foundation for Educational Research (NFER).

Swiss Conference of Cantonal Ministers of Education (CDIP) (2006) *Simplified Diagram of the Swiss Education System*. Available at: http://www.edk.ch/PDF_Downloads/Bildungswesen_CH/BildungCH_e.pdf. Accessed 7 March 2006.

Sylvia, R.D. and Hutchinson, T. (1985) 'What Makes Ms. Johnson Teach? A Study of Teacher Motivation', *Human Relations* 38: 841–56.

Vallerand, R.J. and Thill, E.E. (1993) 'Introduction au Concept de Motivation', in J. Vallernad and Thill, E.E. (eds) *Introduction À La Psychologie De La Motivation*, pp. 201–38. Laval (Quebec): Editions etudes vivantes.

Ward, J.H. (1963) 'Hierarchical Grouping to Optimize an Objective Function', *Journal of American Statistical Association* 58: 236–44.

Wright, P.M. and McMahan, G.C. (1992) 'Theoretical Perspectives for Strategic Human Resource Management', *Journal of Management* 18: 295–320.

Zimmermann, B.J. and Schunk, D.H. (2001) *Self-Regulated Learning and Academic Achievement: Theory, Research and Practice*. Hillsdale, NJ: Erlbaum.

Zuckermann, M., Porac, J., Lathin, D., Smith, R. and Deci, E.L. (1978) 'On the Importance of Self-Determination for Intrinsically Motivated Behavior', *Personality and Social Psychology Bulletin* 4: 443–46.